The
Minister's Manual

SEVENTY-SIXTH ANNUAL ISSUE

THE MINISTER'S MANUAL
2001

Edited by

JAMES W. COX

JOSSEY-BASS
A Wiley Company
San Francisco

Editors of THE MINISTER'S MANUAL

G. B. F. Hallock, D.D., 1926–1958
M. K. W. Heicher, Ph.D., 1943–1968
Charles L. Wallis, M.A., M.Div., 1969–1983
James W. Cox, M.Div., Ph.D.

Translations of the Bible referred to and quoted from in this book may be indicated by their standard abbreviations, such as NRSV (New Revised Standard Version) and NIV (New International Version). In addition, some contributors have made their own translations and others have used a mixed text.

Jossey-Bass is a registered trademark of Jossey-Bass Inc., A Wiley Company.

Jossey-Bass books and products are available through most bookstores. To contact Jossey-Bass directly, call (888) 378-2537, fax to (800) 605-2665, or visit our website at www.josseybass.com.

Substantial discounts on bulk quantities of Jossey-Bass books are available to corporations, professional associations, and other organizations. For details and discount information, contact the special sales department at Jossey-Bass.

 Manufactured in the United States of America on Lyons Falls Turin Book. This paper is acid-free and 100 percent totally chlorine-free.

Library of Congress Cataloging Card Number

25-21658
ISSN 0738-5323
ISBN 0-7879-5002-5

FIRST EDITION
HB Printing
10 9 8 7 6 5 4 3 2 1

CONTENTS

PREFACE

In an earlier annual issue of *The Minister's Manual*, I tried to show the variety of ways in which this volume has proven to be of help to different readers. Some of what I said then needs to be repeated.

Certain ministers find the prayers the most useful feature of the book. Congregations that have sat through the so-called "free" prayers of a pastor who prays the same prayer Sunday after Sunday, with only minor variations, will welcome these varied expressions of pastoral concern. The prayers in the *Manual* reflect a wide scope of interests, needs, and feelings. They express more of what a congregation actually experiences and are not limited to the pastor's understandably personal concerns. Through the centuries, priests, pastors, and rabbis have used the actual works of prayers composed by others, even with no changes, to voice the petitions of their people. Every hymn that a congregation sings is such a prayer. The best use of the prayers in this book, however, may be to let them teach us to broaden the scope of our own prayers and to improve the language in which we couch our petitions. Of course, some may wish to use certain prayers exactly as they stand.

Other ministers utilize the Scriptures in the Call to Worship and the Offertory Sentence. One outstanding minister customarily came on the radio each week with the same call to worship—"Behold, I stand at the door and knock . . ."—and that was cumulatively impressive in its own way. However, variety, such as the *Manual* offers, has its uses also.

Perhaps the sermons are the most useful feature of all, although preachers may be reluctant to admit it. Edgar Allen Poe once wrote that "most writers—poets in especial—prefer having it understood that they compose by a species of fine frenzy—an ecstatic intuition—and would positively shudder at letting the public take a peep behind the scenes." Even preachers as original as Frederick W. Robertson have often needed the flame of someone else's thought to light their own candles. Of the sermons of Robertson himself, Harry Emerson

Fosdick said, "We modern preachers still prime our pumps with his sermons, because they contain so much permanent suggestiveness." The conscientious preacher today can gain much help from the *Manual* and yet produce sermons that bear his or her own image and superscription. The fact that there are sermons for each Sunday of the year in this book is intended to suggest that they were deemed appropriate for the particular Sunday and season, not that they should constitute the preacher's complete worship program.

I am grateful to many individuals and publishers for quotations from their material, and it is hoped that the rights and wishes of no one have been overlooked.

Many contributors from many different denominational backgrounds have made this volume possible. They share our common faith and enrich our personal understanding and devotion. The Southern Baptist Theological Seminary, where I have taught since 1959, has provided valuable secretarial assistance in producing the manuscript. I wish to thank Linda Durkin and the several others who helped her in word-processing and preparing the manuscript. I wish to thank all of these people and the authors and publishers from whose works I have quoted. Again, I am deeply grateful.

James W. Cox
The Southern Baptist Theological Seminary

SECTION I

GENERAL AIDS AND RESOURCES

CIVIL YEAR CALENDARS FOR 2001 AND 2002

2001

January	February	March	April
S M T W T F S	S M T W T F S	S M T W T F S	S M T W T F S
1 2 3 4 5 6	1 2 3	1 2 3	1 2 3 4 5 6 7
7 8 9 10 11 12 13	4 5 6 7 8 9 10	4 5 6 7 8 9 10	8 9 10 11 12 13 14
14 15 16 17 18 19 20	11 12 13 14 15 16 17	11 12 13 14 15 16 17	15 16 17 18 19 20 21
21 22 23 24 25 26 27	18 19 20 21 22 23 24	18 19 20 21 22 23 24	22 23 24 25 26 27 28
28 29 30 31	25 26 27 28	25 26 27 28 29 30 31	29 30

May	June	July	August
S M T W T F S	S M T W T F S	S M T W T F S	S M T W T F S
1 2 3 4 5	1 2	1 2 3 4 5 6 7	1 2 3 4
6 7 8 9 10 11 12	3 4 5 6 7 8 9	8 9 10 11 12 13 14	5 6 7 8 9 10 11
13 14 15 16 17 18 19	10 11 12 13 14 15 16	15 16 17 18 19 20 21	12 13 14 15 16 17 18
20 21 22 23 24 25 26	17 18 19 20 21 22 23	22 23 24 25 26 27 28	19 20 21 22 23 24 25
27 28 29 30 31	24 25 26 27 28 29 30	29 30 31	26 27 28 29 30 31

September	October	November	December
S M T W T F S	S M T W T F S	S M T W T F S	S M T W T F S
1	1 2 3 4 5 6	1 2 3	1
2 3 4 5 6 7 8	7 8 9 10 11 12 13	4 5 6 7 8 9 10	2 3 4 5 6 7 8
9 10 11 12 13 14 15	14 15 16 17 18 19 20	11 12 13 14 15 16 17	9 10 11 12 13 14 15
16 17 18 19 20 21 22	21 22 23 24 25 26 27	18 19 20 21 22 23 24	16 17 18 19 20 21 22
23 24 25 26 27 28 29	28 29 30 31	25 26 27 28 29 30	23 24 25 26 27 28 29
30			30 31

2002

January	February	March	April
S M T W T F S	S M T W T F S	S M T W T F S	S M T W T F S
1 2 3 4 5	1 2	1 2	1 2 3 4 5 6
6 7 8 9 10 11 12	3 4 5 6 7 8 9	3 4 5 6 7 8 9	7 8 9 10 11 12 13
13 14 15 16 17 18 19	10 11 12 13 14 15 16	10 11 12 13 14 15 16	14 15 16 17 18 19 20
20 21 22 23 24 25 26	17 18 19 20 21 22 23	17 18 19 20 21 22 23	21 22 23 24 25 26 27
27 28 29 30 31	24 25 26 27 28	24 25 26 27 28 29 30	28 29 30
		31	

May	June	July	August
S M T W T F S	S M T W T F S	S M T W T F S	S M T W T F S
1 2 3 4	1	1 2 3 4 5 6	1 2 3
5 6 7 8 9 10 11	2 3 4 5 6 7 8	7 8 9 10 11 12 13	4 5 6 7 8 9 10
12 13 14 15 16 17 18	9 10 11 12 13 14 15	14 15 16 17 18 19 20	11 12 13 14 15 16 17
19 20 21 22 23 24 25	16 17 18 19 20 21 22	21 22 23 24 25 26 27	18 19 20 21 22 23 24
26 27 28 29 30 31	23 24 25 26 27 28 29	28 29 30 31	25 26 27 28 29 30 31
	30		

September	October	November	December
S M T W T F S	S M T W T F S	S M T W T F S	S M T W T F S
1 2 3 4 5 6 7	1 2 3 4 5	1 2	1 2 3 4 5 6 7
8 9 10 11 12 13 14	6 7 8 9 10 11 12	3 4 5 6 7 8 9	8 9 10 11 12 13 14
15 16 17 18 19 20 21	13 14 15 16 17 18 19	10 11 12 13 14 15 16	15 16 17 18 19 20 21
22 23 24 25 26 27 28	20 21 22 23 24 25 26	17 18 19 20 21 22 23	22 23 24 25 26 27 28
29 30	27 28 29 30 31	24 25 26 27 28 29 30	29 30 31

Church and Civic Calendar for 2001

January

1	New Year's Day
5	Twelfth Night
6	Epiphany
10	League of Nations and United Nations General Assembly Anniversaries
13	Baptism of the Lord
15	Martin Luther King, Jr. Day
17	St. Anthony's Day
25	Conversion of St. Paul

February

1	National Freedom Day
2	Presentation of Jesus in the Temple
11	Race Relations Sunday
12	Lincoln's Birthday
14	St. Valentine's Birthday
18–25	Brotherhood/Sisterhood Week
19	Presidents' Day
22	Washington's Birthday
24	St. Matthias, Apostle
27	Shrove Tuesday
28	Ash Wednesday

March

4	First Sunday in Lent
9	Purim
11	Second Sunday in Lent
17	St. Patrick's Day
18	Third Sunday in Lent
25	Fourth Sunday in Lent
	The Annunciation

April

1	Fifth Sunday in Lent
	Passion Sunday
8	Pesach
8–14	Holy Week
8	Palm Sunday
	Passion Sunday (alternate)
12	Maundy Tuesday

13	Good Friday
15	Easter
22	Law Sunday
25	St. Mark, Evangelist

May

1	May Day
	Law Day
	Loyalty Day
	St. Philip and St. James, Apostles
6–13	National Family Week
13	Mother's Day
24	Ascension Day
27	Memorial Sunday
28	Memorial Day (Observed)
29	Shavuot

June

3	Pentecost
10	Trinity Sunday
	Children's Sunday
11	St. Barnabas, Apostle
17	Father's Day
	Corpus Christi
24	The Nativity of St. John the Baptist
29	St. Peter and St. Paul, Apostles

July

1	Dominion Day (Canada)
	Independence Sunday
2	The Visitation (Alternate)
4	Independence Day
22	St. Mary Magdalene
25	St. James, the Elder, Apostle

August

6	Civic Holiday (Canada)
14	Atlantic Charter Day
15	Mary, Mother of Jesus
24	St. Bartholomew, Apostle
26	Women's Equality Day

September			11	Stewardship Day
2	Labor Sunday			Veterans Day
3	Labor Day			Armistice Day
18	Rosh Hashanah			Remembrance Day (Canada)
21	St. Matthew, Evangelist and Apostle		18	Bible Sunday Thanksgiving Sunday
27	Yom Kippur		22	Thanksgiving Day
29	St. Michael and All Angels		30	St. Andrew, Apostle

October			*December*	
2	Sukkot		2	First Sunday of Advent
7	World Communion Sunday		9	Second Sunday of Advent
8	Columbus Day Observed		10	Hanukkah
10	Columbus Day			Human Rights Day
18	St. Luke, Evangelist		15	Bill of Rights Day
21	Laity Sunday		16	Third Sunday of Advent
23	St. James, Brother of Jesus		23	Fourth Sunday of Advent
24	United Nations Day		25	Christmas
28	Reformation Sunday St. Simon and St. Jude, Apostles		26	St. Stephen, Deacon and Martyr Boxing Day (Canada)
31	National UNICEF Day Reformation Day		27	St. John, Evangelist and Apostle
			28	The Holy Innocents, Martyrs
November			31	New Year's Eve Watch Night
1	All Saints Day			
2	All Souls Day			

The Revised Common Lectionary for 2001

The following Scripture lessons are commended for use in public worship by various Protestant churches and the Roman Catholic Church and include first, second, and Gospel readings, and Psalms, according to cycle C from January 7 to November 25 and according to Cycle A from December 2 to December 30 (Copyright 1992 Consultation on Common Texts)

Epiphany Season

Jan. 7 (Epiphany Sunday): Isa. 60:1–6; Ps. 72:1–7, 10–14; Eph. 3:1–12; Matt. 2:1–12
Jan. 14: Isa. 62:1–5; Ps. 36:5–10; 1 Cor. 12:1–11; John 2:1–11
Jan. 21: Neh. 8:1–3, 5–6, 8–10; Ps. 19; 1 Cor. 12:12–31a; Luke 4:14–21
Jan. 28: Jer. 1:4–10; Ps. 71:1–6; 1 Cor. 13:1–13; Luke. 4:21–30
Feb. 4: Isa. 6:1–8 (9–13); Ps. 138; 1 Cor. 15:1–11; Luke 5:1–11
Feb. 11: Jer. 17:5–10; Ps. 1; 1 Cor. 15:12–20; Luke 6:17–26
Feb. 18: Gen. 45:3–11,15; Ps. 37:1–11, 39–40; 1 Cor. 15:35–38, 42–50; Luke 6:27–38
Feb. 25: Isa. 55:10–13; Ps. 92:1–4, 12–15; 1 Cor. 15:51–58; Luke 6:39–49

Lenten Season

Feb. 28 (Ash Wednesday): Joel 2:1–2, 12–17; Ps. 51:1–17; 2 Cor. 5:20b–6:10; Matt. 6:1–6, 16–21

Mar. 4: Deut. 26:1–11; Ps. 91:1–2, 9–16; Rom. 10:8b–13; Luke 4:1–13

Mar. 11: Gen. 15:1–12, 17–18; Ps. 27; Phil. 3:17–4:1; Luke 13:31–35

Mar. 18: Isa. 55:1–9; Ps. 63:1–8; 1 Cor. 10:1–13; Luke 13:1–9

Mar. 25: Josh. 5:9–12; Ps. 32; 2 Cor. 5:16–21; Luke 15:1–3, 11b–32

Apr. 1: Isa. 43:16–21; Ps. 126; Phil. 3:4b–14; John 12:1–8

Holy Week

Apr. 8 (Palm/Passion Sunday): Liturgy of the Palms—Luke 19:28–40; Ps. 118:1–2, 19–29; Liturgy of the Passion—Isa. 50:4–9a; Ps. 31:9–16; Phil. 2:5–11; Luke 22:14–23:56

Apr. 9 (Monday): Isa. 42:1–9; Ps. 36:5–11; Heb. 9:11–15; John 12:1–11

Apr. 10 (Tuesday): Isa. 49:1–7; Ps. 71:1–14; 1 Cor. 1:18–31; John 12:20–36

Apr. 11 (Wednesday): Isa. 50:4–9a; Ps. 70; Heb. 12:1–3; John 13:21–32

Apr. 12 (Holy Thursday): Exod. 12:1–4 (5–10), 11–14; Ps. 116:1–2, 12–19; 1 Cor. 11:23–26; John 13:1–7, 31b–35

Apr. 13 (Good Friday): Isa. 52–53:12; Ps. 22; Heb. 10:15–25; John 18:1–19:42

Apr. 14 (Holy Saturday): Job 14:1–14; Ps. 31:1–4, 15–16; 1 Pet. 4:1–8; Matt. 27:57–66

Apr. 14 (Easter Vigil): Gen. 1:1–2:4a; Ps. 136:1–9, 23–26; Gen. 7:1–5, 11–18; 8:6–18; 9:8–13; Ps. 46; Gen. 22:1–18; Ps. 16; Exod. 14:10–31; 15:20–21; Exod. 15:1b–13, 17–18 (resp.); Isa. 55:1–11; Isa. 12:2–6 (resp.); Bar. 3:9–15, 32; 4:4 (alt.); Prov. 8:1–8, 19–21; 9:4–6 (alt.); Ps. 19; Ezek. 36:24–28; Ps. 42–43; Ezek. 37:1–14; Ps. 143; Zeph. 3:14–20; Ps. 98; Rom. 6:3–11; Ps. 114; Luke 24:1–12

Apr. 15 (Easter): Isa. 65:17–25; Ps. 118:1–2, 14–24; Acts 10:34–43 or 1 Cor. 15:19–26; John 20:1–18

Apr. 22: Acts 5:27–32; Ps. 118:14–29; Rev. 1:4–8; John 20:19–31

Apr. 29: Acts 9:1–6 (7–20); Ps. 30; Rev. 5:11–14; John 21:1–19

May 6: Acts 9:36–43; Ps. 23; Rev. 7:9–17; John 10:22–30

May 13: Acts 11:1–18; Ps. 148; Rev. 21:1–6; John 13:31–35

May 20: Acts 16:9–15; Ps. 67; Rev. 21:10, 22–22:5; John 14:23–29

May 27: Acts 16:16–34; Ps. 97; Rev. 22:12–14, 16–17, 20–21; John 17:20–26

Season of Pentecost

June 3 (Pentecost): Acts 2:1–21 or Gen. 11:1–9; Ps. 104:24–34, 35b; Rom. 8:14–17; John 14:8–17 (25–27)

June 10 (Trinity): Prov. 8:1–4, 22–31; Ps. 8; Rom. 5:1–5; John 16:12–15

June 17: 1 Kings 21:1–10 (11–14), 15–21a; Ps. 5:1–8; Gal. 2:15–21; Luke 7:36–8:3

June 24: 1 Kings 19:1–4 (5–7), 8–15a; Ps. 42; Gal. 3:23–29; Luke 8:26–39

July 1: 2 Kings 2:1–2, 6–14; Ps. 72:1–2, 11–20; Gal. 5:1, 13–25; Luke 9:51–62

July 8: 2 Kings 5:1–14; Ps. 30; Gal. 6:(1–6) 7–16; Luke 10:1–11

July 15: Amos 7:7–17; Ps. 82; Col. 1:1–14; Luke 10:25–37

July 22: Amos 8:10–12; Ps. 52; Col. 1:15–28; Luke 10:38–42

July 29: Hos. 1:2–10; Ps. 85; Col. 2:6–15 (16–19); Luke 11:1–13

Aug. 5: Hos. 11:1–11; Ps. 107:1–9, 43; Col. 3:1–11; Luke 12:13–21

Aug. 12: Isa. 1:1, 10–20; Ps. 50:1–8, 22–23; Heb. 11:1–3, 8–16; Luke 12:32–40

Aug. 19: Isa. 5:1–7; Ps. 80:1–2, 8–19; Heb. 11:29–12:2; Luke 12:49–56

Aug. 26: Jer. 1:4–10; Ps. 71:1–6; Heb. 12:18–29; Luke 13:10–17

Sept. 2: Jer. 2:4–13; Ps. 81:1, 10–16; Heb. 13:1–8, 15–16; Luke 14:1, 7–14

Sept. 9: Jer. 18:1–11; Ps. 139:1–6, 13–18; Philem. 1–21; Luke 14:25–33

Sept. 16: Jer. 4:11–12, 22–28; Ps. 14; 1 Tim. 1:12–17; Luke 15:1–10

Sept. 23: Jer. 8:18–9:1; Ps. 79:1–9; 1 Tim. 2:1–7; Luke 16:1–13

Sept. 30: Jer. 32:1–3a; 6–15; Ps. 91:1–6, 14–16; 1 Tim. 6:6–19; Luke 16:19–31

Oct. 7: Lam. 1:1–6; Ps. 137; 2 Tim. 1:1–14; Luke 17:5–10

Oct. 14: Jer. 29:1, 4–7; Ps. 66:1–12; 2 Tim. 2:8–15; Luke 17:11–19

Oct. 21: Jer. 31:27–34; Pa. 119:97–104; 2 Tim. 3:14–4:5; Luke 18:1–8

Oct. 28: Joel 2:23–32; Ps. 65; 2 Tim. 4:6–8, 16–18; Luke 18:9–14

Nov. 4: Heb. 1:1–4; 2:1–4; Ps. 119:137–144; 2 Thess. 1:1–4, 11–12; Luke 19:1–10

Nov. 11: Hag. 2:1–9; Ps. 145:1–5, 17–21; 2 Thess. 2:1–5, 13–17; Luke 20:27–38

Nov. 18: Isa. 65:17–25; Isa. 12; 2 Thess. 3:6–13; Luke 21:5–19

Nov. 25: Jer. 23:1–6; Luke 1:68–79; Col. 1:11–20; Luke 23:33–43

Advent and Christmas Season

Dec. 2 (Advent): Isa. 2:1–5; Ps. 122; Rom. 13:1–14; Matt. 24:36–44

Dec. 9: Isa. 11:1–10; Ps. 72:1–7, 18–19; Rom. 15:4–13; Matt. 3:1–12

Dec. 16: Isa. 35:1–10; Luke 1:47–55; Jas. 5:7–10; Matt. 11:2–11

Dec. 23: Isa. 7:10–16; Ps. 80:1–7, 17–19; Rom. 1:1–7; Matt. 1:18–25

Dec. 25 (Christmas Day): Isa. 9:2–7; Ps. 96; Titus 2:11–14; Luke 2:1–14 (15–20) *or* Isa. 62:6–12; Ps. 97; Titus 3:47; Luke 2:(1–7), 8–20 *or* Isa. 52:7–10; Ps. 98; Heb. 1:1–4 (5–12); John 1:1–14

Dec. 30: Isa. 63:7–9; Ps. 148; Heb. 2:10–18; Matt. 2:13–23

Four-Year Church Calendar

	2001	2002	2003	2004
Ash Wednesday	February 28	February 13	March 5	February 25
Palm Sunday	April 8	March 24	April 13	April 4
Good Friday	April 13	March 29	April 18	April 9
Easter	April 15	March 31	April 20	April 11
Ascension Day	May 24	May 9	May 29	May 20
Pentecost	June 3	May 19	June 8	May 30
Trinity Sunday	June 10	May 26	June 15	June 6
Thanksgiving	November 22	November 28	November 27	November 25
Advent Sunday	December 2	December 1	November 30	November 28

Forty-Year Easter Calendar

2001 April 15	2011 April 24	2021 April 4	2031 April 13
2002 March 31	2012 April 8	2022 April 17	2032 March 28

2003 April 20	2013 March 31	2023 April 9	2033 April 17
2004 April 11	2014 April 20	2024 March 31	2034 April 9
2005 March 27	2015 April 5	2025 April 20	2035 March 25
2006 April 16	2016 March 27	2026 April 5	2036 April 13
2007 April 8	2017 April 16	2027 March 28	2037 April 5
2008 March 23	2018 April 1	2028 April 16	2038 April 25
2009 April 12	2019 April 21	2029 April 1	2039 April 10
2010 April 4	2020 April 12	2030 April 21	2040 April 1

Traditional Wedding Anniversary Identifications

1 Paper	7 Wool	13 Lace	35 Coral
2 Cotton	8 Bronze	14 Ivory	40 Ruby
3 Leather	9 Pottery	15 Crystal	45 Sapphire
4 Linen	10 Tin	20 China	50 Gold
5 Wood	11 Steel	25 Silver	55 Emerald
6 Iron	12 Silk	30 Pearl	60 Diamond

Colors Appropriate for Days and Seasons

White. Symbolizes purity, perfection, and joy and identifies festivals marking events in the life of Jesus, except Good Friday: Christmas, Epiphany, Easter, Eastertide, Ascension Day; also Trinity Sunday, All Saints' Day, weddings, funerals. Gold may also be used.

Red. Symbolizes the Holy Spirit, martyrdom, and the love of God: Good Friday, Pentecost, and Sundays following.

Violet. Symbolizes penitence: Advent, Lent.

Green. Symbolizes mission to the world, hope, regeneration, nurture, and growth: Epiphany season, Kingdomtide, Rural Life Sunday, Labor Sunday, Thanksgiving Sunday.

Blue. Advent, in some churches.

Flowers in Season Appropriate for Church Use

January: carnation or snowdrop	July: larkspur or water lily
February: violet or primrose	August: gladiolus poppy
March: jonquil or daffodil	September: aster or morning star
April: lily, sweet pea, or daisy	October: calendula or cosmos
May: lily of the valley or hawthorn	November: chrysanthemum
June: rose or honeysuckle	December: narcissus, holly, or poinsettia

Quotable Quotations

1. We can take a lot of physical and even mental pain when we know that it truly makes us a part of the life we live together in this world.—Henri J. M. Nouwen
2. The longest journey is the journey inward.—Dag Hammarskjöld
3. A religion that is small enough for our understanding would not be large enough for our needs.—Arthur Balfour

4. Sin is the turning towards ourselves, and making ourselves the center of our world.—Paul Tillich

5. It is very difficult to preach the gospel honestly. It means to preach the severity of God to the proud, and the mercy of God to the brokenhearted.—Reinhold Niebuhr

6. Never argue with a woman when she's tired—or rested.—H. C. Diefenbach

7. To believe only possibilities is not faith, but mere philosophy.—Sir Thomas Browne

8. The Samaritan helps without dragging in religious reasons.—Hans Küng

9. Action springs not from thought, but from a readiness for responsibility.—Dietrich Bonhoeffer

10. Each day is a little life.—Arthur Schopenhauer

11. Remorse is memory awake.—Emily Dickinson

12. Evil has no substance of its own, but is only the defect, excess, perversion, or corruption of that which has substance.—John Henry Newman

13. Punctuality is the thief of time.—Oscar Wilde

14. Many things are not believed because their current explanation is not believed. —Friedrich Nietzsche

15. A Christian man is the most free lord of all, and subject to none; a Christian man is the most dutiful servant of all, and subject to everyone.—Martin Luther, *Concerning Christian Liberty*

16. What this parish needs, what every parish needs, is a man who knows God at more than second hand.—Thomas Carlyle

17. We . . . have to say, on the basis of our present experience, that evil is really evil, really malevolent and deadly and also, on the basis of faith, that it will in the end be defeated and made to serve God's good purposes.—John Hick

18. Blessed are the young, for they shall inherit the national debt.—Herbert Hoover

19. Love is seeing butterflies inside caterpillars.—Peter Kreeft, *A Turn of the Clock*

20. Life is tons of discipline.—Robert Frost

21. The greatest use of life is to spend it for something that will outlast it.—William James

22. Life is the childhood of immortality.—Daniel A. Poling

23. Repentance may begin instantly, but reformation often requires a sphere of years. —Henry Ward Beecher

24. Experience is not what happens to a man. It is what a man does with what happens to him.—Aldous Huxley

25. The modern idol maker goes not to the forest but to the laboratory, and there with the help of scientific concepts molds the kind of god he will adore.—Fulton J. Sheen

26. Life is too short to be little.—Benjamin Disraeli

27. Community is grounded in God, who calls us together, and not in the attractiveness of people to each other.—Henri J. M. Nouwen

28. Castles in the air—they are so easy to take refuge in. And so easy to build as well.—Henrik Ibsen

29. A life spent making mistakes is not only more honorable but more useful than a life spent doing nothing.—George Bernard Shaw

30. Diligence is the mother of good luck.—Benjamin Franklin

31. If architects want to strengthen a decrepit arch, they *increase* the load upon it, for thereby the parts are joined more firmly together.—Viktor Frankl

32. Most people would succeed in small things if they were not troubled with great ambitions.—Henry Wadsworth Longfellow

33. Show me a sane man and I will cure him for you.—C. G. Jung

34. Even though God speaks to condemn me, it is the God of love who speaks. The only bad news would be that God ceases to speak to me.—Jacques Ellul

35. The sea is the universal sewer.—Jacques Cousteau

36. If my doctor told me I had only six months to live, I wouldn't brood. I'd type a little faster.—Isaac Asimov

37. When I pray, coincidences happen, and when I do not, they don't.—William Temple, Archbishop of Canterbury

38. Age is strictly a case of mind over matter. It you don't mind, it doesn't matter. —Jack Benny

39. Life is an adventure in forgiveness.—Norman Cousins

40. In connection with arson a distinction is made between setting fire to a house in the full knowledge of its being inhabited by many or being uninhabited. But candlemongering is like setting fire to a whole community and is not even regarded as a crime!—Søren Kirkegaard

41. Without soul, science is meaningless; for what need has a lump of flesh, if that is all we are, to discover electrons and classify the farthest stars?—David Seabury

42. God has promised forgiveness to your repentance, but He has not promised tomorrow to your procrastination.—St. Augustine

43. Good teaching is one-fourth preparation and three-fourths theatre.—Gail Godwin

44. One ought to pray for peace even to the last clod of earth thrown over his grave. —The Talmud

45. Love it is—not conscience—that is God's regent in the human soul, because it can govern the soul as nothing else can.—Henry Ward Beecher

46. All mankind is of one Author, and is one volume; when one Man dies, one chapter is not torn out of the book, but translated into a better language; and every chapter must be so translated.—John Donne

47. Take hold of Allah's ropes all together, and do not part in sects.—The Koran

48. The tragedy of life is not so much what men suffer, but rather what they miss. —Thomas Carlyle

49. The vanity of being known to be trusted with a secret is generally one of the chief motives to disclose it.—Samuel Johnson

50. It is easy to know God so long as you do not tax yourself with defining Him. —Joseph Joubert

51. We cannot know whether we love God, although there may be strong reasons for thinking so, but there can be no doubt about whether we love our neighbor or not.—St. Teresa

52. God can't fall in love for the same reason water can't get wet.—Peter Kreeft, *A Turn of the Clock*

Questions of Life and Religion

These questions may be useful to prime homiletic pumps, as discussion starters, or for study and youth groups.

1. Why do Christians worship?
2. Are good works an enemy of faith?
3. What do we mean by "the Word of God"?
4. In biblical history, what are some of the various roles of women in the service of God and humankind?
5. How can one achieve wholeness in personal life and in society?
6. Can wealth serve the purposes of God?
7. Does God call every Christian to a specific vocation?
8. How can we reconcile love of neighbor and the use of force in pursuit of justice?
9. Is lying ever justified?
10. Does the Trinity make sense?
11. What is the role of tradition in shaping Christian doctrine?
12. Can we reconcile evil in its various forms with the love of God?
13. Do the Ten Commandments apply today?
14. How does temptation happen to us?
15. How can we gain self-control?
16. What can we do to help individuals who are depressed and desperate?
17. Can God be glorified by human suffering?
18. How do we determine the proper stewardship of our possessions?
19. What is the meaning of the sovereignty of God?
20. Is it possible to live without sinning?
21. What is the positive place of sex in total human experience?
22. In what ways is secularism a threat to religious faith?
23. What does the inspiration of the Bible imply for its authority?
24. Is our salvation eternally secure in Christ?
25. How is the sacrifice of Christ an example for us?
26. In what ways has God revealed himself and his will to us?
27. Why is the Resurrection of Christ important to our faith?
28. How does repentance differ from remorse?
29. In what ways does the reign (kingdom) of God relate to Jesus?
30. Why is racism wrong?
31. How does the providence of God relate to the individual?
32. Which of God's promises are conditional and which are absolute?
33. What are the purposes of prayer?
34. What can we do to ease the plight of poverty?
35. Is politics essential to carrying out the responsibilities of Christian service?
36. Is peace possible?
37. Why is patience a valuable achievement?
38. Does obedience have to conflict with personal autonomy?
39. How does the New Testament use the word *mystery*?
40. Why does the Bible include miracles?
41. Who are the ministers in the Church Universal?

42. What is the importance of Mary in the Church?
43. What are the God-intended ingredients of marriage?
44. How can we define love?
45. How can we "know" God?
46. What justifies us in the eyes of God?
47. Can God's justice and mercy be reconciled?
48. How are joy and happiness different?
49. What steps can we take to normalize Jewish-Christian relations?
50. What was and is Jesus Christ?
51. In what sense is the Bible inspired?
52. What is the meaning of *incarnation?*
53. In what way or ways are we made in the image and likeness of God?

(These questions were suggested by and treated extensively in *Handbook of Themes for Preaching,* edited by James W. Cox, Westminster/John Knox Press, 1991.)

Biblical Benedictions and Blessings

The Lord watch between me and thee when we are absent from one another.—Gen. 31:49

The Lord our God be with us, as he was with our fathers; let him not leave us nor forsake us; that he may incline our hearts unto him, to walk in all his ways and to keep his commandments and his statutes and his judgments, which he commanded our fathers.—1 Kings 8:57–58

Let the words of my mouth and the meditation of my heart be acceptable in thy sight, O Lord, my strength and my redeemer.—Ps. 19:14.

Now the God of patience and consolation grant you to be like-minded one toward another according to Christ Jesus; that ye may with one mind and one mouth glorify God, even the Father of our Lord Jesus Christ. Now the God of hope fill you with all joy and peace in believing, that ye may abound in hope, through the power of the Holy Ghost. Now the God of peace be with you.—Rom. 15:5–6, 13, 33

Now to him that is of power to establish you according to my gospel and the teaching of Jesus Christ, according to the revelation of the mystery, which was kept secret since the world began but now is manifest, and by the Scriptures of the prophets, according to the commandments of the everlasting God, made known to all nations for the glory through Jesus Christ forever.—Rom. 16:25–27

Grace be unto you, and peace, from God our Father, and from the Lord Jesus Christ.—1 Cor. 1:3

The grace of the Lord Jesus Christ and the love of God and the communion of the Holy Ghost be with you all.—2 Cor. 13:14

Peace be to the brethren, and love with faith, from God the Father and the Lord Jesus Christ. Grace be with all them that love our Lord Jesus Christ in sincerity.—Eph. 6:23–24

And the peace of God, which passeth all understanding, shall keep your hearts and minds through Christ Jesus. Finally, brethren, whatsoever things are true, whatsoever things are honest, whatsoever things are just, whatsoever things are pure, whatsoever things are lovely, whatsoever things are of good report; if there be any virtue, and if there be any praise, think on these things. Those things which ye have both learned and received, and heard and seen in me, do; and the God of peace shall be with you.—Phil. 4:7–9

Wherefore also we pray always for you, that our God would count you worthy of this calling and fulfill all the good pleasure of this goodness, and the work of faith with power; that the name of our Lord Jesus Christ may be glorified in you, and ye in him, according to the grace of our God and the Lord Jesus Christ.—2 Thess. 1:11–12

Now the Lord of peace himself give you peace always by all means. The Lord be with you all. The grace of our Lord Jesus Christ be with you all.—2 Thess. 3:16–18

Grace, mercy, and peace, from God our Father and Jesus Christ our Lord.—1 Tim. 1:2

Now the God of peace, that brought again from the dead our Lord Jesus, that great shepherd of the sheep, through the blood of the everlasting covenant, make you perfect in every good work to do his will, working in you that which is well-pleasing in his sight, through Jesus Christ, to whom be glory for ever and ever.—Heb. 13:20–21

The God of all grace, who hath called us unto his eternal glory by Christ Jesus, after that ye have suffered a while, make you perfect, establish, strengthen, settle you. To him be glory and dominion for ever and ever. Greet ye one another with a kiss of charity. Peace be with you all that are in Christ Jesus.—1 Pet. 3:10–14

Grace be with you, mercy, and peace from God the Father, and from the Lord Jesus Christ, the Son of the Father, in truth and love.—2 John 3

Now unto him that is able to keep you from falling, and to present you faultless before the presence of his glory with exceeding joy, to the only wise God our Savior, be glory and majesty, dominion and power, both now and ever.—Jude 24:25

Grace be unto you, and peace, from him which was, and which is to come; and from the seven Spirits which are before his throne; and from Jesus Christ, who is the faithful witness, and the first begotten of the dead, and the prince of the kings of the earth. Unto him that loved us, and washed us from our sins in his own blood, and hath made us kings and priests unto God and his Father, to him be glory and dominion for ever and ever.—Rev. 1:4–6

SERMONS AND HOMILETIC AND WORSHIP AIDS
FOR FIFTY-TWO SUNDAYS

SUNDAY, JANUARY 7, 2001
Lectionary Message

Topic: The Story of the Future
Text: Luke 3:15–17, 21–22
Other Readings: Isa. 43:1–7; Acts 8:14–17

According to the mathematical purists among us, today is the first Sunday of the new millennium. They viewed the hoopla surrounding the anticipation of January 1, 2000, as misguided nonsense. Regardless of when the twenty-first century began, who can forget the anxiety and excitement that surrounded the change of numbers on the calendar from 1999 to 2000. For some, no doubt, the change of centuries has been exciting; for others it has been disastrous; and for others it has been a mixed bag of hopes fulfilled and disappointed. Do you remember what you did to prepare for the new century? Do you remember how you felt as you anticipated the millennial change in human history?

I. Today's Gospel lesson opens with a sense of anticipation and hope. For centuries the people of Israel had lived with a sense of God's absence. The major religious groups, rather than promising a direct encounter with God, counseled the people on how to be ready for the day when God would deliver the nation and restore the throne of David. It would not be a stretch to say that hunger for God's salvation and longing for the coming Messiah had reached a fever pitch. In addition to the Pharisees, who promoted ritual purity; the Saducees, who advised adherence to the Torah; the Essenes, who advocated complete separation from evil; and the Zealots, who believed they could force the hand of God by guerrilla warfare against Rome, hundreds of claimants to the title *Messiah* popped up throughout the land. With all the ferment, people could not help but believe that God would do something soon.

Into that context, John the Baptist came "proclaiming a baptism of repentance for the forgiveness of sin." His preaching attracted crowds of persons hungry for an encounter with the living God. His message seemed to offer hope. Even those whose expectations had been raised and dashed sensed something different in John's preaching. Luke records that John stirred in their hearts a heightened sense of urgent expectancy. Many began to wonder if this odd prophet might not be the Messiah in disguise. Intense anticipation often leads to unrealistic expectations and imaginations run wild.

II. Aware of speculations, John offers a warning. It is a strange warning. John seems to serve notice that his proclamation, his counsel, is tame in comparison to what they will hear and experience in the days to come. Look carefully at John's warning.

First, John informs his followers that, in comparison to the one who is coming, he is not even worthy to be a household slave who has the job of washing feet. To those who wanted to attach their hopes to John's wagon, he advises them not to follow a lesser guide.

Second, John admonishes his followers not to get comfortable in their view of the future. No doubt many of those who responded to John's preaching had experienced a dramatic change in their lives. Something had begun to be reborn in them. It was easy, at the beginning of their spiritual awakening, to assume that those initial experiences were the pattern for the rest of their lives. John knew better. He alerted his followers to brace themselves for even more dramatic changes. The one whose coming they anticipated would be guided by the wildly creative Spirit of the living God. In the wisdom and power of that Spirit he would gather the faithful and consume the unfaithful. The fate of the world would be in his hands.

A crucial mistake we make about the future revolves around the issue of control. Either we believe we can control the direction and circumstances of our lives, or we believe that fate or sinister forces beyond our control will determine our future. In the first instance, our sense of anticipation is informed by an enthusiasm about what we will do and accomplish to fulfill our vision for the future. In the second instance, our sense of anticipation feels more like dread, because we fear what "they" will do to us.

John's warning reminds us that neither we nor the malevolent forces in our world are in control of our future. God, through his anointed messenger, will direct and determine our future.

III. Luke ends this part of his Gospel with an announcement of fulfillment. Jesus' baptism is a major transition in Luke's Gospel. John had been sent to "prepare the way of the Lord." With power and God's blessing he had enflamed people's sense of hope and anticipation. But his role was not to bring the future but to point to it.

At the end of the Gospel passage today, Jesus comes to be baptized by John. After his baptism, Luke pictures Jesus in an attitude of prayer; when the heavens open, the Spirit descends like a dove and God speaks. With these words from God, Luke declares the fulfillment of what John proclaimed and the people anticipated. Unlike John, Jesus is not only God's anointed messenger, he is also God's Son. With the descent of the Spirit and the affirmation of divine sonship, the long-awaited return of God occurs. The hope of God's deliverance is now a reality.

At this point Luke throws us a curve. The story does not end. While the anticipation of God's presence and salvation is realized, Luke offers us not an ending but a new beginning. The implications of the fulfillment of the promise still need to be spelled out. Jesus signifies not the end of anticipation but a lifelong journey that revels in the anticipation of where God will lead us and in what he will do with us next.

Luke signals that the story of the future is not our story or the story of the malevolent forces that would destroy us. The future is the story of Jesus Christ, the beloved Son of God.—Jim Holladay

ILLUSTRATIONS

VICTORY OF TRUTH.   All the forces of evil and sin were pooled on that day of long ago to win a final victory over goodness and righteousness; and so they nailed upon a cross him who personified these virtues.

They nailed him on a cross and thought that they had won.

That love was lost and goodness dead and truth forever done.

But they forgot that this was God's world. God spoke! Christ arose! And the battle for truth was won!

Do you capture the significance of this truth this morning? It means that truth cannot be forever nailed to a scaffold. It means that love cannot be buried in a grave. It means that the goodness in your friend cannot be covered in a wooden box. It means that "though the cause of evil prosper, yet 'tis God alone stands." This was the faith that enabled those early Christians, and indeed Christians of all ages, to carry on because, regardless of discouragements, reverses, and temporary defeats, they knew that in the end theirs would be the victory, for they labored on the side of God.—Donald E. Lewis and G. Paul Butler[1]

HOPE.   Hope is one of the Theological virtues. This means that a continual looking forward to the eternal world is not (as some modern people think) a form of escapism or wishful thinking, but one of the things a Christian is meant to do. It does not mean that we are to leave the present world as it is. If you read history you will find that the Christians who did most for the present world were just those who thought most of the next. The Apostles themselves, who set on foot the conversion of the Roman Empire, the great men who built up the Middle Ages, the English Evangelicals who abolished the Slave Trade, all left their mark on Earth, precisely because their minds were occupied with Heaven. It is since Christians have largely ceased to think of the other world that they have become so ineffective in this. Aim at Heaven and you will get earth "thrown in": aim at earth and you will get neither.—C. S. Lewis[2]

SERMON SUGGESTIONS

Topic: Gratitude Expressed
TEXT: Eph. 5:20
(1) Its recipient: God the Father. (2) Its seasons: At all times. (3) Its scope: For everything. (4) Its means: In the name of our Lord Jesus Christ.

Topic: Something to Be Proud of
TEXT: Rom. 1:16–17
(1) It is good news. (2) It brings salvation. (3) It reveals the righteousness of God, as related to faith.

CONGREGATIONAL MUSIC

1. "How Firm a Foundation," "K" in Rippon's *Selection* (1787)

    FOUNDATION, Anon. American; Funk, *Genuine Church Music* (1832)

    Rippon's title for this strong hymn of faith adequately describes its basic message—"exceeding great and precious promises." The pentatonic melody with its basic tom-tom rhythm can appropriately be sung without instrumental accompaniment. The stanza begin-

[1] *Best Sermons* (New York: McGraw-Hill, 1955), p. 339.
[2] *Christian Behavior* (New York: Macmillan, 1944), p. 55.

ning "When through the deep waters," sometimes omitted, is a direct paraphrase of Isaiah 43:2, making it eminently suitable for use in connection with the Old Testament reading.

2. "When Jesus Came to Jordan," Fred Pratt Green (1973)

   COMPLAINER, *The Southern Harmony* (1835)

Appropriate to be sung either before or after the Gospel reading concerning the baptism of Jesus, this excellent contemporary text set to a Southern shape-note tune should be sung simply and in unison. For contrast, a stanza could be sung unaccompanied by choir or soloist.

3. "Sweet, Sweet Spirit," Doris Akers (1962)

   SWEET, SWEET SPIRIT, Doris Akers (1962)

This contemporary popular song affirms the presence of the Holy Spirit. It could be suited to use with either the New Testament reading from Acts (the Samaritans received the Holy Spirit through the ministries of Peter and John) or the reading from Luke (John the Baptist proclaims Jesus, who will baptize with the Holy Spirit).

4. "To God Be the Glory," Fanny J. Crosby (1885)

   TO GOD BE THE GLORY, William H. Doane (1875)

A gospel hymn that uncharacteristically ascribes glory to God, this song of praise by Fanny Crosby, the "queen of gospel song writers" could appropriately follow the Psalter reading for this day (Psalm 29).—Hugh T. McElrath

WORSHIP AIDS

CALL TO WORSHIP.   When thou passest through the waters, I *will* be with thee; and through the rivers, they shall not overflow thee; when thou walkest through the fire, thou shalt not be burned; neither shall the flame kindle upon thee.

For I *am* the Lord thy God, thy Holy One of Israel, thy savior (Isa. 43:2–3a).

INVOCATION.   Gracious Father, as we stand at the threshold of a new year, we confess our need of your presence and your help for the journey ahead. You have promised that you will never fail us or forsake us, so we put our trust in you, come what may. Through Jesus Christ our Lord.

OFFERTORY SENTENCE.   "And the king shall answer and say unto them, Verily I say unto you, inasmuch as ye have done it unto one of the least of these my brethren, ye have done it unto me" (Matt. 25:40).

OFFERTORY PRAYER.   Our heavenly Father, we bring to you some of the fruits of our labor that you have permitted us to do. Use these tithes and offerings for your honor and glory, whether to strengthen us who believe or to witness to those who do not yet know you or to meet any kind of real need suffered by any of your children. Help us to get a new vision of our partnership with you in what you are doing among us who gather here and in the wide world around us.

PRAYER.   O God, you have been our help in ages past and are our hope for years to come; this is the day you have made—we rejoice and are glad in it. We are glad for the opportunity of a new beginning, when the failures and hurts of yesterday can be erased, and with a fresh clean page we venture forward again in faith. You are a forgiving God and through the voice of Jesus each contrite heart can hear, "Your sins are removed, go now and sin no more." We know from the assurance of your Word that if we come to you believing, none of us will ever go away desolate or unheard. Especially do we face this New Year with brave expectancy for we know that through the saving name of Jesus all those who are possessed by him will themselves possess abundant life.

As we stand upon the threshold of another year, we pray you, our Father, to deepen and increase our faith. Call us into ever new endeavors and achievements and supply us richly with insight to make them useful for human needs and with vision for us to win through. May the focus of our faith tomorrow be the strong Son of God whose triumph over sin and death proved the finality and integrity of your goodness and power. Above all we ask for grace commensurate with the demands and struggles of the days and months ahead. By ourselves we would never get on in this bewildering world where the good is discredited and the wrong has usurped its throne. Establish now within us your dwelling and may your inner reign reflect from us an outward radiance that will encourage those who have lost their fire and nerve. Underwrite all our doings with your eternal hope and may we prevail because we believe even when we cannot see.—Donald Macleod[3]

SERMON
Topic: Under New Ownership
TEXT: Rom. 6:12–23

Paul was writing to insiders, people who already counted themselves part of the community of faith. They were, as the Book says, "God's beloved in Rome, who are called to be saints." Paul wasn't doing evangelism to the unconverted here—open-air preaching that's the equivalent of today's seeker-sensitive service. I am making a similar assumption about you who have come today—that most of you would identify yourselves as Christians. You've already claimed an allegiance to Jesus; you thought of yourselves as disciples before you came to worship this morning.

Our outward appearance isn't so different from most of our nonreligious neighbors. We're part of a tradition that doesn't call us to dress in a distinctive way or to eat only certain foods. It is only when someone gets closer, hears us speak, or watches the way we act that they know what policies direct us, who really owns us.

There are only two owners, says Paul in verse 22. One owner is sin and the other is God. True, we don't often identify the first owner by its proper title anymore. Instead, we use one of its subsidiary names, or appeal to its advertising slogans: Have it your way. A woman's right to choose. Different strokes for different folks. Don't ask, don't tell. Look out for number one. The end justifies the means. God along to get along. Everybody's doing it. We live in an age whose attitude is not unlike the one described in the book of Judges, when "every man did what was right in his own eyes." All these catchphrases are disguises worn by a powerful conglomerate whose CEO and ruling force is sin. They are marketing strategies for a company whose number one product is death.

The Bible teaches that in Jesus Christ we were set free from the ownership of sin. We're no longer bound to its policies or subject to its sales pitch. The man or woman who believes in Jesus is liberated from compulsory service to the life-killing, peace-robbing, inconsistent, and cruel dominion of sin. We are given a choice for the first time: a choice between being owned by the Lord of Life or by the powers of darkness.

Given this choice and this freedom, it must grieve the Spirit of God to see disciples of Jesus trying to serve two masters, or falling back into slavery to sin. The apostle Paul was nearly driven to despair, not simply be seeing others returning to their old owner but by experiencing his own struggles to overcome the guilt and power of sin. As he wrote in chapter 7, "For I do not do the good I want, but the evil I do not want is what I do. . . . I delight in the law of God, in my inmost self, but I see in my members another law at war . . . making me captive to the law of sin which dwells in my members." It isn't easy to hold fast to the new owner, even though a Christian has the choice.

I am reminded of a man I knew several years ago. His nickname was Tex, and as he was growing up on the Texas-Oklahoma border during the Great Depression, his family had only the poorest food to eat: lard spread on white bread, boiled greens with fatback—stuff that might keep you from starving, but no one's idea of a healthy diet. Tex grew to manhood, got married, and got a good job. He learned about nutrition, and now he had the means to choose what to put in his mouth. So he tried lean cuts of meat and fish, and sampled freely the fruits and vegetables available to him, but he didn't stick with it long enough to cultivate a taste for them. Pretty soon he was back to eating lard spread on white bread. Tex loved having a choice. He understood what was good for him, and he enjoyed seeing healthy, attractive bodies—but he didn't live out of his new freedom. And you can guess what happened. Tex died before his time—the victim of the consequences of slavery to his old appetites.

This man found that he couldn't combine the eating patterns of his old life with the nutritional diet available to him and remain healthy. Nor can we who claim to belong to Christ yield ourselves *even occasionally* to the ownership of sin and expect anything resembling spiritual wholeness. Paul speaks plainly about the danger of sin reigning in our mortal bodies, making us obey our bodies' passions. He perhaps knew that the sins we commit with and against our own bodies are those most likely to tempt a Christian back into slavery. You don't have to abuse alcohol every day to endanger others on the road: driving drunk just once can kill a child or wreck a future. A solitary sexual transgression can result in AIDS or a problem pregnancy. It takes only one lapse to destroy unbroken fidelity or rob you of the purity required by your rightful owner. A single instance of gossip by an unbridled tongue can ruin a reputation or break a heart or split a church. It was the peril of bondage to bodily sin that led John Donne to pray, "Wilt thou forgive that sin by which I've won others to sin and made my sin their door? Wilt thou forgive that sin which I did shun a year, or two, but wallowed in a score? When thou has done, that hast not done; for I have more." Or as the apostle Paul put it, "Wretched man that I am! Who will deliver me from this body of death?" (Rom. 7:24).

Who indeed but the new owner? Jesus, the one who in every respect has been tempted as we are but is without sin (Heb. 3:14), has broken the chains of sin and hell through his death and Resurrection. Christ, the rightful owner enthroned within us, is greater than he that is in the world (1 John 4:4). He cancels the power of the old owner to enslave and destroy. A neighbor once phoned our house, frantic because her washing machine was over-flowing and the kitchen was flooding. When my brother went over to see if he could help, he simply turned off the supply valve behind the machine and the water stopped. Was there still pressure in those pipes? Yes! But now it was contained. It would do no further damage. Jesus is the one who can bring a halt to the destructive force of sin that would otherwise overwhelm and drown us. And all we need to do is make the call.—Carol M. Noren

SUNDAY, JANUARY 14, 2001
Lectionary Message

Topic: When God Does the Unexpected

TEXT: John 2:1–11

Other Readings: Isa. 62:1–5; 1 Cor. 12:1–11

C. S. Lewis, British philosopher, theologian, and Christian apologist, married late in life. After only a few years he lost his wife, Joy, to cancer. Reflecting on his marriage, he wrote a brief but powerful book entitled *Surprised by Joy.* An account of the love and happiness his wife had brought to his life, it is also a parable of the way God surprises us with his presence, grace, and joy.

Throughout the Gospel of John, Jesus testifies to the unpredictable, surprising nature of God's love and grace—to the unexpected places and ways in which God breaks into and transforms ordinary events. The Gospel lesson for today speaks of the first of those moments in Jesus' life. John calls what happened at the wedding in Cana the "first of [Jesus'] signs." It was the first of what would be many occasions in which people would be surprised by the glory and grace of God.

I. By all accounts the wedding in Cana was not to be a place for God to reveal himself. In a matter-of-fact way, John records that Jesus and his disciples had been invited to a wedding. Although our current wedding ceremonies make much of Jesus' presence there, chances are that neither Jesus nor his disciples anticipated anything out of the ordinary. Most of them were from Galilee, where Cana is located. It would be safe to assume that Jesus, and perhaps a few of the disciples, knew one or both of the persons getting married. Jesus did not attend expecting to work a miracle or to be the center of attention. He and the disciples were simply guests at a wedding. Jesus had no intention of turning this family celebration into his coming-out party.

This attitude is evidenced by his response to his mother. Realizing that the family had miscalculated the amount of wine needed, she asked Jesus to help. His answer revealed his intention: "Mom, this is not our business, and besides, this is not the place nor the time to reveal who I am."

II. At this point in the story, surprising events began to unfold. Despite Jesus' gentle rebuke, his mother turned to the servants standing nearby and said, "Don't worry. He will help, just do whatever he tells you." Jesus could not have been clearer. The lack of planning on the host's part was not his concern; nor did helping in this situation fit his understanding of his mission. Yet Mary expressed a surprising confidence that Jesus would act. With no evidence that he intended to do anything, she directed the servants to follow Jesus' instructions. Where did she get that confidence? Certainly not from the immediate context.

For whatever reason, Jesus changed his mind and decided to get involved. He turned to the servants and told them to take the six stone jars used for a ceremonial rite of purification and fill them with water—nothing unusual so far. However, when the chief wine steward tasted the contents of the jars, it was not water he tasted but wine. Although John relates the events in an understated manner, surprises abounded.

The first surprise was actually a shocking development. By using the ceremonial pots to hold wine, Jesus participated in defiling them! He seemed to show an astonishing disregard for the ritual practice and sensitivities of the family and the community.

Raymond Brown, a noted expert on John's Gospel, calls this incident in Jesus' life a "story of replacement." By using these particular vessels, Jesus demonstrated that he intended to replace the barrenness of the Jewish purification ritual with the joy of God's saving presence. As a sign of God's Kingdom, Jesus demonstrated that the time of preparing for an encounter with God was over. It was now time to experience God directly through the Son.

Yet the surprises kept coming. When the chief steward tasted the wine he was amazed. His experience dictated that people serve the best wine first and the cheaper wine last. This, however, was among the best wines he had ever tasted. To bring it out toward the end of the party was an unbelievable act of generosity, or foolishness.

As astonishing as the miracle of water to wine may be, the real surprise is what Jesus communicated through the act. Throughout the prophetic writings, wine served as a symbol of the joy of the messianic age, a sign of transformation from old to new. The abundance and quality of wine Jesus provided on this occasion was a sign that the joy of God's salvation is both vast and unrivaled.

III. The enduring significance of this story goes far beyond the fact that by his attendance and miracle Jesus blessed marriage as an institution to be held in high esteem. For John, this was the first of many signs that revealed Jesus' glory and aroused belief. George Beasley-Murray defines a sign as a parable of the Kingdom. That being the case, this sign reminds us that without warning God often breaks into the ordinary events of life, transforming them into moments of insight into his glory and our place in his purposes. In those moments he gives us the opportunity to believe. May we be open to the signs of the Kingdom so that in surprising us with his joy God may claim us as his own.—Jim Holladay

ILLUSTRATIONS

NEW POSSIBILITIES.   When Emily Brontë was about eight years old, her clergyman father took her for a walk out across the moors from their little village of Haworth. He tried to tell her of the wonders of creation and growth and asked, "What is here which was not here a hundred years ago?" Emily answered, "Me." It was a good answer. God is always bringing new forces into His world and upsetting the old. Not for us the sad French proverb that the more it changes the more it is the same. Every new person is a new possibility for a new creative act of God.—Gerald Kennedy[4]

COMING TO FAITH.   I will not live long enough to see the unforeseeable changes and improvements that are bound to occur; but on one point about the future I may be excusably

---

[4] In G. Paul Butler (ed.), *Best Sermons*, Vol. 8 (New York: Van Nostrand Reinhold, 1962), p. 68.

blind. I do not foresee future progress in our scientific knowledge that will require any advances in philosophical theology. I feel secure in my rational affirmation of God's existence and of my understanding of the chasm between that philosophical conclusion and belief in God. I thank God for the leap of faith that enabled me to cross that chasm.—Mortimer J. Adler[5]

SERMON SUGGESTIONS

Topic: The Wisdom of God's Foolishness
TEXT: 1 Cor. 1:18–31
(1) Seen in the wisdom of the cross. (2) Seen in God's choice of people like us to receive and proclaim the message of the cross.

Topic: From Weakness to Strength
TEXT: 2 Cor. 12:1–10
(1) Paul's temptation: pride. (2) God's strange remedy: a thorn in the flesh. (3) Paul's frustration: unanswered prayer. (4) Christ's victory: through Christ's promise, power, persistence, and presence.

CONGREGATIONAL MUSIC

1. "Come to Us, Creative Spirit," David Mowbray (c. 1977)
   ANGEL VOICES, Edwin G. Monk (1861)
   Taking as its theme the multiplicity of gifts bestowed by the one creative Spirit, this contemporary hymn can suitably accompany the Epistle reading in which the apostle Paul teaches about differing spiritual gifts.
2. "Jesus, Come! For We Invite You," Christopher Idle (1979)
   SICILIAN MARINERS, Sicilian Melody (eighteenth century)
   This is a modern response to the incident recorded in the Gospel lesson (John 2:1–11). If sung with meaning and conviction, this hymn brings the worshipping singers into the drama of the miracle that Jesus performed at the wedding in Cana. The tune makes antiphonal singing between choir and congregation effective.
3. "Great Is Thy Faithfulness," Thomas O. Chisholm (1923)
   FAITHFULNESS, William M. Runyan (1923)
   The faithfulness of God proclaimed in Psalm 36:5 is echoed in this popular gospel hymn. The refrain could appropriately be used as an antiphon sung before and after the Psalter reading.
4. "O for a Heart to Praise My God," Charles Wesley (1742)
   RICHMOND, Thomas Haweis (1792)
   As a Christian response to Zion's new name that God bestows (Isa. 62:2), this great Wesleyan hymn could be sung. It calls for Christ to write a new name of love on the heart of the signer.—Hugh T. McElrath

---

[5] In Kelly James Clark (ed.), *Philosophers Who Believe* (Downers Grove, Ill.: InterVarsity Press, 1993), p. 221.

WORSHIP AIDS

CALL TO WORSHIP.   "How excellent is thy loving kindness, O God! Therefore the children of men put their trust under the shadow of thy wings" (Ps. 36:7).

INVOCATION.   In the midst of so many things that disturb us and that threaten our faith in you, O God, you continue to assure us of your love. So we find our security in you. Strengthen us today in our resolve to put our trust in you whatever may come.

OFFERTORY SENTENCE.   "They feast on the abundance of your house and you give them drink from the river of your delights" (Ps. 36:8 RSV).

OFFERTORY PRAYER.   Gracious Lord, you bless us far beyond all that we deserve. Grant that we may share our abundance in our stewardship of offerings for those causes dear to your heart.

PRAYER.   Guide us, O God, through the mysterious ways of life. Save us from thinking that we can storm the gates of life and pick for ourselves its fruit. Give us rather the tranquil spirit of waiting and watching, that we may go about our ways quietly so that when the great experiences of life come we may be ready to receive and enjoy them, through Jesus Christ our Lord.—Theodore Parker Ferris[6]

SERMON
Topic: Just Like Jesus
TEXT: John 11:32–46

Something in me is troubled by these reminders to consider how we may be "just like Jesus" and by the concomitant assumptions about the theological significance of the earthly Jesus. It isn't just evangelicals who are giving renewed attention to the Incarnate Messiah. Some mainline denominations place far greater emphasis on the life and teachings of the Jesus of history than on faith in the Risen Christ. The three years of Jesus' public ministry then become the model for the Church. Liberation theologians study the Scriptures to identify our Lord's solidarity with the oppressed, and they take their cues from Jesus' concrete acts in the first-century, seeing them as a paradigm for their mission today. Some feminist scholars struggle with the male particularity of the Incarnation and quote Julian of Norwich, among others, to find a gender balance in naming the sacred. All of these, in one way or another, are attempts to answer the questions, What would Jesus do? How are we or how can we be just like Jesus? and How is Jesus just like us?

Today's reading from the Gospel makes these hard questions to answer! John places this episode immediately before the triumphant entry into Jerusalem, the Passion, and the death of the earthly Jesus. We can approach the text from a number of angles—but ministers and laity who want to follow in his steps should be reluctant to emulate most of what Jesus did as recorded in this narrative.

---

[6] *Prayers*

Be just like Jesus: Disappoint the people who need you. Both Martha and Mary reproached him: "Lord, if you had been here, my brother would not have died."

Be just like Jesus: Speak in riddles so your congregation can't understand you. The apostles were mystified by his enigmatic statements before they reached Bethany. They didn't know what the Master was talking about.

Be just like Jesus: Go to pieces in moments of crisis. Jesus wept, and people standing by the tomb asked one another, "Couldn't he have done something?"

Be just like Jesus: Raise the dead.

These are clearly not satisfactory responses to the question, What would Jesus do? But there are other answers that I've heard pastors and laity give that are equally troubling.

Be just like Jesus: Be a good pastoral counselor. Notice how he lets Mary and Martha talk out their grief. He validates their experience and doesn't shame them. Active listening—that's what it's all about.

Be just like Jesus: Be someone who authentically owns their real feelings. Forget about professional distance and socially constructed hierarchies; let people see the genuine you, as he did. Share your pain.

Be just like Jesus: Trust God to act and exhort others to pray with expectation. These analogies may sound reasonable, even praiseworthy. They seem to identify common ground and experiences we share with the Son of God.

Yet we recognize that even if we put into practice these sample lessons drawn from John 11, we may wear our What Would Jesus Do? (WWJD) caps with pride but do violence to the text. Add these up—listening skills, genuineness, and the ability to pray in public and encourage faith in others—and you may have a partial job description for a pastoral search committee but only a pale imitation of Jesus as depicted in this narrative. You don't have the King of Glory, the Resurrection and the Life, the Alpha and the Omega. The theological significance of the earthly Jesus is more than slogans and simplistic thinking can apprehend. The truth is, we cannot be just like Jesus—neither in what he does nor in who he is.

If we forget the hard-won debates at the ecumenical councils of Nicaea, Constantinople, Ephesus, and Chaleedon, we can at least remind ourselves what the Gospel of John assumes about Jesus. In the prologue, the writer sets forth the mystery of the person of Jesus: fully God and fully human, the Word made flesh and dwelling among us. We cannot separate the two natures, human and divine, without distorting the truth. John records real events, such as the raising of Lazarus, and presents them as signs pointing to greater and eternal realities. And those realities, in our text, are beyond mortal imitation.

1. For starters, the text points to Jesus as the Resurrection and the Life. The itinerant rabbi says to Martha, "He who believes in me, though he die, yet shall he live, and whoever lives and believes in me shall never die." In Lazarus we are given a sign of Jesus' dominion over the powers of sin and death. Martha's confession of faith and trust in Jesus suggests the means by which humanity may attain the resurrection of the body and life everlasting through Jesus the Christ. As in Adam all die, in the one who calls forth Lazarus shall all be made alive (1 Cor. 15:22).

2. A second eternal reality about the earthly Jesus is found in Martha's confession of faith. She says to her friend Jesus, "Lord, I believe that you are the Christ, the Son of God, he who is coming into the world." Her confidence in his messianic identity is revealed earlier in the conversation, when she pauses in her lament to hint, "Even now I know that whatever you ask from God, God will give you." We may debate the nature of Martha's first-century Jewish

understanding of the promised Messiah. It is evident, however, that she and Mary attribute theological significance to Jesus that is not perceptible to the physical eye.

3. If we continue in the reading, we come to Jesus' promise to Martha and the others by the tomb: "Did I not tell you that if you would believe, you would see the glory of God?" Jesus, not Lazarus, is the one in whom God's glory is revealed. Poor Lazarus is shown wrapped up like a mummy, shuffling out of the cave, with people probably sniffing the air before they got too close to him. The mourners were challenged to believe not in Lazarus but in the one who raised him. Paradoxically, in an ordinary-looking rabbi on his way to arrest, trial, and execution, the magnificence and power and love of Almighty God are revealed. The prologue of John (1:14) asserts that "we have beheld his glory, glory as of the only Son from the Father," and Colossians 1:19 reminds us, "in him the fullness of God was pleased to dwell." It's there, but it requires the eyes of faith to see it.

The Resurrection and the Life, the Messiah, the Son of God, the one in whom the glory of the Father is revealed: these are only some of the divine realities about the earthly Jesus in this episode. They make any notion of being *just like Jesus* ridiculous, if not presumptuous. What would Jesus do? is not the thing to ask in this text or in the Church. What has Jesus done? is a better question. The answers are found as we read John's account of what happened at Bethany and in the days that remained in the life of the earthly Jesus. What Jesus has done is promise eternal life to all who believe in him. Jesus has revealed the glory and power of the Triune God. Jesus has initiated a new covenant, sealed in his body and blood. What Jesus has done is accomplish the work that the Father gave him to do (John 17:4). Jesus has given his life on the cross to "gather in the children of God who are scattered abroad" (John 11:52). Jesus has done all this—and we can't. So what *shall* we do?

Some of Jesus' words in this story suggest how we should respond. Twice he exhorts Martha to have faith. "Do you believe this?" "Did I not tell you that if you would believe you would see the glory of God?" Martha was challenged to trust the earthly Jesus she knew before her brother was raised, before the Crucifixion and Resurrection, before the end of the story was told. How much more should we, living on this side of the cross, believe in him as the Resurrection and the Life: our strength and our song, our salvation? (Isa. 12:2).

What shall we do in light of what Jesus has done? We can, in a manner of speaking, take away the stone as he commanded the mourners at Bethany. We can remove the barriers that keep those who are dead in their trespasses from hearing the voice of Jesus calling them to new life. We cannot be *just like Jesus,* but he graciously allows us to participate in his ongoing work of salvation. Our faith may not be such that moves mountains, but the people of God can nevertheless move the boulders of culture and custom, the stumbling stones of indifference or disdain, which we've routinely placed between a perishing world and the God who so loved it he gave his only begotten Son.

What shall we do in light of what Jesus has done? At the end of this passage, the Savior says, "Unbind him, and let him go." Lazarus, once fettered by a winding burial sheet, captive in a tomb, and bound by death, is freed for new life by Jesus. Once unbound, and let go by the marveling onlookers, surely his life would never be the same. The story says that Mary and many of the Jews who saw what Jesus had done believed in him. Liberated from bondage to sorrow and unbelief, they received the miracle as a sign of who Jesus is and what he will do. No longer wracked with grief, they're freed to look toward that day when God shall wipe away every tear and death shall be no more.

Beloved, we are God's children now, if we believe in Jesus the Christ. Living between the empty tomb and the new heaven and new earth, we have been freed for service to the great life-giver. Knowing him by faith rather than by sight, let us wait with joy for his return, confident that when he appears we shall be like him, *just like Jesus,* for we shall see him as he is (1 John 3:2). To the same Jesus, our Savior, our friend, our bridegroom, and our King, be glory now and forever. Amen.—Carol M. Noren

SUNDAY, JANUARY 21, 2001
Lectionary Message

Topic: The Ministry of Liberation
TEXT: Luke 4:14–21
Other Readings: Neh. 8:1–3, 5–6, 8–10; 1 Cor. 12:12–31a

Every four years a newly elected president of the United States stands before the American people to deliver his inaugural address. Typically he calls on us to rededicate ourselves to the principles, dreams, and spirit of the founders of this nation. We are challenged to stand with those who stand for freedom.

The inauguration of the president is an occasion filled with hope and new beginnings. We are inspired to look to the future, ready to accept the challenges and reap the rewards of our efforts. Inevitably we are disappointed. The man who challenges and inspires us will become all too human and the future will be a mixture of success and failure rather than steady progress toward utopia.

Today's Gospel text speaks of another inauguration address. Some of the themes sound familiar—freedom, a new spirit, preservation of human dignity, a new beginning, and so on. But the thrust is different. Rather than a new commitment to an old ideal, a new reality is offered. Rather than a dream awaiting consummation, we are told, the one who is speaking the hope is reality. In Jesus' inaugural address, the words of the prophet Isaiah serve as an outline for the life and mission of Jesus. This address is the thesis sentence for Jesus' ministry. Within it we can discern two things: the persons to whom Jesus is sent and the nature of his ministry to those persons.

I. Who are the persons to whom Jesus is sent? Luke calls them the poor, the captives, the blind, and the oppressed. Some say that Luke is using these terms in a spiritual sense. But to spiritualize the definition of the people to whom Christ is sent is not fair to the life and ministry of Jesus. The people listed here are not symbols. They are real people.

They are socially excluded. They are those who by circumstance of birth are not allowed to fit into the mainstream of society. In Jesus' day they were Gentiles, Samaritans, lepers, women, and tax collectors. In our day they are blacks, Native Americans, the handicapped, the elderly—all people who are not allowed a full role in society because they are not like us.

They are the religiously excluded. In Jesus' day they were the uncircumcised, the women (again), the Samaritans (again), the publicans, the sinners, and woman taken in adultery, whom the Pharisees would rather stone than redeem. In our day they include murderers, abusers, alcoholics, pornographers, and others we would rather condemn than redeem.

They are the economically excluded. In Jesus' day and in ours they are the poor—those who are dependent on others for support. We label them lazy, shiftless, and of no account.

Because of their economic plight they have no power, no influence, and no real place in society. They are easily discounted, dismissed, and defeated.

But what of those who do not fit easily into these categories? Where do we fit into Jesus' ministry? Martin Luther King Jr. reminded us that as long as there are poor people who feel the heel of oppression, and as long as we participate in or allow that oppression, we are not free. So we too are a part of those who need deliverance.

II. This leads to the second dimension of Jesus' inaugural address: the nature of Jesus' ministry. Freedom and liberation are two concepts that ring through this passage. The Isaiah passage is rooted in the Hebrew tradition of the Jubilee year. As spelled out in Leviticus, the tradition is a reminder that God wants people to be free.

The freedom that Jesus proclaimed in this address is built on two pillars. First and foremost is a relationship with God. The only way to overcome the brokenness of the human condition is by binding oneself to the one who overcomes the world. Freedom ultimately rests on a redemptive relationship with God. Freedom to live comes basically from committing one's life to the ultimately free one.

Second, personal freedom does not exist in a vacuum. The redemptive relationship with God includes being in a redemptive relationship with others. Throughout Scripture there is a strong sense of the togetherness of all persons. What one person does affects all persons. We cannot be free if others are not. We cannot be free if we do not join Jesus in attempting to free others.

III. So, in his inaugural address Jesus offers us freedom. He offers us the freedom to be God's children. He promises freedom from enslavement to sin, freedom from social pressures to conform to the world, and freedom from the power of institutional oppression. Only one who is open to God's Spirit can be free in this world.

But Jesus also makes it known that he will bring freedom to persons in society. He will liberate persons from the tyranny of discrimination, economic deprivation, and religious chauvinism. Those who hunger will be freed from want. Those who thirst will be given to drink. Those who are bound will be set free. God wants people to be free.

To make our freedom possible, God anointed Jesus Christ to be the proclaimer and bearer of liberation. Jesus was the freest person who ever lived. He seeks to free all persons. He seeks to establish a community of free persons who will carry out this mission and in whose midst freedom will be a reality.

As long as one person is not free, the work of God's liberation is unfinished. He has chosen us to join Christ in this ministry of liberation. How will we respond? Proclamation is more than words. Proclamation is incarnation.

We are Jesus' people. Our mission is to join Jesus in fulfilling the prophecy of Isaiah.—Jim Holladay

ILLUSTRATIONS

OUR DEEPEST LONGING.   Imagine a man invested with every form of human power that you can think of: the destructive power of a Hitler, the analytic power of a Freud, the creative power of a Shakespeare, the economic power of a J. Paul Getty, the moral and philanthropic power of a Schweitzer, and so on. Then try to imagine what he could do and what he could not do. He could conquer the world very likely, but could he satisfy the deepest longing of his own soul or your soul or mine? Could he satisfy the deepest longing of just one single human being out of all the millions that we can imagine him having conquered, and by "the deepest longing" I mean the longing for love, for deep peace, for meaning? I believe that he could not. This is something that no man has power to do either for himself or for anyone else. So in terms of what every man needs most crucially, all man's power is powerless because at its roots, of course, the deepest longing of the human soul is the longing for God, and this no man has the power to satisfy.—Frederick Buechner[7]

WHEN IS ONE FREE?   If we are free, it is because Christ loves us. If Jesus is free, even in temptation, it is because he loves his Father. If we live out the freedom which is given us, we are led to love the one who frees us. If we love our brother, it is because we are fully free in relation to every alienation. If we are free with this freedom that is given by Christ, we see in the other the neighbor who himself is also called to be free, and this can be so only in and by love. In Christ there is no freedom without love, for without love freedom would be incoherent and a turning back upon itself. How can we believe that self-admiration or self-centeredness is freedom when all that we have is enslavement to what is most immediate and alienating, our body, our opinions, our needs, and our passions?—Jacques Ellul[8]

SERMON SUGGESTIONS

Topic: A Mighty Standing with God
TEXT: Gal. 4:1-7

(1) It goes back to the coming of God's Son. (2) It means that we are God's adopted children. (3) It results in heartfelt experience of the Spirit of Christ.

Topic: Paul's Prayer for Us
TEXT: Eph. 3:14-21

(1) That we may find inner strength. (2) That Christ may dwell in us. (3) That we may know and be filled with the all-encompassing love of Christ.

CONGREGATIONAL MUSIC

1. "The Heavens Declare Thy Wisdom, Lord," Isaac Watts (1739)
   DUKE STREET, John Hatton (1793)
   Watts, the great liberator of English hymnody, uses the entire Psalm 19 with its dual emphasis on the glory of God's nature and the virtues of God's law to create this majestic hymn. Ideally it could be sung before any of the readings appointed for this Sunday because of its emphasis on the supreme significance of the Word of God.
2. "O for a Thousand Tongues to Sing," Charles Wesley (1739)
   AZMON, Carl G. Glaser (1828); arr. Lowell Mason (1839)
   This powerful hymn of praise is ideal as a response to the Gospel lesson in which Jesus reads from the prophecy of Isaiah in the Nazareth synagogue about the Spirit of the Lord which will bring good news, freedom, sight to the blind, and so on. Stanzas 3 and 4 especially speak of the prophetic passage Jesus reads and bring glad praise to Christ as its fulfillment.

---

[7] *The Magnificent Defeat* (New York: Seabury Press, 1966), p. 33.
[8] *The Ethics of Freedom* (Grand Rapids, Mich.: Eerdmans, 1976), p. 207.

3. "Like the Murmur of the Dove's Song," Carl P. Daw Jr. (1982)
   BRIDEGROM, Peter Cutts (1969)
   Especially in its second stanza, this contemporary hymn invoking the Holy Spirit relates to the Epistle reading (1 Cor. 12:12) about the members of the body of Christ. It could function appropriately as a sung invocation.
4. "Of All the Spirit's Gifts to Me," Fred Pratt Green (1979)
   THREEFOLD GIFTS, Austin C. Lovelace
   Nehemiah's exhortation to the Israelites not to grieve "for the joy of the Lord is thy strength" (Neh. 8:10b) is echoed in this modern hymn that could serve admirably as a closing act or benediction.—Hugh T. McElrath

WORSHIP AIDS

CALL TO WORSHIP.   "The heavens declare the glory of God; and the firmament sheweth his handywork" (Ps. 19:1).

INVOCATION.   O Lord, our God, we are saved by what we can see of your creation, to say nothing of what is beyond our sight and understanding. Grant to us today the faith and willingness to follow with faithfulness what your love revealed as our contribution to this purpose of it all.

OFFERTORY SENTENCE.   "And Moses spake unto all the congregation of the children of Israel, saying, This *is* the thing which the Lord commanded, saying, "Take ye from among you an offering unto the Lord: whosoever is of a willing heart, let him bring it, an offering of the Lord" (Exod. 35:4–5).

OFFERTORY PRAYER.   Gracious Lord, you have given to each of us something of eternal value to your Kingdom, even though this gift is of the earth and earthly. With such gifts grant to us open and loving hearts to share joyfully these blessings.

PRAYER.   Lord, teach us to pray. How do we pray for one another as we should? In the course of the day we hear of another's need but our knowledge of them is limited and we do not seem able to pray for them from the depths of our hearts. Lead us by your Spirit as we seek to become more adept in praying for others. Stir compassion within us that we may feel their anguish and pain. Ignite pity in our souls for them that we might be stirred to action on their behalf. Magnify love in our hearts that we might see all others in the light of the redeeming love of Christ. Remind us that praying is more than words, more than feelings; it is acting in Christ's name on behalf of another. Call us to you this morning and teach us to pray.

Lead us to commitment today, Father. Procrastinating drifters, we need that extra push to make lasting commitments to you, to Christ, to his Church, and to the work of the Church in the world. Take us beyond the thinking stage to the acting point and guide us that we may enter the gates of commitment with all our heart and soul. Give us the dogged faithfulness needed to follow our commitment to serve in your name with single-mindedness and determination, no matter what diversions may tempt us across the days ahead. Lead us this morning to lasting and faithful commitment.

Lead us out to service in Christ's name. Keep us faithful to the commitment we have made to the Church, to teaching, leading, and empowering. But inspire us to serve Christ beyond the doors of the gathered Church as we go out into the world, where need and lostness meet us everywhere. Wherever we go, make us aware of the call we have accepted to be servants of the Lord, for it is in his name that we pray.—Henry Fields

SERMON
Topic: Faith of a Child
TEXT: Matt. 19:13–22

Children have a unique perspective on God, a perspective that we could all use. You can see this clearly in the way they talk to him. On issues of doctrine and Scripture: "Dear God, I read the Bible. What does *begat* mean? Nobody will tell me." "How did you know you were God?" "Dear God, are you really invisible or is that just a trick?" "Dear God, I would like to know why all things you said are in red."

Or questions of a little less eternal significance: "Dear God, who draws the lines around the countries?" "Dear God, I am American, what are you?" There are always honest statements of life in general: "Thank you for the baby brother but what I prayed for is a puppy." "Why is Sunday school on Sunday? I thought that was supposed to be our day of rest." "Dear God, if we come back as something please don't let me be Jennifer Horton because I hate her."

And of course no one can give praise and thanks like a child: "I think the stapler is one of your greatest inventions." "Dear God, I don't ever feel alone since I found out about you." "Dear God, I don't think anybody could be a better God. Well, I just want you to know, I am not just saying that because you are God." "Dear God, I didn't think orange went with purple until I saw the sunset you made on Tuesday; that was *cool.*"

The simple questions are not difficult to ask, the honesty is not held back, and the admiration and worship pours from genuine hearts. Can this be said of us adults?

I. *Jesus rebukes the disciple* (vv. 13–14a). Jesus was very busy while he was here on Earth. Between teaching in the Temple and on the hillside, between the private time he had with his disciples explaining to them what was going to happen and his public ministry to the masses, he completely understood what it feels like to work seventy hours a week. Besides his general schedule, one should not overlook the healings of the demon-possessed, the lame, the leper, and the paralytic; his amazing display of power over the unquenchable powers of nature; his claim over the people of the world as his lost children; his strenuous traveling schedule (from town to town on foot); his intellectual and spiritual battles with the Pharisees, scribes, and Sadducees; and his condemnation of the moral decline of first-century Palestine. From the extremes of feeding five thousand hungry to giving living water to a neglected woman, we see that no opportunity was too big or too small for the careful attention of the Master. Such conviction and persistence caused his friends to worry about him. His slowing pace, his heavy eyes accented by their overbearing bags, and his blistered feet urged his disciples to prioritize his time and let only the important people approach. We can almost hear them agree as the children were carried to him for blessing, "The last thing Jesus needs is to be bothered by a bunch of whining, screaming, pinching, clawing, dirty-diapered, slobbering kids." Anyone could understand that. It is how we feel after a difficult day, let alone a difficult week or year. However, Jesus' indignant words of rebuke rang in the ears of the well-meaning disciples as he commanded that the children be brought forward.

Don't let the familiarity of this story take away from its amazing implications. Jesus wanted to be near the children. He loved them! Always! They were people needing his grace and forgiveness. They were the epitome of faith and hope. He ironically rebuked those protecting him and reached for those who "burdened" his already-busy schedule.

II. *Jesus reaches for the children* (vv. 14b–16). Why? the disciples wonder. Because their faith is to be modeled by all. How? By faith, perhaps even blind faith. Simple faith that hopes to learn more and develop into the type that is able to move mountains. Faith that is trusting enough to think that the God of creation wants us to sit in his lap. If you do not understand this type of faith, get involved in vacation Bible school or teach a Sunday school class. We have much to learn about how a Christian is to accept the Kingdom on Earth. This wide-eyed and open-hearted approach not only works with Jesus but is commanded by him. The confused disciples thought to themselves, "Everyone who has faith believes like a child. To believe in God is to exercise this. It is not as complex as he makes it out to be." However, Jesus' next move startled them even more, shaking the very foundation of their theology.

III. *Jesus rejects the offering of the rich young ruler* (vv. 17–22). The final character in this scene explains Jesus' actions to an even greater degree. Here is a rich man, young, strapping, and outwardly intelligent. He believes in God, he offers obedience to a point, he even displays his society's understanding of *blessed*. However, he chooses himself over Christ. His wealth and intelligence serve only to make him ignorant and poor. He walks away with all he desires and at the same time walks away with nothing. Compared to children, he has nothing to offer the Master because his faith has limits. Does ours?

Who are you? The rich young ruler whose faith went only so far? The overprotective disciples who thought they understood the Messiah's needs and wants more than anyone else? Or the children who just longed to be close to him? The child who knows the Lord always has time to talk, laugh, cry, and hear the confessions of a sincere heart. Our duty here on earth is filled with paradox. We gain wealth by giving all away, we become wise by buying into what the world calls foolish, we become strong by admitting our weakness, and we grow up by becoming more childlike (not childish) in our faith. Christians do need to grow up! We are immature and nonproductive. However, the road to maturity must come through faith. It was the child's faith in the father that brought the prodigal son home. Will our faith in the Father do the same?—Jeffrey Dale Brown

SUNDAY, JANUARY 28, 2001
Lectionary Message

Topic: Radical Inclusiveness
TEXT: Luke 4:21–30
Other Readings: Jer. 1:4–10; 1 Cor. 13:1–13

Today's Gospel lesson is actually the second half of Jesus' inaugural address. If last week was good news well received, then this week is good news not well received. In the first half of his inaugural sermon, Jesus addressed themes that would have been popular to the largely poor and devalued population of Nazareth. (Can anything good come out of Galilee?) He promised God's presence and deliverance. He spoke directly to their need. So far, what he had to say had been well received. After all, he proclaimed a God who was on their side.

In the middle of the sermon, something went awry. He offended their sensibilities, or should we say, their sensitivities.

I. *Everyone spoke well of Jesus.* Sermons in the synagogue took a bit different form than we are used to. Normally someone would be called to read a portion of Scripture and offer a brief commentary. He would then sit down and engage the worshippers in a dialogue about the Scripture and his commentary.

Luke records that on this occasion Jesus' friends and neighbors were impressed not only by his choice of Scripture but also by his commentary. They heard in his words the fulfillment of God's promise to deliver them from every oppression—physical, spiritual, and political. No wonder they were "amazed at the gracious words that came from his mouth."

At first blush, Jesus' message of love, freedom, grace, and inclusion is good news. Who could argue with a God who will heal diseases, free the oppressed, and bring love to the loveless? We all long to hear from God that we are loved and wanted. We are impressed when Jesus assures us that we are accepted "just as we are." The message of love, mercy, and healing is appealing. We are more than eager to respond to a gospel that promises us freedom.

II. *Jesus clarified himself.* No one was more aware of the human propensity to misunderstand God's will and ways than Jesus. As he listened to the dialogue in the synagogue that day, he realized that the worshippers had not understood the full impact of Isaiah's prophecy or Jesus' commentary on it. What Jesus did in response was jarring. Rather than demurely accepting their praise and adoration, he told them that their love would turn to hate and their adoration to disgust.

Then he moved to clarify the radical nature of his message of liberation by using the stories of Elijah and the widow of Sidon and of Elisha's healing of Naaman the Syrian. From a homiletical standpoint, one could criticize Jesus for bringing in an illustration from out of nowhere. On closer examination, however, it unequivocally suited his purpose. Jesus reminded his friends and neighbors that God's promise of salvation includes not only the people of Nazareth and Israel but all the peoples of the world who are beaten down, alienated, and enslaved. To push the envelope further, Jesus reminded the worshippers that in the cases of Elijah and Elisha, God had acted to preserve the lives of people who were enemies of Israel.

Make no mistake about it, Jesus wants to free us from all that oppresses us. He wants to forgive our sins and heal our brokenness. He will act to deliver those who suffer innocently at the hands of others. We are all invited to share in God's blessings. That is easy for us to accept and believe. The hard part is Jesus' insistence that our enemies are also included in God's liberating grace. The difficult, if not offensive, part of Jesus' message is that God intends to embrace those persons we find repugnant. The truly odious aspect of Jesus' declaration is the radical notion that God may work harder to save those outside our circle of respectability than he does to save those within it.

Mass murderers can be forgiven and set free. Impossible! Child molesters can be redeemed and restored. No way! Those who are twisted with hate and guile can be reconciled to God. Impractical! If God is in that business, we are not sure we want any part of it.

No wonder Jesus felt a need to clarify the radical nature of God's inclusive grace and mercy.

III. *Jesus' message was rejected.* Though Galileans had a reputation for being ignorant and unlettered, those who heard Jesus' clarification got the message loud and clear. Luke records that they "were filled with rage." No wonder. For years they had lived as a fringe element of God's people. Jesus had proclaimed their inclusion in God's redemptive plan. Now he was proclaiming that they would have to share their status with the Gentiles! This is not what they wanted to hear. It was more than they could bear. They not only rejected the message, but they also decided to get rid of the messenger.

The radical inclusiveness of God's grace and mercy is hard to swallow. If God would limit himself to healing and saving those with a measure of respectability, we would not have any trouble with Jesus' message. But God insists on reaching out to those who live far beyond the boundaries of acceptability.

We are not likely to resort to violence in our rejection of Jesus' message of radical inclusiveness. We either ignore it or look for loopholes. We hide behind a holy revulsion, asserting that some folks commit such reprehensible acts that they place themselves outside God's freeing grace. Or we develop theories of redemption that justify excluding persons based on God's choice to exclude them. That God would look far beyond our boundaries is hard for us to accept.

IV. *Jesus responded.* The last verse in the passage is troubling. Jesus would have no part in their narrowness of vision or spirit. Nor did he attempt to persuade them to think otherwise. Luke records that Jesus' response to the people's refusal to join him was to pass "through the midst of them and [go] on his way." Jesus will continue God's mission of radical inclusiveness. The only question left is, will we join him?—Jim Holladay

ILLUSTRATIONS

TOTAL LOVE.   Only Love, Charity, in its deep peacefulness and abiding joy, can embrace all human inconsistency and imperfection and see within it the stirring of the Perfect. But so God loves the world. Not its more spiritual inhabitants. Not its church wardens and sacristans and pious old ladies—but the world.—Evelyn Underhill[9]

THE BEST ARGUMENT.   "The people I have dealt with all my life," said Maud [Ballington Booth], "have needed the two great Commandments, and the knowledge that someone loves and cares for them, more than they have ever needed any of the intellectual arguments of theology."—Susan F. Welty[10]

SERMON SUGGESTIONS

Topic: A Model for Working Together
TEXT: Phil. 2:1–11
(1) The Son of God enjoyed the most exalted status with the Father. (2) The Son of God willingly emptied himself of his privileges and lived the humblest life in order to do the will and work of the Father. (3) The Son of God achieved glory for God the Father and indescribable significance for himself.

---

[9] *An Anthology of the Love of God*
[10] *Look Up and Hope: The Life of Maud Ballington Booth*

Topic: If You Belong to God

TEXT: Col. 3:12–17

(1) Practice the everyday human virtues (v. 12). (2) Do the uncommon thing when interpersonal problems occur (v. 13). (3) Go the unlimited way of love (v. 14). (4) Enjoy the peace of Christ in your heart (v. 15). (5) Share the special blessings you have received (vv. 16–17).

CONGREGATIONAL MUSIC

1. "Lord of All Hopefulness," Jan Struther (1931)

   SLANE, Trad. Irish Melody

   The hopeful note in the first verses of Psalm 71 is extended in this classic contemporary song. Its words of hope, strength, love, and peace portray God as the answer to all our needs throughout life. This is the burden of the Psalter lesson.

2. "Though I Speak with Bravest Fire," Hal Hopson (1972)

   GIFT OF LOVE, English melody, adapted by Hopson (1972)

   This modern paraphrase of parts of 1 Corinthians 13 could be sung following the Epistle reading. The final stanza becomes a simple prayer for the spirit of love to control our hearts.

3. "We Are Called to Be God's People," Thomas A. Jackson (1973)

   AUSTRIAN HYMN, Franz J. Haydn (1797)

   Following the reading of the call of Jeremiah (Jer. 1:4–10), the singing of this hymn that reminds us all that we are called would be appropriate.

4. "I Have Decided to Follow Jesus," Anonymous

   ASSAM, Garo Christians (India)

   This anonymous song could be sung in dramatic response and contrast to the scene of the rejection of Jesus and his message recorded in the Gospel lesson. It would be most effective if sung unaccompanied.—Hugh T. McElrath

WORSHIP AIDS

CALL TO WORSHIP.   "I will go in the strength of the Lord God: I will make mention of thy righteousness, even of thine only" (Ps. 71:16).

INVOCATION.   O God, our Creator and our Lord, you have granted to each of us this human life and the promise of eternal life. Let your praise fill our hearts today and forever.

OFFERTORY SENTENCE.   "Thou art worthy, O Lord, to receive glory and honor and power: for thou hast created all things, and for thy pleasure they are and were created" (Rev. 4:11).

OFFERTORY PRAYER.   All things are from you, O Lord, our Creator. We would glorify you; we would honor you; we would bow before your power. Yet humbly we would offer to you these gifts, the labor of our hands, and pray that thy would further glorify you in this world of your creation.

PRAYER.   O god, immortal and invisible, forgive the faltering faith of those whose dwelling is among the mortal and the seen. We have no sight for unseen things, and we may have missed thee at every turn. Every common bush may flame with fire, but we have no time to turn aside, and our hardened feet do not apprehend the holy ground. The heavens may declare thy glory, but our eyes are too earthbound to read their story of infinity and peace. Day unto day may utter speech, but our ears are deaf with inward strife, and we hearken not nor understand. We have brooded long on the pain and anguish of the world, but we can read no redemption in the cross to which humanity is nailed; we have looked into the faces of our fellows, but discern no divine impression there; we have found little to love in the brother whom we have seen, how can we hope to love the God whom we have not seen? And now the awful fear has crept upon us that we are blind.

O Lord, that we might receive our sight.—W. E. Orchard[11]

SERMON
Topic: Let There Be No Poor Among You
TEXT: Deut. 15:4–11

Here in Deuteronomy we see the last words of Moses to the Israelite people. In this second giving of the Law, something has changed from the first giving in Exodus. Yahweh has chosen to describe specific instances, reasoning, and personal motivation. The goal was and would always be the holiness of his people—a holiness that would be comparable to God's own holiness. The weight of this Deuteronomic discussion is seen clearly in its eighty New Testament uses and in the fact that Jesus quotes it more than any other book.

The subject at hand in this chapter is the care of the poor. The goal is that there would be no poor. The motivation was the remembrance of the Israelites' slavery in Egypt. "That is why I give you this command today." This is a passage in which God ordains the Sabbatical Year. He wants to have the financial and social playing field as level as it can be. God knows that money means power and that power corrupts. A choice must be made between the two masters—God and money.

I. *God wants a level playing field.* "There should be no poor among you." This is a simple statement. It is an excellent assessment of the way things should be. Are there poor among us? Of course there are. The promise of an ever-existing poor population is mentioned in this passage as well as in Jesus' words, "The poor you will always have." However, this passage gives direct commands concerning everyone's treatment of the poor. God is promising the people of Israel not only prosperity but also self-sufficiency. The blessing for obedience is specific: "You will lend to nations and borrow from none" (v. 6).

II. *God holds the prosperous responsible for keeping the playing field level.* Because of the prosperity that is promised to the nation in verse 6, God makes a strong statement about the treatment of the poor in the following verse. God commands the people of the land to avoid being two things: "hard-headed and tightfisted." This is one Israelite's expression of love for another, much like the love that has been shown to them by God. Needless to say, love for one's neighbor has tremendous social implications.[12] To an Israelite, a sign of God's presence is charity to those less fortunate than oneself. One of the last things that Moses wishes to convey is this: simply serve one another unselfishly.

---

[11] *The Temple*
[12] Walter Elwell, *Evangelical Commentary on the Bible* (Grand Rapids, Mich.: Baker, 1989), p. 120.

It is one thing to ask someone not to be greedy, but Yahweh takes it a step further in verse 8. He actually commands the people to be extremely generous and give liberally to the poor, "lending them whatever they need." In today's society we have two groups of people who do not work: the very poor and the very wealthy. We have both heard and spoken much about the lazy, multigeneration welfare system. Although this phenomenon cannot be denied, the greed of the wealthy is never acceptable to God. Some are poor because of laziness—a sin. Others are poor because of age, ill health, a death in the family, or abandonment. These are the salt of the earth with whom Jesus ate and drank. God will judge both laziness (we cheer) and greed (we cringe).

Verse 9 brings about an interesting twist. Imagine you are hearing this for the first time. If a modern-day prophet like Moses were to read this oracle to us and read the first part of verse 9, "Be careful not to harbor this wicked thought," we would immediately expect a warning to the poor not to take advantage of handouts. This is what I expected when I read this text for the first time in a while. What we get, however, is another warning to the rich not to be greedy. You want us to what? If someone asks for a loan a month before the seventh year, you want me to give it to them? This is unfair by society's standards, but considered just by God.

III. *If the field is unlevel, God will usually side with the poor.* As the wealthy cringe and grow red in the face, the words ring true, "Be holy as I am holy, remember you were a slave in Egypt." Then the Law begins to make sense: this is God wanting us to treat others with the same grace that he has shown to us. He who owned the cattle on a thousand hills gave liberally to his children. We must model this. The response of the crowd to Moses' command was untypically mild. There wasn't a riot, a stoning, or a hazing of Moses. Probably most people saw the message as irrelevant, perhaps because there were most likely no rich among them. They went to Egypt with little, they left with stolen goods, and they suffered their biggest droughts in the wilderness. Most wealth went into a golden calf. Yahweh knew, however, that things would change. Just as life is today, so it was back then: some would remain poor and others would find success in the Promised Land, but before they received their wealth God wanted them to put their priorities in order.

IV. *God will bless generosity.* Finally, God promises a blessing to those who give. He will bless you "in all your work and in everything you put your hand to." The secret to success is not in wealth but in obedience. The material concerns are the Lord's. We are not owners of his wealth; we are only stewards.

God says that there will always be poor people in the land, so the opportunity for ministry to them will always be there. We Christians today have some serious soul-searching to do. If we trust the Bible as our authority, then we as God's people should take the initiative to care for the poor instead of appointing the government to do it. Our actions, however, should be concerned not only with doing the right thing but also with being the right kind of people. We should be giving, loving, fair, and just. What kind of stewards are we?—Jeffrey Dale Brown

SUNDAY, FEBRUARY 4, 2001
Lectionary Message

Topic: Tell Me Again About the Resurrection
TEXT: 1 Cor. 15:1–11.
Other Readings: Isa. 6:1–8 (9–13); Ps. 138; Luke 5:1–11

Shortly after her father died, a close family friend requested, "Tell me again about the Resurrection." She had been going over the events surrounding the Resurrection of Jesus and was trying to relate them to what had happened to her father. We have all been there, or will be before we die. Our last enemy, death, drives us back to what is important. "Tell me again about the Resurrection."

The church at Corinth was also struggling with the events that surround death, and the apostle Paul wrote to them to remind them of what they already believed about the Resurrection. Their reminders are ours.

I. *We need to revisit the part that the Resurrection plays in our conversion.*

(a) *We have heard the good news and received it* (15:1). We became Christians because of it.

(b) *We have taken our stand on it* (15:1). This is what it means to be a Christian.

(c) *We are being saved if we hold firmly to the message of the Resurrection* (15:2). Salvation has three tenses: we were saved, we are being saved (emphasized here), and we will be saved.

(d) *If we turn back now or if the Resurrection is not true, it has all been in vain* (15:2). That is the difference the Resurrection makes.

II. *We need to revisit the Resurrection as the core of the gospel.*

(a) *It is of first importance* (15:3). Do not dwell on peripheral issues or pet themes. Only the core of the gospel is powerful enough to conquer the last enemy: death.

(b) *It begins with the cross.* "Christ died for our sins according to the Scriptures" (15:3). It was not enough that Christ died; he died for our sins. All the meaning of Calvary is distilled in those words.

(c) *It includes Christ's burial for three days* (15:4), the length of time that the ancients believed it took a body to begin to decompose. He did not swoon a few hours and then revive. He was dead.

(d) *It declares that Christ was raised on the third day according to the Scriptures* (15:4). Note that Paul does not say Christ raised himself from the dead. "He was raised," the Bible says, and it was God who raised him (Acts 2:32). Towering above the cross and the empty tomb is God, who is master over death.

(e) *It insists that all this happened according to the Scriptures* (15:3,4). It finally dawned on Paul that the whole Old Testament, with which he had been saturated as a rabbi, recorded God's movement through history toward the cross and empty tomb of the promised Messiah.

III. *We need to revisit the evidence of the Resurrection.*

(a) *The post-Resurrection appearances of Christ* (15:5–8). Paul does not include all of the appearances listed in the New Testament, but he does include a wide variety of appearances to different people at different times.

1. He appeared to Peter.

2. He appeared to the Twelve.

3. He appeared to more than five hundred brethren at one time, most of whom were still living when Paul wrote.

4. He appeared to James, the Lord's brother, who had originally rejected him as the Messiah but had now become a key leader in the Jerusalem Church.

5. He appeared to all the apostles, evidently a much larger group than the Twelve, who are usually remembered as the apostles and held a special commission to carry the good news.

6. After his Resurrection, Christ appeared to Paul on the road to Damascus and called him to be a chosen vessel to the Gentiles. Paul testified as to how this appearance had changed his life (Acts 9, 26).

We all need objective evidence that what we believe is not a private delusion. The wide variety of Christ's post-Resurrection appearances has given Christians that assurance for twenty centuries.

(b) *Testimonies of changed lives.* But there is another kind of evidence just as powerful as Jesus' post-Resurrection appearances—the testimony of changed lives. People may argue with us about our beliefs about Christ, but they cannot argue with how he has changed our lives. This change is still one of the most powerful testimonies to the Christian faith.

1. Paul gave a special name to everything he had had to say about the gospel. He called it God's gift of grace. We are what we are in Christ by God's grace (15:11).

2. Paul was an apostle by God's grace. He called himself less than the least of the apostles (his name means "little") because he had persecuted the Church and because he had been called later than the others. But he worked harder and produced more fruit than any of the others, and he attributed it all to the grace of God working through him. Everything was God's grace from beginning to end.

IV. *Conclusion.* It strengthens our faith to revisit the Resurrection of Christ. We follow him not only because of his sinless life, matchless teachings, and atoning death. We also follow him because he is the only religious leader in history with an empty grave. Little did Joseph of Arimathea know that the Lord was only going to borrow his tomb for three days. Someone ought to write on the grave of every Christian, "Borrowed only until he comes." God has promised to do for us what he did for Jesus, and he expects us to live like it.—Wayne E. Shaw

ILLUSTRATIONS

FAITH TO LIVE BY.   When the pressing times of life come and our coping capacities are not sufficient, where do we turn? Or when we need support with energy merely to make sense of life day by day, on whom do we call? The answer you would expect to hear from a Christian pulpit—especially on a Sunday morning—is "God." And most of us would want to give that answer, but are we really convinced that God is our strength? I think many of us have had evidence of God as strength in our lives, and we likely wish we could appropriate this reality more consistently. So how do we come to the point of living in such a way as to find our strength in the Lord? Well, coming to the point has something to do with the degree to which we believe that God can be our strength; this fact becomes a conclusion by which we live.—David Albert Farmer[1]

WHAT WE ARE.   This is our Gospel. For this is what Christianity essentially is—*a religion of Resurrection.* This is what every worshipping congregation is intended in the purpose of

---

[1] *Basic Bible Sermons on Hope* (Nashville, Tenn.: Broadman Press, 1991), p. 57.

God to be—a community of the Resurrection. This is the basic character of every act of public worship—a proclamation of the Resurrection. And this is what the Gospel offers to our dark and ruined chaos of a world, where men peering into the future are daunted by the well-nigh impossible task of creating order out of confusion and life out of death: the power of the Resurrection. "O rejoice that the Lord is arisen!"—James S. Stewart[2]

SERMON SUGGESTIONS

Topic: When a Person Goes to Church

TEXT: Isa. 6:1–8

That person (1) should see the holiness of God; (2) should see his own true nature; (3) should see the necessity and availability of cleansing; (4) should see God's will for his life; (5) should see his own level of commitment—Edward D. Johnson[3]

Topic: The Opening Chapter of a New Life

TEXT: Rom. 8:10–11

(1) As a Christian, I am addicted to a new hope (1 Cor. 16:15). (2) I am adopted into a new family (Matt. 12:49–50). (3) I am adorned with a new appearance (Isa. 61:10–11; Titus 2:10). (4) We adorn ourselves with Christly virtues and attitudes (1 Pet. 3:3).—Richard Bennett Sims[4]

CONGREGATIONAL MUSIC

1. "God Himself Is with Us," Gerhardt Tersteegen (1729)

    ARNSBERG, Joachin Neander (1680)

    The sense of awe and mystery attending the prophet Isaiah's experience of worship in the Temple (Isa. 6:1–8) is reflected in the mood of this venerable hymn of gathering. Singing it reverently as a call to worship would be effective.

2. "Sing Praise to God Who Reigns Above," Johann J. Schutz (1566)

    MIT FREUDNE ZART, Bohemian Brethren *Kirchengesange* (1566)

    The singing praise called for by the psalmist (Ps. 138) is echoed in this great seventeenth-century hymn of adoration and exaltation of God's glory. It would be suitable for the opening of corporate worship.

3. "This Is the Threefold Truth," Fred Pratt Green (1980)

    ACCLAMATIONS, Jack Shrader (1980)

    In impressive form this contemporary hymn acclaims the ancient refrain of Christian worship that is set forth by the apostle Paul in 1 Corinthians 15:1–11. The singing of it could either introduce or follow the reading of the Epistle lesson.

4. "Footsteps of Jesus," Mary B. C. Slade (1871)

    FOOTSTEPS, Asa B. Everett (1871)

    This gospel song reflects the spirit of the first disciples who forsook all and followed Jesus. Therefore it could appropriately accompany the Gospel reading for this day.—Hugh T. McElrath

---

[2] *A Faith to Proclaim* (London: Hodder and Stoughton, 1953), p. 110.
[3] *Award Winning Sermons*, Vol. 4
[4] *The Righteousness of God*

WORSHIP AIDS

CALL TO WORSHIP.   "The Lord will perfect that which concerneth me: thy mercy, O Lord, endureth for ever; forsake not the works of thine own hands" (Ps. 138:8).

INVOCATION.   Our Father, you have created each of us through the mysterious chain of events that has brought us to this day and this moment. Help us to see more clearly and believe more boldly that you came to work out your plan for our individual life and destiny.

OFFERTORY SENTENCE.   "Then said Jesus unto his disciples, 'If any man will come after me, let him deny himself, and take up his cross and follow me'" (Matt. 16:24).

PRAYER.   We know, O Lord, that this human life is full of problems and that we would avoid difficulty if we could. Yet you have challenged and called us to a life of service to you and to others that often requires added burdens but promises joys that make all difficulties and sacrifices worthwhile. In that spirit may we serve your Kingdom with our self-denying love and with our tithes and offerings.

SERMON
Topic: A Community of Refuge
TEXT: Eph. 2:13–22

William Keucher relates a news story that describes the situation of the Church in our world. In a small hospital in Kansas, the electrical power was interrupted and the elevator stopped between floors with passengers aboard. One of the passengers began to beat on the door and to shout at the people in the hallway above to do something quickly to get him out. Obviously following company policy, one of the employees attempted to calm the man until help could arrive. He shouted, "The hospital has a generator system to back up the power. The passengers need to be patient and try to remain calm. The maintenance man will soon have power restored to the building and the elevator will be opened." Then the anxious passenger shouted back, "But I am the maintenance man!"

I. *We live in a community of stress.* Sometimes we all feel trapped between floors with a box full of strangers with no way out. I sometimes see myself in the maintenance man. I am supposed to be "out there" saving the world, and I find myself caught up in the same frustrations and fears that possess everyone else. The elevator Church is supposed to be about the business of lifting people out of the basement of materialism into the higher reality of spiritual maturity, but the Church herself is sometimes trapped between floors, caught in a limbo of irrelevance. The problem of stress is not just a private, personal thing. If nothing else brings us together, our common anxieties will. "Physician, heal thyself!" always fits the mission and ministry of Christ in the hands of mere mortals. At best we are what Henri Nouwen calls "the wounded healer." God did not send the world a telegram from a safe distance with instructions on how to behave until the elevator is opened, nor did he send spiritual visions of life outside the elevator. God sent the Son into the middle of our conflict and crises to establish a community of refuge and peace. Thus the Church cannot sit at a safe distance from the anxieties and fears of the world, tossing platitudes at problems. We are citizens of this world, often trapped in the same elevator, always in need of the same salvation.

II. *The Church lives on the battle line.* Paul conceived of the Church as a community in which common hostilities familiar to the world are abolished. The apostle may have been influenced by the vision of Isaiah of a messianic age in which nature's predators and prey would coexist in perfect harmony. If the coming of the Messiah were the occasion for the wolf and the lamb to share a bed of straw, Christ brings Gentiles and Jews together as siblings in the family of God. Only Paul addressed historical experience rather than distant hope. The violent death of Jesus was a dominant reality in the Church of the first century. The irony of the cross is a violence that leads to peace. That violence was not without cause or without impact on the world. The cross was like dynamite in the culture wars of the world. The wall of hostility is abolished by the violence done to the Christ.

A war was raging in jungles far from our national borders. Parents and children were at odds with one another over the political climate that was sending our youth into battle. The prevalence of narcotic drugs on the streets and on the battlefield was so significant that the term *drug culture* emerged to capture the phenomenon. We were entering a global age, where everything we did or thought was connected to the rest of the acts and thoughts on the planet. One of the deacons commented that he wanted to find peace when he came to church. Conflict and criticism were constant in the rest of his life. He wanted to come to church to escape from it all. This was more of a cry for help than a shout of condemnation. Sometimes we just need a place of retreat.

Just as Christ entered our battlefield to bring peace. His Church is never more like Christ than when she takes residence on the boundary between the hostile powers of our world. I still hear the appeal of my friend and I share his desire for a community of peace. Churches do not always manifest that spirit of grace that so characterized the work of Christ. Some of us have a historical reputation for divisions and fragmentation that constantly raise into question our authenticity as the body of Christ. Before we can bring peace to the world, we must have peace within the body of Christ. The Church must live on the border. As the Church was the community of peace between Gentile and Jew, it must be a place of healing for torn families, labor and management, racial fragments, and political hatreds.

III. *The Church is a community of refuge.* In the vigilante justice of early Judaism, six "cities of refuge" were established to protect people who found themselves in the gray area of the Law. The rules required a family to seek revenge for the death of one of their own. The eye-for-an-eye system of justice tended to be too simple and sometimes the cause of terrible injustice. The difficulty was reflected in the kind of limbo defined as the cities of refuge. People who committed manslaughter by accident were not to be hunted down and executed like intentional murders. These refugees from vigilante justice were allowed to live in special cities that were to be sanctuaries protecting them from the families they had injured. In Christian history a similar role was played by the Church. *Sanctuary* was the protected environment of the church building. Bounty hunters, soldiers, and policemen were not allowed to violate the sacred place even if it harbored a known felon.

The Church is still a sanctuary, not as a tool to protect the evil of this world but as a community in which the hostility must cease. The people who come together in the name of Christ come together in a community of peace, the dwelling place of God. We are no longer fragments of society meeting in conflict. The Church forms and the new people of God are bound not by language, race, gender, culture, or nationality. This is the body of Christ bound together by the Spirit of God. The Church is to be a community of refuge from the warfare that is constantly waged in the world. Here the factions that divide us must be left at the door and abolished from our lives. Here we can come together in the healing atmosphere of peace, and out of the positive witness of peace that identifies Christ's body, the world will find the peace that passes understanding.—Larry Dipboye

SUNDAY, FEBRUARY 11, 2001
Lectionary Message
Topic: Tell Me Again About the Difference the Resurrection Makes
TEXT: 1 Cor. 15:12–20
Other Readings: Jer. 17:5–10; Ps. 1; Luke 6:17–26

As human beings, most of us have an incurable optimism about life beyond the grave. Unfortunately, like the Church at Corinth, many of our beliefs are neither biblical nor Christian. For example:

(a) Many believe in reincarnation. Borrowed from Eastern religions, the idea is that we keep coming back to Earth again and again in another life form determined by how well or poorly we live in this present life form.

(b) Others believe this life is all there is. Their philosophy is, "Eat, drink, and be merry, for tomorrow you may die."

(c) Like the Corinthians, some people believe in existence after death, but not in the bodily resurrection of believers. The Corinthians believed that they had been given special spiritual gifts (1 Cor. 12–14) and that as soon as they got rid of their inferior physical bodies they would arrive at perfection.

Any claim about the resurrection of the body was repulsive.

In our text the apostle Paul says, in effect, "Alright, if there is no resurrection, then Christ was not raised from the dead, and I want you to see the consequences."

For most of us, the question, What if Christ be not risen? is horrible. Why even bring it up? we argue. Of course we believe he rose from the dead. It is at the heart of our faith. You would just as well tell the sun not to rise or the tide not to come as try to barricade the tomb of Jesus! But in this passage Paul forces us to think through what the consequences would be if Christ had not been raised.

I. *The consequences for those of us who preach.*

(a) If Christ has not been raised, our preaching is useless (15:14). For me personally this would be a double tragedy. I have preached the gospel for nearly fifty years. If Jesus has not been raised, I have wasted all those years. Further, because I have taught preaching for a third of a century, I have prepared hundreds of preachers to preach the gospel, have mentored seventeen homiletics professors who are currently teaching, and through them have helped to educate many others to do something totally useless. Not only have I wasted my life, but I have taught others to waste theirs and to pass it on to hundreds more.

(b) But Paul does not stop there. He goes on to accuse us of being false witnesses (liars) about God if Christ has not been raised from the dead (15:15). Not only have we wasted our lives, but we have lied about God to all who have heard us.

II. *The consequences for those who believe the Resurrection gospel.*

(a) Our faith is futile (15:17). Why? If Christ's complete trust in God did not get him through death, what chance do we have when we have a faith that sometimes falters? If Christ has not been raised, our faith is futile!

(b) We are still in our sins (15:17). Why? Because if Christ did not rise from the dead, then death and evil have won and Christ went down in defeat, taking all that is good and righteous along with him. The promise of remission of sins and the gift of the Holy Spirit at our repentance and baptism (Acts 2:38) is just wishful thinking and fantasy. If his sinlessness did not carry him through the grave, what chance do we poor sinners have?

(c) Then those who have fallen asleep in Christ are lost (15:18). If there is no resurrection and if Christ has not been raised as the gospel claims, then all those who have died trusting in Christ for eternal life have perished. They are gone forever. We can dream and fantasize all we please, but if the bones of Jesus are still in his grave, our bones and the bones of our loved ones will stay in our graves. The dead are lost forever.

If Christ has not been raised, the consequences are horrible. Paul concludes with these words: "If only in this life we have hope in Christ, we are to be pitied more than all men" (15:19).

Many of us would be shocked if someone suggested that we do not believe in the Resurrection, but when we live mainly for this life and thus treat our faith in the Resurrection casually, Paul warns us what is at stake.

III. *Then comes his ringing affirmation: "But Christ has indeed been raised from the dead, the first fruits of those who have fallen asleep" (15:20).*

(a) First fruits were associated with the Passover. The first barley was brought to the Temple to be offered to the Lord; only then could the barley harvest be gathered and processed.

(b) The order of the resurrection is clear: first Christ was raised; we will follow later. He is the first fruits of the harvest to follow.

IV. *Conclusion: Paul's conclusion is ours.* If you share this hope through the Resurrection, then stand firm. "Let nothing move you. Always give yourselves fully to the work of the Lord, because you know that your labor in the Lord is not in vain" (15:58).—Wayne E. Shaw

ILLUSTRATIONS

INTERNALIZED RELIGION.   I once heard Dr. Wayne Oates use the story of Pinocchio to illustrate this process. As you may remember, Pinocchio was a wooden marionette who came to life but who at first did not have his own conscience. Little Jiminy Cricket tried to function in that role, telling Pinocchio what to do and what not to do, but the only problem was that Pinocchio would get away from him and into trouble. "If I could only get inside of him," Jiminy Cricket would say, "then I could be with him all the time and help him." Dr. Oates pointed out that this is the goal of personal maturing; concepts of right or wrong, which are at first external to us through our parents and society, should become internalized so that we want to do what is right on our own.—John Claypool[5]

RESURRECTION.   The findings of the Society for Psychical Research bring double dismay: that loved ones should visit us through mediums previously unknown to them and us seems an outrage on love's intimacies; and furthermore, the heaven described is not heaven but

---

[5] *Glad Reunion* (Waco, Tex.: Word Books, 1985), p. 147.

only a drearier extension of this earth with a drearier chitchat and even less consequential doings. Resurrection is precisely *not* the "wages of going on," but the lifting of personal life into a new dimension of light and power. It is resurrection. It is the harvest field, not the continuance of seed in the bin.—George A Buttrick[6]

SERMON SUGGESTIONS

Topic: No Continuing City

TEXT: Heb. 13:14

What should be our relation to this world as we pass through it? Three possible attitudes: (1) We may become absorbed in it. (2) We may renounce it. (3) We may use it: (a) This world can never satisfy the deepest needs of our spirits. (b) Our ideals can never be fully realized in this world. (c) The nature of human personality requires another world. (d) Our communion with God in this world only does not satisfy.—Leslie J. Tizard[7]

Topic: Why Be a Christian?

TEXT: Deut. 33:29

(1) The Christian life is happier than any other. (2) The life in Christ is harder than any other. (3) The Christian life is holier than any other. (4) The Christian life is more hopeful than any other.—James S. Stewart[8]

CONGREGATIONAL MUSIC

1. "How Blest Are Those Who Fear God," Psalter (1912)

   ST. ANNE, William Croft (1708)

   This paraphrase of the first Psalm could readily replace the Psalter reading for this day. Any common-meter (86.86) metrical psalm tune could be substituted for ST. ANNE if desired. An unfamiliar tune could be "lined out," following older methods of psalm singing.

2. "This Joyful Eastertide," George R. Woodward (1902)

   VRUECHTEN, *Psalmen* (1685); harm. Charles Wood

   Though primarily an Easter carol, the truth of Woodward's refrain precisely reflects the teaching of the apostle Paul in 1 Corinthians 15:12–20 and thus is ideal to accompany its reading. The vibrant refrain could be sung as an antiphon, alternating with every verse or two of the Epistle reading.

3. "Search Me, O God," J. Edwin Orr (1936)

   ELLERS, Edward J. Hopkins (1869)

   This gospel hymn would be an appropriate response to the Old Testament reading in Jeremiah in which the prophet asserts that the Lord searches hearts (Jer. 17:5–10) and rewards humankind according to conduct and deeds.

4. "How Blest the Poor That Love the Lord," Mollie Knight (twentieth century)

   WAREHAM, William Knapp (1738)

---

[6] *Sermons Preached in a University Church* (Nashville, Tenn.: Abingdon Press, 1959), p. 189.

[7] *Facing Life and Death*

[8] *The Gates of New Life*

A modern paraphrase of the Beatitudes recorded in Matthew 5, this hymn nevertheless captures the spirit of some of the sayings of Jesus found in Luke 6:17–26 and could well be used with the Gospel lesson.—Hugh T. McElrath

WORSHIP AIDS

CALL TO WORSHIP.   "Blessed is the man that walketh not in the counsel of the ungodly, nor standeth in the way of sinners, nor sitteth in the seat of the scornful. But his delight is in the law of the Lord; and on his law doth he mediate day and night" (Ps. 1:1–2).

INVOCATION.   O God, by your help we will refuse to live by the destructive advice of those who have no regard for you. Let our worship today brighten the path of truth and make your Word to us clear and unmistakable.

OFFERTORY SENTENCE.   "As ye have therefore received Christ Jesus the Lord, so walk ye in him: Rooted and built up in him and established in the faith, as ye have been taught, abounding therein with thanksgiving" (Col. 2:6–7).

OFFERTORY PRAYER.   Because of all that you have done for us, gracious Lord, our gratitude follows in the way we live and the way we give. Now we have another opportunity to thank you. Bless what we bring of the work of our hearts and hands that our gratitude may overflow.

PRAYER.   God of forgiveness, we bow before you this morning. Not one of us can stand and declare that we are without sin and need no forgiveness. All have indeed sinned and fallen short of your purpose, the fulfillment of your glory through us. We have hated. We have cheated. We have told and lived the lie. We have thought evil about another. We have ignored calls for assistance that we could have given. Truly, we have in multitudes of ways created problems and pain, intentional and unintentional. We are ever in need of forgiveness and we cannot create it ourselves. We can only come to the author of forgiveness pleading that its power will meet us where we are, cleanse our hearts and souls, and send us away renewed for better life along the journey of faith. How could we but bow before the God of forgiveness and restoration?

God of inward strength, we come to you this morning. Inner weakness so many times is the culprit causing outward wrongs to be done by us. We need the renewing of the inner person, the acquiring of a brave spirit, the power of Godlike courage so that your strength will find its outlet to the world through us. This morning we ask for the indwelling power of your Spirit so that strength from beyond ourselves may flow into us and make us truly useable in doing truth and right in all of the circumstances we meet. In a world needing high moral, ethical, and spiritual strength, how could we not come to you, the giver of such strength?

God of Christ, we worship you this morning. Gratitude fills our hearts when we recall all that Christ has done for the world and for us. To enumerate the blessings we enjoy because of his coming to Earth would be more than we could do in many lifetimes. All we can do is express in words and deeds and lifestyles the gratitude we have for him who is indeed Lord of Life.

So we are here in your presence this morning, seeking to offer praise, adoration, and worship fit for your glory. Pray, Father, take our time before you and give us the blessing you want us to have, even as we renew our commitments to follow him whom you gave to save the world and all of us.—Henry Fields

SERMON
Topic: Happiness Is . . .
TEXT: Luke 6:17–26

A few years ago, people were easing around town to a reggae tune that told us, "Don't worry, be happy." The song suggested that life is too complicated and that things will be much better if we slow down and enjoy things more, preferably in the Carribean. "Hey, 'mon,' take it easy—be happy!" But it is interesting to note that most people have a very poor idea of what it means to be happy. If you ask a person the question, What does it take to make you happy? the answer you will probably get will have a lot to do with things that bring security: enough money, a roof over one's head, a job, perhaps insurance. Some might add a few less tangible things like fulfillment or accomplishment, but in general our ideas of happiness are just about as vague as the reggae song. We're happy when we don't have to worry. But is there anything else? Is there anything more to life?

When Jesus addresses the crowds in today's Gospel story, he gives them a series of propositions, each of them beginning with "Blessed are you who . . ." and then adds a description: "You who are poor," "You who are hungry," "You who weep now." These sayings are sometimes called the Beatitudes, from the Latin word that begins each of the things Jesus talks about. But "blessed" has a kind of technical, religious sound to it. We seldom tell someone that they're blessed unless we're saying that God has done something very special: "You've been blessed with a new baby."

But Jesus wasn't using a technical, religious word when he spoke to the people. The Greek word that is used to translate what Jesus said about all these kinds of blessed people is *makarios* (ma-KAH-ree-os), which means "happy." But the things that Jesus is talking about are not the kind of things we usually think about when we use the word *happy:* the poor, the hungry, those who weep, people who are hated and excluded. These things are pretty guaranteed to make people *unhappy!* Yet Jesus calls these people happy. What is he talking about, and what in fact does *happy* mean?

Rather than go into the fine points of each of the statements of the Beatitudes, I would like to state the obvious about Jesus' words: each of these types of people *lacks* something. The poor have little or no money, the hungry have no food, those who weep have lost their joy, and those who are persecuted have no peace. What can possibly be happy about not having all these things? Well, one answer is that those who have nothing have nothing to lose, and that means they have everything to gain. It also means they are not burdened with the problems and preoccupations of those who are weighed down with things. Over and over in the Bible Jesus says that those who are rich are really in the worst shape because they are so concerned with hanging on to what they have that they don't give any thought to the really important things, like the relationship we have with God, with our families, and with one another. Being poor does not in itself bring happiness, of course. Not having enough to eat or shelter or security can be as debilitating as a disease and can keep a person from being the fully functional child of God that each of us is called to be. Being concerned for the really poor is part of our Christian responsibility, and Jesus makes that very clear in the Bible, too.

But for most of us, the concern is not to escape poverty but to get more of what we already have—more *things* to own—and this can easily stand in the way of giving time and energy to the really important things. Most people, *most* people, think that if they only had a lot of money, or even just a bit more money, they would be generous and benevolent and give money to all kinds of people and charities, but it doesn't usually work that way. While some rich people *do* give generously to charity, many others are far more concerned about hanging on to what they have. Their souls become very closed and hard and the words of Jesus about priorities and relationships sound distant and irrelevant. Jesus' image was that it is easier for a camel to go through the eye of a needle than for a rich person to enter the Kingdom of God, and I think that for the sake of understanding what Jesus means, all of us here might be considered rich, because we all have our priorities in the wrong place most of the time.

When Jesus tells us to be happy under these circumstances, he is not telling us that we have nothing to worry about in this life. God knows very well that life can be hard, dangerous, painful—in short, unhappy. But if we simplify our lives to emphasize what is important, Jesus is saying, we have a greater likelihood of getting things straight—of finding our priorities and setting goals of *quality,* not *quantity.* The happiness that Jesus promises is not the passive kind that sees fulfillment as a lazy life under a palm tree. It is instead a life that has purpose and that is important. Happiness, *blessedness,* is therefore more than a *lack of care;* it is the *overcoming of care by trust and resolve.*

There is an interesting phrase in today's Gospel story that I never picked up on before. The Gospel is about the Sermon on the Mount, but in this version it is Jesus who looks *up* to his disciples as he teaches them. It is almost as if he is saying, "You lucky, lucky people. You have so little, yet you have the potential, the possibility, of being the richest people on Earth—people rich in the things that matter—rich in faith, rich in courage, rich in love. You are the ones who are blessed. You are the ones who are truly happy, because you will recognize the true happiness I have come to give you when it comes." Simplicity is not just something for peasants in first-century Palestine: it is something for all of us, and right now.

Are you truly happy? And if not, why not? Is it perhaps because you haven't gotten your priorities quite right? And what do you think God wants you to do about it? It's all right to worry a little about that, because it just might lead to decisions that will make you happier than you've ever been before.—Tyler A. Strand

SUNDAY, FEBRUARY 18, 2001
Lectionary Message
Topic: Tell Me Again About the Promise of Life Beyond the Grave: Resurrection
TEXT: 1 Cor. 15:35–40, 45–50
Other Readings: Gen. 45:3–11, 15; Ps. 37:1–11, 39–40; Luke 6:27–38

The question, What happens to us after we die? has haunted the human race from the beginning of time. The apostle Paul words it like this in our text: "But some may ask, 'How are the dead raised? With what kind of body will they come?'" Then he goes on to make two comments about it that set the boundaries for our message.

(a) The first comment is literally "foolish man"—not one who has taken leave of his senses but one who, in the Old Testament sense of the word, has left God out of the equation. The Corinthian believers rejected the resurrection of the body because they found the notion of resuscitated corpses repulsive. We do, too. We would not want our loved ones back with disease-ravished bodies. But when we speculate beyond what the Bible clearly states, we limit the power of God and are foolish men and women.

(b) In the second comment Paul uses the term *mystery* to talk about the future beyond the grave (15:51). In the hands of Paul, mystery means an open secret—that which was hidden and is now revealed. God reveals only a fraction of what we would *like* to know, but he tells us all we *need* to know. He takes us beyond the cemetery to discover some things about the other side.

Paul is faced with explaining the mystery in terms we can understand, so he chooses two metaphors that give us fleeting images of what lies ahead for us. The first metaphor is from nature—the seed the farmer or gardener plants in the ground—and the second is the contrast between the two Adams. The point of both metaphors is to emphasize the transformation that takes place when we die and are resurrected. Notice the things that change and the things that do not change in resurrection.

I. *Our resurrection will transform us beyond anything we can imagine.* We will be radically different from what we are now. God has made us in the image of the first Adam for the environment of earth. We must exist within a certain temperature range and have sufficient food, liquid, and oxygen or we die physically. Our physical bodies were created to exist in our environment. But through our resurrection God will transform our physical bodies into spiritual bodies that will bear the image of the second Adam, Jesus Christ, so that we can exist and thrive in the spiritual atmosphere of the life to come.

(a) *The image of the seed and the plant.* The illustration Paul uses is the unrecognizable difference between the "dead" seed that the farmer or the gardener puts into the ground and the vibrant plant that grows from the seed. One could never guess the plant's appearance from looking at the seed, and we can never guess what our transformed spiritual bodies will look like by gazing at ourselves in the mirror. We would never in a thousand years guess that a tomato seed would look like a tomato. At death we are planted as a corpse and we will be resurrected as a spiritual body.

1. We are planted perishable; we will be raised imperishable (15:42).
2. We are planted in dishonor; we will be raised in glory (15:43).
3. We are planted in weakness; we will be raised in power (15:43).
4. We are planted as a natural body; we will be raised as a spiritual body (15:44).

(b) *The image of the two Adams.* If there is a natural body, there is also a spiritual body (15:44).

1. The first Adam was made a living being out of the dust of the Earth; the last Adam is a life-giving spirit (15:45). The order is first the natural, then the spiritual (15:46).
2. As we have borne the likeness of the earthly, we will bear the likeness of the heavenly (15:49).
3. At our resurrection we will not have the first-Adam-body that was buried. We will be raised with a transformed second-Adam-body like Christ's glorified Resurrection body because "flesh and blood cannot inherit the kingdom of God" (15:50).

II. *Our transforming resurrection will also preserve our identity.* Despite all these unbelievable, unknowable changes that will take place through the transforming power of the resurrection, we will still be who we are, but we will be glorified and perfected, without flaws and weaknesses. Our buried physical bodies will dissolve and be raised in a radically different form, but we will be raised the same person even though our spiritual bodies will be different. We will continue as persons; we will still be ourselves.

We do not know what we shall be like but we shall be like him, for we shall see him as he is.

III. *Conclusion.* What happens to us when we die depends on two things: what happened to Christ when he died and what we have done with Christ in this life. We can reject him and hear him say, "Depart from me, I never knew you," or we can hear him say, "Enter into the place I have prepared for you." The choice is ours; the consequences are eternal.—Wayne E. Shaw

ILLUSTRATIONS

LIMITS.   A short time ago I participated in the funeral of a friend who had been a professor of the Old Testament in the seminary where I serve. As always, the funeral ended at the graveside, where we read Scripture and prayed. I have been to the cemetery many times to conclude the funeral services of friends and family, including my grandparents, my parents, and a son. No matter how old or wise we are, we can go as far as the cemetery in this life, but no farther.—Wayne E. Shaw

THE KEY.   Leslie Weatherhead got the idea for a sermon from a house for sale that was all locked up. It had a note taped to the front window that read, "Key Next Door." The point is that we can see some things dimly through the front window, but if we really want to see all God has for us, we will have to wait to get the key next door.—Wayne E. Shaw

SERMON SUGGESTIONS

Topic: When Is Anger Sinful?
TEXT: Matt. 5:21–22
(1) When it is given without any just provocation. (2) When it is aimed not at any good end. (3) When it exceeds due bounds.—Matthew Henry

Topic: A Practical Cure for Loneliness
(1) Something to question: Is my loneliness my own fault? (2) Something to remember: You belong to God, to the Christian family; you can belong to a church. (3) Something to feel: You are sent. (4) Something to do: It must include some kind of service to others.—Leslie D. Weatherhead[9]

CONGREGATIONAL MUSIC

1. "Give to the Winds Thy Fears," Paul Gerhrdt (1635); trans. John Wesley (1739)
   DIADEMATA, George J. Elvey (1868)

---

[9] *Key Next Door*

The eloquent expression of confidence in a loving and provident God in this noble hymn from the pen of Paul Gerhardt, the most beloved of all German hymnists, echoes the spirit of the psalmist (Ps. 37:1–11, 39–40). It could be used as a response to the Psalter reading.

2. "Now the Green Blade Rises," John M. C. Crum (1928)

NOEL NOVELET, French carol; harm. Martin Shaw (1928)

This is a vibrant contemporary hymn on resurrection that would be appropriate for use with the Epistle lesson (1 Cor. 15:35–38, 45–50). Alternately, it may be used as a choral call to praise or as a processional with the choir singing the stanzas in unison and the congregation joining in to sing the refrain.

3. "Forgive Our Sins as We Forgive," Rosamond E. Herklots (1966)

DETROIT, Bradshaw in *Supplement to Kentucky Harmony* (1820)

The Gospel reading could be appropriately accompanied by the singing of this contemporary hymn set to one of the old shape-note tunes of early America. The hymn reflects the spirit of the Lukan passage incorporating some of the teachings of Jesus in the Sermon on the Mount.

4. "Christian Hearts, in Love United," Nicolaus L. von Zinzendort (1725)

CASSELL, trad. German Melody (c. 1735)

This Moravian hymn is a good one with which to open worship that will focus attention on the readings in Genesis and Luke, which emphasize love, forgiveness, and brotherly (and sisterly) concern.—Hugh T. McElrath

WORSHIP AIDS

CALL TO WORSHIP.   "Delight thyself also in the Lord; and he shall give thee the desires of thine heart. Commit thy way unto the Lord; trust also in him; and he shall bring it to pass" (Ps. 37:4–5).

INVOCATION.   O God, we take refuge in you. In the baffling trials of life, you are our true security. Strengthen us by the hymns we sing, by your Word read and proclaimed, and by the decisions we make in your holy presence today.

OFFERTORY SENTENCE.   "Although the fig tree shall not blossom, neither shall fruit be in the vines; the labor of the olive shall fail, and the fields shall yield no meat; the flock shall be cut off from the fold, and there shall be no herd in the stalls. Yet I will rejoice in the Lord, I will joy in the God of my salvation" (Hab. 3:17–18).

OFFERTORY PRAYER.   Times may be tough for some of us, our Father, yet we are rich in grace. We bring before you what we have and make our offerings accordingly, knowing that you know both our needs and our abilities.

PRAYER.   As we delight in this particular day, Father, make us aware of your creative Spirit making all things new. Grant us the discernment to see what new thing you are doing in our day, and the willingness to be a part of what you are making to happen for the good of all mankind.

Deliver us from being so caught up in the trivia of life that we fail to experience your presence and thereby miss our opportunities. Help us to be open to your call, ready to do your will, and eager to engage in eternal enterprise.

Thank you Father, for one another. May we be understanding of each other in our foibles and encouraging of one another. Help us to more fully understand what it means to be a part of the body of Christ. We do not all possess the same responsibility, but remind us that your Spirit equips us for ministry according to our ability. Remind us that we complement one another as we dedicate our abilities to your Kingdom work, and that the fullness of your life can be made known through our life together.

Make us more faithful to your Church. Call us anew to the joy of praying for one another and by this means touch each life of the Church family. Help us to realize that we have a responsibility peculiar to us alone. Give us the grace to seek out those closest to us and minister to them according to their need. May those who are shaken because life has been difficult gain poise to handle creatively whatever life holds for them. Where the ache of loneliness persists, may you minister the Balm of Gilead—the sense of your presence. Free from fear those who are ill so that they may be free to receive your grace no matter what the outcome of the illness. We do ask that healing be the gift of those who have yet another appointed earthly task to perform. And let healing come to those who can be healed only by entering your nearer presence of complete freedom from disease and illness.

Now in this hour call us from sins to salvation, from darkness to light, from chaos to calm certainty, we pray in Jesus' name.—Henry Fields

SERMON
Topic: Purity of Heart
TEXT: Matt. 6:24–33

Living with stress is being stretched on a modern medieval rack with the principal players in your life's drama pulling you in opposite directions, each demanding your individual attention and loyalty, each requiring 100 percent of your time and energy. Stress is living between the demands of your boss and the needs of your family. It is choosing between your child's piano recital, a church committee meeting, a deadline at work, and a bowling game featuring your favorite team. Stress is a family problem. Young parents must learn to nurture both marriage and children without neglecting either. The "sandwich generation" has reached the stage in life when the needs of adult children and aging parents often pull them in opposite directions. Senior adults are in constant tension between their unfulfilled dreams and continuing responsibilities and accepting physical limitations in their energy and mobility. Vocational stress is the norm rather than the exception in this age of economic competition and organizational downsizing. We live in tension between our vocational dream and the reality of daily work, between the conflicted demands of conscience and authority, and between a sense of personal worth and economic necessity. Given the peculiar combination of demands on our lives, most of us can sign our names to the picture of stress.

I. *Stress is the norm for responsible people.* What does the gospel say to people on the rack? Is the Church a part of the problem or a place of refuge from the storm? Linda Doyle came into the office a few days ago to talk with Stuart about the seminar they were planning. I greeted her with a bit of sarcasm. "What is this about? I don't have stress. I am a Christian, and Christians don't have stress." She responded with a knowing smile and the simple response, "Good." Now, we do have a problem here. The counsel of Jesus in the Sermon on the Mount is often summed up in the simple exhortation, "Don't worry!" If being Christian is the simple cure for stress, the clergy ought to be immune, yet clergy stress is one of the hazards of our calling. Medical insurance statistics reveal a high level of stress-related ills among ministers. John Killinger described the pressures of pastoral ministry as living in a piranha bowl. The pastor is seldom devoured by one monstrous demand. Rather, he is nibbled away into oblivion by a multitude of needs: "No one wants all of you, but everyone wants a piece of you."

Stress is the disease of responsible people who take seriously their care and concern for others. Right out of high school Uncle Don went to work for Southwestern Bell Telephone Company in Austin, Texas. In the early 1950s he installed phones and climbed poles. One day he was working just outside the fence at the large mental hospital in the city and one of the residents came to the fence to start a conversation. They exchanged greetings while Don went about his work. Then the man at the fence asked, "I'll bet you think I'm crazy?" Don was made uncomfortable by the question and mumbled something like, "I don't know." The man went on, "Look at you, climbing poles and struggling to feed your family. I get three meals and a bed, and I don't have to worry about a thing. Who do you think is crazy?"

The man had a point. Stress comes from taking on responsibility, not from being evil. It is about growing up, becoming an adult, accepting legitimate roles of parenting and mentoring. Folks who cannot manage stress are sometimes crushed into psychotic escape from the pressures of life. Wayne Oates tells about a devout Christian friend who was involved in a serious automobile accident. Another friend was deeply disturbed at a God who would let this happen. Oates told the friend that we are living in a "morality of risk," not a "morality of safety." Our friend could have stayed at home, or walked, or caught a bus, but he chose to drive. He took the risk of learning to drive and then driving, thus greatly increasing the risk of an accident. Most of us live somewhere between emotional omnipotence and emotional impotence. We are doomed to collapse when we assume our ability to do everything, and we are doomed to failure when we refuse to take the risk of taking on the essential responsibilities of living.

II. *Stress is essentially a question of managing priorities.* Jesus spoke directly to our generation. In his counsel about worry, we often overlook the economic context of striving for the material things of life. Trying to serve two masters, God and mammon, is an impossible division of loyalty. The redemptive good news of Christ is that life can be focused on that which is essential. Let's be honest in our confession within ourselves. Much of the stress of this generation is economics-based; it's about paying the bills and keeping up with material desires. Jesus called for a focus on the Kingdom of God, that "all these things will be given to you as well." I doubt that Jesus was promising sweepstakes wealth for the faithful. He was affirming the power of human choice. Kingdom priorities set the value of everything else, and you have the God-given power of choice.

Søren Kierkegaard called his generation in Denmark into the tension of the gospel. He did not find ease and relaxation in the calling of Christ. He described a gospel that demands a leap of faith beyond intellectual exercise to personal committed decision. He believed in the primary claim of God on every person. He preached a demanding gospel of complete sacrifice. He believed in the God who called Abraham to sacrifice Isaac on the altar of total obedience. He was highly critical of the church leadership of his time for taking the demand out of the gospel. Rather than a soothing tranquility, the gospel leads into the crisis of decision. Kierkegaard believed that Jesus literally came to bring not peace but a sword into our existence, that the Bible is the last place to turn for relief from stress in life; but in the demand of God on our existence is a redemptive focus. His message for harried Christians was, *Purity of heart is to will one thing.* Invest all that you are in the pearl of value. Set aside all of the barriers to the ultimate value in life. Will one thing. Put first things first. Seek first God's Kingdom.—Larry Dipboye

SUNDAY, FEBRUARY 25, 2001
Lectionary Message

Topic: The Awesome Glory of God
TEXT: 2 Cor. 3:7–4:6
Other Readings: Exod. 34:29–35; Ps. 99; Luke 9:28–36 (37–43a)

I. *Move 1: Evidence of God's awesome glory.* Evidence of the awesome glory of God is all around us if we have eyes focused to see and ears tuned to hear. Sometimes this evidence has an impact on us when it happens and sometimes it affects us later, when our memory banks kick in.

(a) *God reveals his awesome glory in the beauty of his creation* (Rom. 1:20). Not only do the heavens declare the glory of God and the firmament show his handiwork, but all nature sparkles with beauty in awesome variety. Some of my memories may remind you of your own: Old Faithful geyser at Yellowstone National Park; the grandeur of the Grand Tetons; the bluff at Scottsbluff, Nebraska; Cape of Two Oceans, where the Atlantic and Pacific come together; Table Mountain towering above Cape Town, South Africa; the view from the mission compound in Bandung, Indonesia; the sunset on the Zambesi River; and Victoria Falls. Add the wonder of a newborn baby and one would have to be completely credulous to believe that beauty has happened by chance.

But there are also tornadoes, hurricanes, floods, and droughts. All is not unlimited beauty in a fallen universe. God's revelation of his glory in nature is limited.

(b) *God embeds his awesome glory in our conscience* (Rom. 2:13–15). Because we have been created in his image, God put eternity in our hearts, as our conscience bears witness. It reminds us that we live in a moral universe even though creation fell when Adam fell. God made us in his own image to live clean lives of high moral purpose because his character is the moral standard of the universe.

But we know too well that conscience can be rationalized, misinformed, and violated enough times until the corners get rounded off and the policeman in our soul starts accepting bribes.

(c) *God reveals his awesome glory in the covenant that he made with Moses.* It may have been a covenant that led many to trust in the outward forms of religion and in the righteousness of their own works, but Paul insists that this covenant came with such glory that the Israelites could not look steadily at the face of Moses (2 Cor. 3:7, 8). Awesome as they are, however, the Ten Commandments lead to faded glory and finally to condemnation and death (3:7–11). They demand perfect obedience and pronounce death on the disobedient.

(d) *God reveals his awesome glory best in Jesus Christ through the new covenant* (3:14–18).

1. This glory does not fade but lasts forever.

2. It does not condemn but makes us righteous.

3. It does not chain us to endless rules or fleshly license but sets us free in Christ.

II. *Move 2: Why we resist God's awesome glory.*

(a) Paul took the congregation in Corinth back to Exodus 34:29–35 to tell them that God's glory was so filled with splendor that Moses put a veil over his face after he had been in God's presence. Then Paul shifted the picture twice. First he said that the veil kept the Israelites from knowing that the glory faded the farther Moses got from God. Second, he said that if we hear the Scriptures without seeing Christ, we have a veil over our eyes. We cannot see that Christ is God's finest revelation of his glory (4:4–6).

If the glory of the new covenant in Christ is so awesome, why do we often resist it by trying to worship God while wearing veils?

1. Veils can cover our prejudices when we go to the Bible to support our views rather than to discover the truth.

2. Veils can allow us a vague commitment to God without having to surrender our lives to Christ.

3. Veils can allow us to be morally blind and disobedient to God.

4. Veils can conceal a closed mind and an unteachable spirit.

III. *Move 3: How we reflect God's awesome glory.*

(a) By being honest with the Scriptures.

1. We reflect his glory when we obey the intent of the Scriptures and not just the letter of the law.

2. We reflect his glory when we interpret the Old Testament in light of the finished work of Christ on the cross. This happened for Paul on the Damascus Road when the light from heaven blinded him. In that act God ripped the veil from Paul's eyes and he saw God's glory clearly for the first time. That glory never again faded for him.

(b) By practicing the presence of Christ in our daily lives.

1. Because we have this hope, we let nothing hold us back (3:12). Otherwise, we would not risk sharing the gospel as we do.

2. We are becoming more and more like Christ as we experience the splendor of his daily presence and allow him to change us from glory to glory (3:18).

As a result:

(a) There is no veil between us and God; therefore we do not quit God's call because of hard times (4:1).

(b) There are no veils between us (4:2).

1. We refuse to wear masks and play games.

2. We refuse to manipulate behind the scenes.

3. We do not twist God's Word to suit ourselves.

(c) One day we will stand before him in all his awesome glory and the most important question for us will be, Have we thrown away our veils that separated us from him?—Wayne E. Shaw

ILLUSTRATIONS

DAWN OF THE ESCHATON.   This, then, was the disciple's immediate experience of the resurrection of Jesus: not as a unique mighty act of God *in the course of* history hastening towards its end (though this is what it must have seemed to them after a short interval), but as the dawn of the eschaton. They saw Jesus in shining light. They were witnesses of his entry into glory. In other words, *they experienced the parousia.*

It is no exaggeration if I say that in my view the life of faith in the early church can only be understood in the light of the results that have been achieved here. For the earliest community, to believe meant to live here and now in the consummation of the world. The pre-Pauline Easter *Haggadah* in 1 Cor. 5:7b–8 says that the believer stands in the Easter of the time of salvation; he has been snatched out of a corrupt generation, doomed to destruction (Gal. 1:4; Acts 2:40); he has been saved through the waves of the flood (1 Peter 3:20) and the Red Sea (1 Cor. 10:1ff.); he is a new creation. These eschatological indicatives, and many like them, presuppose that a real experience of the dawning of God's new world stood at the beginning of the history of the church.—Joachim Jeremias[10]

VISIBLE GLORY.   Throughout the [New Testament] Christ is presented as the glory of God made visible on earth to those whose eyes are opened to see it; but it is perhaps in the Fourth Gospel that this conception is most strongly stressed. Behind the Johannine *doxa* (GK., glory) we must recollect the full biblical richness of the word, as we have described it above. "We beheld his *doxa,* glory as of the only-begotten from the Father" (John 1:4). The miracles of Christ manifested his *doxa* (2:11). His *doxa* is not the glory of men but of God (5:41, 17:5, 22). The great high-priestly prayer of Jesus (John 17) is dominated by the idea of *doxa,* and the entire Passion of Jesus is presented to us as his "glorification" (17:1): he goes to the cross not as a helpless martyr to his agony, but as a victorious king to his crowning. In the Passion and Resurrection of Christ the utter glory of God is revealed.—L. H. Brockington[11]

GLORY IN THE CHURCH.   The knowledge that the glory dwells already in the Church may betray its members into the ancient sin whereby Israel ascribed the glory to itself, unless they are mindful of two warning truths of the apostolic teaching. (1) The first of these truths is that the glory in the Church is an invisible glory. Though the Church is visible, the glory is not to be confused with earthly majesty and splendor, for it is a glory discernible without and realized within—only through faith. It is hidden from the eyes of the unbelieving world and can never be displayed for that world's admiration; and it is hidden also from the members of the Church and can never be enjoyed by them in a quasi-worldly manner. (2) The second of these truths is that the glory in the Church is but a foretaste of the glory that is to

---

[10] *New Testament Theology* (New York: Scribner, 1971), p. 310f.
[11] In Alan Richardson (ed.), *A Theological Word Book of the Bible* (London: SCM Press, 1950), p. 175f.

come, and therefore the Church's sense of possession is mingled with the Church's sense of incompleteness. *Here* the powers of the age to come are at work within the Church's humiliation: *there* the open vision of a glory awaits the Church in the day when judgment will begin at the house of God. It follows that the Church's claims are ratified by the Church's humility, and the Church's riches by the Church's hunger for what she lacks.—Arthur Michael Ramsey[12]

SERMON SUGGESTIONS

Topic: Rejoice in the Lord

Text: Phil. 4:4

(1) The grace commanded: "Rejoice." (2) The joy discriminated: "In the Lord." (3) The time appointed: "Always." (4) The emphasis laid on the command: "Again I say, rejoice."—Charles Haddon Spurgeon[13]

Topic: Christ Above All

TEXT: Eph. 1:17–23

(1) Christ above all powers. (2) Christ above all priorities. (3) Christ above all persons.— Robert C. Shannon[14]

CONGREGATIONAL MUSIC

1. "The Lord God Reigns in Majesty," Psalm 99, vers. Psalter (1912)

 ELLACOMBE, *Gesangbuch,* Wittenberg (1784)

 This paraphrase of Psalm 99 could be sung in place of the Psalter reading of the day. It could easily and effectively be sung line by line antiphonally between choir and congregation.

2. "Christ upon the Mountain Peak," Brian Wren (1962)

 MOWSLEY, Cyril V. Taylor (1985)

 This is a fine modern hymn describing the Transfiguration of our Lord (Luke 9:28–36) and voicing the praise of the worshippers in song. It would be effective sung immediately following the reading of the Gospel lesson.

3. "Christ, Whose Glory Fills the Skies," Charles Wesley (1740)

 RATISBON, Werner's Choralbuch (1851); harm. W. H. Havergal (1861)

 A glorious song for the opening of worship, this fine Wesleyan hymn relates particularly to the Epistle lesson in 2 Corinthians (3:12–4:2) in which believers with unveiled faces are to reflect the radiance of Christ.

4. "Holy, Holy," Jimmy Owens (1972)

 HOLY HOLY, Jimmy Owens (1972)

 A contemporary praise song that magnifies the transcendent holiness of the Triune God, this could be used in connection with any one of the readings for this Sunday, whether the Old Testament reading, the Psalm, the Epistle, or the Gospel.—Hugh T. McElrath

---

[12] *The Glory of God and the Transfiguration of Christ* (London: Longmans, Green, 1949), p. 88f.

[13] *My Sermon Notes,* Vol. 4

[14] *Christ Above All*

WORSHIP AIDS

CALL TO WORSHIP.   "Exalt ye the Lord our God, and worship at his footstool; for he is holy" (Ps. 99:5).

INVOCATION.   We would worship you, holy God, in an attitude that is worthy of you. Cleanse our hearts and our thoughts, so that we can worship you in spirit and in truth.

OFFERTORY SENTENCE.   "Let your conversation be without covetousness; and be content with such things as ye have: for he hath said, I will never leave thee, nor forsake thee. So that we may boldly say, The Lord is my helper, and I will not fear what man shall do unto me" (Heb. 13:5).

OFFERTORY PRAYER.   Give us, O God, the confidence in you that will free us from idolizing money as if it were the be-all and end-all of life. At the same time, remind us of the many good things that our money can do when we bring it to you with a grateful and cheerful heart.

PRAYER.   "Blessed are the pure in heart for they shall see God." O Father of all light, you call us from blindness to sight, from darkness to light, from illusion to the real. In this place may we have such a vision of your presence in all of life—of your oneness—that we may see life clearly, that we may see it whole. That the eyes of faith in us have been opened by your grace, that we should know you, the only true God, and Jesus Christ, whom you have sent, we praise you. For those who have been faithful stewards of your Word in our behalf, we are grateful.

With what love you love us that we should be bold to call you "Father"—that we are your sons and daughters and it "does not yet appear what we shall be."

As we are challenged to walk again in the battlefield of faith, may we hear your call renewed by our elder brother in his "Follow me." May we have the courage to follow, if even from afar. In the wilderness of our temptation may your Word dwell so richly in our minds and hearts that we may resist the world's conforming ways and experience the transformation of your Spirit from within.

For the meaning of *church* that we are privileged to experience in this time and place, we praise you. For the support and encouragement of comrades on the way, we are grateful. We pray for one another. For those in need of your healing grace, we pray. We are thankful for where healing is already taking place. It is such a mystery how the body is refined and renewed.

As we find ourselves in the valley of the shadow of death may we have the faith to know that you do not leave us there but lead us through. Comfort us in our bereavement that we may be able to comfort others in their time of crisis.—John M. Thompson

SERMON

Topic: Your Way, My Way, God's Way
TEXT: Rom. 14:1–12

Sometimes we idealize the first Christians, as if they were super saints living lives of faith and harmony far beyond our reach today. But the truth is that even under the leadership of

Jesus' original companions and under founding apostles like Peter and Paul, the people had their conflicts.

When Paul wrote his letter to the Roman Christians in the late fifties A.D., the major division was between Christian believers of Jewish background and non-Jewish, or Gentile, believers. Many Jewish Christians were still wedded to traditional dietary laws and holy days; Gentile believers resented any such imposition on their lifestyles. It would seem that Paul, despite his own deeply rooted Jewish heritage, would have sided with the liberals in this conflict. Didn't he say, "For by grace are you saved through faith . . . and not as a result of works, lest anyone should boast" (Eph. 2:8–9)? But in our text he takes a conciliatory approach on this issue that seems so near to the heart of his understanding of the gospel.

One person regards one day above another, another regards every day alike. Let each person be fully convinced in his or her own mind. For the one who observes the day observes it to honor the Lord, and the one who eats does so for the Lord, giving thanks to God, and the one who eats not for the Lord abstains and gives thanks to God (Rom. 14:55–56).

Paul, as he thinks aloud about this issue that was every bit as vexing and divisive then as the issues that exercise us now, exemplifies that scriptural mode so dear to me: scripture as an *invitation to conversation* rather than a declaration that closes off conversation.

I remember vividly an encounter I overheard several years ago in the small room that served as a faculty lounge at the Moscow Theological Seminary. A pastor from Texas had a Russian student over in the corner and was pounding into him the Scriptures that suggest "once saved, always saved," or "the perseverance of the saints," as theologians call it. The Russian student, in his imperfect English, was hard pressed to access the companion Scriptures that lift up our need to "endure to the end" and "hold fast to our salvation." Russian Baptists have traditionally taken the Wesleyan stance that it is, tragically, possible to "fall from grace," because of their bitter experience of trusted leaders who turned out to be, in the end, KGB agents. For them, apostasy was real. A conversation needed to take place here, exploring Scripture in the light of two different ranges of experience. But the American was interested not in mutual understanding but in maintaining and justifying his own position.

Even deeply committed disciples differ, sometimes on major issues. But whether in agreement or principled disagreement, "not one of us lives for himself, and not one dies for himself; for if we live for the Lord, or if we die, we die for the Lord" (Rom. 14:7–8).

Agreeing or disagreeing, we must lift up Jesus. Especially in disagreeing, we must be like Jesus, who wept over the very city that crucified him.

As Jesus taught us in his Sermon on the Mount, we can take responsibility for ourselves and practice fidelity in relationships, simple truth telling, compassion—even (especially) for our adversaries, generosity and simplicity. And we should abstain from judging our brother or sister, for God will take care of the judging.

"So then each one should give account of himself [only] to God" (Rom. 14:12).

It fascinates and troubles me that in the current debate dividing American Christianity so much emphasis is placed on questions of sexual ethics and so little on the economics of Jesus, which desperately needs a hearing in this glaringly unjust and economically segregated world of ours. We cite Jesus, chapter and verse, on lust, adultery, and divorce, but we ignore or rationalize away his commands to give away the shirts on our backs to those who ask (Matt. 5:40), to lend freely with no thought of return (Matt. 5:42), and to abstain from piling up possessions (Matt. 6:19–21). How good it is that many rich Christians are appropriately chaste or faithful in their intimate relationships; how sad it is that we judge others when we stand judged by Jesus himself in our economic practices!

We say that we are saved by grace and therefore free in Christ. But when we exercise a Godly liberty in our Christian lifestyle, we must never ridicule the one who abstains or observes a discipline. Indeed, as Paul teaches the Corinthians, sometimes it is better to relinquish our privileges than maintain them to someone else's hurt.

"Therefore if food causes by brother to stumble, I will never eat meat again, that I might not cause my brother to stumble" (1 Cor. 8:13).

And when we do stand on principle, we can do it in a way that is winsome and inviting rather than off-putting or judgmental. For example, the most effective proponents of a Godly chastity for Christian youth—as in the "true love waits" emphasis—do not play on the guilt chord but rather emphasize the freedom that comes to young people who have a settled commitment to sexual purity and self-discipline and can therefore build and enjoy multiple friendships with members of the opposite sex without worrying about being exploiter or exploited.

In all of these examples, the point is not whether your way or my way prevails, but rather that we mutually seek God's way, which is that all should be included, affirmed, lifted up, forgiven, sanctified, and glorified. For the Lord "is patient toward [us], not willing for any to perish but for all to come to repentance" (2 Pet. 3:49). Finally, whether right or wrong on any given issue, all of us who cling to Christ are nothing more or less than beggars saved by grace.—David L. Wheeler

SUNDAY, MARCH 4, 2001
Lectionary Message

Topic: Faith on Trial
Text: Luke 4:1–13
Other Readings: Deut. 26:1–11; Ps. 91:1–2, 9–16; Rom. 10:8b-13

We begin Lent with this monster story known as "The Temptations." What we see in this stark and ominous imagery of the lonely Jesus amid desolation and wilderness is not a solitary never-to-be-repeated encounter. We see an incessant claim on Jesus' life and mission—a claim made no less persistently on you and me who would follow this challenging Galilean.

I. What, then, puts faith on trial in this wilderness encounter? When the Tempter approaches Jesus with the promise of turning stones into bread, we see a deal so right and decent that to deny it appears irrational. We ask, Why did Jesus see this proposition not as a promise from heaven but as a bargain from hell?

Why, for instance, didn't Jesus see this as an opportunity to fulfill the prophet's vision of a successful "war on hunger"? Perhaps he detected the temptation to substitute the expedient good for the courageous best. Perhaps Jesus remembered his forebears marching from Egypt into the wilderness pleading for manna, receiving it from God's hand, and then finally, with full bellies, asking, "Who needs this liberating mission? Get us out of this wilderness. Return us to Egypt. The risks out here are killing us. We want security, even if it is the security of slavery. To hell with risking anything more of being a light to the nations." Here we witness a complacent people ready to trade an expedient good for a courageous best.

II. The Tempter's second proposition provides for sovereignty over the nations of the world. In this day and age, what a temptation that is! We have witnessed a terrible chaos of races, nations, and tribes in these last years, slaughtering one another with nihilistic virulence. Were I offered the power to stop the current violence I would say, "It's a deal! With manic terror across the world, and so that this chaos and national pride will not overwhelm us, we crave divine intervention immediately."

So, of necessity we may be tempted by the insidious voice of realism to cut international development and build missiles. The expedient good for the courageous best? Could it be that in face of these enormous temptations to maintain what the editorialist calls "Pax Atomica" we might better listen to Martin Luther King Jr., who wondered, "Where do we go from here?" and who warned that as we build our prisons, plead for antiballistic missile systems, and plug in our electric chairs that "returning violence for violence multiplies violence, adding deeper darkness to a night already devoid of stars. Hate cannot drive out hate, only love can do that."

Here we see the tension between truth and relevance. But it may be that the ethic of purity is in truth the very root of survival and the most relevant ethic for our time. Amid the violence of our own time the courageous best may be the only expedient good. And when Jesus says, "Thanks but no thanks" to the devil, he opts for the ethic of purity—the only ethic that can truly save us.

III. Finally, the Tempter takes Jesus to the top of the Temple and promises for God's sake to keep him out of harm's way. Here we confront the ultimate bargain. It goes like this: For our sake, Jesus, if you won't feed the hungry, if you won't bend the nations to your will, then somehow prove to us you are in God's camp. Show us truly who you are, what you are about, and why we should believe there is any connection between you and the will, the love, and the purposes of God?

Here we get the gospel straight. Now hear this: The will and love of God make themselves visible and present in our common life not by some arbitrary act of power intervening and bending our distorted lives together into some preordained design, but through vulnerability and by not violating our freedom. The will and love of God are such that even as we violate them in order to do things our way, we realize that God's love will not violate us. We have been given the choice to eliminate hunger—if we want to. We have the choice to unify the nations into the human family—if we will. We have the choice to follow the one who lives and loves, not for the expedient good but for the courageous and loving best, but mostly we don't make that choice. We know that in this world of reason and realism—this world in which our basic principle seems to be that a person's got to do what a person's go to do— the proof of God's love for us rests in Jesus' readiness to risk his life for us and never count the cost, for love's sake. There is no way to protect love from harm's way. That's where love finds itself—right in harm's way. It is open-handed, open-hearted, high risk, and highly vulnerable, even to crucifixion. It's no sellout to the expedient good as a reasonable substitute for the courageous and loving best!

So you see, friends, the Christian life is no easy task. It is a matter of courage, risk, and hope. It makes claims on us. It puts our faith on trial, not once, not twice, but a thousand times over. Yet be assured, it asks not more of us than we have already been given. Therefore, as we begin Lent together, I pray that we will heed that sublime admonition of Charles Wesley's hymn:

Leave no unguarded place,
No weakness of the soul,
Take every virtue, every grace
And fortify the whole.

From strength to strength go on;
Wrestle and fight and pray;
Tread all the power of evil down
And win the well-fought day.

—James W. Crawford

ILLUSTRATIONS

REBUTTING SATAN.   Say to Satan, "In the name of God I dare believe." "Thou art a great sinner," says he. "Yes, but I believe he is a great Saviour." "But thou hast sinned beyond all hope." "No, there is forgiveness with him, that he may be feared." But he says, "You are shut out." "No," say you, "Though he slay me, yet will I trust him." "But your disease is of long standing." "Ay," but say you, "If I but touch the hem of His garment, I shall be clean." But saith Satan again, "How dare you! Would you have the impudence!" "Well," say you, "If I perish I will trust Christ, and I will perish only there." Have it in your soul fixed that in the teeth of everything you will trust Christ—that be you such a sinner or no, still you will trust Christ—that whether Satan's accusations be true or false, you mean to have done answering them and simply trust Christ. Ah, soul, then thou shalt have such joy and peace that nothing shall be like it. O that thou wouldst believe on Jesus *now*! Leave thy feelings, leave thy doings and thy willings, and trust Christ.—Charles Haddon Spurgeon[1]

COURAGE, MEANS, AND STRENGTH.   If our faith in God and in His moral law can be revived, a faith in and allegiance to a Power that is greater than the state, greater than any or all forms of human organization and authority, then we shall come to know beyond the peradventure of doubt that human despotism and cruelty and hate and the destruction of the weak cannot triumph in the end, and we shall find the courage to challenge evil, the means wherewith to destroy evil, and the strength to endure until the victory is won.—Abba Hillel Silver[2]

SERMON SUGGESTIONS

Topic: Faith's Progression
TEXT: Deut. 26:5–11
(1) Blessing (v. 5). (2) Affliction (v. 6). (3) Petition (v. 7). (4) Response (v. 8). (5) Abundance (v. 9). (6) Gratitude (v. 10). (7) Celebration (v. 11).

Topic: Heart Religion
TEXT: Rom. 10:8b–13
(1) The inner and the outer belong together (vv. 8–11). (2) The insider and the outsider belong together (vv. 12–13).

---

[1] *Metropolitan Tabernacle Pulpit*, Vol. 7 (Pasadena, Tex.: Pilgrim Publications, 1969), p. 552.
[2] *Therefore Choose Life* (Cleveland, Ohio: Word, 1967), p. 66.

CONGREGATIONAL MUSIC

1. "Sing Praise to God Who Reigns Above," Johann J. Schutz (1675)

    MIT FREUDEN ZART, Bohemian Brethren Kirchengesang; trans. Francis Cox (1864)

    An excellent selection for the beginning of worship, this German hymn also relates to the central theme of Psalm 91, which magnifies God's power to shelter, protect, and comfort in the storms of life.

2. "O Jesus, Joy of Loving Hearts," twelfth century Latin; trans. Ray Palmer (1958)

    QUEBEC, Henry Baker (1854)

    This fine hymn, translated by one of America's best nineteenth-century hymnists (author of "My Faith Looks up to Thee") relates to the Epistle lesson in Romans. Stanza 2 especially echoes the truth of Romans 10:13.

3. "Lord, Who Throughout These Forty Days," Claudia F. Hernaman (1873)

    LAND OF REST, American folk melody; harm. A. M. Buchanan (1938)

    Relating directly to the temptation of Jesus recorded in the Gospel lesson (Luke 4:1–3), this hymn could be sung with its stanzas interspersed with the reading. The American folk tune to which it is set lends itself to a mood of reverence and penitence.

4. "On Eagle's Wings," Michael Joncas (1978)

    ON EAGLE'S WINGS, Michael Joncas (1978)

    This popular refrain of a contemporary hymn written on the occasion of the death of a relative of a friend of the author could be suitably sung as a response (antiphon) to the verses of Psalm 91.—Hugh T. McElrath

WORSHIP AIDS

CALL TO WORSHIP.   "He that dwelleth in the secret place of the most high shall abide under the shadow of the Almighty. I will say of the Lord, he is my refuge and my fortress, my God; in him will I trust" (Ps. 91:1–2).

INVOCATION.   We have put our trust in you, O God, and we have found shelter amid the storms of life. In the safety of your sanctuary, among your people, you have made us more and more aware of your love. Help us now to share that love with one another in harmony with your Spirit.

OFFERTORY SENTENCE.   "Therefore, my beloved brethren, be ye steadfast, un-moveable, always abounding in the work of the Lord, for as much as ye know that your labor is not in vain in the Lord" (1 Cor. 15:58).

OFFERTORY PRAYER.   We thank you, O God, for the great victory over sin and death that you give us through our Lord Jesus Christ. Now help us to translate this victory into loving and generous service to Christ in every way.

PRAYER.   Our God, we are thankful that you have not only known us but you have made yourself known to us. That you know us and still love us is amazing. But the fact that you have made yourself known to us is proof of that love.

So we come to you with the confidence born of that knowledge and with the joy that comes from being loved by the one who knows us intimately. So often our prayers seem to be only a shopping list of requests; we seem so slow to acknowledge that all we have and all we are is a gift from you, so today we ask not for more but for the grace to be better stewards of what we have.

We who have so much in the way of worldly goods, may we be generous to those who have little. We who have received the gift of forgiveness abundantly, may we be forgiving and kind. Rather than praying for peace in the world, may we offer to the world the Prince of Peace and be ourselves ambassadors of your reconciling love to the nations.

It's not a matter, our Father, of a shortage of gifts and resources; it's a problem of distribution. So forgive us our greed and our tendency to put our goods in locked barns and our light under a bushel. Help us to be your ambassadors to the world.

This prayer is then our pledge to you that because of your love for us, made manifest most eloquently in your Son, we now abandon all in favor of the quest of being your people in the world. The world is skeptical of religiosity and doctrine but is still hungering for authentic love.

We thank you, our Father, for the opportunity to be your children and your emissaries of love to the world. We pray this in the name of him who was our model of how life ought to be lived.—Robert Morley (Sept. 29, 1985)

SERMON
Topic: The Unknown Christian
TEXT: Mark 9:38–50; James 4:13–17, 5:7–11

A little girl came home from her first day at school and told her parents she had met a new friend. Her parents asked questions about the new friend: What's her name? Where does she live? Is she a Methodist? The little girl said, "No, she belongs to a different abomination."

We assume she meant denomination. Christians are divided into denominations, as you know. That has happened for historical and geographical reasons, and sometimes even for theological reasons, but the reasons are lost to most of us and are no longer very important. But denominations still continue, and probably always will, for what could be called psychological reasons, or whatever it is in human nature that needs to identify with a group—something to which we can give our allegiance, something in which we can feel the pride of belonging. That's a tremendous drive in human beings; we need a label we can wear and be proud of, something distinct without being too different.

That's why you see those bumper stickers now that say "California Native." I drive alongside those cars. Their drivers don't look Hispanic to me. They certainly don't look like San Dieguito Indians either. In fact, they look like young Ohioans. They were born here so that gives them an identity; they're "native" Californians. We need to belong. That's a powerful drive in every human being. It's as old as the tribe, I suppose—the need to belong. And it's all right, and it's necessary, and it's good—until it becomes chauvinistic.

That's the adjective that the feminist movement claimed some time ago and applied to males who feel that there is something naturally superior about males relative to females. But the origin of the term, of course, is in politics and it refers to patriotism that can't tolerate criticism, is arrogant and prejudiced, and assumes a natural superiority over other groups of people. That's what chauvinism is.

Chauvinism is always a temptation in groups because the groups to which we belong are an extension of our self, and if they're an extension of the self that includes the ego, we get our image from the group. The image of the group is in a real sense the image we have of ourself. So, if my ego is so fragile that I need to be right all the time, or virtuous above any blame, or infallible, then I'll make that claim for myself. It's ugly. It's ugly wherever it appears. But when it appears in the Church, denomination is pronounced "abomination."

Jesus taught us to see it that way. As Ephesians puts it, Jesus came into the world to break down "the diving walls of hostility" that separate us in this world. Religion, in Jesus' day, was really no different than it is today. The names were different: they called themselves Pharisees and Sadduces instead of Methodists and Baptists, but it was the same mentality, the same denominational mentality that degenerated into chauvinism. Whether we are Jews or Christians—or Muslims for that matter—it's more our own need that makes religion intolerant and arrogant than anything intrinsic to any of those religions. It's the extension of our ego that leads us to emphasize our differences from other people, to build walls, to shut others out, and to condemn other people, and even in the sorriest instances, to abuse them in one way or another. Someone said that half the harm done in this world is done by those who want to feel important, and when those people are religious they are going to use their religion as their means of feeling important. That's the problem.

Nothing could be clearer than that Jesus condemned this attitude. That's why so much of his teaching is about humility, because it is so hard for religious people to be humble. But Jesus was that way; he humbled himself, in the words of Philippians, and became a servant, the least among us, so that we would do the same. And he did more: he spent time with those to whom you and I wouldn't give the time of day, he ate with those with whom we wouldn't even think of sharing our table, he forgave those whom we routinely condemn, and he touched those whom we consider to be untouchable. He came to break down the dividing walls in this world, especially those walls that have been constructed by religion.

To do this he said, in one instance, "He that is not against us is for us." That's our text for this morning. In the context of a whole lot of sayings thrown together, this one jumps out at you: "He that is not against us is for us." Here's the scene: The disciples are walking with Jesus. They haven't even started the Church yet and already they're beginning to build walls. John, one of the disciples, says to Jesus, "Teacher, we saw a man casting out demons in your name and we forbade him because he was not one of us." And Jesus says, "Do not forbid him, for he that is not against us is for us." That's about as inclusive as you can get. That takes in a whole lot of folks, some of whom, I'm sure, we would also say, "They're not one of us." I know I've said that, I've done that: "He's not one of us." I've made that kind of division. I bet we've all said that. We see people whose style of being Christian is different than ours—"They're not one of us!"

I'll be specific here, and I hope I don't offend anybody. I don't listen to religious broadcasting. I hear there's one guy on the radio who's quite extraordinarily good, but besides that there's not much out there. We don't have cable television in our house and most religious programming is on cable television so I don't have to watch that either. But what I have seen does depress me; I just don't like it. So someone says to me, "Did you ever see Reverend so-and-so on television?" I say no, but I really have, a little bit, anyway. I say no because I don't want to talk about it. And then he says, "Oh, he's terrible!" I say, "Tell me more about it"—like Alice Roosevelt Longworth, about whom it was said that when she was at parties she would say to somebody, "If you can't say anything good about anybody, sit next to me."

There's something of that in me, I suppose. You see, I know what I like in religion. What I like in religion is the way I do religion. And there are an awful lot of religious people out there today who are not like that. They're not like us. If you have nothing good to say about them, sit next to me; but if you're going to praise them, I'd just as soon not hear it. They're not one of us.

Not that I'm narrow-minded. I'm an ecumenist. I believe in Christian unity. I participate in the ecumenical movement. Some of my best friends are in other denominations. Of course, those other denominations are like us. There's not that much difference anymore among the mainline Protestant churches, and not that much difference, as a matter of fact, between Catholics and Protestants anymore. I can confess that I have been instructed more richly by Roman Catholic theologians and biblical scholars lately than I have by Protestants. So you see how broad-minded I am! It's just those others—you know who I'm talking about. You know them. They're really strange. They're not like us. Surely Jesus didn't mean to include them when he said, "He that is not against us is for us." But he did; he meant to include them. That's what it says. Read it: "He that is not against us is for us." That includes a whole lot of folks.

If anyone ought to know that God is bigger than any creed or institution, it ought to be the Church. If anyone ought to know that we in the Church don't have the right to boast of our righteousness, it ought to be those of us who live in the Church. We ought to know, those of us in the Church, that God is the one who is beyond our knowledge, that his ways are not our ways and his thoughts are not our thoughts. We ought to know that. That's why we ought to be humble in all we do.

It's a lesson I learned a long time ago in my family. I grew up with a whole bunch of sisters—three of them. My older brothers were gone from the house early on, so I was left as the younger brother of those sisters. I lived under an oppression, a conspiracy is what it was, to get me in trouble all the time. And when our parents would arbitrate the dispute between me and that gang of terror, I was always outnumbered. I always lost. Sometimes I would plead my case in a loud voice in order to be heard, and invariably the parental decree was this, "The one who shouts the loudest is probably wrong!" I heard that so often that I have remembered it all these years, and as I matured I came to appreciate its wisdom. I think it's true, and not just of adolescent quarrels. It's true of the way we communicate the gospel. It's true of the way we talk to one another about our faith. It's kind of like, when in doubt, shout. Those who are confident in what they believe can say it in a whisper. Better yet, those whose lives are firmly rooted in the ground of existence, those who trust God sufficiently to govern things in this world so they don't feel they have to control everything themselves—they're the people who can be tender and loving and humble without feeling diminished. That's the image of the Christian in the New Testament.

People with strength can let other people be who they are. They don't worry that they are not one of us. They can let them be. They can allow that the exorcist, whose behavior is an embarrassment, or the agnostic, whose questions are an affront, may in fact be unknown Christians.

Teacher, we came across a man who is casting out demons in your name. He was not one of us, so we built a wall and shut him out.

You shouldn't have done that, for he that is not against us is for us.—Mark Trotter

SUNDAY, MARCH 11, 2001
Lectionary Message

Topic: Can We Make the Most of a Second Chance?

TEXT: Luke 13:1–9 (31–35)

Other Readings: Gen. 15:1–12, 17–18; Ps. 27; Phil. 3:17–4:1

Luke points this morning to a barren fig tree. We find the tree planted in the lushest of garden spots. The gardener treats it with tender care: he waters, mulches, and fertilizes it before anything else in the garden. He anticipates that the tree will provide abundantly. But after three years: nothing! The owner expresses disappointment and frustration. He finally gives up and demands that the gardener dump the tree.

The gardener's reply? "Oh, chief, not so fast! Let's give the tree another year. Maybe I've failed to do everything necessary to nourish it. Maybe I could enrich the soil, or change the irrigation. In any case, let's give it another chance, and if next year it fails we'll get rid of it."

I. Luke's point is clear. He compares those of us in the churches to the barren fig tree. It is time, he says, for the people of God to bear fruit or be cast aside. He suggests that, like that tree, we have inherited a tremendously rich spiritual heritage and we tend to squander it. He tells us we receive so much from the grace of Christ, yet we fritter those promises and mandates away. Like that fig tree, we're barren of fruit, and the garden might be better off without us.

II. Do you sympathize with the owner? Do you share his frustration with the fig tree— with the Christian Church? with this church? No doubt many of us nod our heads in agreement with the owner. Some of us look at our church and say, "Cut it down."

But the gardener? I prefer to identify with him. His tool is not the axe but the trowel. The fig tree we call the Church of Christ, for all its blight and canker, gains the advocacy of the gardener: just one more chance—irrigation, compost, no axes or chainsaws; just loam, perlite, and peat.

III. What do we want to care for in our churches? What do we want to flourish? What do we want for our worship and music, education, outreach, and pastoral care—the major ministries of a local church? For our church? I hope that through whatever we do here, and in spite of all our limitations, pretensions, and imperfections, those who seek the presence of the one who heals amid illness and reconciles amid brokenness can find that presence here.

IV. I hope we are a people who live from a vision: We remember our future. We live out of hope. We remember the wonderful promise in the book of Revelation where John of Patmos sees a new city in which the caprice of nature, the stupidity of nations, and our own unsettled selves resolve into a harmony radiant in friendship and solidarity. Dr. Martin Luther King Jr. calls this the vision of a "World House," lifting neighborhood concern beyond one's family, tribe, race, class, creed, and nation into an unconditional and all-embracing love for all human beings.

V. If we live from such a vision, then we live also to see it blossom in God's world. And that calls forth from us a ministry of justice and of peace. That means we bear a public agenda. That means we think, pray about, and act on matters of human rights and equal justice. We care who holds power: how they accumulate it, sustain it, use it, and abuse it. If as Christians we find ourselves united to follow one who tilts toward the poor, the maimed, and those who find themselves socially crippled, we will be advocates and discover ourselves joining the struggle against a complacent, resistant, well-heeled political or economic status quo. Ours is a covenant with the God of the prophets and with the Christ to confront poverty—to feed the hungry, clothe the naked, and care for the sick and imprisoned, and to do it not only as an act of charity, which seldom alters an unjust status quo, but even more persistently as an act of justice, seeking to alleviate the root causes of poverty.

VI. Finally, as a community of gardeners, this church needs people who love it. We need people in this church who will be claimed by the vision of Christ's new world and join us in making possible little outposts of it. We need people who see this house, this congregation, and its location not as ends in themselves but as vessels to pass on the treasure of the gospel to new generations, to the curious and the spiritually hungry; to exercise leverage on behalf of the suffering and the bound. I have heard it said that no one builds his life into an institution anymore. Perhaps not. Maybe we muddle along with a nineteenth-century anachronism. But a church like this needs people to invest in it—"loving critics, critical lovers"—loyal to Christ and to what that loyalty means for our pilgrimage together.

It is said that green is the color of hope. We're gardeners working on a glorious fig tree. We want it, in every way, to flourish, blossom, and bear fruit.—James W. Crawford

ILLUSTRATIONS

THE CALL OF NEED.   To Isaiah, the voice said, "Go," and for each of us there are many voices that say it, but the question is which one will we obey with our lives, which of the voices that call is to be the one we answer? No one can say, of course, except each for himself, but I believe that it is possible to say at least this in general to all of us: we should go with our lives where we most need to go and where we are most needed.—Frederick Buechner[3]

THE SECOND CHANCE.   This parable tells us of *the gospel of the second chance.* A fig tree normally takes three years to reach maturity. If it is not fruiting by that time it is not likely to fruit. But this fig tree was given a second chance. It is always Jesus' way to give a man chance after chance. Peter and Mark and Paul would all gladly have witnessed to that. God is infinitely kind to the man who falls and rises again.—William Barclay[4]

SERMON SUGGESTIONS

Topic: When Fear Strikes
TEXT: Ps. 27
(1) The reality of fear. (2) The promise of relief from fear. (3) The plan for routing fear: (a) trusting providence (vv. 2–3); (b) cultivating communion with God (v. 4); (c) plunging with courage and expectation (v. 14).

Topic: Making a Success of the Christian Life
TEXT: Phil. 3:17–4:1
(1) Choose the right examples (vv. 17–19). (2) Remember that we are "a colony of heaven" (Moffatt) with a faith and an ethic to share (v. 20). (3) Stand firm in your faith that God will do in and for us what we cannot do ourselves (vv. 3:21–4:1).

---

[3] *The Hungering Dark* (New York: Seabury Press, 1969), p. 31.
[4] *The Gospel of Luke* (Saint Andrew Press, 1956), p. 180.

CONGREGATIONAL MUSIC

1. "God Is My Strong Salvation," James Montgomery (1822)

    CHRISTUS, DER IST MEIN LEBEN, Melchoir Vulpius (1609)

    James Montgomery's fine paraphrase of Psalm 27 could be used effectively with its stanzas sung intermittently with the verses of the psalm.

2. "O Jesus Christ, May Grateful Hymns Be Rising," Bradford G. Webster (1954)

    CHARTERHOUSE, David Evans (1927)

    This excellent contemporary text and tune relates beautifully with the Gospel reading for this Sunday. The third stanza of Webster's hymn specifically refers to Jesus' weeping over Jerusalem.

3. "Great Is Thy Faithfulness," Thomas O. Chisholm (1923)

    FAITHFULNESS, William M. Runyan (1923)

    This familiar song could be appropriately sung in connection with the Old Testament reading about God's covenant with Abraham. It magnifies the trustworthiness of the God who makes firm promises and holds faithfully to covenants.

4. "Be Strong in the Lord," Linda Lee Johnson (1979)

    FETTKE (STRENGTH), Tom Fettke (1979)

    The Epistle lesson ends with "you should stand firm in the Lord, dear friends" (NIV), to which this new gospel song could be a suitable response.

WORSHIP AIDS

CALL TO WORSHIP.   "One thing have I desired of the Lord, that will I seek after; that I may dwell in the house of the Lord all the days of my life, to behold the beauty of the Lord, and to inquire in his temple" (Ps. 27:4).

INVOCATION.   Gracious God, open our minds and hearts and all our senses to the wonder of delight that is possible to us as we meet in worship, await your loving deeds in the world, and live day by day in courage and expectation.

OFFERTORY SENTENCE.   "Every man according as he purposeth in his heart, so let him give; not grudgingly, or of necessity: for God loveth a cheerful giver" (2 Cor. 9:7).

OFFERTORY PRAYER.   We are assured that it rejoices your heart, O God, when we give ourselves and our offering to you. So we bring to you the fruits of our labor, trusting that our contributions will in some measure reflect your own generosity toward us.

PRAYER.   Most merciful God, we confess that we have sinned against you in thought, word, and deed, by what we have done, and by what we have left undone. We have not loved you with our whole heart; we have not loved our neighbors as ourselves. We are truly sorry and we humbly repent. For the sake of your Son Jesus Christ, have mercy on us and forgive us; that we may delight in your will, and walk in your ways, to the glory of your name. Almighty God have mercy on us, forgive us all our sins through our Lord Jesus Christ, strengthen us in all goodness, and by the power of the Holy Spirit keep us in eternal life.— *The Book of Common Prayer*

SERMON
Topic: Getting or Seeking?
TEXT: Deut. 34:1–12

Have you ever wondered how we know what happened up there on that mountain? The story says that Moses went up Mount Nebo alone, and he did not come back. How do we know what happened up there on that mountain?

We have a 120-year-old man wandering around in the wilderness, and the story says that he was not impaired or feeble, his eyes were clear, and his "natural force had not abated." And nobody has seen a trace of him since. They can't even find a freshly dug grave. The story wants us to understand that Moses did not die from old age or by accident. God was involved in this decision. The story wants it clearly understood that Moses died because God willed it so. Moses' work was done; his service was fulfilled and Moses had come to his end.

There are Jewish traditions, according to Elie Wiesel, that suggest that Moses did not die peacefully. There are traditions that suggest that Moses wanted to go on living, that Moses refused to die, refused to act out the role of saint or martyr; he wanted to go on living and he said so. Throughout the story of Moses in Deuteronomy, this question about Moses—about the Promised Land, about God, and about the issue of Moses' death and new leadership—is discussed. There are so many reasons, so many bad reasons, given in the stories as to why Moses was not permitted to enter the Hold Land that one begins to get the feeling that there is no good reason for Moses *not* to enter the Promised Land—no good reason that the children of Israel were willing to put into the story. No good reason, except that God did not want Moses to go into the Promised Land. In God's providence and love, Moses is not scheduled to enter into the Promised Land.

Moses goes for a walk up the mountain. How do we know what happened next? We are told that while he is up there, God shows Moses all the Promised Land. Moses dies. God buries the body and nobody knows where Moses is buried. There is no shrine, no statue, no marker for the most important man in Jewish history.

What do you think? If God did show Moses all of the promised lands that God was going to give the children of Israel and said, you can look but you better not touch, you can see it but you can't have it, is God being kind to Moses or is God teasing Moses in some kind of cruel game? After all Moses and God have been through together, is God being gracious to Moses to let him see the Promised Land, or is God jerking Moses around and being cruel?

Again, there are Jewish traditions that suggest that God is being terribly kind to Moses. "Who knows," says Wiesel again, "Perhaps God's decision not to let Moses enter the Promised Land was meant as reward rather than as punishment." When you consider all that Moses has had to endure—the griping, complaining, rebellion, disobedience, and disrespect—maybe God was being kind to Moses to end it there and then. "Moses, I won't make you put up with any more. Look at the Promised Land; you got them here, now you can rest."

But others suggest that it is rather cruel to let Moses get so close to the Promised Land—so close that he can see it, he can almost taste it, he can feel the breeze coming off the land—yet not let him go over and touch it. Picture God dangling the Promised Land before Moses and pulling it away when Moses reaches out to take it. We tease our animals and sometimes our children with such games and know it is cruel.

Showing Moses the Promised Land but refusing to let him have it—Is that a reward or a cruel trick? This is what is so wonderful and powerful about the biblical stories: they make us discover who we are and what we think. The answer to that question, reward or punishment, depends so much on whether you believe that the purpose, the glory, and the uniqueness of the human spirit is in having or seeking. Is the dignity of human life found in acquiring, owning, having, and holding, or is the great uniqueness of our human lives found in reaching out for the impossible dream? Is the measure of human life found in the sum of all you have, or in the measure of the vastness of your longings unfulfilled? Is life evaluated by what you have, or by what you are hoping and working for?

So much of our culture keeps trying to tell us that the value of our lives is rooted in what we have, and in that mind-set it was cruel of God not to let Moses have a little piece of the Promised Land. The biblical story seems to affirm that the beauty and power of human life is found in seeking: "Seek ye first the Kingdom of God, and all these things shall be added unto you." Life more abundant is found in the seeking. "What does it profit a person to gain the whole world and lose his soul?" The greatness of the human heart is discovered in the pursuit of the Beatitudes: blessed are the peacemakers, blessed are the merciful, blessed are those who hunger and thirst after righteousness. It is the reaching for the unreachable star that gives us our status as children of God.

Even as Madison Avenue advertisers want us to buy more stuff, they understand this deep hunger inside of us to reach, to seek to go beyond the limits to explore the unknown, to drive where there are no boundaries. They understand that the greatest power of the human race is that we have the power to dream and then to seek to make dreams happen. "I believe I can fly" was one of the Grammy-winning songs a year ago. No fear, no boundaries, no limits. St. Paul suggests that we can do all things through Christ who strengthens us.

Is God being kind or cruel to Moses? The answer to that question lies in whether you believe that the greatness of human life is in seeking after the righteousness of God, in praying for the coming of the Kingdom of God so that mercy and grace might become real for all people; or whether you believe that life really is found in the judgment that the one who has the most toys at the end wins. Are we here, living, to use our lives striving to reach the Kingdom of God, or are we here to get as much stuff and to accumulate enough junk that it fills up our homes as it does in the stories on TV?

Is the glory of life found in seeking or in getting? If the dignity and glory of human life is in seeking, then God did Moses a great kindness in showing him the Promised Land. If life is valued by what you get, then God was playing games with Moses to show him he was close but no cigar. Moses does not get the Promised Land.

If life is in the seeking, then God blessed Moses by showing him the reality of the Promised Land. The sight of the Promised Land was a gracious affirmation for Moses that all of his efforts, all of his dreams, all of his struggles had not been for some imaginary pipe dream.

Moses had spent his life pushing, pulling, and corralling the children of Israel toward a piece of land, a land he had never seen. All of his life he had been struggling and working and taking the abuse of the children of Israel toward a place to which he had never been. How many times do you think he must have wondered whether or not there was such a place? What could be more devastating than to spend one's life seeking after that which it turns out does not have even the possibility of existing? To spend all of one's life seeking after that which turns out to be nothing but a mirage or an illusion? Nobody wants his dream destroyed by a reality. God showed Moses the Promised Land so that Moses would die knowing that the Promised Land existed. That for which he yearned and sought at the very center of his life really did exist.

As Christian people we are invited to come together in hunger and thirst after the Kingdom of God. We are invited to find our life, and life more abundant, by repenting and living as if the Kingdom of God has already come. God has shown us already in Jesus Christ what that new reality, that new creation, that new life would look like. He has invited us to find our joy and glory, to be a royal priesthood, a chosen people. We keep being asked to invest more and more in the support and continuation of the seeking, of the striving, and lots of times we wonder whether we are wasting our money. Could we do something better or get better results with our dollars in different ways? It is giving to and supporting this community that declares that you continue to long for and seek the coming of the Kingdom of God.

God showed Moses the Promised Land. God showed Moses the Promised Land out of great love and compassion for Moses. "Moses, there really is a land that the children of Israel will live on. There is a reality that matches and fulfills your striving." Great comfort and peace comes in knowing that we strive for that which indeed can and will exist. "It doesn't matter about me anymore. I have been to the mountain. I have seen the Promised Land. It is enough." Life isn't really found in getting a lot of stuff and then doing nothing. The whole notion of accumulating lots of stuff and then doing nothing in retirement is foreign to the nature of our lives in Scripture. Remember the farmer who said to himself that he had enough and he was now going to enjoy himself, and then he died. For God created us so that our human dignity, our greatness as a people, is to be found in that for which we yearn, for which we seek, for which we struggle. In Jesus Christ God has shown us that there is the possibility of a new life, a new creation, a new reality, a new Kingdom, and it is as we work, as we give, as we continue as a people to seek to become the children of God in this place that we find our greatest blessing.

Cruelty or grace? Punishment—you can look but you will never touch—or reward? To me the answer seems to be whether you believe God made us for getting and holding and acquiring stuff or whether you believe that we were made for seeking the will and purposes of God.—Rick Brand

SUNDAY, MARCH 18, 2001
Lectionary Message

Topic: A Faith for Tough Times
TEXT: Luke 13:31–35
Other Readings: Isa. 55:1–9; Ps. 67:1–8; 1 Cor. 10:1–13

Can you live the Christian life? Can I? Can this beloved Church of ours? How do we live out our faith in these times?

Our passage this morning offers a clue, but we will find little that suggests some sort of typical religious practice. No spiritual disciplines, no special religious ritual. Luke shows us Jesus being warned by some religious leaders—bishop types—against Herod's murderous designs. Did the warnings come from friends who wanted Jesus to stick around and fight for another day? Or did the warnings come from enemies seeking to scare Jesus into silence? We do not know. In any case, they sound a strident note: "Get out of here! Head for the hills! Herod's death squads mean to kill you. Your silence will keep both the peace and your life."

Do you recall our Lord's response? Does he turn tail, cut and run? Hardly. He replies, "Tell that conniving, two-faced charlatan Herod that Jerusalem remains my objective. I will confront that city with a new way of life. And no doubt the city will treat me with the same contempt and rejection it inflicted upon all who sought to save and transform it down through the ages."

What does Luke show us here? What do we see about the life lived from faith? On the one hand, Herod and his threats and demands will in no way deter or erode Jesus' mission. We see loyalty to a living God that will not be brooked or distracted by any human claims. On the other hand, we see a God who remains loyal to us through everything, who amid all our trouble and failure wants nothing more than to gather us in order to save us. Our loyalty to God and God's loyalty to us: the grounds for faith in tough times.

I. First, then, our loyalty to God. A basic question: Where do our loyalties lie? Who makes the greatest claim on our lives? What, finally, do we worship?

There are of course many things and people in whom we place our confidence and trust: our bloodlines, our credentials, our income stream. But this morning, because of Herod's claims on Jesus, I suggest a loyalty that is making a claim on all of us, our nation, the United States of America.

I beg us, be wary of confusing—as the Herods of this world always do—be wary of confusing what those in power define as the national interest with the will of God. I caution us against identifying any privileged status with the favor of almighty God. Our faith enables us to avoid this trap in two ways: it insists that God be God, and that all of our human constructs—all of them—are frail, finite, and conditioned by the moment, the times, the perspective, the interests of those who design those constructs. What we make, what we decide, and what we speculate are not God, and the claim to be Christian frequently bears a presumption that we creatures dare seldom assert. Bishop Tutu says it best: "You are not God," he said to those South African leaders claiming God for racial oppression. "You are not God. You are just ordinary human beings. Maybe you have a lot of power now. But watch it! Watch it! Watch it!"

Notwithstanding our resistance to the nationalistic claims of Herod in this world, we do hear the prophetic words of Israel and Jesus, and trusting a divine disposition not so much toward Herod and Caesar, we do discover one to the disinherited, the poor, the marginalized, the outsider. We do act from confidence and faith that the God of compassion and justice rules the world and uses even our warped vision and our choices corrupted by self-interest to take baby steps toward healing and hope.

Nevertheless, in nation and politics, only God is God. That is where our loyalties lie.

II. Luke not only urges from us a first loyalty to God, but he also affirms the amazing grace and loyalty of God to us. Luke's picture of this loyalty comes through Jesus' lament over Jerusalem.

I want to say just a few brief words about this lament. We have here one of the Bible's most vivid images of God: a hen gathering a brood under her wings. We see here an intimate God, a God whose wings surround the weakest and the strongest, the most vulnerable and the most secure.

I remember years ago my own mother calling my sisters and me her "little chicks." She uses the same expression for her grandchildren today. I suppose if you were to ask me who God is like, I might begin by saying, "God is like Jesus," but then I would probably begin describing Jesus as a lot like my mother—and I would not be surprised if my own children used *their* mother as an image of God. Fancy that! In my case, my mother was fixing up, bailing out, backing up, filling the need, supplying the difference, sending the check, greasing the wheels, applying the Band-Aids, running interference, communicating, coordinating, surprising, chauffeuring, nursing, teaching, financing, listening, healing, weeping, praying, and always eager to gather and nurture us under wings—and still is to this very moment. Could it be that God is someone like her?

I think so.

Thus is our faith for tough times! It is faith sustained through thick and thin, pinning its loyalty on the sovereign God, betting its life on the intimate God.—James W. Crawford.

ILLUSTRATIONS

THE CONTINUING SELF-DISCLOSURE OF CHRIST.   The Christ who holds the fate of the universe in His hands, both in His earthly and in His continuing disclosure of Himself, has chosen to make Himself known through the pangs of the hungry, the desperation of the sick, the exposure of the naked, the loneliness of the stranger, and the self-defeatedness of the prisoner. Christ continues to reveal Himself anew in the extreme needs of "the least of these His brethren." In them we do not find the mere footprints and fingerprints of where He *has* been. Here we find His feet and hands themselves. Here we do not hear an echo of his voice, but the voice of the Christ Himself. Here we find the Christ Himself achingly involved in the destiny of human beings.—Wayne E. Oates[5]

BIBLICAL REALISM.   At the end of the war in 1945, I wrote in a Christmastide article that peace on earth, on which at that moment the hopes of so many were set, was not at all realizable in the immediate future and hardly to be expected. For this unforgivable pessimism protests rained down upon me and many of my own friends were very discontented with me. So great is the power of desire that it blinds us to the real state of affairs.

But the Bible is through and through realistic. It sees things as they are and never blurs our vision by a blue haze. It never tells us things are getting better and better but warns us in advance: terrible times are coming, times of trial which everyone would like to avoid if possible. And the Johannine Revelation above all does not spare to paint these times of crisis in the darkest and most frighteningly gruesome colours—not to scare us but to make us prepared. If we know that evil times are coming we can be prepared beforehand. Just as we store food supplies for the times when our country, cut off from the outer world, will be in want, so also the soul can, so to speak, make emergency preparations for dark days ahead. For this reason alone the seer John or rather the Lord Himself speaks about what is to come.—Emil Brunner[6]

---

[5] *The Revelation of God in Human Suffering* (Philadelphia: Westminster Press, 1959), p. 17.
[6] *The Great Invitation* (Philadelphia: Westminster Press, 1955), p. 72f.

SERMON SUGGESTIONS

Topic: The Missionary Call of the Old Testament

TEXT: Jonah 1:1–3, 3:1–2

Truths that stand in need of constant reinforcement: (1) God's love and compassion reach out to all. (2) All are capable of receiving that love and responding to it. (3) Some who themselves enjoy the knowledge of God are often strangely and amazingly unwilling to share it with others.—J. D. Jones[7]

Topic: Three Groans

(1) "The whole creation groaneth" (Rom. 8:22). (2) "We ourselves groan within ourselves" (Rom. 8:23). (3) "The Spirit himself maketh intercession for us with groanings which cannot be uttered" (Rom. 8:26).—W. E. Sangster[8]

CONGREGATIONAL MUSIC

1. "Guide Me, O Thou Great Jehovah," William Williams (1745); trans. Peter Williams (1771)
   CWM RHONDDA, John Hughes (1907)
   This great Welsh hymn relating to the struggles of the Israelites in the Wilderness (1 Cor. 10:1–4) would be quite appropriate as an opening hymn of worship.
2. "God Is My Great Desire," Timothy Dudley-Smith (1982)
   LEONI, Synagogue melody, arr. Meyer Lyon (1770)
   A contemporary paraphrase of the Psalter reading (Psalm 63), this hymnlike version is effectively set to a venerable Hebrew tune. The melody reflects the bittersweet sense of thirst for God. It would be effective if its first stanza were sung by male voices alone.
3. "Give to the Winds Thy Fears," Paul Gerhardt (1696); trans. John Wesley (1737)
   ST. BRIDE, Samuel Howard (1762)
   The theme of this fine hymn bears out the teaching of Isaiah 55:8 that God's thoughts are far higher than ours and unfathomable to our finite minds. But this is the basis for the exercise of our trust in his mercy and grace.
4. "Rescue the Perishing," Fanny J. Crosby (1869)
   RESCUE, William H. Doane (1869)
   This gospel song could appropriately follow the Gospel reading with its warnings that all must repent or perish.—Hugh T. McElrath

WORSHIP AIDS

CALL TO WORSHIP.   "Because thy loving-kindness is better than life, my lips shall praise thee. Thus will I bless thee while I live: I will lift up my hands in thy name" (Ps. 63:3–4).

INVOCATION.   Gracious and loving God, what can keep me from praising you? Even amid the trials and tragedies of life we find tokens of your care and providence. Teach us once more as we worship you that you will never leave us or forsake us.

---

[7] *Richmond Hill Sermons*
[8] *Can I Know God?*

OFFERTORY SENTENCE.   "Therefore as ye abound in everything, in faith and utterance and knowledge, and in all diligence, and in your love to us, see that ye abound in this grace also" (2 Cor. 8:7).

OFFERTORY PRAYER.   O God, in the midst of our many comings and goings in our life of faith and service may we remember the causes of your Kingdom that need and use our monetary support. So bless our offerings and bless us in our giving.

PRAYER.   Father, how can we know your mind when we come to you so often from so many directions and with so many petitions? Yet to whom can we go but you? We have indeed found that you do have the words of life. So we gather, folks with many separate agendas, many differing ideas of what you desire, but all in need of your listening ear and directing Spirit. Help those of us who feel that we have hit rock bottom to realize that we have landed on the Rock of Ages. Help us to understand that when we cry in our lostness, feeling abandoned and alone in this universe, "Take not your Holy Spirit from me," that we are really nearer to you than we may have been for months or years. Remind us anew that when we have touched the depths of life we have also touched the everlasting arms.

We have come here this morning for many reasons, Lord. But all of us gather in this quiet, sacred place because we have broken vows we once made, we have frequently failed to live to the highest we know, and we have done that which would long ago have justified your removing your Spirit from us once and for all. Yet the very fact that we are here in this holy place is evidence that your Spirit is still operating in our lives. Otherwise we would not have been moved to be here. Therefore, to the most distressed and troubled among us as well as to those of us who have ignored our sins and shames may the Word of Jesus be plainly heard again, that Word he spoke to his depressed and distressed disciples so long ago when he said, "Look up and lift up your heads, for your redemption has come nigh!" May that be our experience now, Lord, as we wait and worship before you. We pray in Christ's matchless name.—Henry Fields

SERMON
Topic: Master of Wind and Wave
Text: Matt. 8:23–27

They are just four verses in the Gospel according to Matthew, yet they have dramatized for all time the plight of man and the power of God, and the exciting promise of a new world of confidence and courage made possible by faith!

The voice of the disciples is the voice of fear, the voice of Jesus is the voice of power. The disciples knew the sea too well not to fear it. Several of them were fishermen with a fisherman's respect for the sea. They knew their plight; they had yet to learn the power of the Savior who delivers us from the deepest peril. The familiar chorus dramatizes this contrast—the fear of the disciples and the power of the Savior.

This is no isolated incident. It is one in a whole series of incidents in this portion of the Gospel, each one of which speaks of the power of Jesus Christ as not something that man generates but as something that God gives. There is the healing of the Gadarene maniac, the man who thought he was possessed by six thousand devils and who could burst strong chains asunder. But Jesus healed him. There is the story of the healing of the sick woman whom doctors could not help. There is the account of the restoring to life of Jairus's twelve-year-old daughter. These stories tell us of God's power. It is a power that comes to us from God, to hearten us and bless us on our way in this earthly sphere, a divinely given power in which we can trust and put our confidence.

It must be said that if you had looked at Jesus you would not have thought of power. You would have thought of anything else, for the Son of God was weary. He was sleeping the sleep of exhaustion. Even the violent movement of the boat and the great noise of the storm did not wake him; he was so tired. Looking on him in that situation, sunk in slumber, tired and weary of body, you would not have thought of power. In fact, I think the disciples were a little annoyed with him, a little irritated, perhaps disappointed. This man was their Master, yet he was a picture of fatigue, sleeping in the stern of this little fishing boat.

How little we know about the power of God! How obsessed and dominated our minds are by appearance when we should be seeking out realities! For all the power of the universe was personified in Jesus Christ, the Son of God, who was collapsed in the stern of that little fishing boat. We can cling to our confidence in him no matter what the appearance, for he has the power to say, "Peace, be still" and to quiet the fiercest of life's storms!

God is present in storms as well as in calm. He counts on us for courage in experiences of distress. "Where is your faith?" He challenges us to receive his peace. God is present in power, even in the storms of life. Part of our mortal experience will be stormy—you can be sure of it. With the eyes of faith we see the power of God, whose loving purpose fills us with hope, no matter how threatening the storm. "Well roars the storm to those who hear a deeper voice across the storm!"

For the power of God is in the service of his love. The Christ who is master of wind and wave is the Savior whose love rescues the perishing. His love gives the peace that conquers panic, a peace that is strong and confident because it rests on the character of God.

"Where is your faith?" he asks of you and me. If the outlook is bad, have you tried the uplook? You have seen the storm; have you seen the Savior who is stronger than the storm? The Master of wind and wave is our hope and our peace, no matter how fierce the storm!

Matthew 7:21 is a wonderfully practical teaching that strikes an immediate response from everyone. "Not everyone who says to me 'Lord, Lord' shall enter the kingdom of heaven, but he who does the will of my Father who is in heaven." What we profess is judged by what we perform. As Emerson said, "What you do sounds so loudly in my ear, I can hardly hear what you say." There are two atheisms, not one. There is the atheism of unbelief and there is the atheism of conduct. Each atheism is perilous, but the atheism of conduct is the less obvious, and it can betray us before we are aware of it. As James (1:22) warns, "But be doers of the word, and not hearers only, deceiving yourselves." Like Chaucer's parson, he who teaches Christ's love must first live it. The quality of our life is more convincing than the quantity of our professions. People are looking at Christians all the while and asking themselves, "How are they different from anybody else?" Not just creeds but deeds have impact as Christian witness.

The world is watching us—idly, curiously, critically, sometimes earnestly. What they are watching is our conduct. Are we different from other people? Better? More competent to cope? Is there in us a quality of spirit so intriguing that others looking at our lives want to know the secret of our confidence and our peace? Or do the sheep look like the wolves in the actual world of deeds?

The Gospel challenges us to make life and religion one—our deeds and our creeds. By our fruits are we known. People with aching needs may be watching us with wistful hope. Will they know we are Christians by our love?

No matter how enthusiastic our witness of the Word, we are called to a comparable witness of deed. The atheism of conduct can nullify our professions of faith. "Not everyone who says . . . but he who does" is Jesus' word of warning. It is a challenge to vibrant and radiant living, in which the glory of God in whom we believe gives a shining splendor to the life we live among men.—Lowell M. Atkinson[9]

SUNDAY, MARCH 25, 2001
Lectionary Message
Topic: Who Gets a Place at the Table?
TEXT: Luke 15:1–3, 11b–32
Other Readings: John 5:9–12; Ps. 32; 2 Cor. 5:16–21

Who gets a place at God's table? Who is included in the feast of God? Who joins in the joy of the lost being found, the dead gaining life again? This parable about two sons and their father is really about a fantastic party, a gladsome feast, an exuberant banquet thrown by one overjoyed at the recovery of a beloved lost child, a precious life restored.

Luke tells the story amid the virulent hatreds of his own time. Jews and Gentiles found themselves at each other's throats. Indeed, Gentiles coming into the Church caused the Jesus-movement Jews great consternation. Gentiles found themselves unwelcome. They lived outside the pale: rejects, dregs, ethnic and religious outsiders. Unwelcome! And some firmly orthodox folk grumbled about these troublemakers, these sinners, these religious and ethnic rejects making their way into the early Church. So Luke narrates one of our Lord's parables.

I. Luke's parable begins by telling us of a son demanding a share of his father's estate. The father gives his son his due inheritance. The son turns it into cash. He leaves home and heads off into the far country. In that distant land he wastes his inheritance. He goes broke. He cannot find work. He begins to starve. To his family he is lost.

Thus cut off, this lost child comes to his senses. He says to himself, "Even the lowest flunky on my father's payroll gets better than this." So he decides to head home. He practices a mantra of shame on his way, expecting his father to have it in for him. But something else happens. The father recognizes the son's return from far off, and as the boy begins to stammer his confession he finds himself crushed in his father's embrace and kissed—not as a servant, not as a child, but as an equal—and his father saying, "You are my son through everything that has happened."

Then the father, in his overflowing joy, arranges a feast with this son as guest of honor. The father dresses his son in a fine garment, puts a signet on his hand, provides a holiday

---

[9] *Apples of Gold*

calf for the feast, and celebrates "this child of mine who was dead and has come to life, who was lost and is found." Everybody on the estate and those from miles around are in attendance at the feast.

II. Except one! Who is this? Elder brother. Dutiful. Competent. Loyal, hardworking elder brother. He discovers the party. He hears the music. He sees the revelry. He wonders: Why this festive occasion? He learns that his father is throwing the party for that derelict, absent, degenerate child. Is elder brother happy? Is elder brother relieved at the prodigal's return? Not on your life. Elder brother is furious. He refuses to go in.

Why is elder brother so angry? Is it because he hates his brother? No. He's angry because *he* has never known a party like this. He cannot enjoy a feast where everyone, especially the degenerate sibling, is present. *The inclusive party is the issue.* Nothing else. "Never so much as a goat to celebrate with my friends."

The father assures elder brother of his warm acceptance in the house and wonders how elder brother can refuse to participate in the festivities.

So what is Luke doing? He brings together at a great feast the virulent antagonists of his own time. He draws a picture of a jubilant banquet where the most hated and alien enemy of the moment is welcomed, reconciled, and engaged in a festival of peace and joy. Luke leaves behind those grumblers we met at the beginning. They're shocked by Jesus' eating with "tax gatherers and sinners." But Luke leaves those murmurers fuming and whining about who is in and who is out, who eats with whom and who does not, who is welcome at the table and who is not. In this parable Luke says to those calculating religious and ethnic chauvinists, "Hey, you clowns, can't you see that at God's table everyone is welcome? Your strained efforts to divide men and women ethnically, creedally, nationally, and religiously bears no resemblance to the universal festival of reconciliation that God throws. That is the social bash God wants. When it happens, how can we do anything but dance and sing, make music, and like that father, exuberantly share the joy with everyone?"—James W. Crawford

ILLUSTRATION

ACCEPTANCE.   What marks the words *acceptance by God* is the unconditional fact that God accepts precisely the unacceptable. The holy accepts, goes after, and loves the sinner. The one who is the offended party initiates the action so that when we talk of the divine acceptance, that's not the nth power. It is substantially different. That God accepts me is crazy. That I accept my neighbor is an act of humanly understandable generosity. But no understanding of this human meaning of acceptance ever adds up to, or is analogous to, divine acceptance.

You cannot move from the analysis of the ambiguity and partiality of human acceptance to the divine acceptance; but you can move from the divine acceptance to a transformation of the possibilities of our human acceptances. The New Testament instructs us in "forgiving each other as the Lord has forgiven you." This means that the miracle of the divine acceptance, the amazing grace of it, can open us up and make us more generous, charitable, just, and accepting.—Joseph A. Sittler[10]

---

[10] *Grace Notes and Other Fragments* (Minneapolis: Augsburg Fortress, 1981), p. 111.

SERMON SUGGESTIONS

Topic: Honest Confession

TEXT: Ps. 32

(1) The blessedness of being forgiven by God. (2) The burden of the cover-up. (3) The painful process of confession. (4) The new confidence that follows confession and forgiveness. (5) The needed guidance that follows a right standing with God.

Topic: What's New?

Text: 2 Cor. 5:16–21

(1) A new creation: you! (2) A new task: ambassadors for Christ.

CONGREGATIONAL MUSIC

1. "O Love That Wilt Not Let Me Go," George Mattheson (1882)

    ST. MARGARET, Albert L. Peace (1882)

    The compelling love of Christ spoken of by the apostle Paul in 2 Corinthians 5:14 is the basis for this remarkable hymn written from an experience of mental suffering.

2. "Saviour, Teach Me Day by Day," Jane E. Leeson (1842)

    POSEN, George C. Strattner (1691)

    This simple song of prayer and trust for children offers a natural response to the words of Psalm 32:8, "I will instruct you and teach you in the way you should go."

3. "Lord, I'm Coming Home," William J. Kirkpatrick (1892)

    COMING HOME, William J. Kirkpatrick (1892)

    An appropriate response to the Gospel lesson of the parable of the lost son would be this familiar gospel song of invitation.

4. "God Be with You Till We Meet Again," Jeremiah E. Rankin (1880)

    RANDOLPH, Ralph Vaughan Williams (1906)

    This devotional song that echoes the message in Psalm 32:7–8 that God will watch over and protect us would be suitable for the closing of worship on this Sunday.

WORSHIP AIDS

CALL TO WORSHIP.   "I will instruct thee and teach thee in the way which thou shalt go: I will guide thee with mine eye" (Ps. 32:8).

INVOCATION.   O God, our Father, we need your counsel for every step of our living and doing. We pray that we may open our hearts and minds now to hear what you would say to us.

OFFERTORY SENTENCE.   "Now he that ministereth seed to the sower both minister bread for your food and multiply your seed sown, and increase the fruits of your righteousness; being enriched in every thing to all bountifulness which causeth through us thanksgiving to God" (2 Cor. 9:10–11).

OFFERTORY PRAYER.   Lord of the harvest, we anticipate your doing great things with the seed that we sow by bringing offerings to you. Bless these offerings and increase our faith and service, we pray.

PRAYER.   O Giver of every good and perfect gift, driven by great hungers of heart and mind and soul we search the world's mysteries for that bread by which we may be sustained, and we discover in the broken body of your Son the only bread that satisfies. Accept our thanks, O God, for this deep mystery that through his brokenness we are made whole.

The vision present to Peter, James, and John is not denied us but is etched on our minds and hearts in even bolder relief with the validation of nearly twenty centuries of human history.

We pray that the worship of these moments may truly be an epiphany—a mountaintop experience of your glory that will motivate and sustain us in the valley of human need where we are called daily to serve.

In these days of Lent deliver us from all littleness of heart, shallowness of mind, and smugness of spirit that would keep us from entering into the world-embracing love purpose we discover in the life and ministry, the Passion and Resurrection of Christ. Grant us the courage to follow your Word in him wherever it leads us—to follow it when it leads us out of the sanctuary into the marketplace, to follow it when it leads us out of the cozy enclave of some easy security to hazard life on the open road, to follow it when it beckons us to follow him up some new Calvary.

When we do not love, we are false to the purpose to which you are calling us. May your love through us go forth to the ill and their families, to the bereaved in their loneliness, to the failing in their discouragement. Where there is any estrangement among us or among our acquaintances or friends, we pray for the strength to love so that reconciliation may be celebrated. Let us not neglect those resources of your Spirit that you have given for the healing of the nations, so that goodwill and reconstruction may supplant hostility and destruction.

Keep us from going back to business as usual when a day of unprecedented opportunity challenges us to dream and build those structures founded on truth, righteousness, and justice through which your peace can become the blessing of all humankind. With all peoples may we live hopefully in the coming of your Kingdom now present in the world in Christ.— John M. Thompson

SERMON
Topic: Let Faith Look up
TEXT: Ps. 121

Psalm 121 reminds us that our horizon of hope is not the skyline of the city of man; it is the glorious vista of the hills of God. The psalmist's homeland was a land of hills. A mountainous ridge runs north and south through the heart of Palestine, with breathtaking views and startling ravines. Jerusalem, the city of God, is situated atop this ridge. Pilgrims ascended as they made their way to the Holy City. The hill spoke of God to men of faith. "I will lift up mine eyes unto the hills."

How the Hebrews longed for the hills of the homeland when they were exiles in Babylon. In that alien land there were no hills. There was only the flatland of the river plain. The horizon was framed not by the hills of God but by the buildings of man. For Babylon was the business and commercial center of the ancient world, and its great buildings of brick spoke of the achievements of man. No wonder the Hebrew exile yearned for the hills of home! To him they spoke of God, and the cry of longing comes from the heart, "I will lift up mine eyes unto the hills."

"Whence cometh my help?" Not from man. "My help cometh from the Lord, who made heaven and Earth." God's overarching care is ever above us, but we do not enjoy the peace of his wonderful providence until our faith looks up. In our day, too, faith must look up. We are surrounded by the things made by man. Modern Babylons tell of the accomplishments of man in the world of things. Meanwhile, a world impoverished in soul strives desperately to discover from whence cometh help. Corrie Ten Boom tells us what God taught her in a concentration camp. "What did I learn? I learned how futile the things of the world are and how to conquer the things of the world in us. I learned to know the source of strength, and that this source is not in us, but in God." When the outlook is bad, we can trust the uplook.

Where does faith look today? For many, faith looks *in*. Ours is a psychologically oriented age in which many are perpetually holding a mirror to the psyche to discover if all is well. People seek psychological answers to life's real problems. We wonder if perhaps by looking in we may achieve mental health through proper analysis, education, and understanding. The problem of mental health is great. In the hospitals of the United States, one half of the beds are occupied by mental patients. No wonder that in a world of such spiritual disorientation, people feel the need to set things right within. Can we find a successful psychological formula to provide therapy for the multitude of mentally distressed in this great land? Not unless our faith looks up! This is the message of Dr. Robert Schuller, whose training in psychology is dedicated to the service of Jesus Christ, inspiring us to lift up our hearts and look to God in hope. The upward look can save us from the treadmill of perpetual self-analysis and put us on a stairway that leads to heaven. John Wesley wrote to one of his ministers, "You look inward too much and upward too little." We must by all means look inward sufficiently to understand ourselves. But we will never know ourselves only by looking in. We know ourselves when we look up to God and see ourselves as God sees us. When we know *whose* we are, we understand *who* we are!

"Whence cometh my help?" For countless multitudes, faith looks *down*. This may sound bizarre, if not incredible, until we recollect how many people put faith in things the hand can grasp. How many people truly believe that "money talks" and listen eagerly to what it says. We easily say such revealing expressions as, "Money may not be everything but it can get you anything." This is nonsense, of course; yet people say it, believe it, live by it. Here is faith that looks *down*!

Only the touch of God can redeem us from the lure of the material. He has put all things under our feet. He has taught us to respect the dignity of humanity, which is meant to be master of things, not their slave. Persons are more significant than purses in the economy of God. A visitor from another land returned home with the comment, "America is wonderful, but I shall miss only the things that are material." What a terrible indictment! Are our best values in the subhuman realm, below humanity? Must faith look down? No, for God can transfigure our money into human blessing if we look to him in faith. The subhuman world becomes sacramental when faith looks up, and the world of the material serves the purposes of the spiritual world.

Again, faith may look *out*. In our world of highly developed communication, the outward look is universal. The magic of modern electronics makes it not only possible but almost inevitable that news flashes around the globe every day and reaches almost everyone, everywhere. This has a mighty effect on how people feel. If news is good, we feel good. If new is bad, we feel bad. What we see when we look out on our world determines whether we feel good or bad, and multitudes are fluctuating between moods of unwarranted elation and unnecessary despair because they place their faith in the events of the world about us. Our faith as Christians does not depend on the character of current events; it depends on the character of God. Our happiness is not at the mercy of happenings. Men of faith praise God no matter what happens. To be sure, out faith must look out upon our world. We must think in global terms, feel compassion for all peoples, hold the world in our hearts. Because God so loved the world, we must love it, too. This can be done only as faith looks up. Faith in God restores spiritual confidence and zeal when bad news numbs our spirits. The touch of God inspires our missionary outreach and sacrificial service all around the world. The outreach of faith brings the love of God into the lives of mankind everywhere.

"I will lift up mine eyes." Let faith look up and all else falls into place. We can look in, because now we are concerned to give to God a well-integrated personality the better able to do his will. We can look down to the material things with which we have to deal and we can strive for a sound financial life that we may better serve God with the material possessions entrusted to us. Our faith can also look out on our world of tension with courage because our trust is in the God who reigns over all. When faith looks up, it sees the face of the heavenly Father and we never again live without hope. If we look to him, we can never fail; without him, we can never succeed.

Years ago, the Epworth League, the youth organization of the Methodist Church, employed the slogan, "Look up, lift up!" That says it all! The man of faith becomes the man of power. We lift up our eyes unto the hills, and the power from on high that works in us invigorates our lives and we bring the blessings of God into the life of our world.—Lowell M. Atkinson[11]

SUNDAY, APRIL 1, 2001
Lectionary Message

Topic: Not Yet Perfect?
TEXT: Phil. 3:4b-14
Other Readings: Isa. 43:16–21; Ps. 126; John 12:1–8

Not Yet Perfect—question mark! Placing that question mark after the title of this sermon creates a variety of possible responses. Is the question judgmental, critically implying that one ought to be perfect but has not arrived? Or is it a sincere question by a struggling person seeking perfection? Perhaps the question dismisses all one's accomplishments by highlighting life's continuing imperfection. Regardless of how we understand the question, Paul was unequivocal in his understanding: "Not that I have already obtained this or am already perfect" (Phil. 3:12).

Recognizing one's imperfection becomes a prerequisite for achieving emotional and spiritual maturity. Such openness to one's legitimate limitations reminds me of a needlepoint

---

[11] *Apples of God*

wall hanging I purchased overseas some years ago. Inscribed on it is an old Hebrew prayer. Its message has always been a personal challenge:

From the cowardice that shrinks from new truths,
From the laziness that is content with half truths,
And from the arrogance that thinks it knows all truth,
O God of truth, deliver us.

I. *Depending on prior accomplishments* (Phil. 3:4b–6). Persons of significant accomplishment face numerous dangers, especially pride and self-satisfaction. The apostle Paul might well have succumbed to both threats. Indeed, by his own statement he believed, "If anyone has confidence in the flesh, I have more" (Phil. 3:4b). Such pride reflects the twin dangers of a two-edged sword—pride and self-satisfaction destroying one internally while offending others externally.

Pride appropriately affirms personal self-worth and achievement (v. 4b). Doubtless some will think it strange, perhaps even inappropriate, to affirm pride and self-worth. Yet is it not appropriate to affirm those qualities while also recognizing one's limitations? Pity the person who sees herself as a zero, an empty shell with limited or nonexistent worth. Numerous persons see themselves in this way, and they need to discover a new understanding of pride.

Assuming the propriety of pride, we might well distinguish between *positive* pride and *negative* pride. Too often we suffer because we have mistakenly understood that we should suppress pride and minimize individual worth. Nothing could be further from the truth. This conflict between affirming human achievement while avoiding negative pride emerged in the language of a friend who served some years as an executive in a denominational association. Remembering the biblical caution about pride over the years he developed a unique way of congratulating congregations for their accomplishments. "I am humbly proud of your accomplishments." How can one be *humbly proud*? That's positive pride!

Pride's propensity to exaggerate personal achievements threatens authentic spiritual growth (vv. 5–6). Paul might properly have been proud of his significant role in Judaism. His half-dozen signal qualifications merit appropriate affirmation. He demonstrated pride of heritage— "circumcised on the eighth day, of the people of Israel, of the tribe of Benjamin, a Hebrew born of Hebrews." Paul also identified himself with Pharisees, and zeal characterized his persecution of the early Church. Further, he believed himself to be righteous and, under the law, blameless (Phil. 3:3–6).

II. *Dismissing present values* (Phil. 3:7–11).

Discovering Christ as life's transcendent value overshadows pride in human achievements (v. 7). Despite his positive pride, which Paul had in his heritage, as well as his zealous pursuit of his religious convictions and of righteousness through the law, Paul dismissed those values that once held priority in his life. "Whatever gain I had, I counted as loss for the sake of Christ."

Knowing Christ creates a new set of values (v. 8). Conversion created a new situation for Paul in which all that had been of greatest value in Judaism he forfeited to follow Christ. Yet in Christ Paul discovered surpassing worth. For him, values he held prior to his conversion were like "rubbish." Like those of whom Jesus spoke, Paul had discovered the one pearl of great price, a treasure hidden in a field (compare Matt. 13:44–46).

Experiencing Christ personally lifts life to a new level of reality (vv. 9–11). A half-dozen qualities define Paul's discovery of a new reality, which brought with it a new perspective and an ultimate commitment. Notice the six phrases: "gain Christ," "found in him," "know him," "share his sufferings," "becoming like him," and "attaining the resurrection from the dead."

III. *Desiring potential maturity* (Phil. 3:12–14). Pressing on toward perfection requires one's perseverance in faith and a personal demonstration of the gospel. More than anything else, Paul sought maturity in Christ. Two essential prerequisites marked his journey: his awareness of his personal limitations and his personal commitment to achieving God's upward calling in Christ.

Acknowledging limitations clears the way for one to begin the journey toward maximum personal achievement (v. 12). Paul had no illusions about his need for redirecting his life. For each of us a necessary beginning point in our journey toward spiritual maturity is an honest assessment of who we are and have been and a new vision of the person we could become in Christ. How one achieves this goal remains more complex than simplistic exhortations to perfection. Yet for Paul, as for every believer, Christ became the motivational force of his quest. I press on, he said, "because Christ Jesus has made me his own." In the mutuality of this commitment our journey unfolds with excitement and amazing potential: we have made Christ our own and he has made us his own.

Affirming potentialities enables one to run the race toward the goal one adopts (vv. 13–14). Paul's protest against Christian self-satisfaction underscores a virtue to which maturing believers should aspire. The apostle models for contemporary believers a twin objective: a holy discontent with the past and a devoted commitment to the goal. Paul's imagery comes from the sports arena, where athletes stretch every muscle and tendon, straining to complete the race by winning the goal. And what is the goal that Paul envisions? Is it some reward system that he identifies? No, despite how much we might seek to define that goal. Most probably the goal is the journey itself. The prize remains the "heavenly call of God in Christ Jesus"— running life's race with dedication and determination, the full embrace of the power of the Risen Christ being its own reward. The race itself becomes the prize!—Roy L. Honeycutt

ILLUSTRATIONS

BEGINNING SMALL.   It is better to begin from one's feeble state and end up strong, to progress from small things to big, than to set your heart from the very first on the perfect way of life, only to have to abandon it later.—Evagrius of Pomtus (c. 305–400)

THE COMING KINGDOM.   Given the conception of a divine intention working in and through human time towards a fulfillment that lies in its completeness beyond human time, our theodicy must find the meaning of evil in the part that it is made to play in the eventual outworking of that purpose; and must find the justification of the whole process in the magnitude of the good to which it leads. The good that outshines all ill is not a paradise lost but a kingdom which is yet to come in its full glory and permanence.—John Hick[1]

---

[1] *Evil and the God of Love* (New York: HarperCollins, 1966), p. 297.

SERMON SUGGESTIONS

Topic: Son of Destiny

TEXT: Heb. 11:23–29

(1) The story of Moses' life begins in the eternal purposes of God. (2) The providence of God worked throughout his life to prepare him for his great work. (3) The purpose of God operated in Moses' life in spite of Moses' faults.

Topic: A Portion of Thyself

TEXT: Rom. 12:1

(1) God has given himself. (2) God's people through the ages have given awe-inspiring portions of themselves. (3) Your own Christian destiny will be fulfilled through your sacrificial living.

CONGREGATIONAL MUSIC

1. "We Sing the Praise of Him Who Died," Thomas Kelly (1815)

   WINDHAM, Daniel Read (1785) ·

   Here is a great cognitive hymn of hope that expands in transcendental terms the truths uttered by the apostle Paul (Phil. 3:4–14). It would be very suitable for the opening of worship.
2. "When God Delivered Israel," Michael Saward (1973)

   SHEAVES, Norman Warren (1973)

   This modern paraphrase of Psalm 126 could be sung alternately with the verses of the Psalm as follows: read vv. 1–2, sing stanza 1; read vv. 3–4, sing stanza 2; read vv. 5–6, sing stanza 3.
3. "New Every Morning Is the Love," John Keble (1827)

   KEDRON, Elkaniah K. Dare (1835)

   John Keble's memorable morning hymn could be thought of as a devotional reflection on Isaiah 43:19 and thus could be sung in connection with the Old Testament lesson for this day.
4. "More Love to Thee, O Christ," Elizabeth Prentiss (1856)

   MORE LOVE TO THEE, William H. Doane (1870)

   This simple song of love and devotion would be suitable as a meditative response to the Gospel lesson that tells the story of Mary's devotion exhibited in the anointing of Jesus.— Hugh T. McElrath

WORSHIP AIDS

CALL TO WORSHIP.   "They that sow in tears shall reap in joy. He that goeth forth and weepeth, bearing precious seed, shall doubtless come again with rejoicing, bringing his sheaves with him" (Ps. 126:5–6).

INVOCATION.   Lord, it is thy will we would do! Help us to discern what that will is in ever clearer light, through this fellowship of believers.—E. Lee Phillips

OFFERTORY SENTENCE.   "For ye know the grace of our Lord Jesus Christ, that, though he was rich, yet for your sake he became poor, that ye through his poverty might be rich."

OFFERTORY PRAYER.   We bring ourselves and our offerings to you this morning, Lord. Use us as you will to declare the wonder of your grace to all people everywhere. Use our offerings to pave the way for the telling of such grand news. We pray in Jesus' name.—Henry Fields

PRAYER.   O God, how can we thank you for this season of Lent when we are so reluctant to enter into its depths and heights? The challenge of the road less traveled is much too demanding for us who give priority to our own ease, comfort, and security. May the stringent note that Lent sounds awaken us from our complacency lest we miss the narrow way, the discipline of love, that alone holds the promise of life.

You who so loved the world that you have given your only Son, you come to each one of us calling us by name. In the spirit of this love we would pray for one another—those we have called by name and all others in urgent need. You know their names. We pray for our families—how conscious we are of needs there. We pray for our family of faith, that together we may respond to your call to be the Church in this time and place. We pray for the family of humankind in all of its brokenness.

Give to those who rule over us grace to do those things that will invite confidence in their office and trust in them. Let not a spirit of vindictiveness make us vengeful toward those who do wrong, but let us pursue justice with mercy because the wrongdoers know that we ourselves are not without sin.

Grant to world leaders the wisdom and the perseverance to pursue responsibly every possible option to peace. Through faithful prayer and responsible involvement may we seek to sustain those who share this awesome responsibility.

We pray that we may reach up in faith to receive the wholeness that you will for each of us in the fullness of your love.

Through him who teaches us to pray together, saying, "Our Father. . . ."—John M. Thompson

SERMON
Topic: Jesus Wept
TEXT: John 11:17–44

"Jesus wept"—one of the most famous Bible verses ever, but unfortunately not for its *content*, only for its *length*. The New Revised Standard Version, trying (I suppose) to convey even more exactly the original Greek verb tense, has now expanded this famous verse to four words instead of two; but because the original verse actually contains *three* Greek words, I guess we can't complain too much. The point is what the verse tells us about Jesus and his response both to the death of his friend Lazarus and to the reaction of those present. "Jesus wept." But just *why* did Jesus weep? Many different interpretations can be used to explain this event, and each gives a different perspective on our Lord.

Perhaps Jesus wept for his friend. Perhaps Jesus' tears are out of compassion for Lazarus. It is a sign of his love for Lazarus that, after actually delaying his trip to Bethany, he at last faces the reality of his friend's death and is overcome by the atmosphere of mourning and despair that envelopes the scene. Jesus, the Son of God, is also Son of Man; he possesses all of the emotions of a mortal human being. He knows anger and disappointment, frustration, hunger and thirst. He also feels sorrow deep enough for heavy sighs when he must face the obstinacy of the people around him, and tears, as in this case, when he must face the apparent finality of death. Jesus weeps for someone he loves whose life is cut short. It is a normal, human reaction, but it takes on deeper meaning, greater poignancy, to see this reaction in God-made-man, the Creator coming face to face with the most devastating fact of his creation and the fall of man—the end of life.

Perhaps Jesus wept for the world. One of the classic interpretations of this passage is that Jesus is so very disappointed by the lack of faith on the part of even his friends that he breaks down. He has wandered the highways and byways of the countryside, preaching, teaching, and performing the signs that he hoped would establish his credentials as God's Messiah. Now, faced with the challenge of Lazarus' passing, he sees those closest to him, symbolized by Mary and Martha, questioning his ability to challenge his greatest enemy, death itself. "Lord, if you had been here, my brother would not have died," says Mary in sorrow, as if to say, "but *now* you can do nothing and we are lost. Death has won because you did not arrive in time." Jesus wishes, both for their sakes and for his own, that there were enough faith on the part of his followers to face this tragedy with greater trust. He sees their tears, the mourning of the village around them, the perplexity of his own disciples as they have watched the Master delay this trip while knowing full well the seriousness of Lazarus' illness. Martha does admit that her brother will rise on the last day, but it is a pious hope for the future, not a firm faith for the immediate present. The Lord realizes that no one understands who he truly is and what he has come to do, and now they are in despair. Jesus weeps not only out of sorrow but also out of exhaustion. Would they never understand, these poor, pathetic creatures? Would they never realize who he is?

There is a third suggestion that I would like to make, though, and that is that Jesus wept for himself. It doesn't deny the divinity of our Lord or his nature as the Son of God to talk about his humanity and the spiritual growth that we can see taking place in him as his life and ministry progress through the Gospel accounts. He faces a lack of faith, open hostility, and even the ridicule of members of his own family. He confronts sickness, handicaps, and demonic possession and is able to win the day. He has even brought back to life those who have very recently died and were not yet buried. Here, however, in the death of Lazarus, he faces an even greater challenge. This cannot be a case of resuscitation—no, his friend has been dead four days, one day longer than Jewish teaching maintained that the soul still hovered around the body before leaving it for good. Here, in Bethany, at Lazarus' tomb, Jesus faces oblivion—death—in its most corrupt, smelly awfulness. Here he must face for the first time the prospect of *his own mortality,* which he fears is all too near. It is true that John's Gospel rarely shows Jesus as a fallible human being. The fourth Gospel clearly portrays Jesus as the conqueror, the hero, God's champion. When the Lord at last utters the command into the tomb, it is loud and forceful: "Lazarus, come out!" and there can be no doubt in John's writing that any other ending could be possible than that the dead man would come out of that tomb. Yet even in this triumphal Gospel, we are stuck with that little verse that conveys so much feeling and humanity: "Jesus wept." Could not Jesus have stood on the brink of death and been terrified of what he saw, not only for Lazarus but also for himself? What was the point of these three years of hard work? What was God's purpose in creating a world so full of human potential if it all ends like this in a grave? What if there really is nothing else? Jesus faces death and he weeps in terror.

But he doesn't surrender. He conquers. He takes charge of the situation and shows who must cheat death. He does this not only for his friend Lazarus, whom he loves. He does this not only for his disciples and for Mary and Martha, whose faith he must nurture and strengthen. He does this also for himself—to prove to himself that death itself cannot stand in the way of God's power and will, that he can stare death in the face and live to tell the tale. He does this not only for Lazarus, for Bethany, but for the even greater victory to come in two short weeks, when in his own body death will finally be conquered and the promise of even greater life will be made real.

Jesus' tears can tell us a lot today about the Lord whom we love and who loves us. They can impress upon us his compassion, his empathy, his sorrow, and perhaps even his fear and humanity. But ultimately they tell of God's presence in him and of a love so great that it shares all of these emotions and transforms them into something better, something stronger. The story of Lazarus is a tale of two short verses, each important but incomplete without the other: "Jesus wept" and "Jesus conquered."—Tyler A. Strand

SUNDAY, APRIL 8, 2001
Lectionary Message

Topic: Spiritual Role Models
TEXT: Phil. 2:5–11
Other Readings: Luke 19:28–40; Ps. 118:1–2, 19–29 or Isa. 50:4–9a; Ps. 31:9–16; Luke 22:14–23:56

Few persons today would challenge the assumption that positive models influence numerous areas of human activity. They shape personal attitudes, mold patterns of family life, and encourage exemplary professional achievements. Positive role models form a nucleus around which healthy personalities develop, idealism emerges, and individuals achieve maximum potential. Especially dynamic are spiritual role models in shaping believers' lives and leading them to experience a maturing discipleship. Floods of names remind us of the ongoing ministry of persons who significantly influenced our lives. They challenged us by their example and created in us the will to press on toward life's higher callings. More than those persons, however, we look to Christ as our ultimate role model. For every believer there remains the influence of both a cloud of Christian believers and the unshaken presence of Christ.

I. *A mind for the master* (Phil. 2:5). In just this type of context Paul wrote to the early church at Philippi, saying, "Let the same mind be in you that was in Christ Jesus." For Paul's generation, *mind* meant one's attitude, thought, or opinion. Rather than the Greek noun for *mind* (*nous*) Paul used a verb (*phroneite,* from *phronew*) meaning "to have understanding, to feel or think, to direct one's mind to a thing, to seek or strive for something." As used here, the passage speaks of "having the same thoughts among yourselves as you have in your communion with Christ Jesus."[2]

Adopting a collective mind brings into clear focus Paul's concern for the entire congrega-

---

[2] C. H. Dodd, *The Apostolic Preaching,* pp. 106f, cited in Arndt and Gingrich (eds.), *A Greek-English Lexicon of the New Testament.*

tion (v. 5a). Of first importance is Paul's emphasis on the mind: "Have this mind!" The New Testament focuses on mind fifty-one times in forty-seven verses, a massive emphasis suggesting the importance of the mind for Christian attention. Those who may disparage emphasizing the mind should remember that Christ came to take away our sins, not our minds. Yet it is a collective mind to which Paul appeals. The verbs are plural, reminding us that the Christian calling is one of unity, which grows out of the mind of Christ.

Achieving a transformed mind assumes that the mind of Christ creates a new perspective on life (v. 5b). The biblical appeal stresses a unique kind of mind, not just the well-educated or creative mind, as crucial as those may be. Indeed, the mind of Christ takes the finest capabilities of the human mind and transforms them into a new reality. In his affirmation of the mind, Paul focuses on more than mere brainpower. One way of distinguishing the difference between the brain and the mind is to remember that the mind is more than the brain in the same way that the spirit is more than the body.

II. *A model for the masses* (Phil. 2:6–8). As our ultimate role model, Christ demonstrated three stages through which model discipleship continues to progress. He rejected the temptation to cling to his prerogatives as one "in the form of God," he humbled himself by taking upon himself a human form of existence, and through that experience "God also highly exalted him." These three stages—temptation, humiliation, and exaltation—suggest a model for each of us as we seek the high calling of God in Christ Jesus.

Temptation was authentic for Christ and remains so for the twentieth-century person (v. 6). We are left to speculate on how fully Jesus experienced temptation. Yet the biblical answer to this question remains clear. His temptation to cling to the "form of God" and enter into the fullness of humanity surely was as authentic as his other experiences. In the wilderness Jesus' response to temptations set the course for the nature of his ministry. Rejecting the temptation of being a wonder worker and political victor, he chose the role of the suffering servant as the model of his messiahship (Matt. 4:1ff).

Reflecting on the authenticity of Jesus' humanity, the biblical writer underscored the reality of temptation: "For because he himself has suffered and been tempted, he is able to help those who are tempted" (Heb. 2:18 RSV; the NRSV uses "tested by what he suffered, he is able to help those who are being tested"). Like our Lord, we too experience the temptation to grasp or hold on to personal desires that conflict with God's purposes. We who are often tempted to exploit others would do well to hear the biblical declaration, "did not regard equality with God as something to be exploited" (v. 6 NRSV).

Humiliation threatens contemporary surrender to divine purposes, yet Christ's humility remains our challenge (vv. 7–8). Frequently pride precludes confession and subsequent forgiveness, or embarrassment causes one to reject public affirmation of Christ and active congregational participation. Other similar qualities also thwart dynamic Christian discipleship. Perhaps we need to hear again the words of Jesus, urging us to be childlike and trusting in our relationship with him, as with others. The difficulty is not ours alone, however, for one of Christ's signal demonstrations of ultimate commitment to God's will was in humbling himself, becoming obedient unto death, even death on a cross (v. 8).

Exaltation beyond human trials rewards human fidelity while affirming divine justice (vv. 9–11). One of the hazards in speaking of divine reward for human fidelity is the erroneous assumption that there is a divine rewards system that counteracts every human commitment or crisis. A primary theme of the book of Job cautions against superficially emphasizing rewards. For Job stresses that a person of personal integrity will serve God for nothing. The Tempter puts the issue squarely: "Does Job fear God for naught?" For Job, as for every authentic believer, the answer is yes, one will serve God without thought of reward. Yet this should not obscure the reality that, for believers as for the Christ, suffering often is the prelude to exaltation. People may define this reality in a wide variety of ways but for those who resist temptation and accept humiliation there emerges an exaltation into life that defies description.—Roy L. Honeycutt

ILLUSTRATIONS

HUMILITY.   It recalls an event described in a manuscript in the Emory Collection. At a conference session some of the preachers were complaining about their pitiful support and about the problems of sustenance, health, gear, and food. Listening for a time without comment, Asbury suddenly led in prayer: "Lord, we are in thy hands and in thy work. Thou knowest what is best for us and for thy work, whether poverty or plenty. The hearts of all men are in thy hands. If it is best for us and for thy church that we should be cramped and straitened, let the people's hands and hearts be closed. If it is better for us—and for the church—and more to thy glory that we should abound in the comforts of life, do thou dispose the hearts of those we serve to give accordingly; and may we learn to be content, whether we abound or suffer need."—Arthur Bruce Moss[3]

FULFILLMENT.   It is natural and right for a young person to want to be popular with the opposite sex and to marry. It is not easy, but it is possible, to discover that even when this desire is denied, life is not futile. It is natural to want to be healthy. Yet it is possible to struggle with a defective body and still find something worthwhile to achieve. It is natural to want to be well fixed and comfortable. Yet some of the greatest literary and artistic masterpieces have been produced in poverty. If a person has an inner capacity to sublimate desire to chosen ends, no outer disaster can be completely devastating.—Georgia Harkness[4]

SERMON SUGGESTIONS

Topic: Apply This to Jesus
TEXT: Ps. 118:19–29
(1) The coming of Jesus was the answer to many prayers (vv. 20–21). (2) God's answer in Jesus was rejected by many (v. 22a). (3) This rejection became the occasion of salvation in the cross and Resurrection (vv. 22b–23; John 1:11–12). (4) This salvation was celebrated in advance on Palm Sunday (vv. 26–29).

Topic: Why We Do Not Have to Fear
TEXT: Rev. 1:17–18
(1) Because of who Jesus Christ is: "the first and the last, and the living one." (2) Because of

---

[3] In *Zions Herald*, quoted by Gerald Kennedy, *A Reader's Notebook* (New York: HarperCollins, 1953), p. 131.
[4] *Prayer and the Common Life* (Nashville, Tenn.: Abingdon Press, 1948), p. 177f.

God's demonstration of power and approval in him: "I am alive forever and ever." (3) Because he is the answer to the ultimate issues of life: "I have the keys of death and of Hades."

CONGREGATIONAL MUSIC, SET 1

1. "All Glory, Laud, and Honor," Theodulph of Orleans (eighth century); trans. J. M. Neale (1851)

    ST. THEODULPH, Melchoir Teschner (1615)

    Possibly the most appropriate of all hymns in common use for Palm Sunday, this hymn relates the simple story of the triumphal entry in terms of adoration and worship. With or without handbells, this hymn is particularly suitable for the usual Palm Sunday processional.

2. "This Is the Day," Les Garrett (1967)

    THIS IS THE DAY, Les Garrett (1967)

    This scriptural chorus directly quotes Psalm 118:24. Singing it captures the joy and excitement of the Palm Sunday event. The tune lends itself naturally to accompaniment by guitars, tambourines, handbells, or some combination of these.

3. "All Praise to Thee (Christ)," F. Bland Tucker (1938)

    SINE NOMINE, Ralph V. Williams (1906)

    Based on the Epistle reading (Phil. 2:5–11), this excellent twentieth-century hymn with its concluding alleluias in each stanza is a glowing affirmation of the ancient confession that Jesus is Lord.

4. "According to Thy Gracious Word," James Montgomery (1825)

    AVON, Hugh Wilson (1825)

    One of the many fine hymns available for the observance of the Lord's Supper (Luke 22:14–23), this one by the lay hymnist James Montgomery focuses on the idea of remembering Christ in an intimate prayer to the "Lamb of God."

CONGREGATIONAL MUSIC, SET 2

1. "Ride on, Ride on in Majesty," Henry H. Milman (1827)

    TRURO, Thomas William's *Psalmodia Evangelica* (1789)

    Another classic hymn appropriate for Passion/Palm Sunday, "Ride on, Ride on in Majesty," possesses power and challenge by drawing the singers into the center of the triumphal entry event.

2. "At the Name of Jesus," Caroline M. Noel (1870)

    KING'S WESTON, Ralph V. Williams (1925)

    A fine hymn based on the Epistle lesson (Phil. 2:5–11), it can also be used for a Palm Sunday processional.

3. "As He Gathered at His Table," Paul A. Richardson

    STUTGART, Charles F. Witt (1715)

    STUART, Paul A. Richardson

    This contemporary reflection on the Lord's Supper (Luke 22:14–23) concentrates the worshippers' attention on the various actions and symbols, with the possibility of making its observance more meaningful.

4. "I Seek My Refuge in You, Lord," vers. Marie J. Post (1985)

    COLERAINE, Irish melody (1681); arr. Erik Routley (1985)

Stanzas 4 and 5 of this rather long metrical paraphrase of Psalm 31 are the stanzas that parallel the Psalter reading (Ps. 31:9–16).—Hugh T. McElrath

WORSHIP AIDS

CALL TO WORSHIP.   "This is the day which the Lord has made; we will rejoice and be glad in it" (Ps. 118:24).

INVOCATION.   Lord, we pray, open stubborn minds, nudge prideful hearts, stir sinful souls. Shape us in worship for Godly living as here we repent, and believe and dedicate ourselves all over again.—E. Lee Phillips

OFFERTORY SENTENCE.   "Thanks be unto God for his unspeakable gifts" (2 Cor. 9:15).

OFFERTORY PRAYER.   It isn't much that we bring, Lord, when compared to what you have given. Yet we bring these gifts in love and offer them to you that they may be blessed and used as a blessing in your service.—Henry Fields

PRAYER.   Abiding God, you have bid us journey these forty days toward the cross. Forty days—from the time of Noah till our Lord's sojourn in the wilderness, we remember forty days. And now the journey enters Jerusalem: city of destiny and definition. With the triumphant entry this day, O Son of David, we embrace Holy Week, and each day clarifies and sharpens who you are, who by God's love and grace you choose to be.

Help us, dear god, to walk faithfully and gladly these last steps and days with you to the cross. As we revisit the drama of this last week, O Wondrous Love, we see ourself at every turn, in most of the characters of the week. We know we are there, and in our heart of hearts we know that the outcome would not have been different. Whether with Judas or Pilate, the religious leaders or Peter, the hosanna shouters, or the soothsayers who would crucify him, we are there. So it shall be a painful but purifying walk as we live each day, for indeed, it is the season of redemption.

Jesus, keep us near the cross, but even more, keep us near you. Let us truly learn of you this week. We confess that our passion is too self-serving; so let us learn of your passion: sorrow and love flowing down for all God's children, made real in suffering and sacrifice. We confess that our scars are mostly self-inflicted, so let us learn of your pain and wounds, of your hands, feet, and side pierced for us. We confess that when asked to watch and pray, we too fall asleep and are inattentive, and then like Peter, and, unlike you, we find ourselves spiritually unprepared for the demands of the next hours. We fail the test. We confess, O God, our choosing the other Jesus, the Barabbas of our own lives and times. We deny we know you in word and by deed, and then we find ourselves, much too late, left only to bitterly weep alone. Again, too, our sins also pave the path to your cross.

So, Jesus, keep us near the cross and near you this week. We know the test is coming. We know the evil lurks, even in our busyness and private indifference, so help us to keep our hearts and vision set on you and to walk with fresh resolve to the table, to the garden, to the rejection, to the cross, to the death, to the tomb with you. And help us to walk with assured obedience and living faith. Thy kingdom come, thy will be done, in Christ, in us.—William M. Johnson

SERMON
Topic: Surely There's an Easier Way
Text: Zech. 9:9–11; Matt. 21:1–11

Life is difficult for everybody. Where did we get the idea that it was supposed to be easy? Not from the Bible. That's what confuses me about the popular brands of Christianity in our time, the kind that sell faith as if it were some product, telling you that if you will buy this product then good things will happen to you, when Jesus said just the opposite. "If you become a Christian," he said, "you may have to carry a cross. That's the journey that I'm going on, the journey to Jerusalem." And you know what happened to him.

Oh, it's true, he said, that you will find your life if you will follow me. But first you must lose it. And it's true, he said, you will receive, but first you must give. And it's true, he said, that you will have eternal life, but first you must die to this life. In other words, the gifts that Christianity gives are always by-products. You don't get them by going after the gifts themselves. They all come to you when you stop searching for them and seek first the Kingdom of God. And that means going on a journey and maybe enduring suffering. "Seek first the Kingdom of God, and then all these things will be given to you."

I don't know how you can get around that teaching. I guess you can get around it by pretending that it isn't there. But if you do that, then you are asking for disappointment and disillusionment, because life is difficult, for everybody.

What the Bible is trying to get you to do is face it and stop complaining that it's not easy. It's not easy for anybody, not forever it isn't. At some point we all have three choices. We can run away from the difficulty, we can sit where we are and bemoan our fate, or we can move ahead and face it.

Jesus headed for Jerusalem. The text puts it in a marvelous way. It says that at Caesarea Philippi, at that turning point in his ministry, "he set his face steadfastly for Jerusalem." He faced it.

And he did that because someday you and I are going to have to do it, too. I know that some of you have already done it. Some of you do it daily. And you know what it is to face the dragon that guards the treasure and keeps you from the joy and fulfillment of your life. Maybe it's a problem in your life that won't go away, or a burden that you will have to carry. But if you face it, you may not get what you want, but you'll get something better—a new life.

If you read the story of Jesus in any of the four Gospels, you know that someday he has to go to Jerusalem. Even in the story of his birth at Bethlehem, you know that outside the city of Bethlehem loom the buildings of Jerusalem and that someday he's going to have to go there. He goes from town to town, teaching and healing. Everywhere he goes the agents of the government are there, taking notes. You know that they are plotting to do away with him, and you know that someday he's got to face that. Then one day he begins to talk about going to Jerusalem. He talks about carrying the cross and having to suffer. The disciples say "No!" They try to discourage him from that way of thinking. They don't like it.

When the time comes, he seems to know that it is the right time. When the time comes, he sets his face steadfastly for Jerusalem and faces what he could avoid. He doesn't have to go there. He chooses to go there. He goes there because he has come to show us what real life is all about. If that's true, then real life is all about facing the difficult courageously and emerging from it a better person than you are now. Maybe that's what he meant when he said, "You will find your life only by losing it."

Some mess up their own lives, are knocked down and have to crawl back. Others are victims of life. They inherit the mess. They had nothing to do with it. It doesn't matter, according to the Bible. Because everybody, someday, for some reason or another, has to go to Jerusalem. And that's when you see whether they have the stuff heroes and heroines are made of, those who, in a given set of circumstances, act with courage, dignity, decency, and compassion.

All accounts agree that Jesus came riding into the city on Palm Sunday on a donkey. It was a sign of humility. It was staged, you know. He knew they would be expecting him. He knew they would want to greet him as their kind of a hero, as a conquering general on a white horse, throwing the rascals out. So he staged it intentionally to confound them. He came on a donkey in humility. As the wonderful hymn we sang before the sermon put it, he came in "lowly pomp." What kind of pomp is that?

Then, after Palm Sunday, Jesus and the officials maneuvered all week long, like sparring boxers. On Wednesday Judas made it possible for Jesus to be arrested. On Thursday Jesus ate his last meal with his disciples. Then the struggle really began. " 'Tis midnight and on Olive's brow" as the old hymn puts it, he was finally arrested. Friday morning was the trial. At noon, the crucifixion.

It's as if he had marched from Caesarea Philippi, where he had set his face steadfastly for Jerusalem, walked into the city and right up to the Temple to challenge the authorities, to challenge them to do their worst. Then he stood back and waited for it to happen, trusting that God would keep his promise that life would always be good.

Then he walked that Via Dolrosa right into the land where death holds sway. He went there with courage, dignity, decency, and compassion. Even on the cross he had compassion for those around him. And when he descended finally into the deepest depth that you and I will ever travel, into death itself, he conquered it. And on Sunday he returned to bring the gift of new life to those who follow where he has gone.

That's what it's all about, this story. It's clear when you read it that for this he was born. For this he came into the world. It was for this week, from Palm Sunday to Easter, that he came into the world.

He did that not to save us from a similar journey but to give us courage to go bravely into our own.—Mark Trotter

SUNDAY, APRIL 15, 2001
Lectionary Message

Topic: What If?
TEXT: 1 Cor. 15:19–26
Other Readings: Isa. 65:17–25; Ps. 118:1–2, 14–24; Acts 10:34–43 or 1 Cor. 15:19–26

What if Christ was not raised and there will be no resurrection of the body—what if this crucial belief that Christians have cherished through faith for two thousand years is not true? What difference would it make to contemporary believers and their hope for a future that transcends life and death, victory and disaster, joy and sorrow? That this is no idle question becomes apparent when we read Paul's inspired contemplation on resurrection, especially the "ifs" of resurrection.

I. *The futility of resurrection faith* (1 Cor. 15:13–19). Paul's central thesis is on the dynamic relationship between the Resurrection of Christ and the Christian hope of the resurrection of the body. Apparently some in the Corinthian church believed in Christ's Resurrection but rejected the resurrection of individual Christians. Essentially, the biblical revelation emphasizes that you can't have one without the other. It remains a rejection of historic faith to assume belief in Christ's Resurrection while rejecting belief in resurrection for believers. "Now if Christ is proclaimed as raised from the dead, how can some of you say there is no resurrection of the dead?"

On that foundation Paul placed five conditional clauses—the "what ifs" of the resurrection. What if there is no resurrection of the body. What then? If this is true, then Christ was not raised from the dead (v. 13). If Christ was not raised, our preaching is in vain (v. 14). If the dead are not raised, then Christ has not been raised (v. 16). If Christ has not been raised, faith is futile and we are still in our sins (v. 17). Those who have died in Christ have perished (v. 18). We believers, of all persons, are most to be pitied (v. 19). What difference does resurrection faith make? It makes all the difference. For it is the keystone on which biblical faith constructs the arch of Christian hope for future existence. Remove the keystone and the entire archway falls to pieces.

Fundamentally, hope means to wait confidently for the fulfillment of God's purposes. (The word *hope* appears 149 times in the Bible, affirming the widespread belief in its reality.) Yet Paul reminds us that if we have only hope without realization, we are of all persons most to be pitied (v. 19). Should resurrection prove to be no more than a mirage on the desert of our existence, how pitiful has been our faith experience! Indeed, how pitiable would be our position if we should come to the end of life and find that faith had been nothing more than an illusion? (Compare 1 Cor. 13:13.)

II. *The fact of resurrection faith* (1 Cor. 15:20–22). Like a skillful mountain guide leading travelers along the narrow precipice of a hazardous abyss, Paul leads believers to consider the futility of the resurrection. Now, like that same capable guide, he leads us to solid ground with his unshakable conviction, his resurrection faith. "But in *fact* Christ has been raised from the dead" (v. 20).

What are the "facts" of resurrection faith? First, resurrection faith rests on a foundation beyond historical verification. Ultimately, belief in the resurrection, both Paul's and ours, remains an act of spiritual faith and commitment. Simply stated, any proof remains greater than the proven. Second, there is historical evidence that points toward the fact of resurrection. What is some of this evidence? Persons identified in the New Testament were witnesses to Jesus' Resurrection. They had seen the Risen Christ. Paul experienced the Risen Lord following Christ's Ascension (1 Cor. 15:4ff, 8f, 9:1; Gal. 1:16; Acts 8:3, 9:3–6, 15:9). The early Church and its continuance confirmed resurrection faith for two thousand years. Further, contemporary believers have also experienced spiritually the reality of the Risen Lord. While these may or may not be "facts," they are certainly indicators of the factual reality of the Resurrection.

By giving the first fruits of their harvest, Old Testament persons symbolically dedicated the entire crop to the Lord and in the process affirmed the conviction that there was more to come. So here also, by referring to Christ's Resurrection as the first fruits of "those who have fallen asleep," Paul stresses that Christ is but the first to experience resurrection, but the occurrence assures believers that the dead in Christ will also be raised. Like Adam, all humans will die, but in Christ "all will be made alive" (v. 22). Such a glorious promise extends to all believers, not universally to every human as might be implied by the word *all*. (Remember, Paul is writing to Christian believers in the church at Corinth.) Persons are neither automatically condemned nor automatically raised. Rather, each resurrection is a matter of personal decision and commitment.

III. *The finality of resurrection faith* (1 Cor. 15:23–28). Resurrection faith demonstrates an element of finality that remains crucial not only for life but also for death and victory beyond all human experience. The order of the Resurrection moves deliberately toward that point of finality. First, Christ was raised. Then, at his return to Earth ("at his coming"), those who have died in Christ will be raised. (Note the numerous New Testament references to the fact that God raised Christ from the dead, not that Christ himself arose. More than twenty verses describe Jesus the Christ's Resurrection as an act of God.) Finally, Christ will deliver the Kingdom to God after destroying every obstacle to the Kingdom—"every rule and every authority and power" (vv. 23–24).

The climax of resurrection comes with the destruction of death and the accomplishment of God's purpose: "For God has put all things in subjection under his feet" (vv. 25–26). On occasion one hears someone describe death as a "friend," perhaps because death finally has delivered another person from suffering. But make no mistake, death is our enemy, the final enemy to be overcome: "The last enemy to be destroyed is death." Does this mean that believers will not die? Certainly not! Rather, resurrection from the dead has the final triumph over death. Each of us will die. But Christian hope affirms that death does not have the last word. God's final Word is resurrection from the dead. We are not left in the cold, clammy grip of death. Rather, we are raised to a new quality of existence, never fully known in this life but always the promise to those who do not grow weary in their faith.—Roy L. Honeycutt

ILLUSTRATIONS

THE NEW, HEAVENLY LIFE.   For Paul the new, heavenly life is a bodily one. Thus it is precisely not a "mental" body that is contrasted with a "material" one, but the resurrection body—into which one day we will be led whole and unhindered by God's Spirit—that is contrasted with the earthly one, which allows itself to be defined and ruled physically and psychically by all sorts of things. Hence, *body* for Paul means something like our "self" . . . but understood completely as a means of communication. My body is, to be sure, bounded by my skin and always to be found where I go or stay, but it also has, above all, eyes in order to see beyond myself, ears to hear, feet to go to others, hands to receive or to give. Therefore Paul emphasizes both: the fact of a bodily resurrection that transforms, but also preserves, my "self" *and* the totally different nature of the spiritual body, which goes beyond all our imaginings (15:35–50).—Eduard Schweizer[5]

OUR DESTINY.   You man, whoever you are, man or woman, high or low, you have from God one meaning and one goal of your life. You shall not remain what you are, but you will

---

[5] *A Theological Introduction to the New Testament* (Nashville, Tenn.: Abingdon Press, 1991), p. 67.

become what Christ is. For he is the fulfiller and the ideal of human nature. You shall not only become as he is, but you shall take part in him, in his own divine-human nature. To live in him in eternity—that is the true eternal life, that is the fulfillment of human destiny, the destiny of all men, at least of all those who reach their destiny. From eternity we are destined through Jesus Christ to receive in the Son of God divine, eternal life and in this to find our fulfillment, our true human nature. He, Christ, is sent to us by God to awaken us to eternal life from the nothingness of death into which all of us have sunk.—Emil Brunner[6]

SERMON SUGGESTIONS

Topic: True Religion in a Nutshell
TEXT: Deut. 6:4–5; Mark 12:28–34
(1) The demand. (2) The difficulty. (3) The decision.

Topic: Four Judgments on Jesus
(1) Many of them said, he hath a demon (John 10:20). (2) Some said, He is a good man (John 7:12). (3) Simon Peter said, "Thou art the Christ" (Matt. 16:16). (4) Thomas said, "My Lord and my God" (John 20:28).—W. E. Sangster[7]

CONGREGATIONAL MUSIC
1. "Open the Gates of Beauty," Benjamin Schmolck (1732)
   UNSER HERRSCHER, Joachim Neander (1680)
   This is an excellent opening hymn for worship on any Sunday but especially for Easter, with its echo of Psalm 118:19.
2. "Come, Ye Faithful, Raise the Strain," John of Damascus (eighth century); trans. J. M. Neale (1859)
   ST. KEVIN, Arthur S. Sullivan (1872)
   Calling on the faithful to join in exuberant praise of the Triune God, this fine translation from John of Damascus captures the Easter excitement. Its phrases could be joyously tossed back and forth between choir and congregation.
3. "This Joyful Eastertide," George R. Woodward (1884)
   VREUCHTEN, J. Audaen's *David's Psalmen* (1865)
   Another classic hymn of the Resurrection that radiates confidence and overflowing joy in the truth that "Christ (has) arisen!" "This Joyful Eastertide" is really a sprightly carol and should be sung accordingly.
4. "Christ Is Alive," Brian Wren (1968)
   TRURO, Thomas Williams (1789)
   The immanence of the Risen Christ is emphasized in this contemporary Easter hymn as the truth of the living Christ is brought to bear on earthly matters such as justice, conflict, and peace.
5. "Good Christians All Rejoice and Sing," Cyril A. Alington (1925)
   GELOBT SEI GOTT, Melchoir Vulpius (1609)

---

[6] *I Believe in the Living God* (Philadelphia: Westminster Press, 1961), p. 157.
[7] *Can I Know God?*

Each stanza of this modern Easter carol is an encouragement to tell the good news of Christ's victory and to praise the Risen Lord with an alleluia refrain.

6. "Alleluia! Alleluia! Give Thanks," Donald Fishel (1971)

ALLELUIA I, Donald Fishel (1971)

This comparatively new Easter song lends itself to light accompaniment such as flute, recorder, or guitar. The refrain could be used separately to punctuate the reading of the Gospel lesson (John 20:1–18).

WORSHIP AIDS

CALL TO WORSHIP.   "O give thanks unto the Lord; for he is good: because his mercy endureth forever. Let Israel now say, that his mercy endureth forever" (Ps. 118:1–2).

INVOCATION.   Great is thy name and greatly to be praised. Great is thy faithfulness and thy justice to every generation. Mighty thou art, O Lord, and magnificent in all thy ways. Thee we adore and thee we praise, our Creator and our God.—E. Lee Phillips

OFFERTORY SENTENCE.   "For if there be first a willing mind, it is accepted according to that a man hath, and not according to that he hath not" (2 Cor. 8:12).

OFFERTORY PRAYER.   Lord, let our gifts reflect in usefulness this dedication we make with gratefulness, for the cause of Christ in a world of need.—E. Lee Phillips

PRAYER.   Like no other day, this is the day which you have made, O God, which gives significance to all our days. May we receive it in all of its glory and all of its power—this day that affirms that life is going somewhere and that even nails and a cross cannot stop it. As you turned the despair of the disciples into hope, so also give us faith to believe that every good which has seemed to be overcome by evil and every love which has seemed to be buried in darkness and death shall rise again to life and more life.

Christ is risen! Therefore, we verily know that even in our confused and battered world you are bringing life out of death and hope out of despair.

For all of us, let this be a day of rejoicing and great gladness—a day when suddenly we understand that although with men the saving of man is impossible, with you all things are possible; a day when you surprise us with the insight that in our weakness you can make perfect your strength, and through the foolishness of the cross you reveal your wisdom and power.

Christ is risen! Glory, hallelujah! Knowing, Lord, a love that even death cannot vanquish, we are conscious of a fellowship not limited by time or space—the communion of saints. We praise you for the assurance that "life is ever-lord of death and love can never lose its own." May we here and all who are the Church everywhere pursue with renewed commitment your love purpose unmistakably revealed in the life, ministry, passion, and living again of Christ. Bless family and friends with whom we are privileged to celebrate most intimately the goodness of life. Bless the stranger among us with a sense of your love through the hospitality and concern of this fellowship. For those who govern in this nation and all nations, we pray for the enlightenment of that "truth though crushed to earth shall rise again."

We pray through him who is the Resurrection and the Life and who in the experience of this day brings life and immortality to light.—John M. Thompson

SERMON
Topic: Challenge
TEXT: John 20:1–20

The gardener! she supposes. This person so familiar to her Mary now mistakes for the gardener. "Did you snatch his corpse? Where did you hide it?" she demands. The gardener calls her by name. She recognizes the voice, the presence, the person. Not the one she knew. No longer flesh and blood. No longer the countenance familiar from those halcyon days gathering crowds across Galilee and Judea. No longer the one hounding the religious types in their sacred precincts. No longer the one bringing succor and healing to those deemed outside the pale. No longer the parched and dying figure hanging from the cross on that little spit beyond the city wall. Mary turns from the tomb. She directs her gaze from the world of death and crucifixion and confronts—What? A discontinuity? A new quality of existence? An alternative to life as we know it? In this Gospel, through rich metaphor, John shows a dramatic, decisive, radical change breaking in among us. He shows us an alternative world to the one where the likes of Jesus can be crucified. He tells us of a world where human life—yours and mine—rests finally on love and trust. When Mary joyfully acknowledges and rejoices in this new presence, unity, solidarity, and the embracing of our lives by unconquerable love assert themselves as victors over a world laced with the likes of crucifixion—love triumphant over all that would splinter, separate, divide, set us against one another, do us in, kill us.

And yes, John's startling images not only assert and depict such fantastic news, they also challenge us to become *right now* that radically new, loving world-community among ourselves. This narrative challenges us, in a new world, to live differently for one another. Now.

I. Live differently? In what way? Resurrection community means, first of all, dissolving the walls separating us from one another. If anything, the radically new presence of Jesus in John's narrative affirms a promise that we can bring again to one another. What is between us, hobbling us, crippling us in our relationship with one another can be healed, renewed, reclaimed. No relationship is so injured, so broken, so mutilated that it cannot be recreated. Talk about Easter challenge!

I have never forgotten a story Reinhold Niebuhr told of a little boy kicked around from foster home to foster home, incorrigible, a threat to life and limb, a toxic terror. Finally, assigned to a home where he exercised the worst he could muster, tearing the living room apart, making a mess of everything he touched, hurling insults, throwing tantrums, his new adoptive father, in a decisive encounter, took that boy in his arms and told him, "No matter what you do we're never going to let you go!"

Hear that? "No matter what you do we're never going to let you go!" The boy settled down. Is it any wonder? That father's passionate loyalty echoes the Easter promise. The presence in the garden of the resurrected Christ following the Good Friday debacle confirms a divine promise: "No matter what you do, I will never let you go."

Pardoned! So what? In gratitude we offer pardon. It is an Easter challenge.

II. *What does the Easter hope say about war?* Friends, we dare never forget that the Easter moment follows the Good Friday catastrophe. What happens on Good Friday reminds us that our human condition bears a tragic and persistent resemblance to our tendency to have a go at one another. If anything, the crucifixion of Jesus shows us we are capable of doing horrible things to one another—and those bleak, grieving, stunned Kosovo faces peering at us out of railroad cars, staring from the front pages of our papers, weeping as all is lost, tell us again and again what we can find ourselves capable of, about the terrible traps we can stumble into or consciously set for one another through malice and self-deception.

A denial of our Easter faith? A mockery of our music, our prayers, our lilies, our Easter joy today, this grievous and bloody mess in the Balkans?

Not on your life! You see, Calvary and Kosovo and the like demonstrate from what condition we need desperately to be saved. They illustrate the contradiction we present to the kind and quality of life the God of Love wants for us. They show us no one can claim innocence of clean hands; that, if anything, we stand in desperate need of divine mercy. Oh, surely we need to be inspired, urged, even commanded to love one another; but the gospel—and this is what makes it good news—the gospel recognizes that love one another we don't. It understands that we stand in need of mercy, of forgiveness—something we cannot do for ourselves. It offers a savior who can take the worst we can dish out, yet who through love will not let us go, who will heal, reconcile, and restore us to friendship with our God and with one another. What a revelation! The gospel reveals one who weeps over our condition, who shares it with us, whose grace lies in bearing the worst with us, carrying us through, granting us courage, trusting us, loving us, sticking with us, giving us another chance—and another and another—as we muddle and stumble through the lies and brutalities of the likes of Calvary and Kosovo. You see, the Easter moment, that startling presence in the garden after the slaughter of Good Friday, confirms one who hangs in there with us through the dilemmas, the sickness, the blunders, the tragedy of our common life.

But more—and here lies our hope—encountering on Easter Day that transfigured Jesus, broken from the tomb, *different,* a new creation, we find ourselves grasped by the presence of a new community grounded in love, issuing in peace with justice, mutuality, and grace; a new community that we in faith—*in faith* because of this garden encounter—now know is real; a community that we in hope prepare ourselves patiently to invest in and work for; a reconciled, restored community in which we, in love, risk and offer ourselves in order to make it visible now in our families, our churches, our city, our world. In our time and always, an Easter challenge.

The gardener! she believes. No, Mary, a new world of pardon and reconciliation; a new community embraced by divine mercy, renewed by your—by our—commitment, compassion, patience. A glorious, radiant, Easter challenge!—James W. Crawford

SUNDAY, APRIL 22, 2000
Lectionary Message

Topic: Too Good to Be True!
TEXT: John 20:19–31
Other Readings: Acts 5:27–32; Ps. 118:14–29; Rev. 1:4–8

How often have you heard someone respond to a message of good news by saying "that's just too good to be true!" Good news remains a central theme of the New Testament, where the words appear fifty-two times in as many verses. Almost always referring to the gospel, the phrase echoes God's intention for every person, each of whom was created in his image and finds life transformed by being recreated through Christ. The whole of the Christ event—his life, death, and Resurrection—focuses on good news to a world waiting for an encouraging word of affirmation and hope.

How those first-century believers responded to the good news of the Resurrection releases insights into various ways of faith. Some, like Mary Magdalene, responded with fear or amazement. (Matt. 28:5 refers to fear, "Do not be afraid," while Mark 16:6 reports, "Do not be amazed.") For some, Resurrection seemed to be "an idle tale" that they did not believe (as in Luke 24:11: "but these words seemed to them an idle tale, and they did not believe them"). Later, Mary Magdalene responded with tears. ("They said to her, 'Woman why are you weeping?'" [John 20:13].) The biblical text for this service emphasizes doubt as yet another response to the Resurrection: "Unless I see in his hands the print of the nails, and place my finger in the mark of the nails, and place my hand in his side, I will not believe" (John 20:25).

I. *Seeing without questioning* (John 20:19–23). Why Thomas was absent from the room when the Risen Lord appeared to those assembled we do not know. We only know from the biblical record that Thomas "was not with them when Jesus came" (John 20:24). It was on the evening of the first day of the week, the day of the Lord's Resurrection, that he appeared to the gathered disciples. Seeing the Risen Lord for themselves and witnessing the signs of his Crucifixion, the disciples received the Lord without question. They embodied seeing without questioning.

Seeing the Risen Lord replaced fear with peace (vv. 19–20). Although because of their fear the disciples were in hiding, experiencing the presence of the Risen Lord transformed them into an empowered band of zealous believers whose exploits in Christ's name are recorded in the book of the Acts of the Apostles. When we are prone to be afraid, convinced we are powerless to achieve the purposes for which the Lord calls us, we need to hear again his commission and his empowering promise. What a transformation, then, and what a reformation this experience can be for contemporary believers!

Receiving the Lord's commission, the Twelve were called as Jesus' successors (vv. 21–23). "As the Father has sent me, so I send you" (v. 21). Where would one find a more personal and specific calling? If we believe "God sent the Son into the world" (John 3:17), it remains a logical corollary to conclude that the Son has sent not only the Twelve but also every believer into the world. As our Lord became the Incarnation of the Father, so we are to incarnate the Son in and through our lives and witness. To enable us to achieve this, Jesus makes two commitments. He grants peace to those who respond positively and he empowers believers with the strength of his Holy Spirit (compare vv. 19, 23). To them and their successors he said, "Receive the Holy Spirit."

II. *Questioning without seeing* (John 20:24–29). How are we to understand Thomas's doubt, as well as that of our generation and our own personal uncertainty? Because of his response to the disciples' report of the Resurrection he became known as Doubting Thomas. So commonplace has the expression become that one dictionary defines it as "a habitually doubtful person."[8] Yet should we focus on Thomas's doubt, or on the fact that when he heard the good news it was "too good to be true"? We should also consider the "minority view," so to speak, and put in a positive word for the apostle Thomas. The Resurrection was so overwhelming in its stunning good news that it *was* too good to be true!

---

[8] *Webster's Ninth New Collegiate Dictionary*

Doubting can play a positive role in a person's life, especially if it leads to certitude and the resolution of disbelief (vv. 24–25). More often than not we tend to associate doubt with cynical persons who are unwilling to accept truth on faith and faith alone. Doubt becomes more intense in direct proportion to the intensity and authenticity of one's faith. For those who do not take the good news seriously, there is little reason for doubt. Yet for many who experience the good news of God's grace it is simply "too good to be true." Thomas clearly expressed his doubt, refusing to believe unless he could see in Jesus' hands the print of the nails, place his finger in the mark of the nails, and place his hand in Jesus' side. Before becoming too judgmental of Thomas, one should remember that the disciples had already experienced the physical marks of Jesus' suffering: "When he said this, he showed them his hands and his side." Thomas asked for no more than what the disciples had already received—physical confirmation of a spiritual experience.

Believing faith and its example demonstrate renewed commitment (vv. 26–29). Significant for every questioning believer is the assurance that Jesus refused to reject Thomas because of his doubt. Rather, appearing to Thomas, Jesus showed him the signs of the Crucifixion. Although many persons assume that Thomas touched those marks in Jesus' hands and side, the biblical text makes no mention of such action. All Thomas needed was the sight of the Risen Lord and the reassurance that came out of that encounter. Acknowledging Thomas's faith affirmation, the Lord not only commended him but also blessed future generations of believers. It was commendable that Thomas believed because he had seen the Lord. Yet in that context Jesus announces a new beatitude for future believers: "Blessed are those who have not seen and yet have believed" (v. 29).—Roy L. Honeycutt

ILLUSTRATIONS

THE FINAL QUESTION.   What is nature, what is history, what is destiny, if it is true that Jesus rose from the dead on the third day? What *do* we really know about ourselves, about the world, if such happenings really take place in heaven and earth, about which the wisdom of our schools scarcely dreams? Whoever enters into this uncertainty, into this doubt about everything that before seemed so unshakable, whoever ventures out to this frontier where everything ends and something altogether different commences, he stands where Christianity begins. Yes, Christianity is an un-heard-of demand, this resurrection from the dead; but if it is true that Jesus lives—that lifts the world off its hinges.—Eduard Thurneysen[9]

FAITH IN CHRIST.   To have faith in Christ is to know him as an actual presence. It is that trust in him that means openness of life to Christ. It is to be "in Christ" and to have "Christ in you." It is important to believe in the facts, but facts cannot save a person. One is saved by Jesus Christ, our Lord and Saviour. One is saved by Christ when faith is quickened within him, a faith which is also the knowledge of him as a living and transforming presence.—Frank Stagg[10]

---

[9] In Karl Barth and Eduard Thurneysen, *Come Holy Spirit* (Grand Rapids, Mich.: Eerdmans, 1978), p. 167.

[10] *New Testament Theology* (Nashville, Tenn.: Broadman Press, 1962), p. 12.

SERMON SUGGESTIONS

Topic: Guardians of the Springs

TEXT: Prov. 4:20–27, especially v. 23

(1) Our actions spring from our thoughts and feelings, although there are exceptions. (2) However, the wellsprings of action can be poisoned. (a) We are sinful, so it happens. (b) We are poorly taught, by individuals or by our general environment. (c) Even the witness of the Church may become corrupted. (3) However, the springs can be purified through repentance (see Rev. 3:14–22).

Topic: Who Can Please God?

TEXT: 1 John 5:1–5 (John 16:13–33)

(1) Our problem is not that the commandment is too hard; we have liberated ourselves from the duty to do anything unpleasant, especially if someone else wants us to do it. (2) Nevertheless, we *can* do what God wants us to do; the attempt is more important than success. (3) This is the way of victory over all of life's destructiveness.

CONGREGATIONAL MUSIC

1. "Give Thanks to God for All His Goodness," Ps. 118; vers. Stanley Wiersma (1982)
   GENEVAN 98/118, *Genevan Psalter,* (1551)

   This long modern paraphrase of Psalm 118 can be related to the particular section of the assigned Psalter reading (Ps. 118:14–29) by the singing of only stanzas 3, 4, and 5. It is set to the great metrical psalm tune with which it has been associated since sixteenth-century Geneva.
2. "Three Things Did Thomas Count as Real," Thomas H. Troeger (1983)
   MERLE MARIE, Carol Doran

   Troeger's contemporary hymn takes the singer into the mind of doubting Thomas and relates the story as found in this Sunday's Gospel lesson (John 20:19–31). The final stanza becomes a prayer that like Thomas we may be given grace to receive the Risen Christ. The tune BISHOP by Joseph P. Holbrook (1874) may be substituted by those who find Carol Doran's fine tune a bit difficult to perform.
3. "Lo, He Comes with Clouds Descending," Charles Wesley (1758)
   HELMSLEY, trad. English melody (eighteenth century)

   Based on Revelation 1:7, this great hymn on the Second Advent of Christ would be appropriate sung with the New Testament lesson (Rev. 1:4–8). The tune ST. THOMAS by John F. Wade can be substituted for those who find HELMSLEY somewhat too florid.
4. "As Ye What Great Things I Know," Johann C. Schwedler (1741); trans. B. H. Kennedy (1863)
   HENDON, H. A. Cesar Malan (1827)

   A hymn of testimony and witness such as this one would be appropriate for use in connection with the reading in Acts (5:27–32) in which Peter and the other apostles refuse to be silenced in their proclaiming of the good news of the Resurrection.—Hugh T. McElrath

WORSHIP AIDS

CALL TO WORSHIP.   "O give thanks unto the Lord for he is good: for his mercy endureth forever" (Ps. 118:29).

INVOCATION.   O God, you have made joy and praise a part of our life and our worship. Grant that we may realize that all true joy is preceded by dedication, by service, and sometimes by painful sacrifice. Strengthen our resolve to serve you faithfully, whatever the cost, in expectation of joy and fulfillment.

OFFERTORY SENTENCE.   "Every good gift and every perfect gift is from above, and cometh down from the Father of lights, with whom is no variableness, neither shadow of turning" (James 1:17).

OFFERTORY PRAYER.   How rich we are, Father, because of the self-giving poverty of our Lord Jesus Christ! May we remember that as we consider the needs of others and as we now bring our offerings and present them to you.

PRAYER.   Eternal Father, we reach out to feel your presence. The dampness around us sometimes seems to creep into our spirits and brings us low. Sometimes you seem so far from us, O God—so remote, so distant. Yet we read in the Scriptures that you are as near as the breath within us. Teach us to realize that the distance is of our own making and not yours. Open our eyes that we might see you and our ears that we might hear you. There are times we feel so disconnected, anonymous, like a missing person; we long to know, Does anyone care, or love me, or miss me when I'm gone? Most of the time, Father, we feel self-sufficient, but we confess that all of us at some times are discouraged, alone, and lonely. We long for assurance, security, and comfort. Touch us now with your presence. Embrace us with your love. Hug us where we are hurting.

   Thank you for loving us, Father, even when we are unlovable. Love us until we can live and love as we have been loved by you. Help us to love those around us who are hurting also. Work in us and through us to touch them with concern and assurance. Thank you, God, for accepting us. Help us to accept your acceptance of us. With this strong sense of your love, teach us how to live without fear because we are anchored in the strength of your loving presence. Through Christ, we pray.—William Powell Tuck

SERMON
Topic: The Burden of Guilt
TEXT: Ps. 51; Rom. 7:24–8:1

Let the writer of the Psalm 51 enter our thinking. Many scholars believe that this psalm was written by David. This is not certain. But the words could easily be David's testimony. We may be listening to his private confession or reading his personal entry in his journal. His life had become blackened by his conscious sin. He had deliberately taken another man's wife and committed adultery with her. Using his authority as king, he had sent Uriah, Bathsheba's husband, to the front line of battle, where he was killed. Then he had taken Bathsheba as his wife. They had a child who died shortly after he was born. David's conscience was quickened and he was burdened down with his sense of guilt and felt great remorse. He knew that his sin had alienated him from the holiness of God, and he cried for deliverance, cleansing, and restoration. This psalm of David offers us some steps to find relief from the burden of guilt.

The first act is *contrition*. David confessed his sin. "I have sinned and against thee and thee only have I sinned." He had sinned against others but his sin was first of all against God. He openly confessed his sin to God. Repentance is the door into the presence of God's grace. To find forgiveness we begin with an acknowledgment that we have done something wrong. We know that we have missed the mark. We acknowledge that our load is too heavy and that we cannot bear it alone. Our awareness of sin opens the way for us to experience forgiveness.

The second step is *confession*. David frankly acknowledged his sins and accepted full responsibility for them. "For well I know my misdeeds, and my sins confront me all the day long" (v. 3). When the prophet Nathan confronted David through his parable about the little ewe lamb, he touched David's conscience and made him see his guilt (2 Sam. 11:1–12, 15). He then confessed his sin and sought forgiveness. The writer of 1 John reminds us: "If we say that we have not sinned, we deceive ourselves and the truth is not in us. If we confess our sins, he is faithful and just to forgive us our sins and to cleanse us from all unrighteousness" (1 John 1:6–7).

I would encourage you to sit down with a friend, a minister, or a trained counselor and share with him or her whatever heavy burden you may be bearing. Repressed guilt can be released through confession. Find someone with whom you can talk confidentially, who will listen sympathetically, and who will keep your "secret" private.

You begin with contrition, then confession, and the next step is *cleansing*. David prayed, "Wash away all my guilt and cleanse me from my sin" (v. 2). Listen to the verbs: "Purge me." "Wash me." "Cleanse me." Our guilt can make us feel foul and dirty. David felt morally unclean.

You and I affirm that the cross of Jesus Christ provides us with God's forgiveness and restoration in a way that we cannot find anyplace else. God has taken the initiative in bringing us forgiveness. What God has done for us at the cross of Jesus Christ is to restore our broken relationship with him and bring us back into fellowship with him.

Often some *contribution* is essential for real healing to take place. You may need to make amends for the wrongs you have done. Sometimes that is of course not possible. We all know that. The person you hurt may be dead. Reparation might make matters worse. You may not be able to make complete restitution. But on many occasions you can contribute something. You may be able to go to a person and apologize. You may make it possible to pay back some of the money you took illegally. You may start correcting bad habits that cause you to feel guilty.

Then finally there is *consecration*. David prayed, "Create a pure heart in me, O God, and give me a new and steadfast spirit" (v. 10). "O Lord God, my deliverer, save me from bloodshed, and I will sing the praises of thy justice" (v. 14). Having experienced God's forgiveness, David committed his life anew to him. When you and I experience God's forgiveness, then we will commit our lives to him. We will be able to do this when we realize that we are acceptable to God. No matter what your sin is, no matter what your burden of guilt may be, God can release that load.

You can be forgiven. You don't have to bear your burden. That is the good news of the gospel.—William Powell Tuck

SUNDAY, APRIL 29, 2001
Lectionary Message

Topic: The Last Breakfast!

TEXT: John 21:1–19

Other Readings: Acts 9:1–6 (7–20); Ps. 30; Rev. 5:11–14

Some years ago a chapel speaker in a seminary where I served used an intriguing title for this passage of Scripture, one that I shall never forget: The Last Breakfast.[11] Reflecting on that title, I recall numerous parallels between this meal with the disciples and the Risen Lord and the Last Supper in the upper room. How fitting that John should close his writings with this personal experience, and how appropriate that this should now be the direction of our meditation during this Holy Season. During such a time of communion, Jesus calls believers, ancient and contemporary, to be missionaries and shepherds.

I. *Fishing: The missionary calling of the Church* (John 21:1–4). Has it ever seemed strange to you that Jesus began and concluded much of his ministry with a focus on fishing and fishermen? He called his first disciples on the shores of Lake Galilee, entreating them to leave their business and follow him. Each of the four Gospels echoes the same theme: "As he walked by the Sea of Galilee, he saw two brothers—Simon who is called Peter and Andrew his brother—casting a net into the sea, for they were fishermen. And he said to them, 'Follow me, and I will make you fishers of men' " (Matt. 4:18, 19; compare Mark 1:16–20, Luke 5:1–11, and John 1:35–51). Here also, toward the close of his ministry and immediately following the Resurrection, Jesus meets with the fisher-disciples and entrusts to them a magnificent world mission (John 21:15–23). For the Church there is to be both a missionary calling and a pastoral calling.

Returning to an earlier vocation remains a temptation for disappointed disciples (vv. 1–3). Perhaps nothing demonstrates more clearly the disappointment of the disciples than the experience on the road to Emmaus. "But we had hoped that he was the one to redeem Israel" (Luke 24:21). For them it seemed that all hope was gone—"we had hoped." Always the most outspoken, Simon Peter proposed a return to their original occupation: fishing. His invitation may have been only for the night and due to the need for food. From another perspective, he may have seen this path as the return from a failed mission—the death of the Messiah. Peter's invitation may also have been symbolic of the mission of the apostles to be fishers of men (Luke 5:10; see also William E. Hull, *The Broadman Bible Commentary,* p. 372).

Before we condemn those seven disciples for their flight to Galilee and a possible return to fishing as an occupation, we must face our own temptation to turn back when life's circumstances create ultimate disappointments. We too want to "go home again," to abandon crises for the safety of known ways.

Recognizing the transforming Lord creates a new perspective and a different outcome for life (vv. 4–8). Failing to recognize the Risen Lord, the disciples hear only the voice of a stranger on the shore. Yet in the midst of their failure to catch any fish, he gives advice—"Cast the net on the right side of the boat"—with outstanding results. An amazing catch of fish resulted. John recognized the Lord and in response Simon Peter jumped into the sea to

---

[11] Randall Lolley, then President of Southeastern Baptist Theological Seminary.

meet the Savior. The power of the Risen Lord continues to this day to transform persons by creating both a new perspective and a different outcome for life. Leave what you are doing, he calls, then try another side. With such redirection our nights of failure become mornings of benediction.

Renewing prior relationships through a shared meal (vv. 9–14). Not all of the disciples are present. Judas is gone and four others are absent, leaving the seven to witness the wonder of the Risen Christ. In a meal reminiscent of the Last Supper, Jesus takes not bread and wine but bread and fish to celebrate a new communion. A successor to Leonardo De Vinci, who painted the magnificent "Last Supper" in Milan, Italy, might now paint another scene of authentic community: the Last Breakfast.

II. *Feeding: The pastoral calling of the Church* (John 21:15–19).

Demonstrating authentic love through devoted service identifies authentic disciples (vv. 15–17). Following breakfast, Jesus turned to the primary theme of this unique meal, identifying a fundamental role of the Church while also dealing with Simon Peter, who on three occasions had denied the Lord. Three times, one for each time Simon denied him, the Lord asked this probing question, "Do you love me?" The Lord's exhortation following Peter's affirmative response addressed not only Peter but also every contemporary believer: If you truly love the Lord you will feed his sheep. There continues to be a shepherding function for the Church that we should not neglect. It will validate our claim to love the Lord more than any words we might speak.

Demonstrating authentic love despite hostility and persecution characterizes authentic witnesses to the Resurrection (vv. 18–19). With cryptic language Jesus spoke of the persecution and hardship that Peter would encounter in the future, and not Peter alone but all who would remain faithful to the gospel. In veiled language Jesus described crucifixion as Peter's ultimate fate. "You will stretch out your hands, and another will gird you and carry you where you do not wish to go." An editorial comment following this verse suggests that a later writer validated Jesus' statement: "This he said to show by what death he was to glorify God" (v. 19).

When one considers the evangelistic and pastoral command that Christ left for the Church, his words to Simon Peter are all the more encouraging. Accepting the authenticity of Simon's recommitment following his betrayal, Jesus says simply, "Follow me." Not only in this immediate context but later as well, when Peter questions John's future, Jesus provides the same counsel, couched in words of reproach. When we become overly concerned about the relationship of others to Christ, we need to remember the Lord's rebuke and exhortation to Peter: "If it is my will that he remain until I come, what is that to you? Follow me!" (The Greek text uses three words translated "you me follow," that is, "You follow me and do not worry about others such as John. Be concerned with your own following and you will have responsibility enough." Finding, feeding, and following—these three words should mark the ministry of every congregation.—Roy L. Honeycutt

ILLUSTRATIONS

BECAUSE OF GOD.   A businessman returned home one evening with a contract in his hand. It provided him and his wife with an opportunity to make a lot of money. In the quietness of the evening, he sat down and discussed the contract with her. He read it first, then passed it to her and watched the expression on her face as she read it. He waited for her response, which was not long in coming. "Tom," she said, "You and I can't go into this."

"Why?" "Well, because . . . because of God." "Yes, I know," Tom said. "That's what I had decided, too." And so, "because of God," the contract was returned unsigned. Because of God, their lives had boldness at a time when boldness was required. There was no evidence of a "yellow streak."

CHRIST'S LORDSHIP.   Yielding to Christ's lordship opens life up because it brings purpose to our lives. We live in ever-increasing understanding of the great mystery of the ages Paul wrote about. Christ shows us where our places are in His work, and as we take our places we find fulfillment that can nowhere else be found.

Church takes on a new meaning. It is not only a congregation of a caring group who give one another mutual support (though it is that); but it is a body of Christ which exists to do His work His way. Seeking out that work and way is the process of seeking the mind of Christ.—Bill Stephens[12]

SERMON SUGGESTIONS

Topic: No Condemnation!
TEXT: Rom. 8
(1) Do you feel condemned? (2) We may be condemned by the Ten Commandments; by the laws of nation, state, or local government; by neighbors; by conscience. Does God condemn us? (3) We can be free from condemnation. (4) This is a lifelong work of God. God involves himself in everything that happens to us, and his aim is to make us more and more like Jesus Christ. (5) No one can then effectively condemn us if God has acquitted us.

Topic: Why Good Things Happen to Bad People
TEXT: Rom. 2:4; Jon. 3:10–4:11
(1) God is indeed kind, tolerant, and patient toward us human beings. (2) But some things do hinder the working out of God's purpose in our lives. (3) The kindness of God is often questioned and much maligned, yet it is a fact—it wins through, and the miracle of changed lives keeps on happening.

CONGREGATIONAL MUSIC
1. "Alleluia! Sing to Jesus," William C. Dix (1866)
   ALLELUIA, Samuel S. Wesley (1864)
   The heavenly worship around the throne of Christ (Rev. 5:11–14) animates every stanza of this hymn of praise. It could function as a processional hymn for the opening of worship.
2. "Hail, Thou Once Despised Jesus," attr. to John Bakewell (1757)
   IN BABILONE, trad. Dutch melody
   Also based on the passage in the Revelation of John (5:11–14), this older hymn more closely paraphrases the worship acclamations of the Scripture. The hymn can be quite effective when sung phrase by phrase antiphonally.

---

12 In *Discipleship Training*, published by the Sunday School Board of the Southern Baptist Convention, © 1990.

3. "Jesus Calls Us, O'er the Tumult," Cecil F. Alexander (1852)

   GALILEE, William H. Jude (1874)

   This hymn of discipleship and commitment can appropriately follow the Gospel reading (John 21:1–19), depicting Jesus' repeated question, "Do you love me?" and Simon Peter's confessional answers. Stanzas 1 and 3 relate particularly to the crux of the matter of truly loving Jesus.

4. "Heaven Came Down," John W. Peterson (1961)

   HEAVEN CAME DOWN, John W. Peterson

   A modern gospel song such as this one that deals with the sudden, dramatic experience of conversion can be sung in connection with the reading of the account of Saul's miraculous conversion on the road to Damascus (Acts 9:1–20).

5. "Come, Sing to God," Ps. 30, vers. Fred R. Anderson (1985)

   ELLACOMBE, *gesangbuch der H.w.k. Hofkapelle,* (1784)

   It would be instructive to alternate the singing of this fine modern paraphrase of Psalm 30 with the reading of the verses of the psalm according to the following plan: vv. 1–5, stanza 1; vv. 6–7, stanza 2; vv. 8–10, stanza 3; vv. 11–12, stanza 4.—Hugh T. McElrath

WORSHIP AIDS

CALL TO WORSHIP.   "Sing praises to the Lord, O you his faithful ones, and give thanks to his holy name. For his anger is but for a moment; his favor is for a lifetime. Weeping may linger for the night, but joy comes with the morning" (Ps. 30:4–5 NRSV).

INVOCATION.   Your grace and mercy are without end, O God, providing us with forgiveness of our sins, provision of our daily bread, companionship of family and friends, and all good things that bless us. Today help us to know it, to feel it, and to tell it, for Christ is risen.

OFFERTORY SENTENCE.   "Set your affections on things above, not on things on the earth" (Col. 3:2).

OFFERTORY PRAYER.   Lord, we know that what counts with you is not how much we bring when we present our offerings but how faithful we are with what we have. So, show us what we should do, give us grace to do it, and never despise the small gift or begrudge the larger one.

PRAYER.   O you who are in our coming in and our going forth, you who are present not only in the green pastures and beside the still waters but also in the valley of the shadow of death, you are here preparing a table for us not only in the presence of our friends but also in the presence of our enemies; you are present not only in the brightness of the noonday sun but also when the shadows of evening fall. We thank you that you never give up the chase—that you truly are the hound of heaven. Your love pursues us to the far country of our own willfulness and also into the darkest night of the soul.

Grant to us the understanding of the psalmist to know that you are never so present as when you seem most absent.

You are here this morning, present in your Word, calling us as you have so many times before. The question is never about your call but about our response. Make us sensitive and responsive to your call in our common and uncommon tasks and opportunities so that we fail not man nor thee.

O giver of every good and perfect gift, you give us the understanding that to meet you at the throne of grace is to be present with all our brothers and sisters. You are saying to us, as Joseph said to his brothers, "Except your brother [and we add, your sister] be with you, you shall not see my face." You so loved the world that you gave your only Son. Love, your love, looks for ways to be constructive, creative, even to dying on a cross. This is our calling, to love all others as you love us. To be faithful to prayer is to commit ourselves to do what we can do—to make love visible.—John M. Thompson

SERMON
Topic: The Greatest of These
TEXT: Rev. 2:1–7

The ability to remember and the power to love separate us from other living things. The image of God affirmed in Genesis seems to be about relationship. "God created humankind in his image, in the image of God he created them, male and female he created them." We should not be surprised that the figure of marriage emerges in the New Testament figure of the Church as the bride of Christ, and we are called in John's Gospel to love one another as God has loved us. "Love and marriage go together like a horse and carriage." So does love and the Church. Our salvation begins in "God so loved the world." The disciple's response is to love God and to love one another. The "first love" abandoned by the church at Ephesus was the foundation of the family of God.

I. *Love is the essential ingredient to all other qualities of the Christian life.* Although the message to the church in Ephesus is an amazing commendation of the industry, patience, and fidelity of a congregation living in a difficult situation, the striking word is the criticism and threat. This church, which we would probably hold up as an example of organization and orthodoxy, was on the verge of spiritual death. All of the parts of the body were present, but the bond of love was missing, and without love all of the wonderful works of the church were beginning to sound like "a noisy gong or a clanging cymbal."

Ephesus was a center of commerce and wealth and was famous for its corrupt lifestyle. Amid the crosscurrents of religion and immorality, the Ephesian church had held a straight course. In light of the commendations, one is hard-pressed to identify the malignancy within this church.

Like all healthy human relationships, the Church family is a working community. The rewards of the Christian life have often attracted folks who lack the energy or the will to help with building the Kingdom. "Inactive Christian" is an oxymoron, and the Christian mission is no place for lazy or passive people to hide. Yet the Ephesian congregation was active and aggressive in works of ministry and recognized for sustained labor in the face of trial. This was an active, working congregation.

By the second generation of Christians following the time of Christ, despair had begun to take a toll. Some Christians had given up on the return of Christ or had taken an attitude of passive waiting, but not the Ephesian Christians. The congregation was steady as a rock. She endured trial. She had waited patiently and faithfully, not for her own glory but for the sake of her Lord.

As Christianity expanded, false teachers emerged along with bad doctrine. Some immature congregations were safe harbors for false prophets and breeding grounds for corrupt faith; but not Ephesus. She had maintained her orthodoxy against crosscurrents of false doctrine. The Nicolaitans were just one example of false teachings that led to a corrupt lifestyle. This Gnostic sect is believed to have taught the division of the soul from the body, and thus the separation of faith from life. The Ephesians totally rejected this false theology. Give them another gold star.

Only one criticism is presented to the church at Ephesus. They have abandoned their first love, and the body cannot live without a heart. A church without compassion is not the Church of Jesus Christ. We can compensate for anything, but our love for God, our love for the lost, and our love for one another is the body of Christ.

II. *The church can be too good to be true.* Do you have a perfect spouse? If not, let me help you create the image of perfection that you so greatly deserve. Each day you need to make a list of all of your beloved's transgressions. Present your list at breakfast and check for improvement at dinner. If there is improvement in any one area, do not allow this positive move to confuse your ultimate aim of perfection. Constantly dwell on the failures and faults. Be patient in waiting for perfection. Be consistent in your demands. The more you declare your dislikes and hatreds, the more efficient your spouse will become in meeting your high standards. All you have to do to eliminate the stress zones in marriage is to be perfect and demand perfection.

For generations Christians have been scratching their heads in confusion about the Ephesian church. Could it be that the perfection described here is typical of the efficiency that kills marriages and churches? The description of the Ephesian church is too good to be true—probably too good for compassion. There seems to be a connection. Paul advised the Ephesian Christians to speak the truth in love. The truth does not stand alone. Only in love does the truth become the truth of God.

The Church is the Word of God in earthen vessels. The body of Christ consists of very human bodies like yours and mine. Peter Steinke observed that premarriage counseling is futile because you can't talk sense to psychotics. To be sure, love begins with a touch of insanity. People in love cannot see the faults that are glaring to everyone else. But most of us get over this insane blindness. Before long we discover that the bride and the groom have warts, and we have to make a critical decision that affects the rest of our marriage. Do I remind my beloved of her faults until I have shaped her into the perfection that I deserve, or do I just love her as Christ has loved me—warts and all?

Some marriages fail because of infidelity, others because of cynical hopelessness, but by far the greatest cause of marriage failure is disillusionment. When one of us becomes an efficiency expert, attempting to perfect the behavior of the other, we have moved our relationship from the bond of love to the bondage of perfection. The accumulated damage of perfectionist demands can far exceed any single crisis in relationship.

Daniel Day Williams declares, "The goal of love is communion. The experiences of love are experiences of joyful ecstasy, delightful companionship and reconciliation." Love is redemptive. Love accepts the other "just as I am without one plea." The redemptive transformation from the power of love far exceeds the power of condemnation.—Larry Dipboye

SUNDAY, MAY 6, 2001
Lectionary Message

Topic: Who Is Jesus?
TEXT: John 10:22–30
Other Readings: Acts 9:36–43; Ps. 23; Rev. 7:9–17

Like so much of John's Gospel, this passage addresses the question, "Who is Jesus?"

I. It is a subtle irony that this story takes place in the Temple in Jerusalem at the Feast of Dedication or Hanukkah. This eight-day festival commemorates the rededication of the Temple following its desecration by the Greeks under Antiochus Epiphanes. After the Jewish victory led by Judas Maccabeus (164 B.C.), a new altar was dedicated and the Temple light miraculously burned for eight days until a supply of oil reached Jerusalem. Those who know Jesus will understand that his presence in the Temple is its ultimate rededication. Whereas in former times the high priest entered the Holy of Holies to encounter God and atone for the sins of the people, now in Jesus God has come to dwell with human beings in a new way. He himself is the rededicated Temple of God, the place where persons encounter God, and the atoning sacrifice for sin.

Those to whom John first wrote must have known the season in which the Feast of Dedication took place, but John makes a point that "it was winter," the darkest season. Those who know Jesus will remember that he is the Light of the World. Unlike the light in the Temple that lasted eight days until it was replenished, Jesus is the Light that "shines in the darkness, and the darkness did not overcome it."

II. The people who gathered around Jesus asked him, "How long will you keep us in suspense? If you are the Messiah, tell us plainly." One wonders why Jesus did not come right out and say, "Yes, I am the Messiah." Instead, he pointed out that he had already told them plainly who he was. His works spoke for him and there was nothing more he needed to say.

The term *Messiah* (or *Christ*) was a loaded one for those who asked the question. When they heard that word, they associated it with a conquering military hero. The Messiah they were looking for was like Judas Maccabaeus—one who would drive out the armies of occupation and reestablish the political dominance of Israel. By his life and works Jesus was redefining the meaning of *Messiah*. Only by believing could they see Jesus for who he was. Only through faith could they know that Jesus' works were the works of the Messiah.

We sometimes find it vexing that Jesus does not always give clear, crisp answers to the questions we ask him. Our frustration may be because we listen for Jesus' answer through the filters of our expectations. There are times when we feel compelled to take a stand on pressing issues of the day. Our society demands that we come down on one side or the other, using categories that our culture gives us. There are questions we ask Jesus to answer: What do you want me to do with my life? How should I resolve a momentous decision? The easy way is to do as Jesus' questioners did in the Temple: listen for his answer in the terms to which we are accustomed—liberal or conservative, option A or option B. When we are vexed that Jesus does not answer our questions, it may be that we are listening for the answer in our own terms, not in his.

III. Jesus told his questioners, "You do not believe because you do not belong to my sheep." The signs he had performed throughout his ministry should have made it clear who he was. Those who questioned Jesus could not recognize his works for what they were because they did not belong to him.

There are times when you have to belong to see things for what they are. There are things that happen in a family that are of utmost significance to its members yet they go unnoticed by others. Certain gestures, words, or small rituals that a visitor overlooks may communicate important messages to those in the family. Newlyweds soon discover that there are things that mean much more to the new spouse than they ever realized. How the Christmas tree is decorated, for example, or what words are used to express affection carry different meanings in different families.

Those who belong to Jesus see his works and hear his words for what they are—the works and the words of God. Those who do not belong do not understand.

IV. The passage concludes with Jesus' proclamation of what he gives to those who belong to him. He does not give a military or political victory that will prevail until the next world power arises. He does not give a new Temple or new religious practices that will have to be rededicated and renewed with succeeding generations. Instead, he gives eternal life.

Jesus makes it clear where that life is from. Its source is nothing less than the one who is greater than all else. Because that life is from the Father, nothing can snatch it from those who receive it. Soon after this encounter, Jesus' enemies try to silence him by taking his life. They operate from the assumption that there is nothing more powerful than death, so they use death to put an end to Jesus. That is when Jesus proves what he says in the Temple precincts: nothing, not even death, can deprive his followers of eternal life.

Then Jesus makes it clear who he is. He plainly tells the source of his authority. He is able to speak as he does for one simple and profound reason: "The Father and I are one."—Stephens G. Lytch

ILLUSTRATIONS

RESURRECTION. If we are to share the incredible transforming and redeeming power of this risen One with all kinds of people, we need to be able to explain why it is important and what it says about the nature of the universe. Then we can bring the depth of our lives into harmony with the love that made the resurrection possible.—Morton Kelsey[1]

THE IMPACT OF ONE LIFE. All Christian doctrine of the revelation of God in Jesus Christ is an attempt to say how the unity and the power of God's saving activity are experienced in the impact of that one life upon mankind. Christ is the climax of creation, the incarnation of the Logos without which nothing is made, the restoration of the image of God, the divine love made real in a human spirit. But this is also a world in which Christ is crucified. Redemption must come on the other side of the rent in creation, exposed by man's rejection of love. God invades human history at the cost of suffering. Redemption is won as men find themselves judged, forgiven, and brought to repentance through the fact of God's victory on the cross.—Daniel Day Williams[2]

---

[1] *Resurrection* (Mahwah, N.J.: Paulist Press, 1985), p. 30.
[2] *God's Grace and Man's Hope* (New York: HarperCollins, 1949), p. 60f.

SERMON SUGGESTIONS

Topic: If the Lord Is My Shepherd, Then . . .

TEXT: Ps. 23

(1) What the Lord will do: (a) provide for my physical needs; (b) provide for my spiritual needs—renewal, guidance, protection, and divine presence. (2) What I will do: (a) follow the Lord's guidance; (b) refuse to give in to fear; (c) let the worship and service of the Lord be my lifelong and eternal joy.

Topic: A Glimpse of Heaven

TEXT: Rev. 7:9–17

(1) Its inclusiveness (v. 9). (2) Its theme: God, the Lamb, and salvation (vv. 10–12). (3) Its explanation (vv. 13–14). (4) Its occupation (v. 15). (5) Its prospect (v. 17).

CONGREGATIONAL MUSIC

1. "Ye Servants of God, Your Master Proclaim," Charles Wesley (1744)

   HANOVER, attr. William Croft (1708)

   "To be sung in a tumult" was the caption Wesley had for this hymn. What a powerful contrast to sing, as it were, with the great white-robed throng in testimony to the salvation "which belongs to God" (Rev. 7:9, 10) while being assaulted by a violent mob! Read the Revelation passage and then sing this hymn in the spirit of Wesley!

2. "Jerusalem, the Golden," Bernard of Cluny (twelfth century); trans. John Mason Neale (1858)

   EWING, Alexander Ewing (1853)

   One of the great hymns bequeathed to us from the Middle Ages, "Jerusalem, the Golden" is a powerful description of the Holy City and of the worship around the great white throne based on the apostle John's vision (Rev. 7:9–17).

3. "Savior, Like a Shepherd, Lead Us," attr. Dorothy A. Thrupp (1836)

   SICIIAN MARINERS, Sicilian melody (1792)

   BRADBURY, William B. Bradbury (1859)

   Based on the idea of a shepherding God that is found not only in Psalm 23 but also in the Gospel lesson for this Sunday (John 10:22–30), this children's hymn sung to either tune would be effective for this day's worship.

4. "My Shepherd Will Supply My Need," Isaac Watts (1719)

   RESIGNATION, *Beauties of Harmony,* (1719)

   Of the many versions of the Shepherd Psalm available, this paraphrase by the great Isaac Watts is one of the finest and most poetic. Other possibilities generally accessible are "The King of Love My Shepherd Is" by Henry W. Baker, "The Lord My Good Shepherd Is" by Bland Tucker, and the *Scottish Psalter* version, "The Lord's My Shepherd, I'll Not Want."—Hugh T. McElrath

WORSHIP AIDS

CALL TO WORSHIP.   "Even though I walk through the darkest valley, I fear no evil; for you are with me; your rod and your staff, they comfort me" (Ps. 23:4 NRSV).

INVOCATION.   As many of us face trials and difficulties today and as others of us face them in the future, we pray that in these moments together we may be strengthened by your presence and girded with your protection for whatever comes.

OFFERTORY SENTENCE.   "No one can serve two masters. Either he will hate the one and love the other, or he will be devoted to the one and despise the other" (Matt. 6:24a NIV).

OFFERTORY PRAYER.   Free us, O Lord, from preoccupations and idolatries that would keep us from seeing the needs of others and the opportunities we have to advance your Kingdom, beginning in our own hearts and homes and extending to the ends of the earth.

PRAYER.   In an effort to tidy up life, we have gathered some of the events experienced and bring them to you for higher management than we are able to give, Father.

Here this morning we leave the bundle of our failures. Some of them are deliberate, some are the result of neglect, some simply came upon us without warning. Show us how best to manage them, we pray. Help us to correct what we can, to seek forgiveness for the hurts our failures have brought, and to accept responsibility for what cannot be changed. Lead us through the correcting of our failures, we pray.

Here today we bring our sins. Some of them have been committed deliberately, with full knowledge that our actions and thoughts were wrong. Some of them we have simply slipped into because of the many pressures of life and work and social demands. Still others have been committed inadvertently out of ignorance. Yet all break faith with you and cause pain in life and the universe. Forgive us, Father, for all our sins. Strengthen us that we may turn from them and begin life apart from their burden as we move into the future. Fortify us with all the understanding we need to resist the wiles of temptation and guard against the invaders of life that would trap us in the grip of sin in the tomorrows to come.

We bring to you this morning our joys and successes. Thank you for them. Yet guard us from their danger. May we not begin the journey down the road of self-sufficiency nor walk the avenues of pride because of the accomplishments we have been allowed to enjoy in past days. Rather, may we be humbled by their appearance in our lives and be made to realize that joys and achievements are blessings bestowed upon us by a caring and loving Father.

Then we bring to you our hopes. Measure them in your wisdom and fulfill them as they fit your purposes. How we long for peace among all peoples. How we seek enough of the necessities of life for everyone. How we pray for a true spirit of brotherhood to abound everywhere. Let the time before us be enriched for us all as we humbly come to the hope of the world and follow him as the future unfolds by his will and purpose.—Henry Fields

SERMON
Topic: Something About That Name
TEXT: Acts 4:1–22

One of the customs at my denomination's annual meeting is a service of recognition and thanksgiving for the ministries of pastors who are retiring. Each retiring minister is invited to reminisce or exhort the assembly briefly, and depending on how many are retiring, the service of the Word continues with the bishop or someone of the bishop's choice preaching. We had reached that point in the worship service and I was settling down for a little nap when the preacher grabbed my attention with his opening words. He faced the group of retirees and said, "Thank you for each time you have said the name of Jesus. You have served many years, in different places, and with different gifts, but under one Lord and Master. Thank you for all the times you uttered the name of Jesus Christ, our Savior."

I had to stop and think about that. It was a moving moment, certainly, but why did the preacher choose to thank them that way? He could have expressed gratitude to these ministers for diligent service, for laboring for social justice and an end to oppression. The bishop could have acknowledged the sermons they preached or the building campaigns they completed. He could have mentioned any number of things; so why did he thank them for saying the name of Jesus? What is so special about a name?

An answer comes to us from the book of Acts. To understand the reading heard a few moments ago, we have to go back to the event that precipitated the confrontation. It was after Pentecost. Peter and John were walking at the Temple when a lame beggar asked them for help. Peter took the beggar by the hand and said, "I have no silver or gold, but I give you what I have; in the name of Jesus Christ of Nazareth, walk." To the astonishment of witnesses, the man was instantly healed, and he went away walking and leaping and praising God. A crowd gathered, wondering how such a miracle was possible, and Peter saw an opportunity to present the gospel. This upset the priests and Sadducees, and they had Peter and John arrested. Why? Not for healing the man. There were all sorts of itinerant magicians and wonder workers in first-century Palestine. Not for stopping traffic and having a demonstration without a permit—though that would get you arrested very quickly these days in Chicago, where I live. The priests arrested Peter and John anticipating their answer to the question posed in verse 7: "By what power or by what *name* did you do this?"

Any good Jew of the first century knew about the power of names. It was central to his identity and beliefs. From the earliest pages of the Old Testament, naming signifies authority and uniqueness. In Genesis 1 and 2, God said, "Let us make man in our image, after our likeness, and let them have dominion over the fish of the sea and the birds of the air." As a sign of that dominion, the Lord brought all creatures before Adam to see what Adam would name them. When Jacob wrestled with an angel, Genesis 32 says, God's messenger changed his name, which meant supplanter or cheater, to "God rules," and in changing Jacob's name the angel also changed his future. When Elijah had the contest with the prophets of Ba'al on Mount Carmel, it was calling on the name of the Lord God of Israel, rather than on some other deity, that brought down fire to consume the sacrifice. The prophet Hosea gave his children names that announced God's judgment upon Israel, and was later called to change their names to signify God's restoration. Jesus changed Simon's name to Peter, saying, "On this rock I will build my church," and Peter was never the same. Saul's name was changed to Paul when he became a Christian, and in the great hymn recorded in Philippians 2 he reminds us that "at the *name* of Jesus every knee shall bow, in heaven and on earth and under the earth, and every tongue confess that Jesus Christ is Lord."

The Jews knew the power of invoking a name. We should note, as we think about this evening's reading, that the priests and Sadducees did not object to Peter and John healing the man who was crippled. Jesus' disciples were not forbidden to do good but were told to shut up. Stop saying the name of Jesus. Quit claiming and drawing on its power. The combination of letters that forms the word *Jesus* was not at stake, even though the name means "God saves." It was a common enough name in that day. But they told Peter and John, "Do not speak or teach at all in the name of Jesus"—that is, in the name of Jesus the Messiah. Don't talk about the Jesus they crucified, the Jesus people were saying rose from the dead. Don't talk about Jesus as though by his name comes salvation, healing, forgiveness of sins, and the resurrection of the dead. Don't invoke a name with that much power.

What did Peter and John do? They answered, "Whether it is right in the sight of God to listen to you rather than to God, you must judge; for we cannot speak of what we have seen and heard." After their release, they reported to their friends everything that had happened. They acknowledged it was God's hand, not their own, that was stretched out to heal the sick, and that signs and wonders were performed through the holy name of Jesus (v. 29). God gave them boldness, so they were unafraid. They praised God together, and knew the power of the name.

I don't know if the bishop was thinking of this story from Acts when he thanked the retiring clergy for every time they had uttered the name of Jesus. But I can say that this bishop was aware of the kind of world in which the ministers of our conference were working. We don't have priests and Sadducees dragging followers of Jesus into court nowadays—though in the Sudan and other parts of the world a person can be imprisoned, sold into slavery, or put to death for bearing the name of Christ. Even in places where the Church is not persecuted, however, it is a time when many people object to hearing the name of the Messiah.

This is due in part to wildly misinterpreted laws about separation of church and state. For example, it is no longer permissible for children in school to sing Christmas songs with any religious content: the name of Jesus must not be mentioned, nor any reference to his birth. The White House may host its annual Easter egg hunt but may not acknowledge what the holiday really means. Some recent television series that portray religious people in leading roles or as support characters show them to be well-meaning but generally ineffectual. *Seventh Heaven* and *Dr. Quinn, Medicine Woman* come to mind. PBS offers us *The Vicar of Dibley* and *Keeping Up Appearances,* in which clergy may be sexually frustrated comedians but do not utter the name of Jesus, except perhaps as a swear word. They do not communicate the idea that there is power in the name of the Lord. In the weeks before Christmas, the Salvation Army has bell ringers standing by the entrance to every shopping mall and superstore, collecting money for the poor, but when you contribute they say, "Happy holidays" rather than "God bless you," so they don't offend atheists or adherents of other religions in our multicultural society.

Even within our own churches it seems that we are reluctant to utter the name of Jesus Christ or to speak his other titles or present visual reminders of his power and mercy. In many Protestant churches there is a "passing the peace" at some point during the service. Seldom, however, do you hear someone utter, "The peace of Christ be with you." Occasionally someone will say, "Peace be with you," but most often it's "Good morning." We enjoy cultural superiority over people who wear their faith less tastefully than we do, with their sentimental paintings of Jesus at home and their WWJD bracelets on their wrists. We are amused or annoyed by street corner prophets, Christian music with more zeal than appeal, and acquaintances who piously ask us how we met the Lord. Yes, even disciples of Jesus are put off by hearing his name sometimes, coming from the wrong lips, nuanced in certain ways.

What are we to do about this? There is clearly a problem when the name of Jesus causes offense both inside and outside the Church: when a bishop thanking clergy for saying the name of Jesus is newsworthy, when we would more willingly talk about or demonstrate for any number of other good, important things than testify to the power of the risen Savior. I believe that God offers us hope and direction through this story from Acts 4. The passage overcomes most of our objections and invites us to have our Lord's name ever on our lips and in our hearts.

First, for those of us who shrink away from confrontative, in-your-face evangelism, this episode shows that effective witness, like the love of our Savior, is gracious. It is relational. Peter and John were walking to the Temple, going about the business of being faithful disciples, when an opportunity to share Christ presented itself. The lame man asked *them* for help rather than being a captive, helpless audience. After the healing all the people ran *to them* in Solomon's portico; Peter didn't look for ways to exploit the healing as an object lesson. The priests and Sadducees set the apostles in their midst to ask them questions. This account doesn't so much suggest that Christians should stand on their housetops screaming the name of Jesus as it implies that *we should be ready at all times to bear witness.* Opportunities to talk about Jesus come more often than we may think. I remember riding a bus in Stockholm, a city so secular that less than 1 percent of the population attends church. A woman got on the bus a few stops after me and asked the driver for directions. He had difficulty explaining so I leaned forward and said, "I know where you want to go. Sit near me and I'll tell you when to get off." The woman came and sat in the row in front of me—and then, to my surprise, turned around and said, "Do you speak English? Are you a Christian?" When I answered yes to both questions, she said, "Would you talk to me about Christ? My life is a mess and I need help." Your opportunities to talk about Jesus won't come in exactly the same way, but they will come. Can you tell another person who this Jesus is and what he has done?

Peter and John were ready when people approached them and they offered something better than silver or gold. They offered healing (which in Greek has the same root as the word for salvation) in Jesus Christ. And it was offered not just to the crippled man but to the crowds and to those who arrested them. They offered the truth, that there is salvation in no one else, but whosoever will may come and receive God's gift in Jesus Christ. Had Peter and John relied on themselves and been limited to their own resources and ingenuity, they might have said to the lame man, "We don't have any money for you but we feel your pain. We can't give you silver or gold but we'll organize a protest against the local authorities for neglecting you. We don't have any spare change but we'll skip worship to sit down and keep you company for a while." But Peter and John had more than their limited resources and vision. They invoked the powerful name of Jesus, confident that God would work through them to bless others. Are we calling on our Lord, believing that he, by the power at work within us, is able to do far more abundantly than all we ask or think (Eph. 3:20)?

Peter and John drew near to the source of that power. Before they encountered the lame man, they were on their way to worship God. After they were released from custody, they gathered with fellow believers and praised the Lord. Jesus Christ was more than a name or symbol, more than a philosophical framework. For Peter and John, he was the one whose company they sought above any other. *You see, to be ready to bear witness to Jesus, or to draw upon the power of his name, it is necessary to pursue intimacy with him*—to grow into deeper relationship. The New Testament often compares the relationship between Christ and his disciples to that of a husband and wife. In a good marriage, the covenant made on the wedding day is only the beginning. Love and knowledge deepen as the man and woman spend "quality time" together, listen to one another, and look for ways to demonstrate their love for each other. Such a marriage produces joy, security, and confidence as they face whatever adversities may come. So it is in our relationship with Jesus. We can speak his name with boldness if we know the one of whom we speak. We can draw on the power of his name if we are ready to be channels of that power. We can offer hope to a world crippled by sin, through the one who has redeemed us and called us each by name. Then let us praise the blessed name of Jesus and draw near to him who gave his life for us.—Carol M. Noren

SUNDAY, MAY 13, 2001
Lectionary Message

Topic: Love and Glory

TEXT: John 13:31–35

Other Readings: Acts 11:1–18; Ps. 148; Rev. 21:1–6

I. At first glance, it seems odd that Jesus should associate Judas' departure with glorification. Nevertheless, the connection is clear. "When he [Judas] had gone out, Jesus said, 'Now the Son of Man has been glorified. . .'" (v. 31).

The course of events that Judas' departure initiated would ordinarily be understood to produce shame. We feel shame when the reality of our experience falls short of our image of ourselves. Shame occurs when we feel exposed and belittled. In addition to being excruciatingly painful, crucifixion was humiliating. The victim was stripped, his body was mutilated, and he was put on display in such a way that his suffering was a public spectacle. Yet as Judas leaves to betray him, Jesus declares that he has been glorified.

Rather than shame, we experience glory when we are exalted. Usually we glorify those who have achieved some outstanding victory. We often associate glory with winning a sports competition or with bravery in battle. Jesus redefines glory. The glory he received is not due to heroic acts. It was bestowed on him as a result of perfect obedience to the Father. He displayed that obedience by washing the disciples' feet and he perfected it by dying on the cross. Thus the eternal glory of God is seen in him. That glory is glimpsed in the beauty of creation, in the mighty acts of God's deliverance, and in the miracles Jesus performed. It is seen perfectly in his death and Resurrection.

II. Jesus prepared the disciples for the fact that he was going to leave them. As he was betrayed, humiliated, and killed, it seemed to them that things had gotten completely out of control. They likely asked him the same questions we ask when evil seems to have the upper hand: Where is God in this? How could God let this happen? Jesus was clear that his death was something to which he willingly submitted. Far from being evil's triumph over good, Jesus' Passion marks God's victory over sin and death. For now, Jesus' followers carry on his earthly work of revealing the Father and calling to the Father those who belong to him.

III. Jesus' followers carry on his work as they love one another. When Jesus calls this a new commandment, he does not claim that love is a new concept in the Bible. The Old Testament is filled with evidence of God's love. What is new is the character of this love. Jesus' followers love one another the same way Jesus loves them, which is how the Father loves Jesus. Just as the Sermon on the Mount presents the Ten Commandments in a way that goes beyond the technicalities of the law to the underlying meaning, so Jesus' new commandment to love redefines the meaning of love. His followers' love for one another goes beyond doing kind and generous things for one another. It is love like Jesus' love, which lays down its life for others.

The words Jesus spoke throughout his ministry had power, but they were accompanied by signs that showed the source of that power. His works of healing the sick and feeding the hungry showed the love he proclaimed. His followers' love for one another shows the gospel we proclaim. If the communities in which we worship and serve him are contentious, divided, and unkind to fellow believers, how can anyone see Jesus in our midst? Our words, no matter how eloquent, are like clanging brass or noisy cymbals unless they are accompanied by acts of love.

IV. We should not infer that Jesus' love is limited to the community of his followers. Elsewhere Jesus has told us to love our enemies. He told Nicodemus that God so loved the world that he gave his only Son. Jesus looked with compassion on Jerusalem, whose inhabitants would and did kill him. God's love knows no bounds and God showers it on the world whether we are aware of it or not.

There is something unique about the love among the Father, Jesus, and Jesus' followers. In Jesus' love, we know the Father's love. Not only does God's gracious love create us and sustain us, but in Jesus that love transforms us. Through him we know God's love in a particular, personal, and mutual way. God's love is no longer just something we receive. It is something in which we participate. We practice God's love as we love one another.

Our love for one another is also a sign to the world that Jesus will come again. There is an eschatological aspect to it. In Jesus' death, Resurrection, and return to the Father we see the depth of God's love for us and know with certainty that the creation that God made in love is headed toward a culmination of that love when Jesus returns in glory. That glory is foreseen in the love Jesus' followers have for one another.—Stephens G. Lytch

ILLUSTRATIONS

DISILLUSIONMENT AND DISCOVERY.   "We cannot really speak of God," says Eckhardt; "when we would speak of Him we do but stammer." "We are like young children learning to speak," exclaims Luther, "and can use only half words and quarter words." So Paul felt, whenever he tried to set down in words the great decisive experience of his life. All the resources of language could not communicate it. Strive as he might to express it, the inmost secret remained inexpressible. Once he fell back on the word "unspeakable," "God's unspeakable gift" (2 Cor. 9:15), and the adjective there was no mere vague hyperbole, as often in our modern usage: it was the literal conclusion to which the failure of all attempts to capture in words the glory of the fact had driven him. The thing could not be spoken; and the apostle, like the poet, was always conscious of

"Thoughts hardly to be pack'd
Into a narrow act,
Fancies that broke through language and escaped."

—James S. Stewart[3]

---

[3] *A Man in Christ* (London: Hodder Stoughton, 1935) p. 81.

WHAT IS LOVE?.   Love is immortality struggling within a mortal frame, and all the mortal pains that flesh is heir to become golden with immortal life as they are touched by love.—A. Victor Murray[4]

SERMON SUGGESTIONS

Topic: The Alpha and the Omega
TEXT: Rev. 21:1–6
(1) God: Creator of a new heaven and a new earth. (2) God: homemaker supreme, dwelling with us mortals (Gen. 1:26–27; John 1:14). (3) God: Maker of all things new.

Topic: The Final Test
TEXT: John 13:31–35
(1) God glorified in the crucifixion-bound Jesus. (2) God glorified in the love-bound follower of Jesus.

CONGREGATIONAL MUSIC
1. "Praise the Lord, Ye Heavens Adore Him," *Foundling Hospital Collection* (1796)
   HYFRYDOL, Roland H. Prichard (1830)
   A free rendering of Psalm 148, this anonymous hymn is a magnificent summons for all the hosts of heaven and earth to join in the praise of God. It should be sung either preceding or following the reading of the psalm.
2. "I Want to Be Ready," African American Spiritual
   I WANT TO BE READY, African American Spiritual
   Inspired by the apostle John's vision of the New Jerusalem (Rev. 21:1–6), this spiritual is in "jubilee style" and should be sung in a lively manner using the call-and-response method.
3. "Christian Hearts in Love United," Nicolaus L. von Zinzendorf (1725)
   CASSELL, trad. German melody (1735)
   Jesus' command to love one another (John 13:31–35) can be accompanied by this great Moravian hymn that magnifies the love that Christians should manifest for one another and thus "by this, all men will know that you are my disciples."
4. "In Christ There Is No East or West," John Oxenham (1913)
   MCKEE, African American Spiritual; harm. H. T. Burleigh
   ST. PETER, Alexander Reinagle (1836)
   In connection with the reading in Acts (11:1–18) in which the revelation came to Peter that the gospel was for all people, not just the Jews, this classic hymn is ideal. It should be sung to either tune with enthusiasm and conviction.—Hugh T. McElrath

WORSHIP AIDS
CALL TO WORSHIP.   "Both young men, and maidens; old men, and children: let them praise the name of the Lord: for his name alone is excellent; his glory is above the earth and heaven" (Ps. 148:12–13).

---

[4] *Personal Experience and the Historic Faith*, 1939.

INVOCATION.   Open the hearts of all of us, O Lord, so that we can give you the praise that is due your holy name. Let our prayers, our hymns, and our every gesture bring us closer to you and make us more loving toward one another as your people.

OFFERTORY SENTENCE.   "The children of Israel brought a willing offering unto the Lord, every man and woman, whose heart made them willing to bring forth all manner of work, which the Lord had commanded to be made by the hand of Moses" (Exod. 35:29).

OFFERTORY PRAYER.   Our hearts have been made to be willing to bring our tithes and offerings to you, O Lord, because you have given your best, even Jesus Christ our Savior, to us. Now use these gifts, we pray, that we may be strengthened in our resolve to serve you and that others may be brought into the circle of faith, hope, and love.

PRAYER.   Forever God, Lord of the beginning and the end, we know it is true: you are our Creator, our Sustainer, our Lord, our Eternal Life.

Gracious God, Master Designer, as the warm sun touches the budding rose, so your Son reaches into our lives with light and love. We know it is true: You are the Lord of goodness and mercy. Giving Father, the gift of children has come among us today, and we know it is true: you are our Father and we all are your children. In praise and worship we embrace you and in our own way say, Thanks be to God.

Timeless God, Lord of seasons, we are called to serious discipleship, to the uncommon walk to the cross. We stumble for relief. We seek other options. But your Christ will not relent. He beckons our all. We are reluctant, then ashamed. We know our deprivations are few; our scars, if any, are mostly self-inflicted; our passion is self-centered; and our resolve is shaky at best. But in our unsureness, your mercy comes like an unexpected gift from home. We are reminded that Christ has gone before. The victory has been won. So in faith and obedience, with quiet small steps, undergirded by your grace, we venture onward. Continue to lead us, O Lord of the cross, to that saving and redeeming hill where Christ gives flesh and blood to the meaning of love and forgiveness.

May our worship this day enable us alone and together for the journey with you. With Christ, we pray.—William M. Johnson

SERMON
Topic: Faithful Mothers—Stewards of Life
Text: 1 Sam. 1:27–38

When one preaches every Mothers' Day, what is new for one to say? Well, along my journey through the Bible I met a sister named Hannah and I'd like you to meet her, too. Her role, however, is not a typical mother's role. We might call her a faithful mother, a steward of life.

Elkanah, the husband of Hannah, loved her dearly, even though she could not have any children. He finally took a second wife, Peninnah, who bore him many children, both boys and girls. Through these years, poor Hannah grieved and prayed and prayed and grieved. She was especially hurt when it was time to go to the annual service at the tabernacle at Shiloh. Because Peninnah had so many children, she received a much larger portion of everything.

Every year at Shiloh, Peninnah would laugh at Hannah, making her cry so much she had a hard time even eating dinner. Elkanah worried about Hannah's grief.

Elkanah said, "Why make such a fuss over not being able to bear children? Isn't having me better than having ten sons?" For dear Hannah it *wasn't*. Hannah prayed and wept so much that at one point the priest in the temple thought she was drunk. Her mouth was moving but no sound was coming out. Hannah's often-inaudible prayers may have gone something like this: "O Jehovah, Creator and Sustainer of us all, if after all these barren years you would overcome my many bodily handicaps and give me a child, I'd be so careful to give you the praise *and* the child. Lord, if you will make a special provision for this lady growing old and send me a child, I will make a special effort to see to it that he is given every encouragement to be the special person you want him to be. But you will know, Lord, that I will love him more than life itself. I will consider your will with utter awe and deepest respect. And if you say so, I'll even place him in the Temple, where he can finish growing up under high priest Eli. He'll be quite literally your child, not mine. Thank you, Lord, Amen."

As time went on, Hannah was finally blessed by God to have a son, a child of her very own. She gave him the name Samuel. Hannah's fervency of prayer and seriousness of care for a child were honored by God.

Hannah had promised Samuel to the Lord. However, her prayer and care were now as if Samuel were only hers. Her entire self-esteem seemed to be tied up in being a mother, a natural mother by birth and a nurturing mother by function. By this means she hoped to be completely fulfilled; she would make up for all those years of pain and embarrassment.

Hannah's care was total. She had servants and money, but her *personal* investment in her child meant she did everything for her son by her own hand. Throughout his early years, she tenderly sewed every stitch of his clothing, and it was the very best. His new wardrobe was her creation all the way.

But now she was under oath to place the child in the Temple as soon as she had weaned him. This sounds strange to our ears. What high priest—especially a man Eli's age—would dream of baby-sitting a child of even two years? But wait: I think my African roots suggest an answer. Mothers in many cultures, including some in Africa, nurse their babies to the age of five or six years. It could be that Samuel was six or seven when he was weaned and surrendered at last to God. Hannah dragged her feet as long as she could.

There is also an African parallel to this whole process. The Akan people believe that each child has a "KRA" (the Yoruba call it "ORI"). It is the word used for the unique personality given to every child. It is set by God, and God is very strict about not allowing people to tamper with a child's KRA. So the Akans keep babies out of danger and remove from them any articles that might harm them. After that, the child can be and do what the child is inwardly driven to do, because the child is believed to belong to heaven and never actually to the earthly parents. Mothers are just stewards of life, protecting the child's KRA.

No wonder Hannah could feel so strongly about having a son and still surrender him readily to God's plans.

I don't suppose I need to remind you that each child still has a KRA. God still has unique personalities and matchless plans for every child brought into the world. In the divine provision, we are each created unique in the sight of God. God still blesses parents who raise their children to love and trust God. A KRA is no luxury; it is the very stuff of each person we know, and it needs to be expressed.

Hannah was a steward of life given by God. The esteem in which we hold Hannah today is partly because of her praying, but also because of her respect for her promise to God. As mothers, no child belongs to us. Even after giving birth, no child is ours for keeps. They all belong to our Creator.

Hannah never regretted her faithfulness. I don't know how much of her son's career she lived to witness, but I am sure she praised God. Samuel was the last of the judges in Israel and the greatest, towering over his times!

I pray for children and grandchildren without ceasing, but I leave them to the Lord, to do what is placed in them to do. Mothers, grandmothers, surrogate mothers, "wannabe" mothers, expectant mothers, and any other mothers: we are stewards of lives with undreamed-of possibilities. May our faithful stewardship free our children to join the ranks of the Samuels of human history. Amen.—Ella Pearson Mitchell

SUNDAY, MAY 20, 2001
Lectionary Message

Topic: Our Teacher Forever
TEXT: John 14:23–29
Other Readings: Acts 16: 9–15; Ps. 67; Rev. 21:10, 22–22:5

I. A prominent theme of this farewell discourse is the unity of Jesus with God, God with Jesus, and Jesus' followers with Jesus. Thus it follows that our love for God is modeled on God's love for us. From the beginning of time, God's love has involved creative activity. Out of love God made the universe. God loved the world so much that he gave his Son. God's love for us is not passive. Neither is our love for God.

The love Jesus commands motivates us to do things we would not do were it not for our love of God. It is like the love a mother has for her child that leads her to do things she would not choose to do if she did not love the child. One finds joy in the trials of parenting not because those trials are enjoyable but because of the joy that comes from serving the child who is loved. A husband and wife can feel deep love for one another, but unless that love is expressed in acts of kindness and affection, the love grows cold.

Those who love Jesus keep his command to love one another as he loves. That love is defined on the cross where Jesus gave himself for the world.

II. Jesus promises the Holy Spirit, who will teach his followers everything and remind them what he has said. Nothing that the Holy Spirit teaches will differ from what Jesus said to his disciples in his earthly ministry, yet the Holy Spirit will make Jesus' teaching continually fresh and new.

There are few things more powerful than memory. Memories of ancient conquests have fueled ethnic rivalries in the Balkans in recent years. Some people have personal memories that wreak as much havoc on their souls as the memory of a lost battle wreaks havoc on a nation. There are some memories that cause so much trauma that we use up all the psychic energy we can muster to keep them repressed. That is energy we could use to excel in a career or thrive in a relationship, but it is depleted because it takes everything we have to keep certain memories under control.

But memories are also a source of strength. When a student feels that school is more than he or she can handle, memories of affirmation received from a teacher can keep the student from giving up and slumping to the bottom of the class. The memory of Passover has sustained Jews for over three thousand years. When Americans remember the ideals set forth in the Declaration of Independence and the sacrifices their forebears made for liberty, they are prodded to confront the lingering racism that keeps them from fulfilling those ideals of equality that are at the heart of their identity as a people.

Fred Craddock[5] has pointed out that there are three times when we know an event: in anticipation, in the event itself, and in remembrance. Our anticipation is based on expectations, not on the reality of the event itself. The actual event often loses us in a blur of activity. In memory we are able to see the event in the context of the rest of life. It is in memory that we come to understand an important trip, a wedding, a gathering with friends, or the words of the Risen Lord.

Memories are powerful, but they are not static. Sometimes something happens that transforms memories and gives them more significance than you ever knew they had. When you realize you are in love, you see that the conversations you had on long walks with your beloved were more than just ordinary talk between friends. You were revealing your souls to each other, seeing how much of yourself you could entrust, and bringing to life feelings you never knew existed. Memories can be transformed by the birth of a child because your life becomes focused on a person who did not even exist a year ago. You see your parents in a whole new way. You feel the demands your baby puts on you, and you are overwhelmed with gratitude for what your mother and father gave up for you. Or perhaps you realize for the first time how much you needed from your parents but did not receive and you are overcome with sadness. Understanding how hard it is to be a parent, perhaps you can forgive them for their failures and heal some of the painful memories you have carried for years.

The Holy Spirit recalls to our memory the life and ministry of Jesus and guides us as we discern the Lord's Word to us in the present. The Spirit of truth keeps us true to Jesus as the Spirit protects us from projecting our preconceptions and prejudices onto Scripture, keeping our memory true to the Risen Lord.

III. Jesus leaves us his peace, which is different from any peace we can know apart from him. He tells the disciples not to let their hearts be troubled or afraid.

One of the foremost causes of fear is not knowing what to expect. Before surgery a physician may describe as precisely as possible what the patient can expect. The doctor may warn that there will be moments of pain. During the recovery there will be good days and there will be difficult days. The more the patient knows what is ahead, the less fear he or she will have.

Jesus tells his disciples that traumatic times are ahead, but there is no need to fear because what will happen is in accordance with the Father's will. Although it may seem that Jesus has abandoned them, he will be even more accessible to them through the Holy Spirit, whom he will send. Even though they do not know precisely what the future holds, the Spirit will

---

[5] Fred Craddock, *Luke* (Louisville, Ky.: John Knox Press, 1990), p. 287.

give them courage as it assures them that God, whom they know through Jesus, is still in control.—Stephens G. Lytch

ILLUSTRATIONS

THE HOLY SPIRIT TODAY.   What does Holy Spirit mean today? We can start by putting it very simply: the Holy Spirit makes us receptive to Jesus. The early church believed that, to begin with, the Holy Spirit could be seen only in Jesus. Then the church emphasized that it was Jesus, the risen One, who gave it the Spirit. And finally Paul, and still more John, perceived that the one all-important work of the Spirit was to make Jesus come alive for them. Once a person begins to understand that the way Jesus lived and died, which at first sight is so meaningless, is what brings us to order and restores us to communion with God—then the Holy Spirit is at work. "What no eye has seen, nor ear heard, nor the heart of man conceived . . . God has revealed to us through the Spirit . . . Christ crucified, a stumbling block to Jews and folly to Gentiles, but to those who are called, . . . the power of God and the wisdom of God" (1 Cor. 2:9–10; 1:23–24).—Eduard Schweizer[6]

THE HOLY SPIRIT AS TEACHER.   The Fourth Gospel and the Synoptic Gospels as well are all . . . examples of what the Holy Spirit taught the disciples after Jesus' resurrection. Their faith in Jesus, undimmed by the cross and supported by the resurrection, gave a place to stand, a perspective from which what they themselves had seen and heard and what others had experienced could be evaluated and reported. All of this was related to the traditions and scriptures that had nourished the faith of the community into which they were born, so that these primary witnesses were in truth scribes for the Kingdom of heaven, bringing out of the treasure "what is new and what is old" (Matt. 13:53, NRSV). What they announced these early witnesses related to the perceived needs and even peculiarities of those to whom they spoke and wrote, as the Holy Spirit taught them what to say and write under the circumstances. How this worked out is most obvious in the Fourth Gospel, where thematic arrangement and theological interpretation are main concerns. To a lesser degree, but just as surely, the Synoptic writers express the individuality and uniqueness of their own concerns, as they were taught by the Spirit.

In our own times the same principle must prevail, always under the discipline of the Christian community and its scriptures and under the imperatives of the need of those to whom the message is directed.—James W. Cox[7]

SERMON SUGGESTIONS

Topic: The ABC's of Being Human
TEXT: Various
(1) Awakening (Rev. 1:17–18; John 1:1, 4–5, 3:5). (2) Believing (Luke 6:47–48, 12:15; Mark 9:24; Rom. 10:17). (3) Caring (1 John 3:16–18).—Landon B. Saunders[8]

---

[6] *The Holy Spirit* (Minneapolis: Augsburg Fortress, 1980), p. 126f.
[7] In *Review and Expositor*, 1997, *94*(1), p. 90f.
[8] *The Power of Receiving*

Topic: Exodus at Jerusalem

TEXT: Exod. 33:12–23

There is (1) the Word of Command, in every generation—the Bible's first answer to the riddle of human existence: "Speak unto the children of Israel, that they go forward"; (2) the Word of Promise—no situation is hopeless, precisely because in no situation is anybody ever helpless: "My presence shall go with thee; (3) the Word of Victory—for all who can bear it: "This day have I brought thee up out of the land of Egypt. Be of good cheer; I have overcome the world."—Paul Scherer[9]

CONGREGATIONAL MUSIC

1. "God of Mercy, God of Grace," Henry F. Lyte (1834)

   IMPACT, David G. Wilson (1973)

   LUCERNA LAUDONIAE, David Evans (1927)

   This free paraphrase of Psalm 67 could be sung to either tune in alternation with the Psalm verses as follows: read verses 1–4, sing stanza 1; read verses 5–7, sing stanza 2.

2. "Shall We Gather at the River?" Robert Lowry (1865)

   HANSON PLACE, Robert Lowry (1865)

   Based on Revelation 22:1, this classic gospel hymn has achieved the status of a true folk song. It would naturally be sung following the reading of the day's lesson in Revelation.

3. "Saviour, Again to Your Dear Name We Raise," John Ellerton (1866)

   ELLERS, Edward J. Hopkins (1869)

   This hymn, eminently suitable for the closing of worship, nevertheless has as its predominant theme a petition for Jesus' word of peace to be granted as recorded in the Epistle lesson (John 14:23–27).

4. "We've a Story to Tell to the Nations," H. Ernest Nichol (1896)

   MESSAGE, H. Ernest Nichol (1896)

   The singing of this vibrant hymn of mission would be a suitable response to the reading in Acts where the gospel story is shared by the apostle Paul in Philippi, leading to the conversion of Lydia and her household.

WORSHIP AIDS

CALL TO WORSHIP.   "God be merciful to us and bless us, and cause His face to shine upon us. That Your way may be known on earth, your salvation among all nations" (Ps. 67:1–2 NKJV).

INVOCATION.   Lord, as we pause to worship and praise your name, help us to find ourselves through your grace and give ourselves through your love, God's mercy to proclaim.—E. Lee Phillips

OFFERTORY SENTENCE.   "The whole earth is mine, but You will be my chosen people, a people dedicated to me alone" (Exod. 19:5–6a TEV).

---

[9] *The Word God Sent*

OFFERTORY PRAYER.   Lord of life, we consecrate this offering to the doing of your will in this place and to the uttermost parts of the world, in Jesus' preeminent name.—E. Lee Phillips

PRAYER.   Amid plenty and beauty we come before you this morning, Father. Everywhere we turn there is a ready reminder of your creativity and provision for both our need and our pleasure. Abundance appears all about us. Even in the most abandoned spot some manifestation of creativity is found. Thank you for all that comes to us to make life not only livable but useful. May we never become so used to the wonder of your world that we fail to pause and appreciate the intricate patterns of your creation and the marvel of your provision for our physical, mental, and spiritual needs.

Thank you, also, Father, for the Church. We are so quick to forget the importance of its presence in our lives and the purpose you have for its mission in the world. Lead us to a more noble commitment to this living body of Christ. Make us aware of our own need to follow him as we reach out to others in the Church's name. Recall us to a devotion to prayer, to discovering firsthand the wonder of the Word, to sustaining strong support for the mission of Christ's Church, and to defending it against all that would weaken it, use it for wrong reasons, or destroy it. Thank you for the foundation the Church has provided for our journey in time, for the truths it has imparted to strengthen our minds, souls, and hearts. Thank you for the comfort it has given us in times of distress and grief, of confusion and misunderstanding. Thank you for the salvation story that has been sounded throughout its history, calling us to a reunion with rightness, honesty, eternity, and God.

Thank you for the lasting friendships we have found in the company of the committed, those strangers and pilgrims who have faced in the right direction and extended a hand to us to help us walk the road that leads to wholeness and usefulness in the world. Thank you for the challenge they have given, the chastisement they have provided, the understanding they have shared, and the love they have poured out on us at all stations and in all periods of life. May we who have received so much from God's people be moved to share in kind what we have gained so that his Kingdom may at long last become the Kingdom of this world where Christ truly reigns among men and women forever.

Now we offer this hour to you and, standing on tiptoe, listen for your call to all of us and each of us, in Jesus' name.—Henry Fields

Sermon
Topic: Rich Man
TEXT: Mark 10:17–31

The story before us today begins with a job interview. Jesus has been out advertising, cold calling, networking—and he gets a bite. Up runs a guy who seems like the ideal recruit for Jesus' mission. He volunteers, runs up, kneels down before Jesus—you have to admire his spunk. He addresses Jesus with great respect, which Jesus shakes off, and asks what he has to do. We don't see that very often in the gospels. Plenty of naysayers, plenty of critics, but only a handful of folks who just walk up and say, "OK, you've sold me on this Kingdom of God thing; where do I sign?"

Jesus quizzes the man, gives him the full interview, and asks him whether he can live within company policy. And the guy gives an amazing answer! "I have not broken any of these rules since I became a man." How many adults do you know who can say that truthfully?

Jesus clearly is impressed. The text says, "Jesus, looking at him, loved him." I would sign him up right then and there; tell him to sit tight and drink a cup of coffee while I go get the contract, and get him inked in and on the payroll before he gets a chance to change his mind. But Jesus isn't done with the interview. "You lack one thing; go, sell what you have, give the money to the poor, and you will have treasure in heaven; then come, follow me."

I. Now, let's put this in perspective. Nobody among the disciples, so far as we know, has done this. True, Peter and Andrew, James and John have all left their family businesses to follow Jesus; but they haven't sold their boats and nets. Earlier in Mark, in fact, Jesus and the gang go to Peter's house, Jesus heals Peter's mother-in-law, and she serves them dinner. Levi the tax collector quit his job, but he didn't sell his home; in fact, he gave Jesus a big party and invited all his rowdy friends. Why is Jesus making discipleship so hard for *this* guy, who may even be a better person, overall, than any of the twelve? Couldn't Jesus take him on and try to work with him a little? Does he really have to sell everything? I mean, the guy is very religious; he probably gives generously to the charitable fund at his synagogue. Why does he have to give it all away?

The twelve are just as perplexed. Jesus tells them it will be very hard for wealthy people to enter the Kingdom, and they are puzzled. But when he tells them that a camel will slip through a needle's eye easier than a rich man can walk through the door into God's great banquet, they are befuddled. See, I could understand it if the rich man in question were Zacchaeus, the rich tax collector, who made his fortune by keeping other people poor. But this rich man is clearly not like that: he doesn't lie, he doesn't cheat, he doesn't steal, and besides, he's good to his mom and dad. Isn't that what God wants? Aren't we supposed to be good people, and in that way enter God's Kingdom?

Here's the real nub of the issue. Getting into God's Kingdom is really hard, says Jesus, but not in the sense that the rich man thinks. The rich man wants a list of things to do: commandments to keep, oaths to make, pilgrimages to take, financial pledges to commit. He wants to know what he must *do* to enter God's Kingdom, and that's not the right question; if it were, he'd already have been there. The issue is more what he'd be willing to *give up* to enter God's Kingdom, and his answer to that question is clear: there are some things more important to him than being in God's Kingdom, some things he'd not be willing to surrender.

I have a great deal of sympathy for this man. Ask me to give to a charity—no problem. Ask me to give some time for a worthwhile project—I don't have all the time in the world, but I can make some adjustments and give some time for some things. Ask me to give away extra clothes, or contribute cans of food, or even give the last five dollars in my wallet to help someone who really needs a meal—that's really not that hard. You all know this; this church is full of giving people. But there's a point where giving begins to cut into my control of my life, and that's where giving becomes giving up, or surrender, and that's what I find hard. I don't like to commit to endless tasks that take an unspecified amount of time; I'd like to know that I still have control of my schedule. Same with my money: the only good thing about money, it seems to me, is that if you have enough of it, it gives you some control over things. Having money set aside, having more coming in than you have going out gives you a feeling of security, a sense of control over your future.

II. It's not *giving away* that's such a problem, but *giving up,* surrendering, that's so hard. The rich man's stronghold, deep within himself, the fortress he'd not surrender to God was his money. Maybe most of us here, if not all of us, would have the same problem surrendering our possessions completely if we felt God asking us to do so. But the same would be true for other things as well. Could I walk away from my career after investing so much in it? Could I give up my family, walk away from my home like Peter and the other disciples? How many items are there on the list of things I would not surrender?

The crazy thing is—again, I know this and you do, too—that our control of all these things is just an illusion. I don't really control my time, my money, my family; I can't guarantee that disaster or disease won't take them away in an instant. Think of the rich man. He walked away from Jesus, grieving because he could not give up his money. If he was still alive about forty years years later, chances are he lost all his money anyway when the Roman army sacked and burned the cities of Galilee and sold the inhabitants into slavery. We like to think we control our lives, but we don't, and that's why Jesus, who always tells the truth, didn't soft-pedal the message for this man who said he'd never lied since he became a man. "You think you control your money," said Jesus. "OK, show me; give it away and come follow me." But the rich man preferred an illusion to the truth; he would rather hold onto his fortune—or maybe it's more correct to say he preferred that his fortune would hold onto him and his heart.

III. Suppose, though, the rich man had followed Jesus' advice, had given instructions for his business manager to begin selling his property, and had followed Jesus. What then? Well, Jesus says he'd have gotten back a hundred times what he gave away. To make sense of this, look at Jesus. He owned a home in Capernaum, but he seemed to spend as much time in other people's homes as in his own. He had a family back in Nazareth, but he was constantly surrounded by people he called his mother and brothers and sisters. If you give up your illusions of control over your life, put your life into God's hands, and follow Jesus on the Kingdom road, then what you get back is the company of the other disciples. What a deal, right? Would the rich man really trade in his wealthy lifestyle for membership in the Twelve?

He would if he knew what we know. This group of people following Jesus on the road to the Kingdom is here to tell you the truth when you need to hear it, to make the hard calls and tell you that you've gone off track. But they won't leave you out there in despair. Jesus yelled at the disciples when they were being selfish or willfully disobedient, but he never left them, even when they ran away from him.

Walk the road with us and we'll tell you the truth; we'll gently lead you back to where you need to be; and when the disasters come, as they must, we will gather you into a sanctuary, and we'll stay with you until you can get up and go again. Did you notice that little addendum to Jesus' promise? Surrender and you'll get back a hundred times what you gave away— with persecutions. Had the rich man given away his possessions and had he lived another forty years, he'd still have suffered when the Romans invaded his country. Being a Christian doesn't immunize you against disease or heartache or depression or tragedy. But it does mean that you have a place, a safe place, in which to weather the storm and recuperate.

I don't really understand how this happens but it does. God takes a bunch of weak, selfish, irritable, headstrong fishermen and small businessmen and plants them in the thin soil of Palestine, and up grows the great tree of the Church. God takes this bunch—and don't make me enumerate our shortcomings because we'd be here all day—and plants us on this street corner and up grows a community of faith that nurtures children, supports missions, heals broken hearts, and makes us all better together than we were alone. Knowing myself, and knowing some of you—no offense, mind you—I'd have bet on the camel through the needle before I'd have predicted some of the amazing things that have happened here in this community of faith. But then Jesus said that with God all things are possible.

Surrender. Look inside your heart for strongholds, for the places you want to keep tightly clutched, and give them up to God. Then join us and help us to do the same, and together we'll walk down the road toward the Kingdom. That's the gospel, brothers and sisters.— Richard B. Vinson

SUNDAY, MAY 27, 2001
Lectionary Message

Topic: Our Unity in Christ
TEXT: John 17:20–26
Other Readings: Acts 16:16–34; Ps. 97; Rev. 22:12–14, 16–17, 20–21

I. The last words we hear from Jesus before he is betrayed by Judas are his prayer for us. Having prayed for his disciples and commended them into God's care, he now lifts up to God those generations of followers who are to come. His concern for them—and for us—is as deep as it is for those who sat at table with him in the upper room.

Jesus asks the Father to bring about the unity of those who belong to him throughout the ages. That unity is inherent in Jesus' relationship with his followers. Here Christology informs ecclesiology.

Throughout John's Gospel we see how Jesus is one with the Father. That unity is the source of Jesus' authority and power. It is in his followers' unity with Jesus that they have access to the Father, the creator and sustainer of the universe.

The world sees that unity of Jesus with the Father in the unity of the Church. One can summarize the purpose of Jesus' ministry as the restoration of right relationships. He came to restore humanity's relationship with God. Those who live in a right relationship with God ipso facto live in a right relationship with one another. The world sees the proof of Jesus' claim to be one with the Father in the unity of Jesus' followers with one another.

The unity of believers is not something Jesus commands us to achieve. It is something he asks God to perfect. Thus it is not an ideal toward which we strive but a reality in which we live.

II. For two millennia Christ's Church has lived with the tension of maintaining both its unity and its purity. Since Paul wrote his letter to the Galatians, Christians have disputed with one another over questions of doctrine and practice. Jesus warned his disciples to beware of wolves in sheep's clothing who would try to snatch them away from the Good Shepherd (John 10). As long as we see God "through a mirror, dimly," (1 Cor. 13:12) there will be disagreements among Jesus' followers.

Our hope is in the fact that our unity does not rest in organic unions of denominations or in resolution of theological disputes. Those endeavors have their place, but Jesus makes it clear that our unity is elsewhere. "The glory that you have given me I have given them, so that they may be one, as we are one" (John 17:22).

The place Jesus was glorified was on the cross. It is in the cross that Jesus' followers receive the glory that unites us. Various branches of Christ's Church may explain what the cross means in different ways. We may draw differing, even conflicting conclusions about the implications of that cross for our life together. But it is in sharing Jesus' suffering on behalf of the world that we find what unites us. We know that his pain and death, and his Resurrection and eternal fellowship with the Father, are what all Christians have in common. Thus we can see him in the brokenness of the world. We see him suffering with us and giving hope where there is despair. We see him in the midst of the brokenness of the Church, renewing our hope that his body is one, even when it seems hopelessly divided. That unity is a gift from God, not an achievement of human will.

III. Jesus' prayer for us helps us see our life and ministry in proper context. The unity Jesus shares with the Father exists from the beginning of time and will endure until the end. There are times when Jesus' followers despair that the work they do and the words they speak have little effect. There are times when we expend our energies on disputing with one another instead of showing God's love to the world. No matter how futile our efforts as Jesus' disciples may seem, we have the assurance that our unity with him is eternal, just as his unity with the Father is eternal. That fellowship is sealed on the cross, and nothing, not even our own fractiousness, can overcome it.

IV. In last week's Gospel, Jesus promised the disciples that God would send the Holy Spirit. As we read this prayer, we realize how much we rely on the Spirit for its fulfillment. To anyone who looks at Christ's Church, it is obvious that the unity of his Church is impossible apart from the presence of the Holy Spirit. It is the Spirit that gives us the ability to discern truth from falsehood in our midst. Without the Spirit's guidance, we are victims of our ideologies and prejudices. The Spirit reminds us of the unity God has given us that transcends our differences. We cannot set aside our unity and still remain faithful to our Lord. That realization makes us slow to reject those who come to us as sisters and brothers in Christ, even when our consciences make it difficult to commune with them.—Stephens G. Lytch

ILLUSTRATIONS

A FELT PRESENCE.   The paradox is: By opening your heart to others you will *experience* the peace of Christ that is there, *feel* his real presence. Otherwise the peace of Christ may become a cold theological truth: He is our peace and he is within me. Away with cold theological truths! Do you want to feel the peace of Christ, glow with it? Then share it, give it away!—Walter J. Burghardt, S. J.[10]

THE RIGHT PERSPECTIVE.   Suppose that a curtain were drawn across the nave of this chapel. I could not see you in the rear pews. But there is a way by which I could see you. If there were a mirror in the ceiling, I could look up into that mirror and it would enable me to look down into your places. That is a parable. The world is curtained off. We cannot see through on the sidewalk level. But when we go into our houses of worship and look up to God who is the Father of all men, it is like looking up into a mirror of compassionate love and thereby we can see into the places of those whose creed and culture and color may dif-

---

[10] *Sir, We Would Like to See Jesus* (New York: Paulist Press, 1982), p. 79.

fer from ours. And if we do it sincerely enough and repeatedly enough we sensitize our judgments and imaginations into the likeness of him who said, "Whosoever hath done it unto one of the least of these has done it unto me."—Ralph W. Sockman[11]

SERMON SUGGESTIONS

Topic: A Marvelous Outcome
TEXT: Acts 16:16–34
(1) From a conversion to a prison cell. (2) From an earthquake to a baptistery.

Topic: The Right to the Tree of Life
TEXT: Rev. 22:12–14
(2) The blessing of the Lord's reward (v. 12). (2) The authority for his judgment (v. 13). (3) The means of the assurance of the blessing (v. 14).

CONGREGATIONAL MUSIC

1. "And Can It Be That I Should Gain," Charles Wesley (1739)
   SAGINA, Thomas Campbell (1835)
   Wesley's great testimony in this hymn is made against the backdrop of the prison experience of Paul and Silas at Philippi. The hymn sings of Wesley's conversion in terms of being liberated from jail (particularly stanza 4). It bears a natural relation therefore to the narrative in Acts 16:16–34.
2. "Filled with the Spirit's Power," John R. Peacey (1767)
   FARLEY CASTLE, Henry Lawes (1638)
   This hymn relates to the burden of Jesus' prayer in the Gospel lesson (John 17:20–26) that all his followers may be one with one another and with him.
3. "Christ Is the World's True Light," George W. Briggs (1931)
   DARMSTADT, Ahasuerus Fritsch (1679)
   A hymn that relates to both the Gospel reading and the passage in Revelation, "Christ Is the World's True Light" is one of the finest mainline hymns of the mid-twentieth century. The author has carefully crafted his stanzas so that they may be effectively sung between choir and congregation antiphonally.
4. "Rejoice, the Lord Is King," Charles Wesley (1746)
   GOPSAL, George F. Handel (1752)
   DARWALL, John Darwall (1770)
   The first and last verses of Psalm 97 are reflected in this grand Wesleyan hymn that Christianizes the idea that the Lord God reigns. Its singing would be appropriate in connection with the Psalter reading.—Hugh T. McElrath

WORSHIP AIDS

CALL TO WORSHIP.   "A harvest of light has arisen for the righteous, and joy for the upright in heart. You that are righteous, rejoice in the Lord and praise his holy name" (Ps. 97:11–12 REB).

---

[11] In G. Paul Butler (ed.), *Best Sermons*, Vol. 9 (New York: Van Nostrand Reinhold, 1964), p. 23f.

INVOCATION   O Lord, you have made this day for yourself and for us. It is your day and we share in its meaning. As our lives are entwined with your purposes, let us lift our praise to the heavens and rejoice.

OFFERTORY SENTENCE   "The Lord is good to all: and his tender mercies are over all his works" (Ps. 145:9).

OFFERTORY PRAYER.   No gift of ours, O God, can begin to compare with the gift of your Son, our Lord, yet we dare to bring with love our offerings and thank you for every gracious gift that blesses our lives.

PRAYER.   On this day of remembering, Father, our minds and hearts roam the past recalling fond memories and frightening moments. As we think of the many who have given their lives in the name of freedom on this memorial day, we are led into the halls of sadness, which remind us that lives had to be sacrificed on the altar of war to preserve the fragile gift of freedom you have bestowed upon us. As we remember the sacrifices that have been made by family and friends so that we might live freely, give us, we pray, a determination to continue to ensure that this precious gift will remain inviolate for those who come after us, even if it means continued sacrifice from us. Thank you for brave souls, stout hearts, and courageous spirits, those whom we have known and the host of the unknown who have paid the ultimate price for the privileges we enjoy today. This morning, encourage families who will be especially aware of loss because of lives laid down on the altar of freedom. Give us the caring heart that calls us to express personal and collective gratitude to them, even as we share in the sorrow of their loss.

Here before us this hour are those who look back with a sense of accomplishment and forward with a spirit of expectation and hope. They have traveled a pathway that has led them to this commencement time in their lives, this point of new beginnings. Thank you for them, for their accomplishments, and for their inspirations to us during the early growing up years we have shared with them. Only yesterday they were children beside us awaiting our direction and approval. Today they have entered the segment of life reserved for the emerging adult. As they travel this well-worn yet ever-new pathway, grant them a sense of accomplishment, a realistic vision of how to use their abilities and skills in future days, and a determination to pay the price necessary to become all that is possible for them. Keep them true and honest to your highest call and values. Comfort them in momentary failure, that they may learn well from its visit. Bless them in passing success so that they will reach higher to grasp ever nobler purposes. And one day, when they look back across the years they have traveled, may it be with a sense of worthy accomplishment and inward pride that they view their journey.

For those for whom this becomes a time to loose them and let them go, make this a moment of pride and joy. Enable them to cherish the memories molded through the years, but may they not seek to relive with these emerging adults the events that have come and passed. Give parents and family the ability to look forward with hope, expectation, joy, and pride as they walk with their child through these days of the commencement of new beginnings.—Henry Fields

SERMON

Topic: Love Is Not a Feeling

TEXT: 1 Cor. 13; John 13:31–35

I heard about a man who was bitten by a dog suspected of having rabies.[12] They rushed the man to the doctor. The doctor examined him and confirmed that indeed he probably had contracted rabies. The man immediately asked for a pencil and piece of paper. The doctor thought that the man, thinking he was going to die, was going to make out a will. So the doctor told him, "There's no reason for undue alarm. You're going to be all right. We've got serum to counteract rabies. You're not going to die, no need to make out a will." The man said, "I'm not making out a will. I'm making out a list of all the people I'm going to bite."

Ramon Narvaez, the Spanish patriot, was asked on his deathbed by a priest if he wanted to forgive his enemies before he died. Narvaez said, "Father, I have no enemies. I shot them all."[13]

As Christians we are taught there is a better way, and our two texts proclaim it. First Corinthians 13 says, "I will show you a more excellent way," and the more excellent way that Paul is going to show us is love. "Love is patient and kind; love is not jealous or boastful; love is not arrogant or rude; love does not insist on its own way; it is not irritable or resentful; it does not rejoice in the wrong but rejoices in the right. Love bears all things, believes all things, hopes all things, endures all things."

There is no better definition of what Christians mean by love than 1 Corinthians 13. It has always stood over against the spirit of enmity and hatred that exists in our world and claims to be the more excellent way.

As Christians, if 1 Corinthians 13 was all we had about love, then we could accept it as just a beautiful poem and not worry about it. But we also have John 13:34, where it is laid down to us as a command. John says that love is not an optional way of life for the Christian; it's not an alternative lifestyle, nor is it a higher standard of morality for a minority of Christians who aspire to be saints, nor is it a rule for nuns and monks who remove themselves from the harsh realities of this world in some secluded convent or monastery. It's a command for all disciples. It's an unqualified mandate. You can't read it any other way. You can squeeze by some passages in the Bible, but not this one. This one comes to us with the force of an order. "A new commandment I give you, that you love one another even as I have loved you. By this all men will know that you are my disciples, if you have love for one another." These lines reiterate the command that we are to love one another.

I want you to see that in the New Testament love is not a feeling. Love is a command. Love is a strategy for changing the world. The message of the New Testament is that the world does not have to be the way the world is now. It doesn't have to be. There is a more excellent way. In the New Testament, those passages that talk about loving your neighbor don't refer to your feelings about your neighbor. Nowhere do they talk about your feelings. They talk about your *behavior* toward your neighbor.

---

[12] Thanks to Clarence Forsberg via Rodney Wilmoth.
[13] Thanks to Buzz Stevens.

The Samaritan found a Jew beaten and robbed and left to die by the side of the road. Samaritans had nothing to do with Jews. They didn't like them. They were enemies. Samaritans had no warm feelings toward Jews. You've got to remember that to get the point. And that means that the Samaritan did not act on the basis of his feelings. He acted on the basis of the strategy of love. He did the right thing in spite of his feelings. That's the point of the parable. If there was going to be peace between the Jews and the Samaritans, then somebody was going to have to create a new situation. Somebody was going to have to use the strategy of love instead of perpetuating the cycle of violence.

You reap what you sow in this life. Everybody knows that. That's why with violence there's always more violence. So the question that Christianity poses to the world is, If you reap what you sow, what would happen if you sowed love instead of violence? That's what lies behind Jesus' command to the disciples. He says, try it. Why don't you try it? Be the example for the world that love is going to win, just as I have been that example for you.

Love is a strategy designed to change the situation. That's why love can be commanded, because it's not a feeling, it's a strategy. Jesus is not asking us to change our feelings about other people; he's asking us to act on the basis of love in spite of our feelings—because love is a strategy designed to change situations so that feelings can then change.

Sometimes I think that you and I have been duped into thinking that we can't create new situations in this world, that there's nothing we can do but accept the way the world is. Sometimes I think we believe that because we are victims of the new sciences that embarked a century ago on a mission to free us from what was called "religious superstition." The result has been a new kind of bondage just as dangerous. They tried to free us from an overidealized, overrationalized image of human nature. They stressed that we are motivated primarily by feelings and by hidden urges, and that we ought to express those feelings rather than suppress them. Now that's good advice; I myself have given it and it has liberated many people. I still advise some people to be more honest about their feelings. But what has happened is that a whole new bondage has been created, a bondage of feelings in which we have forgotten that we also have a power called willpower, the power to control our feelings and urges and to choose what kind of life we want to live in this world.

I believe that it is by the grace of God that we've been given time to do those things that make for peace. We know what they are and we're commanded to do them, because love is not a feeling. Love is a strategy for changing the world.—Mark Trotter

SUNDAY, JUNE 3, 2001

Lectionary Message

Topic: The Spirit and the Children of God—A Pentecost Sermon

TEXT: Rom. 8:14–17

Other Readings: Acts 2:1–21 or Gen. 11:1–9; Ps. 104:24–34, 35b; John 14:8–17 (25–27)

Pentecost was a tremendous, life-changing experience for the first disciples. In Acts 2:1–41, Luke states that after a period of waiting the church received the Holy Spirit. Tongues of fire came down from heaven. The believers spoke in foreign languages they had never studied. Pilgrims to Jerusalem heard the gospel in their own tongue, and three thousand persons were converted after Peter preached the gospel. Afterwards the church was aflame with the Holy Spirit as they preached, taught, healed, and helped.

This Sunday we mark that day. It is Pentecost and we are the Church. We no longer wait for the Spirit, for he has come. We are no longer a new religion. Today we are a worldwide body with millions of members.

So why is Pentecost important now? Pentecost is still vital to Christianity because it reminds us that the Church is powerless without the Spirit's quickening. This special day reminds us how the Spirit fills us, empowers us, challenges us, and guides us.

Today's text addresses the Spirit's work in our lives and in the church as a whole. Paul reminds the Romans how the Spirit assures Christians of their salvation as they live for the Lord. He has already stated that believers are not condemned by God (8:1–8), asserted that Christians have the Spirit dwelling in them (8:9–11), and declared that they are obliged to serve the one who died for them (8:12–13). Now the apostle shows the personal way the Spirit works in Christians to make them certain that they belong to God.

I. *The Spirit leads the children of God* (8:14). Throughout the book of Romans, Paul defines who are God's children and who are not. This distinction has much to do with the work of the Spirit.

(a) *Those who are not God's children.* Those who are not God's people live according to their sinful desires (1:18–32) and refuse to receive God's gracious offer of forgiveness (3:10–23). Sadly, they do not live by faith, so they never have their sins removed (4:1–25). They never experience peace with God (5:1). Clearly, they do not have the Holy Spirit in them (8:9).

(b) *Those who are God's children.* Those who are God's children have confessed their sins and received Christ by faith. Thus they have peace, patience, endurance, confidence, and hope (5:1–5). They also have the Spirit (8:9). He personally leads them in the way they should go and in the way they should act. He dwells in them, caring for them and compelling them to serve the Lord. This leadership is personal and it is practical.

II. *The Spirit gives us assurance that we belong to God* (8:15–17a). Even the best Christian can become discouraged, because of either circumstances or personal failure. In these times the Holy Spirit reassures us that we belong to God the Father through the work of his Son.

(a) *The Spirit removes our fears* (8:15). Paul states that "a spirit of slavery" leads to fear. He means that if we know we are hired or enslaved, then we are aware that we are not entitled to the privileges given to family members. Those who have trusted Christ and have therefore been given the Holy Spirit know that they have a personal relationship with God and can speak intimately with the Lord. They can rest, fearless about their standing in God's family.

(b) *The Spirit testifies to our spirit* (8:16). Few things are more encouraging than to be told we are loved. Having written that the Holy Spirit pours out God's love within our hearts (5:5), Paul now states that the Spirit testifies alongside our spirit that we belong to God. The Spirit makes sure that we not only know God's love but feel it as well. He does so in different ways for different believers—there is no set way—but he does so for those who belong to God's household. How can we remain in fear when we have an intimate relationship with God and his love is poured out in our hearts?

(c) *The Spirit reminds us that we are joint heirs with Christ* (8:17a). So far Paul has emphasized our current standing before God. Now he stresses our future. Astoundingly, we are joint heirs with Christ! Our future is to share Christ's rule over all things. How can we fear the future if we will share Christ's glory? We truly have the highest privileges a member of God's family can possess.

III. *The Spirit sustains us as we suffer with Christ* (8:17b). It is sometimes easy to get caught up in all the good times God promises us. The Bible also promises that we must share in Christ's suffering. Suffering with Christ is also confirmation that we belong to God, and it is the Spirit who makes certain that we endure such times.

(a) *We will suffer with Christ.* Early Christians considered it a privilege to suffer for Christ's sake (Acts 4:41). Paul believed that suffering helped him be more like Jesus (Phil. 3:10). Christians do suffer, both for Christ's sake and as part of a sinful world. These experiences are proof that we belong to Christ. In crisis times we can expect that the Holy Spirit, who leads us and assures us and loves us, will sustain us.

(b) *We will share Christ's glory.* Sometimes we may wonder what good it does to serve God. In those moments the Holy Spirit reminds us that we will live in God's presence forever and that nothing can compare to possessing such a bright, hope-filled future (2 Cor. 4:16–18). At that time all our hopes will be realized. All our fears will disappear forever. The Holy Spirit's work on our behalf will be complete. Once we share Christ's glory, the children of God will be one with the Father, Son, and Holy Spirit forever. Let us take heart, then, for the Holy Spirit is leading us toward that day.—Paul House

ILLUSTRATIONS

ASSURANCE.   But Paul means that the Spirit of God gives us such a testimony that when he is our guide and teacher, our spirit is assured of the adoption of God: for our mind of its own self, without the preceding testimony of the Spirit, could not convey to us this assurance.—John Calvin

SPECIAL LIGHT.   There is a light that comes and overpowers a man's soul and assures him that God is his and he is God's, and that God loves him from everlasting. . . . It is a light beyond the light of ordinary faith.—John Owen

SERMON SUGGESTIONS

Topic: By the Grace of God
TEXT: 1 Cor. 15:10
(1) I am not what I ought to be. (2) I am not what I hope to be. (3) I am not what I once was. (4) By the grace of God, I am what I am.—Anonymous[1]

Topic: The Theology of Money
TEXT: Deut. 8:18; 1 Cor. 16:2
If the plan of the Apostle is carried out with all willingness and diligence, what results would follow? (1) The fickleness and fitfulness of benevolence would be terminated. (2) The benev-

---

[1] Reported by John A. Broadus.

olent operations of the Church would be immensely facilitated. (3) The gratitude of the individual Christian would be kept in lively exercise.—Joseph Parker[2]

CONGREGATIONAL MUSIC

1. "O Worship the King," Robert Grant (1833)
   LYONS, Johann M. Haydn (1815)
   This classic Romantic hymn is the best paraphrase of Psalm 104 in Christian hymnody. It could be used to introduce the Psalter lesson.
2. "O Spirit of the Living God," James Montgomery (1823)
   MELCOMBE, Samuel Webbe (1791)
   A fervent prayer for the descent of the Holy Spirit, this fine hymn by the greatest laywriter of hymnody would accompany naturally the reading from Acts (3:1–21) concerning the Day of Pentecost.
3. "Come Down, O Love Divine," Bianco da Siena; trans. R. F. Littledale (1867)
   DOWN AMPNEY, Ralph Vaughan Williams (1906)
   This medieval hymn of mystic enthusiasm relates to both the Acts reading and the Gospel lesson, in which Jesus promises the Holy Spirit. The broad sweep of the masterful tune enhances the devout appeal for the Holy Spirit's presence.
4. "For Your Gift of God the Spirit," Margaret Clarkson (1982)
   BETHANY, Henry Smart (1867)
   This long contemporary hymn by an outstanding woman author can be used in connection with the Epistle reading (Rom. 8:14–17). Stanza 5 is particularly appropriate for Pentecost Sunday.—Hugh T. McElrath

WORSHIP AIDS

CALL TO WORSHIP.   "I will sing unto the Lord as long as I live: I will sing praise to my God while I have my being. My meditation of him shall be sweet: I will be glad in the Lord" (Ps. 104:33–34).

INVOCATION.   You have given us your Spirit, O God, and you fill our hearts with joy. May our worship today be in spirit and in truth.

OFFERTORY SENTENCE.   "But you will receive power when the Holy Spirit comes on you; and you will be my witnesses in Jerusalem, and in all Judea and Samaria, and to the ends of the earth" (Acts 1:8 NIV).

OFFERTORY PRAYER.   As you receive our offerings, O God, grant that they may be used by your Spirit in believing hearts to further your message of love to all people everywhere.

PRAYER.   How glad we are that we can come into your presence, Father. Some enter on the wings of joy, having experienced life at its best. These have watched as blessings have

---

[2] Hidden Springs

materialized and circumstances have flourished for their benefit, as well as for the benefit of those whom they love. For them the future gleams with sunlight and life is filled with hope. Thank you for the joy they have found. May it multiply and reach others, to lighten many dark corners with renewed rays of your glory.

Some enter this morning, Father, in a spirit of somberness. They have not been blessed with good news and joyful moments that overrule the struggles in which they find themselves. There are those who this morning are the victims of another's sin. Wrongs have multiplied until, like creeping vines, they have almost choked the life out of those near and dear. Others have had to hear bad news about health and loved ones' futures. Still others have been recent visitors to graves, where a part of their very lives has been laid to rest in the solitude of the quiet hills. Somehow in this sacred place let them find renewed faith and hopeful vision, that they may go out of here encouraged and strengthened to live above and beyond the sources of their concern.

Others enter this place today, Father, seeking truth and new life. They are tired of the road they are traveling and want, more than they can tell, to be invigorated by the power of redeeming faith. Today they need to meet the Savior, to understand his love for them and experience his redemption of their souls. Let some word be fitly spoken, some expression be rightly given, that will open the door for them to walk into your glorious presence and find new life and salvation. By the tender presence of Your Holy Spirit, enter their hearts and claim them for your own, we pray.

This is your special hour, Father. We pause and wait on tiptoe for the wooing of your Spirit as you move among us, touching our hearts and lives and making us fully yours in Jesus' name and power.—Henry Fields

SERMON
Topic: Honoring the Holy Spirit
TEXT: Eph. 4:30

How should Christians honor the Holy Spirit? Let's consider three areas: *recognition, communication,* and *participation.*

I. *Recognition.* The first, most basic aspect of honoring the Holy Spirit is recognition—realizing he's there inside you and recognizing him for who he is. Nothing is more grievous than to ignore someone as though he's not even there.

Honor the Holy Spirit by realizing he's present inside you. The only case in which he's not present is if you don't belong to Christ at all. The Bible says, "Examine yourselves to see whether you are in the faith; test yourselves. Do you not realize that Christ Jesus is in you—unless, of course, you fail the test?" (2 Cor. 13:5). If you have no sorrow for sin, no faith in Jesus' blood to cleanse you, no love for the Lord, no longing to serve and obey him, then you fail the test. But if these signs of true faith are evident, then Christ is in you by his Spirit.

The Spirit isn't just a thing or an abstract power; he is a person, and we must relate to him as a person. We must honor the Spirit by treating him as a real, personal companion and having a relationship of love with him.

But perhaps you find the Holy Spirit's personality mysterious and hard to know. In that case, keep in mind that the personality of the Spirit is just like the personality of Jesus Christ. In the mystery of God's being, God the Father, Christ the Son, and the Holy Spirit are three persons united as one God—the Holy Trinity. Although we can't understand this completely, one thing it means is that when the Holy Spirit lives in us, Christ himself lives in us.

If we're unclear about what sort of personality the Spirit has, we just need to know what Jesus is like. Whatever offends Jesus offends the Holy Spirit, and whatever honors Jesus honors and delights the Holy Spirit.

The Spirit unites believers with Christ and, through Christ, the Spirit connects us with God the Father in a relationship of love.

II. *Communication.* When someone is always around you and is dear to you, you want to hear what the person thinks and you want that person to hear what you think. So it is with the Holy Spirit.

The Spirit speaks to us from the Bible, which was written under the Spirit's direct guidance. When we read the Bible, the Spirit impresses various truths on our hearts and helps us hear him speaking to us personally. The Spirit also prompts certain thoughts in our minds to deal with particular situations in our lives. If we stay alert, we'll hear his voice and feel his nudge.

Communication involves listening and speaking. It involves talking to God in prayer and expressing what's on our hearts. He knows our thoughts before we think them! Smart moms and dads can often tell what's bothering their children or what they're excited about without the kids telling them, but they still want the their kids to tell them about it. If we don't know what to say at times, the Spirit himself speaks on our behalf in ways that no human language can express but which God fully understands (Rom. 8:26–27).

III. *Participation.* If you take part in the holiness and mission of the Spirit, you honor him. But if you resist his holy influence or try to accomplish things without his power, you grieve him.

It's no accident that the Spirit is called the *Holy* Spirit. He is holy, and he intends for everyone in whom he lives to participate in his holiness. This means that in everything you think, say, or do you must ask yourself how the Holy Spirit is affecting you and how you are affecting the Spirit.

It's not just that God always sees whatever you do. God isn't just watching you; he's living in you. You're not just breaking his commands; you're breaking his heart. This applies to all your actions, words, and attitudes. Don't drag the Spirit into sinful activities. Instead, depend on him to lead you into imitating Christ.

Participation in the Spirit's work also includes making use of the Spirit's gifts and power in you. The Spirit gives every Christian gifts and talents for doing God's work. Find out what your spiritual gifts are, make the most of them, and be open and eager to receive any further abilities and power that the Holy Spirit may choose to give you. Also, respect and value gifts that the Spirit may give to other Christians but not to you. Don't think that any spiritual gift is unimportant.

The Holy Spirit is the one who gives life and power to each believer and also to the whole Church. We honor the Holy Spirit when we depend on his divine power and keep asking him to fill us with more. We honor the Spirit when we overflow with his love, joy, and peace and participate in his great work of making Christ known to the world.—David Feddes[3]

---

[3] *The Back to God Hour*

SUNDAY, JUNE 10, 2001
Lectionary Message

Topic: Our God and Our Rejoicing

TEXT: Rom. 5:1–5

Other Readings: Prov. 8:1–4, 22–31; Ps. 8; John 16:12–15

All the great confessions and creeds of Christianity confess that God exists as three persons. God the Father, God the Son, and God the Holy Spirit are all God, yet are only one God. Of course, this is a great mystery, one that has challenged the best minds Christianity has ever produced.

This doctrine has very practical implications. Doctrine helps us know how to live. Romans 5:1–5 celebrates the joy that knowing God in three persons brings to our lives. Here Paul, himself no stranger to life's hurts and challenges, encourages us with the prospect of joy—great joy. This joy comes from our God, whose personality is comprehensive enough to meet all our real needs.

I. *God the Son gives us peace* (5:1). Paul spends most of Romans 1–4 expressing the need for and means of salvation. In Romans 4 he focuses on justification by faith, on how we can be right with the holy God who created the universe. In doing so he uses three words that express what God the Son does to bring us joy.

(a) God the Son *justifies* us. Romans 1–3 establishes that all human beings sin and need forgiveness from the Lord, the Holy One. We can hardly have peace in our hearts when we are not at peace with our Creator. Without God's forgiveness we are guilty of all our sins.

But Paul claims that we are justified, that we are "not guilty" in God's sight. We are forgiven. We can live free from guilt. We can have peace and we can rejoice in our standing before God.

(b) God the Son justifies us through *faith.* Unquestionably, human beings are capable of extraordinary achievements. We relieve suffering, work for justice, and do other noble deeds. Still, we cannot save ourselves, because to earn our own salvation we must reach God's level of perfection (Rom. 3:23; see Isa. 6:1–13).

The gospel, the good news, is that through faith we may be forgiven. Though we will work for the Lord when we commit ourselves to him, it is faith that makes us right with God. We can rejoice that faith in Christ—not good works, as important as they are—is the means of salvation.

(c) God the Son gives us *peace.* Human beings desire peace of all types: peace between nations, peace in relationships, and peace of mind. No peace is as important as peace with God. Because Christ puts us at peace *with* God we can have the peace *of* God. This peace endures in all situations. This peace surpasses all understanding (Phil. 4:7). This peace allows us to rejoice even when other sorts of peace are not available to us.

II. *God the Father will give us glory* (5:2). Christ's work does not just help us feel better about our present lives. Jesus made us right with the Father so that we might be in God's presence forever. We have access to God now and throughout eternity.

(a) *God gives us access to grace now.* Grace sustains us right now. We live by grace as believers. Because of what God the Son did, God the Father accepts us and makes grace possible for us. Therefore, we have a delicious taste of future glory now.

(b) *God gives us the hope of eternal glory.* Right now we live on Earth, where pain and sorrow are normal events. Joy and glimpses of God's glory occur regularly, but they are only hints of what we will experience in eternity. God has made us citizens of heaven (Phil. 3:20). When we die he will change our bodies (Phil. 3:21). We will see God's glory as we relate to him "face to face" (2 Cor. 3:18). We will live where sickness, sadness, and death do not exist (Rev. 21:1–8). The promise of such glory gives us cause for joy.

III. *God the Spirit sustains us* (5:3–5). It is natural to rejoice in salvation, peace, and the hope of eternal life. For the average person, however, the same cannot be said for experiencing difficulties. Paul notes that Christians are not average people. They rejoice even in trouble, for the Holy Spirit enables them to do so.

(a) *The Spirit helps us gain endurance* (5:3). Suffering is part of life. All sorts of injustices can happen to us. Paul's life demonstrates that even those who are faithful to God are not immune from trouble. Indeed, faithful persons may be more susceptible to persecution. But a Christian, who has the promise of eternal life, can view suffering as the means to endurance. That which seeks to harm us thereby becomes the way we get stronger.

(b) *The Spirit gives us character and hope* (5:4). Endurance results in character. Those who endure through the power of the Holy Spirit become persons of character. They are able to live well because they have the proven personal integrity and grit to do so. Therefore they are able to live in hope, knowing that whatever they must face will be faced in the power of the Holy Spirit.

(c) *The Spirit pours out God's love in our hearts* (5:5). No one whose hopes are based in the Lord will be disappointed. He has both a sound present and a bright future. The Spirit gives present assurance by pouring out God's love in the hearts of the faithful. This pouring out comes to each believer in a manner appropriate to him or her. There is no set pattern, but this assurance of love does come.

Given such love, we can rejoice confidently. God the Son brings us to the Father and thus gives us peace. God the Father gives us present and future glory. God the Spirit sustains us through trial by the pouring out of love in our hearts. May we rejoice today in the fact that the doctrine of the Trinity leads to the experience of joy.—Paul House

ILLUSTRATIONS

OUR ULTIMATE PURPOSE.   The ultimate purpose of human life is to render to God worship and service, in which both he and we will find joy. This is what we were made for and what we are saved for. This is what it means to know God and to be known by him and to glorify him.—J. I. Packer

OUR GOD.   And so we see that the glorious truth . . . is just this, that this infinite, absolute, sublime, transcendent, glorious, majestic, mighty, everlasting being who is Spirit, who is truth, who dwells in light no one can approach, this God has been graciously pleased that you and I should know him, that we should talk to him, and that we should worship him.—D. Martyn Lloyd-Jones

SERMON SUGGESTIONS

Topic: Forget to Remember
TEXT: Various
(1) Forget the past (Phil. 3:13); (2) forget yourself (Phil. 3:7); (3) forget the cost (Phil. 3:8, 13–14).—Jack Finegan[4]

---

[4] *Clear of the Brooding Cloud*

Topic: Inside Information

TEXT: John 4:5–42

We Christian believers are "in the know" concerning the greatest things in this life and beyond it. (1) We ought not be in any doubt regarding the fundamental underlying meaning and ultimate purpose of this universe and our relationship to it. (2) God has spoken objectively, universally, for all to know and understand in Christ the Savior and Lord—the historic person. But more than that—now, today, at this very moment, God is speaking to you and to me in our own hearts and minds.—John Trevor Davies[5]

CONGREGATIONAL MUSIC

1. "Spirit Divine, Inspire Our Prayer," Andrew Reed (1829)
   GRAEFENBERG, Johann Crueger (1647)
   Based on the day's Gospel reading (especially John 16:13), this prayer hymn could be sung as a response to that lesson.
2. "How Majestic Is Your Name," Michael W. Smith (1981)
   HOW MAJESTIC, Michael W. Smith (1981)
   The praise chorus that sets the first verse of this hymn makes an admirable antiphon to be sung during the reading of Psalm 8.
3. "How Great Our God's Majestic Name," Timothy Dudley-Smith (1989)
   DUKE STREET, John Hatton (1793)
   This modern paraphrase of Psalm 8 could be sung in lieu of reading the psalm. If the chorus were transposed to the key of DUKE STREET, it could be used as a response alternating with the singing of the stanzas of the hymn.
4. "Alas, and Did My Saviour Bleed," Isaac Watts (1707)
   AVON, Hugh Wilson (1825)
   An appropriate response to the Epistle lesson (Rom. 5:1–15) would be the singing of this classic hymn on the Atonement.—Hugh T. McElrath

WORSHIP AIDS

CALL TO WORSHIP.   "O Lord, our Lord, how excellent is thy name in all the earth! Who has set thy glory above the heavens" (Ps. 8:1).

INVOCATION.   Our praise, O God, can never match your glory and majesty, yet we cannot withhold our feeble attempt to worship you in spirit and in truth. By your grace you give worth to the least of our efforts, so accept and use for your heavenly purposes what we do here today.

OFFERTORY SENTENCE.   "But this I say, He which soweth sparingly shall reap also sparingly; and he which soweth bountifully shall reap also bountifully" (2 Cor. 9:6).

OFFERTORY PRAYER.   We gladly give our offerings today, Father. May they prosper in your care and glorify your name.—Henry Fields.

---

[5] *Lord of All*

PRAYER.   O the depth of the riches and wisdom and knowledge of God! How unsearchable are his judgments and how inscrutable his ways! Eternal God, as we contemplate your being—your presence, your absence—we discover ourselves marveling at your transcendence, your beyondness, your immanence, and your nearness.

We are amazed, too, at your timelessness—"Before the mountains were brought forth or ever you had formed the Earth and the world, even from everlasting to everlasting, you are God." We marvel at your timeliness—"In the fullness of time you sent forth your only Son" for our salvation and the salvation of the world.

You are "the great God and the great King above all gods," yet you are the Word who became flesh and dwelt among us.

As in this place we are awakened to a new vision of your glory. Who among us does not discover herself, himself, exclaiming, "This is none other than the house of God; this is the gate of heaven"? We praise you that your Spirit is at work among us, and that we have been awakened at depths and challenged to heights we have never known before.

What a new vision, or renewed vision, of your grace in the gift of this new day, and in the gift of your Word, perennially fresh as the living bread. For your Word of grace, present from the beginning and now fully manifest in Jesus the Messiah, creating and nurturing the Church among us and in us, we praise you.

What an amazing grace that all things work together for good to those who love you! It is the mighty power of your grace that you can use even the sufferings in life to our good and to your eternal glory. It does not always happen—we do not let it happen. We become hostile, embittered, rebellious, cynical. Save us from ourselves, O God, lest we become part of the problem rather than being part of the cure.

In these moments as we pray for one another, we pray that each of us may be present in such love and trust, in such faith and openness, to receive Christ in the fullness of your grace, to make whole whatever the brokenness.

Your Word of grace declared so conclusively in Christ is not only for our health but also for the healing of the nations. We pray for world leaders, that they will have the humility that leads to the wisdom to know that wealth and power are a stewardship from you so that all peoples may enjoy their inalienable right to freedom and the blessed bounty of the good Earth.

We pray through him who is your Word from the beginning and is now present in Resurrection power, calling persons and nations in every time and place to pray and live.—John M. Thompson

SERMON

Topic: Many Things to Say

TEXT: "I have still many things to say to you, but you cannot bear them now" (John 16:12)

What are the words we can't bear to hear? What are the sounds that make us live day after day with our ears closed—the things we can't bear to see or touch?

We can't bear too much talk of our mortality. We can't bear to speak of our aloneness and fragmentation. We're not good at listening to the reality of our world and church. Even less can we bear to look within, at the pain and fearfulness of our hearts. It's hard to face our stumbling in the dark, our feeble attempts to be anything but what we really are. That kind of speech is altogether too hard to hear.

Instead, we create a speech all our own: colorful, attractive, soothing, closing those dreadful gaping doors. Let's level things out, pull down the mountains, cover the black holes. Let's cower together in a corner, away from the things that frighten us, and call it "community," pretend it might actually be the Christian gospel, the body of Christ.

The Spirit will guide us into all truth, the Johannine Jesus assures us in his farewell discourse. The Spirit will speak, bringing what belongs to God and handing it over to us.

What would it mean if we began to listen to the Spirit—if we were to hear, perhaps for the first time, real, truthful words? Not escapist words dressed up in pious clothing. Not harsh, judgmental words that are a hundred miles away from love. And what if these words came, not from a solitary, judgmental God, enthroned on high to oversee us (the God of our speaking), but from another God entirely, a God who in our present state we might hardly recognize?

The Christian celebration of the Trinity is perhaps the Word, beyond all others, that we need to hear today. The truth into which the Spirit leads us is the journey we have followed from Lent to Easter, from Easter to Pentecost—the journey of Jesus Christ, bringing our humanity to speech. It is the Spirit of this Christ who speaks what is true about our human experience, who names the unnamable: the unbearable reality of our suffering, the unspeakable terror of our aloneness and nakedness. But this divine naming is not done with harshness; it does not take pleasure in tearing down our defenses. Instead, the words are laced with mercy and understanding. In graceful terms the Spirit names the truth about ourselves.

There is more, however, to this naming. The Spirit's revelation is about God as well as about us. In embracing our mortality and brokenness, the Spirit unfolds the mystery of a divine communion, present before the world had even dawned—a community of persons preceding and undergirding us, lying at the heart of all the reality we could ever fathom—past, present, or future.

The God-and-me equation of most of our Christianity is a distortion of the gospel. It is pathetically meager, leaving us in the ditch, cold and hungry and desperately alone. And whether we have a God-and-me relationship that's focused on Jesus or one that's focused on the Spirit or whether it's some vague, intellectually respectable faraway God makes no difference at all. Such a God, in whatever guise, is a projection of our unexamined fears, our superficial desires, our tragic individualism. The God of our speaking merely confirms us in our alienation and isolation; this God has nothing to say to our wounded, desolate souls.

The speech of God is not empty, abstract words that demand mere intellectual attentiveness and assent. Nor are God's utterances imperious, commanding words, dictating to us. They are not didactic words pointing a bourgeois finger and lecturing us on upright living. We are not children in an old-fashioned classroom when we listen to these words, nor timid servants listening for the Master's voice, afraid that our obedience will always be fatally flawed.

God's speech is far more awesome than that. The God into whom the Spirit draws us is the God whose speech is never alone, never in isolation, never autonomous; who speaks from a fullness of life and love that we can barely begin to imagine; indeed whose very being is sociality, relationship, intimacy. And this God speaks lovingly out of that rich communion into the heart of our fragmentation, into the echo of our isolation. God's Word comes to us in our flesh, our mortal frames, our weakness, our vulnerability; in the life we live and in the death we die. And in that unlikely place, that tiny space represented by our human flesh—tiny in comparison to the vastness of the cosmos—God comes as community, a communion that is bigger and richer and deeper than the whole of the universe put together.

Only this Word, at the end of the day, can open our ears and our eyes. Only this Word of grace can help us bear the unbearable, name the unnamable. Over perhaps a lifetime this loving speech slowly unfolds within and around us, in a love that is already of our flesh and blood.

This is the Word spoken to us, above all, in the Eucharist. In the person of Jesus Christ, dying and rising, in the body and blood, we are caught up into this divine community. We are drawn into the embrace of the Trinity, into the truth about ourselves and our own humanity that God speaks to us, with us, and for us. This speech may lead us into suffering, because the cross cannot be bypassed and there is no other way to resurrection and transformation. But ultimately the Spirit's gracious speech leads us into communion, into the joy of God' society, into the bliss of God's delight.—Dorothy Lee

SUNDAY, JUNE 17, 2001
Lectionary Message

Topic: God's Forgiveness and Our Faith
TEXT: Luke 7:36–8:3
Other Readings: 1 Kings 21:1–10 (11–14), 15–21a; Ps. 5:1–8; Gal. 2:15–21

True forgiveness is always difficult. After all, repentance and confession are prerequisites for forgiveness (1 John 1:9–10), and they are hard to face. It is easier to act as if we have done nothing wrong than to admit we were wrong. It feels simpler to hide our sin than to confess it.

True forgiveness is also hard to seek from God because we have been treated badly by unforgiving, legalistic people. We have encountered their meanness and we are afraid that God acts like them. Happily, the Lord has a strong spirit of forgiveness. We may come to him and find grace.

This passage conveys three attitudes related to forgiveness. Each one reveals God's way of understanding sin and forgiveness. The final two attitudes provide hope that by faith we may find healing and wholeness through Christ's forgiving spirit.

I. *The spirit of condemnation* (7:36–39). Condemnation is an ugly attitude that virtually every human being exhibits at one time or another. This attitude encourages us to think more of ourselves than we ought. It allows us to gloss over our sins so that we may consider ourselves holier than the next person. Simon the Pharisee's attitude represents all that is wrong with condemnatory behavior. In effect, those who condemn make certain statements to the world.

(a) *She is a sinner* (7:37, 39). Simon saw a sinful woman wash Jesus' feet. He knew that the woman had done things she should have avoided. Given her failures, Simon thought she had no right to approach or touch Jesus. He thought she would never change. How often do we fail to believe that people can be changed if they turn to the Lord?

(b) *I am righteous* (7:39). By condemning the woman as an irredeemable sinner, Simon could then consider himself righteous. He then had no reason to improve. After all, in comparison to *that woman* he was as pure as wind-driven snow. He could make himself feel better by putting down someone else. He could hide the fact that he was also a sinner.

(c) *Jesus should not waste his time with sinners* (7:39). Simon clearly believed that Jesus was wasting his time with this woman. In fact, he thought that Jesus must not have been all he was reported to be if he did not mind being touched by such a person. Those who condemn often pity or judge those who try to reach sinners with the gospel.

II. *The spirit of forgiveness* (7:40–50). Forgiveness is often defined today as being let off the hook with no consequences attached. Though God is kind, such forgiveness is nothing less than the fantasies of the irresponsible. God could not forgive in this manner with integrity. To be holy, God has to balance high standards and mercy. Thus his spirit of forgiveness includes realism, freedom, and openness.

(a) *God is realistic about sin* (7:40–43). When Jesus confronted Simon he did not say that the woman had not sinned. In fact, he spoke as if she had done many sinful acts. He also noted that Simon had been forgiven at least a few things! God does not gloss over our sins. He is not sentimental about our nature or lackadaisical about our failures. Therefore he is able to help us.

(b) *God is generous with his grace* (7:40–43, 47). God does not decide to forgive or judge based on the number or type of our sins. The woman in the story had sinned ten times more than the "average sinner." Yet Jesus forgave her. God is never stingy with grace. Indeed, it would not be grace if it were not unmerited forgiveness regardless of the extent of the sin.

(c) *God is open in his relationships* (7:44–8:3). In this account Jesus related to a Pharisee, a disgraced woman, sick persons, demon-possessed folks, and run-of-the-mill human beings. Social standing, gender, or previous spiritual condition never affect God's willingness to forgive. God will aid anyone who repents and turns to him in faith.

III. *The spirit of faith* (7:37–38, 50). It is important to note that the Lord did not forgive the woman without a proper attitude on her part. She responded to her sin and to Jesus appropriately. Her broken spirit and giving spirit characterize how we all ought to repent.

(a) *The woman came to Jesus humbly.* This sinful woman came humbly to Jesus. She wept over her sins but did not simply offer an emotional response. Rather, she cleaned and perfumed his feet. In other words, she acted like a servant. Her action reminds us of Jesus' subsequent washing of the disciples' feet. We sinners can come to a holy God only humbly, for we have nothing to commend us. The God to whom we come is kind and never abuses our humility.

(b) *The woman gave herself and her resources.* Not only did the woman act as Jesus' servant, but she also gave her financial resources for the anointing oil. This perfume was probably quite expensive. But expense did not matter to one who longed for forgiveness. It did not matter to one grateful to Jesus.

(c) *The woman acted by faith.* Jesus praised the woman's faith and love (7:50). She showed her faith by coming to Jesus and she showed her love by anointing Jesus' feet. Only faith can lead to forgiveness. If we do not trust God we will not ask him to forgive us, nor will we believe we are forgiven. Only faith in God and love for God lead to the relationship that God requires and that we need. Only faith opens the door to true forgiveness.

Have we faced our sins realistically? Have we realized that God is not unwilling to forgive?

Have we embraced the Lord's grace by faith? If not, we can do so. We can discover that we have been forgiven much and that we can love much.—Paul House

ILLUSTRATIONS

LOVE AND SELF-GIVING.   But loving is giving, self-giving. Therefore, to be myself I have to deny myself and give myself. To be free I have to serve. To live I have to die to my own self-centeredness. To find myself I have to lose myself in loving.—John R. W. Stott

FORGIVENESS AND THE WOMAN IN LUKE.   How beautiful the woman is, for she has been forgiven. Though her sins were as scarlet, she is now pure as snow (Isa. 1:18). And she *feels* the freedom and joy of her forgiveness. If you understand the gospel, you understand what has happened inside her.—R. Kent Hughes

SERMON SUGGESTIONS

Topic: He Obeyed
Text: Heb. 11:8
Abraham, as the story shows, at first met the call of God with a mingled and partial obedience, and then for long years neglected it entirely. (1) At first, then, Abraham's obedience was only partial (Gen. 11:31; Acts 7:4). (2) Abraham's obedience was rendered possible by his faith (Gen. 12:5a; Heb. 11:8). (3) Abraham's obedience was finally complete (Gen. 12:5b).—F. B. Meyer[6]

Topic: God's Bottom Line
Text: Mic. 6:8 TEV
What does the Lord require of us? (1) To do what is just. (2) To show constant love. (3) To live in humble fellowship with our God.

CONGREGATIONAL MUSIC
1. "Alleluia, Alleluia! Give Thanks," Donald Fishel (1971)
   CHURCH STREET, Donald Fishel (1973)
   This contemporary song finds its scriptural basis in the Epistle lesson for this Sunday (Gal. 2:15–21). The refrain could be used as an antiphon before the reading and the entire song could be sung after the reading.
2. "As Morning Dawns," Fred R. Anderson (1986)
   WAREHAM, William Knapp (1738)
   This contemporary paraphrase of Psalm 5 could be used as an opening hymn for this Sunday's worship.
3. "Thou Hidden Love of God," Gerhard Tersteegen (1729); trans. John Wesley (1749)
   VATER UNSER, *Geistliche Lieder*, (1539)
   An appealing, mystical sort of hymn, "Thou Hidden Love of God" would be appropriate

---

[6] *Lord of All*

with the Epistle lesson (Gal. 2:15–21), on which it may be partially based, and with the Gospel lesson (Luke 7:36–8:3). It is a musical expression of the kind of self-denying devotion that was exhibited by the woman who anointed Jesus' feet.

4. "Lead Me, Lord," Psalm 5:8

    LEAD ME, LORD, S. S. Wesley (1867)

    This prayer chorus based on one verse of the Psalter reading (Ps. 5:1–8) could be effective if sung both before and after that reading.—Hugh T. McElrath

WORSHIP AIDS

CALL TO WORSHIP.   "But because of your great love I can come into your house; I can worship in your holy Temple and bow down to you in reverence" (Ps. 5:7 TEV).

INVOCATION.   In our Lord's cross, O God, you have demonstrated for all time your wonderful love. May this love be exalted in our worship today and in our lives every day as we obey your will and reach out to others in concern and compassion.

OFFERTORY SENTENCE.   "Upon the first day of the week let every one of you lay by him in store, as God hath prospered him, that there be no offerings when I come (1 Cor. 16:2).

OFFERTORY PRAYER.   Often, O God, our giving is a measure of our faith and love. If we are reluctant stewards, increase our faith and our love so that we can enter into the joy of our Lord.

PRAYER.   Lord, to be with you is to be at home. Today we thank you for the concept of family and for specific persons who have blessed us as family members. Thank you for the love and care we share with one another and for the ongoing concern we share with the larger family of humanity.

Even as we are thankful for the families we love and appreciate, we know that the family has problems. That is not your fault but the fault of our failure to live up to the calling you have given to govern families. Throughout all your revelation you have given us good examples to follow. In ways unnumbered you have guided our steps. Yet even among those who worship regularly and who love the Lord, there are problems that bring pain and heartache to us. So often we take what you have meant for good and mess it up. We quarrel with one another over insignificant matters and allow the incident to build walls of separation in the family. We too often do not make the effort to get along. We forget the older generation, leave out relatives, and allow varying abuses to exist unchecked.

Help us, Father, we pray. Enable us to recognize and deal with the factors and fatigues that allow us to alienate loved ones. Spare us that horrible drive for success that focuses on the things that pass and ignores the things that last eternally with others. Still the surges of jealousy and envy that pour into us and leave us empty while destroying longed-for close relationships. Teach us understanding, patience, forgiveness, and caring such as Jesus knew. Help us to love deeply and profoundly the ones entrusted to our care and responsibility. We desire and even dare to request from you families that emulate, at least in part, your family. We pray, fulfill that desire today as we wait before you in Jesus' name.—Henry Fields

SERMON
Topic: Why Try This Again?
TEXT: 1 Sam. 15:34–16:13

Walter Brueggemann, an Old Testament professor at Columbia Theological Seminary who was one of the previous Rosyter speakers, tells his seminary students that the safest place for a minister to hide is behind the Bible. Just tell the congregation what the Bible says and when they come and complain about all the mean things you have said about them—the people of God—the minister can say, "I agree with you. I find what I have been saying most offensive. I do not like it either, but that is what the Bible says. It makes me uncomfortable too, but I didn't make it up."

Previously God, through Samuel, told the people of Israel that if they wanted a king they would have a king, but God would not try to fix things when the king did what kings do. Yet here we are a few chapters further into the story and the story is telling us about how God has used Samuel to select Saul as king. Saul, the tall, strong, handsome young man, the Arnold Schwartzeneger of the children of Israel, was picked to be king. God picked Saul, who had all the right military credentials, to be king. The God who had said he didn't want to have anything to do with the children of Israel if they wanted a king had picked Saul, and Saul had done very well as king. Saul and the children of Israel had prospered under the king.

According to Walter Brueggemann, "It's not my job to try to explain this inconsistent behavior to God. It is in the story. I didn't make it up." You can no more explain why God made that rash threat and then turned right around and got smack dab in the middle of things again than you can explain why the mother and father of a sixteen-year-old boy in Texas went out to the garage to cover the smashed back windshield of their son's car to protect his stereo equipment. The boy had been rushing to school. His windows were up and his stereo was blasting as loudly as normal. He did not hear the train that hit his car and put him in a coma for six weeks. The parents blasted, cursed, blamed, and vilified that stereo system. The engineer and others said that the whistle had been blowing. The bells at the crossing had been ringing. If Kerry hadn't had his stereo on so loud, he wouldn't have been hit. The parents threatened to pull the whole system from the car and throw it away, but when the weatherman predicted rain for the next day, mom and dad were out at the junkyard with a large tarp to cover the exposed back seat where the speakers were set. You can't explain that.

God had said he didn't want to have anything to do with them if they wanted a king, and now the story reports that God picked Saul and Saul has prospered, and now God is ready to reject Saul.

The big battle with the Amalekites was coming up and God told Saul that when the battle was over, Saul and the children of Israel were to destroy everything. The children of Israel weren't supposed to prosper by this battle at all. No spoils, no slaves, no animals—everything was to be burned and destroyed. But after the victory Saul did not kill all the leaders and he saved some of the prize-winning animals. When confronted by Samuel about this change in plans, Saul said he had been planning to sacrifice the animals to God.

God, who was going to have nothing to do with kings, said to Saul, "You're history. It's over. If you can't listen to instructions, then you can't be in charge. What does the Lord require of you? Obedience, not sacrifice. Obedience is better than a thousand sacrifices." Because Saul had disobeyed the Lord, the Lord rejected Saul.

You will notice that Samuel is in the same place you and I are. Samuel understands the difficulties Saul is experiencing. Samuel can see the temptations that come from being God's anointed. The more you succeed, the more authority is given to you. The better you do, the more credit is given to you. Pretty soon you slip over the line and begin to believe your press clippings. Moses in the wilderness had just slapped that old rock and ordered water to come out and forgot to acknowledge that his authority for that action came from God, and he was excluded from the Promised Land. Saul made his own decisions as to what was appropriate after the battle; he decided for himself what was good and what was not, and God said, "That's the end."

Funny how it happened. His father brought him up to have confidence in himself, to believe in his ability, to be mentally tough, and to believe he was going to win. Saul got too arrogant. He began to make his own decisions.

But Samuel understood that. Samuel was sitting there thinking, "Can't you work something out with Saul, God? Why do you have to be so mean? Why do you have to be so rigid? Why can't you forgive and forget? Where is all that talk about grace and mercy and forgiveness?"

And God said to Samuel, "How long are you going to mope around here in the past? How long are you going to look back and grieve about what has been? How long are you going to sit here being sorry for Saul? We have work to do. We have got to get with it. You have got to get up and go out and instigate a revolution. You've got to anoint a new king."

God is ready to get on with his work. There is no time to stand around and wring one's hands and regret past decisions and talk about cherished hopes that have died. God has something in mind. God has a vision, an intention, a purpose for creation, a creation to bring to fulfillment, and he has got to get on with the work. Saul did not work out. There are other ways by which God can accomplish his work.

Every morning on WPTF radio there is a talk show host called Dr. Laura and as you may have heard she is very aggressive, blunt, and confrontational. She is also very focused and very wise, but when people call in and ask her for advice and she tells them what she believes is the ethical way to respond, when they try to argue with her, when they try to defend themselves, when they begin to play "Yes, but," she won't put up with it. She simply says, "This is not a debate show. If you want a debate show, call Montel or Revera. You call me for advice. I give you what I think is the best solution. I tell you what is my ethical understanding of your problem and that is the end of it. This is not a debate show."

Well, as much as we might be surprised by the idea, the Kingdom of God is not a debate show either. This is God's creation and God has a vision and a purpose for that creation. Redemption and the cross and forgiveness and reconciliation are all means by which God is at work trying to bring creation into the fulfillment of his vision. The vision is not up for debate. The values of the Kingdom are not subject to a vote. As the slogan says, "The Ten Commandments are not the Ten Suggestions." God calls people to be part of his work and part of his creation, and where they refuse to participate, God moves on and can find other ways. But God invites and works for the redemption of those who want to be a part of the Kingdom, because God's Kingdom needs all the workers God can get.

The foreman of the Hoover Dam project came into town every morning and paid the fines of all the laborers who had spent the weekend in town and were arrested for being drunk and disorderly. It was not that he liked to rescue them. It was not that he liked to pay his share to the city fathers. It was not that he liked those men and wanted to help them. He had a dam to build and he needed all the skilled workers he could get. He redeemed them in order to accomplish his creative purpose. God redeems in service to his creation.

God said to Samuel, "Get up! We still have a people to create; we still have a creation to redeem by the blessings to be given by these chosen people. We have work to do and we haven't time to sit around and feel sorry for Saul. That is a harsh sound—tough love. It is a fiercer and more demanding God than most of us have confronted. The idea is that God has created the world and all that dwells therein and he is out to preserve his creation and his universe. The cross of Jesus is that harsh, demanding love doing what is necessary to redeem the workers to get on with the work of fulfilling creation.

God's redemption of us by his fierce love is in order to call us back to the task of being his stewards and faithful servants of all creation so that our garden might bloom as God intends it to bloom. If we don't want to help, God moves on. If we want to be a part of that great Kingdom, then nothing in the past is so evil that it will keep us from making a contribution and being a part of the people now. "How long are you going to sit around and feel bad about what happened yesterday? There is a Kingdom to be built today that God needs your help with."—Rick Brand

SUNDAY, JUNE 24, 2001
Lectionary Message

Topic: Faith and the Family of God

TEXT: Gal. 3:23–29

Other Readings: 1 Kings 19:1–4; Ps. 42; Luke 8:26–39

Families can be a vital part of our lives. At their best they provide physical, spiritual, and emotional nourishment. They can teach us how to live. Of course, everyone does not enjoy a wonderful home life. This fact heightens the need for good family experiences and relationships.

Paul often speaks of the Church in family terms. For instance, he calls the Church God's household (Eph. 2:19) and compares marriage bonds to the relationship between Christ and the Church (Eph. 5:21–33). He clearly considers the family a positive model for what believers should be to Christ and for one another.

In this passage Paul stresses how we come into God's family by emphasizing special members of God's household. Each of these members has a specific role in the Lord's family.

I. *The Law is our guardian* (3:23–24). In Paul's day, wealthy families appointed a servant to act as a child's guardian, or custodian. This servant protected, guarded, and sometimes taught the child. Obviously this responsibility was given not to just anyone but to the most trusted servant. Though not technically a member of the family, this person was definitely important to the family. Paul states that the laws revealed to Moses fill this purpose in our lives until we trust Christ.

(a) *The law of Moses restrains us* (3:23). One of the guardian's functions was to keep young people out of mischief. Not even the best guardian can guarantee good behavior, but the wisest ones at least inhibit foolish activities. Through its authority and wisdom, Moses' law keeps us from sinning more than we otherwise might.

(b) *The law shows us we need God's grace* (5:24). More important, Moses' law teaches that we need salvation, for it shows us that we are sinners in need of God's grace. We do not keep all God's commands, so we need to make peace with God. In this way our guardian is our friend. The law is a means of helping us understand what God expects and how God makes it possible for us to have a relationship with him.

Today many people have the wrong idea about Moses' law. They think it is stern, harsh, and hard to keep. They think it is our enemy. The truth is that the law is God's kind way of making us come to the end of our self-sufficiency. Anything that brings us to God is ultimately for our good. No doubt many first-century persons did not come to appreciate their guardian until they became adults. So it is with the law and us.

(c) *The guardian's job is done* (5:25). Paul does not mean that we no longer need standards for living godly lives. He means that the law's role in bringing us to faith in Christ is done when we accept Christ by faith. We no longer need to be convinced of our sin or of our need for forgiveness in Christ. The guardian has done his job well and by faith we are ready to be responsible members of God's family.

II. *God is our Father* (5:26). The Bible teaches that God desires an intimate relationship with us. He is our Creator (Gen. 1:26–31). Christ is our Savior (John 3:16). The Holy Spirit lives in us (Eph. 1:13–14). Perhaps the most important of all these images is God as our Father (see Hos. 11:1–9).

(a) *God is our Father.* Our earthly fathers may not be all they should be, but our heavenly Father is loving, kind, appropriately stern, caring, just, and holy. He sent Jesus to save us (John 3:16). All good gifts come from him (James 1:17). Thus he merits our love and trust.

(b) *We are God's children.* As God's children we have tremendous privileges. In both Romans 8:12–26 and Galatians 4:1–7 Paul stresses that we are adopted as God's children. So we are heirs of God's blessings and joint heirs with Christ. The Holy Spirit lives in us now and we look forward to heaven in the future. We pray to our Father (Matt. 6:9–13) and he meets our daily needs (Matt. 6:25–33). Our Father guides and sustains his children.

(c) *We are God's children through faith.* We do not merit such a loving Father. We receive him by believing in Jesus Christ. As we trust him we grow in our relationship with him. The tutor helped us know our Father, and this Father exceeds all our expectations.

III. *God's people are our brothers and sisters* (3:27–29). When we become God's children, we gain brothers and sisters from all races and nationalities who trust Christ. We share with our brothers and sisters a love of the Father and a love for one another that transcends our differences (1 John 3:11–24). This unique family has certain vital features that let the world know who we are.

(a) *Our family has been baptized into Christ* (3:27). Our family practices many types of baptism, yet it agrees that baptism is a mark of God's child. We are happy to submit to baptism so that the world will know that our sins are buried with Christ and we are raised to be new people (Rom. 6:4; Col. 2:12). We are equally happy when someone else is baptized because of faith in Christ.

(b) *Our family transcends race and gender* (3:28). Our family has no use for racial or gender prejudice. We are from many nations and races. We have both brothers and sisters. Our love for Christ unites us and our love for one another identifies us to others. Whenever we fall short of these standards, we are not acting like God's family.

(c) *Our family transcends time* (3:29). Our brothers and sisters stretch back in time. They are literally as old as Moses, Abraham, and Sarah. Like Abraham, we entered the family through faith (Gen. 15:6). Like Sarah and Hagar, we suffer as we serve (16:1–16). We can learn from our older brothers and sisters as we follow their example and avoid their mistakes.

Being part of God's family is a great experience. Let us embrace our family, our heritage, and our future. May we find our place in the family and encourage others to join us as heirs of God!—Paul House

ILLUSTRATIONS

CHRISTIAN ONENESS.   In other words, it is a oneness because such differences cease to be a barrier and cause of pride or regret or embarrassment and become rather a means to display the diverse richness of God's creation and grace, both in the acceptance of the "all" and in the gifting of each.—James D. G. Dunn

THE CHURCH'S IMPERFECTIONS.   The ideal is beautiful. The Church is the chosen and beloved people of God, his own special treasure, the covenant community to whom he has committed himself forever, engaged in continuous worship of God and in compassionate outreach to the world, a haven of love and peace, and a pilgrim people headed for the eternal city. But in reality we who claim to be the Church are often a motley rabble of rather scruffy individuals, half-educated and half-saved, uninspired in our worship, bickering with each another, concerned more with our maintenance than our mission . . . needing constant rebuke and exhortation, which are readily available from both the Old Testament prophets and New Testament apostles.—John R. W. Stott

SERMON SUGGESTIONS

Topic: Four Judgments About Jesus
TEXT: Various
(1) "He is possessed, he is out of his mind" (John 10:20 REB). (2) "He is a good man" (John 7:12 KJV). (3) "You are the Messiah" (Matt. 16:16 NRSV). (4) "My Lord and my God" (John 20:28 KJV).

Topic: The Best Exercise
TEXT: Gen. 5:24
Enoch walked with God. You can walk with God. Walking with God means (1) to go in God's direction, (2) to proceed at God's pace, (3) to progress as God leads, (4) to share God's companionship, (5) to arrive at God's destination.—Harold T. Bryson and James C. Taylor[7]

CONGREGATIONAL MUSIC

1. "Dear Lord and Father of Mankind," John G. Whittier (1872)
    REST, Frederick C. Maker (1887)
    REPTON, Charles H. H. Parry (1924)
    This great unintentional hymn written as part of a longer poem on "The Brewing of Soma" makes specific reference in its stanza beginning "Breathe through the heats of our desire" to

---

[7] *Building Sermons to Meet People's Needs*

the experience of the prophet Elijah on Mt. Horeb (1 Kings 19:11–15a). It would be suitable to sing this hymn following the Old Testament lesson.

2. "Silence, Frenzied, Unclean Spirit," Thomas H. Troeger (1984)

AUTHORITY, Carol Doran (1984)

This gripping contemporary hymn is a natural choice to be sung with the Gospel lesson on Jesus' healing of the demoniac (Luke 8:26–39).

3. "As the Deer Pants for the Water," Martin Nystrom (1983)

AS THE DEER, Martin Nystrom (1983)

This contemporary praise song could be suitably sung following the Psalter reading. Accompaniment by a guitar would be appropriate.

4. "In Christ There Is No East or West," John Oxenham (1908)

ST. PETER, Alexander Reinagle (c. 1830)

The fact that we are all one in Christ (Gal. 3:28) is beautifully expressed in this fine hymn of Christian fellowship.—Hugh T. McElrath

WORSHIP AIDS

CALL TO WORSHIP.   "As the heart panteth after the water brooks, so panteth my soul after thee, O God. My soul thirsteth for God, for the living God: when shall I come and appear before God?" (Ps. 42:1–2).

INVOCATION.   Lord of life, hear our prayers as we come in from the wilderness of grief and suffering, as we return from paths we ought not to have taken, as we leave the petty to contemplate the profound. Fill our humanity with the spirit of Christ that our worship might be pleasing unto God.—E. Lee Phillips

OFFERTORY SENTENCE.   "What good is it, my brothers and sisters, if you say you have faith but do not have works? Can faith save you?" (James 2:14 NRSV).

OFFERTORY PRAYER.   Lord, we would be faithful. We would give because we care, care because we love, and love because God first loved us and sent his Son to die on the cross for our sins. Let that be the message of these gifts today.—E. Lee Phillips

PRAYER.   How can we bring glory and honor to your name, Father? Is our commitment to Christ sufficient? Will our service to our fellow man be enough? Can our deeds of kindness suffice? Will our acts of worship fill in any gaps that are left? Where does the reading of the Scriptures and personal prayer fit in? What are you waiting for, Father, as an indication of our true praise and adoration? Can it be that all you want is still a humble and contrite heart, a sense of unworthiness that fosters need that can be met only in your presence and by your power? Whatever constitutes our giving glory, honor, praise, and adoration to you, teach us how to begin, we pray. May this hour not pass until we have found our personal way to express all that we must if we are ever to fulfill our need to be near you and loved by you.

To the end that such may happen we commit our time and talents, our hearts and souls to you. Do with us as you will. Reshape our lives that we may follow your pathway for us. Remake our maps that we may find the way without failure. Remold our loves that we may love what it is right and holy to love. Show us how to have our deepest need filled. Lead us to the deep waters of truth. Declare to us the Word of hope and salvation from failure and sin. Welcome us, we pray, with all our scars and bruises, which are the results of our failure to trust and follow you on this journey of life. Lead us home, Good Shepherd, we humbly pray.

And carefully tend the wounded among us today. Sorrowing young parents, folks broken by life's insurmountable circumstances, people scarred with wounds inflicted by others, children neglected and mistreated, races pitted against each other by senseless hatred. All of us marred by our mistakes, sins, and misdeeds await the gentle ministering that only your love can supply and that alone brings healing. Blessed Father, let the Holy Spirit do in us today what we cannot do for ourselves or for each other. Let him save us and restore us that we might know the renewed wonder of being your children, free and joyful. So in expectation we wait, knowing that we will not be disappointed by the one who loves us and has given himself for us, even Christ our Lord, in whose name we pray.—Henry Fields

SERMON
Topic: Happy Feet?
Text: Rom. 10:5–15

Paul is quoting from the prophet Isaiah. He says, "The scriptures say it is a beautiful sight to see even the feet of someone coming to preach the good news." What is this message of good news that makes the coming of the messenger so wonderful that people will think even his feet are beautiful?

For Paul the story of the good news is a story about a God who has revealed his love and grace for creation in many ways and most clearly and most powerfully in the life and Resurrection of Jesus Christ. All who are willing to believe that God can do what God has promised to do for us, which is to make us acceptable to himself by the love shown in Jesus Christ, are welcomed by God. Paul says that no one who has faith will be disappointed, no matter if that person is a Jew or a Gentile. There is only one Lord and he is generous to everyone who asks for his help. The story to be told is, "All who call out to the Lord will be saved." There is a gracious God who cares about his creation and desires to be the agent of transformation working in us and for us. All who are reaching out, calling out to God to save them, will be saved. That is the story we live by. That is the story we are encouraged to tell others. It is the story of invitation. That is the liberating, exciting, good news of the happy feet that bring it.

The beautiful and happy feet of the storyteller are always welcomed, which means that the story of faith and hope is more than just mental assent to fixed propositions about an abstract God. God is more than theological doctrines. So often the tellers of the story come as imposters of theological correctness on others and it is not good news. God is not a problem to be solved. God is not a mystery to be explained. God is not just the explanation to be given for all unexplained situations. God is a power, a love, a joy, and a hope that is involved in creation. God is a presence at work in our world.

The good news of the beautiful feet is that God is at work within our history, that God cares for all creation so much that he came into creation to show us that care. God loves creation and all humanity so much that God would not let the Crucifixion of Jesus destroy that love. God continues by his presence in the Holy Spirit to work by love to lure, to beckon, to summon, to entice, to woo, to urge, to push us forward toward his purpose and will. God loves life and people so much that he will not abandon us and will not give up. God is so much at work in history and the life of creation, in my life, and in your life that the story says that no one who has faith that God will bring each of us to the fulfillment and purpose in our lives will be disappointed. No one who has faith that God loves her and is at work in her life to move her toward God's purpose for her will be disappointed. That is the promise that makes the feet of the storyteller beautiful.

The good news is that faith does not see life as sectioned or divided or fragmented into different compartments. The amazing grace of God does not work just in the sections of life we want to call sacred. The good news of God's amazing grace is that God is involved and active in all aspects and in all times of our lives. Faith has to do with the way we look at and respond to all of life.

We have wanted to say that faith has to do with such questions as Do you believe in the Bible? Do you believe in prayer and do you go to church? or Do you believe in an afterlife? Yet faith in the God who is active in all creation, who is at work in all parts of creation, and who makes his power and grace shimmer in all places of creation and in all moments of history is convinced that there are no moments in our lives that are not part of the struggle toward either the good or that which diminishes life. He is also convinced that there are no thoughts and feelings that are not helping time and life move toward God's will and purpose for all of us, nor are there thoughts and feelings contributing to those forces that keep life contrary to God's intention and will. Faith is convinced that no one who calls out to God to bring her to the fullness of her purpose in God's love will be disappointed.

The storyteller does not come with the message that what we do does not matter. That kind of unconditional acceptance is not good news. The storyteller does not come and tell us that only what we do in certain areas of life is what matters, that we are ritually pure when we bring our offerings, and that what we do with widows and orphanages in the marketplace doesn't matter. The prophets Amos and Hosea were among the first to refuse to let us compartmentalize faith that way. The one with the beautiful feet comes and reminds us that in all parts of our lives, in every day and in every way, everything we do matters and is part of God's holy work, and we are working with and for the Kingdom of God even when we let someone merge into traffic who has been a jerk. But the great news is that no one who believes that God is involved and a part of all of life will be disappointed in the end. Faith is calling out for God to save us and redeem us. That kind of humble faith and recognition that we aren't going to save ourselves enables us to recognize joyfully that there is a God who is at work with us and in us to save us. When the storyteller brings that kind of faith, it comes as good news and the feet of the one who brings that story just might reach the level of being beautiful.—Rick Brand

SUNDAY, JULY 1, 2001
Lectionary Message

Topic: How to Miss Heaven
Text: Luke 9:51–62
Other Readings: 2 Kings 2:1–2, 6–14; Ps. 77:1–2, 11–20; Gal. 5:1, 13–25

Heaven is a gated community with strictly limited access. The Messiah is heaven's "open house" and open door. To miss the Messiah is to miss heaven. To miss the Messiah is to miss your best destiny. To meet the Messiah is to meet your best destination. In the twelve verses of Luke 9:51–62, the Gospel writer has compacted numerous cautions about meeting the Messiah.

I. *Caution 1: Meeting the Messiah is at God's discretion.* Jesus practiced his ministry and life with an awareness of limited time. He knew when his round-trip ticket back to heaven was due. He knew that the way of the cross in Jerusalem would lead him home. Timing is everything. This immediacy meant that Jesus would take the direct route through Samaria. His commitment to the timing of God's mission meant an unexpected opportunity for one village to meet the Messiah and to meet their destiny. God comes only in the now. His coming and presence call for decision.

II. *Caution 2: Meeting the Messiah means deciding to follow his direction.* Jesus ever set the cross before the crown, suffering in service before sweetness of reward. Note Jesus' caution concerning the costs of missionary discipleship in verses 57–62.

(a) *Comfort zones will need to abandoned if we are to be faithful messengers* (v. 58). Because the mission of God is a movement, the Church must ever see itself in temporary housing. The missionary member must prefer the hardship of the road to the relaxation of the homestead.

(b) *Expected obligations will need to be neglected if the message is to be served* (v. 60). The gospel is time sensitive. People must open it or be open to it within certain time frames set by God. Because the time is short, the messengers and the missionary Church must neglect some traditions and customs whenever there is not time for them. The gospel and the Kingdom must be served first or they will not be served at all.

(c) *Family hospitalities will need to be delegated to others if we are to be faithful to the Messiah* (v. 62). Grace is free but not cheap. Discipleship costs. Jesus bids us to come and die for the sake of the Messiah and his mission. No wonder Jesus always put a high value on the hospitality received by his messengers.

III. *Caution 3: Meeting the Messiah depends on the reception of his messengers* (v. 53). The Savior is often missed or dismissed for reasons of race, relationships, or religion. The Samaritans expressed rage at the road Jesus intended to travel. They assumed that because he was Jerusalem bound he must also be anti-Samaritan. Effective missionaries and churches must learn to overcome false assumptions about Christ and his people or many will miss heaven. However, once people know you care, then they care to know what you know.

IV. *Caution 4: Dismissing the Messiah begs for God's retribution.* The disciples became indignant when there was no room in the inn in that Samaritan town. They begged Jesus to punish this rudeness by bombing the town with brimstone. In their minds, as perhaps in our own, such retribution was the appropriate way to make people responsible for their close-mindedness to the gospel. After all, had not Jesus taught them that if he was acknowledged before others, reciprocal acknowledgment would be made before the Father by the Son? Conversely, if Jesus was denied before others, he would in turn deny his relationship with that person before the Father. "If you honor me, I will honor you. If you dishonor me, then I must dishonor you," taught Jesus. Humanity is responsible for its right response to God's presence and invitation.

V. *Caution 5: Dismissing the Messiah receives delayed retribution because his mission is mercy.* Jesus refused to give the order for an angelic air force to bomb the village. His mission was mercy and so is ours. Later, John, one of the voices for a just destruction, returned to Samaria and this time the messengers of the Messiah were well received. John must have been grateful that the Messiah withheld holy judgment until the mission of gospel mercy had run its full course through the hands, feet, and mouths of the disciples.

VI. *Conclusion*. Now the mission of the Messiah is in the hands of the Church under the authority and leadership of the Spirit. Two responses are possible. First, will we be responsible messengers of the Messiah by neglecting our comforts in order to comfort others with the hope of heaven? Either the Church is operating under messianic orders to carry out the preaching and healing mission or it is in disorder and disobedience. We must be finding new neighborhoods in which to post heaven's "open house" signs. Second, will we bring sufficient mercy to that mission to overcome resistance and prejudice against Christ? Authentic missionaries of the merciful one will ultimately prove irresistible to those whom God is calling to salvation.—Rodrick K. Durst

ILLUSTRATIONS

BILBO BAGGINS'S GREAT ADVENTURE.   In the 1960s, university students around the West became enchanted with the fantasy Middle Earth world described in the books of J.R.R. Tolkien, who incidentally participated in the translation of the Good News Bible published by the American and British Bible Society. The unexpected heroes of the Tolkien books were small, slightly hairy, humanlike creatures called hobbits. Hobbits invariably dwelt in well-furnished, comfortable holes in the ground and rarely traveled far from home. They never went on adventures and those who did were suspect and not perceived as reliable of character. The books tell of Bilbo Baggins, the hobbit who accepted a mission to turn back dark evil and went on a great adventure by abandoning the hole of his comfort. Christians too must go on an adventure by abandoning our habit to "hobbit" in only familiar paths.

ANSWERING HATE WITH A HUG.   Following her release from a World War II Nazi concentration camp, the Dutch Christian Corrie Ten Boom felt called to preach forgiveness in Christ to the guilt-ridden in Germany. In her messages she always shared the witness of mercy expressed toward their German captors by her sister, who had shared Miss Ten Boom's cell in the camp before she died. Following one such speech, a former camp guard at that very camp stepped forward and identified himself to test the genuineness of Miss Ten Boom's mission. Overcoming her desire to strike out against one who had brought about the painful death of her beloved sister, Corrie Ten Boom gave the former soldier a hug. That hug healed her own heart as well as that of the former guard. Forgiveness became real and heaven and earth became one.—Rodrick K. Durst

SERMON SUGGESTIONS

Topic: You Are a Preacher, Too
TEXT: Acts 8:35
(1) As a Christian, you have an experience to share. (2) In this world, there are people who need what you can give them. (3) As we live from day to day and go here and there, unexpected opportunities to witness come to all of us.

Topic: Bold Service
TEXT: Eccles. 11:1
(1) Some of us, God's servants, may have an eager, even impatient drive to do great things for God. (2) But life tests us with (a) failure, (b) delays, (c) criticism, (d) a sense of unworthiness. (3) Nevertheless, opportunity is always before us, demanding (a) beginning again;

(b) patience; (c) learning from criticism; (d) living by God's acceptance of us, despite our infirmities; (e) believing that God's purpose in and through us will win out for his glory and our good.

CONGREGATIONAL MUSIC

1. "My Song Is Love Unknown," Samuel Crossman (1664)
   LOVE UNKNOWN, John Ireland (1919)
   This exquisite matching of text and tune can be a vehicle of intimate worship when used in connection with the Gospel lesson in Luke (9:51–62). Stanza 5 relates to verse 51 and stanza 6 relates to verse 58, but the entire hymn sums up the loving mission of Jesus.
2. "Like the Murmur of the Dove's Song," Carl P. Daw Jr. (1981)
   BRIDEGROOM, Peter Cutts (1968)
   As a response to the Epistle lesson, especially Galatians 5:22, the singing of this beautiful contemporary prayer for the coming of the Spirit would be meaningful.
3. "Take Up Thy Cross," Charles W. Everest (1833)
   GERMANY, William Gardiner's *Sacred Melodies* (1815)
   The summons of Christ to follow him regardless of the cost is strongly set forth in this American hymn that could be used to respond to the reading of the Gospel lesson (Luke 9:51–62).
4. "God Moves in a Mysterious Way," William Cowper (1774)
   DUNDEE, *Scottish Psalter* (1615)
   The first stanza of this magnificent hymn on the theme of God's providence takes its inspiration from the last verse of Psalm 77. It could be sung to introduce the Psalter reading quite effectively.—Hugh T. McElrath

WORSHIP AIDS

CALL TO WORSHIP.   "I will remember the works of the Lord: surely I will remember the wonders of old. I will meditate also on all thy work, and talk of thy doing" (Ps. 77:11–12).

INVOCATION.   We realize that we have a promising rendezvous with the Creator of all that is, the Lord of all. Grant that we may remember your works of love and grace and that after we have worshiped we may go from this place to witness to all your mercies.

OFFERTORY SENTENCE.   "If you have ears, then listen to what the Spirit says to the churches: 'to those who win the victory I will give the right to eat the fruit of the tree of life in the Garden of God'" (Rev. 2:7 TEV).

OFFERTORY PRAYER.   Lord, give deeper meaning to our giving than at first we thought and wider use to our gifts than we ever imagined, through the unlimited and loving power of the Holy Spirit.—E. Lee Phillips

PRAYER.   Holy God, Holy Christ, Holy Spirit, early in the morning may our song rise to thee. All your works do praise your name, on the earth, in the sky, and on the sea. May we, your best creation, praise and worship you, too. Great is your faithfulness, strong and gentle God, as sure as the dawning of the sun, as steady as the coming of this hour. In worship and praise, adoration and thanksgiving, in obedience and service, may we your children be faithful, too. Stir your cleansing and edifying Spirit among us, O God, and clarify and strengthen our language and love to you.

Holy Spirit, light divine, burn and shine within our hearts and show forth as we worship and serve you this day. For the beauty and blessing of this day and hour, we give you thanks.

Lord God, Creator, Redeemer, Sustainer of all nations and all believers, today we thank you for our country, land of the free and those becoming free, home of the brave and those striving to become brave. We pause to whisper prayers of thanks for those who have given life and limb that we might be here today. Let us never assume or embrace freedom casually.

Liberate us, O God, not to be selfish or shortsighted in our freedom; rather, empower us to work diligently for the freedom and justice of all people and all nations. May we see and know purpose beyond ourselves and our land, and in Christ remind us properly that we are first and always citizens of your Kingdom, your Reign, and that your Kingdom is not of this world. So as we pray for your Kingdom to come, your will to be done, may our worship and our freedom guide us to be about Kingdom work and holy will. Grant us wisdom, discernment, courage, and vision for the serving of these days, in Christ.—William M. Johnson

SERMON
Topic: Considering Our Worth
TEXT: Matt. 6:25–26, 10:29–31

"I feel like my life is worthless," the young woman sobbed on the other end of the telephone line.

I. *I am here to tell you today that you are a person of great worth.* The great value and worth of the human soul is one of the messages Jesus is trying to get across in the two passages that were read from Matthew. "You are of more value than many sparrows," Jesus says (Matt. 10:31). This message regarding the value and worth of ordinary humans was a radical teaching in Jesus' day, and it was a message the people were desperately needing. Our value and intrinsic worth are inherent in our nature in that we have been created in the image of God. The Judeo-Christian faith teaches the great worth and dignity of every human person. Concepts that portray humans as being "totally depraved," "wretches," "worms in the dust," and the like may appeal to some people, but they are inconsistent with the grand design of the Creator. To reiterate, to be created in God's own image means that God has breathed into us his own Spirit; we have been given a touch of the Creator's own creativity, intelligence, and ability to reason and make wise choices. It has not been put any more succinctly than by Robert Schuller in his book *Success Is Never-Ending:* "I am somebody. I am a child of God. I am a friend of Jesus Christ. . . . I am God's chance to do a wonderful thing" (p. 72). There is no way to put a value on the worth of every human soul. As Harriet Beecher Stowe observes in *Uncle Tom's Cabin,* "One soul is worth more than all the money in the world" (p. 42).

Coupled with our self-worth is the fact that we are unconditionally loved by God. As the apostle John put it, "See what love the Father has given us, that we should be called children of God; and that is what we are" (1 John 3:1 NRSV). Now, if God loves us so much, surely he wants us to love ourselves. But sometimes we don't think that way. We are tempted to think that we aren't very important, or we may think that we don't matter, or we may think that others are of more worth or importance to God than we are. But I believe it is necessary for us to love ourselves, because unless we properly love ourselves, how can we possibly love God and others?

II. *A sense of self-worth is necessary for a wholesome, healthy life*—or in the words of M. Scott Peck in *The Road Less Traveled,* "The feeling of being valuable—'I am a valuable person'—is essential to mental health" (p. 24). The absence of self-love and self-worth often results in self-denying, destructive behavior: obsessions, various addictions, aggressions, and violence. Depression and eating disorders also often accompany poor self-esteem.

Persons who have a clear sense of identity and who love and appreciate themselves have inner peace and joy. By nature they tend to be more creative and productive in society than those who do not love themselves. I suspect they may even live longer than persons who have poor self-esteem and low self-worth and who lack of self-confidence.

III. *A sense of self-worth is one of the most critical needs of our day.* Young persons especially often struggle with self-identity, self-esteem, and self-worth. There is first the process of maturing and the physical changes that take place so rapidly. There is also peer pressure to experiment with drugs, alcohol, and premarital sex. There are fashion trends that teenagers feel they must keep up with so they may be in the "in crowd." It is tough being a teenager today. Our kids really have their work cut out for them. Physical changes and appearance, peer pressure, and fashion trends all conspire to try our young persons' sense of self-worth.

But the need for self-esteem and self-worth is not limited to teenagers. Almost everyone—television and magazine beauty queens included—feels inferior and self-conscious about something. You need only walk through the major department stores and see all the beauty products that are sold to cover up our human imperfections to get an idea of our attempts to hide what we don't want people to see.

Too many people are walking around in our world who, because of their appearance, physical or mental challenges, painful life experiences, mistakes they have made, and so on, have no sense of self-worth and no love and appreciation for themselves whatsoever. I believe it is our task, our calling, our joy as a church, to enable people to see their worth in the eyes of God, to assist them in striving to be all God created them to be, and to help them acquire for themselves inner wholeness and the abundant life that Jesus promised.

So, what I am trying to say to you today is this: one of the first steps in living an abundant, productive, successful life is to consider our worth; that is, to see ourselves as we really are: persons of great worth and value in the eyes of God and deserving of love—the love of God, the love of others, and the love of ourselves. To paraphrase the words of Jesus, you are of more value to God than you will ever know.—Randy Hammer

SUNDAY, JULY 8, 2001
Lectionary Message

Topic: The Missionary Methods of Jesus
TEXT: Luke 10:1–11, 16–20
Other Readings: 2 Kings 5:1–14; Ps. 30; Gal. 6:1–6

Bible reading is a great adventure for the believing community. It becomes an adventure whenever we come to Scripture with a prior commitment to obey. Reading Luke 10:1–16 is particularly threatening. It would require the Church to practice the missionary methods of Jesus. Every congregation or believer who has dared to investigate and implement these methods has thereby managed to turn their world upside down.

I. *The master of the harvest is Jesus.* Note that Jesus taught his disciples to pray to the Lord of the harvest to send out more workers and then immediately sent out these seventy disciples to towns and villages of his choosing. Doesn't that imply that Jesus is the Lord of this harvest?

(a) *Jesus thrusts out workers into his mission field.* Remember, we don't take Jesus to people. Jesus takes us to people. We never go to where God has never been. We go only to where God is already at work. Effective disciples are ever alert to what God is already doing in the lives of the lost.

(b) *The number of workers sent out provides clues about the Master, his mission field, and his missionaries.*

1. Seventy is the membership of the religious supreme court in Jerusalem over which the high priest held court. This religious court was called the Sanhedrin. Jesus faced this court on his way to the cross. Peter, James, and John faced the same seventy members in Acts 4. Because the New Testament challenges us to join God in recognizing Jesus as high priest (Heb. 4:14), are not these seventy meant to be the new Sanhedrin over which Jesus rules as high priest?

2. Seventy is also the number of nations listed in Genesis 10. These seventy nations were the way the Hebrews understood the totality of humanity on earth. So, don't the seventy sent by Jesus alert us also to his intention for the Church to take the gospel to the nations? Nothing less will fulfill his mission vision.

3. Seventy is also the number of elders on which the Spirit of prophecy came in Numbers 11:25. In that moment, Moses was spiritually "cloned" as the Spirit empowered the seventy elders to witness with divine unction just as Moses did. Jesus sent out his seventy disciples with the same authority and unction. Jesus is the new Moses, who shares His spirit as ordination for messianic ministry. The sending out the seventy to evangelize and minister in the Palestinian towns foreshadowed the Pentecost to come, which would empower the Christian community to be a prophetic force in the world, which needs Jesus and the Kingdom. Jesus bestows this unction on each of those who are his own.

II. *The main missionary qualification is commitment to discipleship.* The leaders of the Kingdom mission are to be learners. Disciples are those submitted to the Lordship and leadership of Jesus. His words are their words. His ways are their ways. Jesus entrusts the mission of the Kingdom to those who are submissive and obedient. Commitment to Christ enables adherence to his harvest methods.

III. *The missionary method of Jesus involves at least five practices.*

(a) *Go out two by two.* We do ministry and mission best in community. Community brings with it fellowship, worship, accountability, and healing. The missionary band is the tie that should bind us to the great commission of Jesus to disciple the nations.

(b) *Practice defenseless evangelism.* Jesus sends out his workers "as lambs in the midst of wolves." The lamb cannot provide its own defense, so it must rely on the shepherd for protection. The message of Christ gets distorted when the messengers are too defensive to listen to the real needs and concerns of the people to whom they would minister. In the rush to win a debate, the soul is sometimes lost.

(c) *Live close to the culture by trusting the culture to provide your daily needs.* Rich missionaries would never be a problem if the method of Jesus were practiced. Closeness to the people is how God provides for mission. If the message is truly good news to the people, then will not the people respond with sufficient hospitality to sustain the messenger? Besides, if the mission of the Kingdom is about faith, then Kingdom workers must live by faith that God will provide without everything being known in advance. Too many times in the name of planning and preparation, mission adventures are abandoned in disobedience to the Lord of the harvest. God does not lead where he cannot supply. However, we must also practice the missionary principle of Jesus to "eat whatever is set before you."

(d) *Seek the man or woman of peace in the community and make their home your local headquarters.* Every neighborhood has its influencers and opinion leaders. These men and women determine the direction of the community or family. If these people can be won to Christ, they will bring their household or neighborhood with them. Jesus saves individuals but he prefers to save households, neighborhoods, and groups. He wants the Church to grow by both addition and multiplication.

(e) *Bring healing to the hurts of the community in the name and power of Jesus.* Start a conspiracy of kindness to the wounded as Jesus described in the story of the Good Samaritan later in the chapter.

(f) *Stay focused on sharing the gospel.* Always tell the gospel story. People listen when they hear that "the Kingdom of God is near."

IV. *The message of the missionary Church.* The Kingdom is near; to the believer it means forgiveness. The Kingdom is near enough that one can reach out and receive the King. To the rejecter the Kingdom means judgment. The King is near and real enough to hold one accountable for rebellion.

V. *The moment of decision in the mission field.* Note that the human decision for Jesus involves heaven, Earth, and hell. In verse 18, Jesus describes the effective mission of his disciples as a defeat of Satan and a triumph of heaven. When a person acknowledges the name of Jesus, heaven acknowledges that person's name in the Kingdom's citizenship role call. As the apostle Paul said, "We have been transferred from the dominion of darkness into the Kingdom of God's beloved Son."—Rodrick K. Durst

ILLUSTRATIONS

THAT WOULD BE A LITTLE SLOW WOULDN'T IT?   Ryan and Tawny Williams discovered the incredible results when a "man of peace" comes to Christ. As young missionaries to university students in peninsular Mexico, the Williams couple became regular customers at a local restaurant. The owner became interested in these regulars and through his interest the young couple were able to share about Christ. When the restaurant owner eventually prayed to receive Christ, he asked the Williamses what he should do next. They gave him a copy of the *Jesus* film in Spanish and encouraged him to invite some of his friends to his home to view the movie and to share how he had come to commit his life to Christ. At this suggestion, the new Christian replied, "That would be a little slow, wouldn't it?" He proceeded to rent the largest theater in town and invited all his friends and customers to come and see the film. Almost twelve hundred people came and about five hundred of these people made commitments to follow Christ when the restaurateur invited them to do so even as he had.

DRINKING FROM A DIRTY CUP.   Evangelist Leonard Ravenhill once paid a visit to an elderly woman whose home and sense of hospitality had fallen into disrepair. The woman remembered enough of the etiquette required of a hostess to offer her guest a cup of tea. Glancing around the rather shoddily maintained kitchen, the evangelist remembered the admonition of Jesus to "eat and drink whatever is set before you." The woman reached into a small mountain of dirty dishes barely held captive in the sink. Having briefly immersed the fetched cup under running water, she poured hot tea into the cup and placed it in front of her guest. Dr. Ravenhill said that the tea was hot enough to dissolve the grease remaining in the dirty cup and whatever else resided there, too. He was, however, able to drink when he recalled that he had come in the name of the one who had drunk the cup the Father had given. Even as Jesus accepted the cup of the cross from the Father's hand, so Ravenhill chose to accept the dirty cup of tea.

DECISION AND INCISION.   The Billy Graham Evangelistic Association has long published a monthly magazine about evangelism and discipleship called *Decision*. One reader submitted a letter to the editor of the magazine recommending that the name be changed because the articles included were so spiritually and morally convicting. The reader recommended changing the name from *Decision* to *Incision* magazine.—Rodrick K. Durst

SERMON SUGGESTIONS

Topic: When God Calls
TEXT: Exod. 3:1–12
(1) It may be in ordinary, everyday circumstances. (2) However, God's presence and purpose impart extraordinary significance. (3) With the call comes God's promise of adequate resources to carry out his mission.

Topic: A Hope to Keep Us Going
TEXT: Rom. 8:18–25
(1) The gospel gives us confidence that our future destiny with God outweighs our present difficulties. (2) Therefore we can put up with persecution, physical pain, economic reverses, family problems, anxiety, and depression.

CONGREGATIONAL MUSIC
1. "O Lord, by Thee Delivered," *The Psalter* (1912)
   MEIRIONYDD, William Lloyd (1840)
   This paraphrase of Psalm 30 could well be substituted for the Psalter reading. A fresh touch could be given by lining out a stanza or two as in former days.
2. "Jesus Paid It All," Elvina M. Hall (1865)
   ALL TO CHRIST, John T. Grape (1868)
   Relating both to the healing of the leper Naaman as recorded in the Old Testament reading and to the commissioning of the seventy to heal the sick in the Gospel reading, this gospel hymn captures the spirit of divine healing, especially in its second stanza.
3. "Lord, You Give the Great Commission," Jeffery Rowthorn (1978)
   ABBOT'S LEIGH, Cyril V. Taylor (1941)

Luke 10:9 is reflected in this contemporary hymn that reminds each worshipper of the call to service and of the need for the Spirit's empowerment for faithfulness in ministry.

4. "We'll Work Till Jesus Comes," Elizabeth Mills (1836)

O LAND OF REST, American folk tune (c. 1859)

This gospel song's theme is a response to the apostle Paul's exhortation in Galatians 6:9 not to be weary in doing good.—Hugh T. McElrath

WORSHIP AIDS

CALL TO WORSHIP.   "Sing praises to the Lord, O you his faithful ones, and give thanks to his holy name. For his anger is but for a moment; his favor is for a lifetime. Weeping may linger for the night, but joy comes with the morning" (Ps. 30:4–5 NRSV).

INVOCATION.   O you who are the Great God and the Great King above all gods, we worship and adore you for the freedom to worship without intimidation or censor. We praise you for the liberty that is in Christ, for the freedom to be and become, for the privilege to be among your people: to celebrate your Word of grace in Christ, to sing praises of your mighty deeds in creation and redemption, to hear your Word read and preached, to pray, to know the assurance of sins forgiven, and to share the joy of Christian fellowship—we are grateful!

Let the word of our mouths and the meditations of our hearts be acceptable in your sight, O Lord, our Strength and our Redeemer.—John M. Thompson

OFFERTORY SENTENCE.   "He who loves his life loses it, and he who cares not for his life in this world will preserve it for eternal life" (John 12:25 Moffatt).

OFFERTORY PRAYER.   In all of our giving to you, O God, we lose nothing but gain joy and great reward, both in this life and in the life to come. Thank you for giving us life and more life in your love and grace.

PRAYER.   Grant, O God, that your holy and life-giving Spirit may so move every human heart so that the barriers that divide us may crumble, suspicions may disappear, and hatreds may cease; so that once our divisions are healed we may live in justice and peace, through Jesus Christ our Lord.—*The Book of Common Prayer*

SERMON
Topic: The Commandments of Christ
TEXT: Deut. 6:4–5; John 13:34–35, 15:12–17 (also Matt. 22:34–40)

There is a former Baptist group in Athens, Tennessee, that has given up many of the traditional beliefs of the faith and reverted to Old Testament religion. They call themselves the Children of Noah in that they proclaim and try to live by seven commandments they believe God gave to all humanity through Noah:

1.   Promote justice.
2–4. Don't murder, steal, or blaspheme.

5. Don't worship things other than God.
6. No sexual misconduct.
7. No eating of live animal flesh.

Well, these rules are well and good. But we still claim to be Christians, followers of Christ. What does that really mean? Does it mean we accept everything we have heard about Jesus from our youth without examining it? Does it mean we believe everything we hear about Jesus on television? We must answer no; we have to be careful because so much is preached and taught about Jesus that may or may not be true.

So what does it mean to be a Christian? It means keeping Christ's commandments. "You are my friends," Jesus says, according to John's Gospel, "if you do what I command you" (John 15:14). "A new commandment I give to you. . . . By this all men will know that you are my disciples" (John 13:34–35). We are Christians if we keep the commandments of Christ. But what are they? We are all familiar with the Ten Commandments of Moses. But just what are the commandments of Christ?

It is a good exercise to go through the four Gospels—Matthew, Mark, Luke, and John— and reread all the words of Jesus to see what Jesus has to say and to pick out the explicit commandments he gave us. If you have never done this, I recommend that you do it sometime. If you can, read the red-lettered words of Jesus, one Gospel at a sitting. The next day go to the second gospel, and so on. You might be surprised at some of the things you will learn about Jesus and his teachings. Here is what you will find.

I. *The commandments of Christ (that is, where Jesus explicitly uses the word* command *or* commandment*) are all summed up in the commandment to love.* "A new commandment I give to you, that you love one another" (John 13:34). In another place we read, "This is my commandment, that you love one another as I have loved you" (John 15:12).

Jesus first gives us the command to love God. When questioned by a lawyer about the first commandment, as recorded in Matthew 22, Jesus replied, "You shall love the Lord your God with all your heart, and with all your soul, and with all your mind" (v. 37), which is a quotation from the book of Deuteronomy. "This is the . . . first commandment," Jesus said (v. 38).

Jesus' second command was for us to love one another as we have already seen. "This I command you, to love one another" (John 15:17). Perhaps at this point Jesus was thinking more in terms of loving those of the Christian community, the Church.

But then Jesus goes even further and commands us to love our neighbors—whether they are Church members or not—as ourselves. A second commandment is like the first, Jesus said, "You shall love your neighbor as yourself" (Matt. 22:39), a quotation from the Old Testament book of Leviticus.

II. *Jesus contended that the commandment to love is the greatest commandment in the Bible.* "Teacher, which is the great commandment in the law?" the lawyer pressed him. Jesus' answer was the commandment to love God with all our heart, soul, and mind, and our neighbors as ourselves. "This is the great . . . commandment" (22:38). In other words, no greater, no more weighty, no more deserving of our attention in all the Old Testament is the commandment to love.

III. *The commandment to love fulfills the entire law of God.* It may surprise you that Jesus did not do away with the Ten Commandments of Moses. "One came up to him saying, 'Teacher, what good deed must I do to have eternal life?' And Jesus said to him . . . 'If you would enter life, keep the commandments.' And he said to Jesus, 'Which?' And Jesus said,

'You shall not kill, you shall not commit adultery, you shall not steal, you shall not bear false witness, honor your father and mother. . . .'" In other words, even though Jesus listed only five of the Ten Commandments (at least according to Matthew's recollection), I think we can safely assume that Jesus was advocating keeping all of the Ten Commandments. But the point Jesus tried to drive home was that if you truly love God and your neighbor, all the Ten Commandments are covered. If you truly keep the greatest commandment of love, you don't have to worry about breaking one of the top ten. The commandment of love is the umbrella commandment that includes all of the rest of them. Let me illustrate.

1. If I truly love God, I will have no other gods besides him, that is, I will not let anything else take the place of God in my life.
2. If I truly love God, I will not worship any kind of image or material object.
3. If I truly love God, I will not use his name in vain, that is, in a profane or careless manner.
4. If I truly love God, I will remember the Lord's day and try to go to the house of God to worship.
5. If I truly love my father and mother, I will honor them.
6. If I truly love humanity, I will not kill.
7. If I truly love my spouse, I will not commit adultery.
8. If I truly love my neighbors, I will not steal from them.
9. If I truly love my neighbors, I will not tell lies about them, start false rumors, or give false testimony about them.
10. If I truly love my neighbors, I will not covet or lust after what is theirs.

So you see, Jesus' commandment to love God and neighbor is not only the greatest commandment in the Bible, but it is also the *universal* commandment; it covers all the other commandments and, if truly kept, fulfills the entire Law. As the apostle Paul puts it, "The whole law is fulfilled in one word, 'You shall love your neighbor as yourself'" (Gal. 5:14). And the reformer Martin Luther said, "Love God and do as you please." But oh how much hinges on the meaning of that one word, *love.*

So, lest we be naive and think it is easy to be a Christian, let us be forewarned that to be a Christian, a follower of Christ, is to love God and neighbor completely and sacrificially, even as Christ loved God and humanity. In the words of St. John of the Cross, "At the evening of our life we will be judged on love" (*The Sayings of Light and Love*), the one great commandment of Christ.—Randy Hammer

SUNDAY, JULY 15, 2001
Lectionary Message

Topic: The Conspiracy of Kindness
Text: Luke 10:25–37
Other Readings: Amos 7:7–17; Ps. 82; Col. 1:1–14

Jesus was always asked questions and he always answered them in unforgettable ways. These questions seemed to be about two great issues. They were either entrance questions or ethics questions. They sought guidance either about how to enter the Kingdom of God or about how to live ethically inside that Kingdom. In Luke 10:25–37, Jesus may have given his most unforgettable answer to a Kingdom entrance question.

I. *Signposts to the Kingdom should be sought in the Scriptures.* In this passage, an expert in the first five books of the Bible, what the Hebrews called the Torah or Law, asked Jesus about how to inherit eternal life. Jesus assumed, as would his questioner, that such answers must be sought in Scripture. So the initial response of Jesus to the question was to ask the lawyer to give his own understanding from the books of Moses. The lawyer responded and gave the quality answer that to enter the Kingdom one must love the Lord and love one's neighbor.

II. *God's mission for humanity is that we return his love and that we love the people he has created.* The answers were from Deuteronomy 6:5 and Leviticus 19:18. The lawyer has interpreted these two commands as the hinges holding the two tablets of commandments together. We can love because God has first loved us. That love has been demonstrated historically through the sacrificial death of the Son of God for our sins (see 1 John 4:9).

The expression "inherit eternal life" suggests that one has been favored or found worthy to be included in the divine will and testament. The lawyer added a follow-up to his first question. Luke interpreted this second question as an attempt by the lawyer to validate in public his own worthiness. As the lawyer soon discovered, Jesus never validated self-righteousness. To the question, "Who is my neighbor?" Jesus answered with the story of the Good Samaritan. We might call this the story of the three little pilgrims.

III. *This powerful five-verse story reveals six meanings about love for a neighbor.*

(a) *Love for a neighbor means overlooking the justness of the consequences of someone's foolish behavior.* The road between Jerusalem and Jericho was notorious as the "boulevard of bandits." It was not to be traveled alone or at night. By doing so, had not the half-dead traveler received the reward of his own foolishness?

(b) *Love for a neighbor may mean putting yourself at personal risk.* Jesus' story makes no mention of anyone traveling with either the priest or the Levite. If they are traveling alone, will they not also risk personal injury if they stop to meet the injured man's needs?

(c) *Love for a neighbor means willingness to abandon personal plans to find time to meet that neighbor's needs.* The profession of the priest required him to lead Temple ritual according to specific times. If he stopped to show mercy, wouldn't he possibly be irresponsibly late in attending the ritual and worship? The profession of the Levite required him to maintain the physical plant of the Temple and to provide instrumental and vocal music for Temple worship. If he stopped to help, wouldn't he put himself in danger of receiving the wrath of the Temple choir members? Mercy is not always easy. Loving your neighbor is hard because usually we have more than one neighbor and never enough time.

(d) *Love for a neighbor means bringing to bear personal resources to the extent that the real need is met.* Love is expensive. Kindness is kindness when it goes all the way to restoring the safety of the neighbor. The third little pilgrim, the Samaritan, applied compassion, antiseptic wine, and healing oil to the wounds of the injured traveler. He dismounted his donkey to allow the wounded to ride. He paid two days' wages in advance rent to allow the hurt man to recover strength and then guaranteed repayment if additional days of recuperation were needed. This man neglected his travel schedule and ransacked his own expense account to turn a wounded, foolish stranger into a friend and neighbor.

(e) *Love means turning strangers into neighbors by putting their needs above satisfaction of religious ritual, if necessary.* Jesus had already sent more than one such law expert in the Scripture back to Sabbath school with the command, "Go and learn what this means, 'I desire mercy more than sacrifice'" (see Matt.12:7; Hos. 6:6). Care for people and participation in church services are not necessarily in direct competition. But when they are, God himself would rather we stop the ritual to attend to the relationship.

(f) *Love for the neighbor means that we refuse to exclude anyone from our circle of neighborly love.* Who would ask the question, "Who is my neighbor?" other than a person who wants to have as few neighbors as possible? God wants as many neighbors as possible. Jesus has come down from the heavenly Jerusalem to meet the needs of the estranged and wounded so that they become God's friends and neighbors and children.

Why can't we all get just get along? Because we constantly seek to make our neighborhoods smaller by excluding all kinds of people. But not Jesus! Despite the fresh insult received from a Samaritan village unwilling to grant Jesus and his disciples any hospitality, Jesus made a Samaritan the hero of his story. Jesus' backhanded point is that anyone, even Samaritans, can through kindness turn strangers into neighbors. In many minds, Christians are the despised Samaritans of today's public forum. All that is expected of Christians are narrow-mindedness and judgmentalism. Kind service with no strings attached will cause people to revise their understanding of Christ and his followers. Will you become such a servant evangelist so that unbelievers might experience the love of Christ?—Rodrick K. Durst

ILLUSTRATIONS

DRAW HIM IN.   He drew a circle and drew me out. But love and I had the wit to win; we drew a circle and drew him in.[1]

WHAT THE DEAF CAN HEAR.   Kindness can be heard by the deaf, seen by the blind, and spoken by the dumb.[2]

SAMARITAN-STYLE EVANGELISM.   In the book *Conspiracy of Kindness*,[3] pastor Steve Sjogren defined a "high grace, low risk" approach to evangelism that he called a "conspiracy of kindness." This approach used free car washes, windshield cleaning, leaf raking, free coffee, Christmas gift wrapping, and other ministries of "spontaneous generosity" as practical demonstrations of God's love with no strings attached. Such deeds were often followed by the recipients' asking, "Why?" Gospel sharing then occurred in a natural way.

DEEDS.   Our deeds determine us as much as we determine our deeds.[4]—Rodrick K. Durst

---

[1] Paraphrase of Edwin Markhaur
[2] Paraphrase of C. N. Bovee
[3] Ann Arbor: Vine Books, 1993.
[4] George Eliot, *Adam Bede,* chap. 29.

SERMON SUGGESTIONS

Topic: Take Courage

TEXT: Isa. 40:1–11

(1) At last, God will show his power. (2) God's Word will accomplish its purpose. (3) God will deal with his people with great compassion and tenderness.

Topic: Why God Waits

TEXT: 2 Pet. 3:8–15a

(1) God has his own timetable. (2) God gives us space to repent.

CONGREGATIONAL MUSIC

1. "Jesu, Jesu, Fill Us with Your Love," Tom Colvin (1963)

   CHEREPONI, Ghana folk song; adapt. Tom Colvin (1963)

   After the reading of the Gospel lesson concerning the Good Samaritan (Luke 10:25–37), the singing of this African song of service would be appropriate. A light instrumental accompaniment would be appropriate as well.

2. "Living for Jesus a Life That Is True," Thomas O. Chisholm (1917)

   LIVING, C. Harold Lowden (1915)

   This song of devotion is a testimony of one who has responded by totally committed her life to Jesus. The singing of this hymn would be a suitable response to the Pauline prayerful exhortation of the Epistle lesson (Col. 1:1–14 NIV) that we "may live a life worthy of the Lord and may please him in every way, bearing fruit in every good work, growing in the knowledge of God."

3. "Where Charity and Love Prevail," Latin; trans. J. Clifford Evers

   CHESHIRE, Thomas Este, *The Whole Book of Psalms,* (1592)

   Reflecting the spirit and content of the great commandment to love God with all one's powers (Luke 10:27), this ancient song is a beautiful expression of that love as we work it out in forgiving and loving one another. This hymn offers a natural response to the reading of the Gospel lesson.

4. "I Have Come from the Darkness," Marian Wood Chaplin (1964)

   TO THE LIGHT, Marian Wood Chaplin (1964)

   This modern gospel song could be sung as a testimony to the reading of the Epistle (Col. 1:1–14), particularly as it relates to the last two verses of the lesson.—Hugh T. McElrath

WORSHIP AIDS

CALL TO WORSHIP.   "Let us draw near with a true heart in full assurance of faith, having our hearts sprinkled from an evil conscience and our bodies washed with pure water. Let us hold fast to the profession of our faith without wavering (for he is faithful as promised), and let us consider one another to provoke unto love and to good works" (Heb. 10:22–24).

INVOCATION.   Lord, thou hast withheld nothing we need and given us more than we could ever deserve; therefore we do not withhold our great praise of thee and we sing of thy salvation. Great thou art and greatly to be praised, O Lord of hosts.—E. Lee Phillips

OFFERTORY SENTENCE.   "Thou art worthy, O Lord, to receive glory and honor and power; for thou hast created all things, and for thy pleasure they are and were created (Rev. 4:11).

OFFERTORY PRAYER.   To thee, creator God, heavenly Father, we bring in worship and dedication a portion of the things that thou hast created and put in our care. Bless them that they may continue to fulfill thy purpose.

PRAYER.   We praise you, giver of every good and perfect gift, for the gift of your Word by which the worlds came into being, by which man was created, and by which life is nurtured and renewed. It is the Word of an amazing grace!

That in this expansive universe this planet and its peoples should be the recipients of an eternal love is more than we can fathom. We praise you for the beauty and wonder of nature everywhere about us. How fearfully and wonderfully we are made. For the amazing gift of personality with a uniqueness even to the tips of our fingers, we praise you. You call us to freedom—an awful freedom, an awe-full freedom—by which we are persons and not robots. You call us each by name—"John, I love *you* as though there were no other person in the world to love." Your Holy Spirit at work in us does not make carbon copies or rubber stamps of any of us but stirs up the creativity of your love bestowed upon us in your calling us out as persons.

So you call us to love one another, to celebrate the otherness of the other whoever the other may be—mate, daughter, son, grandchild, friend. Help us to love with such self-forgetfulness that we allow the other person to write the agenda for our meeting. To be there, all there, for someone else according to his or her need is the engagement to which you are calling us.

In these moments we pray for one another as brothers and sisters: for the ill, the bereaved, the infirm, the discouraged, the lonely, the homeless. With the Master we pray that we may be strong for the sake of others, but not so strong that we believe our own weakness and forget that life, all of life, is of your grace.

In this day of unprecedented opportunity, we pray for the faith, courage, and goodwill to relate to enemies as well as to friends, that the power of your grace given for the healing of the nations may hasten the day of world community.—John Thompson

SERMON
Topic: The Be-Glad Attitude
TEXT: Ps. 100; Phil. 4:1–7 CEV

Preacher and writer Lloyd John Ogilvie writes of a clergyman he knew who was twenty-five years old but looked sixty-five. His face was set. He could repeat the New Testament impeccably, but there was no joy or gladness in his life. All of us have known persons whose lives lacked joy and gladness. Yet the apostle Paul points out that gladness or joy should be the hallmark of our lives. "Always be glad because of the Lord!" Paul says. "I will say it again: Be glad" (Phil. 4:4 CEV). Rejoicing or gladness is to be the Christian's very lifestyle.

I. *The basis of our gladness is our relationship with God and God's people.* "Be glad that you belong to the Lord!" the Scripture exhorts (Phil. 3:1). Christians, of all people, should be the gladdest, most joyous, upbeat people. He created us in his own image and we belong to him. The Lord is good to us and his steadfast love and faithfulness will last forever. We have been given a glorious hope of new life with the Resurrection of Jesus from the dead. Christian joy or gladness is an internal reality that results from our relationship with God. "Joy is the echo of God's life within us" (Joseph Marmion).

Another source of gladness is our association with God's people. This is one reason the psalmist could proclaim, "I was glad when they said to me, 'Let us go to the house of the Lord'" (Ps. 122:1). There was real joy for the psalmist in gathering with God's people. A source of Paul's joy and gladness was his friendship with the Philippian Christians who had befriended him, supported him, labored with him, and prayed for him in his ministry. Remembering their kindness brought gladness to Paul's heart and life.

There are times when all of us may come to church not feeling very well. We may not be feeling well physically, or we may be down emotionally, or we may be out in left field spiritually. It would be easy at such times to stay home and not come to church at all. But at these times, when we come to church feeling down we may leave church feeling up because we have been in God's presence and have had fellowship with God's people. In the process we have been uplifted, encouraged, challenged, and affirmed. The experience has filled us with gladness.

II. *The nature of our gladness affects our relationships with others.* Our Christian gladness will lead us to be cooperative. There was a problem in the Philippian Church between two of the members, Euodia and Syntyche. We don't know anything about these two other than what is given in the letter. Evidently there had been a disagreement. Harsh words had been spoken. People may have taken sides. The incident was disrupting the harmony of the congregation. Paul said this is not the way it should be. Our Christian joy and gladness should change our disposition and demeanor and the way we interact with other people. "You belong to the Lord," Paul wrote to these two people, "so I beg you to stop arguing with each other" (4:2).

Christian gladness will lead us to be gentle and easygoing. "Always be gentle with others," Paul exhorts (4:5). You know how it is when we are in a bad, grouchy mood; we are prone to growl at everybody, to snap at anyone we meet, to be harsh with those who have done us nothing but good. Christian gladness will motivate us to do otherwise and be gentle and easygoing with others.

III. *The result of our gladness is a positive outlook on life.* A life of gladness is made possible by a worry-free attitude. "Don't worry about anything, but pray about everything," the apostle said (4:6). Here Paul echoes what Jesus says in Matthew: "Do not worry about your life" (Matt. 6:25). Paul was instructing the Philippian Christians to refrain from unnecessary worry, because worry obstructs inner wholeness and well-being and paralyzes creativity. Even while writing this letter to the church at Philippi from a prison cell floor, Paul could speak of rejoicing and gladness because he had learned how to make the best of a bad situation. Paul could be glad even while facing the prospect that his life might be sacrificed for the cause of Christ (2:17). We likewise can rejoice even when circumstances are difficult because we know that through God we can be victorious.

A life of gladness results in a *thankful* attitude. Paul expressed his thanks to God for the Philippian Christians every time he prayed (1:3). Their prayers for him in return filled his life with gladness (1:18–19). With thankful hearts we are to live our lives and offer up our prayers and requests to God.

Severe thunderstorms moved through town late one night. Bright streaks of lightning lit up the dark rooms of neighborhood houses, loud thunder rattled the windowpanes, and hard rain pelted the roof. But the interesting thing was the presence of songbirds that renewed their singing even before the storms had completely moved from the neighborhood. What a wonderful testimony! The birds can continue to sing even in the midst of the storm. Almost anyone can sing during the sunshine. The real test of our religious faith is if it enables us to continue to be glad and thankful and to sing during the storms.

A saintly woman who had suffered for many months from a painful illness related to her pastor, "I have such a lovely robin that sings outside my window. In the early mornings, as I lie here, he serenades me." As a smile shaped her lips she said, "I love him because he sings in the rain." So it can be with those whose lives are filled with Christian gladness. We can continue to sing even in the rain.

A life of gladness results in a *peaceful* attitude. "Because you belong to Christ Jesus," Paul says, "God will bless you with a peace that no one can completely understand. And this peace will control the way you think and feel" (4:7). There was an article in the newspaper about the Rev. Perry Biddle, a Presbyterian minister of Old Hickory, Tennessee. Rev. Biddle was left for dead after his car struck a roadside monument. His 1988 Volvo was demolished and the police pronounced him dead at the scene, but paramedics revived him on the way to the hospital. "The accident shook me loose," Rev. Biddle testified. "I've decided to have some fun." He says he survived his long ordeal by discovering "laughter therapy." "I'm a lot more jovial, tell more jokes, and don't worry about the future," he said. "For once I'm leaving my life to God." The message that Rev. Biddle has for people who suffer is this: "God is very real and is with you night and day. No matter how much pain I've had, God's presence has been overpowering. God never deserted me." God's presence with us provides peace in the midst of life's storms. This peace of God is so profound that it "surpasses all understanding" (4:7 NRSV).

In conclusion, let us ask ourselves, "Do I have the *be-glad attitude?* Is a be-glad attitude in my life evident to others through my cooperative demeanor and gentle, easygoing personality? Does a be-glad attitude manifest itself through a positive, worry-free, thankful, peaceful outlook on life? If I don't have a be-glad attitude, then why not? Is it because I have not opened myself up to God's presence in my life? Is it because I have not availed myself of the joy and gladness God wishes to impart?

As Johannes Gaertner notes in his book *Worldly Virtues*, "The nearer we are to God, the more we are filled with joy [and gladness]" (p. 23).—Randy Hammer

SUNDAY, JULY 22, 2001
Lectionary Message

Topic: Christianity in the Kitchen
TEXT: Luke 10:38–41
Other Readings: Amos 8:1–12; Ps. 52; Gal. 1:15–28

If Christianity can be practiced in the kitchen, then Christianity can be practiced anywhere. If it fails in the kitchen, it will fail elsewhere, too. Spliced between the parable of the Good Samaritan and the Lord's Prayer is a four-verse scene from the kitchen of Mary and Martha. This story occurs in everyone's home and is repeated many times in our own lives.

I. *Stupidity becomes sinful when we fail to learn from repeated failure.* Jesus knows that all of us are apt to commit the sin of stupidity, which is to repeat the same mistake without gaining any wisdom from the experience. In Luke's account, Mary and Martha have guests, including Jesus as the guest of honor. (Strangely, Lazarus, their brother, is not mentioned in this passage.)

II. *Little is learned from failure when we exaggerate the other person's fault.* It is very tempting to type each other. The Marys of the world love to sketch the Marthas as tyrannical perfectionists who believe that a maximum of panic and activity is the only true test of adequate preparation for guests. The Marthas love to sketch the Marys as impractical types who get drawn into a conversation and forget to keep glasses filled and biscuits warm. (Maybe Lazarus was hiding out in the closet!)

III. *High expectations require major preparation and assistance.* Martha's seven-course feast was about to become five courses short if Mary wasn't immediately forced into service. Yet Jesus had welcomed Mary to sit with the rest of the disciples.

IV. *Hospitality must be practiced because it is difficult.* Luke first honors Martha in this passage by naming her as the woman who "opened her house to him." She was "the woman of peace" for this village. She was the kind of person Jesus had described in verse 6 when he was teaching the disciples how to open up a new community to the gospel. However, Martha's helper had deserted the kitchen to learn at the Lord's feet. After all, how often would you have the opportunity to have the Rabbi in your own home? Mary sought first the King and not the carrots!

V. *Putting your guests at ease is the essence of hospitality.* While Mary was focused, Martha became distracted by all her unmet expectations of her preparations. She was stewing in her own stress! At that point, Martha made three rapid mistakes.

(a) *She abandoned her mission of hospitality.* She interrupted Jesus' teaching: "Lord, don't you care?"

(b) *She allowed circumstances and emotions to color her faith.* Our understanding of God's unfailing love is that he always cares! Perspective about circumstances needs to be revisited whenever we feel ourselves drifting into doubts about God's compassion for us. His love never fails. But Martha spoke before she thought, "Lord, don't you care?"

(c) *She tried to impose her will on the Lord's will.* "Lord, tell her to help me!" Now Martha moved beyond doubt about the constancy of God's compassion and into instructing the Lord how to improve his Kingdom! Martha desperately needed to learn how to talk with the Lord. She prayed, "My will be done," not "Thy will be done," and she thought, "My kingdom come."

VI. *Hospitality must be sized to the present needs of your guest.* "Martha, Martha, you are worried and upset about many things, but only one thing is needed." Having too many expectations causes major distress and results in family fights! The legendary hospitality of Martha of Bethany now failed in its main purpose, to make and keep the guest comfortable. Jesus' days were growing short. He wanted quiet conversation with his disciples. Martha's feast was an intrusion on what her guest really needed. Martha's usual poise should have enabled her to be flexible in realizing that food was secondary during this visit. Instead of seven courses, simple sandwiches would have worked. More than one commentator has suggested that Jesus was saying, "Martha, only one dish is needed, not seven!"

VII. *Hospitality becomes wise when it knows what each hour needs.*

(a) *The need of each hour is to live it in worship.* Worship is the Christian way of life. Worship is insistence on giving to God right "worthship" in each and every situation. Worship relieves stress as we recognize the unfailingness of his wisdom and compassion. Worship relieves stress because it reminds us that nothing is too hard for God and that we can do all things through Christ who strengthens us.

(b) *The need of the hour is to know we can trust in his providence for the hour.* There is but one thing he wills of us in any given hour. Worship tells us that God provides. Therefore I need only to do what I believe he wants in any given hour. The rest is his responsibility!

(c) *The need of the hour is to recognize the one need in this one hour.* It helps to ask, What is the one thing I could be doing right now that will really matter ten years from now? What is done for eternity lasts. What is done in obedience to the Word lasts. Mary had recognized the one real need of that hour and she was doing it. Martha was distracted precisely because she had not recognized or could not recognize the need of that one hour of Jesus' visit. She was stressed by what she perceived as multiple needs and she was unwilling to choose among them.

(d) *The need of the hour is then to work at that one need first until it is finished.* We must not let ourselves be distracted by secondary needs. Priority is the true practicality. Attending to first things first makes life purposeful and productive. Making the main thing the main thing makes the Master protective of our endeavor. "Mary has chosen well and it will not be taken from her."

VIII. *Conclusion.* If you would have Jesus' approval of your use of this hour, have you begun it with worship? Have you honored his worth and counted on his provision, wisdom, and compassion for the hour? Have you prayed, "Not my will be done but your will be done in my kitchen as it is in heaven?" Are you trusting his provision by practicing the practicality of prioritizing?—Rodrick K. Durst

ILLUSTRATIONS

SITTING AT HIS FEET.   The expression "sitting at his feet" is a Semetic idiom describing a person who has been formally accepted as the student of a teacher. Had Jesus formally identified that he had accepted Mary into his seminary? In Acts 4, Luke records the recognition received by those who sat at the feet of Jesus to learn. Common men and women became astonishing communicators because they had "been with Jesus" (see Acts 4:13). Jesus placed only one restriction on enrollees to discipleship. Gender, age, and ethnicity are not limits to learn from Jesus. Anyone may be a disciple if he is willing to learn. Jesus will not teach more than we are willing to obey.

THE REMAINS OF MARTHA'S HOUSE AND LAZARUS' TOMB.   The house of Martha was located in Bethany, two miles from Jerusalem on the eastern slope of the Mount of Olives. Visitors to Bethany today are shown the ruins of what are reputed to be the tomb from which Lazarus was raised from the dead, the twin-towered ruins of the house of Simon the leper where the feet of Jesus were anointed, and the ruins of the house in which Martha, Mary, and Lazarus are said to have lived.

MULTI-TASKING.   In computer language, Martha had opened too many programs and windows, and her attempts to multitask caused her computer to crash due to insufficient Mary!—Rodrick K. Durst

SERMON SUGGESTIONS

Topic: God in the Bible

The Bible presents God (1) as a teacher (Ps. 32:8), (2) as a partner (Prov. 3:6), (3) as our guide (Isa. 58:11), (4) as a Light (John 8:12).—Glenn Clark

Topic: A Blessed Touch

TEXT: Mark 5:21–43

(1) The Savior's touch of grace. (2) The sinner's touch of faith.

CONGREGATIONAL MUSIC

1. "Christ Is Made the Sure Foundation," seventh-century Latin; trans. J. M. Neale (1851)

    WESTMINSTER ABBEY, Henry Purcell (c. 1680)

    Relating to Christ, the Head of the Church (Col. 1:18), this majestic hymn could be used as a processional hymn to set the tone for the day's worship.

2. "Mighty Mortal, Boasting Evil," Helen Otte (1985)

    MADILL, Aubrey L. Butler (1971)

    The denunciatory mood of Psalm 52 is dramatically reflected in both this modern paraphrase and the tune by Aubrey Butler. The declamatory style of the first two stanzas could be moderated in the last stanza by a softer accompaniment and more gentle signing. This song could relate to both the Old Testament reading from the prophet Amos and Psalm 52.

3. "More About Jesus," Eliza E. Hewitt (1887)

    SWENEY, John R. Sweney (1887)

    This gospel song reflects the yearning of Mary for greater knowledge of Jesus and devotion to his will. It could therefore logically be sung after the reading of the Gospel lesson (Luke 10:38–42) as a shared expression of worship.

4. "Thou Art Worthy," Pauline Michael Mills (1963)

    WORTHY, Pauline Michael Mills (1963)

    This praise chorus gives us the reason for declaring God worthy of praise, the truth recorded in the lesson from Colossians 1:16. Because God has created all things for his pleasure, we can sing that he is worthy to receive glory, honor, and power.—Hugh T. McElrath

WORSHIP AIDS

CALL TO WORSHIP.   "I wait for the Lord, my soul doth wait, and in his Word do I hope" (Ps. 130:5).

INVOCATION.   Our Father, we come to this place from our often frantic activities, bent as we are to run ahead of you, sometimes ignoring your commandments, sometimes taking matters into our own hands that would be better left up to you. Quiet our racing pulse and restore our jaded spirit as we once again try to put our trust and hope in you.

OFFERTORY SENTENCE.   "I know thy works and thy labor and thy patience" (Rev. 22).

OFFERTORY PRAYER.   When we have labored on with patience, O God, the reward has come. The joy of honest toil and the products of what we have done have added to our sense of meaning and belonging. Grant that those who have no satisfying work or who can no longer work may not feel that life no longer has meaning or that they are now only in the way. Help them to know that you and we do not forget what they have done in the past, and to know that their presence among us is a precious gift of your providence.

PRAYER.   Patient God, we thank you for time, for our life together, for time over coffee, for our kids' time—listening to their music and talking—for lives intertwined through common tasks, for the inns and resting places of the human spirit, and for special people, special times, and holy places where we take a breather—a restaurant or coffee shop, a kitchen table, a corner at work.

Adorable God, we thank you for the liturgy of our common round, the shape of specialness gracing ordinary days, such as lilacs around a dilapidated home, an evening out, a weekend away, hunting or fishing, a ball game, needlework, a good book. We give you thanks for new faces; forbid that we should assume that they shall find something of worth and warm in us and ours. May we be among them as ones who serve. May we be of some use. We pray for people faithfully tending others, that they may find a pace they can hold, that they may endure, that they may laugh, that they may believe beyond the grave.—Peter Fribley

SERMON
Topic: Don't Quit
TEXT: Rev. 2:8–11

One of the most important questions we will ever answer about ourselves is this: How do we handle adversity? How do we handle situations in which our goals seem to be impossible and our very continuance untenable?

I. Consider the church in Smyrna. In reality this church had nothing going for it. John notes that it suffered from affliction and poverty (v. 9). *Affliction* (*thlipsis*) means pressure, opposition, distress from outward situations. The word is also used in situations where someone is tortured to death. *Poverty* (*ptocheia*) means destitution. The Christians in Smyrna were not just poor, they were on the bottom rung, bankrupt, in situations of starvation and deep deprivation.

Ironically these early believers were living in a city that was among the most beautiful and wealthiest in all of the Fertile Crescent. Smyrna enjoyed a reputation as the most faithful and loyal city of the Roman Empire.

Heads of households from all over this province were required to come annually and burn a pinch of incense on the altar to the godhead of Caesar. Representatives of the Roman Empire were present to witness this offering and to give the person a certificate indicating that they had performed their duty and worshipped Caesar as Lord. The presence of the temple became incredibly lucrative for the residents. People had to spend the night and eat, and while in Smyrna they might as well shop. It was something like having the Olympics year-round and every year. Most citizens performed their duty and received their certificate, and business went on as usual.

However, this was not so with the Christians. Knowing that to declare Caesar as Lord would be to renounce Jesus, they refused to make the offering. In following their consciences, they brought trouble upon themselves.

When John wrote this Word from our Lord, the church at Smyrna was suffering the daily physical abuse and even death of its members. The destitution of the Smyrna believers was due to their being excluded from the economic system because of their refusal to engage in emperor worship. As if all this were not enough, the Christians also suffered slander at the hands of some vengeful Jews. Convinced that Christianity was a heretical form of Judaism, the Jews in Smyrna were particularly vicious in their attacks.

Polycarp's reply is one of the most famous of all Christian martyrs: "Eighty and six years have I served Him, and He never did me wrong; and how can I now blaspheme my King that has saved me?" As the flames leaped up around his body, the bishop prayed, "I thank You that You have graciously thought me worthy of this day and of this hour, that I may receive a portion in the number of the martyrs, in the cup of Your Christ."

II. What about us? What keeps us holding on even in the face of death and destruction? How can we remain faithful in a world that is so unfaithful?

We begin with a command: "Do not be afraid of what you are about to suffer." What is the source of fear? Simply put, fear comes from looking at life and its challenges from our own perspective rather than through Christ. Our perspective is so limited, so narrow, that too often we cannot see the power of God at work in and through a given situation. We become concerned with issues of personal survival, safety, and security, and we fail to see the larger picture. Hear me carefully: these issues are valid concerns, but they are not to be all-consuming. As believers in Jesus Christ, we have, in the words of St. Paul, "died to self and risen to new life in Christ." Elsewhere Paul puts it this way: "Nevertheless, it is not I but Christ who lives in me." As the Smyrnaeans learned, so we must learn that there are larger issues than our personal safety and well-being. There is the issue of what our Lord wants to do in and through our lives.

III. As we lose our fear, we also need to focus on our goal—serving our Lord Jesus Christ. Paul writes of this in Philippians 3:13: "But one thing I do: Forgetting what is behind and straining toward what is ahead, I press on toward the goal to win the prize for which God has called me heavenward in Christ Jesus." As long as our eyes are on ourselves or our situation, we are incapable of fulfilling our calling. However, with our eyes on our Lord we can move steadily toward the goal he has for us.

What is it that God has called you to be and do? Educator? Lawyer? Doctor? Nurse? Businessperson? Accountant? Artist? Mechanic? Whatever it is, know that God has called you to be the best you can be with honesty and integrity and in so doing to bring glory and honor to the name of Jesus Christ. You may not achieve what you dream, but the impact you will have for our Lord will be far greater than you could have ever imagined.

True success is never easy, but it is always rewarding. The particular definition of success depends on our situation and God's calling, but it is always about being faithful and focusing on Christ and on what Christ wants to do in and through us.

IV. To persevere, we need to lose our fear, focus on our Lord, and know that there is a limit to the difficult circumstances in which we find ourselves. John tells those who are suffering, "You will suffer persecution for ten days." We are not sure exactly what symbolism the ten days has, but it seems to refer to a time of testing. (Daniel, in requesting not to eat the rich food of the Babylonian king Nebuchadnezzar, asked to be tested for ten days. The king's steward agreed and Daniel and his friends passed the test!) What is important for our purposes is that the persecution will not go on forever; there will be a limit at which God will stop it.

We need to hear this Word, do we not? In the middle of our suffering and trials, we need to hear that they will not last forever, for sometimes we think they will never end. Have you ever noticed that in times of deprivation and hardship Christians tend to focus so much more on heaven? This is not pie-in-the-sky religion but a deep understanding that one day the suffering will be over. African American spirituals display a deep longing for the Kingdom of God: "Swing Low, Sweet Chariot," "All God's Children Got Shoes," "There Is a Balm in Gilead," "Rock-a-My Soul in the Bosom of Abraham," and on and on. Or consider the old Southern Gospel song "I'll Fly Away":

> One bright morning when this life is over, I'll fly away,
> To a land on God's celestial shore, I'll fly away.

Or perhaps you remember,

> Will the circle be unbroken, by and by Lord, by and by,
> There's a better land awaiting, in the sky Lord, in the sky.

One of the reasons we hear so little about heaven is that we have it so good here we consider physical death loss rather than gain. When your difficulties mount up, remember there is a limit; they will not last forever.—Robert U. Ferguson

SUNDAY, JULY 29, 2001
Lectionary Message

Topic: Living to Pray
TEXT: Luke 11:1–13
Other Readings: Hos. 1:2–10; Ps. 85; Col. 2:6–15 (16–19)

Jesus marks his disciples as his disciples by the way he taught them to pray. When you heard a disciple of Jesus pray, you knew this disciple was trained to pray in a certain way and to do so effectively. We bear Christ's mark of ownership as we submit to him and pray as he instructed.

I. *Praise precedes petition.* Reverence comes before request. "Our Father" presumes a personal relationship with the Triune God through being in a Christ-disciplined community. "Our Father" positions the person and people in an attitude of obedience and dependence on God's care and providence.

Transition: Praise enables us to perceive providence rightly.

II. *Prayer integrates providence into practical living.* God's fatherly provision can and must be trusted for our daily needs. Trust for daily bread is an antidote for anxiety and sets the proper limits of our humanity. The Father serves up fresh provision and fresh mercies daily! As we trust him for daily bread, so the disciples trusted him for daily forgiveness. Forgiveness and repentance were ways of living for the disciples and the believing community.

Transition: Prayer grasps the shield of faith because evil is active in the present world.

III. *Prayer acknowledges our need for the Father's leadership in our decision making.* This petition paraphrases Psalm 23: "Lead us in paths of righteousness for your name's sake." It attends to the Pauline theology of temptation stated in 1 Corinthians 10:13. This petition also anticipates the Christology of temptation in Hebrews 4:15: "He was tempted in all points such as we are, yet he was without sin." Christ's temptation was greater than our own because we give in when he would not. Note that the three petitions in the disciples' prayer echo the three temptations Jesus faced in the wilderness. As he triumphed there, disciples will triumph through faith in him. We surrender to Christ because as a live-in Lord he imparts to us his victory over sin and the world and assures us of forgiveness when we fail.

Transition: The mystery of prayerlessness is answered best by Jesus' story of prayerfulness.

IV. *Prayerfulness is faithfulness.* Prayerlessness is faithlessness. In this quaint story, one neighbor shamelessly disrupted his neighbor's sleep to obtain three loaves to sustain his unanticipated guest. The story shows the effectiveness of appeal to a reluctant giver as an exaggerated contrast to the effectiveness of appeal to an ever-awake, generous heavenly Father.

Transition: Faithful prayer is the scriptural door upon which the asker should knock.

V. *Faithful prayer means finding the right intensity in prayer.* The three verbs in the admonition of Jesus—ask, seek, knock—are attached to three encouraging results: giving, finding, opening. Prayer takes on the look of a journey into a village of providence. Prayer begins humbly yet hopefully by asking for directions to the right "house of appeal." Direction is given. Based on those directions from Scripture or the leading of the Spirit, the proper street and address are sought. Upon arriving at the proper door of appeal, prayer then knocks with insistent trust in the Father's goodness and wisdom, and the door of that prayer's answer is opened.

Prayer is not wearing God down to do our will. Prayer is not overcoming God's reluctance to do something good for us. Prayer is overcoming our reluctance to submit to his timing, wisdom, and will. Real prayer is the willingness to accept God's answer, be it yes, no, or "wait awhile."

Transition: Jesus concluded this teaching on prayer by revealing why the Father answers prayer.

VI. *God the Father always answers prayer by giving himself to the one praying.* Prayer builds our relationship with God. Prayer draws us closer to God as we experience answers to prayer that are too precise to be mere coincidence. God hears! God acts! Good happens! As earthly parents use answers to their children's requests as a way to build trust and overcome distrust, so the heavenly Father uses answered prayer to encourage our trust in him. Every gift *we* give is an expression of ourselves. Jesus indicated that the true goodness of the Father is found in his giving of himself as the Spirit in answered prayer. Calling God "Abba, Father" is evidence that Christ has sent the Spirit of sonship and daughterhood into our lives (see Rom. 5:15). We have not really prayed until we sense the Spirit's stirring within as the answer.

VII. *Conclusion.* Have you been born of the Spirit as you have sought forgiveness of the Father in the name of Christ? Have you taken on the disciple's prayer life through praying the Lord's Prayer? Will you chose to have your life marked as a disciple of Christ by praying to live and living to pray as Christ taught?—Rodrick K. Durst

ILLUSTRATIONS

ABBA, FATHER. The word *father* translates a Greek word that in turn translates an Aramaic word that was probably straight from the lips of Jesus. Aramaic was the heart language of the Hebrew households. Some Aramaic words are still found in the New Testament, but none are more important than this one used by Jesus. *Abba* is the word used in ancient Hebrew households by a child to get the attention of his father. It is the equivalent of *Daddy* or *Papa* and it conveys an incredibly personal relationship between father and child, but not without appropriate respect. Every language has this kind of word and generally it is the first word a newborn learns. Little wonder that it is the first word Jesus wants one of his new disciples to learn (see Rom. 8:15; Gal. 4:6; Mark 14:36).

HINDRANCE TO PRAYER. Pride hinders prayer. The hero in the story of Jesus "shamelessly" knocks on his neighbor's door because of the need to provide hospitality. The English word *persistence* actually means shamelessness.

THE NECESSARY CROSS. The famous English historian Arnold Toynbee was bothered by what he called a "sour note" in the Lord's Prayer. "God cannot be both good and omnipotent at the same time. These are alternate conceptions of God's nature, and mutually exclusive. We have to choose between them." Becoming a disciple of Christ and praying his prayer is no absolute guarantee against hunger, sin, or evil. None are worthy to pray as a disciple who are also not willing to take up the cross. Without the cross there will be no crown. Without a death there would have been no Resurrection. The Resurrection is God's answer to the Toynbees who wish for a crown without the cross.

DIMENSIONS OF BLESSING. Clement of Alexandria, the second-century Church leader, preached, "Ask great things of God and he will give you the small ones as well."

FROM THE MOUTH OF JESUS. In 1963, the New Testament scholar Joachim Jeremais made a lecture tour of several Protestant seminaries in the United States. The title of those lectures was "The Central Message of the New Testament." Against the claim of some biblical scholars that scarcely anything historical is known about Jesus, Jeremias successfully demonstrated that the word *Abba*, for Father, could only have come from the mouth of Jesus himself. The use of *Abba* in prayer clearly marked the disciples of Jesus as persons who were keepers of the new covenant by faith in Christ and his cross.—Rodrick K. Durst

SERMON SUGGESTIONS

Topic: Hastening Lot
TEXT: Gen. 19:15
(1) The righteous need to be hastened. (2) The sinners need to be hastened.—Charles Hadden Spurgeon

Topic: What Made the Good Samaritan Good?
TEXT: Luke 10:25–37
(1) He did not use Scripture to justify hardness of heart. (2) He responded at once with true humaneness. (3) He looked to the victim's continuing welfare.

CONGREGATIONAL MUSIC

1. "Speak to My Heart," B. B. McKinney (1927)

HOLCOMB, B. B. McKinney (1927)

This gospel hymn prays for God's voice to be heard, indicating the attitude of the psalmist (Ps. 85:8) to listen for what the Lord will say. It could be sung before any of the scripture readings as a prayer for illumination.

2. "Revive Us Again," William P. Mackay (1863)

REVIVE US AGAIN, John J. Husband (c. 1815)

This gospel song, with its joyful praise for revival, could be sung as a response to the question of the psalmist (Ps. 85:6).

3. "Our Father," The Lord's Prayer

CONNOR, West Indian Spiritual (1945); adapt. John F. Wilson (1989)

This folk-song setting of the prayer Jesus taught his followers to pray could well follow the reading of the prayer in the Gospel lesson (Luke 11:1–13).

4. "I Lay My Sins on Jesus," Horatius Bonar (1843)

CALCUTTA, Anonymous; Sullivan's *Church Hymns* (1874)

A masterful hymn of confession of sin by the great Scottish hymnist Bonar, "I Lay My Sins on Jesus" acknowledges the truth (Col. 2:9) that the fullness of the Godhead dwells in Jesus (see the second stanza).—Hugh T. McElrath

WORSHIP AIDS

CALL TO WORSHIP.   "Wilt thou not revive us again that thy people may rejoice in thee? Show us thy mercy, O Lord, and grant us thy salvation" (Ps. 85:6–7).

INVOCATION.   As thou, Almighty God, did raise Jesus Christ thy Son from the dead, now quicken our spirits that we may be truly alive unto thee, worshiping thee in spirit and in truth.

OFFERTORY SENTENCE.   "What does a man profit if he shall gain the whole world and lose his own soul? Or what shall a man give in exchange for his soul?" (Matt. 16:26).

OFFERTORY PRAYER.   Give us increasing joy, O God, as we give our time, our thought, and our money to the causes of your Kingdom. May that joy lead us into new depths of experience of your grace.

PRAYER.   Architect and Creator of all that is, was, and shall be, we marvel at the order you brought out of chaos: the balance in nature, the orderly succession of the seasons, the positioning of the sun to bring light and life to this planet. Your grace has from the beginning underlain the foundations of the universe or none would live.

In you we do live and move and have our being—life is of your grace: each breath we breathe, every heartbeat. May we see life and all its relationships through the lens of your grace.

Help us to see that ultimately a society is judged not by its jurisprudence but by its compassion. As Jesus taught, nothing is so immoral as moral outrage that is hypocritical.

O God of grace, may we not become so obsessed with evil in high places that we do not see evil in all places. How can we pray except that we pray, "Deliver us from evil"?

How inclined we are to judge and condemn others to avoid the confession and repentance to which you call all of us. As a nation—as leaders and as a people—may we respond to your call to repentance—that we may discover a new birth of freedom in reconciliation, in compassion, in community.

May the Church's Word be a living Word—a Word with hands and feet intent on getting the message into the mess—to be the salt of the earth and the light of the world.

We marvel at your grace—redeeming, restoring, making all things new—the foundation of all new beginnings.

Awaken us, O God, to this new day of unprecedented opportunity. We have been marking time in the border country long enough. You are calling us to move forward to possess the land of your promise. We believe that there are resources among us that have never been mobilized, dreams that have never been dreamed, gifts that have never been awakened, commitments that have never been made.

For your grace, the grace of our Lord Jesus Christ, which has created the Church and this household of faith, we praise you. As your children, as brothers and sisters, we pray for one another—for the ill among us, we pray. Grant to them faith, love, and trust to be available to receive your healing grace. Where there are physical infirmities that must be lived with, we pray for wholeness of mind and spirit that transcends the brokenness of body. Where there is loneliness because of bereavement or aloneness, we pray for the strength of your love that never lets us go.

We pray through him in whom your grace is fully manifest and who is among us now as risen Lord.—John M. Thompson

SERMON
Topic: Ordinary People
TEXT: Matt. 21:1–11; Phil. 2:5–11

Who are the people God chooses to use? Most of us would answer: great people, gifted people, talented people, holy people. We would answer this way because the people in the Bible have been held up to us as icons of virtue, and we know we are anything but that. Sometimes we even start thinking that our ministers must be holy people who can do no wrong. However, if you are ever close to ministers, you'll soon lose that perspective. The thought remains that if God uses someone, that person must be radically different from the normal person; therefore God cannot use me. Nothing is further from the truth. God is in the business of using normal, ordinary people to do normal, ordinary things that become extraordinary in their impact through his love and power.

I. Look at this scene in our Gospel text: two unnamed disciples are sent to get a donkey from an unnamed owner. The faces in the crowd are of nameless, insignificant people who are just going about whatever it is they are supposed to be doing. If they are disciples, they are following Jesus, something they have done for up to three years, and other than a few miracles, nothing earth-shattering has occurred. The crowd—those anonymous souls going about their daily work of buying and selling—are doing whatever their livelihood requires.

A parade moves toward the people, so they stop for a few moments to see what the commotion is about. They ask who this is and the reply comes: "Jesus of Nazareth."

I can hear their thoughts: "Oh, the prophet from that backwater town—I wonder what he will do this trip." They were somewhat accustomed to kooks showing up every so often and proclaiming themselves the Messiah, so this is nothing new. They watch the parade pass by and then return to their work, not really knowing the significance of what has transpired.

Though it may bother us to think that our Lord was perceived as insignificant, is this not the way God works? Hasn't God always worked through insignificant people at insignificant places in insignificant times doing insignificant things to accomplish the significant?

Abram is out minding his own business and God comes and gets him to move to a new country, promising to make him the father of a great nation. And do not forget, Abram was seventy-five and childless.

Moses was a Jew but he was raised as an Egyptian in the Pharaoh's court. He was in exile on the back side of the Negev when God found him and overcame Moses' objections—and a people was set free from slavery.

David was a small shepherd boy on whom God laid his hand on for reasons known only to God—and a Kingdom flourished.

Mary was a teenage girl in Nazareth. An angel appeared, and her life was never the same.

Simon Peter, Andrew, James, and John were carrying on their fishing business—and Jesus walked by.

Paul was being religious and defending God—and Jesus showed up on the Damascus Road and Paul's life was turned around 180 degrees.

God always works through the insignificant and the unimportant—and in ways that are mysterious and wonderful.

II. Our lives are like that, are they not? We are neither the famous nor the important—at least as far as the world is concerned—yet Jesus continues to show up in our lives at the oddest moments to work his miracles of grace. Day by day, week after week, month after month, year after year, we come to this place and worship, pray, and listen to one another and the Spirit. Day after day, week after week, we go to work, do our jobs, go to our homes, spend time with our families, take our vacations, and literally spend our lives doing the ordinary. Every once in a while, every so often, something dramatic happens, but most of the time we live in the ordinary.

Look where people found Jesus in the New Testament: by the Sea of Galilee or walking along a dusty road, at a well at noontime in Samaria, or on a hillside teaching. We find Jesus most when we look for him in the everyday aspects of life. Someone has said that "the secret to life is doing the ordinary in an extraordinary way." I believe not only that this is true, but also that it is the essence of the gospel. When we know the love of God, when we have been touched and transformed at the core of our being, the ordinary becomes extraordinary.

How could Jesus have accepted those accolades that day while knowing that by Friday the hallelujahs would turn to "Crucify him"? Why did Jesus accept these praises and cheers? He knew he was coming to Jerusalem to die. He had made no secret of that to his disciples. Jesus was not one to seek public attention or acclaim. Could it be that he had accepted this because he knew of the "ordinariness" of life? Could it be that Jesus saw that this moment would be one that, after the Resurrection, the people would look back on and know that God had been with them?

A simple meal with family or friends becomes a special moment as we share together the stuff of our lives—and God is present. A gesture by a neighbor, a visit to a shut-in friend, a helping hand to one who needs it, and before we know it, God has been present and our lives are transformed. How did the disciples on the road to Emmaus put it when they realized they had been walking with the Risen Christ? "Did not our hearts burn within us?" Ordinary moments are made extraordinary by the presence of Christ.

IV. The secret to living an extraordinary life as an ordinary person is to look at life and moments in extraordinary ways. When we pause and look at our lives we can see moments that are pregnant with all sorts of possibilities that we overlooked when they occurred. It is in the eyes of the seer that the ordinary becomes the extraordinary as we perceive the presence of God.

There are two inherent dangers in being a person who wants to accomplish something: one is that we will think that the "big event" is what life is about, so we will ignore all else in trying to achieve that moment. When that moment has passed, we will realize how shallow is that approach to life. The other danger is that we will develop routine lives that have no hills or valleys; everything will be the same: flat. When we ignore the presence of God in the ordinary of life, that life will become flat, boring, and routine. The people who see things this way die at forty and are not buried until they are seventy-five.

In the passage from Philippians, Paul writes of the humility of Jesus. Humility comes not from a poor-me, down-in-the-mouth attitude but from an understanding that the God of the universe, the Holy One, loves me enough to be involved in my life. This fact ought not just bring us to our knees occasionally, but it ought to open our eyes to see the presence of Christ in our lives. Jesus knew what God was doing in and through him, so obedience to the Father was no problem; rather, it was an honor. When I see that God is working—even in ways I never dreamed—then I can and will have open eyes and a humble heart.—Robert U. Ferguson

SUNDAY, AUGUST 5, 2001
Lectionary Message

Topic: Enough
TEXT: Col. 3:1–11
Other Readings: Hos.11:1–11; Ps.107:1–9, 43; Luke 12:13–21

The situation in Colossae that prompted the letter we have in front of us was not all that different from the one in which we find ourselves today. Granted, there was no cyberspace, no broadcasting, no Hollywood—but as far as the older Christians were concerned, problems are problems. The fundamental problems between the older and younger generations of Christians have not changed as much as we often think. In Colossae, there was no TV, but there was plenty of concern about the influence of the Greco-Roman marketplace on younger Christians; no AIDS, but no shortage of life-threatening illnesses; no airstrikes on the nightly news, but plenty of experience with refugees; no AK-47s, but plenty of violent death. When you look at the first century and the twentieth century from the point of view of a parent or a pastor—or from the point of view of anybody who is concerned about the future of the Church—the similarities are more striking than the differences.

I. *The cosmopolitan question.* The Colossians, residents of a cosmopolitan city of diverse cultures, were attracted by some of their neighbors' beliefs. Perhaps they thought that access to God through Jesus Christ was too good to be true or too easy or not enough under their own control. Maybe they were just inquiring minds who wanted to know, wanted to be open to the light and knowledge being offered by first-century Marianne Williamses, Peter Druckers, and Werner Erhardts. Maybe they just thought they needed all the help they could get. For whatever reason, Iranian astrology, Phrygian nature worship, and especially the wisdom teachings of various mystery cults began to look good to them.

The questions faced by the Colossian believers have a familiar ring. Is Christ enough given our growing appreciation for the vastness of the cosmos and our own relative insignificance? Is Christ enough in light of the growing world around us and our desire to be inclusive, diverse, open, and tolerant of these new cultures? Is Christ enough given that others claim to have orderly systems and measurable steps that give them a handle on spiritual things? Is Christ enough in light of the belief of our neighbors in angels and astrology?

We might catch ourselves nodding sympathetically. These are our issues, too. Is Christ enough to meet the questions of a postmodern age about tolerance, diversity, and relativity? Is Christ attractive enough to stand up against the luminous video images of Monica, Tess, and Andrew? Is the ambiguous, ineffable, enigmatic Christ enough when others, doggone it, offer steps—"A Course in Miracles," tantric techniques, kabbalist disciplines?

II. *Colossians Answers.* Not surprisingly, Colossians thunders back a yes! It is an answer for the first millennium and for the third. To the moms and dads and pastors and teachers, to the young and old, the veteran Christians and the neophytes, "Christ is all in all," it says. Colossians is exceedingly confident. The words fly up from the page. The Christ you have—the Christ that is already in you—is enough. Enough—though the heavens above and the world around you seem to be exploding. Enough. Therefore (vv. 5–9) get rid of all that old junk that used to keep you at odds with each other—slander, abusive language, anger, lying. You are not divided anymore. You are all in this together. In fact, Christ is in it with you, and Christ is enough to hold it and you together.

III. *The Colossians Model.* The Colossians were looking for a way to control an out-of-control world. Who can blame them? The need to be protected from the largeness of life loomed at Colossae. It looms today in Columbus, Columbia, Colorado City, and Cologne. It looms. The cosmos is exploding for us, just as it was for the first-century Colossians. The horizons and boundaries that have marked the known world and made us feel secure have expanded and in some cases disappeared.

What is striking about the response to this situation in the letter to the Colossians is its restraint. We might expect such a letter to be filled with lists, charts, diagrams, and lesson plans. We might think it would be helpful to establish categories that make it clear what (and who) is in and out. It seems as though the Colossians need to be introduced to personality inventories and spiritual laws. If it were up to me, I would use every tool at my disposal to give those poor, rattled Christians some nailed-down truths, timeless principles, and practical rules. It is amazing that there is not more of that in this letter.

What there is in Colossians is exhortation. Colossians does not so much recommend as reassure, not so much prescribe as reframe, not so much advise the new and not-so-new Christians as remind them of what they already know to be true. As the new millennium begins, we could do worse than to follow Colossians' example. From age to age the Church has one thing to offer the next generation of Christians. It is the same thing Colossians offered to its original audience: the Christ who is enough. We offer the Christ who brought, brings, will bring, and is bringing into being the reality described in verse 11—a church where there is no longer Greek and Jew, insider and outsider, jock and Goth, people who have the right to approach the Divine Presence and people who don't, spiritual intelligentsia and spiritual trash. The Church of the Ages offers the Rock of Ages to every generation. In the Christ who is everything to everybody we find what we need to hold together and go on.—Jana Childers

ILLUSTRATIONS

GROPING MULTITUDES.   All around us today there are multitudes restless and dissatisfied, groping and hungry, and they do not know what they are groping for. That rebellious dissatisfaction is driving some of them, especially the younger ones, to experiment with all kinds of queer cults that are apt to puzzle and perhaps shock their elders. They do not know what that inner craving is and they would probably laugh if you suggested it had anything to do with traditional religion. But in its own strange way it is indeed a hunger for some real bread of life; it is the longing of the exile to get his head above the suffocating vapors of the world's materialism and to breathe his native air. It is the need for something to worship, someone to adore. It is precisely the psalmist's quest: "My heart and my flesh cry out for the living God!"—James S. Stewart[1]

THE POWER OF LIFE.   God's power for life rightly leaves us speechless. We can be speechless, like the Sadducees, and go back to plot how to stay in control one more day. Or we can be speechless in amazement, like David, able only to say, "thou, thou, thine," because we find no words for the new reality.

The power of life is not a religious fantasy. It is a fresh lease on keeping our baptism in the face of injustice and poverty and alienation. It affirms to us that God has not yet quit and God will have God's way. We are on our way with God, rejoicing, praising, surrendering, and obeying. We will then address this age with care and compassion, knowing that the age to come is quite safe in God's mercy.—Walter Brueggemann[2]

SERMON SUGGESTIONS

Topic: Even in Sardis
TEXT: Rev. 3:4
(1) It is possible to be true and faithful under the most discouraging circumstances. (2) Even in the worst condition there may be some redeeming features. (3) God never confounds the godly few with the ungodly many.—Joseph Parker

Topic: No Condemnation
TEXT: Rom. 8:1–8
(1) We stand guilty before God and powerless to change that. (2) God loves us: through Christ and his Spirit he frees us from guilt and empowers us to obey him.

---

[1] *King for Ever* (Nashville, Tenn.: Abingdon Press, 1975), p. 11.
[2] *The Threat of Life* (Minneapolis: Augsburg Fortress, 1996), p. 150.

CONGREGATIONAL MUSIC

1. "Jesus, Thou Joy of Loving Hearts," attr. to Bernard of Clairvaux; trans. Ray Palmer (1858)

QUEBEC, Henry Baker (1854)

Psalm 107:9 is a good verse to be considered a basis for this classic hymn of devotion. It affirms that Jesus satisfies the thirsty and fills the spiritually hungry with good things. Use this hymn to open this Sunday's worship.

2. "Holy God, We Praise Your Name," Te Deum; trans. 1853

GROSSER GOTT, *Katholisches Gesangbuch*, (1774)

"A Hymn of Glory We Sing," The Venerable Bede; trans. 1978

LASST UNS ERFREUEN, *Geistliche Kirchengesaenge*, (1623)

"Since we have been raised with Christ, we are to set our minds and hearts on things above" (Col. 3:1). These are two of many fine hymns that can help us do that.

3. "Redeemed, How I Love to Proclaim It," Fanny J. Crosby (1882)

ADA, A. L. Butler (1966)

A direct response to "Let the redeemed of the Lord say so!" (Ps. 107:2) is this fine gospel song by the queen of gospel writers, Fanny Crosby. It takes on even greater enthusiasm and urgency when sung to Butler's recent tune for it.

4. "What Wondrous Love Is This," Appalachian folk hymn (c. 1811)

WONDROUS LOVE, *Southern Harmony*, (1835)

The compassionate love of God for Israel set forth in Hosea 11 is echoed in this passionate yet reverent folk hymn of early America. It recalls that God's love for wayward Israel was extended by Christ's love for all the world.—Hugh T. McElrath

WORSHIP AIDS

CALL TO WORSHIP.   "O give thanks unto the Lord, for he is good: for his mercy endureth forever" (Ps. 107:1).

INVOCATION.   O Lord, our God, you have called us to be your people, a people to bring honor and glory to your holy name. You have put us forth into the world as your witnesses. Strengthen us now by your Spirit in our inner selves that we may be and become that special people who call others also to praise and serve you.

OFFERTORY SENTENCE.   "Bless the Lord, O my soul, and forget not all his benefits" (Ps. 103:2).

OFFERTORY PRAYER.   We wandered far, O Lord, but you came near. You delivered us in our time of trouble. You have given us good things to enjoy, which we do not deserve. Now we praise you, not only with our tongues but also with our gifts. Bless and use these offerings that your presence may be brought near to others in their need.

PRAYER.   Sometimes, Lord, it is hard to figure out situations in which we find ourselves. We turn to our knowledge and it is not big enough to give us adequate answers. We turn to the skills of others and find that we still are left without sufficient insight. Indeed, we try every avenue we know, as well as those suggested by others, only to discover that when everything from everywhere is added together, the mystery only deepens and new issues are raised that further frustrate and cause pain. This morning we asked that you be in our head and our understanding. Be in our eyes and in our looking. Be in our mouths and in our speaking. Be in our hearts and in our thinking. Fill us with your truth and give us sufficient abilities to deal with the multitude of issues we must meet in the world as well as the individual struggles that are ours alone to manage.

As only you can, show us the doors of opportunity through which you would have us pass. Lead us to the people you would have us especially serve. Bring us to the purpose which you have designed for us.

In the wake of our passing, may hearts be warmed with the wonder of goodness. May eyes be opened to the glory of eternal truth. May souls be quickened with the impact of eternity. May loneliness be erased in the warmth of divine friendship. May Christ be made real and personal for others as he is born with power in us today.

O Father, we need a new breaking in of your Spirit among us. We cannot generate some substitute for the real thing, nor would we dare try. Yet we do long for renewed strength and power to continue the journey of faith—power that is yours alone to bestow. So, here together we expectantly wait like little children, standing on tiptoe, peering into the moment, anticipating with joy the wonder that will be ours when we experience the gift of your grace and presence in our midst. May it happen, even now, as we wait and worship in Jesus' name.—Henry Fields

SERMON
Topic: Disciples in Difficult Places
TEXT: Phil. 4:22

Although it is always difficult to be a disciple, it is never impossible. Regardless of your age, your geographical location, or your vocation, you can live for Jesus. Even in the hardest of places and in the most unlikely surroundings, people have—and still do—live for him.

I. One verse that assures us of this was written by the apostle Paul to the Philippian Christians. He wrote, "All the saints salute you, chiefly they that are of Caesar's household" (4:22).

(a) These saints were living in an unusual place. They were saints in Caesar's "household." The word *household* refers to either a family or a home. In all probability they were members of his civil service or of his guard, or they were slaves who served in his palace.

Can you imagine a harder place to be a saint than in Caesar's household? To live for Christ under the nose of this cruel and despicable man who hated Christianity must have been extremely difficult. Yet the apostle Paul sends this greeting from some Christians who were doing just that.

(b) There is a message in this for you and for me. It is this: If one can be a disciple in Caesar's household, one can be a disciple anywhere. If it was possible to be a Christian in that place, then it is possible to be a Christian anyplace.

There are at least three places where it is especially difficult to be a disciple today. I want us to look at those places with the understanding that if a person could be a disciple in Caesar's household, then we can be disciples in these places also. The three places where it is hard to live for Christ today are in the schools we attend, in the social circles in which we move, and in the businesses where we work.

II. It is hard for young people to live for Christ today. We are living in a time of unprecedented moral confusion. The prevailing moral philosophy in today's America is, "If it feels good, do it."

(a) People have always violated moral standards. But for the first time in the history of the world, many people are not even sure that there is such a thing as an absolute moral standard. Add to the moral confusion of our age excessive freedom and the problem is volatile.

(b) I am persuaded that it is harder to live for Jesus in the schools and universities today than it has ever been in the history of the world. But as difficult as it is, it is not impossible. If there could be saints in Caesar's household, there can be saints in our schools.

Yet there is a price to be paid. It requires a deep commitment to Jesus Christ and his Word. We cannot survive the pressures of today without being anchored in him.

Absolute freedom is absolute nonsense. It leads to complete frustration and emptiness. It is only as we attach our lives to Jesus that we can ever fulfill our intended purpose. It is only through commitment to him that our lives can produce the beautiful melody that God wants to come from them.

III. The social circles in which we move are also hard places to be a disciple. Young people are not the only ones who face social pressures. Adults also know what it is to be tempted to conform and compromise—to go along in order to get along.

(a) Someone has said that every person is born an original and dies a copy. Life is often a gradual process of whittling away our distinctiveness until we are all alike.

Many Christians today are like the chameleon. The chameleon's ability to change its color to match its environment is part of its defense mechanism.

There are a lot of chameleon Christians today. They are so busy trying to conform to the world around them that they live in nervous exhaustion. They have forgotten the admonition of the apostle Paul that we are not to be conformed to this world (see Rom. 12:1–2).

(b) While it is hard to live for Jesus in the social swirls of our communities, it is not impossible. Listen! If there could be saints in Caesar's household, there can be saints at the country club. In fact, if you cannot live for Jesus at the country club, then you need to get out. Your first calling is to be a saint. It is to live for Jesus Christ.

IV. Another place where it is hard to be a disciple today is in the business world. It is hard to live for Christ there because many people check their Christianity at the door when they go to work.

(a) Many people believe that Christianity should be confined to the sanctuary and practiced most consistently by those in clerical collars or choir robes. The truth of the matter, however, is that it was meant for the smoke-filled office, the mechanic's shop, the construction site, the cab of an eighteen-wheeler, and the executive suite. In fact, Christianity looks best when it is dressed in blue denims, a mechanic's overalls, a housewife's apron, or the executive's business suit.

(b) If there could be saints in Caesar's household, then a person can be a Christian where you work. If these saints could live for Jesus Christ in the hardest of all places, surely you can live for Jesus Christ at your place of employment. It is simply a matter of commitment. If you want to live for Jesus, then you can.

There is no higher calling than to devote your life to the spread of God's Word. If you will see your work in that light, it will transform both you and your work. Your work will no longer be a drudgery. You will suddenly become concerned about both the quality and the quantity of your work. Even the way you do your work will be a means of preaching God's Word to those who do not believe it or practice it.

V. We can live for Christ in those hard places. The hard places, in fact, have always been the places where the most effective witness for Jesus Christ has been carried out.

With which Gospel do you think your friends at school, in your social circles, and at your place of business are most familiar?

Are they closer to the Kingdom of God—or farther from it—because of the Gospel According to You?—Gary C. Redding

SUNDAY, AUGUST 12, 2001
Lectionary Message

Topic: High Fidelity
TEXT: Luke 12:32–40
Other Readings: Isa. 1:1, 10–20; Ps. 50:1–8, 22–23; Hab. 11:1–3, 8–16

Just two verses into today's passage, Luke turns a rather large corner. He has been recounting Jesus' teaching on material possessions when he shifts (v. 35) to the subject of the coming of the Son of Man and to three small stories about watchful servants and householders. Is there a logical connection between Jesus' teaching on material possessions and his stories on watchfulness? One possibility is that the pieces of today's passage are unified by a concern for fidelity in discipleship. The first three verses of today's text show one kind of fidelity—a faithfulness in resisting the lure of the material world; the second section of the passage (vv. 35–38) shows what fidelity looks like in the face of delay; and the third section (vv. 39–40) show what fidelity looks like when taken by surprise.

I. *Fidelity and affluenza.* What does it mean to be a faithful disciple of Jesus Christ in a culture where greed is good? Where the palliative of choice is "retail therapy"? Where all the real successes are about money and the worse kind of failure is not any kind of moral dissolution but financial irresponsibility? What does it take for a contemporary follower of Jesus to break free from the thrall of things? Many a preacher has answered these questions by challenging the congregation to reexamine its priorities. The theory is that if we can get our priorities straight, if we can think intelligently about how we should live our lives, then our hearts (and our actions) will follow. But Jesus knows that usually the heart does not in fact follow the head. Our hearts are quite often not where our priorities are. Our hearts are where our money is. Our hearts follow treasure, not the other way around. Verse 34 does not say, "Where your heart is, there will your treasure be." It says, "Where your treasure is, there will your heart be."

The problem will not be fixed by remembering that our hearts should be set on the Kingdom. The problem is that we are spending our money in the wrong places. Verse 34 says that how you manage your money determines where your heart is. The heart of the person whose treasure rests on the rise and fall of the Dow Jones is located on Wall Street. The heart of the person who invests in the Kingdom of God lives on Kingdom Boulevard. That person is Jesus' idea of a faithful follower. Persons like that have more interesting things to do with their money than buy mothballs and Rustoleum. You want to be free from the anxiety that material possessions bring into a person's life? Jesus recommends that you start spending your money on the Kingdom.

II. *Fidelity's work ethic.* Faithful servants of the Son of Man are known not only by their freedom from anxiety but also by the length of their sleeves. Faithful servants are ones whose sleeves are always pushed up. They are the kind of people whose powder is always dry, whose bags are always packed, whose pilot light is always lit. Their toes and knuckles are on the starting line waiting for the pistol. So eager are they to be onto the next piece of the Kingdom's business that they never get around to unrolling their cuffs. They rarely light on a chair, much less settle in for a nap between jobs.

Faithful servants are more than ready. They are the kind of people who not only leave the porch light on for you but also meet you at the door with warm milk, and when you say that your bride has a craving for anchovy ice cream, they ask whether she would prefer a cup or a cone. Contingencies are covered. Backup supplies are laid in. They are the kind of people who out–Boy Scout the Boy Scouts when it comes to being prepared.

Faithful servants are more than alert. They live their lives on tiptoe, with their ears trained for the call. Before the phone can ring a second time, they answer. Before you can get the words, "Would you please come here, I need you?" out of your mouth, they appear. Before the ink is dry on the announcement in the church bulletin, they appear at the office door. Before the recruitment dinner is scheduled, they have volunteered. Theirs is the first signature on the line for the crop walk, the blood drive, and the bake sale.

Faithful servants are more than patient. No matter how long or how often God keeps them waiting, they do not give up on doing God's business. That's the kind of people they are: ready to work and alert, prepared and patient.

III. *Fidelity and surprises.* Not only do the faithful followers Jesus envisions manage financial resources and personal energies around a Kingdom focus, but they are also people who live with a sense of urgency. In fact, the kind of fidelity Jesus has in mind for his followers involves being able to live constantly with a sense of vigilance. In addition to resisting the temptations of materialism and discouragement, Luke seems to be telling us, Jesus' faithful disciples will also be able to resist complacency. We should not be surprised by the way Luke has arranged his notes on Jesus' lectures. He has been working on this picture of high-fidelity discipleship for several chapters. Who are Jesus' faithful followers? Those who trust in God, conquer hypocrisy, pray constantly, handle resources faithfully, and live with their eyes and ears tuned to the Kingdom.—Jana Childers

ILLUSTRATIONS

THE BURNING HEART.   It is urgent that we should have a religion with the animation and the verve which will fight for the Christian view of life, and fan the Divine spark in human clay into a flame of self-surrender and service. The burning heart makes a victorious influence in evangelizing a world gone wrong.

This glow, this shining quality, need not be confined to a very few. The most commonplace nature, the most ordinary person can become interesting, lovable, vivid with a dash of romance, if lit by the fire of Christ. Religious passion brings splendor of spirit. A piece of iron is dull and plain, but make it red-hot and it glows with all the colors of the rainbow—scarlet and gold, purple, green and blue. There is a shining transfiguration of the pedestrian material through the fire in its heart. To be kindled by Christ is to acquire a colorful personality, with the ruddy hue of His flame.

The burning heart is the great essential and Christ offers it to you, presses it upon you. Take it now, that you may love as He has loved, that you may have the passionate heart of service and be a cheerful blaze at which others will warm their hands and their hearts in a chilling time. Religious passion is required to make a more Christian future for humanity.—Arthur A. Cowan[3]

COMPENSATION.   A young bride joined her husband at an army base on the edge of the desert where life seemed primitive. Living in a dilapidated one-room apartment near an Indian village, the desert heat became almost unbearable, the windblown sands constant, the days dreary. When her husband was ordered farther into the desert on maneuvers, that young bride wrote "Mama" she couldn't take any more and was returning home. Wiser than most, her Mother quickly replied:

> "Two men looked out from prison bars.
> One saw mud, the other saw the stars."—G. Othell Hand[4]

SERMON SUGGESTIONS

Topic: Now Life Has Meaning
TEXT: Mark 14:3–9
Loss of meaning has become our pervasive malady. Christ puts meaning back. (1) He restores meaning in the face of all that defeats personhood. (2) He restores meaning in the face of loveliness. (3) He restores meaning in the face of cynicism.—Merrill R. Abbey

Topic: God's Awesome Challenge
TEXT: Matt. 28:18–20
(1) His power. (2) His commission. (3) His world. (4) His teachings. (5) His presence.—Harrold C. Bennett.

CONGREGATIONAL MUSIC
1. "For All the Saints," William W. How (1864)
   SINE NOMINEE, Ralph V. Williams (1906)
   This great hymn in remembrance of saints such as Abraham would be appropriate accompaniment to any reading from the great "by faith" chapter: Hebrews 11.
2. "Come, Let Us Reason," Ken Medema (1971)
   COME LET US REASON, Ken Medema (1986)
   This contemporary scripture chorus takes its text directly from Isaiah 1:18 and thus could be used to introduce or conclude the Old Testament reading from the prophet Isaiah.
3. "Have No Fear, Little Flock," Marjorie Jilson (1972)
   LITTLE FLOCK, Heinz Werner Zimmerman (1971); arr. by W. J. Reynolds

---

[3] *Bright Is the Shaken Torch* (Edinburgh: T. & T. Clark, 1950), pp. 91–92.
[4] *It's Easier to Win* (Columbus, Ga.: American Family Life Assurance Company of Columbus, 1974), Section 18.

This modern minihymn is based on the gracious saying of Jesus in Luke 12:32, and the four stanzas are a commentary on that saying. These comforting and invigorating thoughts are enhanced by the sprightly melody of the contemporary German church musician Heinz Werner Zimmerman.

4. "The Mighty God and Sovereign Lord," Psalter (1912) rev.

ST. PETERSBURG, Dimitri S. Bortnianski (1825)

This paraphrase of Psalm 50 could be sung in lieu of this Sunday's Psalter reading. The first two stanzas and the last stanza parallel the selected verses of the reading.—Hugh T. McElrath

WORSHIP AIDS

CALL TO WORSHIP. "He honors me who offers a sacrifice of thanksgiving, and to him who follows my way I shall show the salvation of God" (Ps. 50:23 REB).

INVOCATION. Almighty God, our Father, who art holy, who looks upon us, we come to thee because thou art holy, not because we are holy, and because we would be holy. Pity us, we beseech thee, with the influence of thy salvation. O God, restore unto us the joy of thine own holiness.—Frank W. Gunsaulus

OFFERTORY SENTENCE. "For all the law is fulfilled in one word, even in this: Thou shalt love thy neighbor as thyself" (Gal. 5:14).

OFFERTORY PRAYER. Our Father, we would honor you in honoring those who serve in your name. By our tithes and offerings we support and strengthen the work of our pastors, our missionaries, our denominational workers, our local church staff, and others worthily employed in your Kingdom. Help us to support and strengthen them also by our mouths.

PRAYER. O God, Creator of the universe and our Father, your greatness overwhelms us. We press to the outer limits of human knowledge and at last we stand before you alone. Before the mountains were brought forth and before you had formed the earth and the world, even from everlasting to everlasting, you are God. We profess to know nothing of you but that which you have revealed. We trace your works in the things you have made and we stand amazed before your wisdom and your power. We see in the manifold works of your providence, espe-cially in the gift of your Son, our Lord and Savior, your righteousness and your loving-kind-ness. Yet you have hidden so much from our sight and have challenged our hearts with so many mysteries that we must walk by faith and not by sight. When we cannot understand, help us to trust. When we cannot feel, help us to go on believing. And grant that our wilder-ness wanderings may at last be rewarded with new strength of character and greater ability to bless others with the very graces that we ourselves have received from you.—James W. Cox

SERMON
Topic: Why We Work
TEXT: Col. 3:23

In this message I want to consider a small but worthwhile question about work: Why? Why do we work? I believe that if we all clearly understood why we work and if we were all working for a good reason, there would be a genuine improvement in the quality of life in North America.

I. Have you ever asked yourself why you work? Maybe you work just to get a paycheck along with other benefits, such as a pension, vacations, and hospitalization insurance. If it were not for these, would you walk away from your job tomorrow? And when you are old enough to retire, are you going to quit your job with great joy and relief?

(a) I have a feeling you would agree with me that one of the reasons we're in trouble these days is that many people are working only for money—nothing more. As a result, some medical doctors are doing a marginal job, some teachers are doing a lot of damage to our children, some preachers are dishonoring the name of Christ, and some assembly-line workers are turning out products that have to be taken back for repair the day after you buy them.

(b) But the problem is not just that some of the results of work are shoddy and not up to par. What's worse, and even tragic, is that when people don't know why they are working, they lose one of the major joys that human beings can have. Doing work that one feels is significant and important is one of the greatest privileges a human being can have. When a majority of a nation's workforce works only for money and for little else, life in that nation turns dismal.

(c) In dealing with issues like this, we are actually entering the area of religion. Often we do not realize that religion is concerned with mundane, workaday matters. Some religion, of course, has nothing at all to do with ordinary work because it is totally otherworldly, encouraging people to separate themselves from the world of work. But as soon as anyone becomes familiar with the Bible, he or she discovers that the Christian faith has a great deal to do with work.

II. One of the most attractive elements of the Christian faith is that it turns the workplace into a place of worship. In this regard I want to read some sentences from Colossians 3 that were originally addressed to workers in the first century.

(a) These workers, I must say, were actually slaves. Now, before we wonder how something written long ago to slaves could possibly be useful for us today, we must remember that slaves carried out many of the same tasks that our workforce today performs. The Bible, in addressing slaves, is not condoning slavery as such but is simply taking that existing social situation and speaking directly to people who were involved in it.

(b) What the Bible says here in Colossians 3 to the slaves of the first century is also very appropriate for working people today. If slaves were instructed to think of their work as serving Christ, people who are free workers should most certainly consider their work a service to the Lord.

What Colossians 3 says to us is liberating and revolutionary. Viewing ourselves in our work as serving Christ, who is our Master in heaven—this idea jars us. Does this include ordinary work, like driving a truck, building a house, or working at a computer terminal for hours on end? Yes, it does; this principle applies to ordinary, everyday work. But is Christ really interested in our ordinary work? Yes, he most certainly is.

The Bible says that the God who exists has revealed himself fully in the person of Jesus Christ, and this Jesus is so interested in me that he wants me to think of all the work I do as something I do for him.

(c) When this message first came to those first-century slaves, it changed everything for them. Their bosses remained important, but they could now look past their bosses to Jesus

Christ the Lord. When they had a job that was not particularly pleasant, they could do it well because they knew that in doing so they were pleasing the Lord Jesus Christ. You see, Christianity is a force that always frees slaves. These slaves were invited to free themselves from the narrow service they had been giving their masters. They were encouraged to work hard and to view their work as done for God himself.

III. The Bible's message about work, which freed slaves in the first century, can still bring freedom to workers today who believe the Bible and want to serve Jesus Christ.

(a) People who believe in Jesus Christ and who are part of the workforce would have an unusual answer if someone were to ask them, "Why are you working?" They would say, "I am doing this because Jesus wants me to do it. I am doing it for him. I am doing it as well as I can because I don't want to present inferior work to Jesus. Christ has saved me, and he wants me to do everything, even my work, for his glory."

(b) I realize this sounds very different from what we usually hear. But believe me, when you take the entire Bible's message, this is where you come out. Work is one of the greatest goods in the world. The God who is at the center of Christianity is a working God. On the sixth day of his creation work, God made our first parents and put them in charge of the rest of his creation; he gave to people the responsibility of working and taking care of the Earth.

(c) The Bible proclaims a gospel for the workers of the world. Working people, unite around the Bible and discover that your work is as holy as the sacrament of baptism. Your work is significant as the very plan of the Almighty God. Work is good and beautiful. Our work is the best gift we can offer to God, our Creator.

IV. Take a look at your life and ask yourself if you are involved in work that you can offer to Christ. Of course, before you can do that you have to take a look at Jesus Christ himself. Maybe you have never believed in him. If so, what I have been talking about has probably sounded pretty ridiculous to you.

(a) Do you understand that Jesus Christ is the Son of the living God and that he has died on the cross to pay for human sin? Do you realize that if you believed in Jesus Christ and threw yourself on him fully he would save you and bring you to glory when you die? Do you know that when you believe in Jesus Christ he will send his Holy Spirit into your life and change you through and through? He will make your life beautiful and meaningful as never before.

(b) God is interested in your work. He wants you to ask why you do what you do. God wants you to turn to his Son, Jesus Christ, surrendering to him completely so that your life will be changed for the good. This change will surely involve your work, too.—Joel Nederhood

SUNDAY, AUGUST 19, 2001
Lectionary Message

Topic: Moment of Truth
TEXT: Luke 12:49–56
Other Readings: Isa. 5:1–7; Ps. 80:1–2, 8–19; Heb. 11:1–3, 8–16

If there is any time of year that seems to be made for lolling, it is the dog days of August. Just when we are making plans for one last long weekend, shaking our heads over the vacation we didn't get enough of, envisioning a little hammock time, and hoping to wring out of the summer one more precious moment of peace, the Lectionary serves up a moment of truth.

It is not as if Luke has nothing to offer on the subject of peace. The word occurs in strategically important places all through his gospel. It is promised at Jesus' birth (2:14), pronounced over the woman who bathed Jesus' feet with her tears (7:50), bestowed upon the woman with a hemorrhage (8:48), and given to the seventy to share (10:5). It occurs also in two passages that follow today's text: the word is on the lips of those who cheer Jesus' entrance into Jerusalem (19:38) and in the last few verses of the book it is the first word the resurrected Christ says to his disciples (24:36). Peace is hardly an incidental theme in the book of Luke. Why then, in today's text, does Jesus say so boldly, "Oh, so you think I have come to bring peace, do you? Hardly. I have come to bring division."

I. *Jesus is frustrated.* Doesn't he say in verses 49–50 that he is filled with longing? He is chomping at the bit, leaning forward into the not yet, anxious to move on. He is constrained, if we take the connotation of the Greek word into account. Like Jeremiah, he has God shut up in his bones like fire (Jer. 20:9) and he is weary from trying to hold it all in. He is kicking against the restraints. Jesus is frustrated. Perhaps he is indulging in a little hyperbole here.

While it is tempting to soften the blow of Jesus' words by making excuses—it was a hot day, the crowd was being deliberately obtuse, he was hungry, the strain of the wait was getting to him—it is not likely that Luke recorded sayings he did not mean for us to take seriously. The fact is that although peace was the anthem the angels sang over Bethlehem and the song on the lips of Jerusalem, division was a result of Jesus' ministry. Ever since the moment of his coming, the world has been divided into two kinds of people: those who are honest about reading the signs and facing up to them and those who pretend that they cannot see what is as plain as the nose on your face. Apparently there were a lot of the latter in the crowd that day. No wonder Jesus was frustrated. No wonder he called them hypocrites. That's a pretty mild word for people who refuse to admit that they know who Jesus is.

II. *Jesus creates crisis.* Of course the crises Jesus created had little or nothing to do with the fact that during the few moments this text describes he was frustrated. The crisis Jesus created is the kind that could be created by a sleeping baby, a man praying quietly in a park at night, a criminal who is silent in the dock. It could be and was and is. The kind of crisis Jesus created he created with his coming into the world—with his person, his teaching, and his work; with his death and Resurrection. The kind of crisis Jesus created is a moment-of-truth kind of crisis and it is a crisis that faces us all.

"Well," many people say, "it's not so important what you believe as that you believe." To them Luke says, "You have not faced the crisis."

"Oh," some folks say, "every world religion has something important to teach us about peace."

"Yes," Luke answers, "but you have not dealt with the crisis."

"Well," we may say, "I am happy to admit that Jesus is the Son of God."

"Good," Luke responds, "but you have still not met the crisis."

"All right," we may eventually say, "some of his teachings seem a little demanding." Luke remains silent. "Okay," we say, "I repent. I choose him. I want to go his way, not that other way."

"Ah," the cloud of witnesses and the heavenly host join the evangelist. "The moment of truth!"

III. *Jesus brings peace.* Although Jesus is the one who occasions decision, who causes division, and who creates crisis, in Luke he is also the one who knows the things that make for peace (19:41–44). In the Gospel of Luke there is an ironic strand of texts that balance the urgent and threatening images of this passage. So if Jesus is the one who causes the fall of those who oppose God's sign, he is also the one that causes the rise of the many (2:34) who recognize God's plan. He is the one who gives peace to the seventy to share (10:1–12). He is the one who knows the things that make for peace (19:41–44). But the question is whether we are paying attention or allowing ourselves to loll in denial. As Luke 12:49–56 reminds us, Jesus does not force his peace on anyone. It is left up to us to read the signs.—Jana Childers

ILLUSTRATIONS

SOLID GROUND.   I read a letter written by a lady near burning streets and crashing buildings in Liverpool which she declined to leave because she was sure that she had still something to do and something to learn there, some service to render and also some insight to acquire on the boundary of vision. "We must trust in God and not be flurried," her letter concluded. But what ground have we for trusting in God and thinking that we may have a clarifying experience of Him on the verge of life? We have this ground—the resurrection of Jesus Christ. "He shewed Himself alive after His passion," to certify the faithfulness of God beyond the range of sight, to prove that we can lean our whole weight on the invisible without any fear of being let down, and to guarantee the constancy and triumph of Divine love beyond the border of what is seen. The first Easter declared that God had conquered in the crisis on the frontier, and changed the beyond from a great blank into a great revelation and a great promise.—Arthur A. Cowan[5]

WE NEED NOT FEAR.   Christ Himself faces the constricting riddles of life. According to the oldest record, His final word on the cross is the anxious cry: "My God, my God, why hast thou forsaken me?" It is characteristic, however, that He does not address this cry of despair into the night of Golgotha. He calls to His Father: "My God, my God." He holds the Father's hand firmly in His own. He brings the anxiety to His Father. He has brought it once and for all. If I am anxious and I know Christ, I may rest assured that I am not alone with my anxiety; He has suffered it for me. The believer can also know that Christ is the goal of history. The primitive community knows that this One has not gone forever but will come again. It thus has a new relationship to the future. This is no longer a mist-covered landscape into which I peer anxiously because of the sinister events which will there befall me. Everything is now different. We do not know what will come. But we know who will come. And if the last hour belongs to us, we do not need to fear the next minute.—Helmut Thielicke[6]

SERMON SUGGESTIONS

Topic: What to Think About Trouble
TEXT: James 1:2–4
(1) Trials will come. (2) Trials test our faith. (3) Trials can produce spiritual maturity. (4) Joy can permeate the entire process.

---

[5] *Crisis on the Frontier* (Edinburgh: T. & T. Clark, 1943), pp. 3–4.
[6] *The Silence of God* (Grand Rapids, Mich.: Eerdmans, 1962), p. 9.

Topic: Real Religion

TEXT: Gal. 2:20

(1) It is not a life built by rules and regulations, as good as they may be. (2) It is a life infused with the presence of Christ who loved us, died for us, and lives forever, justifying us; a life in which we fulfil the law by truly loving our neighbor (Gal. 5:13–14).

CONGREGATIONAL MUSIC

1. "Hear Us, O Shepherd of Your Chosen Race," vers. Bert Polman (1985)

    YORKSHIRE, John Wainwright (1750)

    A close paraphrase of Psalm 80, this hymn can be sung in lieu of the Psalter reading. Stanzas 1, 3, 4, and 5 parallel the suggested psalm verses for reading.

2. "God, Whose Purpose Is to Kindle," David Elton Trueblood (1967)

    HOLY MANNA, William Moore (1825)

    Based on Luke 12:49–50, this contemporary hymn by Quaker leader and thinker Elton Trueblood is a realistic prayer for deliverance from complacency and indifference to God's purposes in the world. Sing it in connection with the Gospel lesson (Luke 12:49–56).

3. "Guide My Feet," African American spiritual; harm. Wendell Whalum

    GUIDE MY FEET, African American melody (nineteenth century)

    The Epistle reading for this day (Heb. 12:1–2) contains the basis for this African American spiritual. The singing of it would be a powerfully effective accompaniment to the Epistle lesson.

4. "I Sing a Song of the Saints of God," Lesbia Scott (1929)

    GRAND ISLE, John Henry Hopkins Jr. (1940)

    Setting forth the truth that sainthood is a living possibility today, this modern children's hymn could logically be sung following the Epistle reading for this Sunday.—Hugh T. McElrath

WORSHIP AIDS

CALL TO WORSHIP.   "Ye shall know the truth and the truth shall make you free" (John 8:32).

INVOCATION.   God, this could be the day when some truth may dawn upon us with a brighter and surer light. Open our minds and hearts to be ready to hear the old, old story with its timely message for each of us. Through him who is the light of the world.

OFFERTORY SENTENCE.   "The rendering of this service not only supplies the wants of the saints but also overflows in many thanksgivings to God" (2 Cor. 9:12 RSV).

OFFERTORY PRAYER.   O God, some of us are able to give much, yet we give little; some of us would give more, but we have little. As you increase the ability of some, increase the ability of others, to the end that no need will go unmet and not one of us will go unblessed.

PRAYER.   We come to thee, our Father, that we may more deeply enter into thy joy. Thou turnest darkness into day and mourning into praise. Thou art our fortress in temptation, our shield in remorse, our covert in calamity, our star of hope in every sorrow. O Lord, we would know thy peace: deep, abiding, inexhaustible. When we seek thy peace, our weariness is gone, the sense of our imperfection ceases to discourage us, and our tired souls forget their pain. When we return to the task of life, strengthened and refreshed by thy goodness, send us forth as servants of Jesus Christ in the service and redemption of the world. Send us to the hearts without love, to men and women burdened with heavy cares, to the miserable, the sad, the brokenhearted. Send us to the children whose heritage has been a curse, to the poor who doubt thy providence, to the sick who crave healing and cannot find it, to the fallen for whom no man cares. May we be ministers of thy mercy, messengers of thy helpful pity, to all who need thee. By our sympathy, our prayers, our kindness, our gifts, may we make a way for thy love to flow into needy and loveless lives. So also may we have that love which alone is the fulfilling of thy law. Hasten the time when all men shall love thee, and one another in thee, when all the barriers that divide us shall be broken down and every heart shall be filled with joy and every tongue with melody.—Samuel McComb

SERMON
Topic: Five Keys for Winning over the Devil
TEXT: Heb. 12:2; Ps. 144:1

Losers focus on war, but champions focus on the spoils of war.

God has given you a weapon that will defeat every demon in hell.

Everyone is going to be in a war of some kind until Jesus comes. It may be physical, emotional, spiritual, financial, or personal. Spiritual warfare is part of every Christian's life. If you think you're not going to have any struggles or strife, you're in denial. You will never outgrow the need to wage war against the devil. The devil is your sworn enemy. He has a plan for your life. His plan is for you to fail in your pursuit of living a life pleasing to God.

Since the devil has a plan for you to fail, you need to have a plan to defeat him. God's plan for you is bigger than the devil's plan. God wants you to win, and he wants the devil to lose! That's why he has provided five keys to ensure your victory.

I. *Focus on God.* The first key to victory is keeping your eyes on the vision of God and the provision he has made of you to win the war. Many times in the Old Testament, God told people to lift up their eyes. When you are troubled, distressed, depressed, or perplexed, keep your eyes on him. He is your vision. He will see you through.

II. *Use God's weapons.* To defeat the devil, you have a second key: the principles and weapons God has provided. The psalmist said in Psalm 144:1, "Blessed be the Lord my strength, who teacheth my hands to war, and my fingers to fight."

David wrote this psalm, and Scripture shows that he faced both physical battles and spiritual ones. He fought to take land. He fought with his relatives. He fought with his own sin and his own weaknesses. He knew how to fight and come out a winner, not a loser.

The greatest thing that can be said about David is that he was a man after God's own heart. In the battles and crises of your life, maintain the vision that you are a man or woman after God's own heart.

III. *Stand on the Word.* God has given you a third key that will defeat every demon in hell and make you a winner. That key is the Word of God. People who say that they can resist the devil without ever opening their Bibles or spending time in prayer are prime subjects for the deceptions and devices of the devil. The battle you're involved in is a spiritual battle, not a natural one. Without spiritual weapons you cannot win. You must feed on the Word of God.

That is why I encourage you to read your Bible. Get a Bible-reading plan and stay with it, even if it takes you two years to get through the Bible. Be consistent. This will make you victorious. Take the promises of the Bible and make them your lifestyle. Then stand on those promises.

If you stand on the Word, you won't fall for the deceptions of the devil. If you aren't in the Word for yourself, you won't know what promise God has given you to stand on. Once you get that promise, write it in the front of your Bible. Don't forget it. Keep claiming your promise. Keep standing on it.

IV. *Get back up when you fall.* All people fall. Have you ever met anyone who is perfect? You may think they're perfect, but they're not. Great men get back up after they have fallen. The Bible record is full of those who fell but got back up to continue the fight of faith. Abraham was a liar. Moses lost his temper. David committed adultery. These men loved the Lord, though, and fulfilled God's plan for their lives.

V. *Keep your vision.* The fifth key to winning the war is to keep your vision. Losers focus on war but champions focus on the spoils of war. Recently I talked to a woman whose son is in prison. One of the pastors of our church has been ministering to him. Now the woman's son is enrolling in our Bible correspondence course. She believes her son is coming through the bad situation victoriously. She's not majoring on the war; she's majoring on her son coming through!

Warfare always surrounds a miracle. There's a miracle on the way for you. The devil always knows when a miracle is on the way, and he will try to stop you from receiving it. The three Hebrew children refused to worship the image of Nebuchadnezzar and were cast into a fiery furnace. They refused to surrender during the battle. When they were cast into the furnace, someone like Jesus showed up. They focused on his presence rather than on the fire.

He is with you in the fire of your affliction, too. He has promised he will never leave you or forsake you. Lift up your eyes. Keep your vision—"Looking unto Jesus the author and finisher of our faith" (Heb. 12:2).

He's with you in the battle, and you will come out a winner! Remember, the five keys God has given you to win the war are mighty. Using them you cannot fail!—Marilyn Hickey

SUNDAY, AUGUST 26, 2001
Lectionary Message

Topic: Kingdom Signs
TEXT: Luke 13:10–17
Other Readings: Jer. 1:4–10; Ps. 71:1–6; Heb. 12:18–29

This is the third time Jesus has been caught in a controversy on and around the Sabbath (6:1–5, 6:6–11) and it is going to happen again before Luke gets through with his next chapter (14:1–6). Obviously someone is trying to say something about the Sabbath, though it is not immediately clear what particular point is being made. Does this text have something new to say on the subject? Has Luke placed this story at this point in his narrative for a particular purpose? Taken on their own, these seven verses don't tell us much more than that Jesus is compassionate and thinks the Pharisees are legalistic hypocrites. There is nothing new in that.

We might well wish for the kind of hints that other Gospel writers provide. But there is no moral of the story here as there is in Mark—"The Sabbath was made for humankind, not humankind for the Sabbath" (Mark 2:28). There is not even the kind of small clue that Matthew gives—"It is lawful to do good on the Sabbath" (Matt. 12:12). On first reading, this text appears to be a very simple story: a healing, an unsurprising objection from the Pharisees, and Jesus' snappy comeback. What is Luke up to?

It is possible that the evangelist is harking back to a point he was making a few chapters earlier—"The Son of Man is Lord of the Sabbath"(6:5)—but it is interesting that he is so spare in his telling of the story and that there is not a whiff of that line in today's lesson. It seems more likely that Luke has placed this story in this particular spot for a reason—that there is a strategically important relationship between this text and what goes before or comes after, or both.

I. *A sign of the Kingdom.* By the time we reach this point in Luke's Gospel, Jesus has been teaching for a couple of chapters about signs of the Kingdom. In chapter twelve he rails at the crowd and is frustrated with the disciples for their lackadaisical attitude toward the coming of the Kingdom. Some people, he says, are being deliberately obtuse about interpreting the signs. In the first part of chapter thirteen, Jesus uses a technique known to good teachers everywhere—he gives an example of correct interpretation. Though his interpretation is a little oblique—he uses a metaphor to make his point—you don't have to be an A student to get it.

In today's text he repeats the lesson. He gives what is perhaps his favorite kind of Kingdom sign when he heals the bent-over woman. However, although healing is a common sign of the Kingdom, taking the initiative to heal somebody is quite uncommon. In Luke most healings take place at the supplicant's request. In this case, it is as if Jesus is going out of his way to provide a learning opportunity. Then, when the synagogue leader tries to confuse the crowd and detract from the moment, Jesus does not keep silent or offer an oblique interpretation of what has happened; he comes right out and defends what he has done. In taking the initiative to heal the woman, in performing the healing and in interpreting it afterwards, Jesus makes sure that the crowd gets the point—the Kingdom of God is at hand.

II. *Symptoms of the Kingdom.* Not only does Jesus make it clear that the Kingdom is present in our midst, he also gives us a few ideas about what that means. If bondage and hypocrisy and lackadaisicalness are symptoms of the work of the evil one, being untied and honest and attentive are symptoms of those who have crossed over into Jesus' Kingdom. In today's text, *untied* is a big word. Not only does Jesus use it to make his point about the treatment of animals on the Sabbath, but he also uses it to talk about the treatment the woman deserves. "She deserves to be untied from the bondage in which Satan has held her for half of her adult life!" Jesus says. One gets the feeling that she is not the only one who is loosed here. The Kingdom, too, is a bit more "loosed" by the events of today's text. Perhaps even Jesus, in this, his last time of teaching in a synagogue and spurred on by his frustration with this student's slowness, is loosening up his Kingdom teaching a little here.

III. *Smallness and the Kingdom.* In interpreting today's text, it is important to notice not only what comes before but also what follows it. Today's passage sets up the passage that comes after it in Luke's version of the Gospel story. It provides an example of the next point that Jesus is going to make: the Kingdom of God is like something very small that becomes very big.

The story of the healing of the bent-over woman is a small story about a small woman and a small healing. Women were more significant than animals in the New Testament world, but definitely less significant than men. When he defends this Sabbath healing, Jesus makes a "from a lesser to a greater" kind of an argument. Given the point that Jesus makes in the four verses that follow this story, it is almost as if he is anticipating the day when women—their status, their role, their perceived value—will no longer be considered so small. Certainly in referring to the bent-over woman as a "daughter of Abraham" Jesus is ahead of his time. The phrase "daughter of Abraham" used in today's text occurs only once in all of the Gospels! Women go unnamed, unseen, and unheard in the first century—except where Jesus is concerned. One of the remarkable things about the evangelist Luke is that he notices Jesus noticing women.—Jana Childers

ILLUSTRATIONS

GOD'S GUIDANCE.   How does this guidance come to us? we ask. Mostly through circumstances which afterwards you see to have been formed and shaped by His gracious hand. In *Alice Through the Looking Glass* Lewis Carroll tells the story of the remarkable adventures of Alice as she travels through a country divided like a chessboard. What strange, unnerving experiences dog her footsteps! When she stretches out her hand for the egg in the shop, it floats away the moment she tries to take hold of it. The flowering rush at the river's edge is just beyond her reach and when at last she can pick some, it withers in her hand. What Alice didn't know—but we do—is that before her adventure began there was a plan for the chessboard as the player sees it, and the picture of it is on the first page of the book. Here each piece is in its proper place in relation to the whole. This is not a make-believe game but a real one, and each move to be made is a deliberate device for getting Alice, who begins as a pawn, to end as a queen.—Elam Davies[7]

PRODUCTIVE WAITING.   In his *Grapes of Wrath* John Steinbeck, the surrealist, pressed this wine of hope: "Man unlike any other thing organic or inorganic in the universe grows beyond his work, walks up the stairs of his concepts, emerges ahead of his accomplishments. This you may say of man—when theories change and crash, . . . man reaches, stumbles forward, painfully, mistakenly sometimes. Having stepped forward, he may slip back, but only half a step, never the full step back."

The testimony of the most tried is that "tribulation worketh patience; and patience, experience; and experience, hope." They have learned the truth of the psalmist's counsel: "Wait on the Lord: be of good courage, and he shall strengthen thine heart: wait, I say, on the Lord."—Ralph W. Sockman[8]

---

[7] *This Side of Eden* (Westwood, N.J.: Revell, 1964), pp. 23–24.
[8] *Now to Live!* (Nashville, Tenn.: Abingdon Press, 1946), pp. 35–36.

SERMON SUGGESTIONS

Topic: Who Bears the Burden?
(1) "Each man shall bear his own burden" (Gal. 6:5). (2) "Bear ye one another's burdens" (Gal. 6:2). (3) "Cast thy burden upon the Lord" (Ps. 55:22).

Topic: Steps in Following Christ
TEXT: Luke 9:23
(1) Make up your mind. (2) Give up yourself. (3) Take up your cross. (4) Keep up your cultivation. (5) Gather up your loyalties.—E. Stanley Jones

CONGREGATIONAL MUSIC

1. "In You, O Lord, I Put My Trust," vers. Clarence P. Walhaut (1985)
   JUDSON, Roger W. Wischmeier (1974)
   WAREHAM, William Knapp (1738)
   Only the first two stanzas of this metrical paraphrase of Psalm 71 parallel the selected verses of the Psalter lesson. The reading of the psalm and singing of the paraphrase could be meaningfully alternated, as follows: read verses 1–4 of the psalm, sing stanza 1 of the hymn; read verses 5–8, sing stanza 2.

2. "Lord, Speak to Me That I May Speak," Frances R. Havergal (1872)
   CANONBURY, Robert Schumann (1839)
   This prayer hymn asking God to speak through us would be a good one to sing following the reading of the call of Jeremiah (Jer. 1:4–10), who protested that he knew not how to speak, but the Lord put his words in the prophet's mouth.

3. "Thine Arm, O Lord, in Days of Old," Edward H. Plumptre (1864)
   ST. MATTHEW, Tate and Brady, *Supplement to the New Version* (1708)
   With skill and economy, the author versifies the healing miracles of Jesus in this fine hymn. It would be meaningful if sung either before or after the Gospel reading concerning Jesus' healing of the crippled woman on the Sabbath.

4. "Jesus, Your Blood and Righteousness," Nicholaus L. von Zinzendorf (1739); trans. John Wesley (1740)
   GERMANY, William Gardiner's *Sacred Melodies* (1815)
   Jesus, by shedding his blood, was the mediator of a new covenant. The great Moravian hymn by Zinzendorf makes more personal this truth found in the day's Epistle lesson (Heb. 12:18–29). The apostle's thoughts in this passage can sound very abstract apart from the singing of a fervent, subjective hymn like this one.—Hugh T. McElrath

WORSHIP AIDS

CALL TO WORSHIP.   "Lord, who shall abide in thy tabernacle? Who shall dwell in thy holy hill? He that walketh uprightly and worketh righteousness and speaketh the truth in his heart" (Ps. 15:1–2).

INVOCATION.   Spirit of holiness and peace! Search all our motives, try the secret places of our souls, set in the light any evil that may lurk within, and lead us in the way everlasting. Take possession of our bodies. Purge them from feebleness and sloth, from all unworthy self-indulgence, that they may not hinder but help the perfection of our spirits. Take possession of our wills that they may be one with thine, that soul and body may no longer war against each other but live in perfect harmony, in holiness and health. Wake us as from the sleep of death and inspire us with new resolves, and keep us blameless in body, soul, and spirit, now and ever. Let thy light fill our hearts more and more, until we become in truth the children of light, and perfectly at one with thee.—Samuel McComb

OFFERTORY SENTENCE.   "He which soweth sparingly shall reap also sparingly; and he which soweth bountifully shall reap also bountifully" (2 Cor. 9:6).

OFFERTORY PRAYER.   O God, you did not spare your own Son but gave him up for us all. Your daily mercies are beyond our counting. May our joyous giving reflect something of the prodigality of your giving.

PRAYER.   O thou great Father of us all, we rejoice that at last we know thee. Our souls within us are glad, because we need no longer cringe before thee as slaves of holy fear, seeking to appease thine anger by sacrifice and self-inflicted pain; instead, we may come like little children, trustful and happy, to the God of love. Thou art the only true Father, and all the tender beauty of our human loves is the reflected radiance of thy lovingkindness, like the moonlight from the sunlight, and testifies to the eternal passion that kindled it.

Grant us growth of spiritual vision, that with the passing of years we may enter into the fullness of this our faith. Since thou art our Father, may we not hide our sins from thee but overcome them by the stern comfort of thy presence. By this knowledge, uphold us in our sorrows and make us patient even amid the unsolved mysteries of the years. Reveal to us the larger goodness and love that speak through the unbending laws of thy world. Through this faith make us the willing equals of all thy other children.

As thou art ever pouring out thy life in sacrificial father love, may we accept the eternal law of the cross and give ourselves to thee and to all men. We praise thee for Jesus Christ, whose life has revealed to us this faith and law, and we rejoice that he has become the first-born among many brethren. Grant that in us, too, the faith in thy fatherhood may shine through all our life with such persuasive beauty that some who still creep in the dusk of fear may stand erect as free sons of God, and that others who now through unbelief are living as orphans in an empty world may stretch out their hands to the great Father of their spirits and find thee near.—Walter Rauschenbush

SERMON
Topic: The Bigot and the True Believer
TEXT: Gal. 5:6

That's the motto of the true believer—and Paul was surely one, although some have tried to lodge him with the bigots. A bigot, according to a dictionary I consulted, is "a person who is utterly intolerant of any creed, belief, or opinion that differs from one's own."

I am not for a moment denying that there is a lot of bigoted, intolerant, and narrow-minded religion around. Not one of us escapes the danger of letting our religious beliefs congeal like some of my Scottish Presbyterian ancestors, to whom Oliver Cromwell addressed his familiar appeal: "I beseech you, gentlemen, in the bowels of Christ, to conceive it possible you may have been mistaken." It is not often noted, however, that there is such a thing as a bigoted atheist or an intolerant agnostic. I would therefore plead for a new understanding of the phrase *true believer* and maintain that it is perfectly possible to hold firm religious beliefs without any intolerance or disrespect for the sincere convictions of those of other religions—or none at all.

I. Let me briefly sketch the background of this debate and then indicate how this flare-up in a first-century church in what we now call Turkey has something to say to Christians today.

(a) As you know, the first Christians were Jewish and it was about the middle of the first century that Gentiles in large numbers began to be baptized and admitted to membership in the Church. The question at issue was how a Gentile man or woman from a pagan background should be received into the Church. Some, led by Paul, whose Jewish credentials were impeccable, held that all that was required was a declaration of faith in Christ as Lord and Savior and baptism in his name. The opposition party protested that members first had to accept the Law of Moses, one of whose requirements was the rite of circumcision of all males.

(b) For a while the debate raged across the expanding Church, and it was mostly thanks to Paul that it was finally settled. If Paul seems obsessed about the question of circumcision, it was because that rite was for him a symbol of the legalism from which he believed the gospel had set us free. So here he says that the demand that a Gentile convert should be circumcised undermines the freedom of the Christian believer. It might seem a minor matter, but he argues that one who receives circumcision is under obligation to observe "the whole Law."

II. Well, where do we come into this ancient argument? Simply as the beneficiaries of Paul's success in eliminating the requirement that a true Christian believer must first accept the requirements of the Jewish Law.

(a) If the other side had won, the Christian advance would probably have ground to a halt, and you and I would not be worshiping here today. Paul tells us in this letter that he squared off with none other than the apostle Peter, who had visited the Galatian church and at first had mixed with the Gentiles but later withdrew from them because some ardent Judaizers had arrived from Jerusalem. "I opposed him to his face," said Paul, "because he was clearly in the wrong." We don't get Peter's side of the argument. But there is nothing obscure in the words he later uses in this Epistle in his attack on the Judaizers: "They had better go the whole way and make eunuchs of themselves."

(b) I think when he wrote that he had forgotten his own reminder to the true believer that "the only thing that counts is faith active in love." He had the faith, but like us he was at times somewhat lacking in the love that should animate the true believer.

III. Are you a true believer? Your answer to that question—and mine—will depend on the kind of picture this phrase conjures up.

(a) If we are inclined to see quotes around the words *true believer* and to start thinking about people we know who wear their religion like a cloak—hugging it tightly so that we never seem to reach the real person inside this cloak covered with conventional pieties and so thick that no new idea ever seems to penetrate, a cloak that seems to shield them from sharing in the activities of normal human beings, the kind of person who makes you uncomfortable because you fear you may offend and cautious in your conversation—then you may want to say, "Thank God I'm not a true believer: I don't want to be a bigot."

(b) On the other hand, your answer would, I am sure, be totally different if the phrase *true believer* evoked for you the picture of one who is, as we say, "a real Christian." That is what a true believer really is. Sometimes that faith is expressed in enthusiastic church activity; sometimes it is shyly concealed; but always it is expressed in deeds rather than words.

IV. There are two points that have come home to me with special force as I have tried to answer the question, Am I a true believer?

(a) One point is that our chosen way of life must rest on a quite specific set of beliefs. Everyone acts on some basic convictions, whether they are specifically religious or not. The true believer is one who is not reluctant to say, "Credo: I believe; I have made my choice." And the true Christian believer is one who can say with Paul, "To me to live is Christ and to die is gain." "I am persuaded that neither death nor life . . . nor things present nor things to come . . . shall be able to separate me from the love of God, which is in Christ Jesus our Lord."

(b) That leads me to the next truth that we miss. To be a true Christian believer does not involve dismissing or despising all other religions. On the contrary, a total yielding of ourselves to the call of Christ from the heart of God will mean an expansion of the mind beyond the narrow limits of this material world and expansion of the heart into the mysteries of a love that breaks all barriers and dissolves the bigotries. The true believer can never claim to possess here and now all truth about God and human destiny, but he expects and welcomes new truth from whatever direction it comes.

V. The true believer knows that the closer we come to Christ, the less intolerant and the more loving, the less arrogant and the more humble, the less bigoted and the more truly human we must become. For when we say, "Credo: I believe," we are turning to the light "that lighteth everyone who comes into the world" and "shines more and more unto the perfect day."—David H. C. Read

SUNDAY, SEPTEMBER 2, 2001
Lectionary Message

Topic: Front-Back, First-Last
TEXT: Luke 14:1, 7–14
Other Readings: Jer. 2:4–13; Ps. 81:10–16; Heb. 13:1–8, 15–16

There wasn't a single time that either my son or my daughter ever forgot to yell, "Front! Front! I get front!" when we'd go somewhere in the car. It didn't matter whether the ride was twenty minutes or two hours. What did matter was being in the front. At first I thought it was about being near the air conditioner or the radio. I soon realized that, all those perks aside, deep down it had everything to do with primacy—with being first. It had to do with being near the power center, next to the parental "big cheeses," a reflected honor conferred by proximity and access.

Elbowing one's way to the center of power and jockeying for position are unfortunately not limited to the insecurities of childhood. In our society it's standard operating procedure for many adults. In today's Gospel the Lord says, once again: "God's ways are not your ways." Jesus is not playing Miss Manners here or giving us the Palestinian version of "How to Get Ahead in Business." It is a foretaste of ultimate reality—the reality of the coming Kingdom of God. Watching the other invited guests scratch and scramble their way to the front tables, Jesus warns us all, "Time out. Reality check." So begins another one of his downside-up reversal parables that prefigure the way things will be—come, Kingdom, come. It's what scholars call a "Kingdom pronouncement," and for believers those pronouncements always go beyond a "heads up" to "straighten up and fly right!"

Our Lord is not just foretelling here. He is demanding advance obedience to his Kingdom reality in the here and now. The Kingdom's first-last, front-back reversal is supposed to impinge on our present behaviors, Jesus says. Invite outsiders inside today? Count in society's "no accounts"? Yes, says our Lord, right *now*. The new reality that this parable invites us to embrace goes against everything we've been taught in this world. Nevertheless, the Kingdom lens must change the way we look at everything, and then it must change our priorities. It must change on a daily basis our whole way of being in relation to others. I think that the more the earthly hierarchy of front-back and first-last fades in obedience to the Kingdom reality, the less there will be of the them-us polarity in society. Instead, what we will experience will be God's emerging Kingdom of *we*. Even now I get glimpses of it, don't you? Our God is arranging the place settings at the messianic banquet. In the muddle of the meantime, where we find ourselves between the First and Second Coming, our job is to practice, practice, practice the topsy-turvy, arms-wide-open hospitality of the Kingdom—obediently, until he comes again.—Georgine Buckwalter

ILLUSTRATIONS

REVERSAL.   Further exploration of "My ways are not your ways, says the Lord" with regard to the reversal themes could include a reference to popular self-help books like *Swimming with the Sharks Without Losing Your Shirt*, or *Looking Out for Number One*. There's a popular country song that boasts about "having friends in low places." These friends, the song goes on to say, "aren't much on social graces." Entrance to the Kingdom is not about social standing or social graces, but grace itself.—Georgine Buckwalter

THE BEST GOOD NEWS.   This has to be the best Good News ever heard on earth—that God is like this, that "while we are yet sinners" and continue to be sinners, he still loves us and is willing to work with us in building a relationship. Let me remind you that He does not have to be that way. There is nothing in us or the universe that decrees that the Everlasting One has to be merciful or that mercy has to be everlasting. That He is this way is a sheer and joyous miracle which we cannot explain but can only celebrate. What Hosea overheard in the heart of the Most High came to its clearest expression on the cross and in the resurrection of Christ, where the Lover whom we had forsaken proved that He would not forsake us.—John Claypool[1]

WE CAN KNOW.   The values of life which are supreme and lasting rest upon the secure basis of personal experience. I know that fire burns—I have been burned. We all know the fragrance of a hayfield freshly mown—some of us grew up on farms. I know that the Matterhorn, and the Taj Mahal in India, and Fujiyama in Japan, are inspiring sights—I have seen them all. If some blind man should stand at Zermatt, or in Agra, or in Tokyo, and insist that there are no such sights, I should feel sorry for his misfortune. But his inability to see them

---

[1] *Glad Reunion* (Waco, Tex.: Word Books, 1985), p. 129.

would not dim the visions of beauty which I have enjoyed in those places. Nor can anyone tell me that there does not come a great succession of power for the living of a right life through faith in God and through prayer. I have been trusting in Him and praying for more than three score years, and I know. If corroboration were needed, there are millions of people in the world who have had exactly the same experience.—Charles R. Brown[2]

SERMON SUGGESTIONS

Topic: The Clemencies of God

TEXT: John 16:32; 2 Tim. 1:2

(1) Ours is a God who never leaves or loses us. (2) He has set great purposes before us in the doing of which he translated loss into love. (3) God surrounds life with a realm of spirit that is able to sustain even life's greatest loss and most adverse denial. (4) In Jesus Christ we find the promise that in and through every denial and lonely crucifixion of love there is a redeeming power at work.—Robert E. Luccock

Topic: Reciprocal Indwelling

TEXT: John 15:4

(1) As to fellowship (John 6:56). (2) As to obedience (1 John 3:24). (3) As to confession (1 John 4:15). (4) As to love (1 John 4:15).—F. B. Meyer

CONGREGATIONAL MUSIC

1. "All My Hope on God Is Founded," Robert Bridges (1899); after J. Neander (1680)
   MICHAEL, Herbert Howells (1930)

   In response to the teaching of the apostle Paul that we offer a sacrifice of praise that confesses our hope in his name (Heb. 13:15), this great hymn is more than adequate. Based on a fine German hymn by Joachim Neander, this twentieth-century expression takes wings with the excellent tune MICHAEL by Herbert Howells.
2. "If You Will Only Let God Guide You," Georg Neumark (1657); trans. C. Winkworth
   WER NUR DEN LIEBEN GOTT, Georg Neumark (1657)

   Of the many hymns that relate to the various exhortations in the concluding chapter of Hebrews, this one certainly is a good one to be used with Hebrews 13:5. It elaborates on the idea that God will not leave us nor forsake us.
3. "Sing a Psalm of Joy," vers. Marie J. Post (1948)
   GENEVAN 81, *Genevan Psalter* (1562)

   The stanzas of this contemporary metrical paraphrase of Psalm 81 that parallel the verses selected for reading are stanzas 1, 5, 6, and 7. They follow the original so closely that they could be sung in place of the Psalter reading.
4. "Lord God, Your Love Has Called Us Here," Brian Wren (1973)
   SURREY, Henry Carey (c. 1723)

   Here is a cognitive hymn containing a rich store of prayerful thoughts that can be appropriately expressed in worship that gathers about the Word of God. It can relate to any of the

---

[2] *Dreams Come True* (Old Tappan, N.J.: Macmillan, 1945), p. 107.

lessons but especially to the Gospel reading, which suggests lessons in unselfishness and humility.—Hugh T. McElrath

WORSHIP AIDS

CALL TO WORSHIP.   "Peter began: 'I now see how true it is that God has no favorites, but that in every nation the man who is God-fearing and does what is right is acceptable to him'" (Acts 10:34–35 NEB).

INVOCATION.   God of the universe, Creator of the whole human family, enlarge our minds and open wide the doors of our hearts that we may think your thoughts after you and pattern our love after yours. So may we worship you in spirit and in truth.

OFFERTORY SENTENCE.   "Each one, as a good manager of God's different gifts, must use for the good of others the special gift he has received from God" (1 Pet. 4:10 TEV).

OFFERTORY PRAYER.   Father, help us to do good not only to the household of faith but also to all who have true need. Bless these offerings to that end.

PRAYER.   O God, our heavenly Father, we do not know how to pray as we ought. We acknowledge that we often come to you so driven by our selfishness, our prejudices, and our ignorance that a direct answer to what we have asked would mean only that we would get things that would harm us, that would harm others, and that would generally frustrate your loving purposes. So we pray that you would increase our love for one another as well as our self-regard, that you would broaden our understanding of one another, and that you would open our eyes to new ranges of truth that we have not known before.

SERMON
Topic: What Was Wrong with the Older Brother?
TEXT: Luke 15

"A certain man had two sons." These two sons were raised in the same home, yet how different they were. The younger son rebelled against his father. The older son remained faithful. The younger son ran away. The older son stayed home. The younger son was undisciplined. The old son had his life closely ordered and rigidly regulated. The younger son was a playboy. The older son was a plowboy. How different these two sons were.

Yet they had this much in common: As the story develops we discover that both of the boys come under Jesus' judgment. Why? It is obvious to all why the younger son would be labeled a sinner, for he openly rebelled against his father, wasted his father's money, ran with a fast crowd, fell into every conceivable kind of immorality, and ended up a physical and spiritual wreck. But why does the older brother come under Jesus' condemnation?

I. First, the older brother had the *wrong attitude.*

(a) Picture the scene. For months the younger brother had been gone. No word had come from the far country about the wayward son. Perhaps he was in desperate need. Maybe he was dead. Every morning when the father got up he would go out on the porch and scan the horizon for any sign of his son coming back home. In the evening, just before the sun set, the father would follow the same ritual. Each day the lines of despair deepened in his face.

Then one day as the older brother returned home from work, the good news was given to him. "Your brother has come home. He is safe. He's back with us now."

How did the older brother respond? Did he say, "Fantastic. Where is he? I've really missed seeing him." No, verse 28 tells us, "But he became angry and was not willing to go in." That's what was wrong with the older brother. He had the wrong attitude.

(b) The message of this parable is that the measure of your Christian maturity is not the actions of your life but your attitude toward sinners who have found their way back into the Father's house. Are you critical or compassionate? That is the key.

II. Notice this second thing in the story. The older brother not only had the wrong attitude, he also had the *wrong focus*.

(a) Listen again to verse 29: "For so many years I have been serving you and I have never neglected a command of yours; yet you have never given me a kid that I might be merry with my friends." Five times in that one short verse the older brother uses the words, *I, me,* or *my.* He was so occupied with casting glances at his own righteousness that he never had time to be concerned about anyone other than himself.

(b) In times past we would say that the older brother was self-centered or selfish. Now we would diagnose him as narcissistic. This term, *narcissistic,* comes from the Greek legend of a man named Narcissus who fell in love with his reflection in a pool and pined away in rapture over it.

(c) The older brother was in love with himself. He was so busy patting himself on the back for his own righteousness that he was unable to feel anything for his wandering brother who had come back home. Underneath the outer facade, his only concern was for himself.

III. Look at the story again and notice this third thing about the older brother: he had the *wrong motive*.

(a) When he complained that after having kept the commandments of his father the father had never given him a kid that he might be merry with his friends, he was revealing the motive behind his actions. The older brother did not stay home because he loved his father. He did not follow his commandments because he wanted to please his father. He stayed home and obeyed his father's commandments for what he could get out of it.

(b) We've often heard the question, If you were put on trial for being a Christian, would there be enough evidence to convict you? But take the question a step further and ask, What if they had to establish motive? Why do you do the things you do? Why do you go to church? Why do you read your Bible? Why do you pray? Why do you give your money? Why? What is your motive?

(c) Why do you do the things you do? Are you pushed by a desire for attention or by fear or by outside pressure? Or do you do the things you do because the "love of Christ constrains you"?

IV. In verse 30 we see something else. The older brother had the *wrong understanding*.

Speaking of this prodigal brother who had just returned home, the older brother called him "this son of yours"—not my brother but your son. The father caught that comment and tried to correct it in verse 32 when he called the prodigal "this brother of yours." What the older son failed to understand is the meaning of brotherhood. The men and women around us are not just God's children. They are also our brothers and sisters.

V. Ultimately the problem with the older brother was that he had the wrong relationship with his father.

(a) He was devoted to his father's law but he was not in sympathy with his father's heart. He stayed in his father's house but he was not at home with his father.

(b) Jesus' parable of the older brother is a reminder that the heart of Christian faith is not a matter of rules or rituals but of relationship. When your relationship is right, when you really love the Father, then your understanding will be right, for you will recognize others as your brothers and sisters; your motive will be right, for you will want to please God; your focus will be right, for you will be more concerned about others than about yourself; and your attitude will be right, for you will rejoice with those who come back to the fellowship of the Father. The key is your relationship with the Father.

(c) Hear this final thought: Verse 28 says that just as the father went out to welcome the prodigal home, he also went out to the older brother to exhort him and encourage him to come back home. That is the word that comes to you this morning. Whether you are like the prodigal who is lost in the far country or like the older brother who is lost at home, you can come back to your Father's house. He loves you now as much as he ever did. His arms are outstretched to you. If you will acknowledge him again as your Father, then you too can come home.—Brian L. Harbour

SUNDAY, SEPTEMBER 9, 2001
Lectionary Message

Topic: Wide-Eyed Discipleship
TEXT: Luke 14:25–33
Other Readings: Jer. 18:1–11; Ps. 139:1–6, 13–18; Philem. 1–21

Over and over in the Gospels the in-breaking Kingdom's "how much more" reality predominates: spikenard extravagance and abundance (even twelve baskets left over). So it may come as a surprise when our Lord recommends a downright prudential ethic. In today's Gospel, Jesus asks the wannabes who were following him around to stop and consider what they were getting themselves into. After all the descriptions of how God will rule over the Earth with justice and compassion when the Kingdom ultimately comes, Jesus calls a time-out and says, "Consider the cost of signing up with me." Truly following in his footsteps will be expensive. Whether it's time, talent, or treasure, real Christian discipleship always costs.

While this passage concentrates on material possessions, it's not just about money. Obedient discipleship is expensive in terms of all kinds of daily priorities and in terms of any number of things longed-for but forgone in his Holy Name. True disciples have to give up all kinds of attitudes and behaviors—maybe even some long-cherished beliefs—to be obedient. "Don't go into this with your eyes closed," our Lord says. Wide-eyed discipleship! That's the ticket. But given humanity's drive to accumulate earthly treasures and bigger and better barns, it's a wonder anybody signs up at all, isn't it? The rich young ruler's response was loud and clear: "Heaven costs too much." Maybe he was really saying: "I'm too afraid to trust in God's providential care to share my wealth with others. I don't think there's enough to go around." He didn't want to take the chance, it seems.

Our Lord says, "Be prudential but take the chance anyway." There's no way to avoid the reality that following Jesus Christ in any age, in any situation, means dropping all kinds of safety nets as well as a portion of one's net assets. "Take that chance with your eyes wide open, and think twice if you want to build a life that towers over the ordinary—no matter what the circumstances. Consider the entire cost of life's long project, not just the fizzy new-convert buzz. There are crosses ahead," Jesus says. "And that king who waged a war? Don't start something you're not willing to finish." You see, our Lord already had an inkling that even kings get nailed crossways. It shouldn't surprise us, then, that enduring through to the end of our lives involves much giving up, much sacrifice, and much suffering. It shouldn't surprise us, because he never promised us anything else this side of heaven—except one important thing: *presence.*

Wise old French monk Jean-Paul Claudel once said, "Jesus didn't come to remove suffering or to explain it away. He came to fill it with his presence." That's what he promised us along with those inevitable crosses: his presence, his life-giving, saving solace. That and only that gives us the strength to trust and to drop our nets and net assets. That and only that gives us the strength to shoulder our individual crosses. Because Christ keeps his promise of presence through the power of the Holy Spirit, co-carrying the crosses of our pain, fatigue, dread, and dreariness, we can even begin to embrace the costs of discipleship. "I have decided to follow Jesus. No turning back. No turning back."—Georgine Buckwalter

ILLUSTRATIONS

RISKY FAITHFULNESS.   Following Jesus requires that we risk faithfulness, including, and gracefully beyond, a legal or moral formula. It may require taking the chance of being accused of unfaithfulness by the purist and the compulsive hunter of motes in others' eyes. And it requires growing in faith until we can say, with all the saints, that we fear no one but God, even though that is unimaginable to those who rely on human power.

But finally, more than anything, being a minister today requires trust. Trust that Jesus will once again draw in the dust and confound our accusers until they have dropped their stones and walked away in shame. And trust that somehow, sometime, those who accuse us falsely will be confronted by God with their own sin. Can we trust that there in the temple, humiliated by the dishonorable behavior of others, we will look up into the loving eyes of a Savior who says, "There is no one left to accuse you. Go in peace and the forgiveness of sin"?

And though we might resist the idea, there will be days when we are just sitting somewhere teaching and preaching and someone will be brought to us for judgment. Out of the darkness created by fear, the morally self-righteous at either end of a polarized spectrum will demand our decision. We may find ourselves in a situation where none of our traditional rules seem to apply.—Mary Zimmer[3]

SIMPLE DISCIPLESHIP.   A sound theology demands the severity of thinking and childlike faith that can unite a genius with one who is mentally handicapped in a common discipleship. I experienced this in my student days when I studied under the great theologian Rudolf Hermann at Greifswald. He had spent an entire semester lecturing on the many abstract and complex thoughts of great thinkers and he had not made it easy for his students. His final

---

[3] In James W. Cox (ed.), *Best Sermons*, vol. 7 (New York: HarperCollins, 1994), p. 215.

lecture closed with this observation: "Gentlemen, all that we have dealt with in these lectures has said nothing other than what the old children's hymn says so simply and beautifully":

> Jesus' blood and righteousness
> Clothe me in a radiant dress
> Which makes me fit, our God to meet
> Before his heavenly judgment seat.

Professor Hermann's great knowledge did not stand between him and discipleship.—Helmut Thielicke[4]

SERMON SUGGESTIONS

Topic: Shadows
TEXT: Acts 5:15
(1) The most potent influence is silence. (2) It is unconscious. (3) It is conditioned by a man's relationship to Christ.—W. A. Cameron.

Topic: Self-Control
TEXT: Gal. 5:23
(1) Recognize the problem for what it is. (2) Act on the knowledge you have. (3) Set some goals for your life. (4) Challenge your feelings occasionally. (5) Find someone who has the kind of difficulty you are going through and share your life with him.—Dan Baumann

CONGREGATIONAL MUSIC
1. "Lord, You Have Searched Me," vers. *Psalter* (1912); rev. Marie J. Post (1986)
   FEDERAL STREET, Henry K. Oliver (1832)
   This metrical version of Psalm 139 would make a good sung prayer of confession to be used after the Psalter lesson.
2. "Wherever He Leads I'll Go," B. B. McKinney (1936)
   FALLS CREEK, B. B. McKinney (1936)
   This hymn of consecration would be appropriately sung following the reading of, or a homily on, the Gospel lesson (Luke 14:25–44) concerning the demands of Christian discipleship.
3. "Have Thine Own Way, Lord," Adelaide A. Pollard (1902)
   ADELAIDE, George C. Stebbins (1907)
   This hymn of discipleship could be effectively used to respond especially to the reading concerning the potter in Jeremiah (18:1–11).
4. "Help Us Accept Each Other," Fred Kaan (1985)
   BECK, John Ness Beck (1977)
   This contemporary hymn voices present-day concerns of the same nature as those expressed by the apostle Paul in his plea to Philemon for the salve, Onesimus. Christian con-

---

[4] *Faith: The Great Adventure* (Minneapolis: Augsburg Fortress, 1985), pp. 139–140.

cern and acceptance of one another is expressed in this prayer hymn that would be appropriately used in connection with the lesson in Philemon 1:21.—Hugh T. McElrath

WORSHIP AIDS

CALL TO WORSHIP.   "Be strong and of a good courage, fear not, nor be afraid of them: for the Lord thy God, he it is that doth go with thee; he will not fail thee, nor forsake thee" (Deut. 31:6).

INVOCATION.   Give us to know, Holy God, in the worship of this hour that we are creatures of purpose and that there is divine meaning for our existence. Sober us with the reality of thy constant watch and care and generous strength, through the Holy Spirit and the Savior Son.—E. Lee Phillips

OFFERTORY SENTENCE.   "And walk in love as Christ loved us and gave himself up for us, a fragrant offering and sacrifice to God" (Eph. 5:2 RSV).

OFFERTORY PRAYER.   Bless our offerings of love, O God, as we remember Christ's sacrifice for us, but bless our offerings in any case, O God, that others may discover and rejoice in your salvation.

PRAYER.   Take us all into thy embrace. Be with the children that come up from the gates of the morning. Let them not by wrong training, evil example, or disastrous circumstance be turned away from thy purpose for them. Steady our boys and girls in their tumultuous years amid the waywardness of this generation. Keep their self-respect unsullied. Save them from the contagion of this unclean world, and may they be strong to offer thee valiant service in the years ahead. Be with the mature in the floodtide of their power. Let no prosperity spoil them, no disappointment crush them, no faithlessness overtake them. Keep them true to knightly vows they took in their chivalrous years, and let their strength be glorified in thy service. Support the aged, now drawing near the river across whose flood they see in vision the shining battlements of the heavenly city. Establish them in their going and give them a triumphant welcome on the other side.

So encompass us in all our varied needs, we pray thee, and in thine everlasting arms enfold us, every one.—Harry Emerson Fosdick

SERMON

Topic: The Gospel and Our Work
TEXT: Ps. 90:16–17; Matt. 20:1–16

This parable is not an economic tract, although some people have tried to press it in that direction. There are some great religious truths that we can draw from the parable for our work.

I. One of the things we need to understand in this story is that the men who were sitting around the marketplace were not being depicted as lazy. This was the place where individuals were supposed to go when they did not have a regular job or trade of some kind or did not own land. The marketplace was the spot for workers to gather who wanted to work.

Maybe a new beatitude could be coined in which we might say, "Blessed are those who give others work because they give them self-respect."

II. It is interesting also to observe the attitude reflected in the men who had worked.

(a) Notice the anger that one man felt toward another when he thought he should have received more wages. Think about how often that happens in our work relationships today. In this parable one man became angry because the owner sought to pay another the same wage for less work than he had done.

(b) In our society today there is no question that our attitudes toward our work often indicate the kind of work we do.

(c) Our work requires of us responsibility and commitment to do the very best we can while we engage in it. In the eyes of God, if each does his work to the very best of his ability, that work before God is equal.

III. One of the unfortunate things in our society is that sometimes people view work as a curse. Many believe that work is the curse that God placed on us at the fall of Adam and Eve. But this is not the biblical attitude toward work. When you read the Genesis account carefully you find that in the story man was placed in the Garden to till the garden before the curse was given. Man was set to work naming the animals and caring for the garden. Man and woman are involved in work as cocreators with the Creator. Work is not a curse but a blessing. Work is a gift to us from God, who invites us to engage with him as his workers in the world.

IV. When we reflect on this parable, we want to declare quickly that it seems so unfair for God to be like this. One of the central truths that comes from this parable is that God is extravagant in his generosity. God does not love us more because some of us work harder or because some of us have superior minds or superior backs or superior jobs. God's love to us is an expression of his grace and does not depend on our own efforts to earn it.

V. It is also interesting to observe in this parable that the men worked with the opportunities they had. "Why are you standing in the marketplace idle?" they were asked. "Lord, no one has given me work to do," they responded.

(a) Some people do not have greater opportunities because they simply have not had doors open for them. But whatever doors of opportunity open before us, small or large, each of us is to use the abilities and talents we have to the very best of our ability.

(b) Not all of us have the same opportunities nor the same abilities. If you give to God your very best from what you have, in God's sight it is of equal worth to what others give. We serve God; we don't labor in our work for reward or recognition from him. We cannot separate the sacred and secular, because God is involved in both our work and our worship. We worship through our work and work through our worship.

VI. God who is the Creator loves us and seeks companionship with us.

(a) Our only real compensation for our labor, we are told through this parable, is God's companionship. Jesus told this parable right after Peter and the others wanted to know what rewards they would receive for following him. To those who labor long and hard this parable might sound unfair. Jesus declared that one could not say that only those who labored long count with God. We cannot pile up merit before God or win his favor. Our relationship to God is not purchased; it is a gift.

(b) God is generous and loving. He is extravagant. If we are concerned because some brother comes into the Kingdom late and is loved graciously by God, the problem is not with God but with us. If we are jealous because a sister or brother is received by God when he or she is elderly and experiences the grace of God, then the problem is not with God but with us. We respond to God's extravagant goodness toward others not begrudgingly but with thankfulness that not only they but we have been treated not as we deserve but according to the graciousness of God.—William Powell Tuck

SUNDAY, SEPTEMBER 16, 2001
Lectionary Message

Topic: Restoration Joy
TEXT: Luke 15:1–10
Other Readings: Jer. 4:11–12, 22–28; Ps. 14; 1 Tim. 1:12–17

If we asked each of the Gospel evangelists just why Jesus came, we would be given four different theological answers. Today's passage parabolicly presents what is more forthrightly stated in the nineteenth chapter: "The Son of Man came to seek out and to save the lost." That's it! There you have it, according to Luke. The Pharisees didn't believe that the intimate honor of sharing a meal should include the no-accounts, the lost causes in society. "This fellow" Jesus disagreed. In the following lost-and-found stories we discover the heart of what has been called "The Gospel to the Outcast"—and it is very Good News indeed!

In Jesus' position on table fellowship we learn important things about the nature of God. In this glimpse of the inclusive, no-outcasts banquet promised at the end of the age we also learn that it's God's nature to take the initiative in seeking the lost ones. That salvation comes from divine initiative is vividly shown in the culmination parable, in which the Father's prevenient grace forgives the prodigal son before any repentance is voiced. The heavenly search party is on! Whether we get trapped in high, craggy places through sloth or sinful slippage, or get lost in sandy wastelands through mindless sins of accommodation, capitulation, neglect, or omission, the search party is on. God is on a treasure hunt as the housewife in this parable turns over every couch pillow and sweeps out every corner in search of one ordinary, tarnished, and pitted coin. We learn it is God's nature, then, to see sinners as lost treasure. And when we're found? It's party time! The clapping and stomping in heaven must sound like a rescue chopper landing. The heavenly ramparts must rock with God's restoration joy. Nothing makes God happier, Luke's Gospel tells us. Nothing.

Robert Fulghum, in his bestseller *All I Really Need to Know I Learned in Kindergarten,* tells of writing at a window desk and watching kids outside playing hide and seek in the approaching dark. One kid hides too well. He's forgotten under a pile of leaves and the others go home. Fulghum finds himself thinking about all the adults he knows who hide themselves too well in life and he has the burning desire to call out the window, "Get found, kid. Make some noise or something. Get found." I think of that often when I see folks lost in all kinds of self-destructive behaviors. Nothing in our earthly experience can compare with being found by the one who came to seek and save the lost. Nothing. There is no joy deeper than having a contrite heart filled with a new spirit and being turned round and round till you "come round right" and righteous by God's saving grace. The beloved hymn *Amazing Grace* got it right. It's almost the Christian's alma mater because it's the sung parable of joy from the sinner's side of today's Gospel. "Get found, friends. Repent. Get found." Nothing makes God happier.—Georgine Buckwalter

ILLUSTRATIONS

IT IS YOU!   Several years ago I once set my little son down in front of a large mirror. At first he did not recognize himself because he was still too young. He quite obviously enjoyed seeing the small image that smiled at him from the glass wall. But all of a sudden the expression on his little face changed as he began to recognize the similarity of the motions and he seemed to be saying, "That's me!"

The same thing may happen to us when we hear this story. We listen to it at first as if it were an interesting tale with which we ourselves have nothing to do. A rather odd but fascinating fellow, this prodigal son. Undoubtedly true to life, undoubtedly a definite type of person whom we have all met at some time or other. And certainly we are all objective enough to feel a bit of sympathy with him.

Until suddenly *our* face may change, too, and we are compelled to say, "There I am, actually. This is I." All of a sudden we have identified the hero of this tale and now we can read the whole story in the first person. Truly this is no small thrill. This is the way we must move back and forth until we have identified ourselves with the many people who surrounded Jesus. For as long as we fail to recognize *ourselves* in these people we fail to recognize the Lord.—Helmut Thielicke[5]

WHY HE CAME.   When the son went astray nobody went after him. How is that? Remember who told the story. Nobody went for him. How is that? Because he was a man, because he was a moral agent, because he was accountable to God for his own act. Why did the father not gather his servants with the elder brother, why did he not gather his neighbors together, and say, "Look here, I have lost my boy, let us go and find him and bring him back in spite of himself"? Why did he not? Because if they had brought him back again he would have been a prodigal still, he would have been a rebel inside the house as well as out of it, for no man comes till he returns; and heaven and the Bible, Christ and Calvary, the Holy Ghost and eternity stand absolutely defeated before the citadel of the human will. Do not forget it. Listen. The prodigal went astray, took every step from the homestead of his own deliberate choice, step by step away up into the far country, and he had to come to himself, and he did not send a letter home to his father and say, "If you will send the old chariot I will come home," and he did not ask anybody to give him a lift. He had to walk back every inch his own self, step by step, with bleeding feet and aching head, and broken heart. He had to do it. "But," you say, "the father ran to meet him, did he not?" Yes, he did, and he will run to meet you when he sees you coming, but you must come. Come in repentance. It is the response of the will. Repentance is the response of the enlightened, redeemed man to the call of God, the "I will" of the soul. It is putting your hand on your heart and getting hold of what has been your curse, the thing that has chained you. It is getting hold of the thing that has made hell of Earth for you, the sin of your heart—for I have discovered that there may be a dozen sins in a man's

---

[5] *The Waiting Father* (New York: HarperCollins, 1959), pp. 17–18.

life, but there are not a dozen that predominate; there is one overmastering, predominating, all-prevailing sin that enslaves and damns, and if that sin goes, everything goes.—Gipsy Smith[6]

SERMON SUGGESTIONS

Topic: When You Feel Alone and Helpless

TEXT: 1 Kings 19:15–21 (compare Rom. 11:4–5)

(1) That very feeling puts you in good company; it is a common experience. (2) God always has a network of human resources on whom he can depend, who can bless and strengthen you in your dark hours. (3) Rejoice in the grace of God who is with you in ways and to a degree that you may not know.

Topic: Living by the Spirit

TEXT: Gal. 5:1, 13–25

(1) It is not self-indulgence. (2) It is not legalism. (3) It is a style of life full of good fruits.

CONGREGATIONAL MUSIC

1. "Immortal, Invisible, God Only Wise," Walter Chalmers Smith (1867)
   ST. DENIO, Welsh folk melody; adapted (1839)
   The apostle Paul's great ascription of honor and glory to God (1 Tim. 1:17) is reflected in this venerable hymn. It would be a splendid selection for the opening of worship.
2. "The King of Love My Shepherd Is," Henry Williams Baker (1868)
   ST. COLUMBA, Irish Melody; harm. (1906)
   DOMINUS REGIT ME, John Bacchus Dykes (1868)
   This meditative hymn, while based principally on Psalm 23, also refers to the parable of the lost sheep (Luke 15:1–7) and therefore would be appropriate for singing in connection with the Gospel lesson.
3. "The Foolish in Their Hearts Deny," vers. Marie J. Post (1983)
   MAPLE AVENUE, Richard L. Van Oss (1984)
   A contemporary paraphrase of Psalm 14, this song lends itself to antiphonal singing, phrase by phrase, between choir and congregation.
4. "God Hath Spoken by the Prophets," George W. Briggs (1952)
   EBENEZER, Thomas J. Williams (1890)
   This strong hymn affirming the righteous power of the Triune God could be appropriately sung in connection with the Old Testament lesson for this Sunday (Jer. 4:11–12, 22–28).—Hugh T. McElrath

WORSHIP AIDS

CALL TO WORSHIP.   "Having therefore, brethren, boldness to enter into the holiest by the blood of Jesus, by a new and living way, which he hath consecrated for us, through the veil, that is to say, his flesh; . . . Let us draw near with a true heart in full assurance of faith, having our hearts sprinkled from an evil conscience and our bodies washed with pure water" (Heb. 10:19–20, 22).

---

[6] *As Jesus Passed By* (New York: Revell, 1903), pp. 37–28.

INVOCATION.   O God of Love who settest the solitary in families, grant that we who have felt the chill loneliness of guilt and estrangement may rejoice in thy gracious mercy and in the warm encouragement of the community of faith and concern in which we have been placed, to the end that thy will may be done in us and that this world's wanderers may find their way home, through him in whose face we see thee.

OFFERTORY SENTENCE.   "And whatsoever ye do in word or deed, do all in the name of the Lord Jesus, giving thanks to God and the Father by him" (Col. 3:17).

OFFERTORY PRAYER.   Almighty God, from whom all good gifts come, accept our offerings today, meager or generous, and multiply their good for thy use and the work of the Church for which Christ died.—E. Lee Phillips

PRAYER.   O God, whose Spirit searches all things and whose love bears all things, come with truth and mercy to us today. We are often blind to the ways that lead to the hearts and needs of others and to thy throne. Give thy light, O God, and take away our darkness. But when we see ourselves as we are, leave us not to stand confused and helpless in our guilt. Give us thy grace, O God, to take away our fears and to strengthen our laggard hearts. Grant, O Lord, that thy Word may give us increased understanding of the scope of our task as servants of Jesus Christ. May we be encouraged to seek new depths of dedication. May we be inspired to take more seriously our opportunities for preparation for the task of witnessing to thy truth to the ends of the Earth.

SERMON
Topic: Jesus' Prayer List
TEXT: John 17:1–11

You can tell much about a person from his or her prayer list. Some people have on their prayer lists the hungry and starving of the world while other people pray only over their own full plates. Some people put at the top of their list "freedom and justice for the poor and downtrodden"; other people place "a raise and a new car" at the top of theirs. Some prayer lists are full of names—Jane, who is fighting cancer; Bob, who needs to find work; the Smiths, who have a new baby—while other prayer lists are only blank sheets. Some people put themselves on their prayer lists under "confession" ("God be merciful to me a sinner"). But others enter their own names under "adoration" (God, I thank thee that I am not like other people"). You can tell a great deal about people from their prayer lists.

Taken in this light, Jesus' own prayer list is something of a shock, perhaps even a scandal. In the passage for today, Jesus, nearing the end of his life, prays a long and beautiful prayer of intercession. In this prayer He gives thanks, praises his Father, and pleads for his followers, but he also—and this is the shock—refuses to pray for the world. "I am not praying for the world," Jesus says, "but for those whom thou hast given me" (John 17:9 RSV).

We have always been taught that it is the duty of Christians to care and pray for the world. What are we to make of the fact that our Lord himself, in his high priestly prayer, refused to put the world on his prayer list?

I. Some would suggest that Jesus refused to pray for the world because the world is evil and has been rejected by God. There is plenty of evidence for this idea, of course. A glance at the newspaper headlines would seem to reveal a world beyond even the power of prayer: government by bribery, business by greed, and public life by violence. Given the kind of world we live in, it seems a small wonder that Jesus said, "I do not pray for the world."

But this suggestion is simply not true. The world has not been rejected by God. Indeed, John himself has told us that God loved the world so much he gave his only Son (John 3:16). There must be some other reason why Jesus refused to pray for the world.

II. Another possibility is that Jesus wanted his followers to make a clean break from the world, wanted them to be "church people" uncontaminated by involvement in the world. But this suggestion is wrong, too. Later in the very same prayer Jesus says that he is sending his disciples "into the world" just as the Father has sent him into the world.

III. In the final analysis, the ironic truth is that Jesus refused to pray for the world at that moment not because he hated the world or rejected the world but because he deeply loved the world and finally saved the world. What Jesus was doing in this prayer was offering gifts to the Father. He offered the gift of himself because his earthly ministry was complete. He also gave his disciples to the Father, for "they are thine." But the world was not yet ready to give as a gift. One day the world will cease to be in rebellion, will cease its hating and its violence against God. Until that day, though, Jesus sends us—his disciples—into the world he loves, just as the Father sent him, so that "the world may believe." The promise is that by God's mercy to the world through our service and love, one day the world will come to the light of Christ and Jesus' prayer will finally be finished: "I pray now for the world, offering it at last to thee, for it is thine."—Thomas G. Long

SUNDAY, SEPTEMBER 23, 2001
Lectionary Message

Topic: Kingdom Prudence
TEXT: Luke 16:1–13
Other Readings: Jer. 8:18–9:1; Ps. 70:1–9; 1 Tim. 2:1–7

The guy was a crook. He was an embezzler, a grafter. How can it be that our Lord praised him? This is probably the most reread of all the parables. But the story always turns out the same way: the bad guy got away with something and came out smelling like a rose. Our Lord's approval can be most perplexing. One interpretive option is that Jesus told it just this way for its shock value. He did that sort of thing. When he wanted to shake up the contented and complacent, he'd tell some Kingdom parable that called the establishment's smug little world into question, all the while turning the exclusive discriminatory value system of Israel on its ear.

Yet as we read and reread this parable, one word starts to stand out: *shrewdness.* Would we consider shrewdness to have Kingdom value? We would probably be more likely to list patience, love, compassion, justice, and mercy. Shrewdness seems too close to craftiness and we often think of craft as deceit. However, craft and shrewdness are not always negative. Jesus wants the "children of light" to learn that from this story.

Maybe our initial reluctance comes from misunderstanding our call to "be wise as serpents and innocent as doves." We pedestalize innocence as if it only meant godliness or sexual purity. However, the Hebrew word for innocence contains the implication of harmlessness when used in the Hebrew parallelisms so common in Scripture's sacred poetry and prose. Here a harmful reptile is set parallel to the harmlessness of the dove. The one telling bit of discipleship wisdom in this parable is: be smart as a whip but be a person in whom there is no harm for others.

Besides, innocence too often means ignorance, and ignorance is not a Kingdom value. Naivete can be downright dangerous. Rollo May, in his seminal work *Power and Innocence* makes a convincing argument that not knowing what we ought to know can lead to complicity with evil. There is no way that being "dumb and dumber" about the ways of this world advances the coming of God's Kingdom.

There is a certain prudential ethic here that is not dissimilar from Jesus' earlier parables in which he cautions the king who wanted to go to war and another who wanted to build a tower. It is, then, also a matter of stewardship. Indirectly our Lord is saying in all of these parables: Don't squander my precious resources. Children of the light are not supposed to be in the dark when it comes to money matters. We are to be reliably resourceful and prudent for the Master's sake. Ignorance is never bliss for God's people. Sadly, it is not uncommon for there to be mismanagement of funds in our churches and squandering of all kinds of resources through sins of omission as well as commission. Naivete has its consequences. Kingdom shrewdness has its benefits.—Georgine Buckwalter

ILLUSTRATIONS

SELF-SEEKING.   The core of man's unfreedom is his self-imprisonment. He is a slave because he permits himself to be enslaved to his self's tyrannical power. When Luther declared that "Man seeks himself in everything, even in God" he observed the core fact of all human life. And in this observation he really understood the tragic context and demand of our Lord's saying, "If any man would come after me, let him deny himself . . ."—Joseph Sitter[7]

STEWARDSHIP.   John Wesley one day exclaimed: "Some of you Methodists are twice as rich as you were before you were Methodists; some of you are fourfold as rich; some of you are tenfold as rich; now, if whilst you get all you can and save all you can you do not give all you can, then you are tenfold more the child of hell than you were before."—Charles A. Wallis[8]

SERMON SUGGESTIONS

Topic: God Keeps His Distance
TEXT: Exod. 19:16–24
(1) In the mystery of his person. (2) In the reverence due his name. (3) Yet he reveals as much of himself as we need to know for our salvation, our joy, and our service (Eph. 3:8–12).

Topic: Christians and the Law
TEXT: Rom. 13:1–10
(1) We citizens of the state are obligated as Christians to obey the law and its authorities.

---

[7] *The Care of the Earth* (Minneapolis: Augsburg Fortress, 1964), p. 146.
[8] *A Treasury of Sermon Illustrations* (Nashville, Tenn.: Abingdon Press, 1950), p. 268.

(2) We citizens of God's Kingdom are obligated to live by the law of love, which surpasses and fulfills all worthy laws, rules, and regulations.

CONGREGATIONAL MUSIC

1. "There Is a Balm in Gilead," African American Spiritual

    BALM IN GILEAD, African American Spiritual

    A positive answer to the plaintive rhetorical questions of Jeremiah (8:22) as to whether there is any healing for a crushed and mourning people is this popular spiritual. Singing it is a reminder that we are to "tell the love of Jesus" by life as well as singing and to affirm the truth that "he died for all," which is the message of today's Epistle lesson (1 Tim. 2:1–7).

2. "Lord of Our Life," Matthaeus A. von Loewenstern (1644)

    The last verse of this day's Psalter reading (Ps. 79:9) finds its echo in this earnest prayer-hymn seeking God's help and deliverance. It would be a logical sung response to the Psalter lesson.

3. "All Hail the Power of Jesus' Name," Edward Perronet (1779)

    CORONATION, Olive Holden (1783)

    MILES LANE, William Shrubsole (1779)

    This grand hymn of the coronation of Jesus makes reference in stanza 2 to the ransom paid for our salvation from the fall (1 Tim. 2:6). It would be an ideal hymn to sing as a vibrant call to worship.

4. "Take My Life and Let It Be Consecrated," Frances R. Havergal (1874)

    MESSIAH, Louis J. F. Herold (1839)

    YARBOROUGH, Anonymous (1830)

    HENDON, Henri A. C. Malan (1827)

    This hymn of stewardship would be a natural accompaniment to the reading of the Gospel lesson (Luke 16:1–13) concerning the shrewd steward and the admonition that one cannot serve both God and money.—Hugh T. McElrath

WORSHIP AIDS

CALL TO WORSHIP.   "Let us draw near with a true heart in full assurance of faith" (Heb. 10:22).

INVOCATION

> Within these walls let holy peace,
> And love, and concord dwell;
> Here give the troubled conscience ease,
> The wounded spirit heal.
> May we in faith receive thy word,
> In faith present our prayers,
> And in the presence of our Lord
> Unbosom all our cares.

—John Newton (1769)

OFFERTORY SENTENCE.   "Though I have all faith, so that I could remove mountains, and have not love, I am nothing" (1 Cor. 13:2).

OFFERTORY PRAYER.   O Lord, let the outworking of our faith find its way to expression in support of loving service to all the causes dear to your heart, whether at home or abroad.

PRAYER.   O Lord, we remember with sadness our want of faith in thee. What might have been a garden we have turned into a desert by our sin and willfulness. This beautiful life that thou hast given us we have wasted in futile worries and vain regrets and empty fears. Instead of opening our eyes to the joy of life—to the joy that shines in the leaf, in the flower, in the face of an innocent child—and rejoicing in it as in a sacrament, we have sunk back into the complainings of our narrow and blinded souls. O deliver us from the bondage of unchastened desires and unwholesome thoughts. Help us to conquer hopeless brooding and faithless reflection, and the impatience of irritable weakness. To this end, increase our faith, O Lord. Fill us with a more complete trust in thee, and with the desire for a more wholehearted surrender to thy will. Then every sorrow will become a joy. Then shall we say to the mountains that lie heavy on our souls, "Remove and be cast hence," and they shall remove themselves and nothing shall be impossible unto us. Then shall we renew our strength and mount up with wings as eagles; we shall run and not be weary; we shall walk and not be faint.—Samuel McComb

SERMON
Topic: The Secret Followers of Jesus
TEXT: John 19:38–42

Joseph of Arimathea was a disciple "secretly," for fear of the Jews, and so was Nicodemus. How many others, one wonders, were also secret followers? Make no mistake about it: there are many and there always have been. We would like to be followers openly—to speak for him in the marketplaces of life, to witness by our piety and devotion—but we do not dare.

I. Poor Joseph and Nicodemus! We sympathize with them.

(a) Two men of distinction, members of the most august body of Jewish men in all the world. What would their colleagues think if they knew that Nicodemus had visited Jesus secretly at night or that he and Joseph entertained the possibility that the Galilean might really be the Savior of the world? What would the masses think?

(b) Life can be terribly complex at times, can't it? And those with the most responsibility find it most complex. It was easy enough for the disciples to follow him—they were simple men, men with few friends, men without political alliances. But Joseph and Nicodemus were well connected. They had others to think about. They had the entire country to think about. That's the way it is with us, isn't it? It's all right for the young and the ill-connected to be fully committed to Jesus. But those of us who are older and more involved and deeply respected—we have to be careful, don't we? Joseph and Nicodemus were disciples secretly, because there were areas of their lives in which Christ wasn't welcome. And we are the same way!

II. Joseph's and Nicodemus's biggest problem, of course, was that they couldn't decide what they really believed about Jesus.

(a) If they had believed for sure that he was the Messiah he claimed to be, and that many of the people said he was, they would certainly have thrown in their lot with him and taken the consequences, whatever they might have been. But they weren't sure. They were clever enough to understand all about delusions and that sort of thing. Suppose Jesus was mistaken about himself and not really the Messiah. Then where would they be? They would have stepped into a ship with no bottom in it! They had to try to befriend Jesus secretly while maintaining their appearance and work as members of the Sanhedrin. In their position they couldn't afford to do more. The leaders of society have to be cautious.

(b) Again, we understand, don't we? Most of us are never really sure of what we believe. There is so much at stake that we seldom take the time or spend the effort to decide what we truly believe. We can't afford to make a mistake, to make a wrong move, so we're committed to not making any drastic moves at all.

III. But something happened to Joseph and Nicodemus. That is the truth to which our text witnesses. Something shocked Joseph and Nicodemus out of their secret discipleship into open discipleship. When they beheld Jesus on the cross they knew where their loyalties really lay. They couldn't remain secret followers any longer.

(a) It isn't any wonder, is it? There isn't anything in the world like the cross of Christ for bringing out the true loyalties of people. And Joseph and Nicodemus, seeing and hearing all, were wrenched as they had never been wrenched before. He *was* the Christ and they had failed him. He *was* the Messiah, and they had waited too long to acclaim him. Suddenly, though it was too late, they made their move. Having lingered in half-belief while he was alive, they came to his side in death and asked permission to take down his poor, broken body and bury it in a tomb.

(b) It is amazing what they risked by doing this. There were strict laws in their religion. Anyone who touched a dead body must go through long and elaborate cleansing procedures before observing a holiday. Passover was upon them—the most blessed feast of the Jewish people. And these two leaders of the people would be unable to participate. They were defiled, accursed, by touching the body of a criminal. Their discipleship would no longer be secret, for now everyone would know. They were signing their own resignations from leadership in the Sanhedrin. Their loyalties to the Galilean were now declared. They had lost more than Jesus' disciples had lost; they had given up their very positions to acknowledge him.

(c) Joseph and Nicodemus were changed by looking at the cross. They traded their secret discipleship for an open discipleship. What about us? Will we be changed too?—John Killinger

SUNDAY, SEPTEMBER 30, 2001

Lectionary Message

Topic: The Gate, the Gap, and Grace

TEXT: Luke 16:19–31

Other Readings: Jer. 32:1–3a, 6–15; Ps. 91:1–6, 14–16; 1 Tim. 6:6–19

"I was hungry and you said apply for food stamps. I was homeless and you said there is a shelter in town. . . . I was naked and you said a local church has clothes. . . ."[9] The problem

---

[9] *Salt,* June 1994, p. 24.

with the rich man was he didn't get it. Nowhere does the parable say he was wicked just because he was rich. Nowhere does it say he intentionally defrauded or oppressed the poor. The sin of the rich man was that he just didn't get it.

Present-day sympathizers with the rich man would fit right in with the Pharisees to whom our Lord addressed this confrontational story, because some present-day believers still think that Christianity is a form of meritocracy. If the Gospel has any message at all it is that merit does not matter when it comes to salvation. But still Pharisees abound among us. We're not exactly hostile to the radical grace of the Gospel; we just don't get it. Or more realistically, we don't want to accept its social consequences. It's more a matter of hardness of heart than thickness of skull. But the end result is the same now as it was then: people walk past the Lazaruses of this world, tossing crusts and rinds left and right.

The gap between the rich man's uncomprehending luxuriating in all that wealth and the painful, howling poverty around him was what Jesus was getting at. We must remember that at the time of the prophet Amos the nation of Israel was described as "pious, prosperous, and pitiless." Amos said to everyone within earshot, "You're going to be held accountable for the gap between your beds of ivory and the piles of rags on which the poor sleep. You're going to be held accountable for the gap between your feasting and their famine." In today's parable, our Lord basically says, "You're going to be held accountable for what you did not see and what you ignored because you did not want to see." Apparently insensitivity matters. Willful ignorance and careless, callous inattention matters. "I was poor and you said God loves the poor. I was beaten and you said avoid dark alleys.[10] In this "scarifying" parable, our Lord goes farther yet. He says, "Wait till you see the gap that's going to exist at the end of time!" Echoes of the Judgment Parable in Matthew 25 merge here with Jesus' voice: "Don't throw me your scraps and your rinds. Don't pass me by or pass me leftovers."

Real Christian charity shares and cares. It goes outside the gates and gets down into the ditches. It doesn't say, "Chin up" or "Check's in the mail." When America's overclass finally sits down outside the gate with the underclass, holy will happen. When the overclass doesn't say "pull yourselves up" but "let me help you up," holy will happen. When America's overclass never even entertains the question of deserving or merit, holy will happen. Blessed are the ones who get it. Blessed are the ones who embrace and obey in advance the radical reversals of the arrival of God's Kingdom. Blessed are the ones who know that charity isn't leftovers. Blessed are the ones who get it: grace, grace, grace. And that, right abundantly.—Georgine Buckwalter

ILLUSTRATIONS

THE FIRST THING.   Too many church members sit smugly in church on Sunday, some closing the eyes and others eyeing the clothes, and with a dozen other things ahead of God in their lives. Some love a pet dog more than they love almighty God. They are saying, "Suffer me *first* . . . to attend to a hundred other items before I get around to Jesus Christ." But Christ is saying, "Seek ye *first* the kingdom of God and His righteousness and *all these things* shall be added unto you."—Vance Havner[11]

---

[10] *Salt*, June 1994, p. 24.
[11] *Playing Marbles with Diamonds* (Grand Rapids, Mich.: Baker, 1985), p. 34.

COSTLY GIVING.   The thing that puzzles most Christians is this: How far ought we to go in our giving? What measuring line can we apply to our liberality? No minister has a right to tamper with another's conscience in this respect or to attempt to lay down specific rules. Personally I have always shrunk from frantic begging appeals and the use of devices calculated to loosen tight purse strings. Henry Sloane Coffin writes of a well-known New York minister who was told by a wealthy parishioner that while he hoped his pastor would long continue in health and vigor, he had selected a text for his memorial sermon, and the text was: "It came to pass that the beggar died." I want to avoid that! There are those in every church who give to the limit. There are others on small pensions or with heavy financial obligations. It is so easy unwittingly to hurt the feelings of people who lack nothing in desire or will but who lack the means to do what they long to do. No one gains or loses prestige in the church of Christ by the amount of his giving. My plea is simply this: as we make our pledges and calculate our contributions, we do so in the light of the searching word, "I will not offer burnt offerings to the Lord my God which cost me nothing." If we do this prayerfully and honestly, our giving will certainly be adequate; it will probably be generous; it may even be sacrificial.—John N. Gladstone[12]

SERMON SUGGESTIONS

Topic: The Golden Calf

Text: Exod. 32:1–14

(1) The temptation of idolatry is always present among the Lord's people and takes many forms. (2) Respected leaders of thought and behavior, such as Aaron, often play significant roles in apostasy. (3) Spiritual recovery may depend on the concern and action of a special leader, such as Moses, who agonizes with God for his people.

Topic: Narrow Passage

Text: Phil. 1:21–27

(1) Paul's dilemma. (2) Paul's desire. (3) Paul's directive.

CONGREGATIONAL MUSIC

1. "Call the Lord God Thy Salvation," James Montgomery (1822)

   BLAENWERN, William Rowland (1915)

   Montgomery's fine paraphrase of Psalm 91 would be an admirable introduction to the reading from the Psalter.

2. "Onward, Christian Soldier," Sabine Baring-Gould (1865)

   ST. GERTRUDE, Arthur S. Sullivan (1871)

   The apostle Paul's charge to the young Timothy was to fight the good fight (1 Tim. 6:12). This popular hymn takes up that theme, emphasizing not only individual responsibility but also the Church's mission. Accompaniment by brass instruments would be appropriate.

3. "On Jordan's Stormy Bank I Stand," Samuel Stenett (1787)

   PROMISED LAND, American folk hymn in *Southern Harmony* (1835)

---

[12] *The Valley of the Verdict* (Toronto: Welch, 1968), pp. 128–129.

This old hymn, with its folk-tune setting, voices the longing for the peace and joy of heaven "in the Father's bosom" that the poor man Lazarus attained in the parable Jesus told (Luke 16:19–31).—Hugh T. McElrath

WORSHIP AIDS

CALL TO WORSHIP.   "Trust in the Lord. Have faith, do not despair. Trust in the Lord" (Ps. 27:14 TEV).

INVOCATION.   As we have assembled in your presence, O Lord, let no burden of guilt, no spirit of anger, no cloud of doubt hide your gracious face from any one of us. Come with your forgiveness, with your peace, and with your reassurance and dispel every hindrance to our true worship.

OFFERTORY SENTENCE.   "Bless the Lord, O my soul, and forget not all his benefits" (Ps. 103:2).

OFFERTORY PRAYER.   If we let memory run free and unhindered, our Father, we recall mercies too many to number. Yet we do think upon these blessings, lingering on this or that benefit, knowing that if you had not helped us we would not, we could not, be here today. So we bless your name and we bring back to you in offering a portion of what you have graciously given to us, asking you to bless it again.

PRAYER.   O Lord, we would rest in thee, for in thee alone is true rest to be found. We would forget our disappointed hopes, our fruitless efforts, our trivial aims, and lean on thee, our comfort and our strength. When the order of this world bears cruelly upon us; when nature seems to us an awful machine, grinding out life and death without a reason or a purpose; when our hopes perish in the grave, where we lay to rest our beloved dead: O what can we do but turn to thee, whose law underlieth all and whose love, we trust, is the end of all? Thou fillest all things with thy presence, and dost press close to our souls. Still every passion, rebuke every doubt, strengthen every element of good within us, that nothing may hinder the outflow of thy life and power. In thee let the weak be full of might and let the strong renew their strength. In thee let the tempted find succor, the sorrowing consolation, and the lonely and the neglected their supreme friend, their faithful companion.—Samuel McComb

SERMON
Topic: God's Inescapable Nearness
Text: Phil. 4:4–8

Paul tells us, "The Lord is at hand." This is the way the Lord himself says to us, "I am at hand." It is not because we live in his nearness but because he promises that to us. This fact has its source in him, not in us. And why? Because the Lord has a name—Jesus Christ.

I. How near is the Lord? As near as one born as I was born, though probably under much more primitive circumstances; as near as one who has a glass of wine with me under the disapproving eyes of the onlookers; as near as one who passes through the experience of death as I will have to do, but under more horrible conditions. This is how the Lord is at hand. Whether I think about it or not, whether I believe it or not, makes no difference. He is at hand for me anyhow.

(a) Because that is true, because we live on the basis of what has already happened, we therefore live also on the basis of what is to come. We live from Jesus Christ and we live toward Jesus Christ. Paul placed the Lord's coming not very far ahead. Of course he was mistaken about that detail. But what of his belief that the goal of his life and the goal of all the world signifies Jesus Christ? A person with Paul's perspective lives not only in anticipation of the meeting he will attend tomorrow evening, the book he will read this afternoon, the examination he will take in the spring, the trip he will go on next summer, his wedding this year, or the surgery he will undergo next month. He also lives toward the day when God will be all in all, for then neither death nor little faith nor sins will be able to separate us from him any more. And he knows that the entire world moves on toward that day.

(b) What does that mean? It means that God is always out ahead of us. The totality of what is out there is neither the wedding nor death nor meaninglessness; it is God. Such an argument sounds completely different from what we find in the Old Testament. In the Old Testament, when the prophets speak about the nearness of the Lord they mean the near wrath of God (see Zeph. 1:14–18). To be sure, the wrath of God came. To be sure, no one who has not come to grips with the God of the prophets understands anything about God.

(c) However, this wrath fell on the very one who is even now near us as the Lord. He passed through this day of wrath. God now wears the face of Jesus Christ. God lets us look into his own face and heart in Jesus. What, then, is awaiting us at the end? Not darkness, nothingness, or extinction, but God! This hope stands over all the world and over every event. So nothing about that has changed, even if Paul did die before the whole world achieved this goal. For this reason, the Lord is near.

II. We may have trouble believing what Paul says to us in our text, but we can practice it, and that is far more important. In four sentences Paul tells us how to practice it today, tomorrow, and the next day, whether we can grasp its full significance yet or not.

(a) Look at the first of Paul's four sentences: "Rejoice in the Lord always; again I will say, rejoice." The most important thing for us to do is rejoice. Paul is well aware that we need to be told to do it. Why? A person can, surprisingly, will to rejoice. One can work at the problem of seeing what our Lord who is near us gives us day by day.

(b) Consider Paul's second sentence: "Let all men know your forbearance!" Again, we can live by the nearness of the Lord if we take special pains to observe others and their needs and questions—even if it hurts us. We need very much to do that, at least until we can get free from ourselves at a few points and actually see other persons.

Hundreds of our decisions, which we arrived at with wisdom and common sense, would have been different if we had made every effort to see their possible effect on other persons. As wise and sensible as they were, our decisions were wrong after all. How remarkable it is that God's love for us becomes real to individuals only when they begin actually to practice love, to open their eyes and become aware of other persons.

(c) Consider Paul's third sentence: "Have no anxiety about anything, but in everything by prayer and supplication with thanksgiving let your requests be made known to God." Once more we are summoned to practice something. If we refuse to pray until prayer wells up spontaneously within us, we will never learn to pray at all. We have to practice even that. As to anxiety—of course we do worry, and we do not help matters by pushing it down in the subconscious.

1. What did Paul have in mind? Certainly not precaution or provision, so we would give no thought to having something to put on the table for breakfast. He had in mind solicitude, worry, and dread. "What might happen next?" Paul had in mind the sort of calculating and scheming that so often shuts up our hearts.

2. He had an excellent solution to the problem: Pray! But pray in such a manner that thanksgiving is already in your prayer. Then all of the nervous tension will be removed. Perhaps we might experience once again a little foretaste of how it will be sometimes, when God is all in all.

(d) Now consider the last of Paul's four sentences: "And the peace of God, which passes all understanding, will keep your hearts and your minds in Christ Jesus." Those words, dear friends, sum up, of course, all that we experience with the practice that we have been talking about.

In brief, it is always God himself who becomes great and strong in us. We do not keep our own hearts fixed on Jesus Christ—his peace accomplishes that. We do not overcome the tumult and confusion and perplexity of our minds with our own peace—his peace does that again and again.

III. The nearness of the Lord consists in the fact that he takes a firm grip on our hearts and minds a long while before we understand and grasp it. This is the nearness of the Lord: he awaits us with his Kingdom and his Kingdom shines into this life of ours even if we are far from believing it.—Eduard Schweizer

SUNDAY, OCTOBER 7, 2001
Lectionary Message
Topic: Do You Have the Kind of Faith That Pleases God?
TEXT: Luke 17:5–10
Other Readings: Lam. 1:1–6; Ps. 137; 2 Tim. 1:1–14

The life of the Christian is a life of faith. We not only enter the Christian life by faith, but we also endure as Christians by the same faith. The Bible teaches in Hebrews 11:6 that "without faith it is impossible to please God." Not only is it impossible to please God without faith but it is impossible to please God without the *right kind of faith*. In the passage before us, Christ teaches his disciples three qualities of the kind of faith that pleases God.

I. *Faith is powerful, though it be small* (vv. 5–6). The first quality of faith is that it is powerful though it be small. Upon hearing Jesus' teachings on the nature of offenses and the forgiveness required toward the offender (vv. 1–4), the disciples requested an increase in faith. The request was due to the difficulty of the demand to forgive. Such difficult demands can be obeyed only in faith. Like the disciples, we would do well to look to Jesus for faith, for he alone is the source.

(a) However, Jesus responded to the disciples by saying in essence, "It is not the quantity of your faith that is important but rather the quality of your faith that matters most." Even the smallest amount of faith, if it is the right kind, can accomplish great things. We need not wait for the full maturity of our faith before we obey the Lord—faith of the size of a mustard seed will suffice. Are you finding the demands of Christ difficult to obey? Take heart, for God's omnipotent power is available to those with the smallest faith.

(b) Now, this small faith is powerful provided that it is the right kind of faith. Jesus says that our faith only needs to be the size of a small mustard seed. Well, what does the seed teach us about the kind of faith that pleases God? A seed contains life; thus the kind of faith we must have is a living faith. A dead, lifeless faith—no matter how large—can accomplish nothing. So the question is not how large is your faith but do you have a living faith or a dead faith? If it is a living faith, then you can obey Christ's difficult demands. You can even forgive your offenders.

II. *Faith perseveres, though it be strained* (vv. 7–8). The second quality of faith is that is perseveres, though it be strained. Living faith has an enduring quality. It cannot run dry because its fountainhead is the very life of God. This does not mean, however, that the life of faith cannot be strained, for indeed it will be strained. But if it be a living faith, it will persevere under the most intense straining.

(a) Jesus uses the illustration of a slave working in the field. After a long day of plowing and tending sheep, the slave is required by his master to do yet more. It is this more that strains our faith. Our faith may have been at work in the field of this world for many years, and still it must be exercised yet more. Like the soldier on the battlefield who can never lay down his shield, neither can the Christian lay down his shield of faith. We must carry it with us at all times. It must be with us when we are awake and when we are sleeping. It must be with us until the fight is finished.

(b) Jesus says that the slave must continue in service to his master and then he will be permitted to eat and drink. We may grow weary in this labor of faith, but the good news is that our labor of faith has an expected end. It is an end filled with promise and hope. When you grow weary in exercising your faith, remember that there is a feast that awaits you in heaven. There you will lay down the tattered garments worn by your labor in this world. There you will sit at the table of God's eternal blessings and find rest for your soul.

III. *Faith does not seek praise, though it be in service* (vv. 9–10). The third quality of faith that is pleasing to God is the faith that does not seek praise though it be in service. Continuing with the illustration of the slave, Jesus says that the master does not thank the slave for his service because the slave only did that which was commanded of him. In part this saying must be understood as a contrast between earthly masters and our heavenly Master, for our heavenly Master will say to all faithful servants, "Well done." However, like earthly masters, our heavenly Master has the right to command us to do what he wants, and having obeyed our Master's commands, we are still not worthy of thanks.

(a) When Jesus teaches us to say "we are unworthy slaves," he is teaching us not to seek praise for our service. Some people are always wanting to be noticed for their Christian service. The faith that pleases God is the faith that does not seek recognition.

(b) Praise is reserved for those who surpass what is commanded. But no one has ever gone above and beyond the call of duty except Jesus Christ. In fact, we have not always done our duty. Be that as it may, when a person does that for which he was created, he must not think he has done something great. A bucket that holds water has not done anything spectacular. It has only done that which it was created to do. Because we were created for God, we should not seek praise for simply doing what we were created to do.

These qualities of faith are pleasing to God. They are pleasing because faith honors the

Creator and not the creation. Because God is the object of our faith, our faith should be focused only and always on him and not on the circumstances of life. To do that, we must have a living faith, a lasting faith, and a lowly faith. Do we possess these qualities of faith spoken of by Christ? If so, then we have been pleasing to God.—W. Bruce Ostrom

ILLUSTRATIONS

WHAT WE OWE TO FAITH.   Living in the New World of the western hemisphere, do we stop to remember that we owe the discovery of this wonderful New World to one man's momentous faith?

Columbus struggled to be heard over a period of eight years, only to be rejected in his dream of a western passage across the Atlantic. First, the King of Portugal, then Ferdinand and Isabella and their advisers rejected the proposals. After four rejections Isabella yielded to the pleading of Columbus and offered to surrender her jewels to help his voyage of exploration. He had been ridiculed and treated as a fanatic, and his enterprise had been regarded as a jest. But he kept his faith high and secure. Sailing from Palos, Spain, with three small ships—the *Santa Maria,* the *Pinta,* and the *Nina*—his faith confronted the disbelief of his sailors. The captains and crews of the *Pinta* and *Nina* demanded under threat that he turn back. The sailors and crew of his own flagship, the *Santa Maria,* mutinied against him.

But on October 11, 1492, a night of full moonlight, the lookout on the ship *Nina* shouted, "Tierra! Tierra!"

After eight months, Columbus, upon returning to Spain, was escorted to the royal court of Ferdinand and Isabella at Barcelona. He presented his sovereigns with a glorious New World.—Benjamin P. Browne[1]

PRAYING WITHOUT GIVING UP.   *What if our prayers go dry?* All sincere prayer must cross that desert. But if we remember that prayer is not centrally our feelings but an act of our will, prayer still reaches its Promised Land. The saints know "the dark night of the soul," but they find also times of rapture. So it is wisdom to keep on praying; no, not in the pretense that we "feel fine" when actually we are desolate, but in the courage which offers God the weariness and the doubt. In his time he exchanges that bedraggled gift for his own joy. Even in the darkness a lightning flash may light the road, and there will be other times when prayer reaches a cathedral with banners hung, organ diapasons rolling through high arches, and a cross shining clear in chancel praise. Even when we are too spent to pray, we can offer God our helplessness. The New Testament assures us that even our groans are not in vain.—George A. Buttrick[2]

SERMON SUGGESTIONS

Topic: Sharing the Mind of Christ
TEXT: Phil. 2:5–11
(1) By assuming the role of a servant. (2) By willingness to suffer for others. (3) By looking only to God for reward.

---

[1] *Illustrations for Preaching* (Nashville, Tenn.: Broadman Press, 1977), p. 79.
[2] *The Power of Prayer Today* (Waco, Tex.: Word Books, 1970), p. 66f.

Topic: Motive and Mission

TEXT: Eph. 4:32 NRSV

Because God has forgiven you: (1) be kind to one another; (2) be tenderhearted; (3) forgive one another.

CONGREGATIONAL MUSIC

1. "O Thou Who Camest from Above," Charles Wesley (1762)

   HEREFORD, S. S. Wesley (1872)

   This beautiful prayer hymn by the peerless Wesley is an apt response to the admonition of the apostle Paul to Timothy (2 Tim. 1:6–7) to fan into flame the gift of God imparted by the laying on of hands.

2. "By the Babylonian Rivers," vers. Ewald Bash (1964)

   KAS DZIEDAJA, Latvian melody; harm. Geoffrey Laycock

   Here is a fine metrical paraphrase of Psalm 137 set to an appealing folk melody. The singing of it could well replace the reading of the psalm.

3. "I Know Whom I Have Believed," Daniel W. Whittle

   EL NATHAN, James McGranahan (1883)

   The contrast of the "I know nots" of each stanza of this gospel song with the reassuring "But I know" of the refrain is striking and dramatic. It aptly sets forth the truth of 2 Timothy 1:12. It could thus be sung at the conclusion of the reading of the Epistle.

4. "My Faith Looks up to Thee," Ray Palmer (1830)

   OLIVET, Lowell Mason (1832)

   The disciples asked Jesus to increase their faith (Luke 17:5). The same yearning animates our hearts when we sing meaningfully this classic nineteenth-century American hymn.— Hugh T. McElrath

WORSHIP AIDS

CALL TO WORSHIP.   "Grace to you and peace from God our Father and the Lord Jesus Christ" (Phil. 1:2 NRSV).

INVOCATION.   Most holy and gracious Father, who turns the shadow of night into the glory of new dawning, shower us with your mercy that we may rejoice and be glad all the day. Lift the light of your countenance upon us, calm our troubled thoughts, and guide our feet into the way of peace. Let your strength be more than sufficient to meet and manage our weakness and let your guidance lead us into all truth and action. Help us in this sacred hour to worship you in the Spirit and name of Jesus, even as did those first followers whom he taught to pray . . . [the Lord's Prayer].—Henry Fields

OFFERTORY SENTENCE.   "And ye shall be witnesses unto me both in Jerusalem and in all Judea, and in Samaria, and unto the uttermost part of the earth" (Acts 1:8b).

OFFERTORY PRAYER.   O God, let us be the instruments of your grace and goodness as we bring to you the fruits of our labor, the dedication of our time and talents, and our intercession on behalf of those who need our prayers.

PRAYER.   How patient you have been with us, Father. Teach us how to be patient with ourselves. Forgive us when we let impatience lead us astray, making us miss the wonder and majesty of your purpose for us. Forgive us this morning for endless running away from reality into dreams of tomorrow—dreams of the senseless and ceaseless getting more and having less. Forgive us for the impatience that drives us to be what we are not and leaves us bored with what we are.

Forgive us for our impatience with others. Forgive us for demanding that our childish desires be met by others when they are tired and weary, frustrated with burdens bigger than they can bear, and worn with the load of caring for others. Forgive us for demanding too much of others because another has demanded much of us. Forgive us for throwing at them some past mistake that we have not had the grace to forgive and forget.

Above all, forgive our impatience with you, Father. How often we want you to operate on our timetable and follow our schedule. We forget that you are the maker and we are that which has been made. Remind us of the need to let you be Lord rather than trying to be dictator of your thoughts and actions. We are sinners, each of us. We are lonely and afraid to let even you know it. We are often hurt and ashamed to admit it. We so often act foolishly and are afraid to confess it. Heal us this morning, Father, of our pride and fear. Cure us of our sick faith, our tired hope, our thin and tattered trust. Here in this sacred place create in us clean, new hearts, cured and healthy, not only able to bear life's struggles and pain, but also sufficiently strong to reach out in caring love to a waiting world and share with it the glory and love of Jesus, in whose name we pray.—Henry Fields

SERMON
Topic: But We've Never Done It That Way Before
TEXT: Mark 2:18–22

Every summer we have tried to take a family vacation. Our travels have taken us to all forty-eight continental states. One aspect of our summer vacations has been amusement parks. Thus we have been to Disney World and Disneyland, Busch Gardens in Virginia and King's Mountain in Cincinnati, the Mall of America in Minneapolis and Six Flags Mid-America in St. Louis. But it was when we visited Busch Gardens near Colonial Williamsburg that something different happened, something that was to forever change our visits to amusement parks.

My wife and I went one way and our children went another way. In a while we met again and our kids said, "Mom and Dad, come ride this little roller coaster with us." "I don't think so," we replied. For you see, we didn't ride roller coasters. We had never done that before. We would ride the Ferris wheel, but never a roller coaster. "Ah, come on," they pleaded. "It's not very bad at all. You'll like it." Wanting to be good parents, we finally agreed to take a chance and go along, even though we had never done it that way before.

Well, we couldn't see the roller coaster course at the entrance area where we got on. It was hidden. We took our seats and the cars began to move. As soon as we exited the terminal and rounded a curve, we started climbing this very tall incline that seemed to have no end. Once we were at the peak, we could see the entire amusement park. Furthermore, we were staring down a drop-off that looked a mile long. We had been duped by our kids. "Oh no!" we screamed just before we lost our breath. The roller coaster fell down the steep slope and made a sharp turn near a river's edge, so close that it looked like we could have reached out and grabbed a handful of river water had we not been going so fast.

Well, we survived the ride—a little shaken and weak-kneed, but we survived. We chided out children for tricking us. But you know what? The next amusement park we visited, what do you suppose was one of the first rides we visited? If you guessed the roller coaster, you guessed right. Even though we had never done it before Busch Gardens, after that first time we grew to like it. So now whenever we go to amusement parks, we ride the roller coasters. Whenever we go through St. Louis, we almost always stop at Six Flags Mid-America because of the big, white, old-fashioned, wooden roller coaster, which we ride at least two or three times.

"But we've never done it that way before." Have you ever said that? "But we've never done it that way before" is something you will hear a lot in churches, especially older churches that have been around a long, long time. The fact is that most people are resistant to change and trying new things.

So it was with the folk of Jesus' day. Some people came to Jesus and asked him why his disciples were not conducting themselves the way the disciples of John the Baptist and the Pharisees were. The real bone of contention at this point was fasting. Why were Jesus' disciples not fasting like John's disciples were? They were not following tradition. They were doing things differently. People just couldn't understand it. "But we've never seen it done that way before," the people complained to Jesus. Jesus explained that the conventional rules of fasting did not apply to that time and place. He compared himself to the bridegroom and his followers to the bride. No one would think of fasting while the wedding feast was in progress. Weddings are a time of feasting and joy. While Jesus—the bridegroom—was with his disciples they did not need to fast. A time would come when the bridegroom would be taken away from them; on that day they could fast.

So Jesus told the two parables of the cloth and the wineskins. Let's suppose that you have a long-sleeve cotton shirt. You have worn a big hole in the elbow. You have washed and dried that cotton shirt so many times that it has shrunk at least two sizes. You wouldn't think of sewing a brand new, unshrunk cotton patch over that hole in the elbow. For if you did, when you washed and dried it, the new piece of cloth would shrink and pull, making a terrible-looking, puckered mess.

As to the wineskins, they didn't have glass bottles in those days like we do today. Wine was often stored in the skins of animals. When the skins were fresh and new they were pliable and flexible and could expand with the wine as it fermented and expanded. But as the skins got old they dried out and got hard and brittle. You might store water in old skins, but never new wine. For as the wine fermented and expanded, it would burst the hard, brittle skins and be lost. Have you ever forgotten and left a canned or bottled drink in your car and it froze and burst? It's the same principle.

The point Jesus was trying to make was that it was a new day. He had ushered in the Kingdom of God. Things would have to be done differently now. The disciples of Jesus could not be expected to act in the old, traditional ways. God was doing a new thing in the lives of his people. The new era called for a new way of looking at things, even though they had never done it that way before.

Let me tell you folks: the church of our time is changing rapidly. The changes that have occurred in the church since I started preaching twenty-three years ago have been dramatic. Up until 1986 I was typing the Sunday bulletin on blue stencil paper on a manual typewriter. The stencil was then wrapped around a drum covered in messy black ink that produced at best a smudgy, blurred copy. For a long time I resisted the idea of bringing the computer into the church office. But now we couldn't do without a computer. I have a computer instead of a church secretary. A lot of ministry and church business is carried on via the Internet.

Also, worship is changing. The days are fast leaving us when the traditional three gospel hymns, responsive reading, offering, Scripture reading, and sermon will be adequate for much of America's population. We are living in a technological society. Technology is making its way into the church sanctuary, and many churches that can't or won't go along are going to be left behind.

One thing appears to be certain: It seems that God is saying to me and to our congregation that a new day is dawning for our church. We may need to be willing to do some things differently. We may have to stop trying to put the new, exciting wine of God into old wineskins, that is, into the traditional way of doing things. God is a God who continues to "make all things new." God is indeed seeking to do a new thing among us.

As Douglas R. Loving has noted, "The quest for new wineskins can open doors to fresh ministries and vibrant witness. . . . Seeking fresh wineskins for . . . new wine challenges us all. The journey can release ingenuity and open doors to new ministries. It may also reconnect us with God's dynamic, transforming movement within each of us."[3]

In other words, God may be calling you and/or your family to new life as well. Perhaps God has shown you that it is time for a new start, a new commitment, a new way of living together in Christian covenant. Perhaps the old ways in which you or your family have been living are not working. Perhaps you need to step out in faith and let God work his newness within you.

Regarding the newness that God wants to impart to our church, our families, and our individual lives, let us be careful that we don't say, "But we've never done it that way before." For as with the roller coaster, we might just like the newness and change that God has in store for us.—Randy Hammer

SUNDAY, OCTOBER 14, 2001
Lectionary Message
Topic: Are Your Blessings Causing You to Forget the God of Blessings?
TEXT: Luke 17:11–19
Other Readings: Jer. 29:1, 4–7; Ps. 66:1–12; 2 Tim. 2:8–15

Everywhere Jesus traveled he encountered sick people. Upon entering a certain village Jesus heard the cry of ten lepers pleading for mercy. Although most people avoided the lepers, Jesus did not. He saw their plight of misery and had compassion. He blessed them with the healing they desired, and with the exception of one leper, all of them forgot the God who blessed them.

---

[3] *Christian Century,* Feb. 16, 2000, p. 177.

I. *The majority's journey toward the blessing* (vv. 11–14). Jesus' response to the lepers' plea for mercy was to send them on a journey to the priests, in accordance with the law prescribed in the Old Testament (Lev. 14). It was the priest who would pronounce them clean.

(a) Due to their leprosy, the journey to the priests would be very painful. The majority of them were determined to get to their blessing. No obstacle would stand in their way. It is interesting, however, that these same people lacked the determination to return and glorify the one who had blessed them. Like the lepers, most people will seek a blessing but they will not seek the Blesser.

(b) The Bible says, "As they went they were cleansed." The blessing they received should have provoked gratitude toward Christ. But sometimes our blessings can blind us to the Blesser. When the lepers were sick they had time to lift their voices to Christ, but when they were healed they had no time for Christ. Are your blessings causing you to forget the God of blessings?

II. *The minority's joy in the Blesser* (vv. 15–16). While the majority was lifted up in pride, the minority was lifted up in praise. All ten lepers had taken the journey toward the blessing; now one of them was returning with joy in the Blesser. He returned to Christ, glorifying God with a loud voice.

(a) The one leper who turned back to Christ was not satisfied with the blessing alone; his satisfaction was in the Blesser. Until God becomes your greatest satisfaction, you will always miss out on the greatest blessing, namely, God. We ought to have the heart of Moses when God was about to lead the people into the Promised Land. Moses said to God, "If your presence does not go with us, do not lead us up from here" (Exod. 33:15). Moses was not satisfied with the blessings of the Promised Land; he wanted the blessings of God's presence.

(b) The one leper's satisfaction in God was expressed by glorifying him with a "loud voice." Two times in this pericope he raised his voice. On the first occasion he raised his voice along with the nine lepers to request mercy. On the second occasion he raised his voice to rejoice in the Master. But according to the Bible, the second voice was greater than the first voice. The point is that a healthy person can raise his voice louder than a sick person. Christ had healed all ten lepers, but only one of them praised him with a loud voice. The other nine lepers could not make a loud joyful noise unto the Lord because they were still sick. Oh, they had been healed in their bodies, but they had not been healed in their souls.

(c) But the one leper could praise God because he had been healed in both body and soul. He left the nine lepers who were still sick in their souls and went back shouting and singing and glorifying God with a loud voice. The majority probably thought he was acting foolishly, but the minority is never ashamed to praise God. If we can raise our voices to request the blessing, then we can raise them to rejoice in the Blesser.

III. *The Master's judgment of those blessed* (vv. 17–19). In the remaining verses Jesus expresses concern over the nine missing lepers and then pronounces the one leper to have been made whole. Because all ten lepers had been healed, all ten lepers should have returned to give thanks to Christ. Where then were the other nine?

(a) This was the question Jesus asked of the one leper. Now, if someone asks us where something is, we presuppose that it is lost. If I ask my wife, "Where are my car keys?" it stands to reason that my keys are lost. Obviously Jesus' question does not carry the exact same overtones, but the implication is the same—the nine lepers were lost. But in what sense where they lost? They were spiritually lost. They were not "found" to "turn back" to "glorify

God" (v. 18). In other words, if a person is going to glorify God, he must repent (turn), and if he is to "turn," he must be "found." Jesus Christ alone can find a lost sinner, turn him from his sins, and give him a new heart to glorify God. This is the "amazing grace" of John Newton's hymn.

(b) The one leper had experienced God's amazing grace. When Jesus said to him, "your faith has made you whole" (v. 19), he was speaking of spiritual healing as well as physical healing. We may be healed in our bodies and still not be whole. To be whole we must have the leprosy of sin cleansed from our spirit. Praise God! Jesus is able to cleanse us from spiritual leprosy.

At the beginning of this pericope, Jesus instructed the lepers to go and show themselves to the priests. The one leper did just that. He showed himself to his High Priest Jesus Christ. And just as priests were supposed to do with lepers, Jesus pronounced him cleansed.

Ten lepers had been blessed, but only one of them remembered the God who had blessed him. Don't let the blessings in your life cause you to forget God. Remember his goodness toward you and praise him for it. But don't just seek the blessing; seek also the Blesser. For whoever has Christ in his life has the greatest blessing of all.—W. Bruce Ostrom

ILLUSTRATIONS
THANKSGIVING.   GRANDPA *(tapping on a plate for silence):* Quiet, everybody! Quiet! . . . Well, Sir, we've been getting along pretty good for quite a while now, and we're certainly much obliged. Remember, all we ask is just to go along and be happy in our own sort of way. Of course we want to keep our health, but as far as anything else is concerned, we'll leave it to you. Thank You.—Moss Hart and George S. Kaufman[4]

INGRATITUDE.   There is no story in all the gospels which so poignantly shows man's ingratitude. The lepers had come to Jesus with a desperate longing; he had cured them, and nine never came back to give thanks. So often, once a man has got what he wants, he never comes back.

So often children are ungrateful to their parents. There is a time in life when a week's neglect would have killed us. Of all living creatures man requires longest to become able to meet the needs which are essential for life. There were long years when we were dependent on parents for literally everything. And yet the day comes when an aged parent is a nuisance; and few young people ever think of repaying the debt they owe. As King Lear said in the day of his own tragedy, "How sharper than a serpent's tooth it is to have a thankless child!"—William Barclay[5]

SERMON SUGGESTIONS
Topic: Putting the Lord to the Test
TEXT: Exod. 17:1–7
(1) By complaining—as if God did not care. (2) By living loosely—as if God did not judge us. (3) By giving in to despair—as if God did not exist.

---

[4] *You Can't Take It with You* (Act I)
[5] *The Gospel of Luke* (Edinburgh, Scotland: Saint Andrew Press, 1956), p. 226f.

Topic: A Rhapsody of Faith

TEXT: Rom. 11:33–36 NB

We glorify God: (1) though his wisdom and knowledge are beyond us; (2) though we cannot understand all that he does or allows; (3) rather, because he is God—"the source, guide, and goal of all that is"—and because we are willing to let God be God!

CONGREGATIONAL MUSIC

1. "Let All the World in Every Corner Sing," George Herbert (1633)
   AUGUSTINE, Erik Routley (1960)
   ALL THE WORLD, Robert G. McCutchan (1935)
   This grand hymn of praise reflects the spirit and meaning of Psalm 66, especially verse 4. It would be appropriate to sing it at the opening of worship.
2. "Come, All You People, Praise Our God," vers. Psalm 66:8–20; *Psalter* (1912)
   ADOWA, Charles H. Gabriel (c. 1920)
   A free paraphrase of the last section of Psalm 66, this song nevertheless captures the spirit of the entire psalm. It could be sung to complement the reading of the psalm.
3. "The Head That Once Was Crowned with Thorns," Thomas Kelly (1820)
   ST. MAGNUS, attr. Jeremiah Clarke (1797)
   The fragment in the Epistle lesson (1 Tim. 2:11–13) that depicts Christ in the heavenly realm in contrast to his creatures in the earthly realm, and the vital connection that exists between the two realms, has a glorious poetic extension in this great early nineteenth-century hymn. Its six stanzas could be sung alternately by choir and congregation, thus dramatizing the hymn's argument.
4. "Now Thank We All Our God," Martin Rinkart (1636); trans. C. Winkworth (c. 1870)
   NUN DANKET ALLE GOTT, Johann Crueger (1647)
   The story of Jesus' healing of the ten lepers and the thanks of only one of them in the Gospel reading highlights the need and the urge to thank God for all things. No hymn can do this better than this classic from seventeenth-century Germany.—Hugh T. McElrath

WORSHIP AIDS

CALL TO WORSHIP.   "Behold the days come, saith the Lord God, that I will send a famine in the land; not a famine of bread, nor a thirst for water, but of hearing the words of the Lord" (Amos 8:11).

INVOCATION.   God of life, renew in us the joy of our belonging to you. In song and prayer, sermon and silence, revive our souls and give us a holy worship.—E. Lee Phillips.

OFFERTORY SENTENCE.   "Walk in love, as Christ also hath loved us, and hath given himself for us an offering and a sacrifice to God for a sweet-smelling savour" (Eph. 5:2).

OFFERTORY PRAYER.   Bless, O Lord, these gifts of love, a token of our devotion to you and a means of reaching out to those who need the message of your love by word and deed.

PRAYER.   Almighty God, Creator of the universe, Father of our Lord Jesus Christ and our Father, we come to you out of our need and our dependence. You have shrouded so much of yourself in mystery, yet you have revealed to us as much as we need to know through Jesus Christ. We stand in awe in your presence, yet we yield our hearts to you in trust and love. We confess that we often vacillate between faith and doubt. We see the tracery of your hand-iwork and rejoice. Then some experience that baffles and pains us clouds over what we have so clearly seen and felt. Give us always, we pray, such commitment of love that the night and the day will be the same to us in our obedience, so that in even the darkest times we shall be led, as it were, by a pillar of fire. May no duty be left undone, no word of witness left unsaid, because of a wavering heart. Lord, we believe. Help our unbelief.

SERMON
Topic: Risky Business
TEXT: John 3:1–21

Someone once said that there are three types of persons in the world: risktakers—those who are willing to gamble everything; caretakers—those who watch out for others and themselves, playing it close to the vest; and undertakers—those who do so little that they bury everyone and everything around them.

We meet all of these types in the New Testament and there is no doubt as to which group Nicodemus belongs: the risktakers. It is highly risky for Nicodemus to come to Jesus, even under the cover of night. Nicodemus is part of a group—the Sanhedrin, or ruling council—which is in opposition to Jesus. He has obviously been listening to and watching Jesus and has come to the point where he believes that Jesus is God. However, he does not understand who Jesus is because Jesus fits none of the categories of holy men: he is neither prophet nor priest. Nicodemus cannot sit quietly and let his colleagues, the religious authorities, do their work of disposing of Jesus. He must talk to Jesus himself to get answers to his questions. So he dares to risk his reputation, his position, and his standing in society in order to talk with Jesus.

If we would follow Jesus then we must also be willing to take risks, to step out onto ground that is both unsure and uncharted.

Fortunately—or unfortunately, depending on your point of view—Jesus calls us not to be caretakers or undertakers but to be risktakers. He calls us to drop all that we consider valu-able and important and follow him, promising us only that he will be with us as we suffer and are despised, hated, and maybe even martyred for our faith. Is it any wonder that we have tamed the message of Jesus, that we have institutionalized him and watered down the gift of eternal life into going to heaven when we die?

There are risks inherent in following Jesus—risks that we cannot avoid if we would be true followers and not distant admirers.

I. *The first risk is that we will never fully comprehend where the Spirit is leading or what God is about in our lives and world.* Our knowledge of God's will is always after the fact, never before. Paul expressed it this way: "We gaze through a dark, shady glass."

Any religion that is fully comprehensible is too small and is not worthy of the greatness and majesty of Almighty God.

Nicodemus came to Jesus as a representative of the religious rationalists, those who had the matter of religion all worked out in their system of rules and laws. Nicodemus was try-ing to understand Jesus on a rational basis, but Jesus would not answer him on that basis because he knew that this was the problem. Nicodemus wanted a completely rational belief and God would not let him have it.

Jesus said to Nicodemus, "You must be born from above," and this is incomprehensible for Nicodemus. It is a totally new idea for which his religious framework has not allowed, and he is as dumbfounded as you or I would be if an alien from Mars walked into our sanctuary this morning. Spiritual birth was not something he or the other Pharisees could comprehend, and without that birth they would never understand. Jesus said to Nicodemus: "The Spirit will blow where it will" (this is a play on words because in Greek the words for *spirit* and *wind* are the same), and just as you cannot comprehend the wind, so you cannot comprehend spiritual birth unless the Spirit comes upon you. We're like Nicodemus—religious but separated from God—and we need to let the Spirit blow through our lives.

We need to let the wind of the Spirit blow out our hatred, our racism, our greed, our lust, our desire for power, our selfishness, our apathy, and all the other characteristics that are un-Christlike. We need to be born anew and anew and anew until the Spirit finishes its work in our lives. Are we willing to risk it?

II. *If we would follow Jesus, the second risk is that we will never be in control of our lives.* Jesus said to Nicodemus, "The wind blows wherever it pleases. You hear its sound but you cannot tell where it comes from or where it is going. So it is with everyone born of the Spirit." As one who has been trying to follow the Spirit, let me share one word: *unpredictable.* We can never predict what the Spirit will do or how the Spirit will lead or act in a given situation. The Spirit will lead us into some of the most difficult situations we have ever faced.

If we are in control of our lives spiritually, that is, if we have all the I's dotted and the T's crossed, if we have this thing called discipleship down pat, then I have news for us: we are not even on the journey.

III. Following Jesus is risky business because it begins with a leap of faith and is a roller coaster ride from there on out. Jesus said to Nicodemus, "For God so loved the world that he gave his one and only Son, that whosoever believes in him shall not perish but have eternal life." We have taken the verb *believe* and made it into a noun, *belief,* and in doing so have exchanged trust in Jesus for intellectual assent. The phrase would be better translated (because of our usage) "whoever faiths in him." Jesus is not referring here to intellectual assent to doctrinal statements, although those are important as road signs on our faith journey; rather, he is referring to surrendering our lives to Jesus in an act of trust that through him we will find forgiveness and a quality of life that is so drastically different as to exist forever—eternal life.

Following the Spirit is dangerous because we are taught to be in control of our lives from the time we are small: be the master of your fate, the captain of your ship.

For what are you willing to risk your life? At one time in my life I enjoyed roller coasters—but no longer. The last time I was on one we were almost flying through the air and the thought went through my mind: Would I be willing to die for a roller coaster ride, for a cheap thrill? The obvious answer was and is no.

Two thousand years ago a man walked on this earth who was more than a man. He said that if we are willing to risk our lives on the truth that he is the Messiah, then the Spirit will come and blow through our lives and they will be radically different. He said that our lives, though dead and lifeless because of our sin and evil, will be radically born from above through the power of the Spirit. Are you willing to risk your life that Jesus was right? Am I?

Is our church? God will that we might listen to the Spirit and follow, no matter what the risk. Yes, following Jesus is risky business.—Robert U. Ferguson Jr.

SUNDAY, OCTOBER 21, 2001
Lectionary Message

Topic: The Ministry of Prayer
TEXT: Luke 18:1–8
Other Readings: Jer. 31:27–34; Ps. 119:97–104; 2 Tim. 3:14–4:5

Jesus told a parable in which he talked about the need for "always praying and never losing heart" (v. 1 Moffatt). That is, we should be so persistent in prayer that no discouragement will keep us from finally winning the victory that God intends us to get through prayer.

There are many things for which we may pray, and for which some of us do pray, and for which more of us ought to pray. There are great causes for which we ought to pray. For instance, "the Kingdom of God," Jesus said, "should be the supreme object of our prayers." We should pray, "Thy Kingdom come, thy will be done, on earth as it is in heaven."

The rule of God over human lives and affairs was the primary obsession of the heart of the Lord Jesus Christ. The expression *Kingdom of God*—the rule of God in human lives—has application both in this world and in the world to come.

In keeping with his obsession with the Kingdom of God, Jesus prayed for the unity of Christian believers. Uniformity is not necessarily the answer to a prayer for unity. We may have dissimilarities and yet, perhaps, have even greater unity because of those very dissimilarities.

Then again Jesus prayed that the world might know God's truth and love. "I pray," he said, "that the world may know that thou hast sent me, and hast loved them, as thou hast loved me" (John 17:23). Isn't that really what God, down through the ages, has been seeking to do in this world?

We perhaps haven't taken into account as we should the great power of prayer. We have used it after a crisis was upon us, but we have not used prayer enough in advance of a great crisis. We pray during war, but we don't pray often enough before war comes. We pray for God to get us out of the mess we have caused, but we do not pray enough that God will keep us from being selfish as individuals and as nations so we may avoid difficulty.

God gives to us as Christians a great opportunity and ministry through prayer. God's Spirit may be released in our world in greater measure as we pray. His Spirit is here, but how much more effectively his Spirit may work in the world as we pray! We must pray for the success of the preaching of the gospel.

We should pray for the forces of righteousness, for all of the forces that are working in our communities and in our world—not only for those with the name of the churches on them, but also for those organizations and leaders whose influence makes for a better community. We should pray for good government by praying for the leaders of our government regardless of what political party they may be associated with. We should pray for international goodwill to prevail and for all of the forces possible to make it come to pass.

I think that if we pray a clumsy prayer in the right direction, God will answer the prayer nonetheless. Remember that when the son of Monica, the mother of Augustine, who was living a licentious life, prayed to the Lord God of Heaven to stop him from going to Italy, where he would be further tempted to sin and where he would be out from under her influence, which she hoped would eventually win him to Christ and to the will of God. But even while she was on her knees praying, he set sail for Italy. In Italy he met Ambrose, who won him to Christ, and Augustine became the most outstanding Christian leader of his time. The literalness of the prayer of Monica was not answered, but the heart of her prayer was answered in a way that was exceedingly abundant, above all that she could ask or think. I believe that we have depended too much on our own wisdom and too little on the wisdom of God.

Then I believe we ought to pray for persons. We ought to "pray for one another. . . . The effectual fervent prayer of a righteous man avails much" (John 5:16).

Jesus was tremendously concerned with the individual. Because of that, we have the parable of the lost sheep. One sheep was lost and ninety-nine were safe. It was perilous to the shepherd to go out and seek the one that was lost—enemies could be lying in wait, predatory animals could tear him limb from limb—but he went out and got that one lost sheep and brought it back, rejoicing. It was just one, but it was a sheep that the shepherd loved and it was important to him.

Jesus prayed for Simon Peter by name and for the other disciples as individuals of supreme value. Jesus anticipated the fall of Simon Peter and said, "Satan has desired to sift you as wheat: but I have prayed for you that your faith will fail not" (Luke 22:31–32). He had prayed for Simon as an individual person—prayed for him by name. He loved him as an individual.

To us has been given this ministry of intercession. Now love will overcome all of the hesitations we might have, if we really love in the spirit in which Jesus loved.

Then we ought to pray for ourselves as Jesus taught us in his model prayer. We ought to pray for God to give to us, to forgive us, and to deliver us. Prayer for self is a legitimate activity and we are actually admonished to pray for ourselves. If we are so concerned about other people as to pray for them and if we feel that it is God's will that we should pray for them and for their good, can we not see that our Heavenly Father is as concerned about us as individual persons as he is about the others he for whom he has commanded us to pray?

What should we pray for? We should pray for our material needs—for "our daily bread"—whatever is necessary for us to live and serve and do the will of God.

We should pray for forgiveness: "Forgive us our debts." That is an urgent need of us all. None of us is ever perfect.

We should pray for spiritual guidance and spiritual power: "Deliver us from evil." Deliver us from the hands of the evil one, from his stratagems and wiles.

God is available and it is the will of God that we be persistent in prayer. Perhaps we do not know what God's perfect will is. Perhaps we have but a faint intimation of what it is. We do not know the correct details, but we must pray the best we can, and if the prayer is not exactly in detail as God would have it, then he will rearrange our prayer and make it work out for the best. Deep within our hearts ought always be this dedication: "Not my will but thine be done."—James W. Cox

ILLUSTRATIONS

PRAYER IS THE LINK.   Prayer is the link between the hope Christ offers us and the hopelessness of people around us. Actually, we are to spend more time talking to the Lord about people than we spend talking to people about the Lord! When we do, two things happen.

First, we are given the Lord's eyes to see people as He sees them and His heart to love them as He loves them. Because each person is unique, He gives us His special strategy for communicating His hope for each one.

Second, when we pray for someone, the Lord intensifies His preparation of that person to receive His hope. He will arrange circumstances to confront people with their need for Him. He will work in their minds and hearts, creating a new openness.

But we need to remember that the Lord's timing is not always ours. So we must leave the "when" to Him—and also the "how." He may use us or someone else. That's really not important. Our task is to be ready and available while we persist in prayer.—Lloyd Ogilvie[6]

CHRIST PRAYING FOR US.   In the New Testament, all through its shining pages, we are taught that Christ is our great high priest, who "ever liveth to make intercession" for us. Christ praying for us—praying for those who have no one to pray for them, no matter how far-wandering or far-fallen!

Truly there must be hope for all when the Son of God prays for each one!—Joseph Fort Newton[7]

SERMON SUGGESTIONS

Topic: Experiences That Turn One to God
TEXT: Ruth 1:1–9a
(1) Loss. (2) Loyalty. (3) Longing.

Topic: The Kind of Christianity to Be Thankful for
TEXT: 1 Thess. 1:1–10
(1) Faith in action. (2) Love in labor. (3) Hope in fortitude.

CONGREGATIONAL MUSIC

1. "Holy Bible, Book Divine," John Barton Sr. (1803)
   ALETTA, William B. Bradbury (1858)
   This simple hymn enumerates the many uses of Scripture: to teach, to chide, to guide, to comfort, and to witness to one's faith in its triumph over death. It thus can be a useful response to the Epistle lesson (2 Tim. 3:14–4:5) in which the apostle Paul charges Timothy to preach this Word and through it to provide instruction and encouragement.
2. "Teach Me, O Lord, Your Way of Truth," vers. Psalter (1912)
   ST. CRISPIN, George J. Elvey (1862)
   Although the stanzas of this metrical paraphrase do not parallel exactly the verses of Psalm 119 selected for today's reading, the tenor of this hymn is quite in keeping with the central thrust of the psalm to exalt the law, Word, commandments, and precepts of God. The singing of the first three stanzas could precede the Psalter reading, with the last two following it.
3. "Hail to the Lord's Anointed," James Montgomery (1821)
   ELLACOMBE, Gesangbuch der H.W.K. Hofkapelle (1784)

---

[6] *A Future and a Hope*
[7] *Everyday Religion*

The parable of the penitent widow who is promised justice (Luke 18:1–8) echoes in this stately hymn promising God's reign and his new covenant of love. The hymn also relates to the Old Testament reading in which God's covenant to forgive Israel and to put a new law in the people's hearts is set forth. It lends itself admirably to antiphonal line-by-line singing.

4. "Thy Word Is a Lamp," Amy Grant (1984) (Ps. 119:105)

THY WORD, Michael W. Smith (1984)

This popular contemporary song focuses on Psalm 119:105 in its refrain but would be suitable to accompany the Psalter lesson as a response. It witnesses to God's companionship and guidance in life.—Hugh T. McElrath

WORSHIP AIDS

CALL TO WORSHIP.   "Thou wilt keep him in perfect peace whose mind is stayed on thee: because he trusteth in thee. Trust he the Lord for ever: for the Lord Jehovah is everlasting strength" (Isa. 26:3–4).

INVOCATION.   You never change, O Lord, but we are always changing, sometimes for the better, sometimes for the worse. Grant us steadier progress in our life of faith as we contemplate what you are and seek after what we may become through your grace.

OFFERTORY SENTENCE.   "What shall I render unto the Lord for all his benefits toward me? I will take the cup of salvation and call upon the name of the Lord. I will pay my vows unto the Lord now in the presence of all his people" (Ps. 116:12–14).

OFFERTORY PRAYER.   For some of us it is easy and painless to give; for others it is a strain and sacrifice. But it is a source of joy for all who consider all your benefits, O Lord, whether rich or poor. Some would give more who can only give less; some give less who could give more. Yet you are able to use and multiply all that we bring to you. So we bring our offerings and ask you to bless them.

PRAYER.   O heavenly Father, who hast filled the world with beauty, open our eyes to behold thy gracious hand in all thy words; that rejoicing in thy whole creation we may learn to serve thee with gladness; for the sake of him through whom all things were made, thy Son Jesus Christ our Lord.—*The Book of Common Prayer*

SERMON
Topic: Waiting for God
TEXT: Acts 1:8, 12–14, 2:1–4, 14–18

Every Sunday I want to begin the sermon by saying the same thing, "This is a remarkable passage!" Perhaps you have had the same experience of digging deeply into a passage and finding new meanings that are startling and transforming. In this passage we discover the Risen Christ, on the day of his Ascension, giving the disciples the command not to go to the ends of the Earth but to wait.

I. *God does say, "Wait." Wait* is not a good American word. America is a place of restless energy. We get restless if it takes the hamburger joint more than a couple of minutes to determine exactly what we want and then to get it into our hands. This is not just a symptom of our modern society but a national trait seen in our sweeping across this continent and on into the heavens of the moon and Mars. Carl Sandburg caught our spirit in the words of his poem "Chicago": "Fierce as a dog with tongue lapping for action . . . bareheaded, shoveling, wrecking, planning, building, breaking, rebuilding. . . ."

It is hard for us to hear the command "Wait," but that is often God's Word to us. The disciples no doubt were full of energy and excitement and ready to do whatever the Lord said, except wait. The full command was to wait in Jerusalem for the Spirit to come upon them. The reason was that they were weak and could not do God's work without the Holy Spirit.

In the Garden of Gethsemane Jesus had cautioned his disciples, "You think you are ready for what is to come but you aren't. Your spirits are willing but your flesh is weak." The good word on the day of Ascension was that God had a plan and a timetable for the work ahead. We are not to run ahead with our plans and energy but to be willing to acknowledge our weakness and need of spiritual preparation. God will provide in time.

II. *Waiting can be active.* Luke says that the disciples went back to Jerusalem and devoted themselves to prayer. For many of us, myself included, prayer is difficult. I am one of the one's ready to lay hands on a task and make it work out. Being still and doing "nothing" but praying seems indeed to be doing nothing while the task awaits.

But then we remember that Jesus was a man of prayer. Even after a long day, or especially after a long day, and before critical decisions Jesus would often get up a long while before day and go out to a lonely place and pray. He prayed so much and seemed to get so much benefit from it that his disciples said to him, "Teach us to pray as you do." That was the occasion for his giving them the model prayer, which we call the Lord's Prayer. I remember reading of Paul Tournier, the Swiss psychiatrist, that he began his day with an hour of prayer, and before days he knew would be extremely busy, he began with two hours.

In my own life I am convinced that I am powerless for ministry without a life of active waiting in prayer. Prayer is hard work for me. I can be still but my mind restlessly paces while I pray and leaps for joy when it is released to wander as it will. For others I know it is their gift and they can pray for hours each day. Such prayer develops a beauty in their lives that comes through hours of communion with the Spirit of God.

III. *The Holy Spirit comes in power.* In today's passage the Holy Spirit comes with power, disrupting lives, disturbing everything, taking hold of people, causing them to say and do things they would never have done otherwise. Luke could not even describe what happened except in images of a great wind, fire, and strange words.

Again and again Luke says that by the power of the Spirit Peter preached the mighty Pentecost sermon, Stephen gave his powerful testimony as he was being stoned, the Church leaders at Antioch set aside Paul and Barnabas for the first mission trip to the Gentiles, and the entire book of Acts itself is bracketed with the Spirit's work.

Certainly this dramatic intervention is not always our experience of the Spirit, who seeks no self-aggrandizing attention in us. The good word for us is that the Spirit of God is that powerful, that capable, that kind of presence in our lives. We can and must seek this enabling for our lives and ministry. As the disciples were told to wait for the Spirit before going out to do Christ's work, so all Christians are to have this Spirit to empower Christian living.

We were given this Spirit when we claimed Christ as our Savior. We have within us the

God of all Creation. We can ignore this Spirit, to our own spiritual weakness, or we can seek to live in the power of the Spirit. The hard word, *wait*, is also a very good word.—Stuart G. Collier

SUNDAY, OCTOBER 28, 2001
Lectionary Message

Topic: God Accepts the Humble

TEXT: Luke 18:9–14

Other Readings: Joel 2:23–32; Ps. 65; 2 Tim. 4:6–8, 16–18

How can a person be accepted by God? Knowing that all have sinned and consequently fallen short of the glory of God (Rom. 3:23), we readily acknowledge that humans experience separation from God. Most humans who desire to be accepted by God will do good things—such as say prayers, do good deeds, be obedient to commands, and perform religious duties—so that God will accept them.

Attempting to win God's favor by doing religious activities and living outwardly moral lives inevitably results in spiritual pride. The egotism that a mortal could satisfy the demands of a holy God is compounded by the arrogance that such a mortal is better than others.

Our Lord addresses this situation in this parable. To those "who trusted in themselves that they were righteous, and viewed others with contempt" (Luke 18:9 NASB) Jesus reveals that those who trust in God alone will be declared righteous.

I. *We see the pride of self-righteousness.* While pride afflicts all persons, a good case can be made that pride is particularly prevalent among religious people. With religion often comes outward morality and the doing of good works. Such a religious person will often compare himself with others—especially with those who continue in certain sins and neglect religious duties.

Jesus portrays the Pharisee in this manner. Compared with extortioners, the unjust, adulterers, and those who collected taxes for the despised Romans, the Pharisee exhibits a certain smugness that many religious persons share. His performance of religious deeds—fasting twice a week and giving of tithes—provides his assurance that God has especially favored his efforts. Certainly he must be righteous.

Before we condemn the self-righteous Pharisee, we must ask if we are actually any better. Do we look down on those at the golf course as we are driving to our church on Sunday morning? Do we congratulate ourselves for our faithfulness and sacrifice as we examine our financial contribution statement at the end of the year? Do we look down on those who have not yet risen to our level of "spiritual maturity"? Surely God sees us as righteous—look at all we've done. We would do well to remember Christ's rebuke to the church at Laodicea: "You say, 'I am rich and have become wealthy and have need of nothing,' and you do not know that you are wretched and miserable and poor and blind and naked" (Rev. 3:17 NASB).

II. *We see the humility of self-abasement.* The tax collector knows the sting of rejection. Roundly condemned for his betrayal of his people, he understands separation. Even in the temple he stands off at a distance. As great as his separation from humans, however, his separation from God because of his sin is greater still. While there is nothing wrong with the Pharisee's physical posture in prayer, the tax collector dares not look toward heaven. In agony he beats his breast and pleads, "God, be merciful to me, the sinner." The Greek carries the definite article, "*the* sinner." Although all of humanity is guilty of sin, the tax collector does not see himself as merely *a* sinner like all other humans. Neither does he compare himself to those who may appear to be even worse sinners than he is. He designates himself as *the* sinner. He focuses on his sin alone.

The tax collector, though evidently untrained in the study of God's law, gets to the root of the matter. He sees himself in abject poverty of spirit against the lovely holiness of God. Standing in an earlier temple centuries before, Isaiah likewise exclaimed, "Woe is me, for I am ruined! Because I am a man of unclean lips and I live among a people of unclean lips; for my eyes have seen the King, the Lord of hosts" (Isa. 6:5 NASB). Similarly, Jesus taught, "Blessed are the poor in spirit, for theirs is the kingdom of heaven. Blessed are those who mourn, for they shall be comforted" (Matt. 5:3–4 NASB).

This tax collector displays a great truth. The issue is not the sin or sinfulness of others; the issue is our own sin. We must acknowledge that we have sinned against the thrice-holy God. By thought, word, and deed, too often we have done that which God has prohibited and failed to do that which God has commanded.

III. *We see the declaration by the Lord.* Jesus declares that the tax collector, the nonreligious one, went to his house "justified." While we must be careful not to pack the Pauline theology of justification into Luke's usage of the term here, the word *justified* still means "to declare righteous." Whereas the person who saw himself as righteous went to his house unjustified, the person who saw himself as unrighteous went to his house justified. David understood the essence of this truth: "For thou dost not delight in sacrifice, otherwise I would give it; thou art not pleased with burnt offering. The sacrifices of God are a broken spirit; a broken and a contrite heart, O God, thou wilt not despise" (Ps. 51:16–17 NASB).

We, too, need to be reminded of this truth. Comparing ourselves with others, always with the sinners and not the saints, results in a smug, spiritual complacency. Only when we see ourselves as God sees us can we receive the forgiveness and the standing that this outcast tax collector received.

IV. *Conclusion.* Perhaps our familiarity with this parable dulls our sensitivity to its truth. After all, the Pharisee is someone else, someone besides *me.* Yet deep within, the heart knows. I am the one who compares myself favorably against others. I am the one who cloaks the poverty of my spirit with religiosity. I am the one who gives God the indication that he is fortunate that I am on his team. Unfortunately, I am also the one who remains unjustified.

How we need to emulate the spirit of the tax collector in Jesus' parable. God is holy; we are sinful. Yet the holy God forgives the one who approaches the Almighty in humility, recognizing his own sin and trusting in the atoning sacrifice of God's own Son: "He made him who knew no sin to be sin on our behalf, that we might become the righteousness of God in him" (2 Cor. 5:21 NASB).—William G. Moore

ILLUSTRATIONS

WE ARE UNABLE TO PRODUCE A RIGHTEOUSNESS ACCEPTABLE TO GOD.   Augustus Toplady knew well the spirit of the tax collector. The words of one of his poems, "Rock of Ages," was put to music by Thomas Hastings and has been sung by Christians for more than a century. One verse poignantly expresses the thrust of our parable:

Not the labors of my hands
Can fulfill Thy law's demands;
These for sin could not atone;
Thou must save, and Thou alone:
Nothing in my hand I bring,
Simply to Thy cross I cling.

—William G. Moore

THE STANDARD MAKES THE DIFFERENCE.   No doubt all that the Pharisee said was true. . . . But the question is not, "Am I as good as my fellow men?" The question is, "Am I as good as God?" Once I made a journey by train to England. As we passed through the Yorkshire moors I saw a little whitewashed cottage and it seemed to me to shine with an almost radiant whiteness. Some days later I made the journey back to Scotland. The snow had fallen and was lying deep all around. We came again to the little white cottage, but this time its whiteness seemed drab and soiled and almost grey in comparison with the virgin whiteness of the driven snow.

It all depends on what we compare ourselves with. And when we set our lives beside the life of Jesus and beside the holiness of God, all that is left to say is, "God be merciful to me–the sinner."—William Barclay[8]

SERMON SUGGESTIONS

Topic: Why Give Thanks to the Lord?
TEXT: Ps. 92:1
(1) Because of what God is. (2) Because of what God does for us. (3) Because of what we can do for God.

Topic: God's Unrecognized Presence
TEXT: Gen. 28:10–22
(1) *Jacob's experience:* the unbiblical story. (2) *Our experience:* (a) in joyous mountaintop events, (b) in uneventful ordinary life, (c) in times of crisis. (3) *The proper response*—solemn dedication: (a) good—Jacob's vow (Gen. 28:20–22), (b) better—the attitude of the three young Jews (Dan. 3:16–18).

CONGREGATIONAL MUSIC

1. "Fight the Good Fight with All Thy Might," John Samuel B. Monsell (1863)
   PENTECOST, William Boyd (1868)
   This bold, invigorating hymn would be suitable as a response to the reading of the Epistle lesson (2 Tim. 4:6–8, 16–18) in which the apostle confesses to having fought the good fight and kept the faith.
2. "Be Thou My Vision," trad. Irish (eighth century); trans. Mary E. Byrn (1905)
   SLANE, trad. Irish melody

---

[8] *The Gospel of Luke*, rev. ed. (Philadelphia: Westminster, 1975), p. 225.

Joel 2:28 promises that God's spirit will be poured out on all, that daughters as well as sons will prophesy and the people shall have dreams and visions. This hymn that is popular with young people, who may "see visions," would be a natural response to the Old Testament lesson.

3. "Thy Might Sets Fast the Mountains," vv. 7–15, *The Psalter* (1912)

MORNING LIGHT, George J. Webb (1837)

This metrical paraphrase of the last half of Psalm 65 could naturally follow the reading of the first six verses. Set to a familiar gospel tune, it could be sung antiphonally between choir and congregation.

4. "Depth of Mercy! Can There Be," Charles Wesley (1740)

SEYMOUR, Carl M. von Weber (1825)

CANTERBURY, adapt. from Orlando Gibbons (1623)

The prayer of the tax collector in the parable Jesus told of the Pharisee and the tax collector was the one approved by God. This Wesleyan hymn of penitence appropriately voices the theme of that prayer and thus would be suitable for use in connection with the Gospel lesson.—Hugh T. McElrath

WORSHIP AIDS

CALL TO WORSHIP.   "He satisfies those who are thirsty and fills the hungry with good things" (Ps. 107:9 TEV).

INVOCATION.   Today, O Lord, may the water and bread of life that come from you satisfy our deepest hungers and thirsts. May we not be content with a cheap, quick fix for our desires but instead find in you what we truly need.

OFFERTORY SENTENCE.   "I urge that petitions, prayers, requests, and thanksgivings be offered to God for all people" (1 Tim. 2:1 TEV).

OFFERTORY PRAYER.   O God, we pray many prayers for many causes and we thank you for hearing us. Now we pray one more prayer: that you would grant us the grace to give so that these offerings will bless all people.

PRAYER.   Thou all-holy one, if it were not for thy love expressed in Christ Jesus, our Lord, we would be afraid and would cringe and falter and go away from thine altar. If it were not that on thine altar is a sacrifice made not by ourselves to propitiate thee but by thine own self to win us, surely there would be no worshipful heart. Each would go away afraid and forever away. But because thou art holy, thou hast been true to thine own nature and for thy name's sake thou hast redeemed us. Thou hast offered the sacrifice not to propitiate but to woo and win us, to show us what sin costs all the time, and to bring us back by a way that shall make us forsake our sins and sinfulness and make us love thee, thou holy one. It is said that the gift thou didst make upon the altar is the holy one. So we cry unto Thee, "Holy, Holy, Holy, Lord God Almighty, who wast and art and is to come." We adore thy holiness in the love and mercy and brotherliness of our Lord and Savior, Jesus Christ.—Frank W. Gunsaulus

SERMON
Topic: The Right Fit
TEXT: Mark 2:13–22

We should not be surprised to discover that there is a great debate about whether or not the Christian Church is delivering what it is supposed to deliver. Has the Church stopped being the place where people fill up their lives with the new wine of Jesus Christ and become an organization that attempts to offer all kinds of things: entertainment, recreation, group therapy, special-interest study groups, and social action to everybody?

Jesus went to Jerusalem because he could not live with the picture the religious community painted of God.

Without a sense of identity, without a sense of purpose, without a sense of mission, God has put us in this place to preach the good news to a particular part of the world. There are those who will spend their days talking about the days of the church when the pews were full and youth fellowship had thousands. Every minister I ever talked with in Pittsburgh had the same story. They could not get their sessions to stop talking about the 1950s, when every church had a thousand members and held two services—the glory days.

Those congregations that do stop looking back are so quickly tempted to try to be the Wal-Mart of the human condition—megachurches with programs for everybody. Religion is the opiate of the troubled soul, the inspiration for the defeated, the power of positive thinking for the pessimist, the center of friendship for the mobile community, and the moment of rest for the recharging of the batteries of life.

What is it we as the Church are supposed to be that will be important enough for us to risk going to Jerusalem with Jesus? Jesus says that he is something that is radically new. He has not come and is not going to Calvary to patch up old traditions and frayed institutions. The Kingdom of God is not called into being just to calm shattered nerves or to give timid salespeople confidence to go to the next appointment. It is not a bandage to be put over old tears. Jesus says he has come to give life and to give it more abundantly, and to say that new life has all the explosive power of fermenting wine. It will burst the seams of all the old skins. Jesus has come so that we might become a new people and live in the midst of a new kind of community. Jesus did not come to make everything better with Jesus on it, like Bluebonnet margarine. Jesus came that we might be reconciled to God and in that reconciliation become new and different.

To begin with, Jesus declared that in his coming the new was already here. "Repent for the Kingdom of God is at hand." The Kingdom of God is around us and can be enjoyed and experienced now. More times than not when we hear about the Kingdom of God it is something pushed into the future. "I am a poor wayfaring stranger traveling through this world below" hoping to live so I can get to the Kingdom of God. We discount Jesus' words about the Kingdom of God being present with him by making the Kingdom all spiritual. This old world holds us back. The less we can have to do with this world, the more spiritual we think we become and the more fit we think we are for the Kingdom of God.

Jesus tells his disciples that the Kingdom of God is in the future with God in heaven, but it is also open to them right where they are with him. The Kingdom of God is right with us now in his Spirit. The Kingdom of God comes to us in all of the moments of life and death, in sickness and in health, in victory and in failure, in fear and hope, in frustration and anger.

The Kingdom of God is present in your life when your heart is full of joy. It happens when we are confronted with the real questions of life, with the mysteries of life and death, when life comes and life is good and we dance on the ceiling knowing that the coming of the King-dom was not our doing. And the mystery of the Kingdom of God is there when the questions of life and death are so hard and so painful, so full of anguish and sorrow, that all we can do is grab ahold of each other and cry and pound our fists and wall up our prayers and trust that the Spirit of God will pray for us because we do not know what to pray.

The Kingdom of God is here in our midst. In the power of the love and grace of God we can see that in the mixture of the ordinary coming and going of the days there is the pres-ence of the eternal. By the light of the grace of Jesus Christ, the God made human, we can see the sacred and the secular all mixed together, but we can also see the sacred at work in the secular. The gift of God in Jesus Christ is the gift of knowing that we live in the midst and in the presence of the Kingdom of God now, and as we sing and dance around the joys of life and share and hold onto one another in the deep sorrows of life, we find our lives being made new each day. We know that in the working out of the mystery of God in the ordinary there is always the possibility of things becoming new. The water might become wine. The fish and loaves might become enough.

We are much too tempted to talk about the spiritual dimension of the Kingdom as being separate from the flesh of humanity. Over yonder they do not love the flesh hard like God has loved it in Jesus Christ. In so much of our New Age spiritualism and in so many religious communities, the Kingdom of God is split from the messy, ordinary stuff of life. They split apart the saving of souls from the redemption of the ghetto. They want to save souls for heaven but they have no interest in cleaning up the park. They want to pray in school but then want to cut out free welfare programs for breakfast and lunch for students. The King-dom of God is celebrated wherever this good old messy creation, which God keeps going and loves so much that he became a part of it in Jesus Christ, is loved and honored.

We gather in worship to rejoice, be glad, and sing because we have seen, we have felt, we have watched as the mystery of life has happened all around us. Every day is a miracle of life for each of us because heaven knows there are enough germs and dangers to kill us all if God did not give us life. We come to rejoice and to sing praises for the God-given new life, new hope, and new possibility for each of us and for all of us. We gather to read the stories to remind us to keep looking, to keep watch, to be alert, for the Kingdom of God is all around and we are to be ready to celebrate it and enjoy it. We gather to affirm the promises and hopes that come in the Kingdom of God, that darkness does not destroy the light, that defeat is not the end, that death is not separation from God, that sin is not the end of our hopes. God's Resurrection can stand erect against those who have been beaten down by the mean-ness of life.

Jesus says that he has come that we might have new life like new wine because we live in the presence and in the power of the Kingdom of God. Life in the Kingdom of God is dif-ferent. It has a vitality to it like wine. It has a spirit to it like fermentation. The people of God live in the Kingdom of God and we live with two major abiding passions: there is the heart that bubbles out in joy in the wonderful celebration of birth and love, and even in the face of death it is full of celebration of the joy of having been able to share love with the deceased; and there is a deeper and more profound current of peace and hope that bears us up in fel-lowship in times of pain and sorrow.

Jesus invites us to enter into the Kingdom of God. He did not come to make our prayer life better and to leave the business part of our lives alone. Jesus does not say follow me in the Kingdom of God on Tuesday and you can do what you want on Wednesday through Saturday. What Jesus did say is that the Kingdom of God is around you at all times. It is a part of all days. It is available in all places. The Kingdom of God is in every part of life. It is part of your senses, your sexuality, your emotions, your imagination, and your intelligence. The Kingdom of God is not a habit to be added to other habits. It is a way of seeing, a way of responding to all of life. We are invited by Jesus to live in the Kingdom of God.

The Kingdom of God is where we are invited and where we invite others to share a banquet together in the presence of a cross. The Kingdom of God is wherever the joy of life is celebrated in the face of all of the forces that seek to control or put a stop to the sharing of joy. The Kingdom of God is wherever that joy keeps expanding and inviting others to come and share it.

The mission, the work, the way for each Christian community is to find how it can celebrate the joy of Jesus and the presence of the Kingdom of God in its midst and share that joy with others. Our purpose as the people of God is simply to celebrate the goodness of God in the land of the living and to trust ourselves to his future.—Rick Brand

SUNDAY, NOVEMBER 4, 2001
Lectionary Message

Topic: Becoming a Grown-Up Christian

TEXT: 2 Thess. 1:1–4, 11–12

Other Readings: Hab. 1:1–4, 2:1–4; Ps. 119:137–144; Luke 19:1–10

I. *The faith of a mature Christian.* The faith of a believer in Jesus Christ must be steadfast, unmovable, always abounding in the strength that will hold firm in the utmost trials of life. Such faith is difficult to attain and is very costly in terms of experience and testing.

A Christian is very uncomfortable having a little, weak faith; strong faith can be developed in its place. It needs to be fed regularly, especially in times of loneliness, illness, poverty, danger, or temptation. The feeding is done by carrying strong texts of Scripture in one's mind at all times, keeping hold of a text until it becomes clear and permanent in one's mind and heart.

Faith may be weak because of lack of confidence in one's ability to face trials and wants. The believer with weak faith is always uncomfortable around others, fearing that he will slip; he doesn't really belong to God, finds being Christian too confining, and feels he will break his own rules.

Strength in faith comes by noting and remembering one's spiritual successes. To find God supplying life's necessities and being sure to recall that when you are next in need; to call upon God's Spirit to hold you true, honest, loyal, straight, and loving in a time of challenge or taunting, or of silent, private temptation; and always remembering whenever subsequent challenges arise that he has held you true—these are means of growth in faith, of strengthening faith, as Paul commended the Thessalonians for doing to survive their persecutions and distresses. Local unbelievers had been trying to destroy their new faith by calumniating Paul and his motives out of jealousy. Paul had to defend himself against charges of treason, which could have shaken the Church's belief. He knew the trials through which they were required to pass.

II. *Surviving the tests of faith.* Survival of a believer's faith when he or she is thrust into the maelstrom of secular society may be a cause of great concern to fellow believers, to family and friends. Exercise of faith while it is growing is a strengthening process.

The neophyte in any skillful practice is well advised to seek the direction and example, the assurances and reminders, of those who are already mature in the skill. Christians who have gloriously proven the victory of the cross in the ways of their own lives and hardships are excellent counselors to the beginner. Intergenerational association has spiritual advantages for younger believers in growing stronger faith and evolving survival strategies. A young person faced with challenges is wise to observe the problems and solutions of more practiced spiritual warriors, as well as to discuss such things with them. For such an experienced person to share times when God's strength sufficed in face of the person's weakness, when God supported the person's character when it was about to crumble, or when God replaced doubt with renewed trust can be a source of nourishment and encouragement to another who is still needing to grow strong in faith.

III. *The fruit of personal faithfulness.* With such faith comes faithfulness. Possessing such faith you are not going to be disloyal or to deceive or betray your God. You are just as unlikely, in the face of temptation, to surrender your faithfulness to your country, your loved ones, your employment, or your own integrity and your confession.

The commendable faith Paul learned of in Thessalonica was perfected after a period of moral and spiritual ripening. Jesus himself likened faith to a seed that grows. We must not expect neglect, carelessness, abandonment, and indolence to produce a strong, growing, mature fruit of faith and faithfulness. But we look forward to the glory when he fulfills "every good purpose and virtue and work of faith" by his power, in the merciful favor of God, "according to the grace of our God and the Lord Jesus Christ."

The assurance we need to find within ourselves is that "we are ready," we are willing to undergo the challenges of discipline—even of suffering—to receive God's commendation and trust, so that we can say, "We are obliged to give thanks to God at all times for you, brothers, just as is right, that your faith grows exceedingly, and the love of every one of you for each other is abounding."—John R. Rodman

ILLUSTRATIONS

HEALTHY RELIGION.   Healthy religion is the affirming of truth even though it is forever on the scaffold and wrong is forever on the throne. If we arrogantly say that we shall affirm truth only in so far as it triumphs in our workaday world, then we again commit the heresy of cutting God's pattern on the Procrustean bed of our own standards. Healthy religion is the affirming of goodness even though you and I as human beings taste little of it. If we affirmed these values only in so far as they came into expression in our lives and our world, then we should again be affirming only ourselves. It is the central failing of us all that we tend to act like pampered children, willing to "play" only if the universe plays our way, giving fidelity to God only so long as He makes us His most favored children.—Rollo May[1]

---

[1] *The Springs of Creative Living*

CHALLENGES TO OUR SPIRITUAL MATURITY.   It would be easy to be overwhelmed by all the projected changes raised to this point. But as a New Zealand Christian film I saw years ago suggests, "We need to learn to grasp the problems at the near edge." Obviously, none of us in our lives, churches, and institutions can begin to respond to all the changes filling our world. But part of the problem is that many of us are making no effort to engage the emerging challenges at all. I believe all of us can find the "near edge of one problem and engage it for the kingdom.—Tom Sine[2]

SERMON SUGGESTIONS

Topic: The Foolishness of God
TEXT: 1 Cor. 1:12, 25 RSV

(1) There was a divine foolishness about his birth. (2) There was a divine foolishness about his silent years. (3) There was a divine foolishness about the conduct of his ministry. (4) The foolishness culminated in the cross.—J. D. Jones

Topic: Protocol for Banquets
TEXT: Luke 14:1, 7–14

(1) *For guests:* If you are not presumptuous, your proper worth will be recognized and rewarded. (2) *For hosts:* More important, if you recognize the proper worth of the outsiders, your "love will be vindicated."

CONGREGATIONAL MUSIC

1. "My Faith Has Found a Resting Place," Lidie A. Edmunds (1891)
   LANDAS, Norwegian folk melody; arr. W. J. Kirkpatrick (c. 1900)
   Following the Gospel reading in which the story of Zacchaeus's conversion is told and the purpose of Jesus is declared to be to seek and save the lost, it would be appropriate to sing this popular gospel song. Its fourth stanza asserts that "the lost he came to save."
2. "We Walk by Faith and Not by Sight," Henry Alford (1844)
   GRAEFENBURG, Johann Crueger (1653)
   DUNLAP'S CREEK, Samuel McFarland (c. 1816)
   Both the Old Testament reading in Habakkuk and the Epistle lesson in 2 Thessalonians focus attention on the need for patient faith and perseverance. This hymn from nineteenth-century Britain—based on the case of Doubting Thomas in John 20:27–29—voices a prayer to meet that need.
3. "Lord, Be Thy Word My Rule," Christopher Wordsworth (1863)
   QUAM DILECTA, Henry Lascelles Jenner (1861)
   This short hymn could serve admirably as a sung response before and after the reading of the lesson from the Psalter. Its theme is that of the entire psalm: exalting the laws, commands, statutes, promises, and so forth of God's Word.
4. "We Have Heard the Joyful Sound," Priscilla Owens (1887)
   JESUS SAVES, William J. Kirkpatrick (1882)
   LIMPSFIELD, Josiah Booth (1898)

---

[2] *Wild Hope*

"The Son of Man came to seek and save that which was lost" (Luke 19:10). This gospel hymn "rings the changes" on that truth with its refrain, "Jesus Saves!" The two tunes could be sung alternately to the four stanzas of the text.—Hugh T. McElrath

WORSHIP AIDS

CALL TO WORSHIP.   "Ye shall go out with joy and be led forth with peace: the mountains and the hills shall break forth before you into singing, and all the trees of the field shall clap their hands" (Isa. 55:12).

INVOCATION.   "God of grace and God of glory," help us to look in the right places for fulfillment and joy. Let us begin the quest with you and trust your wisdom, so that when the days of opportunity are past we will go out with joy and be filled with peace. To this end, make this a time of beginning for some and a time of beginning again for others.

OFFERTORY SENTENCE.   "Give and it shall be given unto you; good measure, pressed down and shaken together, and running over shall men give into your bosom. For with the same measure that ye mete withal it shall be measured to you again" (Luke 6:38).

OFFERTORY PRAYER.   Dear Lord, as we think today about the hurt and pain of a hungry world, make us hungry for a word from you. Even though our stomachs are full, may we feel a need that goes deeper than any physical hunger, a need to be in a right relationship with you. We come now with an opportunity to reestablish that relationship, to reopen our lines of communication with our Maker and our Lord. We thank you for another such chance and pray that we might seize it in such a spirit of gratitude and worship that we all might be blessed.—James M. King

PRAYER.   She is weary, Lord. For long months she has tried to deal with family problems that seem to have no end. She is tired, bone weary, and ready to give up. This morning let her find the inspiration and strength to continue on with hope and faith.

He has struggled for years with the problem, Father. Many encounters with helping systems have not been able to relieve the drive for alcohol. He doesn't want to be its captive, to be constantly seen as its victim, but the addiction is such that he cannot handle it on his own. Meet him this morning with the cleansing power of your presence. Call him to you in love. Steady his resolve and remove the desire for this demon that has dominated his life almost to the point of complete ruin.

They were not prepared for the child that came, Father. In their dreams and imaginings they had built their lives around the vision of a healthy, normal baby. Now they must deal with a child who will never be like other children but will be deformed and largely non-functional in the world. This morning their hearts are heavy as they take up their responsibility and face the long tomorrows to come. Give them endurance for the journey, courage for living, and love for this child that will enable them all not only to survive but also to triumph in the struggles before them, we pray.

They did not hear the good news they had hoped and prayed would come. The spots turned out to be malignant. While treatment will help, they know that there is no cure and that a young life with still years of promise will soon end on this Earth. This morning they are stunned. All those dreams and hopes of future events have been cancelled and a frightening view of the future has fallen on them like a dark curtain. Give them the light they need to walk through this darkness. Bless them with your presence and comfort as they make their way through this valley to the ultimate light of home.

Thank you for being with us in every circumstance of life. Thank you for renewing our joy and giving us the grace and power to manage the overwhelming issues we meet. Thank you for being able to know your love and for helping us to find rest in Christ, the author and finisher of our faith. Thank you for hope in our desperation and assurance in our darkest hours. Thank you for the joy that is rekindled after the sorrow of the storms. Now in our brokenness and lostness may we be met, healed, and redeemed by your eternal grace, we pray in Jesus' name.—Henry Fields

SERMON
Topic: The Difference Christ Makes
TEXT: Luke 19:1–10; Rom. 8

I. The story of Zacchaeus is quickly told. In fact, it consists of only ten verses (Luke 19:1–10). Yet it gives us an unforgettable picture of life's most important moment, that moment when you come face to face with Jesus Christ. You read the story with vivid interest and then think long, long thoughts about the difference Christ makes.

A few years ago I walked the dusty streets of Jericho thinking of the thousands of years in which caravans and travelers had walked through that subtropical town near the fords of the Jordan, going up the mountainous ascent to Jerusalem or going the other way to the towns of the North—Capernaum, Nazareth, or Damascus. In Roman days it was a lucrative place for tax collectors. I asked the guide the name of a tree by the side of the road. "Sycamore," he said, and suddenly I felt a wave of excitement. I thought of Zacchaeus, chief tax collector of Jericho, who climbed a sycamore tree by this road to see Jesus. Zacchaeus was rich and Jesus was poor, but it was Zacchaeus who was in need. "Short of stature," he had to climb the tree to see Jesus because of the crowd. We all need to do that. When the crowd is in the way and we cannot see Jesus, we must find our own sycamore tree in which to attain that higher perspective. The "crowd" may be family or business or society—no matter what, we must get above it. Though our past may be cluttered with things that give no satisfaction, if we meet Jesus, life can be bright with hope and the promise of new meaning.

Zacchaeus, like many a modern, had succeeded in business only to find it was at too great a price. A traitor to his countrymen, an exactor of taxes as a servant of Rome, he had achieved worldly success without respect or affection. "And he was rich" sums up his life, but it sounds like an epitaph. The people had a word for him: *sinner.*

But he met Jesus! And though everyone else said "sinner," Jesus said "Zacchaeus." The world saw the sinner in the man, but Jesus saw the man in the sinner. Jesus saw the *Zacchaeus who might be,* not just the *Zacchaeus who had been.* Jesus always judges a man by his capacity, not by his history. When Jesus calls us by name, our hearts leap with expectancy and joy.

What happened at the dinner we can only guess, but what happened because of the dinner we know, and how exciting it is! Zacchaeus was a new man. He found a new life. He happily gave away half his goods to the poor and pledged himself to repay fourfold all whom he had defrauded. Once he had sought to be rich toward men. Now he only wants to be rich toward God. What a difference Christ makes! How important to meet him on life's way. Christ renews our past, our present, our future. Whatever form your selfishness takes, Christ can save you from it, if like Zacchaeus you look eagerly to him and respond to his friendly and life-transforming love.

II. Romans chapter 8 is an inspiration to multitudes. It represents Paul's powerful optimism at its best. For me it is a spiritual tonic, giving invigoration, courage, and hope no matter what the besetments and vicissitudes of circumstance. What a treasure of life-giving truths! "For I reckon that the sufferings of this present time are not worthy to be compared with the glory. . . . We know that all things work together for good to those who love God. . . . If God be for us who can be against us? . . . Who shall separate us from the love of Christ? . . . In all these things we are more than conquerors." Paul knew all about the bad news of the world—its persecutions and its pain, but he also knew all about the good news of the world—the glorious goodness of the character of God! The Christian can cope because of his God. In the love of Christ we find the power of going on. Whenever we look to God we find in ourselves some new courage, some new strength. Our faith gives us an inner resilience that enables us to bounce back. What a wonderful way to live! In all things, no matter what happens, we can face forward with courage, more than conquerors through Christ who loves us. We can live strength and serenity, hope and peace, through all the vicissitudes of life because of the power that works in us. Is this not what we need to know—the joy of victory that overcomes the stress and distress that constitute so large a part of our experience? "In all these things we are more than conquerors through Christ who loved us."—Lowell M. Atkinson[3]

SUNDAY, NOVEMBER 11, 2001
Lectionary Message

Topic: Keeping a Stable Christian Mind

TEXT: 2 Thess. 2:1–5, 13–17

Other Readings: Hag. 2:1–9; Ps. 145:1–5, 17–21; Luke 20:17–38

Besides commending the believers at Thessalonica for the growth of their faith and love for each other, the apostle found it necessary to urge them to adopt a cautious approach to rumors that conditions for the return of Jesus Christ had been fulfilled. He warned them that the day of Christ's coming would not occur until after the Great Apostasy and the appearance of the "Man of Sin," the "Son of Perdition," which is Paul's reference to the one who has also been called "the Antichrist." The appearance of such a one seems to embody in one individual the total force of Satan, or Belial, to mislead all God's people and lure them to accompany him into everlasting destruction. Perhaps the reference to such a one (as described in verse 4) was prompted by the recent attempt by Caligula to erect a statue of himself in the Temple at Jerusalem and to be worshiped.

I. *Possible avenues of confusion.*

---

[3] *Apples of Gold* (Lima, Ohio: Fairway Press, 1986), pp. 121–123.

(a) The expectation of Christ's return was paramount in the minds of the apostles, who had heard Jesus himself promise that he would return, to "drink it [the cup of wine] new with [them] in [his] father's Kingdom" (Matt. 26:29), and also, as he answered the high priest, that "ye shall see the Son of man sitting on the right hand of power, and coming in the clouds of heaven" (Matt. 26:64). They also bore in mind the words of the angels at the time of Christ's Ascension: "This same Jesus, who is taken up from you into heaven, shall so come in like manner as ye have seen him go into heaven" (Acts 1:11).

(b) Because these promises were not accompanied by specific time references—and John further confused the matter of timing in his Revelation references, describing the necessary conditions more fully—possibilities of false assumptions were great indeed and have continued to be confusing to many even in our generation, so much so that the doctrine is now generally neglected in our preaching and teaching. Many groups, however, have studied these prophecies and analyzed the conditions and have then made thorough preparations in the full expectation of seeing the great Second Coming of the Lord and being lifted up by him to heaven at a specific time and place.

(c) Paul cautioned the believers that they might be alarmed by spiritual movements either in themselves or around them; that messengers might come and by their words seek to plant bothersome and upsetting convictions among them; also that forged letters, purporting to be from Paul and Silvanus and Timothy might be accepted as giving authentic warning that "the day of Christ is at hand."

II. *Living in the great expectation.*

(a) Using the coming of the Lord Jesus Christ and the great assembly of believers before him as the ground of his argument, Paul urged positive exaltation of victorious living in Jesus' name. The hope and faith that the great event would take place is what was to give assurance to the *Kerugma,* the propagation of the good news, with active effort for the redemption of lives. And the preaching was to be accompanied by personal appeal so that belief would become real and lively.

(b) Although the ministry became more objectified and more formally and officially practiced in the Church of the middle ages, the Reformation and the Counter Reformation of the sixteenth century brought the individual ministry back into focus. John Calvin wrote, "We must not think that our work is confined within such narrow limits that our task is ended when we have preached sermons. . . . It is our part to maintain a vigilant oversight of those committed to our care, and take the greatest pains to guard from evil those whose blood will one day be demanded from us if they are lost through our negligence."[4]

It is no wonder that Ernest Renan called Calvin "the most Christian man of his generation," because he was a martyr himself, poor among the poverty stricken, in order to follow his Lord as closely as possible.

(c) So Paul exhorted the Thessalonians, as we must urge our fellow believers, to stand fast and not being shaken by the winds or cross-currents of doctrine. He prayed that the Lord who had given consolation and hope might establish them "in every good word and work." So we must daily be about our Father's business.—John R. Rodman

---

[4] *La Catechisme Francais,* p. 132.

ILLUSTRATIONS

DON'T GIVE IN.   We ought not to give in to apocalyptic answers too soon—especially not when we are still in the prime of life, when we are in positions of some influence, when we can do things to improve the world, and when there are still wonders of creation to observe and enjoy. There is a sense of inappropriateness when fascination and preoccupation with "the end of the world" emerges among middle-class suburbanites, huddling together to protect themselves from a changing world. They are falling back on this "answer" too soon. When all else fails, when there is no longer anything that we can do, when we face the inevitability of death, then the apocalyptic words of hope for the future can bring a comfort that has sustained the faithful through the most terrible trials.—Daniel J. Simundson[5]

WHAT IT TAKES.   A brilliant young woman was persuaded to take a class of boys, though she herself was not a professing Christian. She worried about it, was persuaded to give herself to Christ and did. She won all nine boys to Christ. On the Sunday they made their profession, a friend said to her, "Bess, I'd give my life to do what you've done." Bess replied, "That's what it takes, but it's worth it."—E. Stanley Jones[6]

SERMON SUGGESTIONS

Topic: The Fullness of the Gospel
TEXT: Rom. 15:29
(1) Don't forget his teaching. (2) Don't leave out his cross. (3) Don't forget his victory.—D. M. Baillie[7]

Topic: The Full Christ
TEXT: John 1:16
(1) Fullness of truth. (2) Fullness of strength. (3) Fullness of grace.—J. D. Jones[8]

CONGREGATIONAL MUSIC

1. "My God, My King, Thy Various Praise," Isaac Watts (1719)
   WINCHESTER NEW, *Musicalisches Handbuch* (Hamburg, 1690)
   This paraphrase of Psalm 145 by the great hymnist Isaac Watts would make a fine call to worship, as well as a musical expression reflecting the Psalter lesson.
2. "Be Strong in the Lord," Linda Lee Johnson (1979)
   STRENGTH, Tom Fettke (1979)
   In the passage from Haggai 2:1–9 is found three times the strong Word of the Lord to "be strong," with the assurance that God's spirit remains with his people. This contemporary text and tune contain the same invigorating message, making them suitable for use with the Old Testament lesson.
3. "Ten Thousand Times Ten Thousand," Henry Alford (1867)
   ALFORD, John Bacchus Dykes (1875)

---

[5] *Faith Under Fire*
[6] *The Way*
[7] *Out of Nazareth*
[8] *Richmond Hill Sermons*

The coming of the desired of all nations (Hag. 2:7) is echoed in the third stanza of this brilliant hymn on the second coming of Christ. On this November Sunday, a pre-Advent glimpse is given in both the Old Testament reading and the singing of this hymn.

4. "Jesus, Thine All-Victorious Love," Charles Wesley

AZMON, Carl G. Glaeser (1839)

The apostle Paul speaks of the coming of the Lord in sanctifying power whereby we are saved to share in the glory of Christ (2 Thess. 2:1–5, 13–17). Wesley's prayer for personal holiness calls on this sanctifying Spirit to come. Though possibly an unfamiliar Wesleyan hymn to many, it can be sung well to the familiar AZMON tune.—Hugh T. McElrath

WORSHIP AIDS

CALL TO WORSHIP.   "The Lord is gracious, and full of compassion; slow to anger, and of great mercy. The Lord is good to all: and his tender mercies are over all his works" (Ps. 145:8–9).

INVOCATION.   Gather us together, O God, in the fellowship of thy faithful people. May we never forget what the Church has done for our world and for us. Keep us ever mindful of the fact that we are the Church, and that if we cease to grow, if we stand stiff in our pride, if we let the flames die, the Church dies with us. Pardon our failures, O God, and give us the will and the power to continue the ministry of Jesus in the world of the future.—Theodore Parker Ferris

OFFERTORY SENTENCE.   "Whatsoever ye do, do it heartily, as to the Lord, and not unto men; knowing that of the Lord ye shall receive the reward of the inheritance: for ye serve the Lord Christ" (Col. 3:23–24).

OFFERTORY PRAYER.   Holy God, may the faith that brings us to give be deepened by the mercy we show the neglected, that Christ may be glorified and thy Kingdom come on earth as it is in heaven.—E. Lee Phillips

PRAYER.   Gracious God, by your providence we live and work and join in families, and from your hand we receive those things we need, gift upon gift, all free. We thank you for the harvest of goodness you supply: for food and shelter, for words and gestures, for all our human friendships. Above all, we praise you for your Son, who came to show mercy and who names us his own brothers. Glory to you for great kindness to us and to all your children; through Jesus Christ our Lord.—*The Worshipbook*

SERMON

Topic: To Whom Much Is Given

TEXT: Luke 12:48

As we begin a new century together, we are aware of our past and future. We owe succeeding generations in proportion as we have received from preceding generations. This obligation is what Jesus was referring to in Luke 12, when he said, "Every one to whom much is given, of them shall much be required; and to whom people have committed much, of them they will ask the more." These words also sum up Jesus' parable of the talents, in Matthew 25:14–29. The word *talent*, used for a valuable silver coin, has often been used literally, so it has meaning for us on this Recommitment Sunday.

Witness the first scene: the wealthy lord, the boss man, has assembled three of his managers to describe what to do in his absence. A sizeable part of investments is to be entrusted to them for management, to justify their wages in the interim. He gives one manager five talents, worth at least $50,000 in today's market. He gives the second manager $20,000, and the third gets only $10,000. He trusts them all, certain that each is capable of doing his part.

The first fellow takes his $50,000 and decides to trade in the commercial world, buying low and selling high. He knows the caravan schedules from Damascus and other trading centers and what he can get and quickly resell to the military. He has doubled his funding when his boss returns, reporting 100 percent profit—nearly $100,000.

Among us are smart investors who can offer the Church amazing and wonderful new ideas for ministry and then put them into practice if we will let them. God is in charge and God passes out the resources to be managed, the talents to be exercised. If we are to anticipate the needs and challenges of the third millennium, we will have to be committed to using the very best talent we have been given. Why waste this precious, God-given talent?

The second manager is a very sturdy and dependable sort of fellow. He is not the sort to work with figures in his head, but he knows how to plow a straight furrow, how to pick good farm hands, what to plant and when to harvest. So he invests his $20,000 in land rent, seed and fertilizer, and well-selected labor. He manages to grow one whole crop and double his money after paying the rent, buying the seed, and paying the hands. When the boss returns, this servant has $40,000, and that pleases the boss.

We are entrusted with talents without which our world would be a disaster. Our homes and churches, our schools, our government, and our industries all depend on the vast host of two-talent people. A profitable lot, we can be counted on to visit the sick, teach all ages, and care for the incarcerated in and after jail. We two-talent types run the every-member canvass for the budget that will underwrite all kinds of ministries for next year—our outreach to a sin-sick and needy world. The talents God gives us do pay off, and there are countless tasks for us to do!

The third servant isn't happy about the amount given to him. He quietly withdraws and decides to play it safe. He has seen money lost on crops and on investments in the market, so he puts his money in a safe place—a hole in the ground. When the boss returns, this brother digs up the talent and gives back the same money that was given to him. He is not ashamed; he thinks the boss needed him to guard the ten-grand deposit. He took no risks while the boss was gone. "I knew you were a hard-hearted, money-grubbing rich man and I didn't want you to fuss at me."

What is so tragic is that too many old, historical churches are full of talent-burying members. They don't think God has any right to expect more than regular attendance at morning worship, or a gift to God like a waiter's tip. They forget that God has given the blessings.

As I think of what has been given to us I am overwhelmed by what God gives in just the churches and schools of our time. What God has provided in the wider worlds of science and industry, engineering and space, business and finance is over and above all we have dreamed. The fields of education and social service and the Christian Church have burst unbelievably beyond where they were. By the grace of God we have for several decades been given the tools with which to claim and conquer in all these fields. We stay stuck in the past and invest our talents everywhere but in the Church.

Here I dare to remind you of the words of Jesus: "Everyone to whom much is given, of them shall much be required; and to whom people have committed much, of them they will ask the more." In other words, if you've got a bunch, you owe it to give a bunch. If you have received a bunch of capability, and an abundance of gifts, you have no choice but to use them for the purposes for which they were given to you.

The third servant took the line of least resistance. The Lord is not gentle in his rebuke: "Wicked and slothful! You're a rascal, and lazy, too. I could have had what is mine with interest." The boss disposes of the single talent as a casual gift to the first servant. "Take that $10,000 and give it to the man with the $100,000. It is the quality, not the quantity, that matters.

The human attitude begets godly gratitude. Whether a $100,000 talent or a widow's mite, the heart full of commitment is the heart that pleases God. We all have gifts, and God requires only that we use what we have. Only of those to whom much is given is much required, and we have only to commit to God what we have been given.—Ella Pearson Mitchell

SUNDAY, NOVEMBER 18, 2001
Lectionary Message
Topic: Two Reactions to the Second Coming of Jesus
Text: 2 Thess. 3:6–13
Other Readings: Isa. 12, 65:17–25; Luke 21:5–19

I. *The belief that keeps Christians alert.* Several principal truths are basic guides for Christian living. The Apostles' Creed, adopted by the apostolic church and never superseded, contains succinct statements of the essential beliefs around which faithful lives are organized. In the last clause of the paragraph about Jesus we read, "From thence he shall come to judge the quick and the dead."

This statement is somewhat amplified in the Scots Confession adopted by the Church of Scotland in 1560, of which Chapter 11, "The Ascension," states, "We believe that the same Lord Jesus shall visibly return for this Last Judgment as he was seen to ascend." The paragraph continues to describe the effects of restitution and refreshing immortality for the righteous in Christ, and the eternal separation and suffering of the unrepentant sinners.

The Westminster Confession of Faith, adopted by the United Presbyterian Church in 1958, was a modernized version of the Confession of the Assembly of 1647 at Westminster. In Chapter 8, "Of Christ the Mediator," in paragraph 4 are the words "And shall return to judge men and angels, at the end of the world." Further, there is in Chapter 33 "Of the Last Judgment," which is more enlarged.

II. *The view of immediacy.*

(a) *Inability to determine the time.* The believers were unable, as all persons since have been, to determine the precise time when the Lord would return for the great day of judgment. Hence they were divided into two fairly distinct groups: those who interpreted the prophetic utterances of Jesus to imply that he would return well within the lifetime of his apostles, and those who, taking him at his word, believed that "about that day and hour no one knows, neither the angels of heaven, nor the Son, but only the Father" (Matt. 24:36 NRSV).

(b) *Assumption of immediate occurrence.* Many concluded that the return would occur soon. The history of Christianity records many times when believers have interpreted the signs of their times as having fulfilled all the conditions Jesus gave his disciples in Matthew 24 as well as Luke 17 and 21. Many in our own times have also concluded that the number of believers must be complete and that the ordinary affairs of life—cultivating, planting, reaping, and evangelizing—are no longer appropriate or required.

(c) *Acting on false assumptions.* The "disorderly" of whom Paul writes were the lazy people who, taking advantage of the love and faithfulness of their fellow believers, made their expectation of the immediate return of Jesus their excuse for becoming indolent and dependent upon the generosity of those who were able to help.

Paul had no tolerance for those who would not enter into the common struggle for daily fare. If any who were able to work did not do so, he thought, they should not eat. Generous as he was with the truly poor and needy, he gave no encouragement for support of the able-bodied but indolent.

III. *The view of imminence of the event.*

(a) *The truth forecast by Jesus.* There is no excuse for the Church of Christ to ignore Jesus' promise of returning for his final judgment and his warning that the event would be a surprise. He was quite careful to promise that the return to judgment was possible at any moment, and by parables, comparisons, and analogies he warned all to be ready.

(b) *The warnings of imminence.* Paul's attitude is that of awareness of the possibility of Christ's return, as Christ promised he would at any time (as described in Matthew 24 and 25). The warning of imminence is prominent: "Watch therefore: for you know not what hour your Lord comes" (24:42); "Therefore be ye also ready: for in such an hour as ye think not the Son of man cometh" (24:44).

IV. *Implications of Paul's concerns for the Church.*

(a) *The need for discipline.* During the history of Christianity, the Church has felt and responded to the need for Church discipline. Paul urgently requests that believers separate themselves from the disorderly ones, for the preservation of the true faith, as a warning to those who err, and as a healthful cleansing and straightening of the accounts of life. Paul puts it on the level of working and earning the right to eat. If the Church allows error to disguise itself in the cloak of righteousness, confusion will render the Gospel useless.

(b) *The use of discipline.* The separation Paul commands has been employed by the Church throughout the ages, to protect truth from deterioration and to prevent meaninglessness from taking over and destroying the truth's purity.

The early and medieval Church practiced what it called excommunication, which is what Paul commands here. The Reformation under Luther and Calvin and others also provided the means for the Church body to protect its witness from corruption by persistent sinners. The practice has been called "fencing the table," which does not mean to exclude faithful penitents who have taken care to examine their lives, but to prevent persons who persistently live carelessly from making mistakes. The implication of the command is that we should "exhort the disorderly," working in love to win them to "well doing," counting them not as enemies but as brothers and sisters to be admonished.—John R. Rodman

ILLUSTRATIONS

THE BIG QUESTION.   Fear death, when death comes one day for you? You need to have no fear of it, any more than your own dear ones feared it when it came. It will be no dark ominous spectre you see coming then to meet you. It will be the King in His beauty.

> Jesus, Lover of my soul,
> Let me to Thy bosom fly.

Do you remember John Bunyan's marvelous description in the *Pilgrim's Progress* of the summons to Mr. Valiant-for-truth to cross the river? "When the day that he must go hence was come, many accompanied him to the river side, into which as he went he said, 'Death, where is thy sting?' And as he went down deeper, he said, 'Grave, where is thy victory?' So he passed over, and all the trumpets sounded for him on the other side." May God give us that vision of the saints for the day of death, that like them we too, in that final hour—in that hour supremely—may endure as seeing Him who is invisible. And then, that day over and that river crossed, we shall indeed see Him face to face, and rejoice in His presence for ever.—James S. Stewart[9]

CHRIST FOR ALL.   In the words of Dr. John Mott: "It was overwhelmingly proved that the more open-minded, honest, just, and generous we were in dealing with the non-Christian faiths, the higher Christ loomed in His absolute uniqueness, sufficiency, supremacy, and universality." "There is no one else," said a prominent Hindu to Stanley Jones, "who is seriously bidding for the heart of the world except Jesus Christ. There is no one else on the field." Already one figure is standing where the roads of all the ages meet; and to those who have once seen Him, and experienced in their own lives His power, this above all else is certain, that a day is drawing near when every gate in the universe will be lifting up its head to let the King come in.—James S. Stewart[10]

SERMON SUGGESTIONS

Topic: Marriage and Divine Providence

TEXT: Ruth 2:1-13

(1) *Then:* The providence of God in bringing together Ruth and Boaz. (2) *Always:* High ethical standards from both parties should prevail in courtship. (3) *Now:* Recognize both the hand of God and personal decision and responsibility. Let love protect and not selfishly exploit the parties in this new experience.

CONGREGATIONAL MUSIC

1. "Awake, My Soul, and with the Sun," Thomas Ken (1692)
   MORNING HYMN, Francois H. Barthelemon (c. 1785)
   Thomas Ken's famous morning hymn to be sung by the boys of Winchester College is an

---

[9] *River of Life*
[10] *The Life and Teaching of Jesus Christ*

excellent one for the opening of morning worship. In its exhortation to "shake off dull sloth" it also relates well to the warning against idleness in the Epistle reading.

2. "Surely It Is God Who Saves Me," Isaiah 12:2–6; paraph. Carl P. Daw Jr. (1982)

THOMAS MERTON, Ray W. Urwin (1984)

This contemporary free paraphrase of all but the first verse of Isaiah 12 could be sung in place of reading the chapter. Alternation of reading and singing would also be effective.

3. "I Am Trusting Thee, Lord Jesus," Frances R. Havergal (1874)

BULLINGER, Ethelbert W. Bullinger (1874)

A simple hymn of trust, "I Am Trusting Thee, Lord Jesus" echoes Isaiah 12:2a and could be sung as a response to the reading of Isaiah chapter 12.

4. "Once He Came in Blessing," Jan Roth; trans. C. Winkworth (c. 1870)

GOTTES SOHN IST KOMMEN, Michael Weisse (1531)

The fourth stanza of this Advent hymn makes the same promise that Jesus did as recorded in Luke 21:19: "By standing firm you will gain life." This would be a good hymn to sing before the reading of the Gospel lesson.—Hugh T. McElrath

WORSHIP AIDS

CALL TO WORSHIP.   "Be not conformed to this world: but be ye transformed by the renewing of your mind, that ye may prove what is that good, and acceptable, and perfect, will of God" (Rom. 12:2).

INVOCATION.   God of renewal and reformation: you raised up brave and able men and women to reform the Church. We confess we have lost our way again and need new reformation. We are content with easy religion, with too many things and too little charity; we cultivate indifference. Lord, let your word shake us up, and your Spirit renew us, so that we may repent, have better faith, and never shrink from sacrifice.—E. Paul Hovey.

OFFERTORY SENTENCE.   "And he said to them, 'Go into all the world, and give the good news to everyone'" (Mark 16:15 N.T. in Basic English).

OFFERTORY PRAYER.   Heavenly Father, thank you for our many freedoms. Help us to use our freedoms not to hide behind our safe walls, where it's easy to be thankful around a table so full of blessings, or in a church so full of resources. Helps us to reach out beyond our walls and ourselves, to share your Word and your steadfast love.—Kenneth M. Cox

PRAYER.   Lord Jesus, teach us to live as they should live who have eternity to live in. Lift us more and more into the steadying exercise of an immortal bearing. Give us the courage this day to sift all that we hold here in our hands, and may we keep fast nothing but that which fits our destiny with thee. For thy name's sake we ask it.—Paul Scherer

SERMON

Topic: When the Winds Are Against Us

TEXT: Job 1:13–22; Acts 27:1–12, 33–38 NRSV

I have a special place in my heart for that little group of religious separatists who left Holland on a tiny vessel known as the *Mayflower* to sail to the New World in search of religious freedom. Many were the trials and tribulations the Pilgrims faced throughout their journey that eventually brought them to America. They had difficulty finding a sea captain who would transport them. After they finally found one, he betrayed them and made off with their goods that had already been loaded on his ship. The Pilgrims' religious dissent and desire to leave their homeland led to imprisonment. Families were separated for a time as some began passage while others had to remain behind.

When all were finally able to set sail, the ship began to leak. There was fear they might sink. They had to return to the harbor and start again. Once they did actually start for the New World, they faced violent crosswinds and many fierce storms at sea. Many were afflicted with seasickness. All the troubles they encountered and delays they endured forced them to start much later in the year than they should have. Thus they didn't arrive on America's shores until late November, after cold weather had already set in. Furthermore, they landed much further north than they had anticipated, on what is present-day Cape Cod, Massachusetts, instead of in Virginia, where they had hoped to land. The Pilgrims found themselves in a strange land in the dead of winter, void of shelter against the elements and winter cold. Those Pilgrim mothers and fathers had the winds against them from the beginning.

We find a similar story in the New Testament book of Acts (Acts 27). Paul, the apostle, was being taken to Rome for questioning. The voyage was fraught with difficulty and in trouble from the start. Violent winds were against them as soon as they set sail. Twice the writer of Acts states that "the winds were against us" (27:4, 7). It was dangerous sailing. There was great loss of cargo. The days were dark. All hope seemed to be gone.

There is a parallel in this story to everyday life. The winds of life will often blow against us. Because of all the difficult experiences some folks have had over the years, they feel as though they have been walking against the cold winds of life. Life's journey is often fraught with difficulty and danger. There are days when nothing seems to go right. There is accident and unexpected illness. We will sometimes suffer the loss of life's possessions, and even our dearest loved ones. Dark days will come that will tempt us to give up all hope. As Robert Frost observed in one of his poems, there are times "when the wind works against us in the dark." But the Scripture passages that were read earlier give us some good advice for facing the adverse winds of life.

I. *We must keep up our courage.* "Keep up your courage," Paul said to his fellow passengers whose lives were endangered by the sea (Acts 27:22, 25). The *Mayflower II,* a replica of the original ship that brought the Pilgrims to America, stays anchored in Plymouth Harbor. It is amazing that 102 persons would climb on such a small vessel (only about 106 feet long) to start across a vast sea—and that they would survive. What courage it took! William Bradford, long-time governor of the Pilgrim settlement who left us the most detailed account of the Pilgrims in his work *Of Plymouth Plantation,* has this to say about setbacks and challenges: "All great and honorable actions are accompanied with great difficulties, and must be both met and overcome with answerable courage." The Pilgrim fathers and mothers faced their challenges, difficulties, and adverse circumstances with undaunted courage. And so must we.

II. *As we face the adverse winds of life we must keep fear in its place.* We cannot let ourselves be controlled by fear. "Do not be afraid," Paul encouraged in the storm-tossed boat (27:24). There was a piece on one of the educational channels about people facing their fears. For instance, one group of people were terrified of spiders. So, little by little they got closer and closer to a tarantula until they were finally able to touch it and hold it in their hands. By facing their fear and dealing with it, they were finally able to overcome it. "Don't be afraid to go out on a limb," someone has observed. "That's where the fruit is." Fear must be kept in its proper place.

III. *As we face the adverse winds of life, we must keep faith in God, the Higher Power.* "Have faith in God," Paul exhorted (27:25). We must never give up on the belief that we are not alone in this thing called life. It is comforting to believe that an unseen power faces the adverse winds of life with us, that there is always a hand on our shoulder guiding us. "To stand in the darkness and yet know that God is light—that is a great and noble faith" (Phillip Brooks).

IV. *As we face the adverse winds of life, let us continue to give thanks to God.* Out on the sea, in the midst of a storm, Paul took bread and gave thanks to God, and they had a miniature thanksgiving celebration, even though their lives were threatened by storm. Shipwreck was still a certainty (27:35), but they gave thanks anyway.

In the book of Job, we have read another story of one who faced the adverse winds of life. The story goes that Job lost his oxen, donkeys, sheep, camels, and servants, and even his children. "Suddenly a great wind came across the desert, struck the four corners of the house, and it fell on the young people," the Scripture relates (Job 1:19). Yet "Job arose, tore his robe, shaved his head, and fell on the ground and worshiped" (1:20). In spite of all his trouble, adversity, and loss, Job did not neglect to worship God and give thanks for his life.

Most people know the story well—how about half of the original Pilgrim fathers and mothers died that first winter from the effects of cold, starvation, and disease. Yet in spite of all the trouble and adversity the Pilgrims had endured, in spite of all their great losses, they enjoyed a bountiful harvest during the summer of 1621. Consequently, they felt moved to hold a harvest feast in order to rejoice, celebrate, acknowledge God's providence in their midst, and give thanks for their present condition.

In spite of the troubles and adversities that may come our way, in spite of the adverse winds of life that blow against us, there are still reasons to be thankful. There is much more good in life than bad. In spite of any troubles that blow our way, God still loves us, our friends and family still love us, and hope for the future is still very much alive.

No life is free of trouble. The strong winds of life blew against Job, and Paul and Robert Frost and the Plymouth Pilgrims. And the cold winds of life will blow against all of us now and again. When the winds of life are against us, what do we do? We keep courage, we keep fear in its place, we keep faith in God, and we remember to give thanks.—Randy Hammer

SUNDAY, NOVEMBER 25, 2001
Lectionary Message

Topic: The Christian's Secret of Joyful Living
TEXT: Col. 1:11–20
Other Readings: Jer. 23:1–6; Luke 1:68–79, 23:33–43

I. *The arena of our lives.*

(a) The situation of the church in Colossae was similar to that which many of us face. It was a power struggle in which no holds were barred between darkness and light, error and truth, suffering and joy—among the unknown mysteries of power attempting to control lives and confuse minds about the true nature of the world and human life.

(b) What is your philosophy of life? There are sufficient strains in the normal pursuit of sustenance, clothing, and shelter to challenge all of anyone's intelligence and healthy strength. At the same time, a person's thoughts may be confused by concepts of impersonal forces, dominant authorities, or even otherworldly influences that must be appeased before one can be safe. In our textual passage, Paul refers to "the power of darkness" as well as to "thrones or dominions or rulers or powers," and later he mentions rulers and authorities that Christ disarmed that would have forced the people to follow dietary restrictions for religious reasons, to observe festivals and new moons, to worship angels and see visions, all of which ignore the spiritual truths of Christ's revelation.

(c) If we are Christians, we must not be confused about what is right; we must not try to live in asceticism or by rules that assume that everything material is evil or wrong, including the human body, so that spells and incantations are necessary to combat evil spiritual emanations; and we must not live as if the body must be made to suffer in order for the spirit to triumph. These practical errors form doctrines of their own and Paul is urgent in getting straight the doctrine by which Christians may "with joy endure everything with patience."

II. *The living power of Christ.*

(a) Living amid the forces of nature—fire, wind, tempest, darkness, hail, thunder, lightning, heat, and cold—we may find our strengths not sufficient for survival, much less for joy and happiness. It is to the overwhelmed ones—to all of us—that Paul brings the truth of our position in Christ.

(b) First he establishes Christ's position, in a time when heresies were beginning to teach that Christ was no more than a gifted man, that some prophets were as great in revealing God as Jesus was, and that many rulers were more powerful over worldly forces than Jesus was.

In the great Christological passage of verses 15 to 20, Paul reconfirms in strong language that Christ was with God in the very beginning, that he was the reason for and means of the entire creation of the universe, which God made into a cosmos, a system of beautiful orderliness, rather than a chaos. Paul restates in most forceful language that he with whom we have to do is God in all his fullness.

(c) When Paul says that Christ is "before all things," he does not mean that Christ simply existed earlier than anything or anyone else in temporal priority, but rather that Christ is the source, the controller, and the utmost power and authority of it all. "All things hold together in him" because he is the continual creative force of it all. The King James Version says, "And by Him all things consist." The Greek root for *consist* or *hold together* means "to have been perfectly framed and permanently supported" and is related to the word for *system.*

III. *Our joyful endurance in Christ.*

(a) By relieving us of false teachings and giving us the truth, Paul helps us live in the strength and joy of Christ, according to what he has done for us. He has equipped us with power, not according to our need but according to the divine supply, so that we can endure everything with joyfulness and patience. Enduring could lead to gloominess and a sour disposition, but with Christ's joy we can meet everything in a transport of confidence. After all, we have a share; we have been given a plot among the holy beings dwelling in the light of God here and now—we are partakers with them.

(b) The great deeds we do in our blessed condition are not of great spiritual heroism, although such deeds are possible. But for every one of us there is the practice of passive virtue so that we may meet the greater stress of ordinary existence. We are in a state of holy living. The invisible God has "transferred" or "translated" us into the Kingdom of his dear Son. This is to be taken not only in the eschatological sense, but also in the sense that the movement into Christ's Kingdom need not be longed for in hope, as something to be taken up later, but rather occurred at the same time as the deliverance. Redemption is already ours. No wonder we can joyfully endure everything with patience!—John R. Rodman

ILLUSTRATIONS

A QUEST FOR JOY.   The more I study people—and myself—the more do I put my faith in God alone. God upsets all our neat intellectual formulae. He always has surprises in store for us. There was, for example, an intelligent and sensitive woman whom psychological disturbances had once brought to me. She had been brought up in a strict religious environment, from which she had withdrawn after our consultations. Her cure seemed to be linked with this liberation from a too religious, religious constraint. It is a case, therefore, that I might well have quoted in support of my theory of the two movements. Then I suddenly received a letter from her. I was pleased, for I had not heard from her for some years. She told me that she had gone back to the church she had left, and that her return had given her more happiness and peace than she had known at the time of her healing. I think this is only apparently contradictory—it is the same God who led her once to free herself from the onerous tutelage of her church so that she could become adult and be healed, and who had now called her back to the church so that she could recover all the religious fervor she had lost during her spiritual isolation. Every person has his own road to follow, and we cannot know what it is beforehand. What counts in the end of the day is what God does, not what we do. The only really important thing is that each of us should come to know him, whatever the unforeseen detours we have to make.—Paul Tournier[11]

JOY EXEMPLIFIED.   The pleasure of that harsh confrontation with reality without which everything is but wishful thinking. The pleasure of taking a risk; the pleasure of suspense and of the supreme current of energy that it releases in us. The joy of procreation and of creation; the joy of bringing a new being into the world, halloed with the mystery of all his unknown future; the joy that springs from bringing forth a piece of creative work, the fruit either of a moment of grace or of long and patient toil. The joy of feeling that what I am doing each moment is absolutely unique, that no one else will ever be me, that no other moment of my life will ever be the same as this one. The joy of each experience, of each act, of each success, as soon as we realize that this is what is meant by being in God's image, that He allows us to cooperate in his work, that he is with us in everything we undertake. It is from Him that we draw our courage to live.—Paul Tournier[12]

---

[11] *A Place for You*
[12] *The Meaning of Life*

SERMON SUGGESTIONS

Topic: The Elements of Christian Community
TEXT: Acts 4:32–35
(1) Unity of spirit. (2) Power of testimony. (3) Generosity in stewardship.

Topic: Toward Fellowship with Christ and Christian Joy
TEXT: 1 John 1:1–2:2
(1) Through the forgiveness of our sins (1:6–10). (2) Through the overcoming of our sins (2:1–2).

CONGREGATIONAL MUSIC

1. "Blessed Be the God of Israel," James Quinn (1982)
   FOREST GREEN, trad. English melody; arr. R. V. Williams (1903)
   This excellent contemporary paraphrase of the Canticle of Zacharias (Luke 1:68–79) could well be sung to replace the reading of this passage from Luke.
2. "Majesty, Worship His Majesty," Jack Hayford (1981)
   MAJESTY, Jack Hayford (1981)
   Coming from the praise and worship tradition, this contemporary song would be suitable for singing on Christ the King Sunday. It could accompany the Epistle reading having to do with the supremacy of Christ.
3. "Rejoice, the Lord Is King," Charles Wesley (1746)
   DARWALL, John Darwall (1770)
   GOPSAL, George F. Handel (1752)
   Those who prefer an older tradition for celebrating Christ the King may use this classic hymn by Charles Wesley. Sung to either tune, it carries the exuberant theme of the supremacy of Christ.
4. "Were You There," African American Spiritual
   WERE YOU THERE, African American Spiritual
   This spiritual could be sung unaccompanied to prepare for the reading of the Crucifixion story (Luke 23:33–43). Its original call-and-response nature could be emphasized by having a soloist sing the questions of the first part and the congregation respond with "Oh! it makes me tremble!"

WORSHIP AIDS

CALL TO WORSHIP.   "I was glad when they said unto me, Let us go unto the house of the Lord" (Ps. 122:1).

INVOCATION.   Lord of the mighty Word, the abiding truth, and the still small voice, come to us in our need and fill us with thy power. As we worship may we be blessed and as we return to our homes may we be fortified with the faith that informs life and outlasts it.—E. Lee Phillips

OFFERTORY SENTENCE.   "He that is faithful in a very little is faithful also in much; and he that is unrighteous in a very little is unrighteous also in much" (Luke 16:10).

OFFERTORY PRAYER.   The Earth is the Lord's as are "the cattle upon a thousand hills." We do not offer to your need, Lord, but because of our need—our need to worship you. This we do with our gifts.

PRAYER.   O great Father of all! We draw near to you as disobedient children to confess our wrong and mourn over it and pray for deliverance from it. We pray that we may live worthy of you. We are your sons and daughters. We are adopted into your family. We are much loved and much forgiven. We are borne with and helped every day and on every side. Grant that every feeling of honor and gratitude and love may conspire to prevent us from receiving all your mercies, so many and so precious, and returning nothing but disobedience.

Forgive the past and inspire the future. Grant that we may never be discouraged. If there be any who have begun to walk the royal way of life and are perplexed and hindered and see little of growth in themselves, still let them go forward. Grant that none may look back and count themselves unworthy of eternal life. We pray that you will quicken the conscience of every one, and grant that all who are named may judge their conduct and their character not by human laws but by the higher law of God. So, by that spiritual and inward measure may we measure their thoughts and their feelings and say, from day to day, "Against thee and thee only have I sinned and done this evil in thy sight." So we pray that you will raise us step by step above temptation, until at last we are prepared for that higher land where they sin no more and are tempted no more and rejoice together forever.—Adapted from Henry Ward Beecher

SERMON
Topic: Your Inheritance Is Waiting!
TEXT: 1 Cor. 15:22

Recently the news media carried a story about a woman who had been working two jobs and struggling to raise her children for years, pinching pennies here and there while she tried to make ends meet. Then one day she read an article about "missing heirs" and discovered that, for years she had been very wealthy! A relative had died and left her a fortune but she hadn't known it. In fact, she claimed she had to read the will over and over just to convince herself it was for real.

If you are a member of the family of Christ, I have a similar news flash for you. You are heir to an immense legacy that Jesus put in trust for you almost two thousand years ago—not when he died but when he rose from the grave and conquered death. When you were born again, this inheritance—far more valuable than mere silver or gold—became yours.

With his Resurrection, Jesus broke a threefold curse of death. Consequently, when you accepted him as your Lord and Savior, you inherited a threefold right to life. When Adam sinned, he died spiritually. Sin separated him from God, and that separation bought spiritual death for the whole human race. Jesus Christ broke that curse and you inherited a *right to spiritual life*. "For as in Adam all die, even so in Christ shall all be made alive" (1 Cor. 15:22).

Additionally, Adam's sin brought the consequence of physical death. Jesus broke that curse also, by literally overcoming his physical mortality. Part of your resurrection legacy, then, is the *right to physical life* in your body—and to eternal life through the Spirit: "But if the Spirit of him that raised up Jesus from the dead dwell in you, he that raised up Christ from the dead shall also quicken your mortal bodies by his Spirit that dwelleth in you" (Rom. 8:11).

Finally, you have inherited a full provision for healing through the Resurrection of Jesus Christ, which guarantees you the *right to a healthy life.* God repeatedly stresses in his Word that Jesus died for our health, too: "That it might be fulfilled which was spoken by Esaias the prophet, saying, Himself took our infirmities, and bare our sicknesses" (Matt. 8:17).

Healing is a major part of the Atonement. The Old Testament shows that the curse included all manner of diseases (see Deut. 28:16–52). By his death and Resurrection, Jesus redeemed us from the curse of the law (see Gal. 3:13). First Peter 2:24 says that Jesus "bare our sins in his own body on the tree, that we, being dead to sins, should live unto righteousness: by whose stripes ye were healed."

By overcoming death, Jesus Christ also willed you the legacy of *resurrection power.* This is one of the most exciting gifts he has for you. Like the threefold gift of life, you received it when you were born again, and it was given to you for the purpose of transforming your soul. No wonder that Philippians 2:13 can say, "For it is God which worketh in you both to will and to do of his good pleasure."

God's work of resurrection within you delights him and benefits you. You are going to be thrilled at how God has put resurrection power to work in your spirit for your soul and your body. The covenant made by the death and Resurrection of Jesus provides for your every spiritual and physical need, including your transformation, purification, eternal life, spiritual energy, and power. It provides emergency provisions, divine protection, reconciliation—and the very presence of God!

What does resurrection power do for you? It gives you the means of rising from the death of your old ways into a new and glorious life in Jesus Christ. Have you ever heard people express doubt about themselves, perhaps when they have fallen back into an old habit or when they feel they are backsliding? They say, "It's hopeless! I'll never be able to change!" Maybe you have even felt that way yourself at one time or another. That's where the legacy of resurrection power gives you a wonderful advantage. Without Jesus, death reigns in your emotions, intellect, and will, but resurrection power guarantees your spiritual transformation. You pass from death in sin to life in Christ—and all things become possible!

From the moment you accept Jesus Christ as your Lord and Savior, the awe-inspiring resurrection legacy is yours. Perhaps, like the woman at the beginning of this sermon you want to reassure yourself that this incredible inheritance is really yours. Well, the Word is your Father's "will," and all his promises and legacies are there for you to read. I encourage you to do so. As a child of God, you became rich beyond measure when Jesus rose from the grave. You can now walk in victory every day of your life because you have the authority, Word, blood, and resurrection power of Christ to guarantee your threefold right to life!—Marilyn Hickey

SUNDAY, DECEMBER 2, 2001
Lectionary Message

Topic: A Balanced Life
TEXT: Rom. 13:11–14
Other Readings: Isa. 2:1–5; Ps. 122; Matt. 24:36–44

Today is the first Sunday of the Advent season, that wonderful season of anticipation and preparation. Traditionally, on the first Sunday of Advent Christians consider the hope Jesus Christ brings to a redeemed heart. But how does the hope of Christ reveal itself in today's complex society? The trouble with hope is that we have little or no basis for understanding it, let alone for using it as a tool for successful living. So it seems reasonable to first ask what hope is and then to examine how we maintain that sense of hope daily.

Spirituality, defined as sensitivity to the work of God and the spiritual powers around us, needs an agent to act as a ballast to give life stability. Otherwise we may find ourselves alternating between indescribable joy in the presence of God and overwhelming sorrow at the evil in the world. Hope is God's ballast bringing balance and stability to life. But if God provides hope as a part of his gracious gift, why are so many Christians so anxious? I believe that constant exposure to an anxiety-ridden society without caring for our personal spiritual needs causes the problem. Paul offers a solution in his letter to the Roman Christians.

I. *Be alert!* With both the force of conviction and the touch of the poet, Paul sounds the alarm for us in verses 11–12. It's time to be sober and careful because it's later than any of us might imagine. In preceding verses, Paul speaks of the Christian's responsibilities in life. With verse 11 Paul starts the meter running. We are not free to take our time considering whether or not we wish to live responsible lives. We don't have the option of promising to start somewhere out in the future. Something hangs in the balance and time is running out.

For Paul this is a good news–bad news story. The bad news is that time is nearly gone and there is much left to accomplish. There are still too many who have yet to hear of God's grace. And all of this has occurred while we Christians have slumbered. Still, there is good news, too. With each passing day our salvation draws nearer. Paul is not suggesting a new concept theologically. He often proclaims that God's grace changes the human heart when the individual accepts the message of Christ. From that point, grace begins the process of changing the individual from the inside out. The process is called *sanctification*, in religious jargon. But like other New Testament writers, Paul looks forward to a time when that work will be finished, when what we often call heaven and our salvation will be finalized.

II. *Choose wisely!* How wonderful it is that God has given us opportunities to make choices in life. But along with these glorious opportunities come corresponding responsibilities. Paul reminds us that our past is littered with the debris of bad choices. Indeed, from his perspective we could hardly keep from making those bad choices. However, now that we are Christians we have the capacity to make proper choices. In this text Paul offers two such choices. First, we are to stop acting as we did before redemption. Verse 13 lists the types of action unredeemed people often make. But our lives are to be different.

Next Paul offers a positive spin. As we stop choosing the negatives we can then begin to choose the positives. For Paul, the best choice of all is to put on the "armor of light." Occasionally I hear someone relate the Christian faith to a type of step program for self-help. You know the type. They're all over the place. And although it's true that many of them are modeled on the Christian values, there is one critical difference. Christianity demands that we put aside the negative components of our lives. This is done in willfully surrendering those issues to God. So too do many of the step programs call on the participant to give up negative aspects of life. But Christianity replaces those negatives with the presence of God's Holy Spirit, the best positive of all. The step programs simply call for giving up, not yielding a lesser in order to gain a greater. Paul is saying make room in your life for what God can do by giving up the deeds of darkness. But how exactly is this accomplished?

III. *Accept the Lordship of Christ.* Everything God has to offer the human heart comes as that heart is submitted to the Lordship of Christ. The best gifts in life, the intangibles we all crave, don't come because we work hard for them. They come because Christ our Lord brings them into our lives as part of his reign. It is possible for us to model hope—not a fake kind of hope that artificially masks life's difficulties and differences, but a genuine hope that creates a ballast for the storms of life. It comes from God as a gift of grace, brought to us in the rule of Christ over us—and it's yours this holiday season.—Robert Long

ILLUSTRATIONS

EXPECTATION.   Expect to have hope rekindled. Expect your prayers to be answered in wondrous ways. The dry seasons in life do not last. The spring rains will come again.—Sarah Ban Breathnach[1]

HAPPINESS.   The grand essentials to happiness in this life are something to do, something to love, and something to hope for.—Joseph Addison[2]

SERMON SUGGESTIONS

Topic: When God Comes on the Scene

TEXT: Mal. 3:1–4

(1) He never appears merely to destroy. (2) He sometimes comes with painful judgment. (3) He always pursues his redemptive purpose.

Topic: Partnership in the Gospel

TEXT: Phil. 1:3–11

(1) Is a reality for all Christians. (2) Has the promise of God's prevailing power. (3) Finds its strength in God's grace. (4) Requires Christian graces to bring it to expression and completion.

CONGREGATIONAL MUSIC

1. "Wake, Awake, for Night Is Flying," Philipp Nicolai (1599); trans. C. Winkworth (1858)
   WACHET AUF, Philipp Nicolai (1599); harm. J. S. Bach (1731)
   The Advent season should not pass without the singing of this classic chorale. Its theme fits perfectly with the Epistle reading for this day (Rom. 13:11–14).
2. "I Want to Be Ready," African American Spiritual
   I WANT TO BE READY, African American Spiritual
   This spiritual offers a natural response to the Gospel lesson (Matt. 24:36–44) in which we

---

[1] *Simple Abundance*
[2] From Lillian Eichler Watson (ed.), *Light from Many Lamps*

are warned to be ready because we know not when the Son of Man will come. A leader-soloist could sing all the stanzas with the congregation responding on the refrain.

3. "With Joy I Heard My Friends Explain," vers. *Psalter* (1912)

GONFALON ROYAL, Percy C. Buck (1918)

This interesting paraphrase of Psalm 122 could be sung stanza by stanza, alternating with the reading of the psalm verses according to the following plan: psalm verses 1–2, hymn stanza 1; verse 3, stanza 2; verses 4–5, stanza 4; verses 6–7, stanza 4; verses 8–9, stanza 5.

4. "Christ Is the World's True Light," George W. Briggs (1931)

DARMSTADT, Ahasuerus Fritsch (1679)

The second stanza of this fine twentieth-century hymn relates directly to the Old Testament reading in Isaiah about the beating of swords into plowshares and spears into pruning hooks (Isa. 2:4). The metaphor of light also relates to the reading in the Epistle (Rom. 13:11–14).—Hugh T. McElrath

WORSHIP AIDS

CALL TO WORSHIP.   "The Lord hath done great things for us; whereof we are glad" (Ps. 126:3).

INVOCATION.   Almighty God, hush our restlessness, still our chatter, calm our fears, silence any anxiety, as we approach thy throne. For thou art the God of the still, small voice, the quiet ways of prayer, and the majesty of peace!—E. Lee Phillips

OFFERTORY SENTENCE.   "Greater love hath no man than this, that a man lay down his life for his friends" (John 15:13).

OFFERTORY PRAYER.   Father of our Lord Jesus Christ, we thank you for the gift of your Son and for his willing obedience to you, which brought him to the cross. We thank you for the love for you and for us in it all. Now may we bring our offerings to you as tokens of our gratitude.

PRAYER.   You are here, O God. You are here in the fullness of your grace and truth in Christ. You have been speaking from the beginning, whenever that was: "In the beginning was the Word, and the Word was with God and the Word was God." You did speak words of creative love and the worlds were formed in all of their mystery—in all of their beauty and bounty. You did stoop down and take the dust of the earth and crown your creation by forming man to bear your image: to think your thoughts, to receive and show your love, to hear and communicate your Word. How fearfully and wonderfully we are made!

When man in his pride has sought to substitute his words for your Word, you have never stopped calling him to return. You spoke to our fathers through the prophets, "Return, return, O man," and in these last days you have spoken, and are speaking, through your only Son: "This is my beloved; hear him and live; there is no other." When we do not listen to him, the very stones cry out—nature speaks your judgment on our wayward ways.

O Father, what a stewardship you have ordained for your Church—stewards of the Word of life. May we be faithful to declare and manifest your Word, for without this center any civilization, no matter how sophisticated technologically, is destroyed from within. "Except the

Lord keep the city, or the nation, or the world, the watchman wakes but in vain." May we be as the light set on a hill to lead people to light and to life, that all humankind may become the family you have ordained from the beginning to glorify and praise you who are the one.

In him who from the beginning was your Word is present your Kingdom, and your power, and your glory, forever and ever.—John M. Thompson

SERMON
Topic: The Irony of Christmas Peace
TEXT: Isa. 9:6–7; Luke 1:57–58, 67–79

The Christmas season is traditionally looked on as the season of peace. That word, *peace*, just keeps cropping up in the Scripture passages having to do with the birth of Christ. The prophet Isaiah, in a passage that Christians have always associated with the birth of Jesus, speaks of the child that is born to us, the Son who is given to us, and who shall be called, as Isaiah puts it, "Prince of Peace" (9:6).

Zechariah, the father of John the Baptist (the forerunner of Jesus), likewise spoke of the one who would "guide our feet into the way of peace" (Luke 1:79). The message of the angels to the shepherds who were out in the fields keeping watch over their flocks by night was "on Earth peace" (Luke 2:14). Many of the beloved hymns we sing during the Christmas season speak of "peace on earth, goodwill toward men."

Yet the four weeks between Thanksgiving and Christmas are probably the most stressful and hectic and *least* peaceful days of the year. That's the great irony—or the exact opposite of what one would expect—of Christmas peace.

For instance, on the day after Thanksgiving many of us start that massive spending frenzy in which we max out our credit cards, running here and there looking for gift after gift until we are so stressed out that the thing we want most is for Christmas to be over so everything can get back to normal. There is little peace to be had at the mall or shopping center.

We get together with loved ones far and wide, packing two, three, or maybe four families under one roof for days in which everyone gets on everyone else's nerves until the tension gets thick, tempers flare, hurtful words are spoken, and family peace and harmony are thrown out the window with the table scraps.

Domestic violence reaches its peak during the Christmas holidays. Stress over money (or lack of it), too much drinking, and so on leads to fights and abuse between husbands, wives, and children.

We buy our children toy weapons of war—tanks and guns and violent action figures.

Relations with and understanding of those of other faiths may become more strained during the holidays as we try to force our beliefs and holiday customs on them.

So, you see, by the time December 25 rolls around there hasn't been much Christmas peace in our lives at all. What irony! What a sad state of affairs. How it must make the Lord feel! As devotional writer Henri Nouwen put it, "Many of us have become so serious and intense, so filled with preoccupations about the future of the world and the church, so burdened by our loneliness and isolation, that our hearts are veiled by a dark sadness, preventing us from exuding the peace and the joy of God's children."[3]

---

[3] *In Joyful Hope: Meditations for Advent*

It appears to me that if we really want to experience the Christmas peace that the Scriptures so often talk about, we will have to make a conscious choice to have it and go the extra mile to make it a part of our lives. There are some practical steps that each of us can take to be more peaceful during the Advent and Christmas season—as we were intended to be:

1. We can sit down with our families and set a limit on how much we are going to spend this year. The amount of joy we will experience during the Christmas holidays does not depend on how much money we spend. In fact, the simpler we can make Christmas and the less we spend, the more joyous our holiday should be.

2. We need to realize from the outset that when you put two, three, or four family units under one roof, nerves are going to get frayed and tempers are going to flare. Perhaps we should consider limiting the time of our visits, or check into a hotel. At the very least we need to approach holiday visits with a conscious attempt to be peacemakers.

3. Let's do whatever we can to put a stop to domestic violence—hitting, shoving, humiliating, and so on. Let's support organizations that seek to intervene and provide a safe haven for victims.

4. Whenever possible, perhaps we should choose peaceful toys for our children and try to avoid war toys, violent action figures, and so on.

5. Let's try to be sensitive to those in the community of other faiths—our Jewish brothers and sisters, Muslims, and others who have their own faith traditions (such as Hanukkah) but who don't look on Christmas in the same way we do. I am reminded of two wonderful stories that illustrate this point.

First, there were all the Christian families in Newton, Pennsylvania, who put menorahs in their windows during Hanukkah a few years ago to show their solidarity with a Jewish family whose home had a rock thrown through the window and whose menorah was smashed to the ground and broken. The Christians and Jews of Newtown stood united during the holidays, in spite of their differing traditions.[4] That's what biblical peacemaking is all about.

And then there was the Jewish man by the name of Albert Rosen who for twenty-eight years volunteered to work on Christmas in the place of Christians so they could be off with their families. In all those years Rosen filled in as a police dispatcher, bellman, switchboard operator, TV reporter, chef, convenience store clerk, radio disc jockey, and gas station attendant. Each year before Christmas he trained beforehand for each job so he would be prepared when Christmas arrived. He did it out of compassion for his fellow men. This too is what biblical peacemaking is all about.

There is one more peace story that I would like to share with you that aired a couple of years ago on the television show *Unsolved Mysteries*. It was Christmas 1944. At a little cabin in the woods in Germany, four American soldiers came knocking. One of them was wounded. The mother of the house and her young son invited the soldiers in for Christmas dinner, in spite of the great danger she was putting herself in from both the American soldiers and the German government. Minutes later there was another knock on the door. There stood four German soldiers. After asking that they leave their weapons outside, the mother invited the German soldiers in. All ate Christmas dinner (chicken soup) together. Christmas spirit and Christmas peace prevailed.

---

[4] *The Tennessean*, Dec. 13, 1996, p. 8A.

When thinking about the irony of Christmas peace—the fact that the season of the year that should be most peaceful is the least peaceful and most stressful—let us determine here and now that we are going to be part of the solution instead of contributors to the problem. In the words of Jack Mendelsohn, "If we were to get down on our knees and pray, 'Oh God, bring peace to our world by helping us to realize that it is we who must wage peace, by our attitudes, thoughts, and acts,' we could pray with a clear conscience."[5]

And let us not forget the words of Jesus himself: "Blessed are the peacemakers, for they will be called children of God" (Matt. 5:9).—Randy Hammer

SUNDAY, DECEMBER 9, 2001

Lectionary Message

Topic: The Foundation of Fellowship

TEXT: Rom. 15:4–13

Other Readings: Isa. 11:1–10; Esther 72:1–7, 18–19; Matt. 3:1–12

As a boy growing up in rural Western Kentucky, I learned the simple truth reflected in the old adage, "Two cats tied together by their tails produce union, not unity." Fellowship is the mysterious lubricant of God's Kingdom. When it is present, God's Church offers a positive witness to a fractured world. When it is missing, the Church looks impotent and hypocritical. But fellowship doesn't just happen. It takes deliberate action on our part. As Paul concludes his letter to the Roman church he gives them this pastoral lesson on building unity.

God gives us everything we need to build the fellowship that marks the Kingdom as special. We have the blessing of Scripture, the example of Jesus, and the presence of God's Spirit. From Paul's viewpoint, that was enough.

I. *The blessing of Scripture.* Unlike our modern textbooks, the Bible has a living dynamic about it. Paul knew that the Christians in Rome had coalesced around their only common denominator, the gospel. Gathered in Rome after being scattered across the empire, their differences were apparent to all. Looking only at the human factor would lead anyone to predict a Church always fractured and divided. But Paul looked beyond the human factors and urged his readers to see beyond them as well. His instructions were simple and straightforward—focus on the hope and peace God grants us as his children.

One question remains: How de we achieve this unity? By searching for a common purpose, is his answer. That purpose needs to be worthy of our best effort. It must be universally and equally important to all involved in the life of that fellowship. For Paul, only one purpose stood up to such a test: the role of the Church as a community charged with the task of glorifying God. Where the Church seeks to bring honor and glory to God, the inevitable result is a movement in the direction of unity. Old wounds die away. Relationships form under desirable circumstances.

II. *Follow the example of Jesus.* But how do we know if we're on target? Paul includes a small test in the seventh verse: We should receive each other as we ourselves were received by God. Paul tells the Roman Christians that they are required to accept each other because they were

---

[5] *Being Liberal in an Illiberal Age*, p. 132.

themselves accepted by Christ. The results will be obvious to anyone looking on: God will be praised. If you listen closely to this verse you will hear an echo of Jesus' own words: "By this all men will know that you are my disciples, if you love one another" (John 13:35).

I love the sessions of groups such as the Baptist World Alliance. Christians from all over the world gather under one roof. They all have different customs. They speak different languages. They each approach living out their faith in different ways. But they share in common a love for the Lord and it translates into a love for and tolerance of one another. It was much the same in Paul's day. The apostle believed that an audience from the world looked in on the activities of the Church. They looked to see if the one common point the members shared was enough to override the differences they brought into the fellowship. Such unity could only be the work of God and it would stand out as a witness to the power of God in the lives of the believers.

III. *The presence of God's Spirit.* Just thinking about that fellowship and all its possibilities caused Paul to break out in a resounding benediction of blessing. A fellowship of unity opens the door to God's great blessings in each of our lives. God, who specializes in hope, fills us with joy and peace when we trust him. The antithesis of hope is despair, a quality of existence with which the world is well acquainted. Despair robs anyone of peace and it is found in every corner of society. We normally expect to discover despair in the overwhelming envelope of poverty. But I've seen it in the wealthiest of neighborhoods. We look for despair wherever folks are suffering from illness and disease. But the high rates of teen violence and suicide remind us that despair reaches those whom we felt were immune, and all too often this despair lurks in the corridors of our churches.

On this second Sunday of Advent, we look for the peace Christ brings. We confess how tired we are, for the world sucks the very peace from our existence. Many times we acknowledge we're so empty that trying to generate peace within ourselves only adds to our emptiness. God's remedy is to provide a safe haven in which the entire community stands ready to give us what we want the most and are least capable of providing for ourselves. Today we give thanks to God for fellowship—a community united.—Robert Long

ILLUSTRATIONS

ENEMIES.   Five great enemies to peace inhabit us: avarice, ambition, envy, anger, and pride. If those enemies were to be banished, we should infallibly enjoy perpetual peace.—Ralph Waldo Emerson[6]

PEACE.   Peace does not dwell in outward things, but within the soul; we may preserve it in the midst of bitterest pain, if our will remains firm and submissive. Peace in this life springs from acquiescence to, not in exemption from, suffering.—Francois de Fenelon[7]

THE RAT RACE.   The trouble with being in the rat race is that even if you win, you're still a rat.—Lily Tomlin[8]

---

6 *The Book of Positive Quotations*
7 *The Book of Positive Quotations*
8 *Slowing Down in a Speeded up World*

SERMON SUGGESTIONS

Topic: The Messiah

TEXT: Isa. 11:1–10

(1) His characteristics (vv. 2–3a). (2) His righteous reign (vv. 3b–5). (3) His new world of harmony (vv. 6–9). (4) His universal magnetism (v. 10).

Topic: Let All the Peoples Praise Him

TEXT: Rom. 15:4–13 RSV

(1) God's will for us: to live in harmony with one another. (2) A pattern for this harmony: mutual welcome in the faith, as Christ has welcomed us, the unworthy. (3) A case in point: God's outreach through Christ to the Gentiles.

CONGREGATIONAL MUSIC

1. "Now Blessed Be the Lord Our God," *Scottish Psalter* (1650)

   CORONATION, Oliver Holden (1793)

   This paraphrase of the last two verses of Psalm 72 could be sung as a response between the read verses of the psalm. It could also make an ideal ascription of praise sung at the conclusion of worship.

2. "O Come, O Come, Emmanuel," ninth-century Latin; trans. Composite

   VENI EMMANUEL. fifteenth-century French; arr. Thomas Helmore

   The stanzas of this ancient Advent plainsong relate to this Sunday's reading from prophecy (Isa. 11:1–10). It would be in keeping with its origins if it were sung in unison and completely unaccompanied.

3. "Hope of the World," Georgia Harkness (1954)

   O PERFECT LOVE, Joseph Barnby (1889)

   VICAR, V. Earle Copes (1963)

   This classic twentieth-century hymn could be sung meaningfully immediately after the reading of the Epistle, which ends with the prayer that the God of hope may by his Spirit bring joy, peace, and hope.

4. "On Jordan's Bank the Baptist's Cry," Charles Coffin (1736)

   WINCHESTER NEW, *Musikalisches Handbuch* (1690)

   PUER NOBIS, Trier Ms (fifteenth century)

   As a natural response to the story of John the Baptist (Matt. 3:1–2), this venerable hymn offers an appropriate vehicle of sung worship.—Hugh T. McElrath

WORSHIP AIDS

CALL TO WORSHIP.   "The voice of him that crieth in the wilderness, Prepare ye the way of the Lord, make straight in the desert a highway for our God" (Isa. 40:3).

INVOCATION.   O God, prepare our hearts for the great things you would do within and among us today. Prepare our lives for the great things you would do for others through us. We await your help.

OFFERTORY SENTENCE.   "Every one of us shall give account of himself to God" (Rom. 14:12).

OFFERTORY PRAYER.   Merciful Father, you open springs in the desert and give good things to us when we least expect them. Grant us now one gift more: the grace of cheerful giving, even when personal circumstances make our stewardship difficult.

PRAYER.   Lord, as we look back over the days just past, we marvel at your mercies. You have blessed us with your presence. You have heartened us with new opportunities. You have strengthened us with the gift of friends. You have helped us turn aside from many temptations. You have assured us of your forgiveness as we have confessed our sins to you and as we have made amends for wrongs done to others.

Show us how to be grateful and how to live out our gratitude. Help us to bring your presence near someone estranged from you, to open new doors for someone deeply discouraged, to share with someone the warmth of our Christian love, to bolster the moral courage of someone sorely tested, to assure someone that you truly will forgive all manner of sin. May we herald your coming with salvation.

SERMON
Topic: Powerful Living
TEXT: Matt. 11:11

I drove into the service station and said, "Fill it up." The young man said, "Can't do it," to which I responded, "You don't have any gas?" He grinned. "We got plenty of gas. We just don't have any power."

There have been many times in my life when I have had that same problem. All the resources needed for an assignment were ready. The opportunity to minister or to serve had presented itself. The gas was there but the power was off. Maybe the circuits were overloaded, or maybe I had become unplugged. Whatever the reason, I was trying to operate without contact with my source of power.

It need not be this way for the Christian. God in his infinite love has made it possible for the Christian to plug into his unlimited power.

John the Baptist is the outstanding example of a life lived in the power of God. Although his life ended in its prime, John powerfully accomplished his purpose. Jesus said of him, "Among those born of women there has not arisen anyone greater than John the Baptist" (Matt. 11:11).

John the apostle introduces John the Baptist (see John 1:6–8). Matthew records his death at the hands of Herod, carrying out the tragic whim of the daughter of Herod's mistress (see Matt. 14:9–12).

John the Baptist lived with power. He died with power. His purpose in life was achieved through power. The cost was no less than everything he had.

What was the secret of John's power? Did he possess supernatural qualities? No, but he did live by three certainties that defined the course of his life.

I. *John was certain that he was sent from God.*

(a) In the prologue to his Gospel, John the apostle introduces Jesus as the Light of the World, the Light that shines in darkness and cannot be put out. Anticipating the difficulty his readers will have in understanding this, the writer at once brings John the Baptist into the story. He is a man and he has come to explain the Light. Because he is a man, men will understand his message.

(b) Apparently John the Baptist never strayed from his strong belief that God had sent him to be a witness. Among his followers were those who never accepted his witness. They accepted John but not Jesus. John constantly proclaimed that he was not the Christ, not even a prophet, but a mere voice crying in the wilderness, a voice sent from God.

(c) Although he was a lonely herald without credentials, he was in touch with the God who had sent him. He was a man obsessed by light when other men were content to live in darkness. He was a man willing to renounce the securities in which others thrived in order to depend entirely on God to vindicate his message.

He was a man sent from God.

II. *He was certain that he had a singular purpose.*

(a) John was not sidetracked by the issues and events of his day. His only purpose was to point beyond himself in witness to Jesus. His only message was repeated over and over again, "The true Light that enlightens every person is coming into the world."

(b) Existing on locusts and honey, John might have been excused if he had delayed his preaching to have lunch in the best local restaurant. Called before the Jewish leaders to explain himself, his ambition might have been acceptable if he had assumed a major religious role. In light of the prominence of Herod and Herodias, surely no one would have condemned John if he had ignored the flagrant sins of the king. Perhaps he could even have become the court chaplain.

(c) Considering all else as insignificant, John gave himself wholeheartedly to his purpose. This is best seen in his encounter with the official delegation from the Jewish religious leadership in Jerusalem. Christians today who labor under opposition or even persecution can take courage from John's unflinching, powerful confession under pressure. Repeatedly "he confessed, he did not deny" his faith. Also repeatedly he negated himself, drawing attention away from himself and to the one person to whom he was a witness.

John's power was not dissipated. He brought it to focus on his singular, abiding purpose.

III. *John was certain of his commitment.*

(a) Toward the end of his ministry John was confounded by his followers. With wounded pride, they told John that all the people were going to Jesus. Why? John himself had baptized Jesus. John had begun his work first. How easy it is for our best efforts to become competitive spirits!

(b) Ever true to his purpose of bearing witness to the Christ, John lovingly witnessed to his own disciples (see John 3:28–30).

(c) All that John had he brought into the service of the Lord. God, who had called him, provided the power that made up the difference between what John had and what he needed. John was committed to receiving and using the power that was available.

Have you experienced that kind of power in your own life? Would you like to? It's possible. It comes from the same strong conviction that God himself has called and commissioned you. It is strengthened by dedication to his purpose for you that supersedes any other opportunity that might come. It requires no less than wholehearted commitment.—Carolyn Weatherford Crumpler

SUNDAY, DECEMBER 16, 2001
Lectionary Message

Topic: A Doorway Marked "Joy"!

TEXT: Matt. 11:2–11

Other Readings: Isa. 35:1–10; Luke 1:47–55; James 5:7–10

Somewhere during the holiday season you will probably encounter someone wondering what all the celebration means. Is there any truth to this business of Jesus? Your inquirer won't be the first to ask such a question. One of the first to ask it was John the Baptist. You have to feel for John. He lived his life as a second banana, always shining the limelight on someone else, living in another's shadow. Yet that was the role God chose for him. In today's text he sits alone in prison with despair an unwanted sidekick riding on his shoulder. Eventually he gives in and sends word to Jesus through some of John's followers. He has only one question—the most important question possible: Are you the one or should we look elsewhere?

Jesus could have answered in a variety of ways. He chose an oblique answer. To John's disciples he said, "Judge for yourselves, then report everything you see and hear back to John." Instead of a simple yes or no, Jesus invites John's disciples to report back that something brand new has occurred. This text sits on the fault line of prophetic history. So, naturally you can understand how John would underestimate Jesus' role as Messiah.

I. *More of the same.* John, alone in prison, despairs that he has somehow misinterpreted the divine activity in which he has participated. The concept of the Messiah had been narrowed down to mean little more than a political figure playing out a part on the international stage. For more than four hundred years that notion had been growing more dominant. But Jesus simply refused to act the part. Now John watches and waits and hopes, and with each passing day he grows more despondent. Fear will do that; it will cause even the strongest of hearts to grow faint.

It's much the same today. Society, with its emphasis on a civil religion, still seeks to define the role of the Savior. Humans still search for a culturally acceptable messenger from God. But in the dark night of one's soul, the yearning can't be silenced. We ask ourselves if the picture we have of Jesus is really the picture of God's answer to our need. The world offers more of the same. We cry out for something more. Then we hear God's answer. Something new, something wonderful, something more than we could possibly imagine is available. It's God's good news.

II. *A new message of joy.* Jesus' answer to John is music to the ears of folks stumbling around in the bleakness of their lives. God hasn't done something expected. He hasn't offered a Band-Aid for our souls. He has provided an answer adequate for our wounds. Blind folks see, lame folks walk, deaf folks hear, the diseased are cured, and the dead now live. That's radical. That's different. That's special. That's Jesus. And best of all, that's joyful. It's celebration music played with all the stops pulled out.

Listen to anyone whose life has been changed by the power of God. They tell a story of redemption, of forgiveness, of joy. Jesus would teach his disciples that it was just like a woman madly searching for the only coin she owned until that lost coin turned up. The desperation rose with each stroke of the broom. Fear grew as inch by inch the search yielded nothing. Then it was found and a wave of relief was released. The single woman's celebration tells us everything we need to know. God isn't content with making our lot better. Better isn't good enough. God sweeps away the old to make room for something brand new.

III. *The doorway of a new day.* Listen once more as Jesus praises John and then adds a curious note. Anyone who participates in the Kingdom God is building is greater than the greatest of the prophets. Why? Because the prophets could only look with longing toward something better. We live it!

We live every day of our lives on the joyful side of Easter. Before that decisive moment, humans could only speculate about God's intentions. Did God know them? Did God care about them? There were many hints but no real answers. Then came Easter. God does know us and cares about us, and God has done something more wonderful than we could believe possible. God isn't just willing to make life more bearable now. God also makes life available, both now and beyond the grave.

So, during this holiday season, when someone asks you what all the celebration is about, tell the story: We celebrate the opportunity to walk through God's new doorway. We celebrate joyfully for we know what it is to have lost something precious and dear to us. Ours is not a worn-out holiday, offering more of the same. God met us when and where we were most vulnerable, empty, lost, ashamed, and hopeless, and God gave us the most priceless gift of all. It comes packaged as a simple message, one tied in a ribbon of joy. That's what Christmas is all about: entering a new life through a doorway marked "joy."—Robert Long

ILLUSTRATIONS

VARIETY.   Live a balanced life—learn some and think some and draw and paint and sing and dance and play and work every day some.—Robert Fulghum[9]

JOY.   Focus on the journey, not the destination. Joy is found not in finishing an activity but in doing it.—Greg Anderson[10]

GIVING.   Joy increases as you give it, and diminishes as you try to keep it for yourself. In giving it, you will accumulate a deposit of joy greater than you ever believed possible.— Norman Vincent Peale[11]

SERMON SUGGESTIONS

Topic: Agenda for Service
TEXT: Isa. 61:1–4, 8–11
(1) It is focused on manifold human need. (2) Its success depends on a faithful God. (3) It brings forth joy and exultation.

Topic: Sanctification in Three Modes
TEXT: 1 Thess. 5:16–24, especially v. 23
(1) In the spirit: your relationship to God. (2) In the soul: your essential self. (3) In the body: your physical being. (4) All of which are an inseparable unity special to God.

---

[9] *All I Really Need to Know I Learned in Kindergarten: Uncommon Thoughts on Common Things*
[10] *The Twenty-Two Non-Negotiable Laws of Wellness*
[11] *Positive Thinking Every Day*

CONGREGATIONAL MUSIC

1. "Hail to the Brightness of Zion's Glad Morning," Thomas Hastings (1822)
   WESLEY, Lowell Mason (1833)

   This nineteenth-century American hymn captures the spirit and message of the Old Testament reading about Isaiah's prophecy (Isa. 35:1–10) in which the joy of the redeemed is foretold in beautiful, symbolic terms.

2. "My Soul Gives Glory to My God," Song of Mary; para. Miriam Therese Winter (1987)
   MORNING SONG, Wyeth's *Repository of Sacred Music, Part II* (1813)

   A modern paraphrase of the Magnificat, the tune gives this glorious Canticle of Mary a vehicle for congregational singing. Accompaniment by guitar would be appropriate.

3. "O for a Thousand Tongues to Sing," Charles Wesley (1739)
   AZMON, Carl G. Glaeser (1839)

   This classic Wesleyan hymn relates to the recital of the miracles of healing that Jesus was performing in the report to the imprisoned John the Baptist (Matt. 11:2–11). Note especially stanzas 5 and 6, in which Jesus's healing powers are celebrated.

4. "My Song Is Love Unknown," Samuel Crossman (1664)
   LOVE UNKNOWN, John Ireland (1918)

   This venerable song relating primarily to Jesus' Passion and death also, especially in stanza 4, relates to his miracles of healing during his earthly ministry. The seven stanzas—one should not be omitted—could be alternately sung and spoken as follows: sing stanza 1, speak stanza 2, sing stanza 3, speak stanza 4, sing stanza 5, speak stanza 6, sing stanza 7.—Hugh T. McElrath

WORSHIP AIDS

CALL TO WORSHIP.   "When they had heard the king, they departed; and, lo, the star, which they saw in the east, went before them, till it came and stood over where the young child was. When they saw the star, they rejoiced with exceeding great joy" (Matt. 2:9–10).

INVOCATION.   Lord, our time of waiting is almost at an end. The celebration of Christmas is nigh upon us and we have precious few opportunities left to prepare our hearts for Christ's advent into our lives. Help us to accept the opportunity we have for preparation today with such dedication and purpose that when Christmas day arrives we can say that we are truly ready for Christ to come into our hearts.—James M. King

OFFERTORY SENTENCE.   "Offer the sacrifices of righteousness and put your trust in the Lord" (Ps. 4:5).

OFFERTORY PRAYER.   O God, thou who hast given thine only begotten Son to be our Savior, our largest gifts are but too small. Yet thou dost receive what we bring. Use our offerings, we pray, to spread abroad the good news of Christ Jesus.

PRAYER.   O God, now comes the time of rebirth: the rebirth of wonder and hope, of grief over wrong, of expectation and judgment, of godly fear, of hunger to do what is right. The time of Advent is upon us, welcome as morning's faint orange over the dark of leafless trees and blue-cold snow. Save us, Father, from the worst of Christmas: the busyness that exhausts and the forced fun. Draw us beyond the tinsel and Santa Claus; draw us out under the stars to behold a stable and a cross, that we may turn home in wonder and hold one another reborn.—Peter Fribley

SERMON
Topic: Humble Servant
TEXT: Matt. 23:1–12

It is hard to say what is wrong with someone without sounding superior. Even Jesus can't avoid that Catch-22. When Jesus starts talking about what is wrong with the Pharisees' conduct, he begins to sound like so many other "holier than thou" people. He says to the crowd, you all need to listen to what they teach for they teach the Torah, but do not follow them in what they do because they are "all hat and no ranch." They are all talk and no show. If you talk the talk, you ought to walk the walk, and they talk but don't walk. They like to talk about compassion, but they don't show any compassion.

Jesus says that the Pharisees don't walk what they talk, and that they are always interested in expanding and adding to the religious ceremonies and obligations but are also very successful in exempting themselves from the obligations they impose. The Pharisees are great at expanding the rituals, rules, and regulations for the laity, but the priesthood does not have to observe them.

When they do observe or fulfill any religious obligation, the Pharisees are quick to get publicity for it. They like being invited to the head table to say grace. They ask for the clergy discount at the stores. They want others to see them fasting, praying, and giving alms. They make sure that their good deeds do not go unnoticed.

The Catch-22 is that by just saying these kinds of things in public you end up looking like you think you are morally superior to others because you do not do these things. Well, I don't talk about my religious activities. I never tell others what they should do. I don't say grace over my meals in public because I don't want people to see me and think I am doing it for show.

But Jesus knows he has to teach his disciples how to live in the Kingdom of God because it is being brought into existence by his presence. Those who recognize that Jesus is the one who has come to bring the Kingdom of God will discover that there are a great number of changes in language, relationship, and attitudes. God is our Father, so all of us are brothers and sisters to each other. Jesus is our Lord, rabbi, and teacher, so we will not call anybody else master. But the most important quality in a disciple is humility. In the Kingdom of God, those who exalt themselves will be humbled.

The primary quality of those who are citizens in the Kingdom of God will be the quality of humility. Those who desire to be great will be humble servants of all. The citizens of the Kingdom of God will humble themselves. But not like the college freshman who was telling his new girlfriend that his humility was his greatest virtue. Rather, it is a humility that comes from the honest recognition of two major realities—a humility that grows out of the recognition that we have been blessed with more than we ever deserve, and a humility that feels the immense obligation to preserve and pass on all that others have given us. The citizens of the Kingdom of God will be humble servants—humbled by the sheer volume of grace, blessings, and gifts given to us by others; and servants of those gifts by accepting the responsibility of preserving them and passing them on.

The Kingdom of God is for those who humble themselves. How do we humble ourselves without it being a kind of self-righteous humility? Humility is discovered in the honest examination of our lives and in the awareness that we are in every respect testaments to our own thoroughgoing dependence. *Thought* that we recognize as wise or witty, *behavior* that is gracious or elegant, and *desire* refined beyond mere hunger and rut are all a portion of an inheritance. No one invents such everyday excellences; we all take them up and make them our own by acting in a way that confirms that we have understood them. We have been recipients of the greatest minds in history. We live in a world where dance, drama, manners, customs, and traditions have all been refined over the course of thousands of years. Excellence, standards, and qualifications have all been set by previous generations.

When we take an honest assessment of who we are and what kind of blessings we have been given, we have to admit that there is very little for us to be arrogant about. For it is not too much to say that there is no good or beautiful or healthy thing in this world that does not depend for its origin and continued existence on the well-being of a whole host of others besides ourselves. This honest recognition that we have been born into such an abundance of blessings, that we are continuously blessed beyond our expectations with the gifts of great music, great laughter, great opportunity, people caring about our education, and people who faithfully take away our garbage; blessed with air, water, land, and fire; blessed by God with a life and resources to develop and use, by those who have preserved the faith to share, and by the devotional writings and thoughts of great minds and hearts, has to make us, like the psalmist, ask the question, "Who in the world is Rick Brand that thou art mindful of him?" How can we not be humbled by all the things we have received that we did absolutely nothing to deserve? O to the grace of God, to the goodness and kindness of past generations, to grace—how great a debtor. Take a look at your life and look at all the things that have been given to you and see how much you want to claim that you are a self-made person. A minister friend I know in Pittsburgh is ready to retire and is in wonderful shape financially, but my friend doesn't know who to thank. He can't take any credit for his financial condition. Pittsburgh Presbytery invites ministers to go to a Certified Financial Planner in Pittsburgh because somebody left an endowment to pay for the fees for the first year. The planner suggested a program. My friend took the advice and it is not his fault that he has lived through fifteen of the most profitable years in the history of the stock market. He can't take credit for his present situation. Look at the vast number of people who have contributed to his situation. The TV ad is right in part—Thank you, Paine Webber.

The disciples of Jesus are humble servants of all because they are humbled by their recognition of the amazing blessings, contributions, legacies, and gifts that have been given to them. The Kingdom of God begins with humble servants who are brought to their humility by the overwhelming impact of gratitude.

When we realize just how many, how wonderful, and how amazing are the gifts and blessings we have been given by others, there grows in us the understanding that as we receive these gifts we accept a responsibility for preserving them and transmitting them. The blessing of being God's covenant people is not just so that we may enjoy the covenant; it is always for the joy of sharing it and passing it on.

Just as in our common life, as citizens of our community, we all rely directly on so many of the common gifts—on a legal system, on an economic system, on the environment, and on a political system—and to the extent that we rely on these systems, their upkeep and preservation become a part of our responsibility. To accept and enjoy the blessings we have been given places on us the responsibility to preserve and transmit them. One of the great concerns of our community and nation is that too many of our citizens seem to be walking away from the responsibility of preserving and transmitting the blessings they have been given.

But Jesus says that those who are citizens of the Kingdom of God will not be like the Pharisees; rather, they will be humble servants of all. They will be humbled by the honest recognition that they have been given far more than they could ever deserve or claim to have earned; they will be humbled by the awesome legacy of gifts, traditions, and blessings they have been given; and they will become servants of those gifts by seeking to preserve and pass on the best, the most beautiful, the most inspiring, the most enriching of those gifts to others.

We have seen those who love to talk a good game but cannot hit a lick, those who have no problem making up rules and obligations for others to keep as long as they don't have to keep them, and those who love to get their pictures taken doing good things. Jesus says, My disciples will be those who have humbled themselves by an honest examination of their lives and who know that they did not make themselves, that they do not keep themselves, and that they cannot save themselves; they are overwhelmed with gratitude for all the gifts that have given them life, blessed their living, and offered them hope; and they are eager to share those blessings with others.—Rick Brand

SUNDAY, DECEMBER 23, 2001
Lectionary Message

Topic: The Greatest Love Story of All
Text: Matt. 1:18–25
Other Readings: Isa. 7:10–16; Ps. 80:1–7, 17–19; Rom. 1:1–7

Of the four Gospels, only two, Matthew and Luke, give us the details of Jesus' birth. All the incredible items of the Christmas story are found there. But in those grand stories, what do you suppose is the one essential component? What must be there for the story to have life? What makes all of this wonderful season ring with truth? Is it the Wise Men who traveled far from the East because they'd discovered a new star and according to their traditions and teachings a new star signaled the birth of a new king? Perhaps you vote for the shepherds quietly tending their flocks. Many children delight in the story of angels coming to sing their announcement of the child's birth. Is that the essential component?

As wonderful as these pieces of the story are, they don't measure up as indispensable. To be indispensable an element must be so remarkable that it alone makes the story unique. As I read this text I'm sure such a piece to the puzzle exists. It's the pronouncement by the angel to Joseph that the little one carried by Mary will be Immanuel. Somehow, in a way we can't fully understand, God has determined to come among us. You don't have to have angels singing to shepherds, Wise Men traveling great distances with expensive gifts, or Joseph and Mary making a hard journey to Joseph's ancestral home in order to have this story be true.

The single indispensable component of the Christmas story is one simple statement: This child is Immanuel. In this child, God does something never before imagined.

I. *It is a story of action.* For more than four hundred years, the chosen people had cried out to God for action. Their pleas were as simple as their sufferings were harsh. "God, do something!" I remember that when I was a small boy my dad could be rather stern at times. He modeled tough love before the phrase was invented. Sometimes I would upset him so he would lift his voice at me. I never liked those moments. But what I really dreaded were the times I had upset him to the point that he would just look at me. That silence was the most dreadful thing I ever endured. Just knowing he was there and that I had messed up was bad enough. But to be cut off, isolated, and alone was a punishment far worse than anything else.

The people of Israel had not received a legitimate word from God in generations. With each passing year the silence grew more difficult to withstand. To be sure, there were impostors, each one claiming to be God's special representative. They gathered a few vulnerable folks around them only to disillusion them in the end. But other than the impostors, there was no word from God. Then, just when, from the human point of view, hope was gone, God announced his intention to act. The proclamation didn't come from the royal palace. It wasn't a press release from the centers of power in Jerusalem. The news didn't come first to the movers and shakers of society. It was given to shepherds and outsiders.

II. *It is a story of redemption.* What was God going to do? Would he send a political leader to set Israel free? Would he send a spiritual leader to renew the old covenant? Would he provide a social leader to build some holy remnant out of the old order? There were spokesmen all over Israel calling for God to act in such ways. There were others who dared to act on God's behalf, some believing that God had called them to the task, others desiring to usurp the role for themselves.

The announcement that God authorized was different than any of these options. God was acting alone. The one whom God had commissioned would be Immanuel. God would come to humanity because it was impossible for humanity to approach God. And when God came as Immanuel, the work was far more complicated and radical than people had imagined. Immanuel would save them from their own sinfulness. The wonder of the Christmas message is found here. God looked at the human condition, impossibly marred by our sinful choices, and acted to redeem us—an accomplishment we couldn't even manage on our own behalf.

III. *It is a story of love.* All this begs the question, Why? Why would God do something like this? God doesn't owe us redemption. We don't deserve it. So why Christmas? The rest of the Bible offers us the answer. God loves humanity, not in general, not in the way you and I love our pets. God loves us with an intense love that yearns to be fulfilled in a relationship with each of us individually. Our sinfulness made such a relationship impossible, but God would not be deterred. Refusing to overlook our sins and unwilling to give us over to them, God devised a plan to redeem us from our sins. The story of Christmas is the first stage of that plan. If Jesus is not Immanuel, what does it matter who he is? If Jesus is Immanuel, then the plan of God is launched. Because Jesus is Immanuel, the greatest love story of all time can be told.—Robert Long

ILLUSTRATIONS

GLADNESS.   There were church bells too. . . . And they rang their tidings over the bandaged town, over the frozen foam of the powder and ice-cream hills, over the crackling sea.

It seemed that all the churches boomed for joy under my window; and the weathercocks crew for Christmas, on our fence.—Dylan Thomas[12]

A SONG.

> I sing the birth was born tonight
> The author both of life and light.

—Ben Johnson[13]

SERMON SUGGESTIONS

Topic: The Glorious Deliverer

TEXT: Isa. 35:1–10

(1) God's glory will appear to all creation (vv. 1–2). (2) God's glory combines judgment and deliverance (vv. 3–4). (3) God's glory reverses the ordinary state of affairs and course of events (vv. 5–10).

Topic: The Judge at the Door

TEXT: James 5:7–10

(1) Guarantees the wisdom of patient waiting for justice. (2) Demands an ethic of patience in dealing with our sometimes unfair and unjust neighbors.

CONGREGATIONAL MUSIC

1. "Hark! The Herald Angels Sing," Charles Wesley (1734)
   MENDELSSOHN, Felix Mendelssohn (1840)
   This familiar Christmas hymn relates to both the prophecy of Isaiah (Isa. 7:10–16) and the Gospel account of the birth of Christ (Matt. 1:18–25). The rousing tune as well as the exclamations of the text make this a fine recessional hymn, often accompanied by brass and/or handbells.

2. "Hear Us, O Shepherd of Your Chosen Race," vers. Bert Polman (1985)
   YORKSHIRE, John Wainwright (1750)
   A fine tune for a processional, YORKSHIRE is an apt vehicle for this modern paraphrase of the psalm of the day. Stanzas 3 and 4 may be omitted in order to parallel the selected verses in the Psalter reading.

3. "God of the Prophets, Bless the Prophets' Heirs," Denis Wortman (1884) and Carl Daw Jr.
   TOULON, *Genevan Psalter* (1551)
   The reference to the gospel promised beforehand through the prophets in the Epistle lesson (Rom. 1:1–7) relates especially to the first stanza of this hymn on the Church and its mission. Worshipers today who follow in the prophets' footsteps need the anointing of God's spirit.

4. "Come, Thou Long-Expected Jesus," Charles Wesley (1744)
   STUTTGART, *Psalmodia Sacra* (1715)
   HYFRYDOL, Rowland H. Prichard (1830)

---

[12] *A Child's Christmas in Wales*
[13] *A Hymn of the Nativity*

Of the many fine Advent hymns, this one by the peerless Wesley is one of the best. It lends itself well to antiphonal singing line-by-line between choir and congregation.—Hugh T. McElrath

WORSHIP AIDS

CALL TO WORSHIP.   "Happy is he that hath the God of Jacob for his help, whose hope is in the Lord his God" (Ps. 146:5).

INVOCATION.   As your pilgrim people, Lord, we sometimes feel lost in the wilderness of this world. You led your people once by a pillar of cloud through the day and a pillar of fire through the night, and they found their way. In this sacred hour lead us beside the refreshing streams of worship and send us on our way again—revived, rejoicing, and guided by your Word and Spirit.—Henry Fields

OFFERTORY SENTENCE.   "Be patient, therefore, brethren, unto the coming of the Lord. Behold, the husbandman waiteth for the precious fruit of the earth, and hath long patience for it, until he receive the early and latter rain" (James 5:7).

OFFERTORY PRAYER.   As sure as the coming of the harvest is your coming, O Lord, your blessings are unfailing, though we have to wait for the greatest of them. Give us patience and make us faithful as we wait. As we give our offerings, we wait in faith for the harvest of our stewardship in lives made happy in hope.

PRAYER.   Almighty God, most holy, in whom we live and dwell and have our being: we adore thee, we praise thee, we lift up our hearts in gratitude to thee. Wonderful have been thy gifts to us and resplendent have been thy blessings.

Hear our intercessions for those who stand in great need, whatever it may be. So many walk through threadbare hours devoid of faith, unaware that at the heart of things thou dost wait and hope lifts and love lives: for them we intercede in prayer.

Draw near to those who cannot come close to others because they were once hurt. Be close to those who are hard on themselves because life is not perfect and neither are they. Help those who toil but do not earn enough to meet expenses. Chastise those who work to degrade others. Call back those who no longer call thy name in prayer but cannot forget that their parents did. Draw those who want to come closer to thee, who are catching a vision, who feel the tug of the Spirit and the call of Christ.

Comfort the bereaved to see beyond the grave to an empty tomb and a place prepared for those who love the Lord.

Allow us, O God, to minister to those who are in such great need. Robe us in Christ's humility to be thy servants, that we might shower on human need thy divine love, sharing again the poured-out life of Christ, in whom we make our prayer.—E. Lee Phillips

SERMON
Topic: A Markan Christmas in Whoville
TEXT: Mark 1:1–19

Quite some time ago, Dr. Theodore Geisel, known to millions as Dr. Seuss, wrote a wonderful story called *How the Grinch Stole Christmas*. His story was made into a television special, the viewing of which has become a perennial aspect of holiday celebration in many house-holds. In the story we become acquainted with the simple folk of a village called Whoville, who cherish time-honored Christmas traditions—elaborate decorations, delicious meals, gifts galore, and especially the singing of an innocuous little Christmas ditty in the town square. The Grinch, a classically Seussian creature who is this story's answer to Dickens's Scrooge, lives high atop a mountain overlooking the tiny hamlet. To put it mildly, the Grinch despises Christmas and every Whovillian observance of the day. So he concocts a fiendish scheme to *steal* Christmas. On Christmas Eve, with the help of his beleaguered canine sidekick, Max, the Grinch slinks into town dressed as St. Nick and takes every light, every star, every gift, every bit of holiday food. Having completed his dastardly deed, he beats a hasty retreat to his mountain lair, there to watch with glee as the village mourns the loss of Christmas and its joys. To his bewilderment, however, as Christmas dawns the undaunted Whovillians spill into the decoration-bereft streets and with unmitigated happiness sing their traditional song. This display so touches the heart of the Grinch that he concludes that Christmas must be big-ger than its trappings; its significance is registered in hearts even in the absence of bells, whis-tles, and bows.

I think Mark would like Dr. Seuss. Mark's Christmas story doesn't seem to be a Christ-mas story at all. There are no virgin mothers, no stars in the east, no Wise Men, no angels—nothing Christmassy in the least! In fact, if we had only Mark's Gospel we couldn't muster up a Christmas play no matter how hard we might try. How then can we even consider Mark's first chapter a suitable Christmas sermon text? Well, now, just what *is* Christmas any-way? Look at verse 12 again. There's the answer! Christmas is "the beginning of the gospel of Jesus Christ, the Son of God."

Dr. James Blevins of the Southern Baptist Theological Seminary is fond of referring to Mark as the gospel writer who "tells it like it is!" Mark's beginning to his story of Jesus is a clas-sic example of his gift for cutting through the frills and trappings and driving to the very heart of the matter. For Mark, the real truth of Christmas does not hinge on the miraculous displays that are so vital to the accounts offered by Matthew and Luke. Like a good Whovillian, Mark knows that Christmas is more than these things, as true and marvelous as they may be. In a day when the meaning of Christmas is all but buried beneath a mountain of trinkets and baubles, maybe Mark's Gospel offers us a very relevant reminder of what Christmas is really all about. Let's look again at the text, this time with Christmas in mind, and be blessed by a Markan perspective on the season.

In the books of Matthew and Luke, the coming of Jesus is foretold by angels and couched in heavenly dreams and visions. Mystery and marvel abound. Mark gives the role of herald to a flea-bitten prophet named John. No shining garments here; John sports a camel-hair suit. Let's not even get into the matter of his diet (and you thought fruitcake was bad). But if Christmas is to be understood as the coming of God's Son to earth, John's message is right on target. It was his job to get the world ready for the arrival of the Lord. Maybe his message will serve also to prepare us to celebrate Jesus' birth. What was John's message? It went like this: "The Lord is coming. . . . Repent! Repent!"

Well, now, I know we don't particularly like to hear that "R word"—especially in the sea-son of good tidings. There it is, though—no punches pulled, if you want to prepare for the coming of the Christ child, *repent.* You know, if we would just grant John a hearing, he has a point. After all, can we really celebrate one called "the Prince of Peace" if we harbor war-prone spirits? Or unless we repent of every grudge that disturbs the peace between us and our neighbors? Or if we don't search our hearts to repent of anything that robs us of peace with God? How can we identify with the humble lifestyle of one born in a stable unless we repent of the materialistic pursuits that fuel the commercialization of the Christmas season? Can we really proclaim the "good tidings which shall be to *all* people" unless we repent of our prejudices against *some* people? Mark's Christmas story calls us to repentance as we look to the coming of our Lord.

But Mark's story is not without "good tidings of great joy." In verse 14, as Jesus begins his preaching ministry, he repeats John's call to repentance but adds, "Believe the good news; the Kingdom of God is here and now!"

The most joyous news that you and I can hear this Christmas season is that which Mark records here. The rule of God is not relegated to the long ago, nor is it only a dim dream for some day in the future. The Good News is ours today! Right here, right now! I think Mark was tickled pink to write that because that is "telling it like it is!" Mangers, stars, and angels are all glorious, but what do they really mean to me? Mark tells us in his story: the coming of Jesus brings God right into the thick of the human condition. The divine breaks into the mundane. God comes to bring salvation, order, and purpose to us as we stumble about searching for meaning in our jobs and in our homes, right where we are! Brothers and sisters, *that* is good news!

Right on the heels of this glad proclamation, Mark records that Jesus called his first disciples. His invitation: "Come follow me!"

Mark calls us to repent, he brings us the joyous news of the here-and-now Kingdom of God, and he calls us to come and follow wherever he leads.

The Christmas season, as we have come to know it, also bids us to come and follow. Come and join the parade of rampant materialism. Follow the throng to the malls. Give us your money, the season cries. Pay off your credit card so your limit can be raised so you can max it out at a higher level. It demands our time: shop, bake, decorate, e-mail, attend every party, every cantata—what's next? Where's my planner? Surely Christmas can't come any other way—every Grinch knows that.

"Come and follow me" is a call to commitment, but not a call to added stress. "Come to me all of you who are burdened and heavily laden," Jesus says, "and I will give you rest." *Rest*—what a wonderful Christmas word.

The Grinch came to understand that the real meaning of Christmas has nothing to do with tinsel and garlands. Mark has shown us that the real story doesn't even depend on shepherds and stars. Real meaning is found in the glad realization that God's Son came to bring salvation, liberation, peace, and purpose to every repentant Who in every Whoville—today. "This," Mark says, "is the beginning of the good news about Jesus Christ, the Son of God."—Michael A. Wyndham

SUNDAY, DECEMBER 30, 2001
Lectionary Message

Topic: The Harsh Sound of Christmas
TEXT: Matt. 2:13–23
Other Readings: Isa. 63:7–9; Ps. 148; Heb. 2:10–18

Before you put away the ornaments and wrapping paper, let's take another look at the Christmas event. From Matthew we learn of the curious Egyptian episode in the young life of Jesus. There is no chronology attached to the text and generally we tightly compress the time to fit our holiday schedule. Actually, the young family might have stayed in Bethlehem for nearly twenty-four months. During this time Herod learned that he had been double-crossed by the Wise Men, who had returned to their homeland via a different route. Enraged, Herod retaliated with characteristic vengeance, killing every male child under two in the Bethlehem vicinity.

But Joseph moved his family to Egypt for protection, returning only after hearing of Herod's death. Propelled by that news, Joseph returned to Nazareth, and quietly the boy grew into a young adult. Although the text brings down the curtain on those early years, there are still important lessons for us. Two of those lessons remain as true today as ever. First, the gospel divides, and second, God always provides.

I. *The gospel divides.* This truth is as difficult as it sounds. To a world regularly overdosing on fairy tale endings and easy religion, this is harsh. We prefer a savior who is at least adored by all. Yet time and again the gospel warns us of its dividing nature.

(a) First, the message itself divides us. We humans have chronically understated our sin problem. We look for cosmetic solutions to serious issues. We just can't see ourselves as hopelessly undone by our bad choices. The apostle Paul would bluntly state how he saw the dividing nature of the gospel's message this way: "For the message of the cross is foolishness to those who are perishing, but to us who are being saved it is the power of God" (1 Cor. 1: 18 NIV). As long as folks can tease themselves into thinking that all they need is a little tweaking, the gospel message will sound severe. And as bad as the message is, the gospel's methodology divides even more.

(b) The methodology divides us. Have you ever considered the method the gospel presents for dispensing grace? Without any help from God in the form of proving the truth of the message, each of us is issued a challenge. Individually, we must personally either accept or reject the message. There's a sense in which God is saying that we can't add anything to the finished work of grace. Look all you wish, there are no human fingerprints. In Christ God has provided us with the only opportunity we will ever have to be reconciled. Even when we slightly acknowledge our neediness, we have this tendency to want to do the work ourselves. If there is the slimmest chance we can do anything to provide for our own needs, then the cross of Christ is a cruel hoax.

II. *God provides for us.* The text doesn't go into any great detail as to how God provided for Joseph. In a matter-of-fact manner it states that Joseph received exactly what he needed precisely when he needed it.

(a) God's provision is adequate. When I was in grade school I learned to look on the wonderful word *adequate* with a kind of disdain. Adequate was just what it said—enough but not any more. As a student at New Orleans Seminary, I studied under Fisher Humphreys in

the area of theology. I'll never forget Dr. Humphreys' lecture in which he taught us to appreciate the simple statement, "God is always adequate." What better way is there to describe
the work of God? Have you ever encountered a time or situation in which the grace of God
was less than adequate? Because God understands economics better than anyone else, the
divine resources are never wasted. What I need is always available to me because God is
always adequate.

(b) God's provision is always timely. American business has discovered a new procedure.
Instead of stockpiling provisions in huge warehouses, businesses today use a distribution practice called *just-in-time stocking*. Using this practice, businesses cut their overhead while maintaining the inventories necessary to conduct their business. God invented just-in-time
management. We have the desire to see the provision of God long before it might be used. But
faith learns to accept God's economical management, and God never misses. The divine timing always finds the right mark.

The Bible teaches that the world is a dangerous place for believers. Knowing that shouldn't
cause us to cringe in fear. It shouldn't make us lead timid lives. No, it should remind us to
be alert, careful, and watchful, but never fearful. Because in this dangerous, toxic world God
always provides what we need when we need it. As we close the book on another holiday
season, look closely at the way God provides for a simple, unassuming man and his young
family. And take courage!—Robert Long

ILLUSTRATIONS
COURAGE.   Courage is resistance to fear, mastery of fear—not absence of fear.—Mark
Twain[14]

RULE OF GOD.   The longer I live, the more convincing proofs I see of this truth, that God
governs in the affairs of men. And if a sparrow cannot fall to the ground without his notice,
is it probable that an empire can rise without his aid?—Benjamin Franklin[15]

SERMON SUGGESTIONS

Topic: A New Name
TEXT: Isa. 61:10–62:3
(1) God's people may suffer humiliation for a time. (2) God, however, will take pleasure and
be glorified in those he at last vindicates.

Topic: The Whys and Wherefores of Jesus Christ
TEXT: Gal. 4:4–7 NRSV
(1) When he came: in the fullness of time. (2) How he came: born of a woman. (3) Why he
came: to redeem us and make us children of God. (4) What is the result of all this? (a) the
experience of the Spirit of Jesus in our hearts, (b) the rewards of being an heir of God.

---

[14] *Pudd'nhead Wilson's Calendar*, in *Pudd'nhead Wilson* (1894).
[15] At the Constitutional Convention, 1787.

CONGREGATIONAL MUSIC

1. "Joy to the World," Isaac Watts (1719)

   ANTIOCH, George F. Handel (1741)

   There are many, many Christmas hymns that would be suitable for singing during Christ-mastide. This classic one is listed simply as representative of the hymns available, both old and new.

2. "Praise the Lord, O Heavens, Adore Him," Anon. *Foundling Hospital Collection* (1796)

   HYFRYDOL, Rowland H. Prichard (1831)

   "Sing Praise to the Lord," Henry W. Baker

   LAUDATE DOMINUM, C. Hubert H. Parry (1894)

   Both of these fine hymns are based on Psalm 148 and could be used in place of reading the psalm. They are both of a festive nature that makes them suitable for the opening of worship and/or processional.

3. "Unto Us a Boy Is Born," Latin carol (fifteenth century); trans. Percy Dearmer (1928)

   PUER NOBIS NASCITUR, from *Piae Cantiones* (1582)

   The escape of the Holy Family from Herod's fury into Egypt is related in this ancient narrative carol (stanza 3). It should be sung simply—in unison and to sparse accompaniment.

4. "Alleluia! Sing to Jesus," William C. Dix (1866)

   HYFRYDOL, Rowland H. Prichard (1831)

   Relating both to the Old Testament reading (Isa. 63:7–9) and the Epistle lesson (Heb. 2:10–18), this communion hymn celebrates the high priestly role of Jesus in redeeming the nations by his blood.—Hugh T. McElrath

WORSHIP AIDS

CALL TO WORSHIP.   "I am Alpha and Omega, the beginning and the ending, saith the Lord, which is, and which was, and which is to come, the Almighty" (Rev. 1:8).

INVOCATION.   Gracious Father, as we stand at the threshold of a new year, we confess our need of your presence and your help for the journey ahead. You have promised that you will never fail us or forsake us, so we put our trust in you, come what may. Through Jesus Christ our Lord.—Kenneth M. Cox

OFFERTORY SENTENCE.   "The poor shall never cease out of the land: Therefore I command thee, saying, thou shalt open thine hand wide unto thy brother, to thy poor, and to thy needy, in thy land" (Deut. 15:11).

OFFERTORY PRAYER.   Our heavenly Father, we bring to you some of the fruits of our labor that you have permitted us to do. Use these tithes and offerings for your honor and glory, whether to strengthen us who believe, to witness to those who do not yet know you, or to meet any kind of real need suffered by any of your children. Help us to get a new vision of our partnership with you in what you are doing among us who gather here and in the wide world around us.—Kenneth M. Cox

PRAYER.   O Giver of every good and perfect gift, we thank you for the gift of Christmas—its beauty—your glory—and its meaning: the Word becoming flesh—its rapture; the joy of your presence—its peace; order out of chaos—its hope; your love—from which nothing can separate us.

We thank you that in this season we have been able to share in so many different ways. As you invaded the darkness of the night on that first Christmas, so you are present in the light of your love in the dark night of every soul. That you are with the human family in all the pain and tragedy of these days is the hope of Christmas—Emmanuel, God with us. "The people who walked in darkness have seen a great light; those who dwell in a land of deep darkness, on them has light shone."

As there were those on that first Christmas who were left wondering about what had come to pass, so may we be left wondering so that there will be room for the mystery of your coming in our every day.

O you who sent your only Son among us that your Word might become flesh, bless with your grace and encourage us in our high calling to "flesh out" your love in this time and place—that we may be truly the Body of Christ.—John M. Thompson

SERMON
Topic: It Is Still Christmas!
TEXT: John 1:14

What does Christmas suggest to most of us? Perhaps it means a holiday and a break from work, being together with the family, buying presents, going to church, setting up the tree and the crib, spending too much money, eating and drinking, putting on weight. . . .

And the spirituality of Christmas: what does that mean to us? Why do those stories still manage to retain their magic, no matter how hard department stores work to make us thoroughly sick of them: the very young woman whose pregnancy is embarrassing, the nervous yet upright fiancé, the charming and rather quaint shepherds, the exotic Wise Men from the East, the mysterious star, the evil king, the angelic chorus. These stories teach us of the birth of a baby who is of immense significance to the world, with their message of universal peace and love. Through them we learn of the importance of giving and sharing with others, especially the poor and needy. We find here a new sense of hope for the future, a hope our world badly needs. We are inspired to follow our star as far as it takes us, no matter how long and difficult the journey.

These themes that are part of the meaning of Christmas are important. But if that's all we think Christmas is about, if that's all that Christmas means to us and our society, then we're in serious danger of missing the main point altogether.

When we celebrate the "Christ Mass," we're not basically telling stories about babies, wonderful though they may be. We're not just retelling fairy tales for children, tales that bring back wonderful memories of our own childhood. What we are celebrating fundamentally is the radical advent of God among us. The prologue to John's Gospel makes it clear that Christmas is about God becoming human, taking on our flesh, sharing our human experience in all its pain and joy, its ambiguity and mortality. God has entered our human drama in all its messiness and glory and, because of that, knows intimately what it means to be human—genuinely human. Jesus of Nazareth was an ordinary human being like ourselves—certainly not a disembodied soul who walked six feet above the ground. God's humanity, in other words, is like ours: contiguous and connected, just as difficult at times and just as joyful and ecstatic at other times.

Christmas means that God in Jesus meets us face to face. God is not "out there," no longer "other," not one who checks up on us from a distance to make sure we're behaving like good boys and girls. We don't need to believe that God is far away or that God doesn't care about us or that God doesn't understand what it's like to be human. God knows—not as a sympathetic outsider but as an insider. There is no one—no poet, writer, painter, or musician—in all the world who understands more than God does what it means to be human. No one is more willing to listen, to understand, to feel with us, to forgive, to help us start again when we mess things up. Being human is part of what it means now for God to be God.

Christmas also means that God took on our humanity, not in a vague or abstract way but concretely, in an actual human body: a body that suffered physical needs, was hungry and thirsty, felt cold and heat, was fully sexual, needed to be hugged and held when he was sad or lonely, enjoyed good food and drink and good company—and that's of enormous importance. Some forms of religion (even forms of Christianity!) imply that the body isn't important, that our physical needs are irrelevant to salvation. But God tells us otherwise at Christmas. In Jesus Christ God has taken on our bodily life and so declared the body and its needs to be sacred—not just the soul but the body and soul together. In taking on a body, God has declared that, along with all of creation, our life in the body was created holy and good.

Christmas reminds us, therefore, that because God has entered our humanity in Jesus, we too are able, like God, to share the humanity of others. This is true not just in our friendships, but also, and particularly, in our relations with those who are poor, lonely, and sick. In the orgy of spending we engage in at Christmas, we are summoned to remember those who lack even the basic necessities of life: those who will spend Christmas hungry and without shelter, those who will feel miserably alone, those who will have no safe home to go to. Just as God entered our human situation, so we too are called to enter the humanity of others, this Christmas, especially those who need our compassion and generosity, and our sense of justice.

Christmas is the blessed celebration of God's coming among us in our flesh and blood. It is an exhilarating thought: our humanity is caught up in the very heart of God! The Church offers us this time to remind ourselves joyfully of God's extravagant grace, on which our very being depends. Christmas is also a time to offer our own small blessing to one other: to celebrate our families and friends, and to turn our minds and hearts to the poor, whose poverty God has chosen to share in Christ.—Dorothy Lee

SECTION III

MESSAGES FOR COMMUNION SERVICES

SERMON SUGGESTIONS

Topic: Reflections on Psalm 100

This psalm calls for all people of all lands to praise the Lord God. The image of people coming to God's house for worship plays on our mind in this call to worship. Following are some reflections on the four sections of this psalm.

I. *"Serve the Lord with gladness"* (vv. 1–2). In calling for all people to worship the Lord, we want to emphasize the joy in doing so. Many Christians unfortunately have the notion that serving the Lord is dull, or to use the modern slang, it "cramps our style." We should want to serve and praise God, and with gladness.

II. *"We are his people"* (v. 3). True worship of God involves recognizing him as Creator and Sustainer of all life. We need to remember that we are not our own and self-sufficient. Rather, we are the "sheep of his pasture." As we affirm ourselves as his, we "know that the Lord is God!"

III. *"Give thanks to him, bless his name!"* (v. 4). We have so much that it is often difficult for us to be thankful as we ought to be. As we come into God's presence in worship, whether privately, with family, or in church, we need to do so with thankful hearts. A very important part of worship is thanking our Lord for all his many benefits and blessings.

IV. *"His steadfast love endures for ever"* (v. 5). God is good and his goodness is unchangeable. To think of the magnitude of God's love overwhelms me. Even though we so often fail to live up to the standard of Jesus Christ, we encounter again and again a God whose love is steadfast. Though our faithfulness may slacken, his faithfulness endures "to all generations." The Lord is good!—C. Kenny Cooper

Topic: Reflections on the Lord's Supper
TEXT: 1 Cor. 11:23–29

It was not until I put the Lord's Supper into the context of the long tradition of the Church's worship and ceased to deal with it as a separate entity that its full efficacy and indispensability broke in on me. It brought, then, a completeness without which the story of the Church's worship would have been, for me, something defective, truncated, and wanting.

I. When we see the Lord's Supper within the context of the Church's worship, we realize that *something complete is given to us.*

We know only too well that preaching by itself falls short because of the very nature of the human words we proclaim. The Word—that is, God's Word—consists not merely of lettered syllables and vocal sounds. God's Word is also action, and we see that action in its fullest expression in a life broken for the sin of man. Therefore, the Word is not completely declared until it is seen in an action, and the closest thing to that action we can have on this

300

earth is when we re-present what Jesus did in the Upper Room as he took bread, offered thanks, broke it, and gave it to his disciples, in anticipation of his death.

Here in the sacrament of the Lord's Supper we see God doing for us what we could not do for ourselves, and the impelling power within it is his love. This is how it works. Love identifies itself with us in Christ so that by faith we may identify ourselves with him. And in this great transaction, the work of love is almost complete. As you and I break the bread and lift the cup, we indicate fully in this great act the eternal fact, "God so loved the world that he gave. . . ."

II. When we see the Lord's Supper within the context of the Church's worship, we learn that *something complete is given by us.*

In the Lord's Supper, all of the emphases of Christian worship are present: confession, thanksgiving, proclamation, consecration, and self-dedication.

What is most significant is that all our human faculties are involved here as in no other religious act. We hear with our ears the Word, we see with our eyes the action, we take into our hands the elements, we taste with our mouths the bread and wine, and we assimilate into our bodies the symbols of a broken body and shed blood. Our memory plays on the words *we do this;* our imagination recalls the garden, the cross, and the tomb; our conscience examines us by asking, "Have you the right to be here?" Our affections rise in eucharistic praise for what God has done, and our will resolves to live in this faith "till he comes again."

III. When we see the Lord's Supper within the context of the church's worship, *something complete is given through us.* Here and now, if our faith is real, something happens *through* us: God's grace claims us one by one and makes us into his great family—the Church—around his table. And he who does this is there as the risen Lord who speaks to the needs of those who come believing.

This table is spread for sinners, but only for those sinful folk who yearn to be made whole. To stay away is to be judged, but to come believing in God's redemptive love is to find peace and joy in the Holy Ghost.—Donald Macleod[1]

Topic: Some Insights into the Lord's Supper
Text: 1 Cor. 11:23–30.

I. *The Lord's Supper.* There are two or three good reasons for calling this meal the Lord's Supper. First of all, it was instituted by Jesus. In the closing week of our Lord's earthly life he said to his disciples, "I have earnestly desired to eat this Passover with you before I suffer" (Luke 22:15). For more than three thousand years faithful Jews have celebrated the fast of Passover, and today they follow exactly the same ritual as they followed in the days of Jesus. It was during this memorial meal that Jesus rose, took a piece of bread, and thanked God for it. Then he broke it, gave it to the disciples, and said, "Take, eat; this is my body which is broken for you." It was a picture of what was to happen the following day when Jesus was crucified. Then he took a cup and gave it to them, saying, "Drink this, all of you, for it is my blood, the blood of the New Agreement (covenant), shed to set many free from their sins" (Matt. 26:28 Phillips). It is the Lord's Supper because he instituted it. Jesus then went on to

---

[1] In *Pulpit Digest*

say, "Do this in remembrance of me." Thus the meal is called the Lord's Supper because it is a memorial to him.

People become like the thoughts they hold, like the memories they cherish. It is the very truth, "As a man thinketh in his heart, so is he" (Prov. 23:7). What do we think about during the Lord's Supper? Jesus Christ! And as we do, our faith is nourished, our hope is kindled, and our strength is renewed.

Our modern way of thinking of memory almost presupposes a sense of absence while the ancient Hebrew concept of memory presupposes a sense of presence. That sense of presence is not a crude, literalistic, Aristotelian concept but a realistic spiritual presence. More is meant than a psychological stimulant, a kind of memory quickener. The Lord's Supper was instituted to keep ever before us the meaning of the death of Jesus and to bring us into a "Holy of Holies" where we can come into his presence.

II. *There is a second name for this feast: Eucharist.* Early in the history of the Church the word *Eucharist* was used to refer to the Lord's Supper. When Jesus instituted the Supper he "gave thanks" (*eucharistesas*). Alone he would go forth to face the malice and hatred of those who falsely accused him. Yet "he gave thanks." Beyond the dark shadows and in the presence of death, Jesus saw that which enabled him to give thanks. The celebration of the Supper has always been the great act of the Church's thanksgiving. Eucharist reminds us that we are attending not a funeral but a feast. We meet not on Friday, the day Christ died, but on Sunday, the day he arose from the grave. Here we give grateful praise in hymn and prayer for all that Christ has brought us—peace with God, the forgiveness of sin, and power to break free from our sins.

III. *A third name by which this feast is known is communion.* As Paul wrote to the Corinthians, "The cup of blessing which we bless, is it not the communion ["sharing," NEB; "participation," RSV] of the blood of Christ? The bread which we break, is it not the communion of the body of Christ?" (1 Cor. 10:16 KJV). The Greek word is *koinonia.* We differ, of course, in how we express this presence. Close your eyes and think of Jesus standing beside you. See the look of calm confidence in his face. Feel the touch of his hand on your shoulder. Note the warm friendliness in his voice as he speaks and says, "Be still and know that I am God. Come unto me and I will give you rest. They that wait upon the Lord shall renew their strength. My grace is sufficient for you." When that happens, this supper will be a real communion.

When we speak of communion, we think not of the past but of the present; not of one who is gone from us but of one who is present with us; not of one whom we remember but of one with whom we have actual fellowship in the present. "Memory is absence felt: Communion is presence realized." Because he knows how difficult it is for us to grasp the unseen, he uses the seen and the material to make his presence real to us. That is the way God works—through the material, the spiritual comes. The incarnation says the same to us: through the material the spiritual comes. The incarnation says to us: through the human the divine comes.

We must believe in his real presence with us at the table. It is the Lord himself who presides at the communion service. As we receive that presence, we find that he is able to do for us all that his disciples found he could do for them. We receive him "with all his benefits." One does not commune with a symbol; one communes with a person. We believe in a real presence because we believe in a living Christ who has risen from the dead and who, though we cannot see him, encounters us spiritually as we participate in the means of grace that he has provided.

IV. *Finally, this feast is called by some a sacrament.* Although sacrament is not a biblical word it may suggest a truth that can add meaning to the observance of the Lord's Supper. It comes from the Latin and is a transliteration of the word *sacramentum*. The sacramentum was an oath taken by the Roman soldier that he could be loyal to the emperor and serve the empire with his life. When we keep the Supper, we pledge ourselves to be good soldiers of Jesus Christ and we receive from him the assurance that he not only will be with us as a guide to lead us but will also enter into us himself so that we are enabled to gain the victory that overcomes the world. When you eat the bread and drink the cup, you are giving your word of honor once again that you will keep your promises.—Myron J. Taylor

Topic: Who Shall Sit at the Table?

Without the reality of that first Easter, this meal we share could consist of nothing more than a portion of bread and a thimble of wine. Easter celebrates the reality of Christ's presence as our Risen and living Lord—here with us and for us, binding us together in one body of which he, and he alone, is the head. At the Lord's table we are all one to Christ, in Christ, by Christ, and through Christ. For whenever we eat this bread and drink this cup we affirm our unity under the Lordship of the Risen, living Christ.

So, who shall sit at our table? Those weighed down by a burden of guilt? Those oppressed by grief? Those with fears and failures eating them alive? Those who feel empty and need to be filled with something more substantial than society can give—something sacred—something to save them from trouble, trial, and temptation? Those who are looking for the Lord of Life?

These are the ones who shall sit at our table, and to them—to you—I say: Come to the table of the living Lord, who loves you and desires that you live life more fully. Come to the table of the living Lord, who looks within your heart and always holds out hope for you. Come to the living Lord, who longs for you to become a faithful follower. Come to the table of our Risen Redeemer—and rejoice. Because that's the promise and the power of Easter!—Albert J. D. Walsh

Topic: A Meal to Remember
TEXT: 1 Cor. 11:23–26

I. My wife and I had a memorable dinner in Florida. I ordered something called "O Sole Mio Trio." It consisted of three filets of sole wrapped around bits of shrimp, crab, and scallops, all smothered in a piquant wine-and-cheese sauce. The satisfaction of the dinner prompted me to reflect on other memorable meals in my life.

What are your memories of favorite meals? Try thinking about them sometime. They provide a wonderful recapping of experiences.

II. Then think about the disciples of Jesus and this meal in the Upper Room. The disciples must have had favorite meal memories, too. Perhaps Philip recalled the dinner he had eaten with a dark-eyed young woman from Capernaum, of sweet, tender fish and light, fluffy wheat cakes served with honey on them. James and John surely remembered the last meal they ate with their father in the boat before they left to follow Jesus in his itinerant ministry: cheese and bread and new wine, and melons afterwards. And maybe Matthew liked to think of the time he and another disciple were in a little village, where Jesus had sent them to declare the coming of the Kingdom, and a family had invited them in for roast lamb and all the trimmings.

But of all their memories, which do you imagine were the best?

For some, surely it was hard to forget that time in the wilderness when Jesus said the blessing over a few loaves and fishes and fed five thousand people. What bread or fish ever tasted better?

For others, it was even harder to top that beautiful breakfast by the sea, when they had fished all night and were tired and hungry and Jesus called to them from the shore, "Let down your nets on the right side," and they did, and the nets became unbelievably heavy and alive with fish. When they rowed to shore, there was Jesus with a fire already going, ready to cook the fish and eat with them. That was a magnificent breakfast!

Yet for all of them, the very best memory, better even than dinner in the wilderness and breakfast by the sea, was the meal they ate with Jesus in the Upper Room the evening before he was crucified.

It was probably a Passover meal. If it was, they had lamb and bread and wine and herbs, and probably some cheese and fruits and nuts. But it was the bread and wine they remembered most vividly. Judas, the traitor, had already left; and Jesus, in a winsome mood, perhaps a touch of sadness in his voice, said the blessing over the bread. Then, as he passed it to them, he said, "Here, this is my body, which is broken for you." He could see ahead into the night, to what Judas would do, and into the events to follow. He would indeed be broken. Then he did the same with the wine. "This is the blood of the new covenant," he said. "Multitudinous seas incarnadine," said Milton; his blood would stain them forever—the Creator dying for the whole creation. And then, almost whimsically, he added, "Whenever you do this, do it in remembrance of me."

III. Memory, to the Hebrew mind, had strange powers: it reinvoked the experience, set it in motion again, brought it into being once more. When they remembered, as they did every time they gathered, Jesus was there. The bread and the wine brought him back to them.

The strangest part is, it does the same for us. We were not there, but when we contemplate that night and receive the bread and cup, we relive it as if we had been there, and Christ is here in our midst, offering himself to us all over again. There are people here who will tell you they have felt it. I have felt it.

When I was a boy, the church I belonged to had a large oak communion table. On the front side of it, carved in deep letters like the letters on a tombstone, were the words "In Remembrance of Me." Sometimes, when no one was around I would trace the letters with my finger. It was a very special table and I knew that something special happened when the church gathered around it.

The same something special happens here when we gather around this table. Christ breaks bread with us and shares the cup with us, and mysteriously we feed on him as he does so. It is a miracle as great as any he ever performed in his ministry—as great as feeding five thousand people in the wilderness. It was his last meal with the disciples, but it never ends.

Most last meals must end. I remember the last time I ever ate with my mother. I shall always treasure the memory of that meal and the talk we had together as we ate it. But that meal is over and I cannot bring it back except in memory.

This meal with Christ comes back every time we gather around the table and remember. It is never finished. It goes on and on. And one day it will be taken up into the great heavenly banquet, when we shall eat and drink with him in the Kingdom.

This is a meal to remember!—John Killinger

ILLUSTRATIONS

THE MAGNETISM OF SACRIFICE.   I cling, I cling with strength and passion to the faith that by His dying Jesus has done something for me that I could never do for myself. In some strange, beautiful way you become aware of this. Jesus has taken your place. "He die or me die," the old African slave declared. "He die, me no die." Possibly a very crude way of putting it, but it is the core of the Gospel and it is the heart of the mystery of the Cross.—Alistair MacLean[2]

NOT MOURNING BUT REJOICING.   As it is a feast and not a fast, we are not mourning over a dead Master but rejoicing in a living Lord. There is a real Presence presiding at this Feast. This is more than a memorial feast. His word to us is not, "Do this in remembrance of my death, but of Me, continuing and persisting through my death." "Here, O my Lord, I see Thee face to face." So this is an occasion for joy and not for sorrow. This is a Eucharistic feast. "This is the hour of banquet and of song." It ought to be stressed that this is the Lord's Supper, not ours. It is His Table which He has spread with His own hands. We are His guests at this Table, invited here by the Lord of the Feast Himself. This is His trysting place where He Himself has chosen to meet with His own. Therefore it is above all an agapé, or love-feast.—Robert Menzies[3]

CHRIST'S MANDATE.   Thursday of Holy Week, the final week of Jesus' life, is often called Maundy Thursday. The word *maundy* comes from the Latin *mandatum,* the same word from which we get the word *mandate.* Christ's command—His mandate—in John 13:34 was that His disciples should love each other. How easy to say but difficult to do! Yet He had already shown how to do it when He donned the towel and knelt before each disciple.

We fear the idea of service because we think it may inconvenience us. Perhaps we fear that we will obligate ourselves to a long-term commitment and relationship which will tax our patience and strength. That might very well happen.—Don M. Aycock[4]

GOD IN THE ORDINARY.   Pavlova, the grand ballerina, was once asked to interpret a dance she had performed. Her reply startled her questioner: "Do you think I would have *danced* it if I could have said it?" This reply makes us pause to reflect on the ballerina's meaning. Some things in life seem too packed with meaning, too shrouded in mystery, to be explained with frail words. A Scottish woman was asked to give an account of her religious faith. She said, "Weel, it can be felt but it cannot be telt!"

---

[2] *High Country*
[3] *The Riches of His Grace*
[4] *Eight Days That Changed the World*

The answers of those two ladies give me a clue about what Jesus was doing when he took a cup and a loaf and shared them with his disciples. The act was symbolic: that is, it was an action which conveyed meaning better than words alone could. Jesus took two ordinary objects of his day, a cup and a loaf of bread, and showed his followers how much of God is in the ordinary things of life.—Don M. Aycock[5]

CHRIST WITHIN OUR PAIN.   I remember talking some years ago to a very brilliant surgeon. For two years, through a finger cut and being poisoned during an operation, she had suffered intense agony and pain. On several occasions her life had been despaired of, but now at last she had recovered. Simply and without melodrama she remarked: "I would not have missed this experience of pain for anything. In it the presence of Christ has been more real than ever before."—Bryan Green[6]

---

[5] *Symbols of Salvation*
[6] *Saints Alive!*

MESSAGES FOR FUNERAL AND BEREAVEMENT

AN ODYSSEY OF CONSOLATIONS

BY JAMES W. COX

These messages were presented at various times during the editor's ministry from the 1950s into the year 2000.

Topic: Basic Living
Service for Mrs. C. S. Crockett

Some of us in our times of need demand attention. Others of us, however, do not demand it yet appreciate it profoundly when it comes. Mrs. Crockett was one to whom our church has had the privilege of ministering from the onset of her illness to the very last.

She loved her Bible and its comforting promises. She welcomed her friends and the strengthening fellowship they brought. She was grateful for the church and its ministry to her deepest needs, and the beauty of flowers spoke a message to her soul.

Mrs. Crockett was one of those who make few demands and yet receive so much.

Her sweet spirit through all her illnesses has been an inspiration to those who have visited her and ministered to her. Those who visited her with the intention of bringing a blessing to her went away with a blessing of their own.

With the apostle Paul we can individually say, "I thank my God upon every remembrance of you."

It is not given to many to achieve immortality through newspaper headlines or through dramatic chapters in the history books, but to many is given the opportunity to know life in its basic dimensions. Their lives are unspectacular, yet they are solid. Their deeds are not flamboyant, yet they are real. Their words are not scintillating, nevertheless they are true.

Actually, most of the best work in the world gets done almost unheralded. Some people live quietly but deeply. They serve God behind the scenes but faithfully. They love humanity profoundly, and that love finds its expression in love for individuals.

Too often, I fear, we measure life by the unusual and extraordinary when life's truest dimensions ought perhaps to be measured in terms of what we can see everyday and what is open to every one of us at every moment.

I. *One of the elements of basic living is the significance of the commonplace.* Frequently, a visitor in a village or in the open country comments, "What do you do around here for fun?" How prosaic seems the making of beds, the cooking of meals, the sweeping of floors, the plowing of fields, the making of gardens, and the like; nevertheless, that is getting close to real living and yet millions of people miss it.

James S. Stewart, the noted minister of the Church of Scotland and Chaplain to the Queen, said that a number of years ago he was in a home in Scotland and walked back to the kitchen. Over the kitchen sink, printed on a card, were these words: "Divine Worship will be held here three times daily."

Brother Lawrence, a member of the Carmelite religious order several centuries ago, showed us how it is possible to do everything for the love of God, even to the picking up of a straw from the floor.

When one sees the significance of the commonplace, this humdrum world can be made a veritable garden of God.

II. *Another important element of basic living is parenthood.*

"A good wife, who can find?" is the question asked in the Proverbs. "She is far more precious than jewels" (RSV).

Again, "She looketh well to the ways of her household, and eateth not the bread of idleness. Her children arise up and call her blessed; her husband also, and he praiseth her."

The human race began with a home.

Our Savior appeared on earth in a home.

The home is the first church many noble Christians have known.

The home may be as simple as the primeval beauty of the Garden of Eden, as humble as the stable where the Christ was born, and as unsophisticated as a dedicated hearth where the Bible is read and prayers are said. Nonetheless, it is the ark of salvation, the cradle of civilization, and the seminary of righteousness.

The life of no one is unimportant who has reared children in the nurture and admonition of the Lord.

Likewise, the life of no one is unimportant who, whether by choice or necessity, has no home of his own yet loves little children and seeks to guide and strengthen their walk in the ways of God and righteousness.

III. *A third element of basic living is the sacrament of friendship.* As a minister of the gospel and a student of Christian history, I know something of the power of the spoken word.

The strident tones of the voice of John the Baptist will linger in his prophetic words for centuries to come.

The incisive message of Jesus and his apostles will linger in their kerygmatic words, though heaven and earth should pass away.

The golden words of Chrysostom, the thunderous words of Savonarola, the courageous words of Luther, the holy words of Wesley, and the convicting words of Spurgeon have led people by the hundreds and tens of thousands to love, trust, and serve Jesus Christ.

But there are people who have never preached a sermon who by the sheer power of their friendship have led people away from unrighteousness and have guided them to the Savior of the world.

IV. *A prayer.* We seem to give them back to thee, dear God, who gavest to us. Yet as thou didst not lose them in giving, so we have not lost them by their return. Not as the world giveth, givest thou, O Lover of Souls! What thou givest thou takest not away. For what is thine is ours if we are thine. Life is external, love is immortal, death is only an horizon, and a horizon is nothing save the limit of our sight. Lift us up then, strong Son of God, that we may see further; cleanse our eyes that we may see more clearly; draw us closer to thyself that we may know ourselves nearer to our beloved who are with thee. And while thou dost prepare a place for us, prepare us for that happy place, that where they are, and thou art, we too may be. Through Jesus Christ our Lord. Amen.[1]

Topic: The Secret Place
Service for W. H. Youngblood Sr.

I don't believe I have ever met anyone who showed more courage in suffering than Hal Youngblood did. His courage came from his undaunted faith in God. Once when I was praying at his bedside, I mentioned in my prayer the will of God. Mr. Youngblood interjected, as if talking to someone in the room just as real as Mrs. Youngblood and I, "Yes, Lord! Whatever you do is all right. That's just the way I want it. Thy will be done!" And God's will was apparently many more months of waiting.

Mr. Youngblood was a man of prayer. He believed profoundly that "more things are wrought by prayer than this world dreams of."

For many years he taught the workers' class in our Sunday school. The men who came Sunday after Sunday looked to him for more than a lesson. He entered into their personal problems and needs. He prayed with them. He counseled them. He stood with them in their trying times.

Mr. Youngblood served as deacon in our church. He was a man of vision and his counsel and recommendations in that capacity reflected his belief in progress in the outreach of the church.

He seemed to me to have the soul of a poet and mystic. At times, when talking of God and his ways, his language was sheer poetry; but more than that, it was sincere devotion.

He loved his home, his church, and his adopted community, and all of his loves were reciprocated.

Throughout his illness he was sustained by the grace of God in many ways, not least of which was the solicitous and strengthening love of his family.

In the Old Testament, there is an expression of haunting beauty that again and again, like a symphonic theme, has returned to my thoughts to bless me. "He that dwelleth in the secret place of the Most High shall abide under the shadow of the Almighty."

Most of us, I fear, care little for the secret place. We love better the public place. We shun the closet of private prayer. We prefer the strenuous activity outside. We spend our days expressing our opinions to others. We are impatient about listening to God.

Nevertheless, the secret place is a most practical and advantageous spot. It is the starting point of spiritual creativity, community building, and world brotherhood. It is the threshold of God's throne.

One who dwells there is a partner in all that God does, and comes ultimately to share in the very nature of God himself.

I. *The secret place is a place of prayer.* The one who prays as Jesus taught us to pray is aware that the things that are seen are temporal and fleeting, and that the things that are not seen are eternal and abiding.

---

[1] *Presbyterian Manual*

The one who prays is able to see life steadily and see it whole, because prayer brings the dimension of eternity into the experience of time.

What enabled our Lord Jesus Christ to live as he lived, to speak as he spoke, to help as he helped, and to die as he died was that from first to last his was a life of prayer. Even as the Son of God, he saw that it was necessary for him to make repeated, even continuous efforts to stay in conscious fellowship with the Father.

How much more do we, children of God in a lesser sense than our Lord, need to make deliberate efforts to breathe the air of heaven and rely on the strong arm of God the Father!

II. *The secret place is a place of concern.* One who truly prays is not exclusively preoccupied with his personal needs. All concern is born of a recognition of our own need. We see ourselves standing in need of the mercies and blessings of God, and we cry for God to help us. Then the love of God causes us to see others in our own plight, and we pray for them, too. We love ourselves aright then we love others aright.

One who experiences real prayer carries the lessons and inspiration of prayer into the marketplace, to the banquet table, to the business office, and to the many areas of everyday living.

III. *The secret place is a place of victory.* Jesus never prayed without gaining a victory. His struggles in the wilderness brought conquest. His agony in the Garden brought triumph.

Those who dwell in the secret place of the Most High through intimate prayer know how to live, how to suffer, and how to die. This they know because they know God.

> But the souls of the righteous are in the hand of God,
> And no torment shall touch them.
> In the eyes of the foolish they seemed to have died;
> And their departure was accounted to be their hurt,
> And their journeying away from us to be their ruin:
> But they are in peace.
> For even if in the sight of men they be punished,
> Their hope is full of immortality;
> And having borne a little chastening, they shall receive great good;
> Because God made trial of them, and found them worthy of himself.[2]

Moreover, those who dwell in the secret place of the Most High are able to witness the living, suffering, and dying of loved ones who have dwelt in the secret place, without being dismayed and defeated.

Elizabeth Barrett Browning showed such a faith and courage when she wrote:

> When some beloved voice that was to you
> Both sound and sweetness faileth suddenly,
> And silence against which you dare not cry
> Arches round you like a strong disease and new,
> What hope? What help? What music will undo

---

[2] Wisdom of Solomon, 3:1–5

That silence to your sense? Not friendship's sigh;
Not reason's subtle count: not melody
Of viols, nor of pipes that Faunus blew;
Not songs of poets, nor of nightingales
Whose hearts leap upward through the cypress-trees
To the clear moon; nor yet the spheric laws
Self-chanted, nor the angels' sweet All hails,
Met in the smile of God: nay, none of these.
Speak THOU, availing Christ! and fill this pause.

This availing Christ, who dwelt supremely in God's secret place, promised us not exemption from battle but victory; not peace, but conquest; not ease, but a cross.

Let us therefore say with Paul the apostle, "But thanks be unto God who giveth us the victory through our Lord Jesus Christ. . . . We are more than conquerors through him that loved us."

Topic: The Witness of a Life
Service for Leslie R. Dennis

The suddenness of the passing of our friend Leslie Dennis has stunned all of us. Every few days we exchanged greetings as he drove past our home. Many of us talked with him only a few days ago. Mr. and Mrs. Anthony only a week or so ago visited with the Dennises in their home. Since I came to Johnson City five years ago, it has been my privilege to be closely associated with Mr. Dennis in his role as a deacon and as chairman of the music committee of our church. In all that he did in his church—as deacon, as committeeman, and as worker in the training union department—he made a rich contribution to many lives. I have been inspired by his courage, his radiant outlook, his love of his home, and his devout faith in God.

A while ago he called me in the night and told me that a loved one had passed away. He asked that I come by and have prayer with him before he left. Furthermore, he was a man who carried his triumphant outlook into the wider community; he made rich contributions to the lives of his many friends and was a trusted and energetic worker in his business. His life was a blessing to all of us.

What we do in life is not so important as who we are. However, the things we do are quite often a clue to who we are.

Actually, who we are may preach a greater sermon than the most eloquent message we might compose. Who we are may result in the accomplishment of more magnificent miracles than the ingenuity of our minds and the skill of our hands could devise.

I believe that one of the most significant things about our life is the witness it bears to certain fundamental truths.

I. *Our life may be a witness to the divine resources.* As many people observe the life and strenuous activities of the apostle Paul, they no doubt marvel that one man could do so much under such adverse circumstances. He took no credit for himself. He rather boasted in another. He declared, "I am what I am by the grace of God." When Paul was imprisoned— hounded by enemies and beyond the reach of the helpfulness of friends—he wrote joyously to a little church in Philippi: "I can do all things through Christ who strengtheneth me. I have power to meet any emergency in life through him who gives me power."

Some of us have passed through serious illnesses, have survived the perils of the battle-front, and have escaped virtually unharmed from many accidents. We can attribute our survival only to the mysterious workings of the providential hand of God. Yet all of us know that there are devout souls who pray and yet die of their illnesses, who read the Bible and believe its promises and yet are slain on the battlefield, who trust themselves into the hands of God and yet die in accidents. What shall we say then? Has God deserted them?

Listen to this throbbing tale by Alistair MacLean:

> Four men I knew sailed upon a summer's evening to an island port in the Hebrides, a father and three sons. Suddenly the sky was blacker than the raven's wing. A north wind churned the sea into a thing of fury. The storm leaped upon them with gleaming jaws. Their boat—in a moment less than a child's toy. The brown sail—a rag. Four men fighting death for life. A desperate, unequal conflict. Yet now and then, clear and high above the hurricane, the father's voice rang forth. "Living or dying," he cried in a kind of calm passion. "God saves his own child." . . . And so it was. With almost miraculous abruptness the gale fell. The water slept. At twilight, when the western rim flamed with gold, four silent men came to harbor. In their hearts was the hush of a great awe.

Living or dying, God saves his own child.

II. *Our lives also bear witness to human possibilities through faith.* We can look at our lives through pessimistic eyes and swear there is exceedingly limited usefulness: the times are not right, we do not have skill in a certain direction, our body is not strong enough to undertake our heavy responsibilities, we do not have enough prestige or pull—on and on we might go, making excuses for ourselves. But when faith comes into play and we begin to see ourselves as God sees us and as God can make us be, the picture changes. The time is always right for someone who is inspired by God. God can develop in us skills that we scarcely dreamed we had. God makes our strength adequate to the responsibility and tells us, "It is not by might nor by power but by my spirit."

In the words of Henry Wadsworth Longfellow:

> Lives of great men all remind us
> We can make our lives sublime,
> And, departing, leave behind us
> Footprints on the sands of time.
> Footprints, that perhaps another,
> Sailing o'er life's solemn main,
> A forlorn and shipwrecked brother,
> Seeing, shall take heart again.[3]

---

[3] "The Psalm of Life"

III. *Moreover, our lives may bear witness to the goodness of life itself.* The idea that some people seem to have, that this life has no real value and that all real value is to be found in the life to come, is not the biblical understanding of life. According to both the Old and New Testaments, this life itself—though nature is red in tooth and claw—has many sublime values and, if it is lived in accordance with the purpose and will of God, is essentially good. William Lyon Phelps, renowned professor of English literature at Yale University, was a man who lived enthusiastically. During his lifetime he knew great sorrows and at times felt the black cloud of depression settle upon him. Yet he said, "I live every day as if it were the first day I have ever seen and the last day I will ever see."

God gives us at best a few years on this Earth. He has made them years in which we have the great privilege of coming to know him in a personal relationship, a relationship in which we may explore what our life was intended to be and live it to its highest usefulness, and in which we may distill from the gift of each day its sweetness and satisfactions—in our homes, at our work, and among our friends.

One who understands life in that way discovers life abundant—a satisfaction not only to oneself but a benediction as well to those about one.

Topic: The Complete Life
Service for Wanda Nally

This afternoon we are confronted with the mystery of why a life so young, so promising, had to be cut off just as it was reaching maturity and adult responsibility.

But Wanda lived and in many ways lived richly in the brief years she had with us. She loved her church and found in it rich fellowship and a wide circle of wholesome friends. She sang in the choir and made a contribution to the beauty and inspiration of the services of the church. She devoutly read her Bible and prayed each day, leaving an example that more of us could follow.

When she was making plans to prepare herself for the work she was doing when she was called to be with the Lord, she shared with me, her pastor, her enthusiastic ambition, which she carried out with loyalty and devotion beyond the call of duty.

Some of us, I am afraid, try to evaluate life by measuring the wrong dimension. We think of life in terms of three score years and ten or even four score years. Perhaps as we think of a man like Methuselah, who lived for nine hundred and sixty-nine years, we say, "Now there is one who really lived." But there are other lives of comparatively short duration that we must take seriously, too: the infant child of King David whose passing tore out his father's heart; and our Lord Jesus Christ, whose years on earth were no more than thirty-three at the most.

If we see life steadily and see it whole, we must reckon with the fact that we must also measure life by the dimension of depth. Indeed, the expression "eternal life" in John's Gospel has to do not with length of life but with depth of life. Eternal life is the life of God himself. It has an enduring quality because it is God's life and not our mortal existence.

I. *This life is never complete in itself.* We see it in what happens to our youngsters: Ambitions are unfulfilled. Educations are incomplete. Marriages do not come to pass. Work is hardly begun and never finished.

But even in the case of those who live to be three score years and ten, or four score years, life is never really completed. There are still letters to be written, friendships to be cultivated, neighbors to be helped, a community to be evangelized, and a world to be set on the right road. I have had people in their sixties and seventies tell me, with a trace of wistful regret, that if they had their lives to live over again, this would be different and that would be changed; they would prepare themselves for a different calling or they would do thus and so.

Life is always a reaching out and a reaching beyond. The poet Browning said, "A man's reach should exceed his grasp or what's a heaven for?"

II. *Really, life's meaning is found in God.* This is a big world with billions of people in it. But God has a plan for every life. Some people fail to enter consciously into the purpose of God for their lives as it is related to his transcendent will for the ages. But others knock at heaven's door, seek the divine plan, and know that they have found the place of service where God intends them to be. It may be a dangerous place. Yet they feel it is a place where God's will is carried out and where they can make a contribution to life itself and to the Kingdom of God. That can be an accomplishment measured not in terms of years and scores of years but in terms of fidelity to duty.

There is no such thing as postponement of real living. You and I are living now and our lives tomorrow or the next year or ten years hence are not likely to have a different quality from the life we live today. Our happiness is here, where we are, in what we are doing, if we only have eyes to see it and hearts to appreciate it. The poet Longfellow wrote:

> Trust no Future, howe'er pleasant!
> Let the dead Past bury its dead!
> Act, act in the living Present!
> Heart within, and God o'erhead!

We may be sure that what life itself lacks, God's grace supplies. In fact, the life of none of us will ever be completed on this Earth. This life itself has value, indisputable value, but it is also as, I believe, Keats put it, "the vale of soul-making." It is the part of faith to believe that the interruption of our personal life and fortunes does not interrupt the unfolding purpose of God. It is the part of faith to believe that our lack is supplied by God's bounty. It is the part of faith to believe also that one moment lived for God is not lived in vain.

> Life is a leaf of paper white
> Whereon each one of us may write
> His word or two, and then comes night.
> Greatly begin! Though thou have time
> But for a line, be that sublime—
> Not failure, but low aim, is crime.—James Russell Lowell

Topic: How God Sees People
Service for Charles Kenneth Slade

Many of us will remember Dr. Slade in many different ways, for he touched our lives at different points. His family will think often of his love and devotion to them. His patients will remember his concern for them as persons and his kindness. His friends will recall his broad interests and his wholesome sense of humor. I think of all these qualities and of his solid

Christian character undergirding them. The apostle Paul said of a friend, "He often refreshed me." I can say that of Dr. Slade: "He often refreshed me"—with his sparkling humor, with his firm convictions, with his stimulating conversation, and with his friendship and hospitality. There was a dimension of depth in his friendship that gave it more than ordinary meaning. We, each of us, meet a few steady, solid people in our lifetimes whose opinions and sincerity we fully trust. Kenneth Slade has been for me a person like that, and I thank God for him.

I heard from his patients and I saw for myself that for him the practice of medicine was more than the doing of certain prescribed procedures. It was also caring for persons as persons.

When Jesus ministered to human need, he did not stop with the offer of a crust of bread or the healing of a disease or the offer of good advice or the forgiving of sins. He was interested in the total life of people. That is why we read this comment of Jesus after some miracle he wrought: "Thy faith hath made thee whole."

The medical profession has been saying, in recent years with increasing emphasis, that it must deal with the total needs of the patient. Not only must the infection be stopped and the diseased organ treated medically, but the inner spiritual attitudes must also be considered.

Jesus Christ, by what he said and actually did, showed us, on the other hand, that not only must one's spiritual nature be redeemed, but one's physical body must also be fed and healed.

I. *To God, the individual is of infinite value.* In recent generations there has been a great deal of shifting our accent "from man to mankind," as Paul Scherer puts it. In the shuffle, humankind is unwittingly becoming the loser, along with the individual person.

Jesus showed in one of his most moving parables that as a good shepherd is solicitous over one sheep that is lost, so God yearns over each individual who needs divine love and mercy.

The Epistle to the Hebrews says, "But we see Jesus, who was made a little lower than the angels for the suffering of death, crowned with glory and honor that he by the grace of God should taste death for everyone."

A distinct point of Christian ethics that the apostle Paul makes stems from the terrible possibility of causing one to "perish, for whom Christ died" (1 Cor. 8:11).

The Gospel invitations are highly individual in their appeal: "whosoever will may come," "whosoever believeth shall not perish."

It is highly significant that Jesus not only addressed the multitudes but also prayed for the crowd, "Father forgive them"; he also sought out individuals such as Zaccheus, Matthew, and Peter, and in his death he turned to a dying man, saying, "Today thou shalt be with me in Paradise."

II. *To God, the human body is of inestimable value.* The miracles of Jesus were not calculated merely to overwhelm human skepticism and cause his contemporaries to believe that he was the Son of God. When Jesus healed people of their diseases, it was inevitable. Where the Kingdom of God was so manifestly present, compassion dictated healing and the power of heaven made it possible.

Some of Jesus' healings were plainly of psychosomatic complaints. Others, however, defy a physical or psychological explanation; a supernatural invasion of the realm of the material and physical is the only satisfying answer.

Nevertheless, Jesus did not place a higher value on one type of healing in comparison with another. The important thing is that the person was made well. Because Jesus did not seek a reputation as a dabbler in the occult or as a worker of black magic, he often used some of the current remedies in connection with his healings. No wonder that Luke, a physician, should take so keen an interest in the life and deeds of Jesus!

The human body, though it is referred to in Holy Writ as an earthen vessel, a body of death, and a temporary house, is also called a temple of God. Those therefore who care for and repair the human body are thinking God's thoughts after him.

III. *But this is certain, too: the kindliest ministrations and the most skilled repair work done to the human body do not—no, cannot—complete the work of God. We go so far, and no farther.* That fact calls for resurrection, a new state and order of being. Paul, in the fifteenth chapter of First Corinthians, shows us that resurrection does not mean the reassembling of the human frame cell for cell and bone for bone. It is rather the establishment of the personality in a new, different, and complete state of happiness that has continuity with the earthly life yet does not duplicate its limitations, its sins, and its infirmities.

For that reason, John, Christ's servant, wrote that in the Apocalypse, "God shall wipe away all tears from their eyes; and there shall be no more death, neither sorrow, nor crying, neither shall there be any more pain: for the former things are passed away. And he that sat upon the throne said, Behold, I make all things new" (Rev. 21:4–5).

Topic: Love's Service
Service for Isham Monroe Cox Jr.
Born October 1, 1924; died January 3, 1978

It is a great comfort to me to realize that the significance of a life is not determined by the length of it. In the mystery of divine providence, even some infants who have died in infancy have blessed homes beyond any human calculations, though few if any human beings could see any meaning whatsoever in such a thing.

The life of our blessed Lord was shorter than forty years, yet the ages have not been able to contain the usefulness of that life. A seed fell into the ground and died and brought forth much fruit.

No other life is worthy of being put alongside our Lord's for comparison, yet a truth is set forth in his dying that has universal application. I often think of some words of the physician-philosopher William James, who believed that "vitality is mightier than size." He said, as I recall his words, that he was against bigness and greatness in all their forms and that his sympathy was with the invisible, molecular moral forces that, stealing down like so many tiny rootlets into the crevices, will, given time, rend the hardest monuments of man's pride.

People have told me of how my brother, in the practice of his profession, brought comfort or health of mind or body to one or another member of their family. I am sure that they were not always aware of his own vulnerability. Human weakness ministers to human weakness. The truest sign of conquest is not a sword but a cross. Thornton Wilder, in one of his plays reminds us: "In love's service, only the wounded soldiers can serve."

In addition to my brother's basic professional competence was his refreshing sense of humor, which I am sure became an important item in his armamentarium as he dealt with patients.

I recall that once when our family physician examined him (he was then a thirteen-year-old boy), Dr. Zirkle laid out some pills for my brother's fever and said, "I want you to take one of these every two hours." Roe answered, "Can I wait two hours before I take the first one?" His personality was a breath of fresh air in our home during years of economic struggle and in times of anxiety and illness. It has also been a source of family pride that in his mature years he has shared himself so deeply, not only with his own immediate family but also with a widening circle of people for whom he cared.

There are other things I could say, but these thoughts are too personal and tender and too close to me to share at this time. I must say this, however: he believed in God and trusted Christ—this experience he and I shared from our boyhood. Eleanor, who shared his life for these latter years, said of him, "He was a good man, a devoted husband, and a wonderful father."

In the words of the apostle Paul, "Blessed be the God and Father of our Lord Jesus Christ, the Father of mercies and God of all comfort, who comforts us in all our afflictions, so that we may be able to comfort those who are in any affliction, with the comfort with which we ourselves are comforted by God. For as we share abundantly in Christ's sufferings, so through Christ we share abundantly in his comfort, too" (2 Cor. 1:3–5 RSV).

Topic: A Life of Praise and Melody

My mother-in-law, Lillian Mitchell Parrent (Mrs. Overton Parrent), the mother of my wife Patty, was born in 1898 and lived into the year 2000. She lived in three centuries! I presented the following meditation at her funeral service and offered the prayer at her grave.

The life of Lillian Parrent—Lillian Golden Mitchell Parrent—is a life that we celebrate today. God endowed her with many special gifts and she was faithful in her stewardship of them all. Although we are saddened by her leaving us, we can rejoice in all that she has meant to us in ways that we could hardly begin to name but to which we must attempt to give proper attention.

Her love for her Lord and his Church was deep and abiding. Her family and friends shared the aura of that devotion. A special love of hers was music. Whereas others found their inspiration in books of various kinds, she found hers in the thoughts and words of hymns she knew by heart and sang as prayers and means of personal devotion.

Looking at her long life and how she spent it, one could say that music was her life. When she was in her early teens, she played the organ in a Sunday morning worship service for the first time. It was at the First Baptist Church of Frankfort, Kentucky, and she remembered that the pastor, Fred F. Brown, came to give her a word of encouragement, and she needed it, for she was so young that her feet could hardly reach the pedals of the organ. This was the early promise of her long career as a church organist in Frankfort, beginning at the age of sixteen at the First Methodist Church, then at the First Baptist Church, and after that at the South Frankfort Presbyterian Church and the Memorial Baptist Church.

Mrs. Parrent was an active member of the Frankfort Monday Music Club and frequently a participant in its various events. Besides her work as organist, she was an accomplished vocalist and accompanist. For several years in the 1940s Mrs. Parrent was a musical therapist at the Kentucky Training Home. In the 1950s and 1960s she was a private teacher of voice, piano, and organ. Over several decades she was organist or pianist at hundreds of funerals in Frankfort and Franklin County.

On the lighter side, Mrs. Parrent was gloriously endowed with the gift of gab and I enjoyed every minute I heard it. Recently I was reading her high school annual—*The Capitolian*. The year was 1916 and she was a senior. On a page listing the "vital statistics" of each senior Lillian Mitchell was listed as "noted for loquacity" and having an aversion to silence. Her idea of a good time, it said, was minding her parents, and her chief occupation was singing in the choir.

On another page in the same high school annual, this partly tongue-in-cheek paragraph appeared along with her photograph: "Airy, fairy Lillian is one of the most popular girls in the class. She is always smiling and her sweet, sunny nature is a constant joy. There is only one drawback about Lillian—her unwillingness to articulate."

Lillian once read, "Let your conversation be 'Yea, Yea' and 'Nay, Nay,'" and she followed that admonition most faithfully thereafter.

> She gives her tongue no moment's rest,
> But talks forever with a zest.

In addition to her musical gifts, she was a beautiful seamstress and a wonderful cook.

In every way, as far as I am concerned, Mrs. Parrent was the total repudiation of all the mother-in-law jokes I have ever heard. If I had loved her more, Mr. Parrent should have been jealous.

However, I must tell you of two incidents that she learned to laugh about later.

The Parrent residence was only one block from the Presbyterian church where she was organist. One Sunday morning, after the choir had sung its anthem and just before the preacher began his sermon, Mrs. Parrent slipped out of the choir loft and hurried home to turn on the oven to warm Sunday dinner. She had plenty of time to get back to the church before the final hymn. But no—the telephone rang or something else happened. When she got back to the church, breathless, the choir and congregation were standing, waiting for the organ—and waiting and waiting. After some gentle ribbing, she lived that down.

The other incident was a bit more difficult. Some years later I was back as interim pastor where I had been pastor several years before. Mrs. Parrent was now full-time organist. The church was observing the Fourth of July with very special instrumental music for the occasion. Mrs. Parrent played the organ, accompanied by Patty at the piano. Because Patty had not done this sort of thing recently, she was understandably anxious and for days had rehearsed her piano accompaniment. It was a long piece of music. During the performance, in the middle of the piece, there was a cacophonous discord, and Patty stopped playing. There I sat on the platform, trying to keep a straight and holy face while two deacons on the front row, friends of ours, laughed and punched each other and winked at Patty while Mrs. Parrent finished the music solo. What had happened? Mrs. Parrent had accidentally turned two pages of the music at the same time.

After the worship service, the congregation gathered around tables in the church dining room for a delightful meal, but Mrs. Parrent missed her meal because she spent the hour going from table to table explaining that what had happened was her fault, not Patty's.

As I have reflected on the life of my dear mother-in-law, my thoughts have turned to the one hundredth Psalm:

> Make a joyful noise to the Lord, all the Earth.
> Worship the Lord with gladness, come into his presence with singing.

God in his providence and grace has given life to each and all of us. That is something to rejoice over, something indeed to sing about. With faith in God's love revealed in our Lord and Savior Jesus Christ we can face the worst that may happen to us and begin to understand why Paul and Silas could sing in prison and Paul could write from prison: "Rejoice in the Lord. . . . For the Lord is good; his steadfast love endures forever and his faithfulness to all generations."

What a privilege it was for Mrs. Parrent to lead the people of God meeting for worship—to "enter his gates with thanksgiving and his courts with praise."

Such service is not always easy to render. However, there is the best of motivations to do it and keep at it. The apostle Paul put it this way: "I appeal to you therefore, brothers and sisters, by the mercies of God, to present your bodies as a living sacrifice, holy and acceptable to God, which is your spiritual worship" (Rom. 12:1 NRSV).

Therefore, because of the mercies of God, we have the best of reasons to try to serve him with our own gifts and talents, large or small, and to take comfort in his glorious promises in Holy Scripture, knowing that those promises are for us. I know of no one more richly blessed in so many ways than the one we remember today, but we have our riches, too, in the one who said, "I have come that they might have life, and have it more abundantly."

Here are some of the Scriptures that tell us so:

Two Deuterocanonical passages: Wisdom of Solomon 3:1–3, 5:15–16.
Three New Testament passages: John 14:16; 1 Peter 1:3–9; Rev. 7:9–10, 13–17.

Prayer at the grave: O God of grace and glory, we remember before you this day our loved one, Lillian Parrent. We thank you for giving her to us, her family and friends, to know and to live as our companion on our earthly pilgrimage. In your boundless compassion, console us who mourn. Give us faith to see in death the gate of eternal life, so that in quiet confidence we may continue our course on earth until, by your call, we are reunited with those who have gone before. Through Jesus Christ our Lord. Amen."[4]

---

[4] *The Book of Common Prayer*

SECTION V

LENTEN AND EASTER PREACHING

SERMON SUGGESTIONS

Topic: The Dilemma of the Cross

TEXT: Matt. 16:21–26

During the holy season of Lent, the Crucifixion event confronts each of us with a heart-searching dilemma and urges us to make up our minds once and for all. The Lenten dilemma, as you might know, is a forced choice between embarrassingly difficult alternatives, and if one chooses the wrong one, the whole structure of faith on which it is built is likely to collapse. Either the way of the cross and the kind of belief about God and life that it calls for is so fantastically false, even when held with purity of thought and devotion, that it cannot stand up to the cruel forces that actually dominate the world and is ultimately crushed by them, or it is so true, so rooted in the facts of life, that it can afford to accept seemingly utter defeat, knowing that in the end God's victory is sure. Either the choice is a grim no to the faith proposition that God is love, or it is a firm, persistent yes.

We can't easily evade the dilemma, with the cross so unavoidably central in Christian faith and tradition. Throughout the New Testament, the cross is mentioned directly forty-seven times, with many collateral references. Dozens of the hymns that Christians have sung over the centuries extol the centrality of the cross in faith.

It is not difficult to accumulate Scripture that makes the case for resolving the Lenten dilemma in the affirmative. "As for me," Paul writes in his letter to the Galatian Christians, "I will boast only about the cross of our Lord Jesus Christ; for by means of his cross the world is dead to me and I am dead to the world." Similarly, in his first letter to the Corinthians he asserts, "As for us, we proclaim the crucified Christ, a message that is offensive to the Jews and nonsense to the Gentiles; but for those whom God has called, both Jews and Gentiles, this message is Christ, who is the power of God and the wisdom of God." For the devout, this may be all that needs to be said; but for many moderns, ambivalence about the cross is not resolved by quoting Scripture. The Word of the cross must be tested by human experience, and here we must in honesty confess that we run into a mixed record.

I. *Let's look at the bad and the ugly first.* These historical situations flow from the perverse use of the cross in ways that tragically betray the message of the cross about our reconciliation with God and one another through our faith in the Risen Christ. In one of the darkest periods in Christian history, eleventh-century monk Peter the Hermit, through his preaching about carrying the cross, led multitudes of peasants to follow him into the great slaughter of the Crusades (named from the Latin for "cross"), in which thousands, carrying the red cross on their tunics, died to rescue the Holy Land from the Muslims and even other Christians. They were encouraged by the offer of indulgences and by the promise of eternal merit, and were quite unmindful of the Master's warning in the Garden to an overzealous disciple, "Put your sword back in its place. All who take the sword will die by the sword."

320

The cross atop the spire of the churches in the middle ages, which blessed the use of instruments of torture to inflict excruciating pain and death on heretics during the frightful days of the inquisition, stood as a sign of the profound contradiction between the love of Jesus and the grim determination of the Church to take violent action against those whose religious beliefs were out of favor with the ecclesiastical leaders. Burnings at the stake and the hanging of alleged witches delivered the same message, as did the notorious St. Bartholomew's Day massacre which began in Paris in 1572 and killed an estimated fifty thousand Protestant Huguenots before it was over. The cross was carried on the ships that transported slaves to our shores in the early days of our nation, and to this day it provides the rationale for a virulent anti-Semitism and a sick racism, with its burning crosses and its emblem of the cross worn on the white sheets of the Ku Klux Klan during its obscene activities.

II. But there is another side to the story. Over the centuries the cross has shed its light to illumine and inspire the vast range of human relationships, revealing the power of sacrificial love to cleanse and heal, to reconcile and bring peace. Tradition holds, and probably correctly, that few of the well-known disciples lived out a normal life span, because Rome began to perceive them as a threat to the Empire. Some are said to have died by crucifixion, but head down so they would not be seen as replicating the manner of death of their beloved Lord. The inspirational power of the cross moved heroic Christians to walk into the arena with their heads erect to face lions and fire and sword unafraid—to the amusement of the jeering crowds. It gave additional courage to the brave Italian reformer monk Savonarola, a forerunner of the Protestant Reformation, who died in Florence, hung from the center beam of a cross.

The cross impelled John Wesley, the eighteenth-century founder of the modern Methodist movement, to travel thousands of miles on horseback throughout England, preaching his gospel of salvation by faith in Christ alone, seeking to win the lost, enduring much opposition and persecution along the way. The cross has been at the heart of the antislavery movement, the struggle against child labor, the modern hospital movement, and special care for the handicapped and aging.

In our time and long before, the cross has challenged missionaries to risk the difficulties and hardships of life in strange places for the sake of the challenges and opportunities to proclaim the Word of the cross to those who have never heard it before. The cross has been held aloft over the civil rights revolution within recent memory. Although there is still much work to be done, because of the dying Christ's remarkable concern for his tormentors, the criminals who hung on their crosses at either side of him, and for his weeping mother, the imprint of the cross is still seen in our efforts to create a "kinder and gentler" future for those who will follow us.

Certainly we do not suffer for our faith the way many of the early Christians did, but reflect for a moment on the good counsel that many of them received from the letter that we have received in our New Testament as recorded in 1 Peter 4:12–16: "My dear friends, do not be surprised at the painful test you are suffering, as though something unusual were happening to you. Rather be glad that you are sharing Christ's sufferings, so that you may be full of joy when his glory is revealed. Happy are you if you are insulted because you are Christ's followers; this means that the glorious Spirit, the Spirit of God, is resting on you. If you suffer, it must not be because you are a murderer or a thief or a criminal or a meddler in other people's affairs. However, if you suffer because you are a Christian, don't be ashamed of it, but thank God that you bear Christ's name."

Jesus didn't dance around the issue with his disciples; instead he talked straight with them about his forthcoming death, though Peter did his best to deny that it would ever happen. Pay attention to these words as we read them from the text for today's sermon, for they are Jesus' words of life-and-death importance to each one of us: "If any of you want to come with me, you must forget yourself, carry your cross, and follow me. For if you want to save your own life, you will lose it; but if you lose your life for my sake, you will find it." There are three conditions: (1) forget (or deny) yourself, (2) carry your own cross, and (3) follow—simple but not easy without the grace of God to lend a hand.

Denial is much more than giving up candy for Lent. It becomes a serious year-round effort to subordinate the ego's claims to comfort, self-indulgence, fame, power, wealth, or other golden goodies to the overarching claims of Christ's Kingdom of righteousness, justice, compassion, love, and peace within our local world and in the whole wide world beyond. This kind of denial includes valuing the public good even more than the private privilege, remembering that the advantaged in our competitive society often enjoy their lofty place at the expense of the disadvantaged below them, and never forgetting that Jesus always had a special place in his heart for the least and the lowliest. And we have promised to follow him.

The cross can be for us a far-off historical event, or a symbol of our faith, or even a dynamic personal reality and obligation when we realize that we too have been given a cross to carry, as Jesus told his disciples they would. The cross may become the means of saving our own life by losing it. If through faith the cross is perceived as a personal reality, his and ours, it offers the potential of becoming a life-changing force in our life, if we follow him. This is the obedience he asked of his disciples.

In Gethsemane's garden, Jesus agonized over the imminent prospect of dying on the cross, praying, "My Father, if this cup of suffering cannot be taken away unless I drink it, your will be done." Fifty years later, the author of the letter to the Hebrews writes, "Let us keep our eyes fixed on Jesus, on whom our faith depends from beginning to end. He did not give up because of the cross! On the contrary, because of the joy that was waiting for him, he thought nothing of the disgrace of dying on the cross, and he is now seated at the right side of God's throne." We are told that those who share in the fellowship of Christ's suffering will participate in the power of his Resurrection.—George W. Hill

Topic: Palm Sunday Sovereignty

TEXT: Matt. 21:1–11

Hosanna! Hosanna! The liberator arrives in triumph. "Hosanna!" shout the oppressed and colonized. The long-sought revolution lies at hand. Rome and its sycophants will be driven from the sacred precincts of the Holy City. With local autonomy restored, religious institutions empowered, and homegrown leaders in charge, Israel will gain again its national identity. Hosanna, indeed!

Except that in five days those Hosannas turn to—what? Crucify him! Crucify him! In five days hope turns to betrayal. Jesus, the liberator, suffers a state-mandated death penalty. The religious precincts, ambivalent about this outsider crashing their party, now perceive him as blasphemer, anarchist, and incendiary amid the *status quo*. By Friday the enthusiastic crowd that lined David Street on Sunday troops to the landfill outside the city walls, cursing, mocking, spitting, and shrieking, "Death and good riddance!"

And that gang of twelve, those so-called disciples, parading by his side on Sunday? Pathetic. Disappeared, slunk off, in hiding, shaken by the sentence and bloody catastrophe. Talk about cruel and unusual punishment, talk about innocents executed—just take a trip through Holy Week, Palm Sunday to Good Friday.

Who do we see in charge of that Holy Week debacle? We see Pilate, the Roman procurator, dispatched to keep the peace and secure the empire. We see the religious elite, sworn to uphold the ethical foundations of a sophisticated religious tradition and structure. On Friday we see that Sunday crowd realizing that their expectations have been betrayed, the surge for freedom has gone down the drain, and their lives have been crushed under the imperial boot. All of these people designed, plotted, and with furious enthusiasm collaborated in ridding their world of this fraudulent king, this heretic, this monumental fake and troublemaker. And the sign of their ultimate royal, religious, and popular sovereignty, the signal of their victory? That ruthless and brutal human invention, the cross. Humiliate the king. Delegitimize any religious claims. Mock him before any rendering of loyalty. Dump him. Defeat him. Destroy him. And just like *that* this world takes care of Jesus—an itch in the empire, never to be heard from again.

Never to be heard from again? Defeat at Calvary? The cross, the end? This morbid, decisive symbol of the powers that be getting their way? Not on your life! What looks to be sovereign at Calvary—the forces allied against goodness—turn out to be ultimately defeated, and what looks to be defeated at Calvary is in truth sovereign. Really? Yes, really, proclaim two thousand years of confession and experience by women and men like you, like me.

So what do we say about the cross in light of the events of Holy Week and Easter? We say, in faith and in hope, that the love of God prevails through the worst that life can do to us, even when it looks as if love has failed. The cross testifies to that!

Take the terrible war in Kosovo, for instance—a Holy Week war. In Kosovo we witnessed violence cut from the same cloth that Jesus encountered in his Jerusalem demise. This Kosovo War told us a lot about ourselves. It was not just about Serbs and Albanians, Croats and Greeks, Brits and Germans and Americans. It was about all of us human beings. This war confirmed what we saw at Calvary: hatred and violence, human desecration and self-deception, the murder we intend for and carry out against one another—all of this still plagues us. Things have not changed in two thousand years. The cynicism, the slaughter, the moral rationale; the asking for God's blessing by the leaders of all factions—Muslim, Orthodox, Catholic, Reformed; the use of overwhelming firepower in the fond but usually futile hope that violence can be controlled; another episode in our bloodstained history, another horrible incident in this most horrible of centuries.

What does our faith say about such catastrophe? Is the burning of villages, the massacre of populations, the rape of teenaged girls a denial of the love and power of God? Is a Holy Week war repudiation of the ultimate rule of divine love? No! No! If anything, the Christian faith recognizes this terrible propensity of human beings to make war with one another, to walk on one another, to exclude one another, to separate ourselves from one another—yes, to kill one another. It recognizes our tendency to cloak our activity in lofty rationale, grounding our choices, or more often morally justifying perceived necessity. We used to call it propaganda; we call it "spin" these days. The Christian faith recognizes our tendency to beat on one another, and the Christian faith insists that it is from precisely this condition that we need to be saved. War and rumors of war show us how badly we need a savior. Holy Week's gruesome Friday crucifixion demonstrates how perverse and deceived our hearts can be. If anything, the cross demonstrates the depths of our tragic condition and our incapacity to escape it by ourselves. But right here—right here—lies the heart, the mystery, the magnetic power of the cross: at the very point where we discover ourselves most profoundly lost, here we discover love's intention and means to save.

Let me put it this way: Does the name George Matheson mean anything to you? Probably not. George Matheson went blind. The woman who had agreed to marry him ditched him because she had not included blindness in her agenda. And Matheson—now blind and abandoned—was he cynical? Bitter? Hopeless? Did he curse God? Forget it. George Matheson sat down and wrote one of our most treasured hymns: "O Love That Wilt Not Let Me Go." How could Matheson affirm such a thing? How could he testify, "O light that follows all my way. . . , O joy that seeks me through my pain. . . , O Cross that raises up my head. . ."? George Matheson could write these affirmations when he looked at the one point in human history where it appears as if God really does let us go. When Matheson looked at the cruelty and abandonment at the cross of Christ—at the very moment when life appears God-forsaken—he discovered that human life is, in truth, embraced, affirmed, loved—*loved!* Right in the middle of what appears literally to be a Goddamned mess.

Are you kidding? Loved in the mess? It is a terrible problem, this matching a good and loving God with all the evil, betrayal, arbitrary injury, and self-inflicted wounds we confront in our world. The crucifixion of the innocent, this war in Kosovo. Susan Gove, the mother of a murdered girl, argued with Cardinal Law about the death penalty. I will never forget her deeply wounded and profoundly despondent rejoinder to his kind and earnest pastoral assertion that one murder does not justify another, even in the name of the Commonwealth. Retreating to sit down she wept, "My heart has been cut out. I'm troubled by God. I no longer speak to God." Are we not all troubled with God when stricken with outrage, or with tragedy, an untimely death, a terrible accident, a devastating illness, a Holy Week war? Where do we turn for an answer? Where can we discover a clue?

Try at the foot of the cross. Ask the question there. If God is good, if God is loving, where is this goodness and love when Jesus dies? Where is God's power when the hate-filled mob-execution snuffs out Jesus' life?

The clue to the answer is closer than you think. You can find it in the millions of crosses crowning our steeples, shining through art, glorifying our music, anchoring our chancels, and yes, hanging around the necks of our loves ones, not to mention the crosses pinned to lapels or on the necklaces of you who are in the pews this morning. The answer speaks from this stunning centerpiece that focuses our worship week after week. An instrument of execution? No! A sign of hope! A tool for torture? Hardly. A vehicle of love!

In Holy Week, at the cross, we discover that God's power resides not in preventing tragedy, not in halting disaster, not in staying injury or injustice, not in intervening and single-handedly stopping our malice or curbing our stupidity. God's power resides in working through and, yes, seeking to transform the worst life can do to us, and granting us the strength and courage, the grace and patience, to handle it. God's power lies in enabling us to testify with George Matheson when it looks as if the world is tumbling in and chaos and evil will carry the day. God's power enables us finally to testify and, yes, to sing, in faith, in hope: "O Love that will not let me go!"

So where is God when Jesus dies? Where is God—God's love, God's power—when the world seems upside down or our lives take a devastating hit? Amid all that denies it—and there's plenty, whether on Calvary or in Kosovo, in your life or in mine—God is there, God is here, and God's love works to restore, to redeem, to recreate. God is there, God is here, all the time. Now, in this kind of world, that is sovereignty!—James W. Crawford

Topic: Just What Are We Doing Here? (Maundy Thursday)

I want to say just a word about what we do here this evening and why what we do in this chapel and around this table is important.

We meet here in a world and moment in which we find ourselves particularly sensitive to the consequences of our human divisions. The headlines screaming at us in our newspapers or in television newscasts alert us to the ultimate results of hatred and vengeance, mob rule and gross lying. We have witnessed the failure of threatened violence to work its stated ends, and indeed, chances are it will generate ancillary and unpredictable terrors. We see confirmed our human condition run amok, innocents slaughtered, propaganda substituting for news, the powers on all sides slicing their rationale to serve their own interests, self-inflicted wounds and lofty strategies turning out to be counterproductive. The fierceness of it all is appalling. The failure of diplomacy is a tragedy. The need for it in the first place is the story of a six-hundred-year-old vendetta.

In that story in Genesis in which Cain kills Abel, the farmer murders the keeper of sheep in a conflict of cultures, traditions, and priorities—even though they are brothers. This primordial murder reminds us of the terrible chasms we dig to separate ourselves from one another.

Thus we have this table. Thank God for it. I remind you it comes to use instituted by our Lord himself, on a night long ago when the bloodiest and most divisive human instincts came into play: bribery, betrayal, fear, cynicism, power abuse, a death penalty couched in high moral terms, religion collaborating with political power to rid the world of a troublemaker. It was a table set where religious and national outsiders were perceived as unclean, and women were considered definitely inferior to men.

Have we come a very long way? Maybe. But what we do at this table together tonight shows us the nature of our mission and purpose in this kind of world—a world not so different from the one in which Jesus lived. We call this sacrament Holy Communion. It demonstrates what it takes to bridge the chasms, to dissipate the hatreds, to dissolve the fears, to bring together this fragmented and fragmenting race of ours.

So we break bread. In doing so we show that reconciliation and community come not from beefing up our forces, seeking shortcuts to self-esteem, saving face, preserving our prestige, or justifying our interests. It shows us that we, for God's sake—for Love's sake—need to risk ourselves for our neighbor, that love puts itself on the line—in Jesus' case, to the extremity of death itself.

And we pour the cup. That act demonstrates, in a world in which we find ourselves separated from one another, the way to reconciliation. The way to community is pouring out our life and our love, taking a chance on forgiveness, risking the things we treasure most in order to bind up the wounds, mend the fissures, bridge the chasms we inflict on one another.

And of course we eat, we drink. We share a meal together. We demonstrate—amid our diversity, meager though it may be—in eating and drinking together our solidarity with one another; we become a sign and symbol of the kind of community we believe God wants for our human family.

So friends, what we do here tonight with one another is terribly important. Be assured that we do not simply share in some abstract and beautiful religious rite. The music, the prayers, the elements, and this beautiful room are not an aesthetic exercise without ethical consequence. No way. We share by our breaking and pouring, by our eating and drinking. We share in a way of life we are prepared to accept for ourselves. What we do here defines our Christian life. What we do here demonstrates the depth and scope of God's commitment to us—and yes, it claims us for a vocation to servanthood in God's world, a vocation for each of us and for this congregation that mirrors the action taken at this table, on behalf of a suffering world, for Love's sake, for you, me, our church: broken and poured out. The world—finally—healed.—James W. Crawford

Topic: Why?
TEXT: John 19:1–37

A parishioner asked me about the tragic event that took place in Arkansas when two boys opened fire on the school playground and killed a teacher and some of their classmates. "How can a person explain this? How is God involved?" he asked. Now this parishioner was not being so naive as to think that I had the answer to these questions, or that he could somehow come to God's defense in the face of all other tragedies of life when they hit. But my friend wasn't asking a purely rhetorical question either. He really wanted to know how he, a believing Christian, could or should face crisis and despair.

The problem is that we want to know the answer to these questions, too. We, like everyone else, regularly have a very hard time dealing with a God who, on the one hand, is supposed to be loving and good and just but who, on the other hand, allows seemingly innocent people to suffer, or even (as was the case with the teacher and children in Arkansas) to die.

In seminary they used to call it *theodicy:* trying to explain how and why God does the things he does—asking the really tough questions.

After enough time in the pastoral ministry, one learns that sometimes it is better to keep a respectful silence in the face of tragedy. More often than you might think there really is nothing to say in the face of awful disease or sudden death. Those who expect their clergy to have answers and to be honest about it are expecting more than any person, ordained or lay, could possibly furnish. Often I have found that the best thing one can do at such times is, quite simply, *be:* be *with,* be *for,* be *present* with family and friends and even complete strangers when life goes wrong. I have done very little preaching in emergency rooms, but I have done a lot of ministry.

Good Friday is perhaps the best time to speak of these things, because in the events of this day we are confronted with an act of unspeakable evil and foolishness on the part of our forebears, the Romans and the Jews, who arraigned this Galilean rabbi on trumped-up charges and then hauled him off to be executed in a long, painful, and humiliating way. How could God allow it? What was he thinking? If Jesus is God's Son, then why end his wonderful story in such a ridiculous way? To the foot of the cross we bring these questions and we dump them there along with all our other unanswerable questions: What about those kids in Arkansas? What about cancer? What about my husband, my wife, my children? What about war and famine, God—huh? What about all these things? Where is the justice, O "just" God, and just how do you expect me to take you seriously if you can't even save your so-called Son?!

I imagine that those who went through the events we have just heard dramatically recounted asked the same questions. They were, after all, not extras hired for a Cecil B. DeMille epic who had to look and sound pious, pure, and holy. These were men and women who were losing a friend. They asked, "Why?" But there is more. If not in John's Gospel, then at least in Matthew's, Jesus himself seems to lose sight of the big picture as he cries, "My God, my God, why have you forsaken me?"

It is a dark moment when Jesus shouts that, but in that moment we see Jesus at his most human: asking God the ultimate question, *Why?* Yet whatever satisfaction may come from hearing Jesus ask the same things we do is more than overshadowed by the awful realization that if God's own Son can ask God this question, then even God himself might not know just why things happen the way they do.

This day does not allow for quick answers. To face the cross is to face our worst fears—fears of meaninglessness, of failure, of suffering and death. And if Good Friday were all there were, then we Christians would be the most depressed and depressing of people on Earth. But that is not the case. Good Friday is only part of the story. So we ask another why question. This time not "Why the tragedy? Why the suffering? Why the death?" but "Why the Church?" How and why did men and women asking the awful questions about the death of their teacher and friend see in the empty tomb in a few short days answers that were powerful and real enough to make them go out and offer humankind a different way of living? How did the world-changing appearance of the Lord in their company on that Sunday night make his death the ultimate parallel to and fulfillment of the concept of sacrifice? Why the church indeed? Why a movement, a people who can affirm joy in the midst of sorrow and resurrection in the face of death?

On Good Friday we can ask God the big questions about the really bad things, but we must also ask about the good things, too. Why *joy*, God? Why the hope that this is not all there is? Why the satisfaction of seeing that awful cross as a sign of love, not hate? If in the events of this good and holy Friday we face the dark side of our humanity, then we must also admit to the divine power that enables us to be part of miracles. That, too, is the gift of the cross to us—the good in this Good Friday.

Contrary to what you might think, especially at hard times, God isn't angry when we ask "Why?" but his answer to us takes imagination and love to understand, because it defies all reason—like tragedy, like joy.—Tyler A. Strand

Topic: They Said It Couldn't Be Done
TEXT: John 20:1–18

There were those dubious souls in the Kremlin who said no one could be rocketed into outer space, yet Yuri Gargarin did it in 1961. It took a lot of help and money, but what they said couldn't be done was done. No one can walk on the moon, they said. "It can't be done," many agreed, including scientists and engineers. Neil Armstrong did not believe it and he set foot on that celestial body in 1969—to be sure, with the genius of thousands of others who figured out how it could be done. That "one small step for man" became, as he said, "one giant leap for mankind."

We hear and see that old adage that "it can't be done" shattered almost daily. Communications; transportation; medical, scientific, and engineering feats—from tall buildings to long tunnels deep under the sea—and now genetic engineering were all once said to be impossible to accomplish. All of these and many more wonders continue to prove that the impossible is only a temporary impediment. Given determination and all the necessary resources, what was once lamented as absurd becomes possible. When we put our heads together, we discover that God created more than an advanced animal when he breathed life into Adam; he created human beings who can emulate their Creator by challenging what can't be done by doing it. We are not God, but we are his children—and to some extent it is "like Father, like Son" for us. We are capable of challenging the impossible.

The Resurrection of Jesus Christ from the dead may be a phenomenon that evokes the same discrediting negativism as everything else that is thought to be impossible, but those who say "It can't be done" don't know God. Their God, says J. B. Phillips, "is too small." It is one thing for God to take on human stature, but quite another thing for human beings to try to play God—and even to comprehend the marvel of other divine miracles, not to mention the Resurrection. Even the greatest human visionaries are blind when it comes to seeing as clearly as God does the possibilities he can create out of nothing, out of the preposterous.

For the one who created life out of lifelessness—or as Genesis teaches us, out of dust—pulling life out of death may prove a stretch of divine power, but we do not need to fear that God's inexhaustible elasticity will collapse with a sudden snap. In the Easter miracle, what the critics and skeptics say can't be done was fully achieved. "He has risen," said the angel to the women who came to the tomb that Easter dawn (Luke 24:5). Ever since, in the Eastern Orthodox rite the chant is echoed aloud, "He is risen," to which the congregation responds with eager enthusiasm, "He is risen indeed!" It is the salutation between friends and family members. There is no doubt in the minds of the faithful, no disbelief or unbelief, for they know that the immense genius of God is that he is a God of constant surprises and endless power. If it can't be done, God doesn't know about it—and God knows about everything!

Dick Imes has told of a student who, at the height of Communism's campaign against religion in Russia, attended a sunrise event one Easter Day. The Marxists had replaced the Easter sunrise services with Communist sunrise rallies. All the people were requested to attend, as were the teenagers. Ten thousand people crowded the area. The speaker asked if anyone else had anything to add as the event drew to a close. The throng was silent. Then a boy came forward.

As he came to the microphone he was told, "You must only tell the truth," which evidently meant the Communist version of it, which happened to be the rally's theme. Then he was told that if he disobeyed he would be shot on the spot. This was Stalinist Russia, when free speech was merely a term, not a reality. As the youngster stood on the podium, he was flanked by soldiers with rifles drawn. After a moment of silence he stood erect, took a deep breath, and shouted at the top of his lungs, "Christ is risen."

As the exploding rifles shattered the silence, the boy collapsed, but the ten thousand people responded, "Christ is risen indeed!" The old Orthodox greeting became a benediction for the lad's tragic death and heroic new life.

"It can't be done! I don't care what you or anyone else says," said a dyed-in-the-wool skeptic sometime before he himself was diagnosed as clinically dead on an operating table. He was being interviewed on television. He'd had the familiar afterlife experiences, he reported. When he was revived and learned that he had been pronounced dead and every bit of evidence in that operating theatre said it was so, he could no longer say, "It can't be done!" Still the skeptic, he now says, "I don't see *how* it can be done—pulling life out of death—but in my case it was."

It's a fact that none of us knows how it is done, but we do know by whom it is done.

That early morning before the first rays of the sun's brilliant light flooded the garden where the tomb was located, Mary Magdalene made her way there, John says. Luke tells us there were more women (24:5). They went to finish the hasty job of burial they had begun that Friday before sundown, when they could no longer work because it was the Sabbath and a high Sabbath at that—Passover. The stone that covered the entrance to the tomb—the golal, an immense, heavy disk that could be rolled down a trough to shut the doorway—had been moved and was standing open. The seals imposed by the Roman and Jewish authorities had been broken (Matt. 27:66). The doorway stood unimpeded. The guards posted there by Pilate had run away (Luke 28:4, 11–15). Mary shuddered to think that Jesus' lifeless body had been stolen by his enemies. Had they not done enough, she may have wondered. Or perhaps that crucified form had been taken by well-meaning friends for some hard-to-comprehend reason.

Mary Magdalene, the one from whom Jesus cast seven demons, was in deep shock (Mark 16:9). She ran to tell Peter and John, who came bounding to the tomb themselves, probably from the Upper Room where they had celebrated Passover with Jesus. John, the younger, got there first. The linen wrappings that had once covered Jesus' body were, he could clearly see, lying there. John hesitated going in until Peter came. Following the big fisherman, they both saw the linen strips, but those strips were seen as still being in the folds in which they had been wrapped around Jesus' body. It was as if his body had evaporated, says one translator of the Greek text. The cloth that had covered his head was not rolled up, as our translation suggests; but according to the original Greek, it was literally "lying apart from them, still in its folds, by itself." In other words, it was where Jesus' head had been. It too looked not as though it had been removed by anyone human—a grave robber or body snatcher—but as if the body under it had simply vanished.

You know the old magic trick of pulling a tablecloth out from under a fully set table and leaving everything as if no tablecloth had been removed? Well, that's what it was like. That's what John describes. If it can't be done, this Resurrection of Jesus, why was it done with such perfection that the Greek wording makes it clear that no human being had removed the burial bandings, nor had Jesus wriggled out of them himself. He had just disappeared from them, leaving the shroud of bandings undisturbed, still "in its folds."

But if that seems an impossibility, what about what happened next? Mary sobbed outside the tomb. It was not enough that Jesus was dead, but now his body was missing. That was the ultimate, stinging hurt. At least in seeing his lifeless form she could deal with her grief and realize it was so, but now that grief cycle was interrupted by this disturbing "theft." Angels were in the tomb when she looked again. They asked her why she wept. She explained, and then she immediately turned and Jesus was before her, but through her tears she did not recognize him. He asked her why she wept, and she explained again, thinking that he was the gardener who had come to tend the flowers.

"Sir, if you have carried him away, tell me where you have laid him and I will take him away," she begged.

And then in one word, one simple word, her tears stopped and her blurred vision cleared up. He called her by her name, "Mary," and that was enough. She knew the Lord Jesus was no long among the dead, for what could not be done, what was utterly impossible, was clearly evident in front of her as having been achieved. Jesus lived.

She went out to exclaim to all the world, "I have seen the Lord."

Friend, I can't prove to you that Jesus lives, but I don't have to. Already in these words I have referred to Peter and John and Mary, who know firsthand that the impossible was fulfilled in Jesus of Nazareth. Not only was it fulfilled in him, but it was foretold about him by the prophets. Abraham acted it out with Isaac as he attempted to sacrifice his only son on Mount Moriah (Gen. 22:1-19). Isaiah declared it (Gen. 25:6-9, 26:1, 19). Jonah portrayed it as he emerged from the great fish (Gen. 2:10). There were countless others who verified what the prophets had foretold and the apostles had seen. Scripture records more than five hundred witnesses. I can tell you I know that Jesus lives not because I was at the tomb but because he has risen alive in my own life.

I too have said, "It can't be done," about many things, only to discover I was wrong. God has healed the sick whom I thought it was impossible to heal, and he has changed impossible situations that everyone doubted could be changed. He has demonstrated repeatedly that for him nothing is impossible. The life Christ won for us by abandoning the tomb is the most precious kind of life of all—and it will never end. And if you believe that can't really be done, just watch, if you have a mustard seed-sized faith, as God summons you beyond this life through the ritual of death (Matt. 17:20). Discover then that the new endless life is precious not because it goes on forever but because God so loved the world that he gave his only Son to make it possible, because God said it can be done—and he did it.—Richard Andersen

ILLUSTRATIONS

THE REAL TRIUMPH.   The Lord had worked a most remarkable miracle; he had raised Lazarus from the dead after he had been buried four days. This was a miracle so novel and so astounding that it became town talk. Multitudes went out of Jerusalem to Bethany, which was only about two miles distant, to see Lazarus. The miracle was well authenticated. There were multitudes of witnesses. It was generally accepted as being one of the greatest marvels of the age, and they drew the inference from it that Christ must be the Messiah. The people determined that now they would make him king and that now he should lead them against the hosts of Rome. Intending no such thing, Jesus nevertheless overruled their enthusiasm so that by it he might have an opportunity to perform that which had been written of him in the prophets. You must not imagine that all those who strewed the branches in the way and cried "Hosanna" cared about Christ as a spiritual prince. No, they thought that he was to be a temporal deliverer, and when they found out afterwards that they were mistaken, they hated him just as much as they had loved him, and "Crucify him, crucify him," was as loud and vehement a cry as "Hosanna, blessed is he that cometh in the name of the Lord."—C. H. Spurgeon[1]

---

[1] In *Metropolitan Tabernacle Pulpit*, Vol. 7

FORSAKEN?   Now that is a sublime sentence in the liturgy of the Greek Church, which I have often pondered with emotion—"thine unknown agonies." Yes! the agonies of our sin-suffering, sin-atoning Lord were unknown. No angle could ever fathom their depth, no finite mind shall ever be able to gauge the breadth, to scale the height, to conceive even of the agony of his soul when he exclaimed, "My God, my God, why hast thou forsaken me? I can bear the abandonment of my disciples: one has denied me, another has betrayed me, all have forsaken me, but O my God, my god, why hast *thou* forsaken me?" We may form some idea of their character, else how can we with Paul have fellowship with him in his sufferings.—Octavius Winslow[2]

THE CROSS MEANS FORGIVENESS.   We must say, "Deliver me from bloodguiltiness, O God, thou God of my salvation" (Ps. 51:14).

God will hear and honor that cry from an anguished heart when it is directed to him through Jesus Christ.

He will forgive, he will make clean.

But something follows—"My tongue will sing aloud of thy deliverance."

There will be a change in our language, in our attitudes, in our actions, in our whole way of life if we are living in praise of God who delivers us from the gnawing inner anguish of sin and failure and betrayal.

We will see fellow human beings not as objects to be used, abused, and misused, but as individuals whose worth and dignity are to be respected, whose true personhood is to be protected and nurtured, whose lives should be better and happier for touching ours, and who, hopefully, will see the reality of Christ and his love as it is revealed in what we are and in what we do.—Robert Howard Clausen[3]

BREAKING BREAD.   Breaking bread is a way of divine revelation, and therefore equally of human reconciliation. Sadly, the history of the Eucharist is one of blood and division; communion seems to demand excommunication, just as church (as in fellowship) seems to imply schism. But the spiritual and historical truth is that either bread is broken and shared or the relationship is ruptured and broken. The embarrassing side of Christian history has originated not in the breaking of bread but in the *refusal* to break bread with certain others. The most awful twentieth-century example of this is that Apartheid in South Africa had its origins in the breaking of table fellowship of Christians of different races.

But breaking bread with others *is* a powerful means of reconciliation. If you can't do this in practice, try it as a prayer for a relationship of yours that has lost its love or peace or well-being. Go to the person with a piece of bread. Break it with them and share it. The spiritual associations of bread are so deep in our understanding that simply to think this through is a prayer for reconciliation. To do it in practice would be a sacrament of love and vulnerability. It would be a risk. It would create something new and reveal something eternal. Jesus knew what he was doing when he broke bread with the disciples at Emmaus. He was terminating trouble as he was revealing himself; he was drawing the companions closer to each other as

[2] In *Metropolitan Tabernacle Pulpit*, Vol. 7
[3] *The Cross and the Cries of Human Need*

he was revealing where he was eternally present. When they saw the broken bread, they perceived it and him in a new and uncreated light. Jesus disappeared, the past came to life, and the broken bread remained.—Stephen Chevy[4]

A PASTORAL PRAYER.   Good Shepherd: the Father loves you because you lay down your life. The Father loves you as the crucified Son because you go to your death giving your life for us. And the Father loves you when you conquer death by your Resurrection, revealing an indestructible life. You are the Life and, therefore, the Way and the Truth of our life (compare John 14:6).

You said, "I am the Good Shepherd and I know mine and mine know me, just as the Father knows me and I know the Father" (John 10:14–15). You who know the Father (compare John 10:15)—the only Father of all—know why the Father loves you (compare John 10:17). He loves you because you give your life for each other. When you say, "I lay down my life for my sheep," you are excluding no one. You came into the world to embrace all people and to gather as one all the children of the whole human family who were scattered (compare John 11:52). Nonetheless, there are many who do not know you. "However, I have other sheep that do not belong to this fold. These also I must lead" (John 10:16).—Pope John Paul II[5]

---

[4] In James W. Cox (ed.), *Best Sermons,* Vol. 6
[5] In James W. Cox (ed.), *Best Sermons,* Vol. 7

RESOURCES FOR ADVENT AND CHRISTMAS PREACHING

BY LARRY DIPBOYE

Topic: The Hound of Heaven
TEXT: Jonah 1:17–2:10

Like Jonah, Francis Thompson was a dropout of life. His poem "The Hound of Heaven" was sheer autobiography. He was a dreamer who could never hold a job. A failure in medical school, he became a friendless recluse, finally seeking comfort in narcotics. But one editor, Wilfrid Meynell, saw his writing and recognized his potential. Meynell and his wife took Thompson into their home, encouraged his gift, and not only rescued him from a miserable existence but also discovered one of England's great minds. Thompson saw God in these acts of kindness and wrote about relentless pursuit:

> I fled Him, down the nights and down the days;
> I fled Him, down the arches of the years;
> I fled Him, down the labyrinthine ways
> Of my own mind . . .

Like Jonah, Thompson encountered the God who transcends not only our existence but also our futile attempts to escape our existence.

I. *Religion is usually understood as the human search for God.* The story of Jonah takes a different twist. This is the story about the God of relentless pursuit. God is not an object to be discovered through human genius and initiative. God is the transcendent subject who reaches out to humanity from creation to the present. One of the great theologians, Karl Barth, insisted that our faith must proceed from the initiative and acts of God in revelation. He viewed all religion as a futile groping for the divine. We do not find God; God finds us. The Word becomes flesh. The God of creation owns all of the initiative. We know God only through revelation, never through human reason or the religious quest.

Jonah does not really have a dog in that fight, and I am not fully convinced that the God who created the human genius did not want us to employ all of our gifts in the religious quest. Yet the story clearly distinguishes the God of Jonah from the deities we manufacture with our imagination or our religion. The problem with the gods we control through the manipulation of either our hands or our minds is that any god whom we control is not the God of the universe. The message is pointed: God is bigger than the nation, even bigger than the human imagination. The lesson was hard-learned by the Jews through a half-century of

333

exile among foreigners and strangers. God is not only capable of crossing Jewish borders, but God transcends all human borders. No matter where we deliberately go to flee from the presence of the eternal Spirit, God is there ahead of us. The God who created the heavens and the Earth, the sea as well as the dry land, is free to dwell among all of his children.

The figure of the divine Spirit is the air we breathe. Thus, the Creator gave life to Adam by breathing air-breath-spirit into him. Jonah suggests an experiment in control. If Jonah can escape the air, perhaps he can hide from God. Where can he flee from the presence of the Creator except in the sea, or perhaps the grave? Here the divine Spirit must be limited and Jonah may remain in control. Jonah takes flight into the one place on Earth where he believes God to be incapable of following, yet ironically he identifies his God to the sailors: "I worship the Lord, the God of heaven, who made the sea and the dry land."

One would suspect that the Creator is not unfamiliar with the sea, but something else is at stake here. Jonah prefers death to the divine presence, and we are reminded of the inescapable presence of God in Psalm 139: "Where can I go from your Spirit? Or where can I flee from your presence? If I ascend to heaven, you are there; if I make my bed in Sheol, you are there."

II. *The message is about the nature of God.* It has occurred to me that if God could deliver Jonah through the agency of a fish, God could also deliver a message to the people of Ninevah without the agency of Jonah. I am consistently finding better ways for God to accomplish his purpose in the world than the Bible describes. Surely there is a consultant role for me somewhere. Or perhaps there is more to Jonah than meets the eye. First, his is a story about the nature of God—the God who never turns us loose. When I was a child, we lived near a creek that was full of snapping turtles. I watched one day with fascination while two men dug the reptiles out of the mud for turtle soup. I was not interested in the cuisine but I was impressed by the warning: "If they bite, they won't turn loose until it thunders." How persistent turtles must be! That is the story of Jonah: How persistent God must be!

The story of the great fish that swallowed Jonah is not a test of how much of the Bible we can swallow; it is a message of the persistence of our God to accomplish his purpose in our world. Someone might find here a sample of Augustine's "irresistible grace of God." I would prefer to speak of the unwavering purpose of God. God called Jonah to proclaim his word to the Ninevites. With or without Jonah, the message would be delivered, but the God of Jonah was determined that Jonah was to be the instrument of the message.

III. *Jonah dwells in most of us.* In the final analysis, Jonah is more than a means to an end. God's grace extends to Jonah. Jonah is indeed a scoundrel, but he is the scoundrel in each of us. At the beginning, this comic Hebrew character is more interested in avoiding than in finding god, and I am not sure that the universal love of God ever really sinks in with this so-called prophet, but the psalm of Jonah from the belly of the fish is the one element of piety in the man, the one evidence that he is worth saving. The only time in the entire story when the man seems to care about anyone or anything is when he is in distress. The God who reaches into every corner of our lives is with us in the darkness. It is a strange phenomenon with universal implications that we often see God more clearly in the darkness than in the light. When all else fails and every possible escape is closed, we become aware of God's persistent grace. Paul Scherer described the death of Jesus in exactly these strange terms: "The only way to win was by losing." The God of the crucified never abandons anyone.

Topic: Scolding the World
TEXT: Luke 3:7–18

The language of "the establishment" is familiar in revolutionary circles. I became aware of the pejorative use of the word in the sixties when the baby-boom generation was entering adulthood and declaring war on the sacred cows of American society. The unpopular war in Vietnam was the occasion for the rebellion, but the revolution may have been fueled more by the radical age shift in the population than by the politics of the time. Never before had young adults been so numerous and outspoken. This generation was angry and threatening. As in most revolutions, the earliest evidence of change was a shift in appearance. Beards, long hair, and sloppy clothing became symbols of resistance. Short haircuts, white collars, and ties were clear evidence of identity with the establishment. The revolution threatened the bastions of power and challenged traditional ways of thinking. Establishments tumbled and our world would never again be the same.

I. *The salvation of the world comes in revolution.* In a totally different context and era, I think I may have met the character who preceded the Christ in the Gospels. John would have qualified for a *Reader's Digest* "most unforgettable character" story. He had the wild look, as though he might belong in a mental institution. Duke Divinity School's Brett Webb-Mitchell suggested that John would be a likely candidate for therapy and a prescription for Thorazine if he strolled into town today. His style of clothing hardly allowed him to blend into a crowd. John came out of the deep wilderness. Even his diet was revolutionary. To ask guests about dietary limitations and preferences is a courtesy in our health-conscious culture, but anyone who dines on locusts and wild honey and smells like a camel is not likely to become any-one's houseguest.

Every element of John's appearance was that of a mad man, and that may well have been the key to his survival. Who really pays attention to a mad man? John challenged the sole authority of the religious establishment in matters of faith. He attacked the ethical behavior of the people and demanded immediate evidence of repentance, symbolized in his rite of baptism. He even questioned the personal life of the local monarch, Herod Antipas. Although John's challenge to the throne had fatal consequences, Herod was never quite sure that he was really done with John. Even in death John was a demanding presence, and Jesus may have been feared as a second coming of John. With all of that, John was a popular figure of his time—so popular that the Pharisees tiptoed around him in their attempt to undermine the mission of Jesus. Like the prophets before him, John stood apart in both appearance and thought, and he stood against the world as it was demanding immediate change.

II. *We cannot have Jesus without John.* John is out in front of Jesus in the Gospels, especially in Luke. Paul Winter makes a credible argument for Luke 1:5–80 as an original document from the "Baptists" that Luke edited to introduce the birth of Jesus. John's Gospel is one of those pieces of the Bible that is too bizarre and too much of a problem to have been an embellishment on the story of Jesus. John is the eccentric cousin whom the early Christians cannot disown, so they are constantly trying to explain him. Jesus never seems interested in disowning John, even when he sends back word to prison to set John straight. Jesus never seems to be threatened by John's popularity or weird behavior, and he never tries to exploit the mystical hold that John seems to have on people. Jesus does not come as a "me too" prophet, playing on John's established following. Just as eccentric Cousin John is going to be who he is regardless of the public's opinion or reception, Jesus is quite comfortable with his own identity in the Kingdom of God.

John has occupied center stage on the second Sunday of Advent much as he dominated the religious scene in the decade preceding Christ's baptism. Why? Who needs him? He has all of the character of a con man, a sensationalist who is out to get attention any way he can. Jesus came without a public relations director. He did not need help to create an image that could be marketed on the streets of Jerusalem. At least on the surface, John appears to be everything that Jesus was not. Even John's message was of questionable value. Did not Jesus challenge us to refrain from judging and condemning others? You have heard the old story about getting more flies with honey, but there was no apparent honey in John's message to the world. He came out of the wilderness scolding, condemning the norms and attacking the establishment.

After attending school from age six to twenty-nine, I met the real world outside the protected environs of academia with mixed emotions. I encountered some discomfort in the responsibility to structure my own time and goals after so many years of living by semesters. At the same time, I found welcome relief from the constant pressure of being graded. My exhilaration was short-lived. I soon found that red pencils exist in the pew as well as the classroom. Actually, no one likes to be judged, and people who seek out pain are not healthy. Why were people drawn to the whipping post of John's pulpit and to the waters of his baptism? We are still enamored of the gospel of positive thinking and we pastors have a serious problem with pressure to please. The trendy church and ministry today sets its standards according to public opinion polls and busies itself carrying coals to Newcastle.

John is about more than truth. John is about integrity. When the church is consistent with internal principles, the world takes notice. A principled life does not often lead to material success, but it brings inner satisfaction and an attitude of hope. The rewards are within us more than around us. John proclaimed the Word of God. The Bible is about revelation. The very word speaks of pulling back a veil to see the bare truth behind the screen of pretense. John drew a clear boundary of transformation. Baptism provided physical evidence of a spiritual change in life. In our world of doublespeak and euphemisms, rites and symbols anchor our faith in action and substance.

III. *We cannot have John without Jesus.* The followers of John were so convinced by him that a group of his disciples was discovered in Acts (18–19) long after Pentecost. In Ephesus, Apollos was among an entire community of John's followers who were rebaptized in the name of Christ. John never preached John. His message always pointed to the one who was to come. The absence of conflict between John and Jesus was rooted in a clear understanding of the difference between the message and the messenger. John is the messenger for whom Christ is the message. Like John, we can never stand alone or stand in the place that belongs to the Christ.

Topic: Let Us Go and See
TEXT: Luke 2:8–20

In 1957, during my first term at Baylor, the Soviet Union launched *Sputnik.* We were torn between the celebration of human achievement and our disappointment at falling behind the

Russians. The whole nation was put on alert, and education in the United States was put on trial. A student on my hall had a shortwave radio. He tuned in the frequency for the Soviet satellite and we gathered around one night to listen to the steady beeps of the space traveler and to express our wonder at the new age that was opening to us. Later the same school year, central Texas was shaken by an unidentified light moving across the evening horizon. For a few hours the whole town went crazy. We were certain that we were witnesses to a visitation from another planet. Military planes scrambled, local radio stations suspended playing the top forty hits to follow the exciting search for invaders, and a group from my dorm jumped in a car and drove twenty or so miles toward the light. I still wonder what we would have done with the thing if we had caught it.

I suspect that *Sputnik* had opened our eyes and ears toward the heavens. The next day we felt a bit foolish when Dr. Packard explained to his introductory physics class that the strange light was an ordinary atmospheric occurrence caused by the reflection of light from Venus on the horizon.

I. *God comes to us.* Advent speaks of the coming God. The shepherds are at home in the fields, doing what their forebears had done for generations, what they had done most of their lives. They were doing the ordinary, but everyone knows that nothing special ever happens around home. This is the place where the same sheep graze on the same grass in the same field under the same sky forever, and nothing ever changes. Expectation is nil around here. Boredom is a way of life. No one is looking for the Messiah. That old saw has been dragged across the same old wood for centuries and nothing really ever happens, so no one is looking for God around here. If God were to be known, surely it would not be in a sheep pasture, and every Pharisee knows that God would not be known to mere shepherds! But this story is perfectly consistent with the revelation of God throughout the Bible. The God of the ages is not a prize to be discovered by searching the universe. God comes to us, as God came to Abraham, Isaac, and Jacob. As God came to Moses and the children of Israel, as God came to Isaiah, God comes to us. Why not open your eyes to the revelation of God right where you live?

II. *Revelation is in the eye of the beholder.* What causes us to drop what we are doing to leave the ordinary to investigate the extraordinary? Shepherds had been camping in fields around Bethlehem for ages. Perhaps even David had once tended his flock on this hill. I dare say that nothing like this had ever happened before. Besides, no one would expect divine revelations to be made to ordinary shepherds. These folks were not counted among religious scholars or the spiritually elite. They were not the sort you would expect to get special attention at the central moment in human history. Shepherds had a reputation for having rough edges. We might associate them with drovers, farmers, or truckers. In Luke, shepherds are special. Not only are they the recipients of a special revelation about the birth of the Messiah, but they also become the messengers of this good news to Joseph and Mary. Only the shepherds receive a direct revelation from the heavens. Only the shepherds hear the "Gloria in excelsis deo." In the choice of Mary and Joseph as well as in the revelation to the shepherds, Luke proclaimed that very common folks are often chosen by God for special moments of revelation. The shepherds also associated Jesus with David, the shepherd king, and he exemplified for them the pastoral image of God in Psalm 23 and the pastoral mission of the Christ, the good shepherd.

No explanation for the response of the shepherds is required. I suspect that the most crass and skeptical witnesses would take notice of a heavenly chorus. Somehow we get the impression that God is not around unless we are hearing voices from heaven and seeing the bright light of divine presence filling our darkness. Maybe this is the only kind of revelation that gets the attention of the characters in the birth narratives of Matthew and Luke. If the glory of God fills the whole of creation, we do not have to hear voices, see lights, and be audience to heavenly choirs.

On Friday afternoon our scout troop traveled to the edge of the big city by car and set out on an overnight hike. I doubt that we were more than ten miles from home, but for city kids something is different out in the woods at night. We set up camp, cooked over an open fire, played games (including snipe hunt), and as the fire died down to embers, our scout master took his big five-battery flashlight and gave us a lesson in astronomy. We sat on the ground on that clear night and discovered worlds we did not know about. We learned to follow the lip of the Big Dipper to the North Star to define our direction in the woods. I still remember some of the constellations we identified that night, but mostly I remember the sense of wonder. Somehow I had missed it in the city, in the rush and busyness of daily events. The psalmist knew that the heavens reveal the glory of God long before the shepherds knew it, and one night I made that wonderful discovery.

John Killinger tells about the night Franklin Roosevelt was entertaining a friend at the White House. Before bedtime, they made their way to the Rose Garden to spend a few minutes admiring the beauty of the night. Their eyes were raised above the Washington skyline to the thousands of stars twinkling in the night. After a while the president said, "All right, I think we feel small enough now to go in and go to sleep."

Jewish scholar of the Old Testament Abraham Heschel wrote of the human encounter with God in the Bible. He taught his students to pray for wonder. One has to look at the world with the eyes of the prophet to see the glory of God. We live by the expectation that we know God only by the miracles we encounter that call us away from the ordinary events at home. One of my favorite lines comes from Elizabeth Barrett Browning, reflecting on the revelation of God to Moses at the burning bush. The nineteenth-century English poet wrote, "Earth's crammed with heaven, and every common bush afire with God; But only he who sees, takes off his shoes." Make what you will of the revelation of the Shepherds; unless they open their eyes to the wonders of God, no revelation takes place, and our world sits and waits for miracles while the wonders of God dance all around us.

Open your eyes and ears to the glory of God, the God who comes to us in the majesty of creation, the Lord of the universe who meets us in the child of Bethlehem.

Topic: Amazing Grace
TEXT: Phil. 1:3–11

The city carried memories of hard times. You remember Philippi. Paul and Silas left the tranquility of Troas for the conflict of Philippi because of a vision from God. There the healing power of the gospel came into conflict with the commercial exploitation of a slave girl, and these early Christian missionaries were beaten and thrown into prison. "About midnight Paul and Silas were praying and singing hymns to God." The songs in the night opened prison doors—not only for Paul and Silas, but also for the jailer whose life they saved. This song at midnight was the beginning of the church at Philippi. I cannot help but believe that midnight for Luke is about something besides time. The message in Acts 16 is about the power of the Christian gospel in the dark night of the soul. Times and seasons are irrelevant. This kind of darkness emerges from our fears and depressions. It is within us. This is the kind of darkness that no sun or laser can begin to penetrate. The midnight of the soul is pierced only by the light of God, which came into the world in Christ. The powerful word of the fourth Gospel rings in our ears: "The light shines in the darkness, and the darkness did not overcome it." And this light of God continued to come into the darkness all the way down to a Philippian jail in the midnight of Paul and Silas. Has the light of God reached you?

I. *No one wants to hear bad news—especially at this time of year.* We live under tremendous social pressure to be happy: "'Tis the season to be jolly." Through the joyous refrain of the angel's song and the laughter of children listen to the silent sobs of lonely souls in the dark night of fear, grief, illness, abandonment, and depression. Every year at this time I rediscover how difficult Christmas is for some of us. Folks who are not exuberant are expected to stay out of sight and sound until the season passes. The myth of Christmas is the expectation of a seasonal island of happiness in the annual sea of sickness, war, famine, and death. The poor soul who happens to be drowning in sorrow either becomes a pariah to our clanging brass and tinkling cymbals or politely stays out of sight until our ribbons and lights have been safely stored.

I have a good word for Scrooge. You know the character, or the caricature, from Dickens's novel. His depressive anger gives us plenty of reason to want to avoid him, and he is certainly blind to all goodwill. We do not save Scrooge by rejection. He has encountered the real darkness out there and it has overwhelmed him. His blindness to the light is no worse than our blindness to the dark.

II. *Advent is more than a season of joy.* Beverly Gaventa comments on hearing a pastor grump about the Christmas season: "I'm sick of the season already, and it's just started." She calls his response "utterly comprehensible." Apart from the increased busyness which seems to be inseparable from the church's Advent celebration, pastoral resistance may stem from the inhumanity of social expectation. I conduct funerals and visit hospitals during Christmas week. The season does not change the reality of sorrow that dwells with us in this world. My frustration rises with the pressure to ignore the darkness. We must present people with a wider range of options than giggling happiness or depressive guilt.

Advent celebrates the gift of God that extends far beyond the historical events about which we sing. The joy we celebrate is greater than the season, or even than a lifetime. The external joy of God underlies every moment of every day of every lifetime of every epoch of all eternity. Until we acknowledge the sorrow in the world, we have no right to the joy. Until we have confronted the darkness, we cannot appreciate the light. Our best songs always arise from the midnight of life. They well up from souls who have found a light that no darkness can overcome. Thus Matthew writes of a child born in poverty in a hostile world surrounded by the sound not only of Mary's lullaby but of the wails of the mothers of Bethlehem whose children have been slaughtered by Herod.

III. *The amazing grace of God reaches the dark dungeons of life.* Paul's message from prison to old friends in the church at Philippi has a deep, somber note of celebration. It bears his trademark greeting, "Grace to you and peace from God our Father and the Lord Jesus Christ." Paul has come full circle. The church at Philippi started with midnight songs in prison. We should not be surprised that Paul's mind lingered on the folks at Philippi as he awaited a new fate from a new judge in yet another jail. Paul had no illusions about the struggle of life on this planet, but he had been given a song to sing and he would not be silenced. The celebration of the gospel was coming from a strange place. The deepest gratitude, the highest celebration, and the most lasting meaning in life came out of a midnight experience. Paul sang a song of hope—God never leaves work undone: "The one who began a good work among you will bring it to completion by the day of Jesus Christ." He sings a song of grace. The shared grace of God is the link that breaks through prison walls and reaches over continents to tie us together in Christian love. Paul may be lonely in prison, but in Christ he sings of an extended family that grows with each new congregation he meets. As his mind lingers on his friends at Philippi, Paul sings of the love of God overflowing from the church into the sorrow of the world.

"Amazing Grace" is not a Christmas carol, but it has the character of a carol. The haunting melody lingers long after the organ has stopped and all of John Newton's five stanzas have been sung. The movies have long identified the hymn with southern Bible-belt religion. Some have suggested that the title might be legitimately changed to "The Baptist National Anthem." "Amazing Grace" is among the hymns in Baptist hymnals that make the cut in every new edition. Bill Moyers's Southern Baptist roots were apparent in the unusual feature program he developed around this hymn. He located a wide variety of arrangements, from classical anthems to freestyle improvisations of jazz, and learned that the hymn had found a home in many distinctly different cultural environs. Mostly he discovered an amazing variety of personal experience linked to this song. Invariably people had personal stories about early memories or original encounters with the hymn. One of my early memories of it was at the Cherokee Indian pageant, "Unto These Hills." "Amazing Grace" was sung by the Cherokee community at the sacrificial execution of Tsali—hero of the tragic "trail of tears." Far from the context of Newton's original intent, the message meets us in every midnight with a song of hope. The grace of God reaches the heights of our joy; but of greater importance, God's grace sustains us in the depths of our sorrow.

Topic: Going Home Again
TEXT: Luke 2:1–7

He was named E.T., for "extraterrestrial," by the kids. He was a loveable space traveler who became the adopted guest of a typical American, single-parent, suburban family. Steven Spielberg reversed George Orwell's nightmare about space invaders with a story about a poor little guy whose spaceship left for home without him. E.T. offers no threat to society. He is not a spy preparing for an invasion of earth. Apparently he is not even a health hazard. He is just a lost kid who wants to go home. Every kid who has been to camp knows what it is like to be homesick, and every child harbors the basic fear of abandonment. E.T. is not really extraterrestrial. He is "inner-terrestrial." He is the little guy within you who is lost and wants to go home.

The same emotional package turns up every year at this time in the cultural celebration of the holiday season. Christmas is about going home. Making the annual pilgrimage has made the holiday celebration as much about place as about time. Christmas is a festival of the family that calls us together with parents and siblings, to a time to reflect on our roots.

The nostalgia we connect with Christmas may offer more disturbance than comfort, and for some folks, it makes this a season to avoid.

I. *The birth of Jesus is rooted in the Old Testament hope for Messiah.* What does all this have to do with the Christian celebration of the birth of the Messiah? Maybe nothing. However, the birth narrative in Luke begins with a journey home. It is hardly a sentimental journey. Rome rules the world, and Joseph and Mary are on the road because of an imperial decree requiring all families to return to their city of origin to be registered, probably for census and taxation purposes. That Mary is forced to travel when her child is due to be born says something about the iron fist behind the decree and the heartless attitude of Rome toward the provinces. Luke says almost nothing about the birth of Jesus—simply that Mary delivered her firstborn child in Bethlehem, wrapped him and placed him in a manger (probably a trough from which the animals ate) because there was no place for the child to be born in the inn.

Why all of the dubious detail about the political purpose of the journey to Bethlehem? Luke writes about what he believes to be important. Somehow the pilgrimage to the City of David is more important than the difficulty or length of labor, the weight of the infant, or how the Holy Family came to be in an animal stall at the time of delivery.

Caesar Augustus and Quirinius are little more than props behind the journey to Bethlehem. This is a pilgrimage of sorts. It is a journey back to family roots. Caesar is not the cause. He is an unwitting tool in the hand of God, bringing together the birth of Jesus with the messianic hope of Israel. Luke reminds us that we cannot understand the coming of the Christ apart from the hope and expectation of Israel. This is a family event. Christ did not appear from nowhere and grow out of nothing. The one sent from God was sent through the family line of David. The main event is Bethlehem. The rest is decoration.

II. *Disillusionment is the child of our illusions.* Much of the nostalgia of the season is a manipulation of our emotions. All of us are driven by emotion. We carry an emotional barometer that registers the high points of life, and we are always in search of the emotional repetition of significant memories. Hallmark Cards has honed the business of pushing our emotional buttons to a fine art, in spite of the fact that nostalgic scenes and professionally written greetings are never as valid as a personal note written from the heart on the back of an envelope. The level of expectation connected to Christmas sets us up for big disappointment. The higher we rise in our emotional expectation, the farther we fall when the perfect mood is not found or recreated. Folks go home for Christmas and find that the memories are not the same. Levels of irritation and even conflict rise with our disappointments.

I have never forgotten a visit I made one December to one of many widows in town. She had family in town. Her son was a member of our church. But she seemed terribly lonely and troubled as we visited. Finally she volunteered that Christmas was not a very happy time for her. The death of a child and later a husband in December dominated her memories. To her, Christmas trees were decorations that had to be removed for personal tragedy. Her emotional association with Christmas was burdened with grief.

Both Matthew and Luke proclaim the essential role of family in the coming of the Messiah, but it is not an idealized message. Although Joseph is of the house of David, he is also of the peasant class and cannot even find hospitality for a pregnant wife in the royal city. Birth is a moment of high anxiety, especially for the young and inexperienced. Joseph and Mary go home to where there is no home for them, no parents or siblings waiting at the door, no warm dinner on the table. If you want to get the hard facts of the story, it is not about going home as much as it is about being on the road. The mentality that Christmas does not happen in strange places is a secular myth that has nothing to do with the birth of the Messiah. The social demand that you always be in a cozy little cottage with family at Christmas does not grow out of the Gospels.

III. *Family is important.* This is the beginning of a new family, a new tradition for the children of Abraham. The story begins, in Luke, with Mary surrounded by family. God has visited not only the Virgin; he has also come to Elizabeth and Zechariah. The celebration begins long before the birth of the Messiah, with the reunion of Elizabeth and Mary and Mary's song of hope. The importance of family is significant to the coming of Christ, but Jesus is born in isolation from this warm and wonderful community of love. The young parents are uprooted and in search of roots. Luke constantly holds before us the need of the world. We are reminded of the words of the Christ when his mother and siblings were at the door waiting for him. He declared, "Here are my mother and my brothers! Whoever does the will of God is my brother and sister and mother" (Mark 3:34ff).

In the Spirit of Christ, our celebration should extend the family of God. The hungry and the homeless are welcome in the family of God. The lonely find family here. The depressed find hope and the lost come home.

ILLUSTRATIONS

D-DAY.   Murdo McDonald, one of the leading preachers of Scotland, was taken as a prisoner of war by the Germans, and because the American prisoners of war didn't have a chaplain, he stayed with them in their camp, which was close by the English camp. Those in the English camp kept in touch with the outside world through an underground radio. A Scotsman, who spoke Gaelic, met daily with McDonald and across a barbed-wire fence told him about the news received from the BBC. McDonald relayed the news to the men in the American camp. Early one morning somebody woke McDonald, shouting in his ear: "The Scotsman wants to see you—it's terribly important!" McDonald put on his clothes as quickly as possible and ran to the barbed wire fence where the Scotsman spoke two words in Gaelic— "They've come!" It was D-day. The word spread rapidly. The reaction was incredible. Men shouted for joy, hugged one another, leaped into the air, and rolled on the ground with abandon. Freedom and deliverance were on the way.

The message of Christmas is not that they've come, but that he's come. And he has come to set us free.—Chevis F. Horne[1]

REFUGEES AT CHRISTMAS.   Our church sponsored a refugee family from Germany who had been caught in the dislocation of war. They arrived during the Christmas season. Our church had rented a house from them, furnished it, and stocked the pantry with food. We even put up a Christmas tree for them. A little girl who had been actively concerned about the family called her father who was away from home. "Daddy," she exclaimed, "I've never had such a happy Christmas!"—Chevis F. Horne[2]

---

[1] *Basic Bible Sermons on Christmas*
[2] *Basic Bible Sermons on Christmas*

A PERSONAL GIFT.   Do you remember in elementary school when you exchanged Christmas gifts with others in your class? In my school we would draw names and then bring the gift the day of the Christmas party. I believe it was fourth grade when this happened. My mother carefully wrapped the present I was to give. I brought it to school and put it under the tree. The time for the party came. I was so exited. What would I get?

The presents were taken from under the tree and the names were called. I kept thinking that I would be next. Finally everybody's name except mine was called. Whoever had my name had forgotten to bring a gift. On her desk the teacher had five or six gifts that were used for emergencies like this. "Here, Chuck," she said, "take one of these." But it wasn't the same. These were "generic" gifts, and nobody wants a generic gift when you can have one with your name on it.

I look at John 3:16. It does have everybody's name on it—"For God so loved the world. . . ." Somebody might say, "Well, if the gift of God is for everyone, it's generic." But when you look at that verse more carefully, you see how beautifully personal it is. So *who* may receive the gift of God's grace? Each of us who responds to the generous offer of God's love.—Charles B. Bugg[3]

REALIZED ESCHATOLOGY.   A young man was arrested for preaching the Kingdom of God, wrote E. Stanley Jones of India. When the fellow defended himself that he was preaching only what Jesus had preached long ago, the prosecutor argued, "But the Kingdom of God has not come yet." "It has for me," the young man replied.—L. D. Johnson[4]

THE MESSAGE OF CHRISTMAS.   How different from the God-man relationship depicted in other religions. In Islam, the Muslim believer urgently desires to make a pilgrimage to Mecca at least once during his lifetime as a part of his search for God. The Buddhist is encouraged to withdraw from humanity and meditate upon his soul until he finds God. The Hindu is challenged to get off the wheel of incarnation through moral living and enter into nirvana, the place of absorption into the divine spirit of the universe.

In every other religion it is man seeking God. In Christianity the message that erupted from the dark Judean night long ago is that God seeks man. His love comes to us where we are. It is an embracing love.—Brian L. Harbour[5]

---

[3] *Getting on Top When Life Gets Us Down*
[4] *Images of Eternity*
[5] *From Cover to Cover*

EVANGELISM AND WORLD MISSIONS

SERMON SUGGESTIONS

Topic: A Witness to Give

TEXT: Matt. 28:16–20; Acts 1:6–8

We have done a magnificent job of domesticating the Great Commission. We live with it fairly comfortably, even in disobedience. Perhaps in these days as we think of witness one of the things we should pray for is that God would bring to us larger dimensions than we have had before of what it means to make disciples. I came with a great deal of interest to study Frank Stagg's commentary on Acts and discovered a thing I should have discovered all along—that is, that when the disciples heard this they did not hear what we hear. They heard him say, "Ye shall receive power after the Holy Ghost has come upon you, and ye shall be my witnesses—to the Jews who are in Jerusalem, to the Jews who are in Judea, to the Jews who are in Samaria, and to the Jews who are in the uttermost parts of the earth."

I would be untrue in what I feel in my heart if I did not say in the very beginning that everything good that has come or is coming into my life really has its source in one truth—that God is in Jesus Christ reconciling the world unto himself. So the love and freedom and purpose and hope I have is related to this. As I begin to think of what God has done for me, I realize that he ministered to me through very ordinary people. I have never heard his voice in the thunder. Through all of these years God has allowed people to be his witness to me. Many of them at the time they were trying to help me see him, love him, trust him, obey him, follow him, probably had little sense of success or awareness that they were the voice of God for me.

I think, for instance, of my Grandmother Smith. During the Depression my family moved to northern Illinois, where my mother and father got jobs in a factory. They worked six days a week. Church was not a big thing with them in Oklahoma, and it was nothing for them in Illinois. Then Grandmother Smith came to live with us. She became God's witness to the Chafin children about church. My mother spent Sunday washing and ironing and doing all the things she could not do because of her job at the factory, and my father went fishing. It was my grandmother who suggested that perhaps I ought to enroll in Sunday school and study the Scriptures. She loved God and believed that his Word and his Church had some-thing to say to life. She pointed me in that direction.

Mrs. Mason, my Sunday School teacher, first taught me the Scriptures. She would write a card when, on some Sunday, I decided to go fishing with my dad instead of coming to hear her teach the Bible. She was a signpost along the way of life for me, pointing me to God, the Church, the Bible, and righteousness.

The thought keeps presenting itself, "Does God surround me with people who point me to him and have no one for me to influence? Does God put me in the world and constantly point me to him through the lives, the interest, the compassion, and the prayers of other people, and have no place for me to witness?" The ministers on our staff are to witness. What about the rest of us? Is there someplace, is there some witness, is there some person? I think so. I think that everyone who knows Jesus Christ not only has a potential for witness but probably also has a field for witness that he may not be aware of. As I approach this, there are many things I need to keep reminding myself.

I. *I need to remind myself that I will never meet anyone who does not really need what God has to offer in Jesus Christ.* You recall that when Nicodemus came to Jesus, with his salutation he put Jesus in a place where few men had stood (John 1:2). Jesus said, "Nicodemus, there is something so wrong with everyone else in the world that unless you have a burden from above, you will not understand sonship; eternal life will evade you." The Scripture says that in his contact with the rich young ruler, "Jesus beholding him loved him." He was an attractive man, a man of culture, a man of obvious intensity. Jesus said to him, "One thing thou lackest." You and I would have trouble with this, especially if Nicodemus lived next door or if the rich young ruler were in our office. If some man comes stumbling into the neighborhood, having made a complete mess of his whole life, we can see how God might help him. But when the fellow comes in and his car is longer than ours, his lot is wider than ours, his house is bigger than ours, and his position is more powerful than ours, we have a tendency to look at him as not really needing the same thing as the man who made a mess of his life. We are wrong.

Let us suppose you are on a train going from Fort Worth to Houston. You look up and getting on the train is the original flapper. She has on a mini-mini skirt. She has on more makeup than she ought to have on for this time of day, or perhaps for any time of day. She is chewing gum and popping it. She comes and plops down next to you without speaking. She proceeds to dig around in her purse and takes out the last cigarette from a pack and throws the pack into the aisle. Then she takes from her bag a popular magazine and begins to read. The thought comes to you that God could bring so many things into her life. You are not an eager beaver or a direct sort of person, so you ask the woman about your friend who is pastor at the Field Street Church. She asks about your church affiliation and you begin to talk. One thing leads to another and you talk about what Christ means to you. You are proud of yourself.

A few days later you are coming back to Fort Worth and you are thinking about this girl and wondering if what you said did any good. You are sitting there again, waiting for them to change crews, and you look up and standing in the door is the flapper's opposite. Here is a girl who someone with taste and money has taken to the best stores and dressed in the peak of style. She has bearing and poise about her. She asks if the seat beside you is taken. She sits down and takes out a lovely silver cigarette case and asks, "Do you mind if I smoke?" You say, "No." She says, "Now really, smoke offends some people. Do you mind?" By now you are saying, "Hurry up and light up!" As she lights her cigarette and offers you one, you are almost sorry that you gave it up. She takes out a magazine and says, "While I was waiting for the train I read the most interesting article on the moral implications of nuclear testing. What do you think about that?" Right away you think, "Wow! Here's a lovely person, well dressed, and cultured and refined," and you have the most invigorating, scintillating discussion. All at once you are in Fort Worth and off the train. On the way home you think, "You know, I never did talk to her about Christ."

Do you know why you did not bring up the subject of religion with her? Because deep down in your heart you find it really hard to believe that her problem is the same as the other girl's problem. Because you and I are so dreadfully middle class, we think that because a person lives in a nice house, wears nice clothes, and is cultured and sophisticated she has discovered everything that God can say to her in Christ. This is not so. If we are to be witnesses, we need to remember that whether we deal with a janitor or the president of the company, we will never be in contact with people who do not need to know God in forgiveness, who do not need to know him to find purpose in their living, who do not need to know him to comfort them in their mortality and their dying.

II. *I do not come across anyone who is not the object of God's love and the object of God's concern.* We have a tendency in evangelism to collect people who are already like us. I constantly need to go back to the Scriptures to realize that the Christian never really comes in contact with anyone who is not the object of God's love and concern.

When the disciples came back to the well of Sychar (John 4) and found Christ talking to the woman of Samaria, they were taken aback that Jesus would be talking with this woman. Why? Because although they had walked with him, they still had not learned that you do not meet people who are not the objects of God's love. The first two or three months in which they were following Jesus they sang the first-century equivalent of "Amazing Grace." They had not been in charge of the intermediate department very long when they began to sing "How Great We Are" and started to look on people as "church type" and "nonchurch type." We are to witness. We are to look at people and we are to be reminded that no matter how we feel about them, they are the objects of God's love and the objects of his concern. We will not be good witnesses of God until we feel about them as he does.

III. *Everyone has worlds where they are responsible and where they have some possibility of being a witness for God.* I think there are times when the enormity of the task that faces us simply tends to paralyze us. One day a dear friend of mine suggested that I needed to retranslate the Great Commission to read, "Go ye into all *your* worlds and make disciples." The real emphasis in the Great Commission is not on the word *go*, for it is better translated *going*. The real emphasis is on making disciples. So why not, just to get a handle on it, translate it like this: "Go ye into all your worlds and make disciples." We do have little worlds, little circles. Some of them overlap and some are miles apart—where we go to school, where we live, where we work, where we do business, or the world of our social life. These are our worlds.

You say, "Well, I've got these worlds and I know who the people are, but I am just not the witnessing type." Let me suggest that the ways of witnessing are as infinite as love will create. Take the case of a woman who was a children's worker—not exactly the hot spot in the church for evangelism, you would think. She was converted in her middle forties and had very little background and training, but she had a marvelous gift from God. She loved children and through the children she loved the parents. She got to know them. She prayed for them. During the five years that I was her pastor I baptized many young couples because this woman had witnessed to them by loving the child.

Another example is a prominent businessman in Fort Worth who was converted. He was very glib and found it easy to verbalize his thoughts and feelings, but he found his new faith difficult to talk about because he was such a baby in his faith and such an old man in the community. He decided that everyone he really wanted to witness to he would bring to the church he attended. He would speak to them, shake hands with them, and say, "I've found something. Go with me to this place," and he would take them. After his death I preached for a week in that church in a pre-Easter series of services. I suppose I met a score of grown men who said, "I am a follower of Jesus Christ today for one reason: That businessman brought me here, and what I felt and what I heard I knew to be true, and I responded." Not a very complicated system, is it?

A young executive attended a Christian Laymen's Forum at a seminary where he heard a faculty member discussing the new American Bible Society's translation, *Good News for Modern Man.* The faculty member said, "If the average person would expose himself to the Scriptures in an up-to-date language, he would discover God saying things to him." The young executive bought a copy of that Bible and read it. It was a very enriching experience. Now, as a part of his witness, he has bought copies and given them to friends and associates with these words, "I read this book the other day and it is changing my life." You may say, "That's not much." You are right. But you would be absolutely amazed at the number of people to whom this has been a witness and a signpost.

During my second year as a seminary student I went to preach in a revival in a ranching community in eastern New Mexico. No one new had moved into the community for about thirty years, and everyone who got old enough and had enough bus fare left. So anybody who was not already a church member had been exposed to a preacher and evangelist every year for about forty years. We made the rounds. I remember we went to see a man named Johnson and you could see the smile on his face as he thought, "Oh, I forgot it's the revival. This evangelist is here to try to convert me." And I tried. When I got through, he grinned and thanked me for coming—and that was it. I thought to myself, "What would it take to get to a man like this?" Living next door to him was my host who had been a neighbor some twenty-five or thirty years. He was a Godly man but not very articulate about it. During the course of this week, sitting there on the back row with Johnson, my host became burdened for him. He reached over and took his neighbor by the elbow and gave it a muscular squeeze, looked at him, and tears came to his eyes. He turned the man loose, turned his head and blushed, and that was it. The next morning, on the crank phone that cranked four times for my hosts' residence, came a call for me. It was Johnson. He said to me, "Kenneth, I have decided to commit my life to Jesus Christ, and if I am alive tonight when you have that service and sing the hymn, I will come forward and tell the whole church that I have decided to commit my life to Jesus Christ." Do you know why he did that? It was not because I went there and quoted the New Testament to him. It was because someone he knew as a part of his world actually cared and in a very nonverbal way made it known. I wonder if you and I do not need to look around and see if there are people in our world whom God sees and we do not—people for whom he cares, people who need to have shared with them what we have come to know. For I believe this is a part of God's plan for each of us: to be his witness in the world.—Kenneth L. Chafin.

Topic: Who Speaks for Jesus? The Importance of Every-Member Evangelism
TEXT: Luke 19:28–40

I. *Evangelism ought to be a vital part of our life.* We tend to take a lot for granted, especially in secure older churches, and we forget that no church was ever built on mere spit and tradition, that somewhere, sometime, someone had to go out into the highways and byways and bring people together in Christ. We are like the lifesavers in one of Merrill Abbey's books—rescuers on a rockribbed seacoast who had done such a tremendous job of saving storm-wrecked sailors that the citizens of their region bought them a splendid house and provided for their every comfort; and then they grew so languid and comfortable that they stopped going out to rescue people! We belong to a big church and we assume that our work is done. Jesus' command to go into all the world and preach the gospel falls on deaf ears—or strikes us as words to ministers and missionaries, not to average Christians.

Part of our trouble is a psychological block. It doesn't take us long, especially in a church with a beautiful sanctuary, to dissociate ourselves from coarser forms of Christianity in which congregations engage in every-member evangelism—knocking on doors, handing out pamphlets, and badgering people about their souls and the end of the world. We are "First Church"—noses atilt—and we don't *do* things like that! We don't, do we? And I will be the first to say I am glad we don't do things like that. I wouldn't for a minute put down the churches that do; somebody probably needs to do it. But I am glad it is not our style.

I have always liked a little story I heard years ago from Kenneth Chafin, who at that time was a professor of evangelism in Fort Worth, Texas. It was about a veteran soul-winner who spent most of his time going around after the unconverted and winning them into the Kingdom. His Bible was as marked up as a novice's travel guide, and there was nobody, but nobody, he couldn't quote and cross-reference into salvation. One day he was out making his rounds with a beginning soul-winner, a young man who was thinking about entering the ministry. The young man was impressed and amazed as, one after another, various persons targeted for conversion surrendered to the Lord. The two had been at it all day when late in the afternoon they pulled up at the curb outside an expensive ranch house in an exclusive subdivision and walked up the flagstone walkway that wound through a carpet of lush, green grass. As the walk wound past a picture window, they saw the man of the house sitting inside. He was in his shorts, lying back in a great reclining chair, watching a football game on TV. He had a can of beer in one hand and the other hand was idly stroking the head of a beautiful Great Dane lying beside the chair. As the old soul-winner reached for the doorbell, the young man stopped his arm a moment. "Before we go in there," he said, "I need to know something." "What's that, son?" asked the older man. "What kind of good news do we have for him?"

There is a lot of truth about evangelism in that little story. Good news begins at the point of our realization of need, and because our needs vary, the way the good news is presented must vary. The method of winning a soul to Christ that worked for a down-and-out gas station attendant in one section of the city would not work for the up-and-out business executive relaxing in front of the TV. The man in the ranch house probably had as much need for Christ as the man in the gas station, but his way of perceiving himself and his need was different and the evangelists should have taken that into account.

II. *Jesus expects his followers to acclaim him to other people.* If they don't, the very stones in the ground will cry out to acclaim him, Jesus once said. There ought never be any shyness in us about confessing the lordship of Christ and what it means in the structuring of our lives and hopes. In fact, there is probably some correlation between such shyness and our failure to lead mature Christian lives. But we are also expected, if our imaginations are converted as well as our mouths, to be able to transcend mere abecedarian approaches to spiritual matters and witness to Christ in an idiom that other people can understand and relate to. Let me give you two or three pictures to show you what I mean.

(a) Picture one: Here is a teenager named Mike who has been in and out of detention several times in the past three years. He comes from a well-to-do home but is constantly in trouble. He is a known user of alcohol and drugs. His parents are at their wits' end with him. A traditional evangelistic approach to Mike—someone going into the detention hall, sitting next to him, and showing him in the Bible that he is lost and damned without Christ, and then asking him to become a Christian—might work, within limits, because Mike is in an extreme situation and will grab at anything. But suppose an interested Christian goes to Mike with love and gifts and says, "Mike, I care about you and I hate to see you screwing up your life this way. I know everything looks bleak from where you sit. I suppose it would be that way with me if I had had to live in your shoes. But thank God I've had some spiritual experiences that have turned me around and set me on a pretty productive path in my life. Let me tell you about them, and then you see if you think something similar to them might occur in your own life." The Bible might come later, as part of Mike's rehabilitation course, but it wouldn't be thrown at him as a magic book without reference to a specific human situation.

(b) Picture two: Here is a young woman named Jill. She is twenty-seven years old, a college graduate, unemployed, mother of two small children, and her husband has just left her for another woman. Jill's life is more in pieces than it has ever been before, but she is managing to keep a stiff upper lip. You can see the hurt in her eyes and in the slow way she moves around the living room, but she is a tough woman and she will hold things together. You know she used to go to church and still attends occasionally, but she has never shown any signs of being strongly committed to Christ. You would like to witness to her about your faith but don't want to offend her. You don't begin by quoting Scripture. Maybe you start by inviting her to lunch day after tomorrow. She needs the new perspective of getting away from the house once in a while. And maybe you say, "Jill, I don't mean to pry but I wonder if any of what we learned in Sunday School as girls is having a special meaning for you these days." Perhaps she says, "Why, what do you mean?" And you say, "Well, I mean about Christ and how he sustains us if our faith in him is strong." And before you know it you are deep into a heart-to-heart talk about faith in which you can make your own personal witness to the significance of Christ.

(c) Picture three: Here is a fifty-three-year-old naval officer named Jim who lives in your neighborhood. He seems to have plenty of money, plays golf at the club, takes nice trips to Nassau and Bermuda in the wintertime, and drives a luxury automobile. His wife attends church but he doesn't. As far as you know he has no faith commitment at all. He is a little like the man in the picture window. How do you witness to him? Perhaps you begin by inviting him into your golf game. You get to know him and what some of his experiences in life have been. You try to discern whether Christ has ever been part of those experiences in any way. Maybe you learn that his parents were avid churchgoers and forced him to attend when he didn't want to; he didn't like the brand of perfervid Christianity forced on him. When he was old enough to join the navy, he rebelled against the church and never had any more to do with it. He can tell you about all the hypocrisies of those who do attend church. And perhaps at this point you say, "Yes, it's true; we don't live up to what we profess to believe. But Jim, I don't know what I would do without Christ in my life. My soul would be an absolute desert without him. I couldn't face growing older and watching the dissolution of everything if I didn't have an eternal hope in my heart. I wonder that you can." The wedge is driven, the goal is in sight.

Note: In every one of these pictures, the church and Christian fellowship are important. We do not go out to evangelize in a vacuum. We do it in the context of a world where people are hurt and lonely and of a church where those who are in Christ come together for healing and fellowship. That's always part of the wider background of a picture. Conversion may begin when people decide to trust Jesus with their lives, but it continues in the shared life of Christians in the church, and it doesn't end until we are finally converted into the Kingdom beyond death. This is one of the problems with television evangelism. It makes cut-flower Christians, Christians who will fade away in a few days because they lack the nourishing soil of a loving fellowship in which to grow and make mistakes and grow some more. All true evangelism begins and ends in the fellowship of the Church.

III. *Your life and your church's life are both incomplete without the witnessing process.* You and your church need to be doing evangelism in order to stay alive in Christ. The minute you receive the good news of Christ and fail to pass it on in the course of daily living, you become like the Dead Sea, that remarkable body of water that is dead precisely because it receives life-giving water and doesn't pass it on. Your church is the same way. Its only life comes through sharing what it has received.

In his book *Portrait of Churchill,* Guy Eden tells the story of the heroic evacuation of Dunkirk during the bleak early days of World War II. Every ferryboat, every trawler, every pleasure craft the English people had was pressed into service to sail across the channel and bring back the remnants of the Allied army that had been forced onto the beaches of Dunkirk. Eden reports that one man, a government servant, rowed his canoe back and forth to Dunkirk three times, under heavy shelling, to rescue people. Imagine that—three times in a canoe! Talk about individual responsibility! And that's precisely what we're talking about when we talk evangelism—every member's responsibility to be a faithful witness to Jesus Christ. If we don't do it, the very stones will cry out to own his lordship.—John Killinger

Topic: Coming to See
TEXT: John 1:46

What could I say to you to persuade you to accept Christ? There was once a man named Nathaniel who needed Jesus as much as you do right now. He had a friend who had just the right words. Read the text: "Come and see."

Jesus found John, Andrew, Peter, and Philip. But Jesus did not find Nathaniel—Philip found Nathaniel on Jesus' behalf. Nathaniel was hesitant but curious; he was critical but practical. So the advice, "Come and see," was perfect for him.

This is the best advice I could possibly give you. I give it to all my friends. You need Jesus, but I cannot compel you to obey him. I want you to come and see Jesus for yourself. You will find that these words are a challenge, an opportunity, an invitation, and an enticement.

I. *"Come and see" is an enticement to you because you are curious.* You are interested or you would not be listening. There is something in you that is pricked. Curiosity? This is the beginning of obedience. For now, I simply say, "Come and see."

(a) I am pointing the way for you without telling you everything.

(b) I am allowing for your human nature, or curiosity, to draw you even further.

(c) I am urging you to become an independent discoverer of Jesus. You must meet him personally.

II. *"Come and see" is a challenge to you because you are skeptical.* And you should be. Jesus sounds too good to be true. Nathaniel was a skeptic. Jesus is always open to the honest skeptic.

(a) He has for you a tangible message.

(b) He has for you a revelation of his wisdom.

(c) He has for you a demonstration of his power.

(d) He will satisfy your skepticism or you are welcome to depart.

III. *"Come and see" is an opportunity for you because you are practical.* I take it for granted that your interest is not frivolous, nor your skepticism unfair. You are honestly interested in personal benefit. What will Jesus do for you?

(a) Jesus will give you a remedy for your sin.

(b) Jesus will give you what you cannot buy from any other source: forgiveness, life, truth, and nurture.

(c) Jesus will give you a place to live, work, and thrive.

IV. *"Come and see" is an invitation to you because you are hesitant.* Nathaniel was hesitant. You might not have believed that you are really welcome. Up to this point you have been an outsider looking in. But this invitation is genuine; it has your name on it.

(a) Jesus often said "Come" to the most unlikely people.

(b) The word is used in many places with all kinds of people, and he is saying to you, "Come."

(c) "Come" is Jesus' last word to an indifferent world, and his first word to those who want him.

(d) Read John 1:18, 4:24, 14:9.

What was the result of Nathaniel's response? He came and he saw for himself. He proclaimed that Jesus was the Son of God! Jesus never fears the honest seeker. So if you are curious or skeptical or practical or merely hesitant, *come and see for yourself.*—David Beavers

Topic: Let God Help You
TEXT: 2 Cor. 12:9

Of this we can be sure: Our need is great, but God's grace is greater. When Saint Paul cried out in anguish at the thorn in his flesh, he was answered with a mighty word of hope: "My grace is sufficient for thee." It is, indeed! But do we know it? God's help is real. Do we want it? God's saving power is there. Will we take it?

I. *What is it?* Theologians have two words for it—prevenient grace—the good help of God that is already present. Before we think to ask for help, God is already there trying to help us.

When we first become aware of life's needs, we are already recipients of God's blessings. We discovered the world, we did not create it. We received the gift of life, we did not begin it.

God the Creator has blessed us from our birth. His providence has sustained us on our way. His help is all about us before we know enough to ask for it.

Underneath us are the everlasting arms. Above us is his overarching care. We are encircled by his compassion. We do not ever need to live outside the circle of his love.

II. *Do we know it?* God's help is here—but do we know it? Never was it more imperative to live fully aware of God's help than now. As civilization advances, so life's hazards increase. In days of great stress we need the help of a great God.

That help is at hand. Do we know it? The person of dependable strength is the one who trusts the character of God rather than the character of current events. In God's strength, goodness, and love are our true hope!

III. *Do we want it?* In the confusion of our times there are some who think that God cannot help. Others think that God will not help. Still others doubt if God can be found.

They are all wrong. God is both able and willing to help, and he is already helping us while we debate about it and wonder where we can find him. The real problem is with ourselves. God's help is here, but do we want it?

Our need calls for God's help, and God's help calls for our willingness to receive it. We are persons, not puppets. God seeks our willing response as persons when he offers his grace. He stands at our door and knocks. Without the willing response that opens the door from within, God's love is rebuffed. A Swedish layman used to pray, "Lord, make us willing to be willing!"

Are we really willing to have God in our lives? To do so may interfere with our desires and change our habits. For God not only comforts the afflicted; he also afflicts the comfortable. His disturbing presence may change everything. His help may convert us—literally turn us around—so that we see things as he sees them and learn to love the things we ought to love.

IV. *Will we take it?* God's help is here but will we take it? We are called to commitment. It is the uncommitted life that lacks God's blessings, not because the blessings are not there but because the individual has never taken them. Such a person is like the naive and economy-minded lady who ate crackers and milk in her cabin throughout an ocean voyage, not realizing that the magnificent food in the dining room was hers for the taking at no extra cost.

Christ calls us to clear and conscious decision: "Follow Me." What a way to live, with purpose and confidence, enthusiasm and power, because we have taken him for our Master and have heeded his call! How can we be casual in the presence of life's greatness?

Some Welsh miners were trapped in a cave-in. The rescuing party worked desperately, knowing that they were in a race against time. At last, in sheer exhaustion and despair, not even sure of their direction, the rescuers lay down their picks. In weariness and deep need they bowed in prayer.

Suddenly they heard a sound—the faint sound of a pick. It was the trapped miners signaling their position. Leaping from their knees with fresh power and enthusiasm, as if only beginning, the rescuers worked with new vigor and hopefulness until they burst through the last wall of rock and their friends were saved.

Is this not a parable of life, that we must let go and let God if our labor is to avail? God's help is here. But to have it, we must know it, want it, take it in simple trust and thankfulness of heart.—Lowell M. Atkinson

ILLUSTRATIONS

NEED FOR REVIVAL.   The great evangelical prophet Isaiah also saw the necessity of revival. He told the people of Judah that God had nourished them, had brought them up as children, and yet they had rebelled against him. He said they were a "sinful nation, a people laden with iniquity, a seed of evildoers, children that are corrupters: they have forsaken the Lord, they have provoked the Holy One of Israel unto anger, they are gone away backward" (1:4). The result of their disobedience was that their hearts were sick and faint, their country was desolate, their cities were burned. God was tired of their multitudes of sacrifices when they were not living sacrificial lives. And the great prophet Isaiah cried out, "Wash you, make you clean; put away the evil of your doings from before mine eyes; cease to do evil; learn to do well; seek judgment, relieve the oppressed, judge the fatherless, plead for the widow. Come now, and let us reason together, . . . though your sins be as scarlet, they shall be as white as snow" (vv. 16–18).—James P. Wesberry[1]

MEETING GOD.   I walked once with a friend down a busy road, and we saw a man with a doleful expression slowly parading up and down, carrying a poster bearing the words: "Prepare to meet thy God." It seemed to me a foolish way of witnessing, and I said: "How awful! Trying to threaten people!" My friend replied, "You interpret those words as a threat. I see them as a glorious hope. How marvelous to meet our God—the God of Creation, of Jesus, of love and mercy! I'm prepared, excited!" The point was well taken. We must all meet God at last. It may seem a threatening prospect—the weak before the Omnipotent, the sinful before the Holy, the mortal before the Infinite. But God has already met us! Rich in mercy, boundless in compassion, He has taken the initiative to give us grounds for confidence on the day of meeting.—John Gladstone[2]

HIS BUSINESS, OUR BUSINESS.   A woman of fashion in Boston was thunderstruck when a stranger, the zealous "Uncle John Vassar," besought her to accept Christ. She told her husband, who said indignantly, "If I had been there, I would have told him very quickly to go about his business." Her reply was empathic: "If you had seen him, you would have thought he was about his business."—George A. Buttrick[3]

WHO WILL FIND US?   Some animals have a fine sense of direction. The pigeon, for example, has a homing instinct. You cannot lose a pigeon.

At the beginning of this century some experiments were being done in animal psychology. In a northern state some pigeons were blindfolded, put in cages, and brought to the town in Virginia where I live. Some of the old-timers who saw the experiment said they took the pigeons out of their cages, removed their blinds, and released them. They flew to a certain height, circled several times as if getting their bearings, and then flew back home. A pigeon can do that but a sheep can't. The Bible tells us that we are like sheep, not pigeons. Somebody has to find us.—Chevis E. Horne[4]

---

[1] *Evangelistic Sermons*
[2] *All Saints and All Sorts*
[3] *Christ and Man's Dilemma*
[4] *Preaching the Great Themes of the Bible*

BIBLE STUDY I

BY EDUARD SCHWEIZER

Topic: The Rich and the Poor
TEXT: 2 Sam. 12:1–15; Mark 2:14–17; John 1:29

I. *"And the Lord sent Nathan to David"* (v. 1a). God's Word upsets us time and time again. Everything was going fine and smoothly for David, and suddenly God's Word broke in and disrupted everything. It might be a good test—certainly more important than the many tests we carry out with detergents and shoe polish and applicants for a job in an office—to ask ourselves whether God's Word really disturbs us. If it does not—if it even simply confirms our personal disposition, our views, our plans; if it brings only peace and rest and higher feelings—then it probably died in our lives long ago. It is precisely because God does disturb us, and sometimes very much so, that the Bible calls God's Word *grace*. Oh, I agree with those who think that a good stroll in the woods on a warm summer day is more refreshing, or a visit to a baseball game on a Sunday afternoon more exciting, than going to a church service. However, neither the woods nor the baseball stadium interferes with our course in life. David's life was not interrupted by the woods on the Mount of Olives, nor did the play of the youngsters in the streets of his capital affect him; but when God's Word came, it broke into his life and changed it.

I am afraid it was not even a particularly good sermon that the prophet delivered. We might hear better ones in our churches. The story of a rich man slaughtering a poor man's only lamb, which had slept with his master, eaten of his bread, and drunk from his cup, is a bit sentimental and not quite credible, but it is courageous enough to call sin *sin* without any embellishment. Therefore, in this sermon God himself comes to David, and I am not sure he always comes to us in the sermons we hear.

II. *"Then David's anger was greatly kindled against the man; and he said to Nathan, 'As the Lord lives, the man who has done this deserves to die; and he shall restore the lamb four-fold, because he did this thing, and because he had no pity'"* (v. 5). David can get angry. This is God's good gift to him—a gift not always easy to live with but a good gift nonetheless. Years ago when the giant Goliath sneered at Israel's God day by day, David got so angry that he left his flock, sneaked into the fighting troops, and finally killed the giant, just as he had killed lions and bears that were attacking his sheep. No, David was not one of those who simply said, "Well, well, it is certainly said, but such is the course of the world—it is getting worse and worse; you cannot change it." He was still able to flare up and get angry—so angry that he was ready to take action. He was not one of those who bear a bag of sand instead of a heart, so that God's word is cushioned and reduced to silence before it can do any harm.

354

III. *"Nathan said to David, 'You are the man'"* (v. 7a). Nathan did not cut the bonds of brotherhood with David; on the contrary, he exercised brotherhood by speaking the truth to him. This is the weirdest part of the story. God caused this short sentence to get inserted into the Bible. Hence it goes on speaking, century after century, until it hits us here. It is a sentence that nobody wants to hear, and there are always excuses for not listening to it. There are always reasons for seeing the whole thing from another angle, for understanding the other person's position. Was not David in his day rather progressive in his social program? Why should we listen to this verdict? Are we not Christians, perhaps even devoted Christians? Have we not built a solid house for our children or given them all the education they need? Are we not caring in a responsible way for our workmen or employees or church members? Have we not given good service to our country? Could anybody reproach us for any negligence in our business? Are we not human with all those for whom we are responsible? Are we not doing more than we should be forced to do? Are we not giving 2 or 5 or even 10 percent of our income to those who have more difficulties than we do?

This, just this, is the way to escape God's Word. We are quite upset by all the injustice in the world. We are furious when we read of those in power who torment the powerless in their prisons. We are angry with a government that expels other races or tribes from its territory. We are terrified by the news about riots or civil wars that we read in our papers. We may even go so far as to sign a resolution against all this injustice, as long as it does not hurt us. Yet we are so far from even imagining that God could mean us when he says, "You are the man." There is not an inkling in our hearts of the possibility that God could be interested in the one person who is suffering in our homes, our enterprises, or our neighborhoods, perhaps simply because of our laziness, which stops us from doing something about the injustice we condemn with horrified exclamations but without deeds.

Unperturbed, God went on: "You have smitten Uriah the Hittite with the sword and have taken his wife to be your wife, and have slain him with the sword of the Ammonites" (v. 9b). Now, was this not a bit unjust? Was this not terribly exaggerated? What happened? True, David saw the wife of Uriah; true, he fell in love with her. This can happen. What did he do beyond this? In a war, someone must fight at the most dangerous place. David shared the terrible responsibility of selection with his general and hinted that he could well put Uriah in this place. Why not? Strangely enough, it was again a noncitizen, an alien, in whom God was so interested. It indeed seems that in the Bible it is always the people outside the normal areas of life who are cared for by God. Uriah was a foreigner from Anatolia who was profiting by the boom in David's empire. It was only right that he should carry his share of the burden and danger of the empire; and if he were not at the most dangerous place, another man would have to be there. Everything sounds absolutely correct—as correct as it sounds in our countries. Someone must do the dirty work. If there are foreigners who will to do it, why not allow them to? This is still better than what they would find in their own countries, and anyway there is nobody of our own nation who would be ready to do it. Someone must produce the goods and others must manufacture and sell them; because cocoa grows in Africa and rubber in Malaysia, it goes without saying that these materials would be grown in these countries and that other countries would manufacture and sell products made from these materials. Someone must rule and others must obey. Why shouldn't our family, our tribe, our country rule over others? This is how we are speaking, and everything we say seems to be so right. The only difficulty lies in the fact that God is not convinced by our plea. He simply goes on saying, "You are the man." We point to other people and other nations whose crimes are a crying shame—to the capitalists or the communists, to white or black governments—in short, to others rather than to ourselves. Then God is not able to speak his Word to us. There is something like a reef in front of our hearts that breaks the waves so that nothing can hit us. We see all the injustice in the world, but only outside, beyond that reef—never in our own port, where we want to see nothing but quiet, unruffled waters. In this case, the four words of God remain outside; they cannot reach us, and we are still sitting happily in our peaceful realm, thinking that God means other people when he says, "You are the man."

We may reduce our own consciences to silence, but we cannot silence God's Word. God went on: "Now therefore the sword shall never depart from your house, because you have despised me and have taken the wife of Uriah the Hittite to be your wife" (v. 10). Indeed the sword does not depart from the Earth. We do not like to be reminded of this, and if our artists or poets or dramatists paint their pessimistic or strange pictures of our world, we call it nihilism. But what if it is the proclamation of God's judgment that comes through these artists in a desperate effort to call us back from our ways and incite us to act? What if it is God who is trying to say to us what he said through Nathan to David? "David said to Nathan, 'I have sinned against the Lord'" (v. 13a). David is able not only to get angry but also to become very quiet in order to listen. This is what made him the blessed king of Israel, foreshadowing Christ's Kingship. The Word of God was not cushioned on a sandbag nor diverted to others by a reef of sharp rocks; it was allowed to reach David's heart. So blessed was he that he learned to accept this Word and to accept himself, saying, "Yes, I have sinned." Again, God may be asking our assembly whether we are able to listen so that his Word gets through to us.

Modern psychology tells us how utterly important it is that we learn to accept ourselves. The question, however, is, How do we do this? We could do it in a cheap way, by following the slogan that there are all types of people, so why not a type like me? If we do this on the level of our individual lives, it is just our family or the workers in our office who have to suffer. If we do it on the level of political systems or social groups, then we simply accept the situation as it is without any hope of change. Maybe you know the old story about the poor bed wetter who went to see a psychologist. Sometime later his friend found him radiating with happiness and asked him whether he had been cured and he answered, "Oh, no, but now I like to do it." Of course no serious psychologist would lead a client to such a cheap solution, to a yes to ourselves that would cost nothing. It is the same as with, let us say, the Internal Revenue Service. We might like to accept our view of our income tax return, but this does not help us any if the tax collector does not agree. Our view is not valid as long as the tax collector thinks that our view is much too optimistic. Similarly, we may have a very optimistic view of our way of life. Twenty times over we may accept ourselves and our ways and tell ourselves that other people are much worse, but as long as God is not convinced by our reasoning, it does not help us.

What the Bible tells us about David is quite different. David's yes to himself was a yes in the presence of God, and therefore it was not a cheap yes. He accepted himself, but as God saw him. Therefore his was a costly yes but a yes that was valid: "Yes, I have sinned against the Lord." Without this yes we will never be able to hear what God wants to say to us, nor will we be able to speak to our brother with the fraternal love with which Nathan spoke to David.

All the beautiful clichés with which David had excused himself broke into pieces in the presence of God, and in this presence all his fine reasoning that somebody must fight in the first rank and why not Uriah, or that somebody must do the dirty work and why not the foreigners, was no longer plausible. Who knows whether God is much more interested in the suffering of one foreign laborer or one man of the so-called wrong color than in the whole established economic system of a nation or in the success of a well-run firm. David begins to learn that it is indeed so.

David's yes to himself was a costly yes. It was not simply a confession of sins repeated every Sunday as part of a liturgy, which costs nothing at all—not even a bit of thinking, because it comes automatically. A sentence like David's—"I have sinned against the Lord"—cannot simply be learned by heart and repeated whenever it seems appropriate, or even by mere force of habit. One must practice such a statement. David has to suffer under God's punishment. His son fell ill and died, and the whole time David, in his grief and misery, was fasting and sleeping on the bare floor. His confession of sin was not a cheap one; he accepted God's way and took the consequences.

"And Nathan said to David, 'The Lord also has put away your sin; you shall not die!'" (v. 13b). Here we see into the innermost circle of what happens when God encounters a person in such a way that the person is able to see himself in the light of God. In that moment, God's freeing judgment takes place. The German word *richten* means both to judge and to set right. Indeed, nothing less than God's judgment is able to set us right—definitely and eternally right. This is what happened to David: God set him right. This meant real freedom—not a freedom that we try to give to ourselves by using standards that are not too strict and by taking comfort in the fact that others are even worse than us. This is the freedom that is valid for eternity, because it is God who grants it to us.

IV. *"Then Nathan went home"* (v. 15a). No, the Word of God is not always available, not always at our disposal. It has its hour, and there is also always the hour when it has passed. Then the decisive question is whether we have listened to it in such a way that it goes with us from that moment on, through the months and years of our lives, into all of the many nonreligious but concrete and practical encounters with other people, with our families and our employees, with other classes and races, with other political systems and foreign nations. This is not simply a question put to individuals; there might also be a time for a whole church to listen to God's Word, which seeks the church's understanding, its anger, its evaluation of itself in the light of this Word, its conversion and action. Here too there might be a time when this Word has passed.

David heard the Word of God so that it began to change his life. We read that he learned to "console" his wife. That is to say, he learned to see other people in their own right, to understand how they felt, and to realize how they suffered.

He learned more than that. "Then David comforted his wife, Bathsheba, and went in to her and lay with her" (v. 24a). So seriously did he take the promise of his God that he slept with the very woman for whom he had sent Uriah into the war and to his death. It would be blasphemy if he did not do whatever was in his power to do, to help those who had to suffer from his crime. If he had not done that, he would not have heard the Word of forgiveness and of justification, because God's word of justification is always a creative word, bringing our whole person under its sway. Just as it is impossible to hear music or to read a love letter in an understanding way without being moved by it, so it is impossible to hear God's

Word of forgiveness without being shaped by it in the whole of our lives, in our thoughts and acts and feelings. This is what happened to David. God's word of justification gave him back his peace and his serenity—so much so that he slept with his wife.

V. *"And she bore a son, and he called his name Solomon. And the Lord loved him"* (v. 24b). Whenever we want to know what justification means, we are to read this verse again and again. I think it was Kierkegaard who once formulated, "Justification means that God makes what we have done in our wicked ways better than it would have been if we had done it well." This is what happens here. Even when this story was written down, the author knew that on this night was born the one from whose descendants the Messiah would come—the descendant of David and Bathsheba and of their son Solomon. This is God's end of the story, and it goes so unbelievably far beyond all that one could hope for. This is what God's forgiveness and justification mean: if we are able to listen to his Word so that it begins to alter and form our whole lives, God's justification begins to change our sinful deeds into his acts of blessing and help.

This is so because only those who are able to accept God's verdict will be able to give, to help, to grant liberty, to promote social improvement without patronizing. This is the unique opportunity of the Church, that she knows of the Word of justification that liberates us from all patronizing and conceit, and from all paralyzing inferiority complexes. It might be one of the urgent tasks of the Church today to lead the world to the serenity of the justified King David, which was founded on the knowledge of being accepted. Perhaps the Church has to believe and pray for the world in order to be able to communicate such serenity, which alone makes us free from all sense of guilt, which leads to inhibition and inactivity, and free from all superiority, by which we humiliate the receivers of our gifts. Maybe this is how God's justification by faith will become meaningful even outside the group of believers.

What finally came out of David's crime? Mark tells us, "And as he sat at table in his house, many tax collectors and sinners were sitting with Jesus and his disciples, for there were many who followed him" (Mark 2:15). It is the outcasts with whom Jesus sat, eating and drinking. Today he means all the outcasts of the world—all those of a different creed, color, race, or nation who are not accepted by the established society. He means all the poor—the individuals and groups, the classes and nations—who are not accepted by the rich. It is those who meet Sunday afternoon where other people do not meet, somewhere under the trees, at the seashore, or in the central railway stations of the big cities in Europe, isolated from the society meeting in the marketplace, in luxurious restaurants and at fashionable cocktail parties. It is with them that Jesus ate and drank. He did not preach to them, did not even speak to them of the Kingdom of God or of sin and forgiveness; but they realized that in his being with them God himself broke vehemently into their lives. In the company of Jesus, God became real in the year 28 A.D. In the company of the disciples of Jesus, God also became real that year, in much the same way. It is only those who have learned to go the way of David who will be able to radiate a bit of this reality of God that overcomes all man-made separation.

We know something more. We know that the established society of Palestine of the year 28 or 30 A.D. did not endure this behavior of Jesus. They felt how much it attacked them and their ways of life. Hence they nailed this troublemaker to a cross, and they did it well enough that he could not come down and trouble them again. But in this very way he began to trouble them and to trouble all those who are too well established and who too easily forget the sufferings of others; for Jesus did not go the way of the rich man in Nathan's story, who slaughtered the lamb of the poor neighbor. Instead, he went the way of the poor man, or rather, the way of the lamb that was slaughtered: "Behold, the Lamb of God, who takes away the sin of the world" (John 1:29). And whosoever wants to become his disciple will have to learn to be ready to go Jesus' way.

BIBLE STUDY II

BY EDUARD SCHWEIZER

Topic: The Young and the Old
TEXT: Luke 15:11–32; Hosea 2:1–3:5

This is a very strange story. The situation, however, is not strange; we can easily understand it. There are strong tensions, even conflicts between the older and the younger generation—between father and son and between elder and younger brothers. This is what we all know all too well. Everywhere in the world, youngsters go their own way, no longer according to the standards that an older generation has set. Impatiently they want to try out new ways and are no longer ready to wait for slow progress, as advised by an older generation. We also know young nations impatiently waiting for their new place in the world, and we know of older nations reluctantly yielding to the younger ones. We know well how many tensions and struggles are caused by these facts in our families, our tribes, our schools. We know particularly well how explosive the situation has grown in some parts of the world where older and younger nations are living side by side. All of this is understandable and not strange at all.

The strange part of the story is as follows: At the end of the story there is this elder brother who was so totally right that everything he said was dreadfully correct: "Lo, these many years I have served you, and I never disobeyed your command; yet you never gave me a kid, that I might make merry with my friends. But when this son of yours came, who has devoured your living with harlots, you killed for him the fatted calf!" (29–30). What the elder brother said was true. Whatever way you look at it, he was right. Twelve hours of labor every day, three hundred days a year equals a minimum of 3,600 hours of labor; and it might have been five years since the day the younger brother left the house of the father to throw away all his father's money for drink and women—which makes about 20,000 hours of hard work. On the other side of the equation, there was not even an occasional kid, let alone festivities with veal and steak and old wine. Right he was, this elder one—perfectly right. Yet at the end of the story he stayed outside the father's house. In all his rightness he was far from the banquet and the old wine and the dances. He was far from his father.

At the beginning of the story there was the younger brother. He was certainly not quite as right as his elder brother was, yet we can understand him. He was eager to see life as it was, not merely the sheltered area of his father's farm. He wanted to see the world—and the world is what he saw! That the world was not so wonderful as he had thought it would be, that there were also very bad experiences in store for him, is not surprising. We all know that this is so, and that, as we say in German, one usually does not eat the food as hot as it is served. But the surprising part of the story is that the younger son realized this, that he did not stick to his view, that he learned something. Some years earlier he had not cared a bit for his father's advice, but he did now. He was no longer so sure that he was right and had always been right. The wild younger brother, with all his revolutionary ideas, who had done so much damage to the father's well-run business, was, at the end of the story, sitting at the banquet in the father's house, eating meat to his heart's desire, drinking the best wine, and dancing merrily.

Shall we start with a look at this younger son? The father gave him plenty of rope; he did not even try to keep him back, although he well knew how extremely difficult it would be for his son and how great would be the danger of losing him for good. He knew that it was impossible to win the love of his son without giving him full freedom—freedom to live in strange and dangerous and painful ways. This is exactly how God acts, setting an example for how we should act with our brothers and sisters, or with our brother and sister nations. This is the first miracle that Jesus, who knew his Father in heaven better than any man on earth, told about in this story. God is the one who gives us full freedom—freedom also to live in strange and dangerous and painful ways. This is the cause of our full responsibility in our personal lives, in our families, in our churches, in our nations—for our individual, social, and political problems. We have to decide, we have to choose, we have to dare to go in the way we consider the right one, and to let others go their own ways. There is no God who could serve as an oracle whenever we wish to consult him. Even more, when his young son went to seed, far away from the father, the father did not call in the police to bring him home. Jesus could have told a story like this, but he did not do so because he knew his Father in heaven too well. He knew that God had decided to win our love and that it would not help to force us to acknowledge his power. It is not so simple that God just sends the police, that he punishes us as soon as we go astray so that we quickly knuckle under his rule, like boys who have tasted the rod so often that they obey like puppets. God is no old-fashioned, harsh schoolmaster; instead, he seeks the free obedience of children who love him. This is God's suffering; he must let us go our own way, he must suffer with us when we go in wrong ways full of pain for ourselves, our families, our churches, our nations, and our world. The father in Jesus' story had the power to call in the police and they would have brought his son home within a fortnight. The only thing that hindered him from doing so was his love for his son, a love that knew that he would win his son only if and when his son returned by his own free will. Therefore no policeman went after the son on his straying ways—only the heart of his father followed him, full of a burning love. Therefore no angel goes behind us, punishing us after each step we take in a wrong direction. It is only the heart of the father, burning with love, that follows us step by step, waiting, always waiting, for our love. Therefore we must go our own ways, we must accept responsibilities, we must make decisions, as we all do. Therefore we must go along with other people, with political parties and groups that fight for social aims. It is at this point that we see one vital difference between Christians and non-Christians. The former know of the heart of our Father and of his burning love. Hence, they will feel time and time again what God's love expects from them, and they can no longer presuppose that they will always be right. Suddenly they will be where they must say no, even if they have gone along with others for a long way. Remember that it was not the righteous elder brother but the wild revolutionary younger one who realized that he was not always right just because he tried to go his own new, untraditional way.

But let us now look at the elder brother. Here the parable of Jesus becomes even more urgent, because it ends with the question put to this elder son about whether or not he still belonged to the house of the father. This is the same question that Jesus puts to us when he leaves us at the end of his story. The elder son was a righteous son; he lived close to his father in the traditional way. This was not wrong. One can accept one's responsibilities and can make one's decisions in different ways—in a usual or unusual way, in a cautious or daring way. God gives us various gifts and various tasks. Some of us must go on revolutionary new roads, some must go on traditional, well-known tracks. This is not the problem in this parable. The problem is precisely the rightness of the elder son. There came a time when the younger son became more and more uncertain as to whether his new ideas were really always right. It was so much more difficult for the righteous elder son to see that, because his course was the generally accepted one with which everybody had always agreed. This was how his father and grandfather had lived. Why should he be wrong?

Why indeed? What did he say about his younger brother? "He has devoured your living with harlots." Now, I wonder how he knew that. Jesus, at least, said only that "he squandered his property in loose living." His righteous brother painted the picture just a trifle blacker. And what did he say about himself? "I have never disobeyed your command." Now, I wonder whether this "never" was not a bit too strong, whether he really remembered every instance over those many years, or was the righteous son perhaps not a trifle too righteous? And what did he say about his father? "You never gave me a kid." Had he really forgotten that everything that was his father's was also his property? Is it really credible that he never made merry with his friends? Or was he exaggerating just a trifle? Nevertheless, on the whole he was no doubt right. On the whole, we are very often right.

There is a husband who insults his wife like a madman because she is again expecting a child from him. All the world sees is just the effective and successful husband, and nobody knows about the quiet and inconspicuous wife. Is she not right, right without any doubt, when she complains of her husband and thinks that nobody could live with such a man?

Some desperate students in a university hospital destroyed the whole card index of all the patients so that all the cards had to be renewed in a long and difficult process because otherwise the patients could not be treated adequately. The doctors were doubtless right when they got extremely angry.

There are certainly also young nations trying to take the first steps on their way of independent existence and making mistakes, and all the older nations watching them are right when pointing to some actual mistakes. All this is correct. On the whole, we are very often right.

There is but one flaw in our reasoning. It was the righteous elder son, who on the whole was probably right, who in Jesus' story was left alone outside the father's house, and it was his younger brother, with all his mistakes and vices, who was sitting in the banquet hall. The question that Jesus puts to us at the end of his parable is not a question put to wild and uncontrollable young people but a question put to righteous people who on the whole are right. Why was the elder brother left outside? He was so righteous and impartial that he did not lie, yet he exaggerated and falsified the story just a trifle, and this was the decisive trifle. There are overtones in his description of the case that show that he was totally incapable of understanding his brother.

Is God's aim today to warn not just the wild, the revolutionary, and the young, but also the older ones among us, the righteous, those who on the whole are quite right in their criticism? This is indeed the question at the end of the story with which Jesus leaves us alone: Are you not also righteous, also incapable of understanding others in their not so righteous ways? Jesus' story that invites us in such an incredible way into the open banquet hall of God, that incites us to joy and happiness, could become the most terrible damnation if we do not hear this question, if we simply go on our righteous way without really seeing the problems and wants of our younger siblings.

The question is whether we who are so correct in our traditional theology may not become the elder brothers of younger groups that do not always conform with the established church or society or world policy. May we who are so correct in our section reports and assembly statements not become the elder brothers of our younger brothers who are living in incomparably more difficult situations than we are?

What do we do? Very often, instead of letting Jesus' parable accuse us, we start accusing God. We ask, Where is God in this world of turmoil and injustice? Where is this God whom the Bible says is love? Patients and wives and whole nations are suffering because of the mistakes and wild ideas of others, and God does not step in. Is God dead? Where is God indeed?

"His father came out and entreated him." Here he was, this father. He was with his elder son and his outrage and accusations. He was with him as he was in his heart day by day with his younger son when that one went to seed, entertaining prostitutes and feeding swine. No, the father was not in the banquet hall in luxury and comfort; the father was where his lost and outraged son was. What did Jesus say? Did we hear correctly? He said that God is not in a golden heaven, in which all problems are solved, far away from the turmoil and all the misery and wretchedness of the world. He said that God is there where a man doubts and rebels against him and other people.

This is, perhaps, the most moving part of Jesus' story. In some way the father in the story was totally helpless; he was not an almighty father. To be sure, if he wanted to he could exercise all his power. It would be very easy to call two servants and drag his son into the house. But this father had decided to love, to seek nothing less than the hearts of his children. Therefore he stayed outside the banquet hall. He could state nothing but his word, for love and joy cannot be forced on anybody. Into this word he put all his love, his graciousness, his readiness to do whatever would help his son. But because he had decided to wait for the heart of his son, to wait for his son to come in of his own free will, he had nothing but this free will, nothing but this word. It was exactly the same with his younger son when he had gone astray; the father had nothing but his burning love and his word of welcome as he waited for the return of the prodigal son, as he was now waiting for the return of the righteous son.

Some centuries before, the prophet had sung God's song of love to his people Israel: "Plead with your mother, plead—for she is not my wife, and I am not her husband—that she put away her harlotry from her face and her adultery from between her breasts, lest I strip her naked and make her as in the day she was born, and make her like a wilderness, and set her like a parched land, and slay her with thirst" (Hosea 2:2–3 RSV). But Israel did not listen. She thought she had earned all her wealth herself, that it was her merit, her skill, her hard work that had made her a well-developed country. "For she said, 'I will go after my lovers, who give me my bread and my water, my wool and my flax, my oil and my drink.' . . . And she did not know that it was I who gave her the grain, the wine, and the oil, and who lavished upon her silver and gold which they used for Ba'al" (2:5b and 8). Thus God had to go with her through hard and merciless times that showed her how utterly uncertain her standard of life was. "Therefore I will take back my grain in its time, and my wine in its season; and I will take away my wool and my flax, which were to cover her nakedness. . . . Now I will uncover her lewdness in the sight of her lovers, and no one shall rescue her out of my hand. . . . And I will lay waste her vines and her fig trees, of which she said, 'These are my hires, which my lovers have given me.' I will make them a forest, and the beasts of the field shall devour them" (2:9, 10, 12). So concrete, so real, so serious is God's Word of life that it might destroy whatever we are so proud of, that it might mean war and famine and misery. Yet even so, it is still his Word of love. It cannot force us to accept him, it can but wait for us. "Therefore, behold, I will allure her and bring her into the wilderness, and speak tenderly to her. . . . And there I will give her her vineyards, and make the Valley of Achor a door of hope. And there she shall answer as in the days of her youth, as at the time when she came out of the land of Egypt. . . . And I will betroth you to me for ever; I will betroth you to me in right-eousness and in justice, in steadfast love, and in mercy. . . . I will betroth you to me in faithful-ness; and you shall know the Lord" (2:14, 15, 19, 20). So incredibly serious is this Word of God's love that it had to become flesh in the life of his prophet, for the sake of Israel. "And the Lord said to me, 'Go again, love a woman who is beloved of a paramour and is an adulteress; even as the Lord loves the people of Israel, though they turn to other gods and love cakes of raisins'" (3:1).

The seriousness of this Word of God's love is even more unbelievable. The Word is not merely of the prophet but of God himself, in the life of whose Son the Word became flesh to call us, to call us back to God's festival meal. Just then its total helplessness became obvi-ous. The people cried, "Where is God?" and looked up to the sky and thought of some golden heaven and a throne with God seated on it. They supposed that he should sit there and play policeman and step in with brutal force when so many outrageous things happen on Earth—when husbands oppress their wives, when children drive their parents to despair, when employers exploit their employees, when nations rebel, and . . . and . . . and. But the Word of God had long ago become flesh and was, in its total helplessness, hanging just above them on a cross and did not descend in a miraculous way. Instead it did nothing but invite, even in its silence, and call us and tell us about the burning love of the Father. This is the power-lessness of God, who is not content with less than our hearts. One may call, invite, even entice to love, but one can never force it on anybody. To be sure, we may tell John, "Listen, my boy, if you behave as you did last time and refuse the welcome kiss to auntie, you will learn it the hard way," and John will probably behave and dutifully kiss his aunt. Love, how-ever, will not be in the kiss. This is God's helplessness, that he decided to create a world in order to share his bliss and joy with creatures that would love him from their hearts, because it is only in the freedom of our hearts that we are able to love and praise and find real joy.

Yet this seemingly helpless Word of God, even nailed to a cross and, as everybody thought, reduced to a deadly and definite silence, is still speaking. It is something like the balance in a clock, which keeps the world on the move. It speaks in Jesus, as it spoke in the prophets for centuries and centuries. It reaches us today, all of us, who might be so dreadfully right in our complaints. It says, "Son, you are always with me and all that is mine is yours." Indeed, we may not have realized it but this is what God means. He has given us his creation to use. We are free to use it or to abuse it. This is our freedom, with all its dangers and all its almost inconceivable hope. And God tells us, "You should make merry and be glad." This is what God invites us to do, this God who is helplessly nailed to a cross yet still inviting us to the banquet.

Let us not forget Jesus' question, which comes to us now with double force from his cross.

God's decisive question is still waiting for us: Do we want to be with him or not? The elder son was standing a few inches from the father, yet he was miles away from him in his heart—the elder son, the one who was so totally right, as right as we may be. Yet in all his rightness he was so far from the father. It is his calculating and arguing that separated him from the father. The people who stood under the cross were perhaps more right than we have been. Doubtless there were Jews who did not care for the laws of God and who behaved in a shocking way. There were also pious ones—for instance, the Pharisees—who donated 10 percent of their income to God every week. But just by being so right they could no longer understand Jesus, who ate and drank with tax collectors and sinners. And in their total righteousness they crucified him.

God does not ask us to become blind to the mistakes and faults of others. If we are right in our criticism, why not utter it? If we have a better idea for solving problems, why not fight for it? There is only one thing only God demands from us: that we may learn to love. I even think that this is the meaning of all life on Earth, even of all the suffering in it: that we learn to love—to love God, whose heart is waiting behind all the wild oats we sow and burning with love. For if we learn this love, we are in the banquet hall of the father, and there we shall meet our younger brother, who is maybe not quite so perfect as we are, perhaps not even by far.

But you see, if we have really learned what the love of the Father means, then it will be absolutely impossible for us to go on adding up all our righteous deeds and all the correct decisions we have made. Then we will learn to tell the story of our younger brother with a loving heart, just changing it a trifle—that decisive trifle—in his favor, because we have understood his misery and his needs. Then we shall learn to understand the younger generation and much of its unrest and its not-always-right ideas. Is it the meaning of all life, and even of all suffering in our world, that we learn to love—to love God and therefore also our sometimes strange younger brothers? I think it is.

PREACHING ON LOVE

BY ROGER LOVETTE

Topic: The Setting of Our Heart
TEXT: 1 Cor. 12:27–31

When Paul sat down in Ephesus to write to his troubled friends in Corinth, he faced a world much like our own. It was a hard time. The divisions were deep. Relationships were frazzled. Fear was in the air. Morality was uncertain. A multitude of pagan faiths converged in that time. Slavery and poverty were everywhere. Great gaps separated the rich and the poor.

In the hard soil of secular Corinth, Paul sowed the seeds of the gospel and planted a church. The first converts came from the city's lowest rungs of society. Some were slaves. Others were poverty stricken wage earners. Yet there were some of great affluence. The city treasurer, Erastus, joined the church. Chloe, a woman of means, and Crispus, who had been president of the synagogue, came into the fold. After eighteen months, under great pressure from the Jews, Paul left Corinth.

It was only after his departure that trouble erupted in that congregation. The congregation's members mirrored the troubled times in the world around them. They disagreed on leadership. There were sexual problems. Members sued one another in the civil courts. They haggled about idols, the role of women, doctrine. They were divided along class lines and almost everything else.

Could they survive? It is an old question. Can we survive shootings in public schools, ineffective leaders in public life, and culture wars over doctrine, social issues, and church direction?

What happened at Corinth was nothing short of a miracle. In the shabbiest of churches with the shabbiest of problems, in the shabbiest of times, Paul put pen to paper and began to write. "Though I speak with the tongues of men and of angels . . . but have not love. . . ." These words would become the glue that would mold the members into a fellowship so strong that nothing could break its power.

Paul began the roll call in the twelfth chapter with an enormous challenge: "Set your hearts on the best spiritual gifts." His antidote for a troubled time and a troubled church was the gift called love. He gave the congregation a vision of a caring that would keep them together and mend their differences, a dream that would send them out into the world different, better prepared for whatever would come.

The challenge of Corinth is a challenge to the Church in our time. That challenge is to set our hearts on a vision so great that nothing can stop its power.

First Corinthians hammers out what this dream of love would mean to a troubled church in a troubled time. To love would mean to care—to care for one another, to put the interests

PREACHING ON LOVE 367

of that little troubled church above one's own interests, to love the world. Paul said that this is the most practical way we can all love God.

The members were to keep that love specific and concrete. They would begin with one another, where they were. They would begin to reach out to the people whose names they already knew. They would touch the needs close at hand. The list would be long but pointed.

When you were little someone may have given you a magnet. You may have taken some metal shavings or some paper clips and placed them on a piece of paper. You may have placed the magnet underneath the paper and a strange thing would have occurred. Those bits and pieces of metal filings or those paper clips would have come together into a whole with a pattern of unity. If you had moved the magnet around, the metal filings would have followed it. If you had taken the magnet away, the pattern would have fallen into its separate parts.

So the apostle Paul, in writing to a splintered, fragmented congregation in Corinth, remembered his days before the Damascus Road experience. He remembered that the Great Magnet had reached down into the broken, cluttered pieces of his life and formed a wholeness. Years later he wrote to his splintered friends in that splintered congregation surrounded by a splintered world, "You set your hearts on the best spiritual gifts, and I will show you a way that surpasses them all." Paul knew that what had happened to him could happen to the church and to the whole world. When we set our hearts on the love that cares, a great change takes place. The splintered fragments come together. The great magnet of love always does its great work.

Topic: What Matters Most
TEXT: 1 Cor. 13:1–3

Howard Thurman tells of a dream a man once had. In the dream the man was on a train. The train stopped and he found himself in a large city. It was early morning and snow covered the ground. As he left the train the man noticed that no one he met wore shoes. They were warmly dressed but the baggage man and the redcap wore no shoes. He thought this was odd for such a cold day. As he moved into the station he noticed that nobody had shoes on. Boarding a bus he saw that everyone on the bus was barefooted. When he arrived at his hotel, everyone he met was shoeless.

Finally he could restrain himself no longer and asked the manager about the practice. "What practice?" the manager said. "The practice of not wearing shoes. Nobody in this town wears shoes and it is very cold." The manager shrugged, "Ah, that's just it. Why don't we?" The man was persistent. "I don't understand. Why don't you wear shoes? Don't you believe in shoes?" The manager said, "Believe in shoes, indeed we do. This is the first article of our creed, shoes. Shoes are indispensable to the well-being of humanity. Why, shoes make things more comfortable. Not to speak of the cuts, sores, and suffering they prevent. Shoes really are wonderful." So the man asked, "Then why don't you wear them?" The manager sighed, "Ah, that's just it. Why don't we?"

After the man checked into his room he went down to the coffee shop and sat down next to a man who wore no shoes. The man was friendly. After the meal he told the stranger he would show him around the city. The first building they came to had a huge sign indicating that shoes were manufactured inside. The man did not understand: "You manufacture shoes there?" The host said, "Well, not exactly. We talk about making shoes. We have one of the most brilliant fellows to lead us you will ever meet. He's quite well known, really. Every week he talks convincingly and movingly about the great subject of shoes. He has enormous charisma. Just yesterday as he talked about wearing shoes people in the audience just broke down and wept. It was one of the greatest things I have ever seen." The man said, "But why don't you wear shoes?" And his guide said, "That's just it. Why don't we?"

They turned down a side street and through the window the man saw a cobbler making a pair of shoes in a shop. He excused himself from his guide and walked into the shop. He asked the shoemaker why his little shop was not overrun with customers. The cobbler said, "Nobody wants my shoes. They just want to talk about them."

The man bought what pairs of shoes the cobbler had and rushed out of the store. He handed one of the pairs to his host and said, "Put them on—you'll feel so much better on this cold day."

The man drew back in embarrassment. He thanked the stranger and shook his head. "You just don't understand, do you. This just is not done. The best people in town would never wear shoes."

The stranger thought he was going mad. "But why don't people in this town wear shoes?" And the tour guide smiled and said, "Ah, that's just it. Why don't we?"

As the stranger left the town, one question kept ringing in his ears: "Why don't we? Why don't we wear shoes?"

Paul could have had that dream about Corinth. Located in a thriving metropolis and surrounded by people from the world over, the little church at Corinth merely floundered. They haggled about everything: sexual conduct, marriage, rich and poor, and what was most important to the church. They met Sunday after Sunday. Often they were moved to tears when the gospel was preached. Yet somehow their lives never changed. They were in utter shambles.

So Paul took up his pen and wrote, "Strive for the greater gifts and I will show you a more excellent way." Adolph Harnack calls the following words the greatest, strongest, and deepest thing Paul ever wrote: "If I speak in the tongues of mortals and of angels but do not have love. . . ."

So the apostle called his friends back to what mattered most. He knew that if they could set their priorities straight, their lives could be ordered in a way that would last.

There is a correlation between the people in the shoeless town, the people in Corinth, and the people of our own time. Paul put his finger on the pulse when he wrote, "If I speak about love but do not have love, it means nothing."

Like the people in that shoeless town, we too confuse faith with words. Neil Postman says in *Amusing Ourselves to Death* that we have reached the point where cosmetics has replaced ideology as the field of expertise over which a politician must have competent control. "Consequently," he writes, "we spend more time with hair dryers than we do scripts."

Paul moved beyond cosmetology. He talked of a doing that would change people's hearts and the world. Not tongues, not eloquence, not prophetic powers or understanding or even knowledge, not even faith, the generosity of giving, or even great sacrifice was enough.

Every gift Paul mentioned is a necessary part of the faith journey. Yet none of these gifts is the main thing. Three times Paul challenges, us in those first three verses, to love. The word is *love*.

In another place he said, "By love all shall know that we are his disciples." Not steeples, not the book, not worship—the centerpiece for Corinth and for us all is love.

Agape love is the glue that holds it all together. It is not this endless talk about love; it is this endless doing of the will of God.

The man who dreamed he was in a city without shoes kept asking the same question over and over, "Why don't we? Why don't we?" This was Paul's great challenge to Corinth: Why don't we love?

Topic: Love Is a Verb
TEXT: 1 Cor. 13:4–7

I have never known a church that did not have trouble with verbs. I have never known a conscientious Christian who didn't somehow have difficulty with the action words of faith.

Nouns have always come easily. *God, Father, Jesus, Holy Spirit, fellowship, cross, baptism, Lord's Supper, Bible, book, blessed hope.* We have battled long and hard over many of these nouns, but they have come easily for most of us.

The adjectives have come even more easily: *wonderful, great, spectacular, lovely, best, Spirit-filled, Bible-believing, verbally inspired, holy, sacred.*

But the verbs have always given us the most difficulty. Verbs connote action. They make things happen in a sentence. My freshman English teacher would say, "That's not a sentence— it doesn't have a verb." Long ago Paul wrote across the miles to Corinth. Like my old English teacher, he chided his friends at Corinth. What kind of a church do you really expect to be with only nouns and adjectives? You won't get anywhere without the verbs.

This is why it took the children of Israel forty years to travel a short distance of four hundred miles. They had difficulty with the verbs. The verbs are everywhere in the gospel: *come, follow me, take up your cross, give away what you have, build a tower, lay down your life, eat, drink, knock, ask, seek.*

The amazing thing about this love chapter is that Paul says over and over that love is a verb. In the Greek text, scholars tell us that *love* is used as a noun only three times in this long chapter. We also discover fifteen verbs in this passage. After the first verse, not a single descriptive adjective is used in the Greek. We encounter only verbs and verbal adjectives. And as Carlyle Marney has pointed out, all the verbs are verbs of relation.

Remember Paul's audience? They were divided and fragmented people. They could not agree on leaders: Paul, Apollos, Cephas. Members dragged one another into the law courts. Sexual sins were rampant in the congregation. Rich and poor did not get along. Jewish and Gentile Christians could not see eye to eye on anything.

So Paul, from Ephesus, took up his pen and began to write. You don't need any more nouns or adjectives. What you need are some action words to build a bridge across the chasms that divide you from one another. Paul believed that this single verb, *love*, had the power to reshape the broken, splintered body in Corinth.

In writing to Corinth, Paul wrote about the specific needs he had encountered in the eighteen months he had served as their pastor. This is what he remembered:

Love is patient and kind.

Love is not jealous or boastful.

Love is not arrogant or rude.

Love does not insist on its own way.

Love is not irritable or resentful.

Love does not rejoice at the wrong but rejoices in the right.

And then, if all that had gone before was not enough, he ends with the incredible verbs: Love *bears* all things, *believes* all things, *hopes* all things, *endures* all things. These verbs are comprehensive. Over and over Paul writes in large letters: ALL THINGS.

Paul would not let his friends off the hook. Love is not something we feel; it is something we do. Every parent knows there are nights when you pad down some dark hall to get a little one a drink of water or change a diaper. You'd rather be sleeping. Who feels warm and mushy at three o'clock in the morning? There is a need and you respond. You do something. A father sits down at the end of the month and writes out a check, sometimes many checks: piano lessons. doctor bills, a new dress, college tuition, a pair of shoes, long-distance telephone calls. He may have a headache and there may not be enough in the checking account for that stack of bills, but he scribbles out a date and an amount and signs his name. Why? Because love is something you do. There is no romance in telephone bills and Visa receipts, but the father knows deep in his heart that love bears, believes, hopes, and endures all things.

Christ did not enjoy touching the leper. The body stank. Infection was a possibility. The man's flesh rotted. His face may have been horribly disfigured. But Jesus touched him and it changed his life. Love is what we do.

Paul reminded his friends that love is not a noun or an adjective. Love is a verb. This was Corinth's task and ours as well: to march back into whatever commitments are ours. We will bear all things, we will believe all things, we will hope all things, and we will endure all things. It is never what we say; that will come later. Love is what we do.

Topic: The Gift That Does Not Fail
TEXT: 1 Cor. 13:8–13

One of the characters in the play *Inherit the Wind* tells of something that happened to him as a little boy. He would stand outside the general store and dream of the rocking horse that stood in the window of that shop. The horse's name was Golden Dancer. The boy said that Golden Dancer became his fantasy. He was seven years old and a very fine judge of rocking horses. He began to say, "If I had Golden Dancer I would have everything I would ever want." The rocking horse had a bright red mane, blue eyes, and was gold all over with purple spots. The boy said that when the sun hit the horse's stirrups, she was a dazzling sight to see. But the boy's family was poor, and though they knew he wanted that rocking horse, they could not afford it. Yet one birthday he woke up and there was Golden Dancer at the foot of his bed. He couldn't believe that his dream had come true. He said he jumped on the rocking horse and began to rock, and a terrible thing happened. It broke. It split in two. The wood was rotten. The whole thing was put together with spit and sealing wax. The boy said, "Bert, whenever you see something bright, shining, perfect-seeming, all gold with purple spots, look beneath the paint! And if it's a lie, show it up for what it really is!"

When Paul wrote to the Corinthians, he wanted to give them something that would last. First Corinthians 13 is about the rocking horses we have longed for all our lives. Paul talked about the transience of so many things. The rocking horses of much of our lives will not endure. Only these remain: faith, hope, and above all, *love*. Paul said that love was the gift that would not fail.

Everybody has a need to be taken into the circle of love. Corinth was falling apart because the congregation had tried to sustain themselves with golden things with purple spots. It did not work. Tongues of men and angels, prophetic powers, understanding all mysteries, knowledge, faith that could even remove mountains, giving that was generous, even the offering up of one's life—Paul said that there is only one gift that will endure. That gift is love.

Love is primary because we all need love. Studies show that infants die in hospitals not because of lack of nourishment but because no one holds them, touches or cares for them; no one loves them. Children shrivel up and die when love is absent. Of one of the characters in *Les Miserables* the doctor says, "He is very, very sick." "What is the matter?" someone asks. "He has all the appearances of someone who has lost a friend. People die of that."

We keep reading *Beauty and the Beast* because when the beautiful princess kisses the ugly beast a miracle takes place. The ugliness disappears. That story touches something primal in all of us. Without love and caring and recognition we cannot survive. No wonder Paul said that love has no equal.

But if the Corinthians were to take in love, they were also to give out love. Not everyone could preach like Apollos. Not everyone had the disposition for unknown tongues. Not everyone could be rich. But like the rocking horse with the bright red mane and the purple spots, these are not essentials.

The preacher said the primary gift is love. The acid test for the faithful stops right here. "By this they will know that we are his disciples, if we love one another." To invest ourselves in some cause bigger than we are, we are never diminished. We stand taller. We give away chunks of ourselves, and miraculously we are the recipients.

One of the great voices of the twentieth century was Marian Anderson. Once she went to Russia to sing. Before she went she was told she could sing no religious songs, no spirituals. But Miss Anderson was a stubborn woman. She said, "If I sing, I sing what I choose. The repertoire remains." Reluctantly they agreed to her conditions. The night of the concert she ended her performance with a medley of Negro spirituals. After she walked off stage and the pianist left, there was pounding and clapping and it sounded as if the whole building would be torn apart. Marian said, "What in the world is going on there?" A Russian woman said, "Come back on the stage and see." Marian came out and all the people who were in the back had poured toward the front, those who were near the front had come closer to the stage, and they all stood around the base of the platform, clapping and pounding the stage and saying in broken English, "Deep River!" "Nobody Knows the Trouble I've Seen!" "Amazing Grace!" They were asking her to sing again some of the spirituals she was not supposed to sing. She stood there and sang in a language they did not understand, but it was a language and a melody that transcended all barriers and all language. She had touched a universal note. The note was love. No wonder Paul said that love is the word that knows no equal.

CHILDREN'S SERMONS

January 7: God Watches Over You
TEXT: Ps. 92:5
Song: "I Need Thee Every Hour"
Object: Clock

Hello, boys and girls. Aren't you glad you came to church today?

Perhaps this object I'm holding in my hand helped you get ready for church? [*Show children the clock and move the hands to several numbers.*] As you know, this is called a clock. A clock has a minute hand, an hour hand, and an alarm button. Will someone tell me why a clock is important? [*Pause for response.*] Yes, a clock helps us get up on time in the morning. Your family may eat breakfast, lunch, and dinner at a certain time. Perhaps you have to be inside from outdoor play at a specific time, and you go to bed at night at another hour. We could say our family needs a clock to live by.

Just like a clock is important for living, Jesus is important for our daily lives. Let us name some ways Jesus takes care of boys and girls throughout the hours on the face of this clock. Will someone tell me how Jesus watches over you? [*Allow time for response.*] Yes, he gives us rest at night. He watches over us when we play. He gives us parents to provide love, food, clothing, and a home.

Throughout this week, thank God for his care over you as you sleep, play, and go to school, and in all parts of your life. Remember, God's clock never stops. He is always there. He wants us to live a happy, healthy life.

[*Read Psalm 92:1: "How great are your works, O Lord, how profound your thoughts!" (NIV). Ask the pianist to softly play "I Need Thee Every Hour" as the children return to their seats.*]—Carolyn Tomlin

January 14: Prayer Is Our Connection to God
TEXT: Matt. 7:7
Object: A cell phone

This cell phone is a convenient way to keep personal connections open. Cell phones can be taken in the car or carried to the grocery store. These phones are intended for two-way communication, that is, both persons can talk and listen to each other.

God has granted prayer as a way of staying in touch with him. We don't need any special equipment. All we need is our faith and knowledge that he wants us to talk with him. We can bow our heads and talk to God wherever and whenever we chose to do so. When our friends are not at home, our telephone calls to their homes go unanswered. God is always ready to take your call to him. Listen to this verse. [*Read Matt. 7:7.*]

We must see prayer as a marvelous privilege. God has opened a way for us to talk to him through the salvation that we have in Jesus Christ. The Lord has promised that we can ask for whatever our needs are. Now, prayer is not like magic. God answers the prayers that are good for us and his Kingdom. If we pray for something that is not appropriate, God does not grant what we wish because he loves us. When we pray correctly we are praying according to God's will. That means we are not asking for things that are good only for us but for things that are good for God and everybody else in the world, too.

Prayer is also a way of listening to God. The best way to hear from God is to read the Bible. But prayer is a way of having a two-way conversation with the Creator of the universe. So we shouldn't just hurry into our prayers asking for this and asking for that. Sometimes we just need to be quiet and still. God is able to impress on us what he wants us to know when we are quiet in his presence.

Cell phones are very handy. If your family owns one you have noticed how much it is used. We need to be able to say the same thing about our prayers. We need to take advantage of the privilege of prayer and pray often. God is waiting to hear your voice. Be sure to pray to him today so he can know you are trusting in him.—Ken Cox

January 21: Saying Nice Things to Others
TEXT: 1 Thess. 5:11; Ps. 30

I want to say some nice things to you. I want you to know that I really like this time with you. I look forward to seeing you up here with me. I love your smiles and your laughter. Your dresses and outfits are so pretty. Your hair looks so nice. I have fun with you and I am glad that you like to be here with me.

I want to tell you these things because I know it makes you feel good to hear me say them to you. I also want to tell you these things because I want to show how nice it is to make others feel good by saying nice things to them.

God uses the Bible to tell us that saying nice things to people is important. It makes them feel special. He also tells us that he likes us to say nice things to him, too. It makes God feel special. When you get home today, will you say something nice to each person who lives there with you? Will you help them to feel special? Let's tell God right now how much we love him and make him feel special too.—Michael Lanway

January 28: Getting the Dirt and Mud Off
TEXT: Rom. 3:23–24; Isa. 53:12

My little boy loves dirt. He really loves dirt when it gets wet and becomes mud, and he loves mud puddles, too. He is always out in the dirt, digging a hole, filling it back in, and digging it out again. He will ride his bike as fast as he can through a puddle so that the mud flies up on his bike and his pants.

But his mama does like dirt or mud, especially not on his clothes, and especially not in her house or on her floors. When she sees her little boy covered with dirt and mud, she makes him take off his clothes right at the door and then sends him to the shower. "And make sure you clean behind your ears too!" she yells. It is important for him to get clean or he will be in big trouble with his mama.

God wants us to be clean, too. That is why he gives us water and soap and mamas, so that we can get clean and stay clean. God knows that if we stayed dirty we could get sick from infections and other things. He doesn't want that to happen to us. He cares about us and wants us to take care of our bodies. Let's thank him for caring about our bodies and us.—Michael Lanway

February 4: A Heart as Hard as a Rock
TEXT: Mark 10:5
Object: A large rock

We describe love as if it comes from our hearts. That's why on Valentine's Day we give away cards with hearts on them. When someone is loving and kind we call them soft or tender-hearted. On the other hand, it is possible for a human heart to be as hard as this rock. A mean person's heart muscle isn't tough. It just means they don't show concern or kindness for others. Listen to this verse. [*Read Mark 10:5.*]

A hard heart doesn't happen overnight. Catching a stony heart occurs through many wrong steps. When unkind steps are taken, like breaking into line at school, calling people names, disobeying your parents, or saying curse words, your heart grows cold and tough. Step by step a heart grows hard, and most persons don't realize how harsh they have become.

The good news is that we can cultivate kind hearts. Because God is love and has a kind and tender heart, we become like the Lord when we develop loving hearts. We grow a kind heart by believing God's Word and planting seeds of kindness in the lives around us. For instance, if I share my M&M's with you, I know that I have been generous. When I do the right thing in obedience to God, I become happy with myself. People who have kind hearts are happy inside and glow with the joy of the Lord.

The Bible warns everyone to guard their heart because it is the wellspring of life (Ps. 4:23). In some special places in Arkansas there are springs where water flows out of the Earth. The water is bottled and sold everywhere because it is crystal clear and delicious. Our hearts are like a spring of water. If our hearts are hard, bad things will flow out of us as naturally as water pours out of a pitcher. If we have loving hearts, good deeds flow out and quench the thirst of a very cruel world.

We have a choice to make. We can make our hearts soft and loving, or hard and angry. I know you want to make the right choice so that goodness from God can flow out of your life.—Ken Cox

February 11: The Greatest Commandment
TEXT: Mark 12:29–30
Object: A valentine

Valentine's Day is this week. On Valentine's Day we give cards with hearts on them to the people we love. Who we love is very important. One day some men asked Jesus which commandment was the most important. Listen to this verse that contains Jesus' answer. [*Read Mark 12:29–30.*]

Jesus said that we are to love the Lord with all of our heart, mind, and strength. That is a very powerful love. We are to love God because he is worthy of our adoration. In the last book of the Bible, thousands upon thousands of angels in heaven are described as singing to Jesus. The words to the angel chorus mention that Jesus is worthy of their love.

I heard a man report once that he had gone fishing and had not caught a single fish. He said that his fishing trip was a lot of trouble. He bought minnows, sat in the boat for hours, and got painfully sunburned. He was very unhappy and said, "It just wasn't worth it!"

Believers who love Jesus never come to the conclusion that Jesus is not worth it. The more we love Jesus and show our devotion to him by keeping his commandments, the more convinced we become of Jesus' worth to us. A songwriter named Bill Gaither wrote a song with a chorus that says, "The longer I serve him the sweeter he grows." That means Bill Gaither is convinced more each day of the worth of loving Jesus. Another song contains the words, "Every day with Jesus is sweeter than the day before." These songs are just like the ones sung by the angel chorus that is described as singing in heaven.

When I was growing up I commented that I loved chocolate cake. My mother corrected me and said that we can only love people, not things. I wondered what she meant and have thought about her lesson often. If we love things, those objects will eventually disappoint us. Only people have eternal life. God is a person and so are we, created in his image. We can know and love God. It may seem hard at first because God is spirit and we are human. But if will try to love God, we will discover that we can. We will also learn, like those thousands of angels in heaven, that God is worth it.—Ken Cox

February 18: Jesus Loves You
Text: John 3:16
Song: "Jesus Loves Me"
Object: One large paper heart and enough small hearts for the children

Boys and girls, I'm holding an object that represents something else. Can you guess what this is? [*Pause for response.*] Yes, this is a large heart made of paper. This piece of paper is something we give a person we love very much. It represents our feelings and tells the other person we care. Have any of you received a heart such as this? [*Pause*] Or have any of you given a heart such as this to a friend or family member? [*Pause and allow children time to respond. Give each child a heart.*]

The Bible tells us that Jesus loves us very much too. He watches over us when we play. He guides our parents as they take care of us. He encourages our church teachers as they prepare to tell us about his love. Can you tell me other ways you know Jesus loves you? [*Allow children time to respond.*] Yes, those are good answers. Thank you for sharing.

Did you know that Jesus loves us so much that he died on the cross for our sins? Listen as I read John 3:16. "For God so loved the world that he gave his one and only Son, that whoever believes in him shall not perish but have eternal life" (NIV).

Would you do something for me when you return home today? Why don't you make a big heart for Jesus and place it in your home. Then every time you see that heart you will be reminded how much Jesus loves you.

[*Have the pianist play softly "Jesus Loves Me" as the children return to their seats.*]—Carolyn Tomlin

February 25: Getting the Rest We Need
TEXT: Matt. 11:28–30; Exod. 20:8–11

Do you ever take a nap? In kindergarten my teacher would give us milk and cookies around 2:00 P.M. We would eat the milk and cookies and listen to a story the teacher would read. Soon I would be yawning, and all the other boys and girls would be yawning, too. When that happened, the teacher would give each of us a small rug to lie on and a blanket to cover up with. We would lie there listening to the rest of her story until we fell asleep.

We all needed the rest, and the teacher was very kind to be sure we got it. She knew that when we were well rested, we would be better students and playmates. She was right.

God knows that we need rest and sleep. That is why there is nighttime, so we can sleep. That is why we can take naps, to rest during the day. In the Bible God tells us to take time to rest and to let him help us get it. He wants us to be strong while we work and study, and having the right amount of rest helps us be strong. He wants us to be careful when we work and study, and being well rested helps us protect ourselves. God wants us to trust him to give us all we need, and not to work and worry ourselves to death. Getting the right amount of rest shows we trust God to take care of us. Let's thank God for caring about us so much that he wants us to get the rest we need.—Michael Lanway

March 4: Conquering Fears
TEXT: Ps. 56:11
Song: "Trusting Jesus"
Object: Flashlight

Boys and girls, I'm holding something in my hand that you may have used on a dark night. [*Turn flashlight on and off several times.*] Being afraid of the dark is a fear some boys and girls experience. Can you name other things children are afraid of? [*Pause for response.*] Yes, those are real fears that others face, too.

I want to tell you a story about a man in the Bible who was afraid. His name was Gideon. For seven years the Israelites had been ruled by the people of Midian. God chose Gideon to lead the Israelites out of bondage. Gideon was no coward, but he feared the power of the Midianites. God said, "I will be with you. Do not be afraid." God instructed Gideon to choose three hundred men for battle. They were to carry torches, shout, blow trumpets, and break jars. When they did what God commanded, they conquered the Midianites. Gideon overcame his fear of the Midianites by trusting in God.

What can we learn by studying the life of Gideon? [*Pause for response.*] We can learn how a frightened young man overcame his fear and grew into a mature, courageous, faithful leader of his people. Can God help you over any fear you may have? Yes, the Bible speaks of many people who were able to conquer their fears. God helped people during Bible times. He continues to help boys and girls with any concerns they may have today.

In Psalm 56:11, we read, "In God I trust; I will not be afraid" (NIV).

[*Lead the children in one verse of "Trusting Jesus" before they return to their seats.*]—Carolyn Tomlin

March 11: What Makes You Happy?

TEXT: Ps. 144:15

Object: Draw a happy face and a sad face on two paper plates.

Boys and girls, do you know the definition of *happiness?* [*Pause for response.*] The dictionary says it is "to have joy, well-being, contentment; to be satisfied or pleased." Can someone tell me how you feel when you are happy? What is the difference between being happy and being sad? [*Hold up faces drawn on the plates. Pause for response.*]

Let us think about some things that make boys and girls happy. Could it be a lot of new toys? What about a new bike? Expensive clothes? These are material things and the Bible says they do not bring happiness. What about not having to do any chores at home? Being part of a family carries a responsibility. Never having to do homework? Just like your parents go to work, school and preparing for your future is your work.

God says that true happiness comes from putting him first in your life, placing the needs of others second, and putting yourself last.

Another way to find happiness is by keeping God's laws. Psalm 144:15 says, "Blessed are the people whose God is the Lord" (NIV). When we follow God's commandments and do what we know is right, we will be happy. This type of happiness comes from within. It is a feeling that lights up our lives. When we have the love of God in our heart, we want to share it with others.

I'm asking you to do something this week. Make a list of ways you can show happiness to others. Think of ways you can please God. And you know something? I believe you will have found the secret of happiness yourself.

[*Pray that God will help each boy and girl find true happiness in their lives.*]—Carolyn Tomlin

March 18: Does God Play Hide and Seek?

TEXT: Isa. 1:15–17a, 55:6

Object: A piece of camouflage clothing

This camouflage shirt is used by hunters to hide from ducks or deer. Camouflage allows the hunter to blend in with the shrubbery so the animals won't see him. The hunter wears camouflage because he wants to stay hidden. Being hidden is fun. One of the favorite games of all times is Hide and Seek.

Have you every wondered if God hides from us? The Bible says that God does hide himself at times. The Bible also tells how God wants us to seek and find him.

Isaiah was a faithful prophet of God who lived about 2,700 years ago. As a preacher of God's word, Isaiah was committed to God's Kingdom, to putting the Lord's interests first in his life. Isaiah lived in a sad time because God's chosen people were not obeying the Lord's commands. God gave commandments to his chosen people to help them, but they were not trusting and following him. Isaiah told the people that they had been so evil that God was hiding from them. Listen to these verses (1:15–17a). Isn't that amazing? God was hiding from his people because of their wickedness.

God is not happy with people who break his commandments. God sent Jesus into the world to show us the way to heaven. Jesus said the way to heaven was to love God and obey his commandments. When we keep the commandments of God we are in fellowship with the Lord and he will not hide from us.

Isaiah also gave the most wonderful news. He preached that God was willing to be found. Those who seek after God will always be rewarded with finding him. Matthew 7:7b reads, "Seek and you shall find." That is a marvelous promise. If you are seeking to know God, he wants you to know that you will find him. Listen to this verse. [*Read Isa. 55:6.*].—Ken Cox

March 25: Who Is the Greatest?
TEXT: Mark 9:35
Object: A magazine with a celebrity cover photo

This is a news magazine. Each week magazines like this are published with pictures of important people on the cover. Some people make it their life's goal to have their picture printed on the front of magazines. It makes them feel important.

Jesus had a group of twelve disciples who walked around Galilee with him spreading the good news. One day some disciples got into an argument about who was the greatest. Jesus insisted they tell him about their silly argument. He then described how to become great in the Kingdom of God. Listen to this verse. [*Read Mark 9:35.*]

In the days of Jesus some very fortunate homes had servants. The servants did all the hard work that nobody else wanted to do. They cleaned, hauled water, cooked, and took care of the children. The head of the servants was the master. In those households the master was considered far greater than the servants. Jesus reversed the definition of greatness when he proclaimed that servants were greater than masters.

We become servants today by taking steps to put others first. When we try to meet the needs of family members, friends, and even those living in foreign lands, we are serving them. In some cases being a servant is as simple as giving a glass of cold water to a thirsty person. In other situations we serve others by patiently listening to them. We don't have to solve everybody's problems. Sometimes just being willing to listen provides all the needed help.

Our picture may never be on the cover of a magazine, but that doesn't mean we aren't great. Whenever we serve others by caring for their needs, we become great in God's eyes.—Ken Cox

April 1: I Want to Go First
TEXT: Matt. 20:26–27; Isa. 53

If you have to stand in line, do you want to be the first in line or the last in line? I always wanted to be first in line when I was in school. We had to get in line for everything—when we went to lunch, when we went to recess, when we went to the library. I wanted to be the leader and be first in line. The first in line got to be the first to get to eat or to get the books you wanted or to get the game you wanted.

But I didn't get to be first all the time. The teacher always let everyone take a turn at being first in line. Being in the middle of the line or in the back of the line was not as much fun—except for one thing: when you were the last person in line at one thing, then you would be the first person in line at the next thing. So I was glad to let others get in front of me, because I knew the teacher would notice that I was last in line again, and she would reward me for letting others go first by letting me go first next time.

In the Bible God says we should not always try to be first in line. He says that if we are nice to others and let them go first, then he will notice how nice we are and will reward us for it. It is God's way of helping everyone get along. Let's thank him for that.—Michael Lanway

April 8: God's Blessings
TEXT: Ezek. 34:26
Song: "There Shall Be Showers of Blessings"
Object: Umbrella

Hello, boys and girls. Seeing your smiling faces makes me happy today. Aren't you glad you came to church?

[*Hold up umbrella.*] Now, we all know what this is, right? Yes, it's an umbrella. How many of you have an umbrella at home? [*Pause for response.*] Can someone tell me the purpose of an umbrella? [*Pause for response.*] Yes, an umbrella is used to keep the rain off your body. It is also used to shield the sun on a summer day. But you know something? An umbrella is only useful when it is open. [*Open umbrella.*] If you forget to bring it with you when it rains, what happens to you? That's right, you get wet! I even had an umbrella that would turn inside out on a windy day. Now that umbrella didn't do me much good.

Like an open umbrella that shields us from the rain or sun, Jesus is our shield. Only when we allow him to use our lives can we receive his blessings. We can become what he intends for us. Jesus wants us to accept him and give every part of our life over to him.

Let's think about some ways Jesus can use boys and girls. [*Allow several responses.*] Yes, being a witness, loving others, obeying our parents, attending Sunday school, bringing friends to church programs with you, and supporting our church through giving an offering.

Listen as I read from God's word. "I shall send down showers in season; there will be showers of blessing" (Ezek. 34:26 NIV).

Boys and girls, the next time you see someone using an umbrella, or you use an umbrella, remember to think about the many blessings God has given you.

[*Lead the children in one stanza of "There Shall Be Showers of Blessings." Invite the congregation to sing with you.*]—Carolyn Tomlin

April 15: A Young Man in White
TEXT: Mark 16:5
Object: An angel

I had to borrow a Christmas angel for our object lesson today. Angels were present to announce the birth of Jesus. They were also present to announce the Resurrection of Jesus from the dead.

Jesus died on the cross on Friday. On Sunday morning some women went to the tomb where Jesus had been placed after his death. They planned to lay some spices near his body. In those days when a person died they were not buried in the ground but put in a place like a cave. When the women entered the tomb they didn't see Jesus, but they did see someone else. Listen to this verse. [*Read Mark 16:5.*]

The young man was clothed in white. White clothing is worn by God's angels because it stands for their purity and righteousness. In other passages the angel has a dazzling appearance, like a flash of lighting. The angel talked to the women and told them what had happened.

The angel's job was very important, because no human being had seen Jesus raised from the dead. No human knew what had happened, so the angels who witnessed the Resurrection had to explain it to the women coming to the tomb. The angel made sure that the women understood what God had done. Listen to what he told them. [*Read v. 6.*] Later the women and other disciples saw Jesus in his resurrected body. Then they knew that the angel's message was true.

We can be like that angel if we tell others what God has done to make Easter special. The plan of God is for us to explain what he has done. The meaning of Easter and the Resurrection is that death will not be the end of life for us. For God's children there is eternal life. Jesus has been raised from the dead, and Jesus has promised that we will be raised just like he was. That is the message of Easter.—Ken Cox

April 22: Jesus' Death Produced Forgiveness
TEXT: Matt. 26:28
Object: A cluster of grapes and a bottle of grape juice

This is a cluster of grapes. Aren't they beautiful? Grapes don't stay tantalizingly delicious for long. If ripe grapes are not gathered, the cluster falls from the vine and rots on the ground. If the grape is harvested and crushed, it becomes delicious grape juice, like this. A grape must perish to become grape juice.

At Easter we express our thanks for what Jesus did for us. He taught us and worked miracles, but he had to die on the cross to save us from our sins. Jesus' life was much like these grapes: he had to perish to become the savior. Jesus' life was not taken from him; he willingly offered himself to be our savior. Listen to this verse. [*Read Matt. 26:28.*]

Our lives are like these grapes. We don't have to be crushed, but we must be willing to be changed by God to be useful in his kingdom. We can't come to God and insist that everything in our thinking and behavior remain the same. We have to be willing to be shaped by God's designing power. We may have to give up selfish wants and needs. We have to be willing to read the Bible to learn how to be obedient to God. When we give something up it is called *surrendering.* A wonderful truth is that when we surrender something to God, he always gives us something better.

For a grape to become special, it must be crushed. For our lives to become special, we must surrender some things so that our lives will be patterned after Jesus' life. That is the meaning of the cross and the heart of Easter.—Ken Cox

April 29: Words of Willingness
TEXT: Isa. 6:8
Objects: "I Love You" and "Here I Am, Send Me" posters

Some of you are beginning to read and write words. There are many words to learn and use correctly. Three little words have been called the most powerful words in English. These words are written on this poster. They are, *I love you.* These words sound pleasant. We should say them often to those we care about.

Isaiah's name is on one of the longest books in the Bible. Isaiah was a mighty prophet and sixty-six chapters are filled with his messages. Out of all his words, Isaiah is best known for a very brief answer he gave to God. It contained only five words.

Isaiah was in the temple of God when he said these five words. God had majestically revealed himself to young Isaiah. Isaiah knew that God was listening to everyone in the world and seeing their every action. God warned Isaiah of the dreadful conditions in Israel brought about by disobedience. When the Lord told Isaiah that the Lord needed a messenger, Isaiah gave him an answer of only five words. Listen to this verse. [*Read Isa. 6:8.*]

I have written the five words of Isaiah on this poster. When we hear of great needs in God's Kingdom, our response should be the same: *Here I am, send me.*

We should say similar words to humans. When a friend is hungry and without money to buy food, we should not wait for someone else to help. We should say, "I have some food; I'll share." When someone is lonesome, we shouldn't hope that someone else will make a difference. We should say, "I'll be your friend." Most needs are not impossible to meet. All that is needed is someone willing to help.

For those we care about, the most powerful words we possess are *I love you.* When the Lord reveals a need in our world, we don't need to say a lot. We only need to repeat what Isaiah said: "Here I am, send me."—Ken Cox

May 6: The Master's Touch
TEXT: Gen. 1:31
Song: "For the Beauty of the Earth"
Object: Painting by Claude Monet

Boys and girls, I'm holding a copy of a famous painting by Claude Monet, a well-known French artist. Look how the artist chose the colors to complement each other. Look at the use of curved and straight lines. Monet often worked in his garden, drawing and painting the plants he had grown himself. The artist often painted the same scene in different weather, in early morning fog or late afternoon sunset. This is truly a great piece of work, and it continues to increase with value over time.

Just like this painting was created by a great master, we also were created by God, our Master. Each of you is different from every other person. We have various skin color, eyes, and hair. Our physical features are not the same. But God made you. You are truly a great boy or girl. God loves you and wants you to grow physically, mentally, and spiritually. He wants you to increase your knowledge in the ways he has provided for you to learn.

Will you do something for me? The next time you look at a great work of art, think about how God made you great too. Thank God for giving you eyes that see, ears that hear, and a mind that thinks. Thank him for your ability to run and play. Some of us may be limited in what our body can do. But we can use the skills that God has provided to praise him.

Please bow your heads as I pray that God will help us see beauty in all of the things he has created. Listen as I read from God's Word: "God saw all that he had made, and it was very good" (Gen. 1:31).

[*As the children return to their seats, have the pianist softly play "For the Beauty of the Earth."*]—Carolyn Tomlin

May 13: Mothers Need Help
TEXT: 2 Kings 4:7
Object: Olive Oil

This bottle contains olive oil. In Israel, where Jesus grew up, olive oil has been used for thousands of years. Olive oil is used for cooking, for lighting lamps, as medicine, and for personal grooming. Olive oil is very valuable. If a large quantity is owned, a person is rich. A story in the Bible about olive oil teaches us that mothers need help. This is Mother's Day and we must remember that mothers need all the help they can get.

The Bible describes the hardship of a family whose daddy died. This daddy had been a believer in God and had faithfully served a prophet named Elisha. When the daddy died he owed a lot of money. The mother of the family was scared for herself and her two sons. In those days, when money was owed the debtors would come and sell the two sons into slavery to pay what was owed. Thankfully this mother knew how to get help.

The first thing the mother did was go to the prophet Elisha to get the help of God. Elisha gave her very specific instructions. He told her to have her two sons help her fill their house with empty jars. Then she was to close the door of the house and start pouring oil, from the little she had left, into all the empty jars. The woman followed Elisha's instructions exactly and soon her house was filled with jars full of olive oil! When she told Elisha, he told her the next step to take. [*Read verse.*] She sold the oil, paid her debts, and had money left over to live on.

This story has a happy ending because the mother received help. Elisha told her how God would help her. She also got help from her two sons. Her two children helped by moving all those jars around. Without the help of her children, she wouldn't have made it.

Your mother needs help, too. We forget that mothers need help because our mothers love us and are able to do so much for us. After making sure your mom has a great Mother's Day, give her a helping hand. It doesn't have to be a big job. It can be picking up your room, or running and getting something she needs. Look for anything you can do and do it to help your mom. When you help, look at her face and you will see a big smile. Mothers are super but they need all the help they can get!—Ken Cox

May 20: Temptations
TEXT: Exod. 17:14–16; Eph. 6:10–18

Have you ever thought about doing something you know you are not supposed to do? That is what the Bible calls a *temptation.* We begin to think, "I can get away with it; nobody will ever know"—like when we think about eating a cookie or something our mommies and daddies told us not to eat, or when we don't want to go to bed when we are told and we think about sneaking out of bed and playing with toys or reading a book, or when the teacher wants us to work on something and we think about just pretending to do it while we daydream or color or scribble.

God tells us that it is important to do what our parents and teachers tell us to do. They are trying to help us and protect us. If we don't do as they say, we are hurting ourselves and hurting them, too. God says that we are also to obey what the Bible says. It is the best thing we can do for ourselves. The Bible tells us that when we are tempted to disobey God or our parents or our teachers and do something we shouldn't, we should pray to God and ask for his help. He can help keep us from doing the wrong thing. Let's pray right now and ask him to help us do the right things.—Michael Lanway

May 27: What the Early Church Did Together

TEXT: Acts 1:14

Object: Praying hands sculpture, prayer shawl, and so on

The book of Acts describes the early Church. The young Church was organized in the city of Jerusalem after Jesus ascended into heaven. The first meetings of any organization are very important. During a group's first meetings a direction is established that is followed for the rest of the organization's life. Some of you are in school; others will start kindergarten in a short time. On the first day of school the teacher describes how the class will function and what learning goals will be accomplished. The first day of school is always important and exciting because everything is fresh and new.

The beginning of the Church was exciting, too. Listen to this verse about the activity of the new Church. [*Read Acts 1:14.*]

The early Church met and prayed. When we come to church we sing, take up the offering, listen to sermons, and of course pray. The early Church met primarily to pray together. The early Church prayed to ask for God's direction. They prayed that they would get started on the right path. Only God can guide us into the perfect direction for our lives. The Church also asked for wisdom and for the selection of leaders. In every need they prayed and prayed.

We still have a great need to pray in the Church. When people ask you what you do in church, you can tell them you pray. You pray for the same things as the early Church: direction, wisdom, and leaders. Each time we pray in church, bow your head and pray with us. On special occasions, like Wednesday night, we devote the whole meeting to praying. In emergency situations the whole city will be called to a time of prayer. When God's Church prays, it's still very special to the Lord. He has promised that when two or three are gathered in his name he is in their midst (Matt. 18:20).—Ken Cox

June 3: Personal Testimonies Spread Like Wildfire

TEXT: John 4:39–41

Object: Pictures of forest fires

This is a picture of forest fires in California. Firefighters in California say that windblown brush and forest fires can cross ten acres in just a few minutes. The flames move so quickly that a person can be taken by surprise, surrounded by flames and in great danger. Don't ever play with fire. If you see a fire, be sure to go for help immediately.

This danger is not just in California. When there has been no rain for weeks, we have to be very careful about burning piles of leaves. I saw a whole field on fire one time. A fireman told me that a man had been burning a small pile of leaves and the fire had spread because the field was so dry. A whole neighborhood could have been burned.

Something else spreads quickly. It is what we tell others we know about Jesus. One day Jesus talked to a lady at a well who had come out to draw water. She believed what Jesus told her and left her water jar and ran to town to tell her friends. Jesus had been alone outside of town but soon a crowd from town was coming out to learn for themselves what the lady had said about Jesus. Listen to these verses. [*Read John 4:39–41.*]

The same thing can happen when we tell our friends about Jesus. We may be afraid that our friends don't want to hear or won't understand. The Bible tells us that they will understand and that they will soon be telling others.

When we tell others about Jesus, the truth spreads rapidly, like a wildfire. Let's be sure we tell others about Jesus.—Ken Cox

June 10: Missionaries Plant Churches

TEXT: Rom. 16:3, 5

Object: Seeds and a picture of a church

To grow a tomato plant, seeds like these are planted in a garden and nurtured. After several days of sunshine, a little sprig emerges from the soil. After more growth the plant buds and produces delicious red tomatoes.

The work of missionaries is often called *church planting.* To grow a church like the one in this picture, a process like gardening is completed. A church field, such as a country or city, is selected. The location for the church is prepared by prayer and preliminary work, such as medical missions. During medical mission trips the people of the new country or city begin to trust the missionaries. Then the seed of the word of God is planted in the hearts of the people by proclaiming the truth about Jesus. As the people believe the message, the church grows and becomes healthy. The fruit of a church is eternal life for believers and a society changed for the better.

Our church didn't just appear. Years ago this church was started as a mission, too. A small group of people began meeting in a house for Bible study. In the New Testament, churches first met in houses, too. Listen to these verses. [*Read Rom. 16:3, 5.*]

As the group that formed our church multiplied, they outgrew the house where they were meeting. A larger building was constructed so that more people could come to Sunday school and worship. Finally this building was constructed. Our church is the result of planting, nurturing, and growing.

Missionaries are working in the United States and around the world to plant churches. Let's pray for them as they do their work. Our hope is that God will bless their cultivation work and allow new churches to grow into thriving fellowships.—Ken Cox

June 17: God, Our Loving Father

TEXT: Luke 15: 11ff

My daddy is a good man who loves me very much. There are so many things I remember about growing up with my daddy. One of my best memories is when I had to ride the school bus home for the first time. The bus was so big and the driver was a strange-looking old man. I was scared! When I got home, I ran to my daddy, who was waiting for me on the front porch. It felt so good to be in my daddy's arms. I was safe now and I knew that nothing could hurt me when he held me tight. Then my daddy took me to Burger Castle and bought me a root beer float and a hamburger and fries. Everything seemed so much better as I sat there and ate with him.

My daddy let me know that he loved me very much. One of the most important things he taught me was that God was my "other daddy" and that God loved me very much, too. I knew that if God loved me like my daddy did, then God was a good God and I wanted to know him better. I started reading my Bible and praying so that I could get to know God better.

God is your other daddy, too, and he loves you very much. Get to know him by reading your Bible and praying, and you will find out what a good daddy he is.—Michael Lanway

June 24: When Someone Does a Bad Thing
TEXT: Matt. 18:21–35; Deut. 15:1–11

The Bible tells us that when people do things that hurt us, we need to forgive them. What does it mean to forgive? It means that we aren't angry about it anymore and that we don't think about it anymore. That can be hard to do.

People say mean things sometimes. A boy in school called me a sissy in front of the whole class. Everyone laughed and others started calling me a sissy, too. That was a mean thing for that boy to do and it made me mad. I wanted to get even. I began to think about mean things I could do to him. Every time I thought about it I got madder and madder. Every time I saw that boy I got so mad that it made my tummy hurt. Pretty soon my tummy hurt all the time.

One day, I told the doctor about how mad I was and that my tummy hurt whenever I thought about it. I thought he would feel sorry for me, but instead he told me that I needed to stop thinking about what the boy had said or my tummy would get worse. The doctor told me I needed to forgive the boy. I decided the doctor was right. When I decided to forgive the boy and to stop thinking about what he had said, my tummy stopped hurting.

Then I remembered that the Bible tells us to forgive. Now I know that if I keep thinking about the bad things people have done to me, it only hurts me. Don't make the same mistake I did. Instead, forgive people when they hurt you. It is the best thing to do.—Michael Lanway

July 1: God Protects Us
TEXT: Ps. 23; John 10:1–21

At our city swimming pool there are really tall chairs with big umbrellas on them. Do you know who sits in those chairs? The lifeguards. Lifeguards are men and women who know how to swim really well and who rescue people who need help in the water. They keep people from drowning or getting hurt in other ways. They blow a whistle to get your attention if you are doing something they know is dangerous for you to do. I have told my children that they must always listen to the lifeguards and do what they say, because I know the lifeguards will keep my children safe while they are at the pool.

All kinds of people protect us. Do you know some of them? The policemen, the firemen, the doctor, the security guard, the soldiers in the army—all these and others protect us in some way.

God is the one who has given us these people to protect us. God cares about you and me very much and he wants us to be safe and protected. Jesus watches over us all the time because he wants to protect us. Let's thank God for loving us so much and for giving us Jesus and others to protect us.—Michael Lanway

July 8: Living Water

TEXT: John 4:13–14

Song: "God, Who Made the Earth"

Object: Two plants, one healthy and one withered (Before the sermon, place the two plants near the children.)

Boys and girls, I am happy to see you today. I want us to talk about something that is very important to all living things. Perhaps if I show you these two plants you can guess what we will talk about during our children's sermon today. [*Pause for response. Allow time for children to see the difference between the plants.*] Now, can you guess what made one plant healthy and one plant wither?

Yes, you are correct. The answer is *water.* Water is necessary for all living things. [*Hold up the appropriate plant.*] This plant has been watered, this plant has not been watered. Have you ever been where you could not get a drink of water? Perhaps you were playing ball and no one remembered to bring a container of water. Or do you live where there is little rainfall? What happens? [*Allow time for response.*] Yes, the grass turns brown, pets and wildlife suffer, and people are asked to reduce the amount of water they use.

Just as the water we drink and use for daily needs is important, there is another kind of water that Jesus talks about.

In John 4:13–14, Jesus told the Samaritan woman, "I am the water. No one who comes to me will ever thirst again." What do you think that means? It means that Jesus will give us eternal life. When our life on Earth is over, we will live forever in heaven with Jesus and with others who have accepted him. Isn't that a wonderful promise? [*Lead the children in one stanza of "God, Who Made the Earth." Invite the congregation to sing with you.*]—Carolyn Tomlin

July 15: How Does the Bible Become Real to Me?

TEXT: Isa. 8:16

Object: A scroll with a wax seal

In the days of Isaiah the prophet, land sales were recorded on pieces of paper called scrolls. A scribe would write a description of the land and its price. He would then bind the scroll with string and seal it shut with wax. The hot wax would be impressed with a unique seal. The scroll would look like this when finished, and it would be placed in a clay jar to keep it safe for many years. Later, if anyone had to look at the scroll, the intact, unique seal in the wax would prove that no one had changed what had been written years ago.

When Isaiah lived, the chosen people were breaking God's commandments. They didn't seem to care about how serious their actions were.

The Lord told Isaiah to select some disciples, or followers, and teach them God's Word. God wanted people to know that his Word didn't change and that it was very important. The disciples were to obey what God had said. The Lord instructed Isaiah as if he was making a scroll. Listen to this verse. [*Read Isa. 8:16.*]

God wanted his people to preserve his law in the way that a deed for a land purchase was saved. Instead of writing words on a page, the disciples would memorize God's commandments. Instead of sealing the scroll with wax, the teachings of God were to be kept through obedience. When anyone is joyfully obedient to God's Word, they become a living document of God's truth. When people see an obedient Christian, they can understand what is written in the Bible.

God still wants his people to keep the Bible in high standing. Let's be sure that we bind up the teachings of God in our lives and let our hearts be the special storage place for God's Word forever.—Ken Cox

July 22: What Does "I Love You" Mean?
TEXT: John 15:12–14

Do you ever say "I love you" to someone? Who do you say it to? I tell my wife, my children, my parents, my brother and sisters, and some friends. Do you think I really mean it, that I really love them? How can they know for sure that I love them? How do you know that your mommy and daddy love you?

What you are saying is, you can tell if somebody really loves you by how they treat you. The Bible says that, too. The Bible says that if we really love someone, we will show it by giving our lives to them. How do we do that? By paying attention when someone is talking to us. By spending time with them, playing with them, reading to them, helping them, and being there when they need us. Do others do these things for you? Do you do these things for others?

God loves us. He says, "I love you" to us all the time, and he really means it. We know he really means it because he is always there for us. He talks to us through prayer and the Bible. He has given Jesus to us. He shows his love to us all the time. Let's be sure that we say to God, "I love you, too," and show him our love by spending time with him.—Michael Lanway

July 29: Ezra Was Dedicated to God
TEXT: Ezra 7:6
Object: Picture of an all-star athlete

This athlete [*give name*] has excelled in his sport because of his dedication. He has special ability, but he had to be dedicated to develop his gift. Star athletes should have daily practice, not eat junk food, and get plenty of rest because they are in training. Athletes must be dedicated in order to become exceptional.

For great things to be accomplished in the Lord's work, God must have people who are dedicated to him, too. At one point in the history of God's people, the Lord was rebuilding the city of Jerusalem. But God was not only rebuilding the city; he was also rebuilding the way the people got along together. To accomplish those tasks the Lord needed a dedicated person to teach the people about God. The Lord was able to use a committed man named Ezra. Listen to this description.

The Bible says that Ezra was "ready" (KJV) or "well versed" (NIV) in the Law of Moses. That means that Ezra had been a dedicated student of God's Word and was able to tell others the truth of the Scriptures. Ezra was a star player on God's team. With Ezra's help, the chosen people were able to rebuild their city and their lives.

I know you want to be dedicated to God. Here are a few things we can do to prepare ourselves to be stars on the Lord's team. One way to show our dedication to God is by keeping

Sunday set aside for Sunday School and worship. It is easy to be drawn away to a multitude of other things, but Sunday is a special, holy day for the Lord. Another way we can be dedicated to God is by reading his Word, the Bible, every day. By reading just a few verses every day we can learn much about God's purpose for our world. The last thing is praying. God's dedicated team members should pray every day. Through prayer, God's guidance and strength come to us.

Teams are able to win when they have dedicated players on their rosters. Our church can do great things only when we are made up of dedicated people. Let's be dedicated to God.—Ken Cox

August 5: Jesus, the Great Physician
TEXT: Matt. 9:12 NIV
Song: "The Great Physician Now Is Here"
Object: Stethoscope

Good morning, boys and girls. I like to see your bright smiling faces. I can tell you are happy about being in God's house.

Today I want to show you a tool that is used by the medical profession. I'm sure your family doctor has used this instrument when you have had a checkup. It is called a *stethoscope.* [*Demonstrate how a stethoscope is used.*] Do I have volunteers to pretend to be a doctor and a patient? A stethoscope is used to listen to a patient's heart. People not trained in this procedure might not find anything unusual about a person's health. But a doctor who has received years of training and practice can detect a faint heart murmur or irregular heartbeat.

When do you usually go to a doctor? [*Allow time for children to tell you when they have seen a doctor.*] Yes, one of your parents usually takes you to a doctor when you get sick. You may also have an annual checkup just to make sure you stay healthy.

Jesus was concerned about healing people, too. One of the names he is called is "the Great Physician." He made sick people well, helped the cripple to walk, gave sight to the blind, and healed Jarius's daughter. People praised Jesus for healing them. Jesus said in Matthew 9:12, "It is not the healthy who need a doctor but the sick" (NIV). In other words, he was saying, "I have come to save sinners—not the righteous."

Today God continues to heal people. He also works through the lives of Christian doctors and nurses to help people get well. Let us say a prayer of thanksgiving for those who have dedicated their lives to helping others.

[*Ask the pianist to play softly one verse of "The Great Physician" as the children return to their seats.*]—Carolyn Tomlin

August 12: Do We Welcome God?
TEXT: John 14:23
Object: A welcome mat

This is a welcome mat. Welcome mats are laid just outside our doors at home so that visitors will know we are glad that they have come to see us. We should ask, "How can I welcome God into my life?"

First, we can welcome God by welcoming Jesus. We accept Jesus as the true and only way to God. We pray in the name of Jesus and we honor him. You may hear some people take God's name in vain, or hear them say Jesus' name when they are angry. That is not honoring Jesus. It is sad to hear someone misusing the name of our savior.

Second, we welcome God by listening to his teachers. Our Sunday School teachers are God's teachers. When we listen closely to them and expect to learn very important truths, we are putting a welcome mat outside the door of our lives. In Sunday School this morning, Jesus was there. He was there in the person of your teacher. Jesus said that if we reject his teachers, it is the same as rejecting him.

Third, we welcome God by keeping his commandments. Listen to this verse. [*Read John 14:23.*] If we are disobedient and break God's commandments, it is the same as telling God that he is not welcome in our lives. But did you hear what happens when someone is obedient to God? When we are obedient, God comes into our lives and lives there.

It is a good thing to have God in our lives. We want him to feel welcome like our other friends. We welcome him by honoring Jesus, by listening to his teachers, and by obeying his commandments.—Ken Cox

August 19: Asking God for Help
TEXT: Matt. 26:39; Ps. 25

There are times when I cannot make up my mind. Sometimes I don't know what clothes to wear, so I ask for help and I get my wife's thoughts about what I should wear. Then I can make up my mind and choose my clothes. Do you ever ask for help?

We ask for help lots of times. When we don't understand a word in the book we are reading, we get help. When we don't understand how to spell a word, we get help. When we can't tie our shoes, we get help. It is good for us to get help when we need it, so we can get things done and so we can learn something new. It is always nice to know that there are others who want to help us—our parents, our brothers and sisters, our teachers, our friends.

Do you know who else wants to help us when we don't understand something or when we are not sure what to do? God. God wants to help us make up our minds. So he made sure that we have this Bible to get the answers we need, and he made sure that we can pray to him and get the answers we need. Ask God to help you make up your mind when you are not sure what to do, and he will help you. He loves you and will always help you when you need it. You can count on him.—Michael Lanway

August 26: God Gives Us the Things We Need

I love to go the grocery store and I have enjoyed it since I was a little boy. I always hope that there will be a lady cooking some sausage that she will ask me to taste, or let me eat a free cookie or two. I love those free food samples!

When I was little I thought the grocery store was where all the food was. I thought there was someone there who made all the cookies and the cereals and the breads. I thought there was someone who somehow made the milk and the meat. I didn't know about farms and cows and pigs and wheat and stuff like that. And I really didn't understand that my mommy and daddy had to pay for whatever we got. I just thought that food magically and wonderfully appeared when I needed it, and that it was free.

Now I know that farms are where all the food is. Now I know that God is the one who makes sure that the farm has enough sun and enough rain and enough shade so that the wheat and corn and stuff can grow and be made into food. Now I know that God is the one who makes sure that the cow can give milk for us to drink, and that that there are enough cows and pigs and chickens so we can have meat to eat. Now I know that God is the one who makes sure that mommies and daddies have jobs where they can make enough money to buy the food for us to eat.

God gives us all the things we need to grow and be strong and healthy. God really loves us! Let's thank him for giving us so much!—Michael Lanway

September 2: Always Tell the Truth
TEXT: Jer. 9:5
Object: Simulated polygraph tape

A polygraph is a machine that discovers when a person is telling a lie. Lie-detecting machines measure changes in the rate of heartbeat, breathing, and other things. A technician attaches painless little sensors to the fingers and body of the one being tested. The machine draws little graphs or lines of the body functions being measured and prints them out on a tape like this. This isn't a real polygraph tape; I have simulated what one looks like.

As we examine this imitation tape, like a polygraph technician would, we can see how a truthful answer looks. See, there is some change in the graph lines when a question is answered. For most people, when they tell a lie they become nervous. Their heart beats more rapidly and their breathing is faster than normal. When a lie is told on the polygraph test the little sensors make the graph lines move erratically, like this, and a skilled worker would catch it.

A person learns how to lie. If one lie is told, telling another story is easier. A second fib may be told to cover up the first lie. On and on lying goes until a person is used to lying and telling the truth is hard to do. There is no such thing as a little lie. All lies are big and dangerous. Listen to this verse. [*Read Jer. 9:5.*]

In the ninth of the Ten Commandments, God forbids the telling of lies. It is natural and right in God's eyes to tell the truth. That's why our heart rates and breathing are normal and don't show up on a polygraph when we tell the truth. God always tells the truth in the Bible, and we are like God when we tell the truth in love.

It is tempting to tell a lie to impress our friends. We could tell our friends that our dad is Superman. But they next time they see Dad, it'll be obvious that Dad is just a regular guy. After we lie to our friends, they reach the point of not believing anything we say. and then when we really need them to listen to us, they won't. So remember, it is best and easiest to tell the truth always, in love, and God is happy with us when we refuse to tell a lie.—Ken Cox

September 9: The Buddy System
TEXT: Luke 10:1–2; 1 Kings 19:21

When I was in school, we would go on field trips to the park, to the zoo, and to other places. Do you do that? My teacher would always pair me with someone because she didn't want me to get lost or wander off somewhere. Whoever she picked for me was my buddy for the day. We ate lunch together, walked together, and even went to the potty together. Have you ever had a buddy for the day?

In the Bible God tells us that we need each other all the time. He wants us to have buddies, too—except not just for the day but forever. He wants us to help each other. He wants us to have someone who will watch out for us.

Who will be your buddy? I will be your buddy. Your Sunday School teacher will be your buddy. There are others, too. We want you to know that you are loved here and that you are safe here. God loves you and he has given you buddies in this church who will look out for you. Let's thank him.—Michael Lanway

September 16: Not Praying Is Wrong
TEXT: 1 Sam. 12:23
Object: Posters of the *no* symbol

This is a *no* sign. It means no to whatever is in the circle and behind the slash. This sign means "No smoking," and this sign means, "No pets."

When we think of sin, we tend to think of not doing things. We could design some *no* signs, like "No lying" or "No stealing." We may believe that if we stop doing a list of wrong things, then we will not sin against God. However, we are also guilty of sin if we fail to do good things.

A man named Samuel is one of my favorite Bible characters. Samuel began serving at the Tabernacle, God's house, when he was a little boy. One night God spoke to Samuel, and the young man became a prophet of God. Samuel served from that very young age until his old age as a faithful prophet. He spent all of those years serving the people of Israel. He taught the people the truth of God, helped them with their decisions, and prayed for them.

A sad time came in Samuel's life when the people rejected his spiritual leadership. The people wanted a king like all the other countries around them. They thought a king would lead them to military victories and provide for all of their needs. This decision broke Samuel's heart. When the people noticed that Samuel was disturbed, they became worried that Samuel would not pray for their protection any longer. Samuel promised that he would continue to pray for them. Listen to this verse. [*Read 1 Sam. 12:23.*]

When we fail to pray, we sin against God. When we pray, God answers and does tremendous good for our world. So always pray, because God has promised to answer. If we fail to pray, we have done the wrong thing in God's eyes. Let's remember Samuel's message that he would never cease to pray for his friends. We can please God by doing good things like praying for our friends.—Ken Cox

September 23: Making Our Hurts Go Away
TEXT: Exod. 15:22–27; Matt. 9:14–38

Whenever I got hurt I would cry for my mother to make it better. Do you do that, too? One day when I was about three years old, I was walking through the yard on a hot summer day and I was barefoot. I felt something go into my foot. Ow! A thorn, and boy, did it hurt! I picked my foot up and hopped toward a place where I could sit, and stepped on another thorn. Ow! So I decided to sit right there and put my hands out on the ground so I wouldn't fall, and my hands got thorns in them! And they were in my bottom, too! Ow! Ow! Do you know what I did then? I cried and screamed for my mommy. My mommy came and picked me up and pulled each one of the thorns out of me. Then she held me until I felt better and stopped crying. Thank goodness for her! I could always count on my mommy to make my hurts go away.

Do you know who gives us mommies and daddies and grandmas to make hurts go away? God! God doesn't want us to hurt; he wants our hurts to go away. We can always ask him to help us when we are hurt and he will help make the hurt go away. Let's thank him for giving us our mommies and daddies and grandmas, and for helping make our hurts go away.—Michael Lanway

September 30: We Are Never Alone
TEXT: Ezek. 48:36; 2 Cor. 6:16

Do you sleep in a room all by yourself or do you share a room with a brother or sister? Is it hard to sleep in a room all by yourself? It is for me.

There are a few times each year when my wife and children visit family or take trips without me because I have to stay home and work. When I am all by myself I have a hard time adjusting to being alone. The house seems darker, the noises are louder, and I am a little scared of all that.

When I feel that way I pray. God reminds me that he is always with me and will never leave me all by myself. That makes me feel so much better because I know that God loves and will protect me. The Bible tells us that God is with us always and that we will be with him forever. That is why Jesus came to Earth, to tell us that. Let's thank Jesus for telling us and for being with us always.—Michael Lanway

October 7: Jesus Came to Help the Needy
TEXT: Mark 2:17
Object: A box of Band-Aids

This is a box of Band-Aids. If we tumble while skating and scrape a knee, a Band-Aid is the first thing we want. When we're hurting we want help, and the sooner the better. The people who are willing to help are very important to us.

Jesus was criticized for making friends with unpopular people. He asked a tax collector named Matthew to be one of his apostles. To celebrate Jesus' presence there, Matthew threw a party at his house. All of Matthew's friends came to the party. Matthew's friends were like him. They were outsiders and unpopular people. Some of the religious leaders said that Jesus shouldn't have anything to do with Matthew and his friends. Jesus told them that he had come to help people who were hurting. Listen to this verse. [*Read Mark 2:17.*]

It is natural to want to make friends with boys or girls who have nice homes and fun toys and are happy. Those positive things attract us. It is also normal to avoid boys and girls who don't have nice things and are unhappy. When adults and children are not popular, they might be hurting very badly on the inside. Some people are not able to fit in and be likeable no matter how hard they try. Loneliness, frustration, and rejection cause feelings to hurt. Folks who are hurting are in need of a Band-Aid for their feelings.

Jesus was drawn to unpopular people. He would help them by smiling at them and talking to them. He was able to miraculously meet their needs. Jesus is the friend of everyone and he meets a special need in the lives of those who are hurting. We can be like Jesus and help, too. We can be friendly to those who don't have any friends. A wonderful change can come about in a boy or girl's life if he or she is able to have some friends to play with. Jesus loved people who were hurting and he showed his love by coming to their parties even when only unpopular people were there.

Jesus came into the world with spiritual Band-Aids. He came to bind up and heal those who had broken hearts and lives. So let's remember never to think that anyone is beyond the touch of God. They are not. When we tell them of Jesus, they might just do what Matthew did—believe and throw a party in celebration of accepting Jesus as savior.—Ken Cox

October 14: The Words We Use Are Important
TEXT: Lev. 11:44, 45; Rom. 6:16–23

I was watching a movie the other day—a movie that was supposed to be good for children. Suddenly one of the little boys in the movie said a bad word and everyone around us in the movie theater laughed. They didn't seem to mind that a bad word had been spoken, probably because it was spoken in a funny situation.

I minded that it happened. My children need to know that it is not good to say bad words, even if others think it is funny.

Sometimes the people around us have different ideas about what is funny and what words are good to use. The Bible tells us that no matter what other people think, we are to let only God decide what is good or bad. God tells us that we should not ever say bad words. God tells us that we should live and act and speak the way God does. God is always good and kind and loving. God is never nasty or mean and he doesn't say bad words. Jesus helps us live in the ways that God wants us to live. Let's ask Jesus to help us live that way too.—Michael Lanway

October 21: We Need More Than Bread to Live
TEXT: Matt. 4:4
Object: A selection of foods, including bread and snacks

Some common foods are in this lunch sack. Here is a slice of bread, an apple, and a bag of M&Ms. I like all of these foods. We are very fortunate to live in an abundant land where we have so much to eat. In some countries there are no supermarkets with long, tall aisles filled with food. We should be grateful for all we have to eat.

The Bible teaches that we need more than food to survive. To live as we should we must hear the truth of God. Jesus once went forty days without food. I can't imagine being without food that long. The devil tempted Jesus to misuse his power and turn a stone into bread. Listen to this verse that contains Jesus' answer to Satan. [*Read Matt. 4:4.*]

We can learn from Jesus' encounter with the devil. Jesus said that we sustain our lives by the Word of God. That means it is essential that we read the Bible and listen to God's messages in Sunday School and church. Listening to God is as important as eating. If we go without food we become physically weak. After not eating for several days it is hard to get up and walk around. The same is true about spiritual food. Without consuming truth we become discouraged and unhappy. Without a steady diet of God's Word we can get lost in our lives, like losing our way on a long trip without a map.

We stay in touch with God through a good spiritual diet. We are fortunate to live in a land where there is plenty of food. We are also blessed to enjoy religious freedom so we can get bread from heaven.—Ken Cox

October 28: We All Are Copycats
TEXT: Deut. 5:8–10

Do you know what a copycat is? When I want to do or have the exact same thing as you do or have. I can copy your answers on a test. I can copy the shoes or the dress you wear by getting the same kind. I can copy your words or your actions when I say the words you say or do the things you do.

I tell Katherine, my oldest child, that she has to be very careful about what she says and does, because her sister and brother will want to say and do it, too. She has to remember that her sister and brother are always watching her.

The Bible tells us that we need to be very careful about what we say and do, because others are learning from us. It is important to remember that. Let's be sure we set a good example for others with what we say and do.—Michael Lanway

November 4: There Are No Secrets
TEXT: Luke 12:3
Object: A megaphone

This megaphone makes voices louder than normal. Cheerleaders use megaphones at football games to be heard over large crowds of fans. Listen to this. [*Demonstrate megaphone.*]

There are times when we don't want to be heard. In those instances we whisper. This is a whisper. [*Demonstrate whisper.*]

We may whisper if we are saying something that would shame us if it were heard by others. I remember whispering a secret in class when I was in second grade. The teacher noticed and made me stand up and tell everybody what I was whispering. I was very embarrassed.

The words we say are very powerful. We may not think that our words are important and that we can tell little "white" lies or say rude things and not hurt ourselves or others. We must keep in mind that God knows everything we say. Listen to this verse. [*Read Luke 12:3.*]

We must be very careful what we say because the Lord is aware of every word that comes out of our mouths. The Lord spoke powerful words when he created the heavens and the Earth. Our words are not that powerful, but they do carry a lot of force. With our words we can tease someone about the clothes they are wearing and hurt their feelings. With our words we can congratulate and encourage a brother or sister for making good grades. Whether hurting or helping, our words make a big difference to those around us. Just think, Jesus said that the words we say in secret will be shouted from the rooftops. That's the Lord's way of warning us about the importance of what comes out of our mouths. Therefore we should always be kind and encouraging. The most important thing we can say is to tell others about the love of Jesus.—Ken Cox

November 11: We Don't Have to Be Afraid
TEXT: Judg. 6:24; Phil. 4:4–9

Are you afraid a lot? It seems that people are afraid of a lot of things a lot of the time. Some are afraid of airplanes, some are afraid of the dark, and some are afraid of cats and dogs. Mommies and daddies get afraid, too. Some are afraid of getting old, some of losing their jobs, and some of losing their health.

We can spend an awful amount of time being afraid. God knows that, and he wants us not to be afraid so much. In the Bible God tells us to "fear not!" He says it a lot of times to a lot of different people. God knows that if we are afraid a lot of the time, we will miss out on the happy and wonderful feelings he wants us to enjoy.

God reminds us that he has planned for us to enjoy life and not be afraid so much. That is why he sent Jesus to us. Jesus reminds us that God can help us not be afraid. When we are afraid, Jesus tells us to pray and to read the Bible. He tells us that we can know for sure that God is right here with us and that he will not leave us, ever. Let's thank God for being here, and for helping us not to be afraid.—Michael Lanway

November 18: No One Can Do It by Themselves
TEXT: Rom. 12:4–8

The other night at the dinner table, my son Robert wanted some ketchup on his plate. He grabbed the ketchup bottle and started to squeeze it to pour the ketchup out. I said, "Robert, let me help you." He said, "I want to do it by myself!" He squeezed it too hard and ketchup went everywhere. "Oops!"

No matter how hard I try to help, there are times when my son wants to do it by himself. And that's good, because there are some things that he needs to learn to do by himself. All of us do. But there are other things that he shouldn't do by himself. Some things he shouldn't do by himself because he isn't old enough yet, like squeezing ketchup out of a bottle. Other things he shouldn't ever do by himself. In those instances, it is important for Robert to realize that he needs the help of others or he could get hurt.

That is why God put us all in this church, so that we can help each other. We can't do everything by ourselves. At times that would be boring; at other times it could even be dangerous. If you need my help, tell me and let me help you. If I need your help, I will tell you and let you help me. Let's thank God for the help we can give each other.—Michael Lanway

November 25: The Bible—A Book for Everyone
TEXT: Ps. 119:11
Song: "Holy Bible, Book Divine"
Object: Several translations of the Bible (Before the boys and girls come to the front, ask them to bring their Bibles.)

Hello, boys and girls. How many of you brought your Bibles to church today? [*Wait for a show of hands.*] Every time we come to God's house we should bring our Bibles. You may have several versions of the Bible in your home. If you check on the outside spine [*indicate where to look*] you will see the version of your Bible. Some of you may have the King James

Version, or you may have the New International Version, Good News for Modern Man, or others.

Regardless of the version, we believe that the Bible was inspired by God. Biblical scholars who have written newer translations work together through prayer and dedication to transcribe the text.

A new version called *The Book* has recently been completed. The purpose of this new translation is to make the Bible easy for everyone to read and understand. This new text will be promoted by such well-known people as singers, actors, and television personalities. Will this promotion be expensive? Yes. Why do you think the publishers are putting so much money into this book? [*Pause for response.*] It is because Christians believe that everyone should hear the message of God's Word. Everyone, regardless of where they live, or their educational level, should hear and understand the gospel message.

Boys and girls, hold up your Bibles. Remember that the Bible is the most important book you will ever read. The writer of Psalm 119:11 says, "I have hidden your word in my heart that I might not sin against you" (NIV).

[*Lead the children in one verse of "Holy Bible, Book Divine."*]—Carolyn Tomlin

December 2: Christmas Decorations
TEXT: Luke 1, 2; Isa. 9:6–7

Christmas decorations are everywhere! Do you have Christmas decorations in your house? There are Christmas lights, Christmas trees, and Christmas wreaths. There are snowmen, Santa Clauses, and reindeer on roofs and in yards.

In our church we have decorations, too. We call them Advent decorations, which means Christmas decorations. There are candles and a tree and poinsettia flowers. There are banners and lights. All these things remind me of Christmas and of Jesus and of how much God loves us. They make me feel warm and wonderful all over.

I like feeling warm and wonderful. I like being reminded about how much God loves us. Do you know what helps me remember those things and feel those things best? It isn't the candles. It isn't the trees. It isn't the banners or the lights or flowers.

Do you know what it is? It's you! You help me remember what Christmas is all about. When I see you I remember that Jesus was born as a baby and was a child, just like you. When I hear you laugh, you remind me that Christmas is about the joy Jesus brings. When I see you smile and hold your hand, you remind me that Christmas is about God's love that was sent with his son, and I feel warm and wonderful all over.

Each of you and Jesus are the best parts of Christmas for me. Thank you, God, for the love and joy you bring through Jesus and these children.—Michael Lanway

December 9: Superheroes and Power
TEXT: Eph. 3:14–20

When I was a little boy I loved to watch my cartoon superheroes because they were so strong and powerful. When Popeye ate a can of spinach, his arms would get huge and he would beat up the bad guys. When he pulled on his belt and said "Shazaam!" he would become the strongest guy in the world. All Clark Kent had to do was take off his glasses and his clothes to become Superman.

I want to be powerful like that. But no matter how many cans of spinach I eat, no matter how many times I say "Shazaam!" no matter how many times I take off my glasses, I don't have the power of my cartoon superheroes. But you know what? No one else does either, because all of it is make-believe.

There is a power that is more powerful than all the cartoon superheroes combined, and it is not make-believe. I am talking about the power of God. Who is more powerful than God? No one! His power is the power of love. His love is so powerful that it beats up the bad guys, like hate and anger and the devil.

In the Bible God tells us that he wants to share his power of love with us. He puts his power in our hearts when we put Jesus in our hearts. If you want to share the power of God's love, put Jesus in your heart. You can do that today.—Michael Lanway

December 16: Let Me Tell You About the Neatest Thing
TEXT: Matt. 28:18–20

What's the best movie you have seen? What is your favorite cartoon? What is your favorite TV show? What is your favorite storybook? What is your favorite thing to eat for breakfast? What was your favorite gift on Christmas [or birthday]?

We tell others about all these neat things all the time, don't we? We like to tell others about these things, and others like to hear about them, too. They may not have read that book or seen that cartoon or seen that movie, but if they hear us talk about it, they might get to see and have those things, too, and enjoy them as much as we have enjoyed them.

Do you know what is the neatest thing that happened to me? I got to know Jesus and I put him into my heart. I want to make sure I tell people about Jesus, too, because I want others to have Jesus in their hearts, too. Have you told people about Jesus? Let's do that so that they enjoy him, too.—Michael Lanway

December 23: How Much Do I Love You?
TEXT: John 3:16; Jer. 30:8–11

I love my children so much and I tell them that all the time. I say to them, "Do you know how much I love you?" and they say, "As big as the ocean?" "Bigger!" I say. "As big as the sky?" "Bigger!" I say. "As big as the whole universe?" "Even bigger than that!" I say. Then I hug them and hold them and kiss them. I want them to know that I love them more than they can ever know.

God feels the same way about his children. Do you know who his children are? That's right—you and me! He wants us to know how much he loves us, so in the Bible he tells us he loves us, again and again. One of the places God says this in the Bible is John 3:16, which says that God loves us so much that he gave us Jesus. Jesus came to earth to tell us that God loves us more than we can ever know. When we get to heaven, God will put his arms around us and hug us and hold us, just like this [hold and hug each child].

God loves you and he wants you to be with him forever. Let's tell him that we love him and that we want to be with him forever.—Michael Lanway

December 30: Saving for Our Future
Text: Rom. 6:23
Object: Piggy bank

[*Ask someone to play "Amazing Grace" on an autoharp or piano as the boys and girls gather. Shake the bank to hear the coins jingle.*] How many of you know what I'm holding in my hand? Yes, I think everyone knows this is a piggy bank. How many of you put money into some type of bank at home? [*Acknowledge raised hands.*] Boys, girls, and their parents try to save money. Think back to something you really wanted. You couldn't possess it immediately but you saved pennies, nickels, and dimes until you had enough to make the purchase. Perhaps some money was given to you as a gift, or you earned it by working. Would someone like to share what you bought with your money? Or how long you saved?

Children usually keep their money at home, but parents usually place their money in a community bank. When placed in this location, it is safer. Yes, we could say a bank is a good place to save our money.

As Christians we must save for a future home. Another name for *heaven* is our "eternal home." When we ask Jesus to come into our life, we want to do good works. We want to help others. Everything we do should be for the glory of God.

Yes, saving is important. It shows others that we are concerned about our future. Jesus gives us the gift of salvation. We place our lives in his care. We please him when we save for our eternal home. The Bible says, "For the wages of sin is death, but the gift of God is eternal life in Christ Jesus our Lord" (Rom. 6:23 NIV).

[*Close by having the pianist softly play "Amazing Grace" as the children return to their seats.*]—Carolyn Tomlin

SECTION XI

A LITTLE TREASURY
OF ILLUSTRATIONS

THE SPIRITUAL DIMENSION.   Evelyn Underhill wrote a treatise on the human soul in which she said, "The soul lives in a two-story house. The upper floor is the supernatural, spiritual life with a capacity for God." The tragedy of life is spending all of one's days, including old age, on the lower level. "For what good is it for a man to gain the whole world," asks Jesus, "at the price of his own soul?" (Matt. 16:26 Phillips).—Batsell Barrett Baxter, *When Life Tumbles In*

MOTHER'S PRAYER.   Thomas Carlyle described the strongest spiritual influence of his youth as his mother's praying. He wrote, "The highest whom I knew on earth, I saw bowed down to a Higher in heaven. Such things, especially in infancy, reach inward to the very core of your being."—Leslie D. Weatherhead, *The Eternal Voice*

A PROUD MOMENT.   I've heard children in church talk about how they wanted to be one thing or another—*anything* but a preacher. I have read youngsters' essays on the black heroes they respected and admired, people they looked up to and wanted to be like, and unless it was a Nobel Peace Prize winner like Martin Luther King Jr. or a presidential candidate like Jesse Jackson or a mysterious movement leader like Malcolm X, almost never did anyone want to be a pastor like Eli.

This is not your most sought-after job. So you know that a daddy looks with pride when one of his own children says yes to the Lord, yes to service, yes to sacrifice, yes to preaching, yes to pastoring, yes to the same number of years in school that a doctor or a lawyer spends with no chance of ever making one-tenth of what those professions pay. When a preacher's kid says yes to preaching, that is a proud moment.—Jeremiah A. Wright, *Good News*

REJECTION.   It's a frame of mind we can understand perhaps. In one of the Charlie Brown cartoons, Charlie is talking to his friend Linus about the pervasive sense of inadequacy he feels all the time. "You see, Linus," Charlie moans, "it goes all the way back to the beginning. The moment I was born and set foot on the stage of life, they took one look at me and said, 'Not right for the part.'"

Another time, Charlie complains to Linus about his publisher. "The publisher sent me a rejection slip," laments Charlie.

"So what," says Linus, "lots of writers get rejection slips."

"Yes," says Charlie, "but I didn't send in a manuscript."—Martin Camroux, *The Times Best Sermons for 1998*

GRIEF.   One of the stops we made during last summer's vacation was to see a good friend, a dear lady, who had lost her husband, Michael, recently to an illness when he was in the prime of his life. He left four children behind and a loving wife whose wounds have not healed yet. As a mending process she often goes out to the cemetery and visits the grave of her late husband. It so happens that her brother is one of the most prominent artists of our time and he has designed a simple brass monument for Mike, so she often goes out there to meditate. She invited us to go with her to the gravesite. After we arrived it was so wonderful to hear how she touched on their life together, recalling the creative experiences of married life that a happy couple share. Recalling years of togetherness was a form of healing, each little detail adding to the mending process.—Laszlo Kovacs

MAKING ROOM FOR CHRIST.   Two friends of mine, expecting their second child, looked in vain for a place to park baby number two. After several lengthy discussions it was decided that the husband's study would have to go and his library would have to be moved to his office or divided up into smaller bookshelves throughout the house. He loved his library dearly, this friend of mine, but there was a new life on the way, and that way had to be prepared. The analogy holds. Whether it is our own baby we are expecting or the baby Jesus, or a grown-up Lord coming in great power and glory, we are called to prepare the way for new life in our lives, to make room for it by letting go of our old ways, even our old loves, as painful as that may sometimes be. It is either that or prepare ourselves for the news that we have been passed over because there was no room in us.—Barbara Brown Taylor

SEEING CHRIST.   The first time that I went from Montevideo to Rio de Janeiro everybody wanted me to see the statue of Christ on the Corcovado. They would tell me during the day as the ship was coming into the port, "You have not seen anything of beauty until you see the Christ." Of course they were referring to the statue. In a different way, in a far different way, you and I have seen nothing until we see the Christ, until we make him the center of our life, until we allow him to guide us and bless us and protect us.—Violeta Cavallero, *The Upper Room Chapel Talks*

CHOICE.   One evening my family and I decided to go eat at a landmark restaurant just west of Chicago. It's been there at least seventy years. Legend has it that Al Capone used to play cards with the owner. The Bohemian decor and traditional menu make it popular with immigrants and descendants of immigrants, and the early-bird specials draw local senior citizens who want good value. But there was still another attraction for my family. The restaurant issued frequent diner cards that would be stamped for each meal purchased. When you had ten stamps, you got a free dinner.

We parked the car and went in through the heavy, ornate front door. Everything looked the same as we remembered it. Songs being sung in Czech or other languages played in the background. There were carved wooden chandeliers and cuckoo clocks. But it quickly became apparent that things had changed. Because my parents are smokers, we couldn't get a table in the room where we were used to eating. The food seemed much the same but the basket of freshly baked breads placed on the table was only half its former size, and when it came time to pay the bill, the server refused to honor our frequent diner card. We asked to see the manager—and were surprised when a man we'd never seen before came to the table. What was going on? Why had the service changed? Why wouldn't they honor the frequent diner card? The answer was simple, said the manager. The restaurant was under new ownership. That was how to account for the changes.

To a person looking at the restaurant's Old World facade, everything appeared to be the same. Even walking inside didn't immediately reveal the differences. The dining rooms looked as they had always looked. The deck of cards allegedly used by Al Capone was still in the display case. But things were not the same. The new owners had different values. Different principles directed the way they did business with the world. They didn't have to keep the same policies as the former owners or honor promises made by others. Some things that were allowed in the past—such as smoking in the nicest dining room—were no longer possible. The owners had every right to make these subtle but substantive changes. After all, the restaurant was theirs.

So the family is faced with a choice. We can continue to patronize the restaurant, accepting its new rules and policies, or we can stay away and have nothing further to do with this once-familiar landmark. But we cannot choose to do both—certainly not simultaneously. Yet this is what many Christians try to do in following Jesus Christ. It has been a problem for disciples since Paul wrote his letter to the Romans.—Carol M. Noren

FROM FEAR TO FAITH.   There was a time in the experience of John Wesley when he was a man literally full of fear. On his trip to this country his little ship had to undergo the ordeal of three violent Atlantic storms. John Wesley found himself terrified. He was a man of devotion. He tried strenuously to discipline his sprit, but he confessed that he was afraid to die. By a curious providence, on that same ship there was a group of Moravian Christians, fine evangelical believers in Christ, courageous and fearless, who had flung all of their cares upon the merciful providence of God. They had lost their fears forever. In the midst of the storm the Moravians sang hymns of confidence and victory. This impressed John Wesley so much that he hardly knew what to think, so he went to their leader and asked him a whole series of questions:

"Are you not afraid?"

"No, we are not afraid."

"But your women and children, they are singing hymns; aren't they afraid?"

"No, they are not afraid because their trust is in Christ."

"But there is real danger!"

"Yes, we know there is real danger, but our lives are in the hands of God and we are not afraid."

Staggered by that confident faith Wesley searched his heart and mind and soul. That was the beginning of his conversion that took place at Aldergate two years later, the beginning of that quest which resulted in a complete surrender to Jesus Christ until he found the confidence that he could not generate in himself. It was given to him as a gift of God, as a result of his faith.—Lowell M. Atkinson, *Apples of Gold*

CHRIST IS DIFFERENT.   Lest students of comparative religion be tempted to believe that to compare them is to discover that at their hearts all religions are finally one and that it thus makes little difference which one you choose, you have only to place side by side Buddha and Christ themselves.

Buddha sits enthroned beneath the Bodhi tree in the lotus position. His lips are faintly parted in the smile of one who has passed beyond every power in earth or heaven to touch him. "He who loves fifty has fifty woes, he who loves ten has ten woes, he who loves none has no woes," he has said. His eyes are closed.

Christ, on the other hand, stands in the garden of Gethsemane, angular, beleaguered. His face is lost in shadows so that you can't even see his lips, and before all the powers in earth or heaven he is powerless. "This is my commandment, that you love one another as I have loved you," he has said. His eyes are also closed.

The difference seems to me this. The suffering that Buddha's eyes close out is the suffering of the world that Christ's eyes close in and hallow.—Frederick Buechner, *Now and Then*

COUNTERFEIT RELIGION.   No enemy is so deeply entrenched from the shafts of God as the man who has a counterfeit religion—the man who follows the custom, knows the jargon, engages in the practices of religion, but who knows no living source of power within the will, whose life has never been transformed, whose ears are no longer sensitive to the voice of Christ. He is the hardest person to win. That is why Jesus used spiritual dynamite to shell such men out of their dugouts and why he was gentle to prostitutes, for the former are in deeper dugouts than lust provides. Ecclesiasticism may be a more effective protection against the shafts of God. "The harlots," said Jesus to religious people, "go into the kingdom of God before you."—Leslie D. Weatherhead, *Personalities of the Passion*

GOD'S BLESSINGS.   The great Reformed Theological Seminary in Debrecen trained many young students since it was founded in 1536. My experience there was as just one of the thousands who attended that distinguished institution of higher learning.

It was customary on Sundays that there was no hot meal served in the dormitory at all. Sunday breakfast was served by the lower classmen, and upon leaving the dining room each student received two sandwiches—one for lunch and one for dinner—and some fruit. Each portion was modest and we usually finished them by midafternoon, and they had to be supplemented as the day passed.

The usual practice was observed on that one Sunday, in the fall of 1956. I had finished my sandwiches and was getting mighty hungry, and by late afternoon I started thinking about satisfying my increasing appetite. There was no sense in staying in the room, so I decided to take a walk. It so happened that just a stone's throw away from the dormitory, right along the Great Reformed Church, there was a bakery, and by sheer instinct I made my way toward the store. Sure enough, there on the shelves, just on the other side of the glass window, there were those magnificent, delicious loaves, all neatly lined up for the customers. It would have been ever so nice to have a generous slice of that bread and take it back to my room. Of course the store was closed on Sundays. Besides, even if it had been open, I had no way of purchasing any of it—there was not a single penny in my pocket. Hungry, frustrated, angry, I returned to my dormitory room and cried myself to sleep. A few weeks later, in the wake of the Hungarian Revolution, I left Debrecen and Hungary.

The following year I entered the United States and became a citizen in 1965. A few years later, in 1970, I was invited to give a lecture at the University of Debrecen, and as I walked through the center of the city I first made my way directly to that familiar bakery again. I entered the store without any hesitation and purchased a magnificent slice of warm bread, carried it out to the street, sat down on a nearby bench next to my suitcase and had a memorable feast. Later that day I went to the Great Reformed Church and—with tearful eyes—thanked God for all his blessings, for the beauty and gift of life, and for the promises of the future.—Laszlo Kovacs

FOR GOD'S GLORY.   The shoemaker who is a church school teacher is not doing a sacred thing only when he teaches his class on Sunday. He is also doing a work of spiritual significance when he puts good leather into shoes and makes them watertight. He is helping God to answer the prayers of His people for health in wet weather, and he is as much a minister of Christ—if he does his work in His spirit and offers it up to God—as the priest or minister who administers the sacrament. He may be even more so, for so-called religious work can be done in a secular spirit, and the sacred mysteries, preaching especially, can be exploited to make a platform on which a secular-minded exhibitionist displays his trivial egotisms. One is reminded of the significant epitaph which reads: "Here lies the body of John Smith, who for forty years cobbled shoes in this village to the glory of God."—Leslie D. Weatherhead, *The Eternal Voice*

THE JERICHO ROAD AGAIN.   On a university campus the parable of the Good Samaritan was repeated, with malice aforethought. A professor, impressed with how much distraction there is in the way of modern students' study, told his class that he wished to find out whether it made any difference in examination results if the students studied quietly and alone in a room or studied on the move in the midst of a distraction. So he gave half the class an assignment to be studied in their rooms in silence for an hour. The other half of the class was given the same textbook assignment and told to study it, also for an hour, while walking around the campus on a specified route.

The teacher was deliberately fooling his students. He really wanted to find out how compassionate they were. So he planted on the walking route a student who was paid to act the part of one in great pain, rolling and groaning about. Well, the long and short of it was that only three out of twenty-eight students who walked the route so much as bothered to slow down or to evidence any concern for the ailing student, so intent were they on reading for their examination. Thus was demonstrated once more what had happened on the road to Jericho.

The students, incidentally, were all members of the same New Testament class at the university's theological seminary.—Walter D. Wagoner, *Mortgages on Paradise*

THE PROMISE OF JESUS.   When David Livingstone went back to Glasgow and addressed the university there, the students had assembled in a spirit of ridicule. But as they gazed upon his face, blackened by the African sun, and at his lion-injured arm limp by his side, they grew quiet. At the conclusion one of them rose and asked, "Dr. Livingstone, what was it that enabled you to keep on out there in Africa?" He replied: "If you would know what it was that sustained me in my loneliness, gave me strength when I could not bear the food which was offered me, was my help among those whose language I could not speak, and gave endurance for all the unspeakable trials which beset me, I will tell you. It was the promise of Jesus to his church: 'Go . . . and, lo, I am with you always.'"—James P. Wesberry, *Evangelistic Sermons*

LIFE'S MEASURE.   Leo Tolstoy tells a story of a Russian peasant who was dissatisfied with his life until he visited a rich relative who offered him, for the price of one hundred rubles, all the land he could cover in a day. This man was to start out early in the morning and run all day, and this he did. He ran and ran, and finally at the end of the day he fell over on his face. When they turned him over, blood gushed out of his mouth, and they felt his pulse and found that he was dead. They went out and dug a hole seven feet long and buried him in it. Tolstoy's conclusion is that all the land a man needs is seven feet.—James P. Wesberry, *Evangelistic Sermons*

QUESTIONS OF CONDUCT.   Many young people want to know if they can read a certain off-color book, or see a certain salacious movie, or engage in a particular questionable conduct without its "hurting them too much." Such a question is exactly backwards! We ought to ask, "What is the *best* book I can read?" or "What is the best movie I can see?" We must do the things which will build up our minds, our spirits, and our bodies—not the things which will fill them with filth and destruction. This principle can be applied to almost any question of conduct, and it would save earnest Christians from many a pitfall.—Wayne E. Ward, *The Word Comes Alive*

BEYOND DEATH.   We find by losing. We hold fast by letting go. We become something new by ceasing to be something old. This seems to be close to the heart of that mystery. I know no more now than I ever did about the far side of death as the last letting-go of all, but I begin to know that I do not need to know and that I do not need to be afraid of not knowing. God knows. That is all that matters.—Frederick Buechner, *A Room Called Remember*

DEATH.   I walked one autumn day on the lonely roads of Vermont. The view was endless. One range of brown and golden hills rose behind the other. The sun was setting before me, casting its bursting light over the whole landscape. Even the trees on the distant hills seemed afire. The glow surrounded me and gave me a wonderful feeling.

The entire scene was a visual parable of human life. In our inner faithfulness toward ourselves, of our inner contact with the incomprehensible, with the Infinite, we approach life's sunset, bathed more and more in the light until the final moment when the earthly sun sets for us all. Just as the outward sun goes down for us, too.

For the people of faith, darkness cannot extinguish the light of eternity. For the Son of God came into the world and became our Savior. He has lifted us up from our fears and trivialities, from our anxieties. He has directed our eyes toward the truth, toward the infinite spirit within us which longs for eternity. "The dust returns to the earth as it was, and the spirit returns to God—who gave it" (Eccles. 12:7).—Laszlo Kovacs

FOR OUR GOOD.   If we belong to Christ, if we present our bodies as a living sacrifice, holy and acceptable to God (Rom. 12:1), we discover that his will is ever directed to his children's good. The moments of greatest happiness in our present life—those times when communion with Christ is experienced with an immediacy and power that cannot be communicated by human language, the encounters with God's majesty as we behold a sunrise or with God's handiwork as we witness the miracle of birth, the experiences of God's mercy as we're reunited with loved ones after a long separation—as wonderful as they are, these are only a foretaste of the glory prepared for those who love Christ and belong to him. We have a limited understanding of what it will be like: a place where God will wipe away every tear and death shall be no more, neither shall there be mourning nor crying nor pain anymore. Revelation tells us that the Lamb's servants shall worship him, and his name shall be on their foreheads, but Scripture evokes rather than defines the joy that is yet to come. As the writer of 1 John put it, it does not yet appear what we shall be, but we know that when he appears we shall be like him, for we shall see him as he is.—Carol M. Noren

DELIVERED.   We labor to be born. All what little we have in us of holiness labors for breath, strains to be delivered of darkness into light. It is the secret, inner battle of every one of us. And through all our laboring, God also labors: to deliver what is whole in us from what is broken, to deliver what is true in us from what is false, until in the end we reach the measure of the stature of the fullness of Christ, Paul says—until in the end we become Christ ourselves, no less than that: Christ to each other and Christs to God.—Frederick Buechner, *A Room Called Remember*

CHRISTIAN RADIANCE.   I also think of my aged aunt, Mrs. Mae Legate. At eighty-three she amazed us by teaching her class of preschool children each Sunday. She not only taught them, she told them Bible stories in such a way that she delighted them. During the week she found time and energy to baby-sit for parents who, for one reason or another, needed to be away from home. She always had a twinkle in her eye and some interesting plan of activity under way. She had a heart condition, and had had major surgery for cancer, but she still outdistanced most of us. When we talked occasionally about her age and about growing old, she liked to say, "I'm still looking for a little bit of sugar in the bottom of the cup." We who knew her and loved her are sure that she found it.—Batsell Barrett Baxter, *When Life Tumbles In*

THE REAL CHURCH.   In John's lovely vision in the last book of the Bible we find that the Holy City has no temple. The Community and the Church are one and the same. He saw "no temple therein," but he saw the Holy City "coming down out of Heaven from God."

The Church *on earth* began when Jesus, in Mark's lovely phrase, chose twelve men "that they might be with him"; and every denomination has developed from that fellowship. But there is no denomination that is not, in a sense, a mere shadow—perhaps a caricature—of that beauteous, holy, and perfect fellowship in the unseen and eternal world which existed before this little insignificant planet began its course, and which will go on when the earth hangs like the moon, a frozen planet in the sky, or is burnt up in the sun which gave it birth.—Leslie D. Weatherhead, *This Is the Victory*

PLODDING.   William Carey, once a cobbler, became a distinguished educator, minister and Bible translator who organized the modern missionary movement among the churches of the world. In Calcutta, Carey left this personal statement: "If after my removal, anyone should think it worth his while to write about my life, I will give you a criterion by which to judge its correctness. . . . If he gives me credit for being a plodder, he will describe me justly. Anything beyond this will be too much. *I can plod—I can persevere in any definite pursuit. To this I owe everything.*"—G. Othell Hand, *It's Easier to Win . . .*

THE BIBLE DID IT.   In recent years the thrilling story of Pitcairn Island and the mutiny on the *Bounty* has been retold and popularized in newspaper articles and books. There is one incident in that story which, indeed, is worth retelling. The mutineers sank their ship and landed with their native women on the lonely island named Pitcairn. There were nine white sailors, six natives, ten women, and a girl of fifteen. One of the sailors discovered a method of distilling alcohol, and the island colony was debauched with drunkenness and vice.

After a time only one of the white sailors who had landed survived, surrounded by native women and half-breed children. This sailor, Alexander Smith, found in one of the chests that had been taken from the *Bounty* a copy of the Bible. He began to teach his fellow exiles its principles, with the result that his own life was changed, and finally the life of that island colony.

In 1808 the United States ship *Topaz* visited the island and found a thriving and prosperous community, without whiskey, without a jail, without a crime, and without an insane asylum. The Bible had changed the life of that island community.

So it has been from age to age: "The entrance of thy words giveth light" (Ps. 119:130).—Clarence Edward Macartney, *Macartney's Illustrations*

GOSSIP.   A full-scale picture of a certain character in a modern story is drawn with this one deft touch, "She nibbled at her salmon and at other people's reputation." In a modern novel this is the best that could be said about one whose portrait is there drawn: "He could whisper away a character by an innocent interrogation. He could destroy a high reputation by a shrug of the shoulders. He could assassinate a soul by silence when silence became the strongest instrument."

An effective sentry, standing guard with fixed bayonet at the tongue where unspoken words struggle for wings, is the triple test: Is it true? Is it kind? Is it necessary?—Frederick Brown Harris, *Spires of the Spirit*

GENERIC AND PERSONAL GIFTS.   Do you remember in elementary school when you exchanged Christmas gifts with others in your class? In my school we would draw names and then bring the gift the day of the Christmas party. I believe it was fourth grade when this happened. My mother carefully wrapped the present I was to give. I brought it to school and put it under the tree. The time for the party came. I was so excited. What would I get?

The presents were taken from under the tree and the names were called. I kept thinking that I would be next. Finally everybody's name except mine was called. Whoever had my name had forgotten to bring a gift. On her desk the teacher had five or six gifts that were used for emergencies like this. "Here, Chuck," she said, "take one of these." But it wasn't the same. These were "generic" gifts, and nobody wants a generic gift when you can have one with your name on it.

I look at John 3:16. It does have everybody's name on it—"For God so loved the world. . . ." Somebody might say, "Well, if the gift of God is for everyone, it's generic." But when you look at the verse more carefully, you see how beautifully personal it is. So *who* may receive the gift of God's grace? Each of us who responds to the generous offer of God's love.—Charles B. Bugg, *Getting on Top When Life Gets Us Down*

FROM TROUBLE TO LOVE.   A friend told me about a teacher who was given the assignment of working with a very difficult young girl. Many had tried to work with this girl, but without success. She was trouble from the word *go*. She would rebel against everything and did so with this new teacher. The teacher tried everything she knew to reach her. The teacher struggled with the child, was patient with her, went places with her, but never thought she was getting anyplace with her.

One day the teacher came into class and saw a little envelope on the desk. She opened it. It was a handmade card. The picture on it was not well drawn, the letters were not well formed, and the card simply said, "I love you." But that gift was unforgettable, for it meant all the love she had poured into the girl was not wasted. Some of it had gotten through.—Hugh Litchfield, *Sermons on Those Other Special Days*

SOME OTHER DAWN.   Famous journalist William Allen White lost his daughter, Mary, while she was a high-school student. Her spirited horse ran beneath a tree limb and Mary died from the injury she suffered. After her death, her father wrote an editorial about her that appeared in *The Emporia Gazette*, a famous newspaper he edited. White told of Mary's love for life, her vivacious spirit, her sense of fairness and equality, and her compassion for people. He closed his editorial with reference to her casket as it was lowered into the grave: "A rift in the clouds in gray day threw a shaft of sunlight upon the coffin as her nervous energetic little body sank to its sleep. But the soul of her, the flowing, gorgeous, fervent soul of her, surely was flaming in eager joy upon some other dawn."

We can write with that kind of hope with confidence if we believe that Easter has rolled away the stone of death at the entrance of life.—Chavis F. Horne, *Basic Bible Sermons on Easter*

WAGES OF SIN.   Death is called here "the wages of sin." It could also be called the pay, the salary, the compensation paid by sin to those who are in its service and work for it. Strange, isn't it? Sin fulfills here the function of the paymaster in the armed services, or of the employer or his cashier in a business enterprise who pays the employees and workers. Here is what is your due, what you have earned through your efforts. Is it the correct amount? Take a good look! Absolutely correct, isn't it? This is what you deserve, and you've got it: death, not more, not less, and nothing else.—Karl Barth, *Deliverance to the Captives*

NEW LIFE.   On a trip to Norway, we cruised along the West Coast of Norway, stopping to visit the various towns that dot the coast. Suddenly it struck me—all the buildings are new! Then I realized what had happened. All these towns had been destroyed by the Nazis and leveled to the ground. But not the people! They had not been crushed, and their resilient and courageous spirit had rebuilt all these towns and created a new life for their land. On the same trip we revisited Rotterdam. Once a great seaport, it had been annihilated by the Nazis. But not the people! They had taken calamity as an opportunity to put their best thinking into the rebuilding of their city, and today Rotterdam is the number one seaport of the world. Failure is not final, and deep in the human spirit God had placed His resurrection power!—Lowell M. Atkinson, *Apples of Gold*

LETTING GO.   I once heard of a child who was raising a frightful cry because he had shoved his hand into the opening of a very expensive Chinese vase and then he couldn't pull it out again. Parents and neighbors tugged with might and main on the child's arm, with the poor little creature howling out loud all the while. Finally there was nothing left to do but break the beautiful, expensive vase. And then as the mournful heap of shards lay there, it became clear why the child had been so hopelessly stuck. His little fist grasped a paltry penny which he had spied in the bottom of the vase and which he, in his childish ignorance, would not let go.—Helmut Thielicks, *How to Believe Again*

A CHANGE OF ATTITUDE.   A young bride joined her husband at an Army base on the edge of the desert where life seemed primitive. Living in a dilapidated one-room apartment near an Indian village, the desert heat became almost unbearable, the windblown sands constant, the days dreary. When her husband was ordered farther into the desert on maneuvers, that young bride wrote "Mama" that she couldn't take any more and was returning home. Wiser than most, her mother quickly replied:

"Two men looked out from prison bars.
One saw mud, the other saw the stars."

Reading those lines over and over, the daughter thought reflectively and set out to make friends with the Indians, asking them to teach her weaving and pottery. She became fascinated with their culture, history, and personal patterns. Gradually the desert changed from a desolate, forbidding place to an awesome thing of beauty as she studied forms of the cacti, the yuccas, and the Joshua trees. Dreary days turned into delightful interests.

But what had really changed? Not the desert nor the Indians—her frame of mind! Likewise, abounding people manipulate their inner feelings to brighten a not-so-beckoning situation, reverse an unfriendly relationship, do a near-hypnotic selling job, and paint golden hues across the horizon of any day.—G. Othell Hand, *It's Easier to Win*

LOVE—UPSIDE DOWN.   A young mother once recounted to me that she had spent much time and expense on new wallpaper for her house. Then, when she had gone out for a moment to shop, little Inge had made an unimaginable mess on the walls with crayons. When she returned, Inge presented her with this product and beamed, "Look what I painted for you, mother!" "For you," she said—and these two words had choked off the anger which was welling up within her. The little girl had, in her own way, painted a declaration of love on the wall, and the mother had recognized it amidst the scribbling, even though the childish scrawl was contrary to rules and orderliness and involved some trouble for the mother. The child had used her freedom (really freedom!) to tell the mother in her own way that she had waited lovingly and eagerly for her to come home. And despite her irritation over the wallpaper, that love was more important to the mother than rigidly channeled obedience and routine good behavior.—Helmut Thielicke, *How to Believe Again*

GREATNESS.   The name William James, who was teaching at Harvard fifty years ago, is known to many. I think that the finest tribute I have ever heard paid to any teacher anywhere was paid to James by one of his students. He said, "You went to other men's lectures here at Harvard and you were impressed, even oppressed, by the lecturer's massive learning, by his greatness as a scholar. But you never came out of James's lecture room feeling what a great man James is. You came out with a strange new thought and feeling, 'If I could only find myself, what a great man I might be.'"—Willard L. Sperry, *Sermons Preached at Harvard*

NEEDED STRENGTH.   Like a house in the rain, books were havens of permanence and protection from whatever it was that as a child I needed protection from. Oz might be full of magic and danger, but even so it was safer than Washington was.

I remember, at the age of five or six, standing in the lobby of the Mayflower Hotel there one day when suddenly everybody around me was saying, "The President is coming, the President is coming," and starting to crowd around. Then slowly the doors of the main elevator rolled back, and there, framed in the opening, was the President himself with braces on his legs and one of his sons on either side of him, holding him up under the arms, and I remember realizing that if they had let him go, he would have crumpled to the floor like a doll. King Rinkitink would not have crumpled to the floor, but President Roosevelt would have crumpled because nowhere in Washington, as far as I knew, was there a blue pearl to confer strength and a pink one for invulnerability and a white one with words wise and helpful enough to sustain him.—Frederick Buechner, *The Sacred Journey*

THE WORK OF THE WORD ALONE.   Where God's Word enters man's heart, there also enters the divine will and intention. God's will and intention has but one meaning: love. Where God reigns, love reigns. And where love reigns, life becomes human, whole, joyful. Self-centeredness yields to love of neighbor. Loneliness is overcome by fellowship. Anxiety gives way to confidence. The bad conscience ceases to exist. God's Word of love and forgiveness obstructs the poisonous fountain and makes flow the waters of childlike love of God. Is this exclusively the work of God's Word, of nobody else, of nothing else? It is indeed the work of the Word alone.—Emil Brunner, *Sowing and Reaping*

IDOLATRY.   This is one of the worst sins that can lay hold of a human life. This covetousness—this desire for things of this world more than for riches in the inner life, is named in the Bible for what it is. God calls it idolatry. It is devotion to things; it comes almost to worship of them. It is native to our hearts unless they are freed from it by the liberating grace of God. And when a profession of religion is used to cover it over, it makes one more guilty than an infidel. To profess to put trust in God, to profess to be devoted to him, and to allow that profession to be simply a screen to hide the actual devotion of our hearts to things of this world is a sin that a man should fear like a cancer. It is a pose, a cover; and the searching eye of the living God sees through it.—John Reed Miller, *Disciples in Disguise, Vol. II*

CONSCIENCE.   Although we must always be bound by conscience, some of the great crimes of our own day have been committed, and are being committed, by an appeal to individual conscience, as though there were no higher norm. But as our Holy Father said in *Veritatis Splendor*, "It is always from the *truth* that the dignity of conscience derives." Consequently, the act of conscience is not arbitrary. Conscience does not make the truth but only discerns and applies it. As St. Bonaventure teaches, "Conscience is like God's herald and messenger; it does not command things on its own authority, but commands them as coming from God's authority, like a herald when he proclaims the edict of the king." As we know, true conscience enables us to see what actions are actually for our good and for the promotion of human happiness.—Joseph Cardinal Ratzinger

GUILT AND SHAME.   In another generation, people might have been ashamed of their poverty and have cringed at the thought of others knowing where they lived. Today, many young people feel ashamed if they do not have the right sneakers or if their pants are not baggy enough. Shame of this kind produces embarrassment of a strictly horizontal sort, and this is mostly how every experience of being unacceptable is understood. As external moral norms have collapsed, being unacceptable has come to mean being unacceptable only to *ourselves*; it is guilt that tells us we are unacceptable before *God*. These two realities, guilt and shame, now need to be illustrated further and their exact relationship needs to be defined more precisely.—Donald F. Wells

SANCTIFICATION.   If Christ did nothing except save us from the wages or results of sin, he would be worthy of our undying obedience and thanks; but our Lord does much more. The one who saves and owns us also shows us, by example, how to live in conformity to the will of our heavenly Father. If any of you have tried to set up a computer or program a VCR, you know that the instruction books in the carton, truthful and comprehensive as they may be, cannot compare with having someone there who knows how it all works to show you the way. Jesus knows how it all works. God became flesh not to cancel the written Word but to show it and fulfill it. The WWJD bracelets worn by many disciples today bear witness to the value of a model: someone whose life provides a pattern for our own.

There is no planned obsolescence in this model, no shadow of turning with him. Jesus Christ, the same yesterday, today, and forever, promised his disciples, "Lo, I am with you always, to the close of the age" (Matt. 28:20). Political systems will rise and fall, leaders may disappoint and mislead us, but our Redeemer is faithful and true. His Holy Spirit is the companion who will support and guide us in every phase of life, through every situation. The Spirit can work within us what is pleasing in God's sight, if we "yield our members to righteousness for sanctification" (Rom. 6:19).—Carol M. Noren

THE BURDEN OF GRIEF.   Through our griefs and sorrows we often come to a brighter, better world. As the Strait of Gibraltar seems to close like a gate behind the ship that has passed through it from the Mediterranean, so death and other of life's crises seem to close us in from life. However, as the broad expanses of the Atlantic open wide beyond the Strait, so do the beautiful vistas of eternity open wide to the Christian beyond death. Christ is our Pilot on a voyage that is often dark and stormy from earth to heaven.—Batsell Barrett Baxter, *When Life Tumbles In*

GREATNESS OF GOD.   Robert Louis Stevenson was no naive believer in secondhand religion, not a contender for orthodoxy. Yet in his long-drawn-out battle against disease, which was sapping his physical strength, he laid hold on the greatness of God. Describing a decisive stage in his soul's career, he testified, "I came about like a well-handled ship. There stood at the wheel that unknown steersman whom we call God."—Frederick Brown Harris, *Spires of the Spirit*

THE DOXOLOGY.   In the decade of the 1660s England passed through a period of unprecedented disaster. In 1665 a great plague swept over London, leaving nearly 70,000 people dead. A year later came the fire that destroyed four fifths of London. Many believed that England would never recover from this double tragedy.

Bishop Thomas Ken lived through these difficult days and endangered his own life in ministering to others. Out of this tragic experience came a song which Bishop Ken wrote. We sing it every Sunday in our worship service. In fact, it is the *only* song that we sing *every* Sunday at our church.

> Praise God from whom all blessings flow.
> Praise Him all creatures here below.
> Praise Him above ye heavenly host.
> Praise Father, Son and Holy Ghost.

The doxology! How ironic that the doxology was born out of disaster. Thanksgiving rose from the ashes of tragedy.—Charles B. Bugg, *Getting on Top When Life Lets Us Down*

AUTHENTIC WITNESSING.   Jesus said to His disciples after His resurrection: "You shall be my witnesses" (Acts 1:8). A witness is one who knows firsthand. He tells what he has seen, heard, and experienced. He does not tell what others have said and heard. He does not theorize and speculate. He tells what he knows.

Authentic witnessing is powerful. It is moving to hear a person say: "I was being destroyed by guilt, and Christ forgave me," or "My life was like a raging sea, and Christ gave me peace," or, "My life was being burned up by hatred, and Christ enabled me to love." You cannot refute that kind of reality.—Chevis F. Horne, *Basic Bible Sermons on Easter*

SAVED BY GRACE.   We dislike hearing that we are saved by grace, and by grace alone. We do not appreciate that God does not owe us anything, that we are bound to live from his goodness alone, that we are left with nothing but the great humility, the thankfulness of a child presented with many gifts. For we do not like at all to look away from ourselves. We would much prefer to withdraw into our own inner circle, not unlike the snail into its shell, and to be ourselves. To put it bluntly: we do not like to believe. And yet grace and therefore faith as I just described it is the beginning of the true life of freedom, of a carefree heart, of joy deep within, of love of God and neighbour, of great and assured hope! And yet grace and faith would make things so very simple in or lives!—Karl Barth, *Deliverance to the Captives*

THE FINAL PROOF.   Is it not true that we constantly bewail secularism when we read the newspapers? How could we do otherwise in the face of the brimful measure of injustice and inhumanity which is evident in our day! As soon, however, as we begin to reflect more deeply, must we not bewail even more ourselves, the Christians, the church, organized Christianity, which for centuries has treasured the gospel and all its gifts and yet has given so little to the world of the new life hidden in the gospel? Time and again I tremble when I think of our church. What a tremendous apparatus of Christian education, groups, meetings, and how preciously little strength and life! Are we truly "in" and the others "out"?

Who is "in"? Those who understand the secrets of the Kingdom of God and—not to be overlooked—who change their ways. For both belong inseparably together in Jesus' eyes. The doing is always the proof of the hearing.—Emil Brunner, *Sowing and Reaping*

CONTRIBUTORS AND ACKNOWLEDGMENT

CONTRIBUTORS

Andersen, Richard. Pastor, Evangelical Lutheran Church in America, former Pastor of International Church of Copenhagen

Atkinson, Lowell M. Retired Methodist minister, Holiday, Florida

Beavers, David. Chairman, Pastoral Department, San Jose Christian College, San Jose, California

Brand, Rick. Pastor, First Presbyterian Church, Henderson, North Carolina

Brown, Jeffrey Dale. Doctoral candidate in homiletics, Southern Baptist Theological Seminary, Louisville, Kentucky

Buckwalter, Georgine. Chaplain, Episcopal Retirement Home, Louisville, Kentucky

Chafin, Kenneth L. Pastor Emeritus, South Main Baptist Church, Houston, Texas

Childers, Jana. Professor of homiletics, San Francisco Theological Seminary, San Anselmo, California

Collier, Stuart G. Baptist minister, Birmingham, Alabama

Cooper, Kenny C. Baptist minister

Cox, Ken. Pastor, First Baptist Church, New Barton, Texas

Crawford, James W. Pastor, Old South Church, Boston, Massachusetts

Crumpler, Carolyn Weatherford. Retired executive director, Woman's Missionary Union, Southern Baptist Convention

Dipboye, Larry. Pastor, First Baptist Church, Oak Ridge, Tennessee

Durst, Rodrick K. Dean of the faculty, Golden Gate Baptist Theological Seminary, Mill Valley, California

413

Feddes, David. Preacher on The Radio Pulpit of "The Back to God Hour" of the Christian Reformed Church

Ferguson, Robert U. Pastor, Trinity Baptist Church, Seneca, South Carolina

Fields, Henry. Pastor, First Baptist Church, Toccoa, Georgia

Fribley, Peter. Presbyterian minister

Hammer, Randy. Columnist and pastor, Franklin, Tennessee

Harbour, Brian L. Baptist minister, Richardson, Texas

Hickey, Marilyn. President of Marilyn Hickey Ministries

Hill, George W. Minister, First Baptist Church, Los Angeles, California

Holladay, Jim. Pastor, Lyndon Baptist Church, Louisville, Kentucky

Honeycutt, Roy L. Chancellor and former president, Southern Baptist Theological Seminary, Louisville, Kentucky

House, Paul. Former professor of old testament, Southern Baptist Theological Seminary, Louisville, Kentucky

Johnson, William M. Associate minister, Crescent Hill Baptist Church, Louisville, Kentucky

Killinger, John. President of the Mission for Biblical Literacy

King, James M. Baptist minister, Atlanta, Georgia

Lanway, Michael. Baptist minister, Bardstown, Kentucky

Lee, Dorothy. Professor of new testament, Theological Hall, Orman College, Melbourne, Australia

Long, Robert. Pastor, Walnut Street Baptist Church, Louisville, Kentucky

Long, Thomas G. Director of Congregational Resources and Geneva Press

Lovette, Roger. Pastor, Covenant Baptist Church, Birmingham, Alabama

Lytch, Stephens B. Pastor, Second Presbyterian Church, Louisville, Kentucky

Macleod, Donald. Retired professor of homiletics, Princeton Theological Seminary

McElrath, Hugh T. Senior professor of church music, Southern Baptist Theological Seminary, Louisville, Kentucky

Mitchell, Ella Pearson. Minister and educator, Emeritus

Moore, William G. Doctoral candidate, Southern Baptist Theological Seminary, Louisville, Kentucky

Morley, Robert. Associate minister, First United Methodist Church, San Diego, California

Noren, Carol M. Professor of homiletics, North Park Theological Seminary, Chicago, Illinois

Ostrom, W. Bruce. Baptist minister, Louisville, Kentucky

Phillips, E. Lee. Freelance author and Baptist minister, Atlanta, Georgia

Read, David H. C. Minister Emeritus, Madison Avenue Presbyterian Church, New York, New York

Redding, Gary C. Baptist pastor, North Augusta, South Carolina

Rodman, John R. Retired Presbyterian minister, Louisville, Kentucky

Schweizer, Eduard. Former professor of new testament and *rektor* (president), University of Zurich, Switzerland

Shaw, Wayne E. Dean and professor of preaching, Lincoln Christian Seminary, Lincoln, Illinois

Strand, Tyler A. Dean of Episcopal Cathedral, Manila, Philippines

Thompson, John. Minister of pastoral care, Venice Presbyterian Church, Venice, Florida

Tomlin, Carolyn. Writer for a variety of publications, specializing in church curriculum materials, Jackson, Tennessee
Trotter, Mark. Pastor, First United Methodist Church, San Diego, California
Tuck, William Powell. Pastor, First Baptist Church, Lumberton, North Carolina
Vinson, Richard B. Dean, Averett College, Danville, Virginia
Walsh, Albert J. D. Pastor, First United Church of Christ, Schuylkill Haven, Pennsylvania
Wheeler, David L. Pastor, First Baptist Church, Los Angeles, California
Wyndham, Michael A. Pastor, Summit Hills Baptist Church, Louisville, Kentucky

ACKNOWLEDGMENT

The sermon by David Feddes, "Honoring the Holy Spirit," is reprinted by permission of *The Back to God Hour* of the Christian Reformed Church in North America, 6555 West College Drive, Palos Heights, IL 60463. All copyrights are retained by *The Back to God Hour.*

INDEX OF CONTRIBUTORS

SERMON TITLE INDEX

Children's stories and sermons are identified as (cs); sermon suggestions as (ss).

SCRIPTURAL INDEX

INDEX OF PRAYERS

INDEX OF MATERIALS
USEFUL AS CHILDREN'S STORIES
AND SERMONS NOT INCLUDED IN SECTION X

INDEX OF MATERIALS USEFUL
FOR SMALL GROUPS

TOPICAL INDEX